Penguin Education

Sociological Perspectives

Selected Readings

Edited by Kenneth Thompson
and Jeremy Tunstall

Sociological Perspectives

Selected Readings

Edited by Kenneth Thompson and Jeremy Tunstall
at The Open University

Penguin Books
in association with The Open University Press

Penguin Books Ltd, Harmondsworth,
Middlesex, England
Penguin Books Inc, 7110 Ambassador Road,
Baltimore, Md 21207, U.S.A.
Penguin Books Australia Ltd,
Ringwood, Victoria, Australia

First published 1971
This selection copyright © The Open University, 1971
Introduction and notes copyright © The Open University, 1971

Made and printed in Great Britain by
Hazell Watson & Viney Ltd
Aylesbury, Bucks
Set in Linotype Times

Contents

Part Five Sociological Perspectives 475

Introduction

The central theme of this volume is indicated in the heading to Part One – 'The Sociological Perspective'; our prime concern is to indicate the distinctive way in which sociology views society and social life. We would like the reader to come to appreciate some of the subtlety and complexity that characterizes all good sociological analysis.

'Sociological Perspectives' is the title both of Part Five and of the whole volume, and this plural version indicates a second theme. Within the broad view of sociology there are at least two (and possibly more) distinctive perspectives. At their crudest the two views differ in that one places the emphasis on 'man in *Society*' whilst the other shifts the emphasis to '*Man* in society'. Sometimes the two views are termed respectively 'the social-system approach' and 'the social-action approach'. Carried to their logical extremes they posit antithetical views of human nature and the relationship between the individual and society. One stresses the constraint that the social system exercises over the individual; the other stresses the role of the individual in constructing his meaningful world. The reasons for the different emphases are to be found in the historical setting in which sociology arose and the opposing problems of social order and individual control that had to be faced. But reasons can also be found in the very nature of society as an entity that is external to the individual and yet depends on individuals for its construction and maintenance.

The contrast between the two perspectives is most apparent in the change from the 'man in *Society*' emphasis of Durkheim at the end of Part One, to the emphasis on '*Man* in society' in Part Two on 'Interaction'. In Part Five the two perspectives are compared and contrasted more explicitly and possible syntheses are suggested.

We assume that our readers will have some previous acquaintance with sociology – the minimum expectation is that the reader will already have absorbed the contents of at least one broad introductory textbook. However, this book is definitely not intended as an advanced or postgraduate level text.

'Sociological theory' is often taught separately from other courses in sociology. We are unhappy about this rigid distinction between sociological theory and 'other' sociology; we believe that the *de facto* distinction does not follow from the way in which sociology teachers view sociology but rather from the requirements of the academic division of labour, examinations and the multiplicity of small courses in many academic institutions. The Open University happens to reverse this trend – by having fewer, but much larger courses – large in terms of resources, numbers of students and student hours per course. In the case of sociology, this compels us to do what we (and many other sociologists) would much prefer to do anyway – to adopt a broad approach to sociology.

Although this is not a reader in sociological theory as such we have nevertheless concentrated to a greater extent on the theoretical than upon the empirical end of the continuum. We aim to present a basic core of both classical and modern theoretical writings which have been, and promise to be, productive of empirical research.

We have deliberately decided to concentrate on certain major sociologists and major sociological themes. Rather than provide small samples from the writings of a long succession of chronologically arranged sociologists, we have concentrated on the work of a few classical writers – especially Weber, Marx and Durkheim. This concentration has allowed us to include larger sections than is the case with some volumes of selections.

We have concentrated in another way – by selecting two main substantive areas, namely stratification and belief. We chose these particular areas because both have been of central importance in sociology and because both are strong in theoretical insights as well as empirical research.

This book originated with a specific purpose – to form part of an Open University 'second-level' course. *Sociological Perspectives* is one component of a course which also includes personal tuition, a basic correspondence text, BBC radio and television programmes and other prescribed books ;[1] we have deliberately avoided including pieces which already appear in these prescribed books. We are also able to send some offprints (for instance of journal articles) to Open University students. Consequently, in editing this Reader we have deliberately kept in mind the requirements both of students enrolled in sociology courses elsewhere and also of the layman who wants to see what sociology has to offer beyond the most elementary level.

1. In addition to this volume the other prescribed texts for the Sociological Perspective course are: Raymond Aron, *Main Currents in Sociological Thought*, Penguin, 1965, vol. 1. Raymond Aron, *Main Currents in Sociological Thought*, Penguin, 1970, vol. 2. André Béteille (ed.) *Social Inequality*, Penguin, 1969. J. H. Goldthorpe, D. Lockwood, F. Bechhoffer and J. Platt, *The Affluent Worker in the Class Structure*, Cambridge University Press, 1969. Robert A. Nisbet, *The Sociological Tradition*, Heinemann, 1967. Roland Robertson (ed.) *The Sociology of Religion*, Penguin, 1969. Arnold Rose (ed.) *Human Behavior and Social Processes*, Routledge & Kegan Paul, 1962.

Editors' Note

This book is the result largely of a collective effort by a number of people involved in the Sociological Perspective course. Our academic colleagues at the Open University played a major part in the planning of this course over the period of a year, and also in the selection of pieces for inclusion here. Ruth Finnegan and David Boswell were largely responsible for the selections in Part Two. Francis Castles was actively involved in the selections for Parts One and Five; Graeme Salaman was similarly involved in Part Three. David Weeks also took part in the selection of Part Three; in addition he performed invaluable labours in library searching, in assessing pieces, in detailed editing and indexing. We are also indebted to our BBC colleagues and especially to Clare Falkner and Ken Patton – not only for their broadcast expertise, but also for their sociological knowledge; they have taken an active part in the meetings from which this book derives. In addition we are grateful for the advice of our two BBC senior producer colleagues, Chris Cuthbertson and John Radcliffe.

At the Open University we have been valiantly supported by the secretarial work of Pam Howell and Kathy Tyrell. We are also similarly grateful to Leslie Lonsdale-Cooper and Roger Lubbock, Director of Publishing and Coordinating Editor at the Open University, for their wise advice and for their efficient handling of this book.

Despite the invaluable assistance of all these people, we ourselves have been the full-time academic core of the Sociological Perspective course, have chosen the majority of the pieces in this volume, have done most of the detailed editing, and we therefore are solely responsible for any mistaken choices or other errors in the pages which follow.

Part One The Sociological Perspective

The central theories and research interests of sociology reflect the circumstances of its emergence in nineteenth-century Europe. The disturbing impact of political and economic changes called into question the viability and legitimacy of all social institutions. What was needed was a perspective that would translate such problems into a new idiom where they could be analysed in the systematic fashion that had brought such success to the natural sciences. The development of such a perspective was the main contribution made by those such as Comte, Spencer, Marx, Weber, Simmel and Durkheim, who gave rise to the 'Classical Tradition' in sociology.

The continuities and conflicts in the nature and aims of that tradition are brought out by the first piece in this section, which was written by a prominent contemporary American sociologist, Alvin Gouldner. In Reading 1 he relates the sociological perspective to the setting in which it arose after the French Revolution. He suggests that the origins of sociology gave rise to a unique contradiction in its vision of society: man is viewed as the controlled product of society and culture, and yet also as the maker of society and culture.

Auguste Comte, who gave sociology its name and much of its programme, emphasized the contribution that sociology could make to the development of a new social order. He saw the purpose of sociology as the uncovering of laws of social order and social progress. Sociology would avoid the fragmentation of social reality perpetrated by other disciplines and it would resolve the social crisis caused by the conflict between rival principles of explanation – the theological, metaphysical and positive/scientific (Reading 2).

Like Comte, Herbert Spencer set out to synthesize the various elements of social order and process into a general model. He made imaginative use of the organic analogy in analysing the nature of social interrelationships and the theory of evolution in explaining the course of social development (Reading 3).

In the case of Karl Marx (Reading 4) the same themes of social interrelationships and development are treated, but in this case the model also prescribes some definite causal relationships between social structures. The mode of production of material-life is seen as a determinant of social, political and even spiritual processes of life. Max Weber does not provide a model of whole social systems, but he does provide models (or ideal types) of parts of such systems. His ideal-type bureaucracy is one such model. Like Marx's concept of alienation, Weber's concept of bureaucratic rationalization throws light on a trend which characterizes the modern era (Reading 5).

Georg Simmel's sociology is akin to that of Weber in its attempt to relate forms of social interaction to larger social structures. He contrasts the social interaction in small-scale communities with that which occurs in the great city (Reading 6).

All the early sociologists were interested in defining the distinctive character of social phenomena, but none more so than Emile Durkheim (Reading 7). His major emphasis is on the constraints which society exercises on the individual, and the pathological consequences which result when such constraints are removed. It is in this light that he analyses the social causes of suicide and rejects explanations which viewed it as a purely individual phenomenon.

1 Alvin W. Gouldner

Sociology's Basic Assumptions

Excerpt from A. W. Gouldner, *The Coming Crisis of Western Sociology*, Heinemann, 1971, pp. 52–4.

The domain assumptions[1] of sociological analysis are embedded in – both expressed and concealed by – its most central programmatic concepts, its most elemental vision of 'society' and 'culture'. The *focal* implications of these concepts stress the manner in which men are shaped and influenced by their groups and group heritage. Yet since the social sciences emerged in the secularized world of the 'self-made' bourgeoisie that surfaced after the French Revolution in nineteenth-century Europe, these concepts also tacitly imply that man *makes* his own societies and cultures. They imply the potency of man. But this vision of the potency of man, in contrast to that of society and culture, tends to be confined to the merely subsidiary attention of Academic Sociology rather than to its focal concerns.

Academic Sociology's emphasis on the potency of society and the subordination of men to it is itself an historical product that contains an historical truth. The modern concepts of society and of culture arose in a social world that, following the French Revolution, men could believe they themselves had made. They could see that it was through their struggles that kings had been overthrown and an ancient religion disestablished. Yet, at the same time men could also see that this was a world out of control, not amenable to men's designs. It was therefore a grotesque, contradictory world: a world made by men but, despite this, not *their* world.

No thinker better grasped this paradoxical character of the new social world than Rousseau. It was central to his conception that man was corrupted by the very advance of the arts and sciences, that he had

1. Gouldner defines domain assumptions as follows: 'Domain assumptions are the background assumptions applied only to members of a single domain; they are, in effect, the metaphysics of a domain. Domain assumptions about man and society might include, for example, dispositions to believe that men are rational or irrational; that society is precarious or fundamentally stable; that social problems will correct themselves without planned intervention; that human behaviour is unpredictable; that man's true humanity resides in his feelings and sentiments.' [Eds.]

lost something vital in the very midst of his highest achievements. This paradoxical vision also underlies his conception of man as born free but now living everywhere in chains: man creates society through a willing contract but must then subject himself to his own creation.

Culture and society thus emerged as ambiguous conceptions, as being man's own creations but also having lives and histories of their own. It is precisely this ambiguity to which the central conceptions of sociological analysis, 'culture' and 'society', give continued expression. Both culture and society are seen, in sociological analysis, as having a life apart from the men who create, embody, and enact them. The concepts of culture and society tacitly predicate that men have created a social world from which they have been alienated. The germinal concepts of the social sciences, then, are imprinted with the birth trauma of a social world from which men saw themselves alienated from their own creations; in which men felt themselves to be at once newly potent and tragically impotent. The emerging academic social sciences thus commonly came to conceive of society and culture as *autonomous* things: things that are independent and exist for themselves. Society and culture were then amenable to being viewed like any other 'natural' phenomena, as having laws of their own that operated quite apart from the intentions and plans of men, while the disciplines that studied them could be viewed as natural sciences like any other. Method, then, follows domain assumption. In other words, sociology emerged as a 'natural' science when certain domain assumptions and sentiments became prevalent; when men felt alienated from a society that they thought they had made but could not control. Whereas European men had once expressed their estrangement from themselves in terms of traditional religion and metaphysics, they now began to do so through academic social science, and scientism became, in this way, a modern substitute for a decaying traditional religion.

The concepts of society and culture, which are at the very foundation of the academic social sciences, are in part based upon a reaction to an historical defeat: man's failure to possess the social world that he created. To that extent, the academic social sciences are the social sciences of an alienated age and alienated man. From this standpoint the possibility of 'objectivity' in, and the call to 'objectivity' by, the academic social sciences has a rather different meaning than that conventionally assigned. The 'objectivity' of the social sciences is not the expression of a dispassionate and detached view of the social world; it is, rather, an ambivalent effort to accommodate to alienation *and* to express a muted resentment of it.

In one part, then, the dominant expressions of the academic social sciences embody an accommodation to the alienation of men in contemporary society, rather than a determined effort to transcend it. The core concepts of society and culture, as held by the social sciences, entail the view that their autonomy and uncontrollability are a normal and natural condition, rather than intrinsically a kind of pathology. It is this assumption that is at the heart of the *repressive* component of sociology.

At the same time, however, the social sciences' accommodation to alienation is an ambivalent and resentful one. It is in this muted resentment that there is the suppressed *liberative* potential of sociology. And it is this total conception of man – the dominant focal view of him as the controlled product of society and culture, combined with the subsidiary conception of man as the maker of society and culture – that shapes the unique contradiction distinctive of sociology.

It is not simply that one or another 'school' of sociology embodies these contradictory domain assumptions about men and society, but that these dwell in the basic charter of Academic Sociology as a discipline. These assumptions resonate certain sentiments about the grotesqueness of the social world that began to emerge during the nineteenth century, and they are rooted in a contradictory personal reality widely shared by men who, then as now, felt that they were somehow living in a world that they made but did not control.

2 Auguste Comte

The Positive Philosophy

Excerpts from Auguste Comte, *The Positive Philosophy*.
freely translated and condensed by Harriet Martineau, John Chapman, 1853, 2 vols.[1]

The positive philosophy [2]

In order to understand the true value and character of the Positive
Philosophy, we must take a brief general view of the progressive course
of the human mind, regarded as a whole; for no conception can be
understood otherwise than through its history.

From the study of the development of human intelligence, in all
directions, and through all times, the discovery arises of a great
fundamental law, to which it is necessarily subject, and which has a
solid foundation of proof, both in the facts of our organization and
in our historical experience. The law is this: that each of our leading
conceptions, each branch of our knowledge, passes successively through
three different theoretical conditions: the Theological, or fictitious; the
Metaphysical, or abstract; and the Scientific, or positive. In other
words, the human mind, by its nature, employs in its progress three
methods of philosophizing, the character of which is essentially
different, and even radically opposed: viz, the theological method, the
metaphysical and the positive. Hence arise three philosophies, or
general systems of conceptions on the aggregate of phenomena, each
of which excludes the others. The first is the necessary point of
departure of the human understanding; and the third is its fixed and
definite state. The second is merely a state of transition.

In the theological state, the human mind, seeking the essential nature
of beings, the first and final causes (the origin and purpose) of all
effects – in short, Absolute knowledge – supposes all phenomena to be
produced by the immediate action of supernatural beings.

In the metaphysical state, which is only a modification of the first,
the mind supposes, instead of supernatural beings, abstract forces,
veritable entities (that is, personified abstractions) inherent in all beings,
and capable of producing all phenomena. What is called the explanation

1. The editors have divided this Reading into sections with their own headings.
Page references for each section are given with each heading.
2. Vol. 1, pp. 1–7.

of phenomena is, in this stage, a mere reference of each to its proper entity.

In the final, the positive state, the mind has given over the vain search after Absolute notions, the origin and destination of the universe, and the causes of phenomena, and applies itself to the study of their laws, that is, their invariable relations of succession and resemblance. Reasoning and observation, duly combined, are the means of this knowledge. What is now understood when we speak of an explanation of facts is simply the establishment of a connection between single phenomena and some general facts, the number of which continually diminishes with the progress of science.

The Theological system arrived at the highest perfection of which it is capable when it substituted the providential action of a single Being for the varied operations of the numerous divinities which had been before imagined. In the same way, in the last stage of the Metaphysical system, men substitute one great entity (Nature) as the cause of all phenomena, instead of the multitude of entities at first supposed. In the same way, again the ultimate perfection of the Positive system would be (if such perfection could be hoped for) to represent all phenomena as particular aspects of a single general fact; such as Gravitation, for instance.

The importance of the working of this general law will be established hereafter. At present, it must suffice to point out some of the grounds of it.

There is no science which, having attained the positive stage, does not bear marks of having passed through the others. Some time since it was (whatever it might be) composed, as we can now perceive, of metaphysical abstractions; and, further back in the course of time, it took its form from theological conceptions. We shall have only too much occasion to see, as we proceed, that our most advanced sciences still bear very evident marks of the two earlier periods through which they have passed.

The progress of the individual mind is not only an illustration, but an indirect evidence of that of the general mind. The point of departure of the individual and of the race being the same, the phases of the mind of a man correspond to the epochs of the mind of the race. Now, each of us is aware, if he looks back upon his own history, that he was a theologian in his childhood, a metaphysician in his youth and a natural philosopher in his manhood. All men who are up to their age can verify this for themselves.

Besides the observation of facts, we have theoretical reasons in support of this law.

The most important of these reasons arises from the necessity that always exists for some theory to which to refer our facts, combined with the clear impossibility that, at the outset of human knowledge, men could have formed theories out of the observations of facts. All good intellects have repeated, since Bacon's time, that there can be no real knowledge but that which is based on observed facts. This is incontestable, in our present advanced stage; but, if we look back to the primitive stage of human knowledge, we shall see that it must have been otherwise then. If it is true that every theory must be based upon observed facts, it is equally true that facts cannot be observed without the guidance of some theory. Without such guidance, our facts would be desultory and fruitless; we could not retain them: for the most part we could not even perceive them.

Thus, between the necessity of observing facts in order to form a theory, and having a theory in order to observe facts, the human mind would have been entangled in a vicious circle, but for the natural opening afforded by Theological conceptions. This is the fundamental reason for the theological character of the primitive philosophy. [. . .]

The Law of human development being thus established, let us consider what is the proper nature of the Positive Philosophy.

As we have seen, the first characteristic of the Positive Philosophy is that it regards all phenomena as subjected to invariable natural *Laws*. Our business is, seeing how vain is any research into what are called *Causes*, whether first or final, to pursue an accurate discovery of these Laws, with a view to reducing them to the smallest possible number. By speculating upon causes, we could solve no difficulty about origin and purpose. Our real business is to analyse accurately the circumstances of phenomena, and to connect them by the natural relations of succession and resemblance. [. . .]

Before ascertaining the stage which the Positive Philosophy has reached, we must bear in mind that the different kinds of our knowledge have passed through the three stages of progress at different rates, and have not therefore arrived at the same time. The rate of advance depends on the nature of the knowledge in question, so distinctly that, as we shall see hereafter, this consideration constitutes an accessary to the fundamental law of progress. Any kind of knowledge reaches the positive stage early in proportion to its generality, simplicity and independence of other departments. Astronomical science, which is above all made up of facts that are general, simple, and independent of other sciences, arrived first; then terrestrial Physics; then Chemistry; and, at length, Physiology. [. . .]

In mentioning just now the four principal categories of phenomena, astronomical, physical, chemical and physiological, there was an omission which will have been noticed. Nothing was said of Social phenomena. Though involved with the physiological, Social phenomena demand a distinct classification, both on account of their importance and of their difficulty. They are the most individual, the most complicated, the most dependent on all others; and therefore they must be the latest, even if they had no special obstacle to encounter. This branch of science has not hitherto entered into the domain of Positive philosophy. Theological and metaphysical methods, exploded in other departments, are as yet exclusively applied, both in the way of inquiry and discussion, in all treatment of Social subjects, though the best minds are heartily weary of eternal disputes about divine right and the sovereignty of the people.

The need for sociology and its relation to other disciplines [3]

The positive Philosophy offers the only solid basis for that Social Reorganization which must succeed the critical condition in which the most civilized nations are now living.

It cannot be necessary to prove to anybody who reads this work that Ideas govern the world, or throw it into chaos: in other words, that all social mechanism rests upon Opinions. The great political and moral crisis that societies are now undergoing is shown by a rigid analysis to arise out of intellectual anarchy. While stability in fundamental maxims is the first condition of genuine social order, we are suffering under an utter disagreement which may be called universal. Till a certain number of general ideas can be acknowledged as a rallying-point of social doctrine, the nations will remain in a revolutionary state, whatever palliatives may be devised; and their institutions can be only provisional. But whenever the necessary agreement on first principles can be obtained, appropriate institutions will issue from them, without shock or resistance; for the causes of disorder will have been arrested by the mere fact of the agreement. It is in this direction that those must look who desire a natural and regular, a normal state of society.

Now, the existing disorder is abundantly accounted for by the existence, all at once, of three incompatible philosophies, the theological, the metaphysical and the positive. Any one of these might alone secure some sort of social order; but while the three coexist, it is impossible for us to understand one another upon any essential point whatever.

[. . .] In all Social phenomena we perceive the working of the physiological laws of the individual; and moreover something which modifies

3. Vol. 1, pp. 14–15, 27–8, 503–4; vol. 2, pp. 63–73.

their effects, and which belongs to the influence of individuals over each other – singularly complicated in the case of the human race by the influence of generations on their successors. Thus it is clear that our social science must issue from that which relates to the life of the individual. On the other hand, there is no occasion to suppose, as some eminent physiologists have done, that Social Physics is only an appendage to physiology. The phenomena of the two are not identical, though they are homogeneous; and it is of high importance to hold the two sciences separate. As social conditions modify the operation of physiological laws, Social Physics must have a set of observations of its own. [...]

Thus we have before us Five fundamental Sciences in successive dependence, Astronomy, Physics, Chemistry, Physiology and finally Social Physics. The first considers the most general, simple, abstract and remote phenomena known to us, and those which affect all others without being affected by them. The last considers the most particular, compound, concrete phenomena, and those which are the most interesting to Man. Between these two, the degrees of speciality, of complexity and individuality are in regular proportion to the place of the respective sciences in the scale exhibited. [...]

The only really universal point of view is the human, or, speaking more exactly, the social. This is the only one which recurs and is perpetually renewed, in every department of thought; in regard to the external world as well as to Man. Thus, if we want to conceive of the rights of the sociological spirit to supremacy, we have only to regard all our conceptions, as I have explained before, as so many necessary results of a series of determinate phases, proper to our mental evolution, personal and collective, taking place according to invariable laws, statical and dynamical, which rational observation is competent to disclose. Since philosophers have begun to meditate deeply on intellectual phenomena, they have always been more or less convinced, in spite of all prepossession, of the inevitable reality of these fundamental laws; for their existence is always supposed in every study, in which any conclusion whatever would be impossible if the formation and variation of our opinions were not subject to a regular order, independent of our will, and the pathological change of which is known to be in no way arbitrary. But, besides the extreme difficulty of the subject and its vicious management hitherto, human reason being capable of growth only in social circumstances, it is clear that no decisive discovery could be made in this way till society should have attained a generality of view which was not possible till our day. Imperfect as sociological study may yet be, it furnishes us with a principle which justifies and guides its intervention, scientific and logical, in all the essential parts of the speculative system, which can thus alone be brought into unity. [. . .]

Sociology and art

[. . .] The same considerations apply to the aesthetic case. The sociological mode must be fittest to regulate the subordination of the sense of the beautiful to the knowledge of the true: and the scientific spirit most disposed to unity must be most suitable to the synthetic character of aesthetic contemplation, which always, perceptibly or not, relates to the emotions of the human being. If the positive philosophy has been often reproached with its anti-aesthetic character, it is owing to the sway of the mathematical spirit for three centuries, the dispersive and mechanical tendency of which affords fair ground for the reproach. By its contrasting character of true and fertile unity, the sociological philosophy will prove itself more favourable to Art than the theological, even in the polytheistic period. The positive spirit, in its sociological form, undertakes to disclose the general laws of the human evolution, of which the aesthetic evolution is one of the chief elements; and the requisite historical process is eminently adapted to exhibit the relation which must ever subordinate the sentiment of ideal perfection to the idea of real existence: and by discarding henceforth all superhuman intervention, sociological philosophy will establish an irreversible agreement between the aesthetic and scientific points of view.

On economics

[. . .] The avowal of the economists that their science is isolated from that of social philosophy in general, is itself a sufficient confirmation of my judgement; for it is a universal fact in social, as in biological science, that all the various general aspects of the subject are scientifically one, and rationally inseparable, so that they cannot but be illustrated but by each other. Thus, the economical or industrial analysis of society cannot be effected in the positive method, apart from its intellectual, moral and political analysis, past and present. [. . .]

As each serious difficulty arises, in the course of industrial development, political economy ignores it. In the great question of machinery this is remarkably illustrated. This is one of the cases of inconvenience inherent in every industrial improvement, from its tendency to disturb, more or less, and for a longer or shorter time, the mode of life of the labouring classes. Instead of recognizing in the urgent remonstrances called forth by this chasm in our social order one of the most eminent and pressing occasions for the application of social science, our economists can do nothing better than repeat, with pitiless pedantry, their barren aphorism of absolute industrial liberty.

On history

[...] Still history has more of a literary and descriptive than of a scientific character. It does not yet establish a rational filiation in the series of social events, so as to admit (as in other sciences and allowing for its greater complexity) of any degree of systematic prevision of their future succession.

The positive method

[...] If we contemplate the positive spirit in its relation to scientific conception, rather than the mode of procedure, we shall find that this philosophy is distinguished from the theologico – metaphysical by its tendency to render relative the ideas which were at first absolute.

All investigation into the nature of beings, and their first and final causes, must always be absolute; whereas the study of the laws of phenomena must be relative, since it supposes a continuous progress of speculation subject to the gradual improvement of observation, without the precise reality being ever fully disclosed. [...]

We have to contemplate social phenomena as susceptible of prevision, like all other classes, within the limits of exactness compatible with their higher complexity.

Statistics and dynamics [4]

The philosophical principle of the science being that social phenomena are subject to natural laws, admitting of rational prevision, we have to ascertain what is the precise subject, and what the peculiar character of those laws. The distinction between the Statical and Dynamical conditions of the subject must be extended to social science; and I shall treat of the conditions of social existence as, in biology, I treated of organization under the head of anatomy; and then of the laws of social movement, as in biology of those of life, under the head of physiology. This division, necessary for exploratory purposes, must not be stretched beyond that use: and, as we saw in Biology, that the distinction becomes weaker with the advance of science, so shall we see that when the science of social physics is fully constituted, this division will remain for analytical purposes, but not as a real separation of the science into two parts. The distinction is not between two classes of facts, but between two aspects of a theory. It corresponds with the double conception of order and progress: for order consists (in a positive sense) in a permanent harmony among the conditions of social existence; and progress consists in social development; and the conditions in the one

4. Vol. 2, pp. 74–84, 127, 132, 140, 149–50, 156–7.

case, and the laws of movement in the other, constitute the statics and dynamics of social physics. [. . .]

The statical study of sociology consists in the investigation of the laws of action and reaction of the different parts of the social system, apart, for the occasion, from the fundamental movement which is always gradually modifying them. In this view, sociological prevision, founded upon the exact general knowledge of those relations, acts by judging by each other the various statical indications of each mode of social existence, in conformity with direct observation, just as is done daily in the case of anatomy. This view condemns the existing philosophical practice of contemplating social elements separately, as if they had an independent existence; and it leads us to regard them as in mutual relation, and forming a whole which compels us to treat them in combination.

The scientific principle of the relation between the political and the social condition is simply this; that there must always be a spontaneous harmony between the whole and the parts of the social system, the elements of which must inevitably be, sooner or later, combined in a mode entirely conformable to their nature. . . . Even during revolutionary periods, when the harmony appears furthest from being duly realized, it still exists: for without it there would be a total dissolution of the social organism. During these exceptional seasons, the political regime is still, in the long run, in conformity with the corresponding state of civilization, as the disturbances which are manifest in the one proceed from equivalent derangements in the other. [. . .]

It is, in fact, true that wherever there is any system whatever, a certain interconnection must exist. [. . .]

It follows from this attribute that there can be no scientific study of society, either in its conditions or its movements, if it is separated into portions, and its divisions are studied apart. [. . .]

Before we go on to the subject of social dynamics, I will just remark that the prominent interconnection we have been considering prescribes a procedure in organic studies different from that which suits inorganic. [. . .]

Now, in the inorganic sciences, the elements are much better known to us than the whole which they constitute: so that in that case we must proceed from the simple to the compound. But the reverse method is necessary in the study of Man and Society; Man and Society as a whole being better known to us, and more accessible subjects of study, than the parts which constitute them. In exploring the universe, it is as a whole that it is inaccessible to us; whereas, in investigating Man or Society, our difficulty is in penetrating the details. [. . .]

Passing on from statical to dynamical sociology, we will contemplate the philosophical conception which should govern our study of the movement of society. [. . .]

Though the statical view of society is the basis of sociology, the dynamical view is not only the more interesting of the two, but the more marked in its philosophical character, from its being more distinguished from biology by the master-thought of continuous progress, or rather, of the gradual development of humanity. [. . .]

The true general spirit of social dynamics then consists in conceiving of each of these consecutive social states as the necessary result of the preceding, and the indispensable mover of the following, according to the axiom of Leibnitz, *the present is big with the future.* In this view, the object of science is to discover the laws which govern this continuity, and the aggregate of which determines the course of human development. In short, social dynamics studies the laws of succession, while social statics inquires into those of coexistence. [. . .]

Though the dynamical part of Social Science is the most interesting, the most easily intelligible, and the fittest to disclose the laws of interconnection, still the Statical part must not be entirely passed over.

Every sociological analysis supposes three classes of considerations, each more complex than the preceding: viz., the conditions of social existence of the individual, the family, and society. [. . .]

As every system must be composed of elements of the same nature with itself, the scientific spirit forbids us to regard society as composed of individuals. The true social unit is certainly the family, reduced, if necessary, to the elementary couple which forms its base. [. . .]

The main cause of the superiority of the social to the individual organism is, according to an established law, the more marked speciality of the various functions fulfilled by organs more and more distinct, but interconnected; so that unity is more and more combined with diversity of means. We cannot, of course, fully appreciate a phenomenon which is for ever proceeding before our eyes, and in which we bear a part; but if we withdraw ourselves in thought from the social system, and contemplate it as from afar, can we conceive of a more marvellous spectacle, in the whole range of natural phenomena, than the regular and constant convergence of an innumerable multitude of human beings, each possessing a distinct and, in a certain degree, independent existence, and yet incessantly disposed, amidst all their discordance of talent and character, to concur in many ways in the same general development, without concert, and even consciousness on the part of most of them, who believe that they are merely following their personal impulses? This is the scientific picture of the phenomenon:

and no temporary disturbances can prevent its being, under all circumstances, essentially true. [...]

If we regard the course of human development from the highest scientific point of view, we shall perceive that it consists in educing, more and more, the characteristic faculties of humanity, in comparison with those of animality; and especially with those which Man has in common with the whole organic kingdom.

The whole system of biological philosophy indicates the natural progression. We have seen how, in the brute kingdom, the superiority of each race is determined by the degree of preponderance of the animal life over the organic. In like manner, we see that our social evolution is only the final term of a progression which has continued from the simplest vegetables and most insignificant animals, up through the higher reptiles, to the birds and the mammifers, and still on to the carnivorous animals and monkeys, the organic characteristics retiring, and the animal prevailing more and more, till the intellectual and moral tend towards the ascendancy which can never be fully obtained even in the highest state of human perfection that we can conceive of. This comparative estimate affords us the scientific view of human progression, connected, as we see it is with the whole course of animal advancement, of which it is itself the highest degree. [...]

Civilization develops, to an enormous degree, the action of Man upon his environment: and thus, it may seem, at first, to concentrate our attention upon the cares of material existence, the support and improvement of which appear to be the chief object of most social occupations. A closer examination will show, however, that this development gives the advantage to the highest human faculties, both by the security which sets free our attention from physical wants, and by the direct and steady excitement which it administers to the intellectual functions, and even the social feelings. [...]

Though the elements of our social evolution are connected, and always acting on each other, one must be preponderant, in order to give an impulse to the rest, though they may, in their turn, so act upon it as to cause its further expansion.

[...] intellectual evolution [is] the preponderant principle. If the intellectual point of view was the chief in our statical study of the organism, much more must it be so in the dynamical case. [...] If the statical analysis of our social organism shows it resting at length upon a certain system of fundamental opinions, the gradual changes of that system must affect the successive modifications of the life of humanity: and this is why, since the birth of philosophy, the history of society has been regarded as governed by the history of the human mind. [...]

As it is necessary in a scientific study, to refer our historical analysis to the preponderant evolution, whatever it may be, we must in this case choose, or rather preserve, the general history of the human mind as the natural guide to all historical study of humanity. One consequence of the same principle, a consequence as rigorous but less understood, is that we must choose for consideration in this intellectual history, the most general and abstract conceptions, which require the exercise of our highest faculties. Thus it is the study of the fundamental system of human opinions with regard to the whole of phenomena, in short, the history of Philosophy, whatever may be its character, theological, metaphysical or positive, which must regulate our historical analysis.

We may now proceed at once to investigate the natural laws by which the advance of the human mind proceeds. The scientific principle of the theory appears to one to consist in the great philosophical law of the succession of the three states: the primitive theological state, the transient metaphysical and the final positive state, through which the human mind has to pass, in every kind of speculation.

The methods of sociology [5]

We must observe, in the first place, that social phenomena may, from their complexity, be more easily modified than any others, according to the law which was established to that effect in my first volume. Thus, the limits of variation are wider in regard to sociological than any other laws. If, then, human intervention holds the same proportionate rank among modifying influences as it is natural at first to suppose, its influence must be more considerable in the first case than in any other, all appearances to the contrary notwithstanding. This is the first scientific foundation of all rational hopes of a systematic reformation of humanity ; and on this ground illusions of this sort certainly appear more excusable than on any other subject. But though modifications, from all causes, are greater in the case of political than of simpler phenomena, still they can never be more than modifications: that is, they will always be in subjection to those fundamental laws, whether statical or dynamical, which regulate the harmony of the social elements, and the filiation of their successive variations.

[. . .] Thus, then, we see what is the function of social science. Without extolling or condemning political facts, science regards them as subjects of observation: it contemplates each phenomenon in its harmony with co-existing phenomena, and in its connection with the foregoing and the following state of human development: it endeavours

5. Vol. 2, pp. 90–106.

to discover, from both points of view, the general relations which connect all social phenomena: and each of them is *explained*, in the scientific sense of the word, when it has been connected with the whole of the existing situation, and the whole of the preceding movement.

As Social Physics assumes a place in the hierarchy of sciences after all the rest, and therefore dependent on them, its means of investigation must be of two kinds: those which are peculiar to itself, and which may be called direct, and those which arise from the connection of sociology with the other sciences ; and these last, though indirect, are as indispensable as the first. I shall review, first, the direct resources of the science.

Here, as in all the other cases, there are three methods of proceeding: by Observation, Experiment and Comparison.... No real observation of any kind of phenomena is possible, except in as far as it is first directed, and finally interpreted, by some theory: and it was this logical need which, in the infancy of human reason, occasioned the rise of theological philosophy, as we shall see in the course of our historical survey. The positive philosophy does not dissolve this obligation, but, on the contrary, extends and fulfils it more and more, the further the relations of phenomena are multiplied and perfected by it. Hence it is clear that, scientifically speaking, all isolated, empirical observation is idle, and even radically uncertain ; that science can use only those observations which are connected, at least hypothetically, with some law ; that it is such a connection which makes the chief difference between scientific and popular observation, embracing the same facts, but contemplating them from different points of view: and that observations empirically conducted can at most supply provisional materials, which must usually undergo an ulterior revision. The rational method of observation becomes more necessary in proportion to the complexity of the phenomena, amidst which the observer would not know what he ought to look at in the facts before his eyes, but for the guidance of a preparatory theory ; and thus it is that by the connection of foregoing facts we learn to see the facts that follow.

[...] [in] social science, there is more need than anywhere else of theories which shall scientifically connect the facts that are happening with those that have happened: and the more we reflect, the more distinctly we shall see that in proportion as known facts are mutually connected we shall be better able, not only to estimate, but to perceive, those which are yet unexplored. I am not blind to the vast difficulty which this requisition imposes on the institution of positive sociology, obliging us to create at once, so to speak, observations and laws, on account of their indispensable connection, placing us in a sort of vicious circle, from which we can issue only by employing in the first instance materials which are badly elaborated, and doctrines which are ill-conceived. How I may succeed in a task so difficult and delicate, we shall see at its close; but, however that may be, it is clear that it is the absence of any positive theory which at present renders social observations so vague and incoherent. There can never be any lack of facts; for in this case even more than in others, it is the commonest sort of facts that are most important, whatever the collectors of secret anecdotes may think; but, though we are steeped to the lips in them, we can make no use of them, nor even be aware of them, for want of speculative guidance in examining them. The statical observation of a crowd of phenomena cannot take place without some notion, however elementary, of the laws of social interconnection: and dynamical facts could have no fixed direction if they were not attached, at least by a provisional hypothesis, to the laws of social development. The positive philosophy is very far from discouraging historical or any other erudition; but the precious night-watchings, now so lost in the laborious acquisition of a conscientious but barren learning, may be made available by it for the constitution of true social science, and the increased honour of the earnest minds that are devoted to it. [. . .]

It might be supposed beforehand that the second method of investigation, Experiment, must be wholly inapplicable in Social Science; but we shall find that the science is not entirely deprived of this resource, though it must be one of inferior value. We must remember (what was before explained) that there are two kinds of experimentation; the direct and the indirect: and that it is not necessary to the philosophical character of this method that the circumstances of the phenomenon in question should be, as is vulgarly supposed in the learned world, artificially instituted. Whether the case be natural or factitious, experimentation takes place whenever the regular course of the phenomenon is interfered with in any determinate manner. The spontaneous nature of the alteration has no effect on the scientific value of the case, if the elements are known. It is in this sense that experimentation is possible in Sociology. If direct experimentation had become too difficult amidst the complexities of biology, it may well be considered impossible in social science. Any artificial disturbance of any social element must affect all the rest, according to the laws both of coexistence and succession; and the experiment would therefore, if it could be instituted at all, be deprived of all scientific value, through the impossibility of isolating either the conditions or the results of the phenomenon. But we saw, in our survey of biology, that pathological cases are the true scientific equivalent of pure experimentation, and why. The same reasons apply, with even more force, to sociological researches. In them, pathological analysis consists in the examination of cases, unhappily too common, in which the natural laws, either of harmony or of succession, are disturbed by any causes, special or general, accidental or transient; as in revolutionary times especially; and above all, in our own. These disturbances are, in the social body, exactly analogous to diseases in the individual organism. [. . .]

As for the third of those methods, Comparison, the reader must bear in mind the explanations offered, in our survey of biological philosophy, of the reasons why the comparative method must prevail in all studies of which the living organism is the subject; and the more remarkably, in proportion to the rank of the organism. [. . .]

To indicate the order of importance of the forms of society which are to be studied by the Comparative Method, I begin with the chief method, which consists in a comparison of the different coexisting states of human society on the various parts of the earth's surface, those states being completely independent of each other. By this method, the different stages of evolution may all be observed at once. Though the progression is single and uniform, in regard to the whole race, some very considerable and very various populations have, from causes which are little understood, attained extremely unequal degrees of development. [. . .]

The historical comparison of the consecutive states of humanity is not only the chief scientific device of the new political philosophy. Its rational development constitutes the substratum of the science, in whatever is essential to it. [. . .]

The prevailing tendency to speciality in study would reduce history to a mere accumulation of unconnected delineations, in which all idea of the true filiation of events would be lost amidst the mass of confused descriptions. If the historical comparisons of the different periods of civilization are to have any scientific character, they must be referred to the general social evolution: and it is only thus that we can obtain the guiding ideas by which the special studies themselves must be directed. [. . .]

On the materialist view of history [6]

One consideration remains, of the more importance: . . . I mean the consideration of Man's action on the external world, the gradual development of which affords one of the chief aspects of the social evolution, and without which the evolution could not have taken place as a

6. Vol. 2, pp. 118, 144.

whole, as it would have been stopped at once by the preponderance of the material obstacles proper to the human condition. In short, all human progress, political, moral or intellectual, is inseparable from material progression, in virtue of the close interconnection which, as we have seen, characterizes the natural course of social phenomena. Now it is clear that the action of Man upon nature depends chiefly on his knowledge of the laws of inorganic phenomena, though biological phenomena must also find a place in it. [. . .]

Human automatism of the division of labour

If we have been accustomed to deplore the spectacle, among the artisan class, of a workman occupied during his whole life in nothing else but making knife-handles or pins' heads, we may find something quite as lamentable in the intellectual class, in the exclusive employment of a human brain in resolving some equations, or in classifying insects. The moral effect is, unhappily, analogous in the two cases. It occasions a miserable indifference about the general course of human affairs, as long as there are equations to resolve and pins to manufacture. This is an extreme case of human automatism; but the frequency, and the growing frequency of the evil gives a real scientific importance to the case, as indicating the general tendency, and warning us to restrain it. [. . .]

3 Herbert Spencer

The Study of Sociology

Excerpts from Herbert Spencer, *The Study of Sociology*. Kegan Paul, Trench & Co., 1873, pp. 385–413 ; *The Principles of Sociology,* Williams & Norgate, vol. 1, 1876, pp. 580–85, vol. 3, 1897, pp. 325, 599.

The study of Sociology [is] the study of Evolution in its most complex form. It is clear that to one who considers the facts societies exhibit as having had their origin in supernatural interpositions, or in the wills of individual ruling men, the study of these facts will have an aspect wholly unlike that which it has to one who contemplates them as generated by processes of growth and development continuing through centuries. Ignoring as the first view tacitly does, that conformity to law, in the scientific sense of the word, which the second view tacitly asserts, there can be but little community between the methods of inquiry proper to them respectively. Continuous causation, which in the one case there is little or no tendency to trace, becomes, in the other case, the chief object of attention ; whence it follows that there must be formed wholly-different ideas of the appropriate modes of investigation. A foregone conclusion respecting the nature of social phenomena, is thus inevitably implied in any suggestions for the study of them.

While, however, it must be admitted that throughout this work there runs the assumption that the facts, simultaneous and successive, which societies present, have a genesis no less natural than the genesis of facts of all other classes ; it is not admitted that this assumption was made unawares, or without warrant. At the outset, the grounds for it were examined. The notion, widely accepted in name though not consistently acted upon, that social phenomena differ from phenomena of most other kinds as being under special providence, we found to be entirely discredited by its expositors ; nor, when closely looked into, did the great-man-theory of social affairs prove to be more tenable. Besides finding that both these views, rooted as they are in the ways of thinking natural to primitive men, would not bear criticism ; we found that even their defenders continually betrayed their beliefs in the production of social changes by natural causes – tacitly admitted that after certain antecedents certain consequents are to be expected – tacitly admitted, therefore, that some prevision is possible, and therefore some subject-matter for Science. From these negative justifications for the belief that Sociology is a science, we turned to the positive justifications. We found that every aggregate of units of any order, has certain traits necessarily determined by the properties of its units. Hence it was inferable, *a priori,* that, given the natures of the men who are their units, and certain characters in the societies formed are pre-determined — other characters being determined by the cooperation of surrounding conditions. The current assertion that Sociology is not possible, implies a misconception of its nature. Using the analogy supplied by a human life, we saw that just as bodily development and structure and function, furnish subject matter for biological science, though the events set forth by the biographer go beyond its range ; so, social growth, and the rise of structures and functions accompanying it, furnish subject matter for a Science of Society, though the facts with which historians fill their pages mostly yield no material for Science. Thus conceiving the scope of the science, we saw, on comparing rudimentary societies with one another and with societies in different stages of progress, that they *do* present certain common traits of structure and of function, as well as certain common traits of development. Further comparisons similiarly made opened large questions, such as that of the relation between social growth and organization, which form parts of this same science ; — questions of transcendent importance compared with those occupying the minds of politicians and writers of history.

The difficulties of the Social Science next drew our attention. We saw that in this case, though in no other case, the facts to be observed and generalized by the student, are exhibited by an aggregate of which he forms a part. In his capacity of inquirer he should have no inclination towards one or other conclusion respecting the phenomena to be generalized ; but in his capacity of citizen, helped to live by the life of his society, imbedded in its structures, sharing in its activities, breathing its atmosphere of thought and sentiment, he is partially coerced into such views as favour harmonious cooperation with his fellow-citizens. Hence immense obstacles to the Social Science, unparalleled by those standing in the way of any other science.

From considering thus generally these causes of error, we turned to consider them specially. Under the head of objective difficulties, we glanced at those many ways in which evidence collected by the sociological inquirer is vitiated. That extreme untrustworthiness of witnesses which results from carelessness, or fanaticism, or self-interest, was illustrated ; and we saw that, in addition to the perversions of statement hence arising, there are others which arise from the tendency there is for some kinds of evidence to draw attention, while evidence of opposite kinds, much larger in quantity, draws no attention. Further, it was shown that the nature of sociological facts, each of which is not observable in a single object or act, but is reached only through registration and comparison of many objects and acts, makes the perception of them harder than that of other facts. It was pointed out that the wide distribution of social phenomena in Space, greatly hinders true apprehensions of them; and it was also pointed out that another impediment, even still greater, is consequent on their distribution in Time – a distribution such that many of the facts to be dealt with, take centuries to unfold, and can be grasped only by combining in thought multitudinous changes that are slow, involved, and not easy to trace. Beyond these difficulties which we grouped as distinguishing the science itself, objectively considered, we saw that there are other difficulties, conveniently to be grouped as subjective, which are also great. For the interpretation of human conduct as socially displayed, every one is compelled to use, as a key, his own nature – ascribing to others thoughts and feelings like his own; and yet, while this automorphic interpretation is indispensable, it is necessarily more or less misleading. Very generally, too, a subjective difficulty arises from the lack of intellectual faculty complex enough to grasp these social phenomena, which are so extremely involved. And again, very few have by culture gained that plasticity of faculty requisite for conceiving and accepting those immensely-varied actualities which societies in different times and places display, and those multitudinous possibilities to be inferred from them. Nor, of subjective difficulties, did these exhaust the list. From the emotional, as well as from the intellectual, part of the nature, we saw that there arise obstacles. The ways in which beliefs about social affairs are perverted by intense fears and excited hopes, were pointed out. We noted the feeling of impatience, as another common cause of misjudgement. A contrast was drawn showing, too, what perverse estimates of public events men are led to make by their sympathies and antipathies – how, where their hate has been aroused, they utter unqualified condemnations of ill-deeds for which there was much excuse, while, if their admiration is excited by vast successes, they condone inexcusable ill-deeds immeasurably greater in amount. And we also saw that among the distortions of judgement caused by the emotions, have to be included those immense ones generated by the sentiment of loyalty to a personal ruler, or to a ruling power otherwise embodied.

[. . .] Recognizing the truth that the preservation of a society is made possible only by a due amount of patriotic feeling in citizens, we saw that this feeling inevitably disturbs the judgement when comparisons between societies are made, and that the data required for Social Science are thus vitiated ; and we saw that the effort to escape this bias, leading as it does to an opposite bias, is apt to vitiate the data in another way. While finding the class-bias to be no less essential, we found that it no less inevitably causes one-sidedness in the conceptions of social affairs. Noting how the various sub-classes have their specialities of prejudice corresponding to their class-interests, we noted, at greater length, how the more general prejudices of the larger and more widely-distinguished classes, prevent them from forming balanced judgements. That in politics the bias of party interferes with those calm examinations by which alone the conclusions of Social Science can be reached, scarcely needed pointing out. We observed, however, that beyond the political bias under its party-form, there is a more general political bias – the bias towards an exclusively-political view of social affairs, and a corresponding faith in political instrumentalities. As affecting the study of Social Science, this bias was shown to be detrimental as directing the attention too much to the phenomena of social regulation, and excluding from thought the activities regulated, constituting an aggregate of phenomena far more important. [. . .]

Having thus contemplated, in general and in detail, the difficulties of the Social Science, we turned our attention to the preliminary discipline required. Of the conclusions reached so recently, the reader scarcely needs reminding. Study of the sciences in general having been pointed out as the proper means of generating fit habits of thought, it was shown that the sciences especially to be attended to are those treating of Life and of Mind. There can be no understanding of social actions without some knowledge of human nature ; there can be no deep knowledge of human nature without some knowledge of the laws of Mind ; there can be no adequate knowledge of the laws of Mind without knowledge of the laws of Life. And that knowledge of the Laws of Life, as exhibited in Man, may be properly grasped, attention must be given to the laws of Life in general.

[. . .] The implication throughout the argument has been that for every society, and for each stage in its evolution, there is an appropriate mode of feeling and thinking ; and that no mode of feeling and thinking not adapted to its degree of evolution, and to its surroundings, can be permanently established. Though not exactly, still approximately, the average opinion in any age and country, is a function of the social structure in that age and country. There may be, as we see during times of revolution, a considerable incongruity between the ideas that become current and the social arrangements which exist, and are, in great measure, appropriate ; though even then the incongruity does but mark the need for a re-adjustment of institutions to character. While, however, those successive compromises which, during social evolution, have to be made between the changed natures of citizens and the institutions evolved by ancestral citizens, imply disagreements, yet these are but partial and temporary – in those societies, at least, which are developing and not in course of dissolution. For a society to hold together, the institutions that are needed and the conceptions that are generally current, must be in tolerable harmony. Hence, it is not to be expected that modes of thinking on social affairs, are to be in any considerable degree changed by whatever may be said respecting the Social Science, its difficulties, and the required preparations for studying it.

The only reasonable hope is, that here and there one may be led, in calmer moments, to remember how largely his beliefs about public matters have been made for him by circumstances, and how probable it is that they are either untrue or but partially true. [. . .]

The illogicalities and the absurdities to be found so abundantly in current opinions and existing arrangements, are those which inevitably arise in the course of perpetual re-adjustments to circumstances perpetually changing. Ideas and institutions proper to a past social state, but incongruous with the new social state that has grown out of it, surviving into this new social state they have made possible, and disappearing only as this new social state establishes its own ideas and institutions, are necessarily, during their survival, in conflict with these new ideas and institutions – necessarily furnish elements of contradiction in men's thoughts and deeds. And yet as, for the carrying-on of social life, the old must continue so long as the new is not ready, this perpetual compromise is an indispensable accompaniment of a normal development. [. . .]

[. . .] From the doctrines set forth in this work, some have drawn the corollary that effort in furtherance of progress is superfluous. 'If', they argue, 'the evolution of a society conforms general laws – if the changes which, in the slow course of things bring it about, are naturally determined ; then what need is there of endeavours to aid it? The hypothesis implies that the transformation results from causes beyond individual wills ; and, if so, the acts of individuals in fulfilment of their wills are not required to effect it. Hence we may occupy ourselves exclusively with personal concerns ; leaving social evolution to go its own way.'

This is a misapprehension naturally fallen into and not quite easy to escape from ; for to get out of it the citizen must simultaneously conceive himself as one whose will is a factor in social evolution, and yet as one whose will is a product of all antecedent influences, social included.

[. . .] An analogy will best show how there may be reconciled the two propositions that social evolution is a process conforming to natural laws, and yet that it results from the voluntary efforts of citizens.

It is a truth statistically established, that in each community, while its conditions remain the same, there is a uniform rate of marriage: such variations in the numbers of marriages as accompany variations in the prices of food, serving to show that so long as the impediments to marriage do not vary the frequency of marriages does not vary. Similarly, it is found that along with an average frequency of marriages there goes an average frequency of births. But though these averages show that the process of human multiplication presents uniformities, implying constancy in the action of general causes, it is not therefore inferred that the process of human multiplication is independent of people's wills. If anyone were to argue that marriages and births, considered in the aggregate, are social phenomena statistically proved to depend on influences which operate uniformly, and that therefore the maintenance of population does not depend on individual actions, his inference would be rejected as absurd. Daily experience proves that marrying and the rearing of children in each case result from the pursuit of exclusively private ends. It is only by fulfilling their individual wills in establishing and maintaining the domestic relations, that citizens produce these aggregate results which exhibit uniformities apparently independent of individual wills. In this instance, then, it is obvious that social phenomena follow certain general courses ; and yet that they can do this only on condition that social units voluntarily act out their natures. While everyone holds that, in the matter of marriage, his will is, in the ordinary sense of the word, free ; yet he is obliged to recognize the fact that his will, and the wills of others, are so far determined by common elements of human nature, as to produce these average social results ; and that no such social results could be produced did they not fulfil their wills. [. . .][1]

Here let it once more be distinctly asserted that there exist no analogies between the body politic and a living body, save those necessitated by that mutual dependence of parts which they display in com-

1. The excerpt from *The Principles of Sociology*, vol. 1, starts here.

mon. Though, in foregoing chapters, sundry comparisons of social structures and functions to structures and functions in the human body, have been made, they have been made only because structures and functions in the human body furnish familiar illustrations of structures and functions in general. The social organism, discrete instead of concrete, asymmetrical instead of symmetrical, sensitive in all its units instead of having a single sensitive centre, is not comparable to any particular type of individual organism, animal or vegetal. All kinds of creatures are alike in so far as each exhibits cooperation among its components for the benefit of the whole ; and this trait, common to them, is a trait common also to societies. Further, among individual organisms, the degree of cooperation measures the degree of evolution ; and this general truth, too, holds among social organisms. Once more, to effect increasing cooperation, creatures of every order show us increasingly complex appliances for transfer and mutual influence ; and to this general characteristic, societies of every order furnish a corresponding characteristic. These, then are the analogies alleged: community in the fundamental principles of organization is the only community asserted.

But now let us drop this alleged parallelism between individual organizations and social organizations. I have used the analogies elaborated, but as a scaffolding to help in building up a coherent body of sociological inductions. Let us take away the scaffolding: the inductions will stand by themselves.

We saw that societies are aggregates which grow ; that in the various types of them there are great varieties in the growths reached ; that types of successively larger sizes result from the aggregation and re-aggregation of those of smaller sizes ; and that this increase by coalescence, joined with interstitial increase, is the process through which have been formed the vast civilized nations.

Along with increase of size in societies goes increase of structure. Primitive hordes are without established distinctions of parts. With growth of them into tribes habitually come some unlikenesses ; both in the powers and occupations of their members. Unions of tribes are followed by more unlikenesses, governmental and industrial – social grades running through the whole mass, and contrasts between the differently-occupied parts in different localities. Such differentiations multiply as the compounding progresses. They proceed from the general to the special. First the broad division between ruling and ruled ; then within the ruling part divisions into political, religious, military, and within the ruled part divisions into food-producing classes and handicraftsmen ; then within each of these divisions minor ones, and so on.

Passing from the structural aspect to the functional aspect, we note that so long as all parts of a society have like natures and activities, there is hardly any mutual dependence, and the aggregate scarcely forms a vital whole. As its parts assume different functions they become dependent on one another, so that injury to one hurts others ; until, in highly-evolved societies, general perturbation is caused by derangement of any portion. This contrast between undeveloped and developed societies, arises from the fact that with increasing specialization of functions comes increasing inability in each part to perform the functions of other parts.

The organization of every society begins with a contrast between the division which carries on relations, habitually hostile, with environing societies, and the division which is devoted to procuring necessaries of life ; and during the earlier stages of development these two divisions constitute the whole. Eventually there arises an intermediate division serving to transfer products and influences from part to part. And in all subsequent stages, evolution of the two earlier systems of structures depends on evolution of this additional system.

While the society as a whole has the character of its sustaining system determined by the character of its environment, inorganic and organic, the respective parts of this system differentiate in adaptation to local circumstances ; and, after primary industries have been thus localized and specialized, secondary industries dependent on them arise in conformity with the same principle. Further, as fast as societies become compounded and re-compounded, and the distributing system develops, the parts devoted to each kind of industry, originally scattered, aggregate in the most favourable localities ; and the localized industrial structures, unlike the governmental structures, grow regardless of the original lines of division.

Increase of size, resulting from the massing of groups, necessitates means of communication ; both for achieving combined offensive and defensive actions, and for exchange of products. Faint tracks, then paths, rude roads, finished roads, successively arise ; and as fast as intercourse is thus facilitated, there is a transition from direct barter to trading carried on by a separate class ; out of which evolves a complex mercantile agency of wholesale and retail distributors. The movement of commodities effected by this agency, beginning as a slow flux to and re-flux from certain places at long intervals, passes into rhythmical, regular, rapid currents ; and materials for sustentation distributed hither and thither, from being few and crude become numerous and elaborated. Growing efficiency of transfer with greater variety of transferred products, increases the mutual dependence of parts at the same time that it enables each part to fulfil its function better.

Unlike the sustaining system, evolved by converse with the organic and inorganic environments, the regulating system is evolved by converse, offensive and defensive, with environing societies. In primitive headless groups temporary chieftainship results from temporary war; chronic hostilities generate permanent chieftainship; and gradually from the military control results the civil control. Habitual war, requiring prompt combination in the actions of parts, necessitates subordination. Societies in which there is little subordination disappear, and leave outstanding those in which subordination is great; and so there are produced, societies in which the habit fostered by war and surviving in peace, brings about permanent submission to a government. The centralized regulating system thus evolved, is in early stages the sole regulating system. But in large societies which have become predominantly industrial, there is added a decentralized regulating system for the industrial structures; and this, at first subject in every way to the original system, acquires at length substantial independence. Finally there arises for the distributing structures also, an independent controlling agency.

Societies fall firstly into the classes of simple, compound, doubly-compound, trebly-compound; and from the lowest the transition to the highest is through these stages. Otherwise, though less definitely, societies may be grouped as militant and industrial; of which the one type in its developed form is organized on the principle of compulsory cooperation, while the other in its developed form is organized on the principle of voluntary cooperation. The one is characterized not only by a despotic central power, but also by unlimited political control of personal conduct; while the other is characterized not only by a democratic or representative central power, but also by limitation of political control over personal conduct.

Lastly we noted the corollary that change in the predominant social activities brings metamorphosis. If, where the militant type has not elaborated into so rigid a form as to prevent change, a considerable industrial system arises, there come mitigations of the coercive restraints characterizing the militant type, and weakening of its structures. Conversely, where an industrial system largely developed has established freer social forms, resumption of offensive and defensive activities causes reversion towards the militant type.

And now, summing up the results of this general survey, let us observe the extent to which we are prepared by it for further inquiries.

The many facts contemplated unite in proving that social evolution forms a part of evolution at large. Like evolving aggregates in general, societies show *integration*, both by simple increase of mass and by coalescence and re-coalescence of masses. The change from *homogeneity* to *heterogeneity* is multitudinously exemplified; up from the simple tribe, alike in all its parts, to the civilized nation, full of structural and functional unlikenesses. With progressing integration and heterogeneity goes increasing *coherence*. We see the wandering group dispersing, dividing, held together by no bonds; the tribe with parts made more coherent by subordination to a dominant man; the cluster of tribes united in a political plexus under a chief with sub-chiefs; and so on up to the civilized nation, consolidated enough to hold together for a thousand years or more. Simultaneously comes increasing *definiteness*. Social organization is at first vague; advance brings settled arrangements which grow slowly more precise; customs pass into laws which, while gaining fixity, also become more specific in their applications to varieties of actions; and all institutions, at first confusedly intermingled, slowly separate, at the same time that each within itself marks off more distinctly its component structures. Thus in all respects is fulfilled the formula of evolution. There is progress towards greater size, coherence, multiformity, and definiteness.

Besides these general truths, a number of special truths have been disclosed by our survey. Comparisons of societies in their ascending grades, have made manifest certain cardinal facts respecting their growths, structures and functions – facts respecting the systems of structures, sustaining, distributing, regulating, of which they are composed; respecting the relations of these structures to the surrounding conditions and the dominant forms of social activities entailed; and respecting the metamorphoses of types caused by changes in the activities. The inductions arrived at, thus constituting in rude outline an Empirical Sociology, show that in social phenomena there is a general order of coexistence and sequence; and that therefore social phenomena form the subject-matter of a science reducible, in some measure at least, to the deductive form.[2]

[...] Like other kinds of progress, social progress is not linear but divergent and re-divergent. Each differentiated product gives origin to a new set of differentiated products. While spreading over the Earth mankind have found environments of various characters, and in each case the social life fallen into, partly determined by the social life previously led, has been partly determined by the influences of the

2. The excerpts from *The Principles of Sociology*, vol. 2, start here.

new environment; so that the multiplying groups have tended ever to acquire differences, now major and now minor: there have arisen genera and species of societies.

[. . .] The cosmic process brings about retrogression as well as progression, where the conditions favour it. Only amid an infinity of modifications, adjusted to an infinity of changes of circumstances, do there now and then occur some which constitute an advance: other changes meanwhile caused in other organisms, usually not constituting forward steps in organization, and often constituting steps backwards. Evolution does not imply a latent tendency to improve, everywhere in operation. There is no uniform ascent from lower to higher, but only an occasional production of a form which, in virtue of greater fitness for more complex conditions, becomes capable of a longer life of a more varied kind. And while such higher type begins to dominate over lower types and to spread at their expense, the lower types survive in habitats or modes of life that are not usurped, or are thrust into inferior habitats or modes of life in which they retrogress.

What thus holds with organic types must hold also with types of societies. Social evolution throughout the future, like social evolution throughout the past, must, while producing step after step higher societies, leave outstanding many lower.

4 Karl Marx

(a) The Materialist Conception of History

Excerpts from Karl Marx, *Preface to A Contribution to the Critique of Political Economy*, 1859, and *German Ideology*, 1845–6, reprinted in T. B. Bottomore and M. Rubel (eds.), *Karl Marx: Selected Writings in Sociology and Social Philosophy*, Watts, 1956; Penguin, 1963, pp. 67–70.

I was led by my studies to the conclusion that legal relations as well as forms of State could neither be understood by themselves, nor explained by the so-called general progress of the human mind, but that they are rooted in the material conditions of life, which are summed up by Hegel after the fashion of the English and French writers of the eighteenth century under the name *civil society*, and that the anatomy of civil society is to be sought in political economy. The study of the latter which I had begun in Paris, I continued in Brussels where I had emigrated on account of an expulsion order issued by M. Guizot. The general conclusion at which I arrived and which, once reached, continued to serve as the guiding thread in my studies, may be formulated briefly as follows: In the social production which men carry on they enter into definite relations that are indispensable and independent of their will; these relations of production correspond to a definite stage of development of their material powers of production. The totality of these relations of production constitutes the economic structure of society – the real foundation, on which legal and political superstructures arise and to which definite forms of social consciousness correspond. The mode of production of material life determines the general character of the social, political and spiritual processes of life. It is not the consciousness of men that determines their being, but, on the contrary, their social being determines their consciousness. At a certain stage of their development, the material forces of production in society come in conflict with the existing relations of production, or – what is but a legal expression for the same thing – with the property relations within which they had been at work before. From forms of development of the forces of production these relations turn into their fetters. Then occurs a period of social revolution. With the change of the economic foundation the entire immense superstructure is more or less rapidly transformed. In considering such transformations, the distinction should always be made between the material transformation of the economic conditions of production which can be determined with the precision of natural science, and the legal, political, religious, aesthetic or philosophical – in short, ideological – forms in which men become conscious of this conflict and fight it out. Just as our opinion of an individual is not based on what he thinks of himself, so can we not judge of such a period of transformation by its own consciousness; on the contrary, this consciousness must rather be explained from the contradictions of material life, from the existing conflict between the social forces of production and the relations of production. No social order ever disappears before all the productive forces for which there is room in it have been developed; and new, higher relations of production never appear before the material conditions of their existence have matured in the womb of the old society. Therefore, mankind always sets itself only such problems as it can solve; since, on closer examination, it will always be found that the problem itself arises only when the material conditions necessary for its solution already exist or are at least in the process of formation. In broad outline we can designate the Asiatic, the ancient, the feudal, and the modern bourgeois modes of production as progressive epochs in the economic formation of society. The bourgeois relations of production are the last antagonistic form of the social process of production; not in the sense of individual antagonisms, but of conflict arising from conditions surrounding the life of individuals in society. At the same time the productive forces developing in the womb of bourgeois society create the material conditions for the solution of that antagonism. With this social formation, therefore, the prehistory of human society comes to an end.

The premises from which we begin are not arbitrary ones, not dogmas, but real premises from which abstraction can be made only in the imagination. They are the real individuals, their activity and their material conditions of life, including those which they find already in existence and those produced by their activity. These premises can thus be established in a purely empirical way.

The first premise of all human history is, of course, the existence of living human individuals. The first fact to be established, therefore, is the physical constitution of these individuals and their consequent relation to the rest of Nature. Of course we cannot here investigate the actual physical nature of man or the natural conditions in which man find himself – geological, oro-hydrographical, climatic and so on. All historiography must begin from these natural bases and their modification in the course of history by men's activity.

Men can be distinguished from animals by consciousness, by religion, or by anything one likes. They themselves begin to distinguish themselves from animals as soon as they begin to *produce* their means of subsistence, a step which is determined by their physical constitution. In producing their means of subsistence men indirectly produce their actual material life.

The way in which men produce their means of subsistence depends in the first place on the nature of the existing means which they have to reproduce. This mode of production should not be regarded simply as the reproduction of the physical existence of individuals. It is already a definite form of activity of these individuals, a definite way of expressing their life, a definite *mode of life*. As individuals express their life, so they are. What they are, therefore, coincides with their production, with *what* they produce and with *how* they produce it. What individuals are, therefore, depends on the material conditions of their production.

(b) Existence and Consciousness

Excerpts from Karl Marx, *Economic and Philosophical Manuscripts,* 1844, and *German Ideology,* 1845–6, reprinted in T. B. Bottomore and M. Rubel (eds.), *Karl Marx: Selected Writings in Sociology and Social Philosophy,* Watts, 1956; Penguin, 1963, pp. 91–5.

Social activity and social mind by no means exist *only* in the form of activity or mind which is *manifestly social*. Nevertheless, *social* activity and mind, that is, activity and mind which show themselves directly in a *real association* with other men, are realized everywhere where this *direct* expression of sociability is based on the nature of the activity or corresponds to the nature of mind.

Even when I carry out *scientific* work, etc. – an activity which I can seldom conduct in direct association with other men – I perform a *social*, because *human*, act. It is not only the material of my activity – like the language itself which the thinker uses – which is given to me as a social product. My *own* existence *is* a social activity. For this reason, what I myself produce, I produce for society and with the consciousness of acting like a social being.

[. . .] It is above all necessary to avoid postulating 'society' once more as an abstraction confronting the individual. The individual is a *social being*. The manifestation of his life – even when it does not appear directly in the form of a *social* manifestation, accomplished in association with other men – is therefore a manifestation and affirmation of *social life*. Individual human life and species[1]-life are not *different* things, even though the mode of existence of individual life is necessarily a more *particular* or more *general* mode of species-life, or that of species-life a more particular or more general mode of individual life. In his *species-consciousness* man confirms his real *social life*, and reproduces his real existence in thought, while conversely species-being confirms itself in species-consciousness, and exists for itself in its universality as a thinking being. Though man is a *unique* individual – and it is just his particularity which makes him an individual, a really *individual* social being – he is equally the *whole*, the ideal whole, the subjective existence of society as thought and experienced. He exists, in reality, as the representation and the real mind of social existence, and as the sum of human manifestation of life.

Thought and being are indeed *distinct*, but they also form a *unity*.

The existing relations of production between individuals must necessarily express themselves also as political and legal relations. Within the division of labour these relations are bound to assume an independent existence *vis-à-vis* the individuals. In language, such relations can only be expressed as concepts. The fact that these universals and concepts are accepted as mysterious powers is a necessary consequence of the independent existence assumed by the real relations whose expression they are. Besides this acceptance in everyday consciousness, these universals are also given a special validity and further development by political scientists and jurists who, as a result of the division of labour, are assigned to the cult of these concepts, and who see in them, rather than in the relations of production, the true basis of actual property relations.

The ideas of the ruling class are, in every age, the ruling ideas: i.e. the class which is the dominant *material* force in society is at the same time its dominant *intellectual* force. The class which has the means of material production at its disposal, has control at the same time over the means of mental production, so that in consequence the ideas of those who lack the means of mental production are, in general, subject to it. The dominant ideas are nothing more than the ideal expression

1. The term 'species' was used by Marx, following Feuerbach, to refer to man's awareness of his general human qualities, of belonging to the 'human species'.

of the dominant material relationships, the dominant material relationships grasped as ideas, and thus of the relationships which make one class the ruling one ; they are consequently the ideas of its dominance. The individuals composing the ruling class possess, among other things, consciousness, and therefore think. In so far, therefore, as they rule as a class and determine the whole extent of an epoch, it is self-evident that they do this in their whole range and thus, among other things, rule also as thinkers, as producers of ideas, and regulate the production and distribution of the ideas of their age. Consequently their ideas are the ruling ideas of the age. For instance, in an age and in a country where royal power, aristocracy and the bourgeoisie are contending for domination and where, therefore, domination is shared, the doctrine of the separation of powers appears as the dominant idea and is enunciated as an 'eternal law'. The division of labour, which we saw earlier as one of the principal forces of history up to the present time, manifests itself also in the ruling class, as the division of mental and material labour, so that within this class one part appears as the thinkers of the class (its active conceptualizing ideologists, who make it their chief source of livelihood to develop and perfect the illusions of the class about itself), while the others have a more passive and receptive attitude to these ideas and illusions, because they are in reality the active members of this class and have less time to make up ideas and illusions about themselves. This cleavage within the ruling class may even develop into a certain opposition and hostility between the two parts, but in the event of a practical collision in which the class itself is endangered, it disappears of its own accord and with it also the illusion that the ruling ideas were not the ideas of the ruling class and had a power distinct from the power of this class. The existence of revolutionary ideas in a particular age presupposes the existence of a revolutionary class. [. . .]

If, in considering the course of history, we detach the ideas of the ruling class from the ruling class itself and attribute to them an independent existence, if we confine ourselves to saying that in a particular age these or those ideas were dominant, without paying attention to the conditions of production and the producers of these ideas, and if we thus ignore the individuals and the world conditions which are the source of the ideas, it is possible to say, for instance, that during the time that the aristocracy was dominant the concepts honour, loyalty, etc., were dominant ; during the dominance of the bourgeoisie the concepts freedom, equality, etc. The ruling class itself in general imagines this to be the case. This conception of history which is common to all historians, particularly since the eighteenth century, will necessarily come up against the phenomenon that increasingly abstract ideas hold sway, i.e. ideas which increasingly take on the form of universality. For each new class which puts itself in the place of the one ruling before it, is compelled, simply in order to achieve its aims, to represent its interest as the common interest of all members of society, i.e. employing an ideal formula, to give its ideas the form of universality and to represent them as the only rational and universally valid ones. The class which makes a revolution appears from the beginning not as a class but as the representative of the whole of society, simply because it is opposed to a *class*. It appears as the whole mass of society confronting the single ruling class. It can do this because at the beginning its interest really is more closely connected with the common interest of all other non-ruling classes and has been unable under the constraint of the previously existing conditions to develop as the particular interest of a particular class. Its victory, therefore, also benefits many individuals of the other classes which are not achieving a dominant position, but only in so far as it now puts these individuals in a position to raise themselves into the ruling class. When the French bourgeoisie overthrew the rule of aristocracy it thereby made it possible for many proletarians to raise themselves above the proletariat, but only in so far as they became bourgeois. Every new class, therefore, achieves its domination only on a broader basis than that of the previously ruling class. On the other hand, the opposition of the non-ruling class to the new ruling class later develops all the more sharply and profoundly. These two characteristics entail that the struggle to be waged against this new ruling class has as its object a more decisive and radical negation of the previous conditions of society than could have been accomplished by all previous classes which aspired to rule.

(c) The Sociology of Capitalism

Excerpts from Karl Marx, *Wage Labour and Capital*, 1849, reprinted in
T. Bottomore and M. Rubel (eds.), *Karl Marx: Selected Writings in Sociology and Social Philosophy*, Watts, 1956; Penguin, 1963, pp. 155–6.

Capital consists of raw materials, instruments of labour and means of subsistence of all kinds, which are employed in producing new raw materials, new instruments of labour and new means of subsistence.

All these components of capital are created by labour, products of labour, *accumulated labour*. Accumulated labour that serves as a means to new production is capital. So say the economists.

What is a negro slave? A man of the black race. The one explanation is worthy of the other.

A negro is a negro. Only under certain conditions does he become a *slave*. A cotton-spinning machine is a machine for spinning cotton. Only under certain conditions does it become *capital*. Torn away from these conditions, it is as little capital as *gold* by itself is *money*, or as sugar is the *price* of sugar.

In the process of production, human beings do not only enter into a relation with Nature. They produce only by working together in a specific manner and by reciprocally exchanging their activities. In order to produce, they enter into definite connections and relations with one another, and only within these social connections and relations does their connection with Nature, i.e. production take place.

These social relations between the producers, and the conditions under which they exchange their activities and share in the total act of production, will naturally vary according to the character of the means of production. With the discovery of a new instrument of warfare, the fire-arm, the whole internal organization of the army was necessarily altered, the relations within which individuals compose an army and can act as an army were transformed, and the relation of different armies to one another was likewise changed.

The social relations within which individuals produce, *the social relations of production, are altered, transformed, with the change and development of the material means of production, of the forces of production. The relations of production in their totality constitute what is called the social relations, society,* and, moreover, a society at a definite stage of historical development, a society with a unique and distinctive character. Ancient society, feudal society, bourgeois (or capitalist) society, are such totalities of relations of production, each of which denotes a particular stage of development in the history of mankind.

Capital also is a social relation of production. It is a *bourgeois relation of production*, a relation of production of bourgeois society. The means of subsistence, the instruments of labour, the raw materials, of which capital consists – have they not been produced and accumulated under given social conditions, within definite social relations? Are they not employed for new production, under given social conditions, within definite social relations? And does not just this definite social character stamp the products which serve for the new production as *capital*?

Capital consists not only of means of subsistence, instruments of labour and raw materials, not only of material products: it consists just as much of *exchange values*. All products of which it consists are *commodities*. Capital, consequently, is not only a sum of material products, it is a sum of commodities, of exchange values, of social magnitudes. [. . .]

Capital therefore presupposes wage-labour ; wage-labour presupposes capital. They condition each other; each brings the other into existence.

(d) Alienated Labour

Excerpt from Karl Marx, *Economic and Philosophical Manuscripts,* 1844, reprinted in Erich Fromm (ed.), *Marx's Concept of Man* (trans. T. B. Bottomore), Frederick Ungar, 1961, pp. 93–109.

We have begun from the presuppositions of political economy. We have accepted its terminology and its laws. We presupposed private property, the separation of labour, capital and land, as also of wages, profit and rent, the division of labour, competition, the concept of exchange value, etc. From political economy itself, in its own words, we have shown that the worker sinks to the level of a commodity, and to a most miserable commodity ; that the misery of the worker increases with the power and volume of his production; that the necessary result of competition is the accumulation of capital in a few hands, and thus a restoration of monopoly in a more terrible form ; and finally that the distinction between capitalist and landlord, and between agricultural labourer and industrial worker, must disappear and the whole of society divide into the two classes of property *owners* and propertyless *workers*.

Political economy begins with the fact of private property ; it does not explain it. It conceives the *material process* of private property, as this occurs in reality, in general and abstract formulas which then serve it as laws. It does not *comprehend* these laws; that is, it does not show how they arise out of the nature of private property. Political economy provides no explanation of the basis of the distinction of labour from capital, of capital from land. When, for example, the relation of wages to profits is defined, this is explained in terms of the interests of capitalists; in other words, what should be explained is assumed. Similarly, competition is referred to at every point and is explained in terms of external conditions. Political economy tells us nothing about the extent to which these external and apparently accidental conditions are simply the expression of a necessary development. We have seen how exchange itself seems an accidental fact. The only moving forces which political economy recognizes are *avarice* and the *war between the avaricious, competition*.

Just because political economy fails to understand the interconnections within this movement it was possible to oppose the doctrine of competition to that of monopoly, the doctrine of freedom of the crafts to that of the guilds, the doctrine of the division of landed property to that of the great estates; for competition, freedom of crafts and the division of landed property were conceived only as accidental consequences brought about by will and force, rather than as necessary, inevitable and natural consequences of monopoly, the guild system and feudal property.

Thus we have now to grasp the real connection between this whole system of alienation – private property, acquisitiveness, the separation of labour, capital and land, exchange and competition, value and the devaluation of man, monopoly and competition – and the system of *money*.

Let us not begin our explanation, as does the economist, from a legendary primordial condition. Such a primordial condition does not explain anything; it merely removes the question into a grey and nebulous distance. It asserts as a fact or event what it should deduce, namely, the necessary relation between two things; for example, between the division of labour and exchange. In the same way theology explains the origin of evil by the fall of man; that is, it asserts as a historical fact what it should explain.

We shall begin from a *contemporary* economic fact. The worker becomes poorer the more wealth he produces and the more his production increases in power and extent. The worker becomes an ever-cheaper commodity the more goods he creates. The *devaluation* of the human world increases in direct relation with the *increase in value* of the world of things. Labour does not only create goods; it also produces itself and the worker as a *commodity*, and indeed in the same proportion as it produces goods.

This fact simply implies that the object produced by labour, its product, now stands opposed to it as an *alien being*, as a *power independent* of the producer. The product of labour is labour which has been embodied in an object and turned into a physical thing; this product is an *objectification* of labour. The performance of work is at the same time its objectification. The performance of work appears in the sphere of political economy as a *vitiation* of the worker, objectification as a *loss* and as *servitude to the object*, and appropriation as *alienation*.

So much does the performance of work appear as vitiation that the worker is vitiated to the point of starvation. So much does objectification appear as loss of the object that the worker is deprived of the most essential things not only of life but also of work. Labour itself becomes an object which he can acquire only by the greatest effort and with unpredictable interruptions. So much does the appropriation of the object appear as alienation that the more objects the worker produces the fewer he can possess and the more he falls under the domination of his product, of capital.

All these consequences follow from the fact that the worker is related to the *product of his labour* as to an *alien* object. For it is clear on this presupposition that the more the worker expends himself in work the more powerful becomes the world of objects which he creates in face of himself, the poorer he becomes in his inner life, and the less he belongs to himself. It is just the same as in religion. The more of himself the man attributes to God the less he has left in himself. The worker puts his life into the object, and his life then belongs no longer to himself but to the object. The greater his activity, therefore, the less he possesses. What is embodied in the product of his labour is no longer his own. The greater this product is, therefore the more he is diminished. The *alienation* of the worker in his product means not only that his labour becomes an object, assumes an *external* existence, but that it exists independently, *outside himself*, and alien to him, and that it stands opposed to him as an autonomous power. The life which he has given to the object sets itself against him as an alien and hostile force.

Let us now examine more closely the phenomenon of *objectification*, the worker's production and the *alienation* and *loss* of the object it produces, which is involved in it. The worker can create nothing without *nature*, without the *sensuous external world*. The latter is the material in which his labour is realized, in which it is active, out of which and through which it produces things.

But just as nature affords the *means of existence* of labour in the sense that labour cannot *live* without objects upon which it can be exercised, so also it provides the *means of existence* in a narrower sense; namely the means of physical existence for the *worker* himself. Thus, the more the worker *appropriates* the external world of sensuous nature by his labour the more he deprives himself of *means of existence,* in two respects: first, that the sensuous external world becomes progressively less an object belonging to his labour or a means of existence of his labour, and secondly, that it becomes progressively less a means of existence in the direct sense, a means for the physical subsistence of the worker.

In both respects, therefore, the worker becomes a slave of the object; first, in that he receives an *object of work,* i.e. receives *work,* and secondly that he receives *means of subsistence.* Thus the object enables him to exist, first as a *worker* and secondly, as a *physical subject.* The culmination of this enslavement is that he can only maintain himself as a *physical subject* so far as he is a *worker,* and that it is only as a *physical subject* that he is a worker.

(The alienation of the worker in his object is expressed as follows in the laws of political economy: the more the worker produces the less he has to consume; the more value he creates the more worthless he becomes; the more refined his product the more crude and mis-shapen the worker; the more civilized the product the more barbarous the worker; the more powerful the work the more feeble the worker; the more the work manifests intelligence the more the worker declines in intelligence and becomes a slave of nature.)

Political economy conceals the alienation in the nature of labour in so far as it does not examine the direct relationship between the worker (work) and production. Labour certainly produces marvels for the rich but it produces privation for the worker. It produces palaces, but hovels for the worker. It produces beauty, but deformity for the worker. It replaces labour by machinery, but it casts some of the workers back into a barbarous kind of work and turns the others into machines. It produces intelligence, but also stupidity and cretinism for the workers.

The direct relationship of labour to its products is the relationship of the worker to the objects of his production. The relationship of property owners to the objects of production and to production itself is merely a *consequence* of this first relationship and confirms it. We shall consider this second aspect later.

Thus, when we ask what is the important relationship of labour, we are concerned with the relationship of the *worker* to production.

So far we have considered the alienation of the worker only from one aspect; namely, *his relationship with the products of his labour.* However, alienation appears not only in the result, but also in the *process,* of *production,* within *productive activity* itself. How could the worker stand in an alien relationship to the product of his activity if he did not alienate himself in the act of production itself? The product is indeed only the *résumé* of activity, of production. Consequently, if the product of labour is alienation, production itself must be active alienation – the alienation of activity and the activity of alienation. The alienation of the object of labour merely summarizes the alienation in the work activity itself.

What constitutes the alienation of labour? First, that the work is *external* to the worker, that it is not part of his nature; and that, consequently, he does not fulfil himself in his work but denies himself, has a feeling of misery rather than well-being, does not develop freely his mental and physical energies but is physically exhausted and mentally debased. The worker therefore feels himself at home only during his leisure time, whereas at work he feels homeless. His work is not voluntary but imposed, *forced labour.* It is not the satisfaction of a need, but only a *means* for satisfying other needs. Its alien character is clearly shown by the fact that as soon as there is no physical or other compulsion it is avoided like the plague. External labour, labour in which man alienates himself, is a labour of self-sacrifice, of mortification. Finally, the external character of work for the worker is shown by the fact that it is not his own work but work for someone else, that in work he does not belong to himself but to another person.

Just as in religion the spontaneous activity of human fantasy, of the human brain and heart, reacts independently as an alien activity of gods or devils upon the individual, so the activity of the worker is not his own spontaneous activity. It is another's activity and a loss of his own spontaneity.

We arrive at the result that man (the worker) feels himself to be freely active only in his animal functions – eating, drinking and procreating, or at most also in his dwelling and in personal adornment – while in his human functions he is reduced to an animal. The animal becomes human and the human becomes animal.

Eating, drinking and procreating are of course also genuine human functions. But abstractly considered, apart from the environment of other human activities, and turned into final and sole ends, they are animal functions.

We have now considered the act of alienation of practical human activity, labour, from two aspects:

1. The relationship of the worker to the *product of labour* as an alien object which dominates him. This relationship is at the same time the relationship to the sensuous external world, to natural objects, as an alien and hostile world.

2. The relationship of labour to the *act of production* within *labour*. This is the relationship of the worker to his own activity as something alien and not belonging to him, activity as suffering (passivity), strength as powerlessness, creation as emasculation, the *personal* physical and mental energy of the worker, his personal life (for what is life but activity?) as an activity which is directed against himself, independent of him and not belonging to him. This is *self-alienation* as against the above-mentioned alienation of the *thing*.

We have now to infer a third characteristic of *alienated labour* from the two we have considered.

Man is a species-being not only in the sense that he makes the community (his own as well as those of other things) his object both practically and theoretically, but also (and this is simply another expression for the same thing) in the sense that he treats himself as the present, living species, as a *universal* and consequently free being.

Species-life, for man as for animals, has its physical basis in the fact that man (like animals) lives from inorganic nature, and since man is more universal than an animal so the range of inorganic nature from which he lives is more universal. Plants, animals, minerals, air, light, etc., constitute, from the theoretical aspect, a part of human consciousness as objects of natural science and art; they are man's spiritual inorganic nature, his intellectual means of life, which he must first prepare for enjoyment and perpetuation. So also, from the practical aspect they form a part of human life and activity. In practice man lives only from these natural products, whether in the form of food, heating, clothing, housing, etc. The universality of man appears in practice in the universality which makes the whole of nature into his inorganic body: (a) as a direct means of life; and equally (b) as the material object and instrument of his life activity. Nature is the *inorganic body* of man; that is to say, nature excluding the human body itself. To say that man *lives* from nature means that nature is his *body* with which he must remain in a continuous interchange in order not to die. The statement that the physical and mental life of man, and nature, are interdependent means simply that nature is interdependent with itself, for man is a part of nature.

Since alienated labour: 1. alienates nature from man; 2. alienates man from himself, from his own active function, his life, activity;

so it alienates him from the species. It makes *species-life* into a means of individual life. In the first place it alienates species-life and individual life, and secondly, it turns the latter, as an abstraction into the purpose of the former, also in its abstract and alienated form.

For labour, *life activity, productive life,* now appear to man only as *means* for the satisfaction of a need, the need to maintain his physical existence. Productive life is, however, species-life. It is life creating life. In the type of life activity resides the whole character of a species, its species-character; and free, conscious activity is the species-character of human beings. Life itself appears only as a *means of life*.

The animal is one with its life activity. It does not distinguish the activity from itself. It is *its activity*. But man makes his life activity itself an object of his will and consciousness. He has a conscious life activity. It is not a determination with which he is completely identified. Conscious life activity distinguishes man from the life activity of animals. Only for this reason is he a species-being. Or rather, he is only a self-conscious being, i.e. his own life is an object for him, because he is a species-being. Only for this reason is his activity free activity. Alienated labour reverses the relationship, in that man because he is a self-conscious being makes his life activity, his *being*, only a means for his *existence*.

The practical construction of an *objective world*, the *manipulation* of inorganic nature, is the confirmation of man as a conscious species-being, i.e. a being who treats the species as his own being or himself as a species-being. Of course, animals also produce. They construct nests, dwellings, as in the case of bees, beavers, ants, etc. But they only produce what is strictly necessary for themselves or their young. They produce only in a single direction, while man produces universally. They produce only under the compulsion of direct physical need, while man produces when he is free from physical need and only truly produces in freedom from such need. Animals reproduce only themselves while man reproduces the whole of nature. The products of animal production belong directly to their physical bodies, while man is free in face of his product. Animals construct only in accordance with the standards and needs of the species to which they belong, while man knows how to produce in accordance with the standards of every species and knows how to apply the appropriate standard to the object. Thus man constructs also in accordance with the laws of beauty.

It is just in his work upon the objective world that man really proves himself as a *species-being*. This production is his active species life. By means of it nature appears as *his* work and his reality. The object of labour is, therefore, the *objectification of man's species-life*; for he no longer reproduces himself merely intellectually, as in consciousness, but actively and in a real sense, and he sees his own reflection in a world which he has constructed. While, therefore, alienated labour takes away the object of production from man, it also takes away his *species-life*, his real objectivity as a species-being, and changes his advantage over animals into a disadvantage in so far as his inorganic body, nature, is taken from him.

Just as alienated labour transforms free and self-directed activity into a means, so it transforms the species-life of man into a means of physical existence.

Consciousness, which man has from his species, is transformed through alienation so that species-life becomes only a means for him.

3. Thus alienated labour turns the *species-life of man*, and also nature as his mental species-property, into an *alien* being and into a *means* for his *individual existence*. It alienates from man his own body, external nature, his mental life and his *human* life.

4. A direct consequence of the alienation of man from the product of his labour, from his life activity and from his species-life is that *man* is *alienated* from other *men*. When man confronts himself he also confronts *other* men. What is true of man's relationship to his work, to the product of his work and to himself, is also true of his relationship to other men, to their labour and to the objects of their labour.

In general, the statement that man is alienated from his species-life means that each man is alienated from others, and that each of the others is likewise alienated from human life.

Human alienation, and above all the relation of man to himself, is first realized and expressed in the relationship between each man and other men. Thus in the relationship of alienated labour every man regards other men according to the standards and relationships in which he finds himself placed as a worker.

We began with an economic fact, the alienation of the worker and his production. We have expressed this fact in conceptual terms as *alienated labour*, and in analysing the concept we have merely analysed an economic fact.

Let us now examine further how this concept of alienated labour must express and reveal itself in reality. If the product of labour is alien to me and confronts me as an alien power, to whom does it belong? If my own activity does not belong to me but is an alien, forced activity, to whom does it belong? To a being *other* than myself. And who is this being? The *gods*? It is apparent in the earliest stages of advanced production, e.g. temple building, etc. in Egypt, India, Mexico, and in the service rendered to gods, that the product belonged to the gods. But the gods alone were never the lords of labour. And no more was *nature*. What a contradiction it would be if the more man subjugates nature by his labour, and the more the marvels of the gods are rendered superfluous by the marvels of industry, he should abstain from his joy in producing and his enjoyment of the product for love of these powers.

The *alien* being to whom labour and the product of labour belong, to whose service labour is devoted, and to whose enjoyment the product of labour goes, can only be *man* himself. If the product of labour does not belong to the worker, but confronts him as an alien power, this can only be because it belongs to a *man other than the worker*. If his activity is a torment to him it must be a source of enjoyment and pleasure to another. Not the gods, nor nature, but only man himself can be this alien power over men.

Consider the earlier statement that the relation of man to himself is first realized, objectified, through his relation to other men. If therefore he is related to the product of his labour, his objectified labour, as to an *alien,* hostile, powerful and independent object, he is related in such a way that another alien, hostile, powerful and independent man is the lord of this object. If he is related to his own activity as to unfree activity, then he is related to it as activity in the service, and under the domination, coercion and yoke, of another man.

Every self-alienation of man, from himself and from nature, appears in the relation which he postulates between other men and himself and nature. Thus religious self-alienation is necessarily exemplified in the relation between laity and priest, or, since it is here a question of the spiritual world, between the laity and a mediator. In the real world of practice this self-alienation can only be expressed in the real, practical relation of man to his fellow-men. The medium through which alienation occurs is itself a *practical* one. Through alienated labour, therefore, man not only produces his relation to the object and to the process of production as to alien and hostile men ; he also produces the relation of other men to his production and his product, and the relation between himself and other men. Just as he creates his own production as a vitiation, a punishment, and his own product as a loss, as a product which does not belong to him, so he creates the domination of the non-producer over production and its product. As he alienates his own activity, so he bestows upon the stranger an activity which is not his own.

We have so far considered this relation only from the side of the worker, and later on we shall consider it also from the side of the non-worker.

Thus, through alienated labour the worker creates the relation of another man, who does not work and is outside the work process, to this labour. The relation of the worker to work also produces the relation of the capitalist (or whatever one likes to call the lord of labour) to work. *Private property* is therefore the product, the necessary result, of *alienated labour,* of the external relation of the worker to nature and to himself.

Private property is thus derived from the analysis of the concept of *alienated labour*; that is, alienated man, alienated labour, alienated life and estranged man.

We have, of course, derived the concept of *alienated labour* (*alienated life*) from political economy, from an analysis of the *movement of private property*. But the analysis of this concept shows that although private property appears to be the basis and cause of alienated labour, it is rather a consequence of the latter, just as the gods are *fundamentally* not the cause but the product of confusions of human reason. At a later stage, however, there is a reciprocal influence.

Only in the final stage of the development of private property is its secret revealed, namely, that it is on one hand the *product* of alienated labour, and on the other hand the *means* by which labour is alienated, the *realization of this alienation*.

This elucidation throws light upon several unresolved controversies:

1. Political economy begins with labour as the real soul of production and then goes on to attribute nothing to labour and everything to private property. Proudhon, faced by this contradiction, has decided in favour of labour against private property. We perceive, however, that this apparent contradiction is the contradiction of *alienated labour* with itself and that political economy has merely formulated the laws of alienated labour.

We also observe, therefore, that *wages* and *private property* are identical, for wages, like the product or object of labour, labour itself remunerated, are only a necessary consequence of the alienation of labour. In the wage system labour appears not as an end in itself but as the servant of wages. We shall develop this point later on and here only bring out some of the consequences.

An enforced *increase in wages* (disregarding the other difficulties, and especially that such an anomaly could only be maintained by force) would be nothing more than a *better remuneration of slaves*, and would not restore, either to the worker or to the work, their human significance and worth.

Even the *equality of incomes* which Proudhon demands would only change the relation of the present-day worker to his work into a relation of all men to work. Society would then be conceived as an abstract capitalist.

2. From the relation of alienated labour to private property it also follows that the emancipation of society from private property, from servitude, takes the political form of the *emancipation of the workers*; not in the sense that only the latter's emancipation is involved, but because this emancipation includes the emancipation of humanity as a whole. For all human servitude is involved in the relation of the worker to production, and all the types of servitude are only modifications or consequences of this relation.

As we have discovered the concept of *private property* by an *analysis* of the concept of *alienated labour*, so with the aid of these two factors we can evolve all the categories of political economy, and in every category, e.g. trade, competition, capital, money, we shall discover only a particular and developed expression of these fundamental elements.

However, before considering this structure let us attempt to solve two problems.

1. To determine the general nature of *private property* as it has resulted from alienated labour, in its relation to *genuine human and social property*.

2. We have taken as a fact and analysed the *alienation of labour*. How does it happen, we may ask, that *man alienates his labour*? How is this alienation founded in the nature of human development? We have already done much to solve the problem so far as we have *transformed* the question concerning the *origin of private property* into a question about the relation between *alienated labour* and the process of development of mankind. For in speaking of private property one believes oneself to be dealing with something external to mankind. But in speaking of labour one deals directly with mankind itself. This new formulation of the problem already contains its solution.

ad (1) *The general nature of private property and its relation to genuine human property*.

We have resolved alienated labour into two parts, which mutually determine each other, or rather constitute two different expressions of one and the same relation. *Appropriation* appears as *alienation* and *alienation* as *appropriation*, alienation as genuine acceptance in the community.

We have considered one aspect, *alienated* labour, in its bearing upon the *worker* himself, i.e. *the relation of alienated labour to itself*. And we have found as the necessary consequence of this relation the *property relation* of the *non-worker* to the *worker* and to *labour*. *Private property* as the material summarized expression of alienated labour includes both relations; *the relation of the worker to labour, to the product of his labour and to the non-worker,* and the relation of the *non-worker to the worker and to the product of the latter's labour*.

We have already seen that in relation to the worker, who *appropriates* nature by his labour, appropriation appears as alienation, self-activity as activity for another and of another, living as the sacrifice of life, and production of the object as loss of the object to an alien power, an alien man. Let us now consider the relation of this *alien* man to the worker, to labour and to the object of labour.

It should be noted first that everything which appears to the worker as an *activity of alienation,* appears to the non-worker as a *condition of alienation*. Secondly, the *real, practical* attitude of the worker in production and to the product (as a state of mind) appears to the non-worker who confronts him as a *theoretical* attitude.

Thirdly, the non-worker does everything against the worker which the latter does against himself, but he does not do against himself what he does against the worker.

5 Max Weber

(a) The Ideal Type

Excerpts from Max Weber, 'Objectivity', *Archiv für Sozialwissenschaft und Sozialpolitik*, 1904, reprinted in Edward A. Shils and Henry A. Finch (eds.), *The Methodology of the Social Sciences*, Free Press, 1949, pp. 89–92, 93–4, 97–9.

We have in abstract economic theory an illustration of those synthetic constructs which have been designated as *'ideas'* of historical phenomena. It offers us an ideal picture of events on the commodity-market under conditions of a society organized on the principles of an exchange economy, free competition and rigorously rational conduct. This conceptual pattern brings together certain relationships and events of historical life into a complex, which is conceived as an internally consistent system. Substantively, this construct in itself is like a utopia which has been arrived at by the analytical accentuation of certain elements of reality. Its relationship to the empirical data consists solely in the fact that where market-conditioned relationships of the type referred to by the abstract construct are discovered or suspected to exist in reality to some extent, we can make the characteristic features of this relationship pragmatically clear and understandable by reference to an ideal type. This procedure can be indispensable for heuristic as well as expository purposes. The ideal typical concept will help to develop our skill in imputation in research: it is no 'hypothesis' but it offers guidance to the construction of hypotheses. It is not a description of reality but it aims to give unambiguous means of expression to such a description. It is thus the 'idea' of the historically given modern society, based on an exchange economy, which is developed for us by quite the same logical principles as are used in constructing the idea of the medieval 'city economy' as a 'genetic' concept. When we do this, we construct the concept 'city economy' not as an average of the economic structures actually existing in all the cities observed but as an ideal type. An ideal type is formed by the one-sided accentuation of one or more points of view and by the synthesis of a great many diffuse, discrete, more or less present and occasionally absent concrete individual phenomena, which are arranged according to those one-sidedly emphasized viewpoints into a unified analytical construct (*Gedankenbild*). In its conceptual purity, this mental construct (*Gedankenbild*) cannot be found empirically anywhere in reality. It is a utopia. Historical research faces the task of determining in each individual case, the extent to which this ideal-construct approximates to or diverges from reality, to what extent for example, the economic structure of a certain city is to be classified as a 'city economy'. When carefully applied, those concepts are particularly useful in research and exposition. In very much the same way one can work the 'idea' of 'handicraft' into a utopia by arranging certain traits, actually found in an unclear, confused state in the industrial enterprises of the most diverse epochs and countries, into a consistent ideal construct by an accentuation of their essential tendencies. This ideal type is then related to the idea (*Gedankenausdruck*) which one finds expressed there. One can further delineate a society in which all branches of economic and even intellectual activity are governed by maxims which appear to be applications of the same principle which characterizes the ideal-typical 'handicraft' system. Furthermore, one can juxtapose alongside the ideal typical 'handicraft' system the antithesis of a correspondingly ideal typical capitalistic productive system, which has been abstracted out of certain features of modern large-scale industry. On the basis of this, one can delineate the utopia of a 'capitalistic' culture, i.e. one in which the governing principle is the investment of private capital. This procedure would accentuate certain individual concretely diverse traits of modern material and intellectual culture in its unique aspects into an ideal construct which from our point of view would be completely self-consistent. This would then be the delineation of an 'idea' of capitalistic culture. We must disregard for the moment whether and how this procedure could be carried out. It is possible, or rather, it must be accepted as certain that numerous, indeed a very great many, utopias of this sort can be worked out, of which none is like another, and none of which can be observed in empirical reality as an actually existing economic system, but each of which however claims that it is a representation of the 'idea' of capitalistic culture. Each of these can claim to be a representation of the 'idea' of capitalistic culture to the extent that it has really taken certain traits, meaningful in their essential features, from the empirical reality of our culture and brought them together into a unified ideal-construct. For those phenomena which interest us as cultural phenomena are interesting to us with respect to very different kinds of evaluative ideas to which we relate them. Inasmuch as the 'points of view' from which they can become significant for us are very diverse, the most varied criteria can be applied to the selection of the traits which are to enter into the construction of an ideal-typical view of a particular culture.

What is the significance of such ideal-typical constructs for an empirical science, as we wish to constitute it? Before going any further, we should emphasize that the idea of an ethical imperative, of a 'model' of what 'ought' to exist is to be carefully distinguished from the analytical construct, which is 'ideal' in the strictly logical sense of the term. It is a matter here of constructing relationships which our imagination accepts as plausibly motivated and hence as 'objectively possible' and which appear as adequate from the nomological standpoint.

[. . .] the ideal-type is an attempt to analyse historically unique configurations or their individual components by means of genetic concepts. Let us take for instance the concepts 'church' and 'sect'. They may be broken down purely classificatorily into complexes of characteristics whereby not only the distinction between them but also the content of the concept must constantly remain fluid. If however I wish to formulate the concept of 'sect' genetically, e.g. with reference to certain important cultural significances which the 'sectarian spirit' has had for modern culture, certain characteristics of both become essential because they stand in an adequate causal relationship to those influences. However, the concepts thereupon become ideal-typical in the sense that they appear in full conceptual integrity either not at all or only in individual instances. Here as elsewhere every concept which is not purely classificatory diverges from reality. But the discursive nature of our knowledge, i.e. the fact that we comprehend reality only through a chain of intellectual modifications postulates such a conceptual shorthand. Our imagination can often dispense with explicit conceptual formulations as a means of investigation. But as regards exposition, to the extent that it wishes to be unambiguous, the use of precise formulations in the sphere of cultural analysis is in many cases absolutely necessary. Whoever disregards it entirely must confine himself to the formal aspect of cultural phenomena, e.g. to legal history. The universe of legal norms is naturally clearly definable and is valid (in the legal sense!) for historical reality. But social science in our sense is concerned with practical significance. This significance however can very often be brought unambiguously to mind only by relating the empirical data to an ideal limiting case. If the historian (in the widest sense of the word) rejects an attempt to construct such ideal types as a 'theoretical construction', i.e. as useless or dispensable for his concrete heuristic purposes, the inevitable consequence is either that he consciously or unconsciously uses other similar concepts without formulating them verbally and elaborating them logically or that he remains stuck in the realm of the vaguely 'felt'.

Nothing, however, is more dangerous than the confusion of theory and history stemming from naturalistic prejudices. This confusion expresses itself firstly in the belief that the 'true' content and the essence of historical reality is portrayed in such theoretical constructs or secondly, in the use of these constructs as a procrustean bed into which history is to be forced or thirdly, in the hypostatization of such 'ideas' as real 'forces' and as a 'true' reality which operates behind the passage of events and which works itself out in history.

There is still another even more complicated significance implicit in such ideal-typical presentations. They regularly seek to be, or are unconsciously, ideal-types not only in the logical sense but also in the practical sense, i.e. they are model types which – in our illustration – contain what, from the point of view of the expositor, should be and what to him is 'essential' in Christianity because it is enduringly valuable. If this is consciously or – as it is more frequently – unconsciously the case, they contain ideals to which the expositor evaluatively relates Christianity. These ideals are tasks and ends towards which he orients his 'idea' of Christianity and which naturally can and indeed doubtless always will differ greatly from the values which other persons, for instance, the early Christians, connected with Christianity. In this sense, however, the 'ideas' are naturally no longer purely logical auxiliary devices, no longer concepts with which reality is compared, but ideals by which it is evaluatively judged. Here it is no longer a matter of the purely theoretical procedure of treating empirical reality with respect to values but of value-judgements which are integrated into the concept of 'Christianity'. Because the ideal type claims empirical validity here, it penetrates into the realm of the evaluative interpretation of Christianity. The sphere of empirical science has been left behind and we are confronted with a profession of faith, not an ideal-typical construct. As fundamental as this distinction is in principle, the confusion of these two basically different meanings of the term 'idea' appears with extraordinary frequency in historical writings. It is always close at hand whenever the descriptive historian begins to develop his 'conception' of a personality or an epoch. In contrast with the fixed ethical standards which Schlosser applied in the spirit of rationalism, the modern relativistically educated historian who on the one hand seeks to 'understand' the epoch of which he speaks 'in its own terms', and on the other still seeks to 'judge' it, feels the need to derive the standards for his judgement from the subject-matter itself, i.e. to allow the 'idea' in the sense of the ideal to emerge from the 'idea' in the sense of the 'ideal type'. The aesthetic satisfaction produced by such a procedure constantly tempts him to disregard the line where these two ideal types diverge – an error which on the one hand hampers the value-judgement and on the other, strives to free itself from the responsibility for its own judgement. In contrast with this, the elementary duty of scientific self-control and the only way to avoid serious and foolish blunders requires a sharp, precise distinction between the logically comparative analysis of reality by ideal types in the logical sense and the value judgement of reality on the basis of ideals. An 'ideal type' in our sense, to repeat once more, has no connection at all with value-judgements, and it has nothing to do with any type of perfection other than a purely logical one. There are ideal types of brothels as well as of religions ; there are also ideal types of those kinds of brothels which are technically 'expedient' from the point of view of police ethics as well as those of which the exact opposite is the case.

(b) Power and Bureaucracy

Excerpts from Max Weber, *Wirtschaft und Gesellschaft,* 1922, reprinted in Talcott Parsons (ed.), *The Theory of Social and Economic Organization,* Free Press, 1947, pp. 324–5, 328–35 and in Hans Gerth and C. Wright Mills (eds. and trans.), *From Max Weber: Essays in Sociology,* Routledge & Kegan Paul, 1948, pp. 214–16, 228–30.

The basis of legitimacy

The definition, conditions and types of imperative control. Imperative coordination ... [is] as the probability that certain specific commands (or all commands) from a given source will be obeyed by a given group of persons. It thus does not include every mode of exercising 'power' or 'influence' over other persons. The motives of obedience to commands in this sense can rest on considerations varying over a wide range from case to case ; all the way from simple habituation to the most purely rational calculation of advantage. A criterion of every true relation of imperative control, however, is a certain minimum of voluntary submission ; thus an interest (based on ulterior motives or genuine acceptance) in obedience.

Not every case of imperative coordination makes use of economic means; still less does it always have economic objectives. But normally (not always) the imperative coordination of the action of a considerable number of men requires control of a staff of persons. It is necessary, that is, that there should be a relatively high probability that the action of a definite, supposedly reliable group of persons will be primarily oriented to the execution of the supreme authority's general policy and specific commands.

The members of the administrative staff may be bound to obedience to their superior (or superiors) by custom, by affectual ties, by a purely material complex of interests or by ideal (*wertrational*) motives. Purely material interests and calculations of advantage as the basis of solidarity between the chief and his administrative staff result, in this as in other connections, in a relatively unstable situation. Normally other elements, affectual and ideal, supplement such interests. In certain exceptional, temporary cases the former may be alone decisive. In everyday routine life these relationships, like others, are governed by custom and in addition, material calculation of advantage. But these factors, custom and personal advantage, purely affectual or ideal motives of solidarity, do not, even taken together, form a sufficiently reliable basis for a system of imperative coordination. In addition there is normally a further element, the belief in legitimacy.

It is an induction from experience that no system of authority voluntarily limits itself to the appeal to material or affectual or ideal motives as a basis for guaranteeing its continuance. In addition every such system attempts to establish and to cultivate the belief in its 'legitimacy'. But according to the kind of legitimacy which is claimed, the type of obedience, the kind of administrative staff developed to guarantee it and the mode of exercising authority, will all differ fundamentally. Equally fundamental is the variation in effect. Hence, it is useful to classify the types of authority according to the kind of claim to legitimacy typically made by each.

The three pure types of legitimate authority. There are three pure types of legitimate authority. The validity of their claims to legitimacy may be based on:

1. Rational grounds – resting on a belief in the 'legality' of patterns of normative rules and the right of those elevated to authority under such rules to issue commands (legal authority).

2. Traditional grounds – resting on an established belief in the sanctity of immemorial traditions and the legitimacy of the status of those exercising authority under them (traditional authority).

3. Charismatic grounds – resting on devotion to the specific and exceptional sanctity, heroism or exemplary character of an individual person, and of the normative patterns of order revealed or ordained by him (charismatic authority).

In the case of legal authority, obedience is owed to the legally established impersonal order. It extends to the persons exercising the authority of office under it only by virtue of the formal legality of their commands and only within the scope of authority of the office. In the case of traditional authority, obedience is owed to the person of the chief who occupies the traditionally sanctioned position of authority and who is (within its sphere) bound by tradition. But here the obligation of obedience is not based on the impersonal order, but is a matter of personal loyalty within the area of accustomed obligations. In the case of charismatic authority, it is the charismatically qualified leader as such who is obeyed by virtue of personal trust in him and his revelation, his heroism or his exemplary qualities so far as they fall within the scope of the individual's belief in his charisma.

1. The usefulness of the above classification can only be judged by its results in promoting systematic analysis. The concept of 'charisma' ('the gift of grace') is taken from the vocabulary of early Christianity. For the Christian religious organization Rudolph Sohm, in his *Kirchenrecht*, was the first to clarify the substance of the concept, even though he did not use the same terminology. Others (for instance, Hollin, *Enthusiasmus und Bussgewalt*) have clarified certain important consequences of it. It is thus nothing new.

2. The fact that none of these three ideal types, the elucidation of which will occupy the following pages, is usually to be found in historical cases in 'pure' form, is naturally not a valid objection to attempting their conceptual formulation in the sharpest possible form. In this respect the present case is no different from many others. Later on the transformation of pure charisma by the process of routinization will be discussed and thereby the relevance of the concept to the understanding of empirical systems of authority considerably increased. But even so it may be said of every empirically historical phenomenon of authority that it is not likely to be 'as an open book'. Analysis in terms of sociological types has, after all, as compared with purely empirical historical investigation, certain advantages which should not be minimized. That is, it can in the particular case of a concrete form of authority determine what conforms to or approximates such types as 'charisma', 'hereditary charisma', 'the charisma of office', 'patriarchy', 'bureaucracy', the authority of status groups and in doing so it can

work with relatively unambiguous concepts. But the idea that the whole of concrete historical reality can be exhausted in the conceptual scheme about to be developed is as far from the author's thoughts as anything could be.

Legal authority with a bureaucratic administrative staff

Legal authority: the pure type with employment of a bureaucratic administrative staff. The effectiveness of legal authority rests on the acceptance of the validity of the following mutually interdependent ideas.

1. That any given legal norm may be established by agreement or by imposition, on grounds of expediency or rational values or both, with a claim to obedience at least on the part of the members of the corporate group. This is, however, usually extended to include all persons within the sphere of authority or of power in question – which in the case of territorial bodies is the territorial area – who stand in certain social relationships or carry out forms of social action which in the order governing the corporate group have been declared to be relevant.

2. That every body of law consists essentially in a consistent system of abstract rules which have normally been intentionally established. Furthermore, administration of law is held to consist in the application of these rules to particular cases; the administrative process in the rational pursuit of the interests which are specified in the order governing the corporate group within the limits laid down by legal precepts and following principles which are capable of generalized formulation and are approved in the order governing the group, or at least not disapproved in it.

3. That thus the typical person in authority occupies an 'office'. In the action associated with his status, including the commands he issues to others, he is subject to an impersonal order to which his actions are oriented. This is true not only for persons exercising legal authority who are in the usual sense 'officials', but, for instance, for the elected president of a state.

4. That the person who obeys authority does so, as it is usually stated, only in his capacity as a 'member' of the corporate group and what he obeys is only 'the law'. He may in this connection be the member of an association, of a territorial commune, of a church or a citizen of a state.

5. In conformity with point 3, it is held that the members of the corporate group, in so far as they obey a person in authority, do not

owe this obedience to him as an individual, but to the impersonal order. Hence, it follows that there is an obligation to obedience only within the sphere of the rationally delimited authority which, in terms of the order, has been conferred upon him.

The following may thus be said to be the fundamental categories of rational legal authority:

1. A continuous organization of official functions bound by rules.

2. A specified sphere of competence. This involves (a) a sphere of obligations to perform functions which has been marked off as part of a systematic division of labour. (b) The provision of the incumbent with the necessary authority to carry out these functions. (c) That the necessary means of compulsion are clearly defined and their use is subject to definite conditions. A unit exercising authority which is organized in this way will be called an 'administrative organ' (Behörde).

There are administrative organs in this sense in large-scale private organizations, in parties and armies, as well as in the state and the church. An elected president, a cabinet of ministers, or a body of elected representatives also in this sense constitute administrative organs. This is not, however, the place to discuss these concepts. Not every administrative organ is provided with compulsory powers. But this distinction is not important for present purposes.

3. The organization of offices follows the principle of hierarchy; that is, each lower office is under the control and supervision of a higher one. There is a right of appeal and of statement of grievances from the lower to the higher. Hierarchies differ in respect to whether and in what cases complaints can lead to a ruling from an authority at various points higher in the scale, and as to whether changes are imposed from higher up or the responsibility for such changes is left to the lower office, the conduct of which was the subject of complaint.

4. The rules which regulate the conduct of an office may be technical rules or norms. In both cases, if their application is to be fully rational, specialized training is necessary. It is thus normally true that only a person who has demonstrated an adequate technical training is qualified to be a member of the administrative staff of such an organized group, and hence only such persons are eligible for appointment to official positions. The administrative staff of a rational corporate group thus typically consists of 'officials', whether the organization be devoted to political, religious, economic – in particular, capitalistic – or other ends.

5. In the rational type it is a matter of principle that the members of the administrative staff should be completely separated from owner-

ship of the means of production or administration. Officials, employees and workers attached to the administrative staff do not themselves own the non-human means of production and administration. These are rather provided for their use in kind or in money, and the official is obligated to render an accounting of their use. There exists, furthermore, in principle complete separation of the property belonging to the organization, which is controlled within the sphere of office, and the personal property of the official, which is available for his own private uses. There is a corresponding separation of the place in which official functions are carried out, the 'office' in the sense of premises, from living quarters.

6. In the rational type case, there is also a complete absence of appropriation of his official position by the incumbent. Where 'rights' to an office exist, as in the case of judges, and recently of an increasing proportion of officials and even of workers, they do not normally serve the purpose of appropriation by the official, but of securing the purely objective and independent character of the conduct of the office so that it is oriented only to the relevant norms.

7. Administrative acts, decisions and rules are formulated and recorded in writing, even in cases where oral discussion is the rule or is even mandatory. This applies at least to preliminary discussions and proposals, to final decisions, and to all sorts of orders and rules. The combination of written documents and a continuous organization of official functions constitutes the 'office' which is the central focus of all types of modern corporate action.

8. Legal authority can be exercised in a wide variety of different forms which will be distinguished and discussed later. The following analysis will be deliberately confined for the most part to the aspect of imperative coordination in the structure of the administrative staff. It will consist in an analysis in terms of ideal types of officialdom of 'bureaucracy'.

In the above outline no mention has been made of the kind of supreme head appropriate to a system of legal authority. This is a consequence of certain considerations which can only be made entirely understandable at a later stage in the analysis. There are very important types of rational imperative coordination which, with respect to the ultimate source of authority, belong to other categories. This is true of the hereditary charismatic type, as illustrated by hereditary monarchy and of the pure charismatic type of a president chosen by plebiscite. Other cases involve rational elements at important points, but are made up of a combination of bureaucratic and charismatic components, as is true of the cabinet form of government. Still others are subject to the authority of the chief of other corporate groups, whether their character be charismatic or bureaucratic; thus the formal head of a government department under a parliamentary regime may be a minister who occupies his position because of his authority in a party. The type of rational, legal administrative staff is capable of application in all kinds of situations and contexts. It is the most important mechanism for the administration of everyday profane affairs. For in that sphere, the exercise of authority and, more broadly, imperative coordination, consists precisely in administration.

The purest type of exercise of legal authority is that which employs a bureaucratic administrative staff. Only the supreme chief of the organization occupies his position of authority by virtue of appropriation, of election, or of having been designated for the succession. But even *his* authority consists in a sphere of legal 'competence'. The whole administrative staff under the supreme authority then consists, in the purest type, of individual officials who are appointed and function according to the following criteria:

1. They are personally free and subject to authority only with respect to their impersonal official obligations.

2. They are organized in a clearly defined hierarchy of offices.

3. Each office has a clearly defined sphere of competence in the legal sense.

4. The office is filled by a free contractual relationship. Thus, in principle, there is free selection.

5. Candidates are selected on the basis of technical qualifications. In the most rational case, this is tested by examination or guaranteed by diplomas certifying technical training, or both. They are *appointed*, not elected.

6. They are remunerated by fixed salaries in money, for the most part with a right to pensions. Only under certain circumstances does the employing authority, especially in private organizations, have a right to terminate the appointment, but the official is always free to resign. The salary scale is primarily graded according to rank in the hierarchy; but in addition to this criterion, the responsibility of the position and the requirements of the incumbent's social status may be taken into account.

7. The office is treated as the sole, or at least the primary, occupation of the incumbent.

8. It constitutes a career. There is a system of 'promotion' according to seniority or to achievement, or both. Promotion is dependent on the judgement of superiors.

9. The official works entirely separated from ownership of the means of administration and without appropriation of his position.

10. He is subject to strict and systematic discipline and control in the conduct of the office.

This type of organization is in principle applicable with equal facility to a wide variety of different fields. It may be applied in profit-making business or in charitable organizations, or in any number of other types of private enterprises serving ideal or material ends. It is equally applicable to political and to religious organizations. With varying degrees of approximation to a pure type, its historical existence can be demonstrated in all these fields.

1. For example, this type of bureaucracy is found in private clinics, as well as in endowed hospitals or the hospitals maintained by religious orders. Bureaucratic organization has played a major role in the Catholic Church. It is well illustrated by the administrative role of the priesthood (*Kaplanokratie*) in the modern church, which has expropriated almost all of the old church benefices, which were in former days to a large extent subject to private appropriation. It is also illustrated by the conception of the universal Episcopate, which is thought of as formally constituting a universal legal competence in religious matters. Similarly, the doctrine of Papal infallibility is thought of as in fact involving a universal competence, but only one which functions 'ex cathedra' in the sphere of the office, thus implying the typical distinction between the sphere of office and that of the private affairs of the incumbent. The same phenomena are found in the large-scale capitalistic enterprise ; and the larger it is, the greater their role. And this is not less true of political parties, which will be discussed separately. Finally, the modern army is essentially a bureaucratic organization administered by that peculiar type of military functionary, the 'officer'.

2. Bureaucratic authority is carried out in its purest form where it is most clearly dominated by the principle of appointment. There is no such thing as a hierarchy of elected officials in the same sense as there is a hierarchical organization of appointed officials. In the first place, election makes it impossible to attain a stringency of discipline even approaching that in the appointed type. For it is open to a subordinate official to compete for elective honours on the same terms as

his superiors, and his prospects are not dependent on the superior's judgement.

3. Appointment by free contract, which makes free selection possible, is essential to modern bureaucracy. Where there is a hierarchical organization with impersonal spheres of competence, but occupied by unfree officials – like slaves or dependents, who, however, function in a formally bureaucratic manner – the term 'patrimonial bureaucracy' will be used.

4. The role of technical qualifications in bureaucratic organizations is continually increasing. Even an official in a party or a trade union organization is in need of specialized knowledge, though it is usually of an empirical character, developed by experience, rather than by formal training. In the modern state, the only 'offices' for which no technical qualifications are required are those of ministers and presidents. This only goes to prove that they are 'officials' only in a formal sense, and not substantively, as is true of the managing director or president of a large business corporation. There is no question but that the 'position' of the capitalistic entrepreneur is as definitely appropriated as is that of a monarch. Thus at the top of a bureaucratic organization, there is necessarily an element which is at least not purely bureaucratic. The category of bureaucracy is one applying only to the exercise of control by means of a particular kind of administrative staff.

5. The bureaucratic official normally receives a fixed salary. By contrast, sources of income which are privately appropriated will be called 'benefices'. Bureaucratic salaries are also normally paid in money. Though this is not essential to the concept of bureaucracy, it is the arrangement which best fits the pure type. Payments in kind are apt to have the character of benefices, and the receipt of a benefice normally implies the appropriation of opportunities for earnings and of positions. [. . .]

Technical advantages of bureaucratic organization. The decisive reason for the advance of bureaucratic organization has always been its purely technical superiority over any other form of organization. The fully developed bureaucratic mechanism compares with other organizations exactly as does the machine with the non-mechanical modes of production.

Precision, speed, unambiguity, knowledge of the files, continuity, discretion, unity, strict subordination, reduction of friction and of material and personal costs – these are raised to the optimum point in the strictly bureaucratic administration, and especially in its mono-

cratic form. As compared with all collegiate, honorific and avocational forms of administration, trained bureaucracy is superior on all
these points. And as far as complicated tasks are concerned, paid
bureaucratic work is not only more precise but, in the last analysis, it is
often cheaper than even formally unremunerated honorific service.

Honorific arrangements make administrative work an avocation and,
for this reason alone, honorific service normally functions more slowly ;
being less bound to schemata and being more formless. Hence it is
less precise and less unified than bureaucratic work because it is less
dependent upon superiors and because the establishment and exploitation of the apparatus of subordinate officials and filing services are
almost unavoidably less economical. Honorific service is less continuous than bureaucratic and frequently quite expensive. This is
especially the case if one thinks not only of the money costs to the
public treasury – costs which bureaucratic administration, in comparison
with administration by notables, usually substantially increases – but
also of the frequent economic losses of the governed caused by delays
and lack of precision. The possibility of administration by notables
normally and permanently exists only where official management can
be satisfactorily discharged as an avocation. With the qualitative increase of tasks the administration has to face, administration by notables
reaches its limits – today, even in England. Work organized by collegiate bodies causes friction and delay and requires compromises
between colliding interests and views. The administration, therefore,
runs less precisely and is more independent of superiors ; hence, it is
less unified and slower. All advances of the Prussian administrative
organization have been and will in the future be advances of bureaucratic, and especially of the monocratic, principle.

Today, it is primarily the capitalist market economy which demands
that the official business of the administration be discharged precisely,
unambiguously, continuously and with as much speed as possible.
Normally, the very large, modern capitalist enterprises are themselves
unequalled models of strict bureaucratic organization. Business management throughout rests on increasing precision, steadiness and, above
all, the speed of operations. This, in turn, is determined by the peculiar
nature of the modern means of communication, including, among
other things, the news service of the press. The extraordinary increase
in the speed by which public announcements, as well as economic
and political facts, are transmitted exerts a steady and sharp pressure
in the direction of speeding up the tempo of administrative reaction
towards various situations. The optimum of such reaction time is
normally attained only by a strictly bureaucratic organization.

Bureaucratization offers above all the optimum possibility for carrying through the principle of specializing administrative functions according to purely objective considerations. Individual performances are allocated to functionaries who have specialized training and who by constant practice learn more and more. The 'objective' discharge of business primarily means a discharge of business according to *calculable rules* and 'without regard for persons'.

'Without regard for persons' is also the watchword of the 'market' and, in general, of all pursuits of naked economic interests. A consistent execution of bureaucratic domination means the levelling of status 'honour'. Hence, if the principle of the free-market is not at the same time restricted, it means the universal domination of the 'class situation'. That this consequence of bureaucratic domination has not set in everywhere, parallel to the extent of bureaucratization, is due to the differences among possible principles by which polities may meet their demands.

The second element mentioned, 'calculable rules', also is of paramount importance for modern bureaucracy. The peculiarity of modern culture, and specifically of its technical and economic basis, demands this very 'calculability' of results. When fully developed, bureaucracy also stands, in a specific sense, under the principle of *sine ira ac studio*. Its specific nature, which is welcomed by capitalism, develops the more perfectly the more the bureaucracy is 'dehumanized', the more completely it succeeds in eliminating from official business love, hatred and all purely personal, irrational and emotional elements which escape calculation. This is the specific nature of bureaucracy and it is appraised as its special virtue.

The more complicated and specialized modern culture becomes, the more its external supporting apparatus demands the personally detached and strictly 'objective' *expert*, in lieu of the master of older social structures, who was moved by personal sympathy and favour, by grace and gratitude. Bureaucracy offers the attitudes demanded by the external apparatus of modern culture in the most favourable combination. As a rule, only bureaucracy has established the foundation for the administration of a rational law conceptually systematized on the basis of such enactments as the latter Roman imperial period first created with a high degree of technical perfection. During the Middle Ages, this law was received along with the bureaucratization of legal administration, that is to say, with the displacement of the old trial procedure which was bound to tradition or to irrational presuppositions, by the rationally trained and specialized expert.

The permanent character of the bureaucratic machine. Once it is fully established, bureaucracy is among those social structures which are the hardest to destroy. Bureaucracy is the means of carrying 'community action' over into rationally ordered 'societal action'. Therefore, as an instrument for 'societalizing' relations of power, bureaucracy has been and is a power instrument of the first order – for the one who controls the bureaucratic apparatus.

Under otherwise equal conditions, a 'societal action', which is methodically ordered and led, is superior to every resistance of 'mass' or even of 'communal action'. And where the bureaucratization of administration has been completely carried through, a form of power relation is established that is practically unshatterable.

The individual bureaucrat cannot squirm out of the apparatus in which he is harnessed. In contrast to the honorific or avocational 'notable', the professional bureaucrat is chained to his activity by his entire material and ideal existence. In the great majority of cases, he is only a single cog in an ever-moving mechanism which prescribes to him an essentially fixed route of march. The official is entrusted with specialized tasks and normally the mechanism cannot be put into motion or arrested by him, but only from the very top. The individual bureaucrat is thus forged to the community of all the functionaries who are integrated into the mechanism. They have a common interest in seeing that the mechanism continues its functions and that the societally exercised authority carries on.

The ruled, for their part, cannot dispense with or replace the bureaucratic apparatus of authority once it exists. For this bureaucracy rests upon expert training, a functional specialization of work, and an attitude set for habitual and virtuoso-like mastery of single yet methodically integrated functions. If the official stops working, or if his work is forcefully interrupted, chaos results, and it is difficult to improvise replacements from among the governed who are fit to master such chaos. This holds for public administration as well as for private economic management. More and more the material fate of the masses depends upon the steady and correct functioning of the increasingly bureaucratic organizations of private capitalism. The idea of eliminating these organizations becomes more and more utopian.

The discipline of officialdom refers to the attitude-set of the official for precise obedience within his *habitual* activity, in public as well as in private organizations. This discipline increasingly becomes the basis of all order, however great the practical importance of administration on the basis of the filed documents may be. The naive idea of Bakuninism of destroying the basis of 'acquired rights' and 'domination' by destroying public documents overlooks the settled orientation of man for keeping to the habitual rules and regulations that continue to exist independently of the documents. Every reorganization of beaten or dissolved troops, as well as the restoration of administrative orders destroyed by revolt, panic or other catastrophes, is realized by appealing to the trained orientation of obedient compliance to such orders. Such compliance has been conditioned into the officials, on the one hand, and, on the other hand, into the governed. If such an appeal is successful it brings, as it were, the disturbed mechanism into gear again.

The objective indispensability of the once-existing apparatus, with its peculiar, 'impersonal' character, means that the mechanism – in contrast to feudal orders based upon personal piety – is easily made to work for anybody who knows how to gain control over it. A rationally ordered system of officials continues to function smoothly after the enemy has occupied the area ; he merely needs to change the top officials. This body of officials continues to operate because it is to the vital interest of everyone concerned, including above all the enemy.

During the course of his long years in power, Bismarck brought his ministerial colleagues into unconditional bureaucratic dependence by eliminating all independent statesmen. Upon his retirement, he saw to his surprise that they continued to manage their offices unconcerned and undismayed, as if he had not been the master mind and creator of these creatures, but rather as if some single figure had been exchanged for some other figure in the bureaucratic machine. With all the changes of masters in France since the time of the First Empire, the power machine has remained essentially the same. Such a machine makes 'revolution', in the sense of the forceful creation of entirely new formations of authority, technically more and more impossible, especially when the apparatus controls the modern means of communication (telegraph, etc.) and also by virtue of its internal rationalized structure. In classic fashion, France has demonstrated how this process has substituted *coups d'état* for 'revolutions': all successful transformations in France have amounted to *coups d'état*.

6 Georg Simmel

(a) The Dyad and the Triad

Excerpts from Georg Simmel, *Sociologie, Untersuchungen über die Formen der Vergesellschaftung*, 1908, reprinted in Kurt H. Wolff (ed. and trans.), *The Sociology of Georg Simmel*, Free Press, 1950, pp. 123–4, 135–6, 145–7.

The dyad

Everyday experiences show the specific character that a relationship attains by the fact that only two elements participate in it. A common fate or enterprise, an agreement or secret between two persons, ties each of them in a very different manner than if even only three have a part in it. This is perhaps most characteristic of the secret. General experience seems to indicate that this minimum of two, with which the secret ceases to be the property of the one individual, is at the same time the maximum at which its preservation is relatively secure. [. . .]

More generally speaking, the difference between the dyad and larger groups consists in the fact that the dyad has a different relation to each of its two elements than have larger groups to *their* members. Although for the outsider, the group consisting of two may function as an autonomous, super-individual unit, it usually does not do so for its participants. Rather, each of the two feels himself confronted only by the other, not by a collectivity above him. The social structure here rests immediately on the one and on the other of the two, and the secession of either would destroy the whole. The dyad, therefore, does not attain that super-personal life which the individual feels to be independent of himself. As soon, however, as there is a sociation of three, a group continues to exist even in case one of the members drops out.

This dependence of the dyad upon its two individual members causes the thought of its existence to be accompanied by the thought of its termination much more closely and impressively than in any other group, where every member knows that even after his retirement or death, the group can continue to exist. [. . .]

The significance of this characteristic, however, is by no means only negative (referring, that is, to what it excludes). On the contrary, it also makes for a close and highly specific coloration of the dyadic relationship. Precisely the fact that each of the two knows that he can depend only upon the other and on nobody else, gives the dyad a special consecration – as is seen in marriage and friendship, but also in more external associations, including political ones, that consist of two groups. In respect to its sociological destiny and in regard to any other destiny that depends on it, the dyadic element is much more frequently confronted with All or Nothing than is the member of the larger group.

The expansion of the dyad

The triad v. *the dyad*. This peculiar closeness between two is most clearly revealed if the dyad is contrasted with the triad. For among three elements, each one operates as an intermediary between the other two, exhibiting the twofold function of such an organ, which is to unite and to separate. Where three elements, A, B, C, constitute a group, there is, in addition to the direct relationship between A and B, for instance, their indirect one, which is derived from their common relation to C. [. . .] Discords between two parties which they themselves cannot remedy, are accommodated by the third or by absorption in a comprehensive whole.

Yet the indirect relation does not only strengthen the direct one. It may also disturb it. No matter how close a triad may be, there is always the occasion on which two of the three members regard the third as an intruder. [. . .]

The sociological structure of the dyad is characterized by two phenomena that are absent from it. One is the intensification of relations by a third element or by a social framework that transcends both members of the dyad. The other is any disturbance and distraction of pure and immediate reciprocity. In some cases it is precisely this absence which makes the dyadic relationship more intensive and strong. For, many otherwise undeveloped, unifying forces that derive from more remote psychical reservoirs come to life in the feeling of exclusive dependence upon one another and of hopelessness that cohesion might come from anywhere but immediate interaction. Likewise, they carefully avoid many disturbances and dangers into which confidence in a third party and in the triad itself might lead the two. This intimacy, which is the tendency of relations between two persons, is the reason why the dyad constitutes the chief seat of jealousy.

The triad

The sociological significance of the third element

What has been said indicates to a great extent the role of the third element, as well as the configurations that operate among *three* social elements. The dyad represents both the first social synthesis and unification, and the first separation and antithesis. The appearance of the third party indicates transition, conciliation and abandonment of absolute contrast (although, on occasion, it introduces contrast). The triad as such seems to me to result in three kinds of typical group formations. All of them are impossible if there are only two elements; and on the other hand, if there are more than three, they are either equally impossible or only expand in quantity but do not change their formal type.

The non-partisan and the mediator

It is sociologically very significant that isolated elements are unified by their common relation to a phenomenon which lies outside of them. [...]

In the most significant of all dyads, monogamous marriage, the child or children, as the third element, often has the function of holding the whole together. [...]

When the third element functions as a non-partisan, we have a different variety of mediation. The non-partisan either produces the concord of two colliding parties, whereby he withdraws after making the effort of creating direct contact between the unconnected or quarreling elements; or he functions as an arbiter who balances, as it were, their contradictory claims. [...]

[...] A third mediating social element deprives conflicting claims of their affective qualities because it neutrally formulates and presents these claims to the two parties involved.

(b) The Metropolis and Mental Life

Excerpt from Georg Simmel, 'Die Grosstädte und das Geistesleben', 1903, reprinted in Kurt H. Wolff (ed. and trans.), *The Sociology of Georg Simmel,* Free Press, 1950, pp. 409–24.

The deepest problems of modern life derive from the claim of the individual to preserve the autonomy and individuality of his existence in the face of overwhelming social forces, of historical heritage, of external culture and of the technique of life. The fight with nature which primitive man has to wage for his *bodily* existence attains in this modern form its latest transformation. The eighteenth century called upon man to free himself of all the historical bonds in the state and in religion, in morals and in economics. Man's nature, originally good and common to all, should develop unhampered. In addition to more liberty, the nineteenth century demanded the functional specialization of man and his work ; this specialization makes one individual incomparable to another, and each of them indispensable to the highest possible extent. However, this specialization makes each man the more directly dependent upon the supplementary activities of all others. Nietzsche sees the full development of the individual conditioned by the most ruthless struggle of individuals ; socialism believes in the suppression of all competition for the same reason. Be that as it may, in all these positions the same basic motive is at work : the person resists to being levelled down and worn out by a social-technological mechanism. An inquiry into the inner meaning of specifically modern life and its products, into the soul of the cultural body, so to speak, must seek to solve the equation which structures like the metropolis set up between the individual and the super-individual contents of life. Such an inquiry must answer the question of how the personality accommodates itself in the adjustments to external forces. This will be my task today.

The psychological basis of the metropolitan type of individuality consists in the *intensification of nervous stimulation* which results from the swift and uninterrupted change of outer and inner stimuli. Man is a differentiating creature. His mind is stimulated by the difference between a momentary impression and the one which preceded it. Lasting impressions, impressions which differ only slightly from one another, impressions which take a regular and habitual course and show regular and habitual contrasts – all these use up, so to speak, less consciousness than does the rapid crowding of changing images, the sharp discontinuity in the grasp of a single glance and the unexpectedness of onrushing impressions. These are the psychological conditions which the metropolis creates. With each crossing of the street, with the tempo and multiplicity of economic, occupational and social life, the city sets up a deep contrast with small town and rural life with reference to the sensory foundations of psychic life. The metropolis exacts from man as a discriminating creature a different amount of consciousness than does rural life. Here the rhythm of life and sensory mental imagery flows more slowly, more habitually and more evenly. Precisely in this connection the sophisticated character of metropolitan psychic life becomes understandable – as over against small town life which rests more upon deeply felt and emotional relationships. These latter are rooted in the more unconscious layers of the psyche and grow most readily in the steady rhythm of uninterrupted habituation. The intellect, however, has its locus in the transparent, conscious, higher layers of the psyche; it is the most adaptable of our inner forces. In order to accommodate to change and to the contrast of phenomena, the intellect does not require any shocks and inner upheavals; it is only through such upheavals that the more conservative mind could accommodate to the metropolitan rhythm of events. Thus the metropolitan type of man – which, of course, exists in a thousand individual variants – develops an organ protecting him against the threatening currents and discrepancies of his external environment which would uproot him. He reacts with his head instead of his heart. In this an increased awareness assumes the psychic prerogative. Metropolitan life, thus, underlies a heightened awareness and a predominance of intelligence in metropolitan man. The reaction to metropolitan phenomena is shifted to that organ which is least sensitive and quite remote from the depth of personality. Intellectuality is thus seen to preserve subjective life against the overwhelming power of metropolitan life, and intellectuality branches out in many directions and is integrated with numerous discrete phenomena.

The metropolis has always been the seat of the money economy. Here the multiplicity and concentration of economic exchange gives an importance to the means of exchange which the scantiness of rural commerce would not have allowed. Money economy and the dominance of the intellect are intrinsically connected. They share a matter-of-fact attitude in dealing with men and with things; and, in this attitude, a formal justice is often coupled with an inconsiderate hardness. The intellectually sophisticated person is indifferent to all genuine individuality, because relationships and reactions result from it which cannot be exhausted with logical operations. In the same manner, the individuality of phenomena is not commensurate with the pecuniary principle. Money is concerned only with what is common to all: it asks for the exchange value, it reduces all quality and individuality to the question: How much? All intimate emotional relations between persons are founded in their individuality, whereas in rational relations man is reckoned with like a number, like an element which is in itself indifferent. Only the objective measurable achievement is of interest. Thus metropolitan man reckons with his merchants and customers, his domestic servants and often even with persons with whom he is obliged to have social intercourse. These features of intellectuality contrast with the nature of the small circle in which the inevitable knowledge of individuality as inevitably produces a warmer tone of behaviour, a behaviour which is beyond a mere objective balancing of service and return. In the sphere of the economic psychology of the small group it is of importance that under primitive conditions production serves the customer who orders the goods, so that the producer and the consumer are acquainted. The modern metropolis, however, is supplied almost entirely by production for the market, that is, for entirely unknown purchasers who never personally enter the producer's actual field of vision. Through this anonymity the interests of each party acquire an unmerciful matter-of-factness; and the intellectually calculating economic egoisms of both parties need not fear any deflection because of the imponderables of personal relationships. The money economy dominates the metropolis; it has displaced the last survivals of domestic production and the direct barter of goods; it minimizes, from day to day, the amount of work ordered by customers. The matter-of-fact attitude is obviously so intimately interrelated with the money economy, which is dominant in the metropolis, that nobody can say whether the intellectualistic mentality first promoted the money economy or whether the latter determined the former. The metropolitan way of life is certainly the most fertile soil for this reciprocity, a point which I shall document merely by citing the dictum of the most eminent English constitutional historian: throughout the whole course of English history, London has never acted as England's heart but often as England's intellect and always as her moneybag!

In certain seemingly insignificant traits, which lie upon the surface of life, the same psychic currents characteristically unite. Modern mind has become more and more calculating. The calculative exactness of practical life which the money economy has brought about corresponds to the ideal of natural science: to transform the world into an arithmetic problem, to fix every part of the world by mathematical formulas. Only money economy has filled the days of so many people with weighing, calculating, with numerical determinations, with a reduction of qualitative values to quantitative ones. Through the calculative nature of money a new precision, a certainty in the definition of identities and differences, an unambiguousness in agreements and arrangements has been brought about in the relations of life-elements – just as externally this precision has been effected by the universal diffusion of pocket watches. However, the conditions of metropolitan life are at once cause and effect of this trait. The relationships and affairs of the typical metropolitan usually are so varied and complex that without the strictest punctuality in promises and services the whole structure would break down into an inextricable chaos. Above all, this necessity is brought about by the aggregation of so many people with such differentiated interests, who must integrate their relations and activities into a highly complex organism. If all clocks and watches in Berlin would suddenly go wrong in different ways, even if only by one hour, all economic life and communication of the city would be disrupted for a long time. In addition an apparently mere external factor: long distances, would make all waiting and broken appointments result in an ill-afforded waste of time. Thus, the technique of metropolitan life is unimaginable without the most punctual integration of all activities and mutual relations into a stable and impersonal time schedule. Here again the general conclusions of this entire task of reflection become obvious, namely, that from each point on the surface of existence – however closely attached to the surface alone – one may drop a sounding into the depth of the psyche so that all the most banal externalities of life finally are connected with the ultimate decisions concerning the meaning and style of life. Punctuality, calculability, exactness are forced upon life by the complexity and extension of metropolitan existence and are not only most intimately connected with its money economy and intellectualistic character. These traits must also colour the contents of life and favour the exclusion of those irrational, instinctive, sovereign traits and impulses which aim at determining the mode of life from within, instead of receiving the general and precisely schematized form of life from without. Even though sovereign types of personality, characterized by irrational impulses, are by no means impossible in the city, they are, nevertheless, opposed to typical city life. The passionate hatred of men like Ruskin and Nietzsche for the metropolis is understandable in these terms. Their natures discovered the value of life alone in the unschematized existence which cannot be defined with precision for all alike. From the same source of this hatred of the metropolis surged their hatred of money economy and of the intellectualism of modern existence.

The same factors which have thus coalesced into the exactness and minute precision of the form of life have coalesced into a structure of the highest impersonality; on the other hand, they have promoted a highly personal subjectivity. There is perhaps no psychic phenomenon which has been so unconditionally reserved to the metropolis as has the blasé attitude. The blasé attitude results first from the rapidly changing and closely compressed contrasting stimulations of the nerves. [...] An incapacity thus emerges to react to new sensations with the appropriate energy. This constitutes that blasé attitude which, in fact, every metropolitan child shows when compared with children of quieter and less changeable milieus.

This physiological source of the metropolitan blasé attitude is joined by another source which flows from the money economy. The essence of the blasé attitude consists in the blunting of discrimination. This does not mean that the objects are not perceived, as is the case with the half-wit, but rather that the meaning and differing values of things, and thereby the things themselves, are experienced as insubstantial. They appear to the blasé person in an evenly flat and grey tone ; no one object deserves preference over any other. This mood is the faithful subjective reflection of the completely internalized money economy. By being the equivalent to all the manifold things in one and the same way, money becomes the most frightful leveller. For money expresses all qualitative differences of things in terms of 'how much?' Money, with all its colourlessness and indifference, becomes the common denominator of all values ; irreparably it hollows out the core of things, their individuality, their specific value and their incomparability. All things float with equal specific gravity in the constantly moving stream of money. All things lie on the same level and differ from one another only in the size of the area which they cover. In the individual case this colouration, or rather discolouration, of things through their money equivalence may be unnoticeably minute. However, through the relations of the rich to the objects to be had for money, perhaps even though the total character which the mentality of the contemporary public everywhere imparts to these objects, the exclusively pecuniary evaluation of objects has become quite considerable. The large cities, the main seats of the money exchange, bring the purchasability of things to the fore much more impressively than do smaller localities. That is why cities are also the genuine locale of the blasé attitude. In the blasé attitude the concentration of men and things stimulate the nervous system of the individual to its highest achievement so that it attains its peak. Through the mere quantitative intensification of the same conditioning factors this achievement is transformed into its opposite and appears in the peculiar adjustment of the blasé attitude. In this phenomenon the nerves find in the refusal to react to their stimulation the last possibility of accommodating to the contents and forms of metropolitan life. The self-preservation of certain personalities is bought at the price of devaluating the whole objective world, a devaluation which in the end unavoidably drags one's own personality down into a feeling of the same worthlessness.

Whereas the subject of this form of existence has to come to terms with it entirely for himself, his self-preservation in the face of the large city demands from him a no less negative behaviour of a social nature. This mental attitude of metropolitans toward one another we may designate, from a formal point of view, as reserve. If so many inner reactions were responses to the continuous external contacts with innumerable people as are those in the small town, where one knows almost everybody one meets and where one has a positive relation to almost everyone, one would be completely atomized internally and come to an unimaginable psychic state. Partly this psychological fact, partly the right to distrust which men have in the face of the touch-and-go elements of metropolitan life, necessitates our reserve. As a result of this reserve we frequently do not even know by sight those who have been our neighbours for years. And it is this reserve which in the eyes of the small-town people makes us appear to be cold and heart-less. Indeed, if I do not deceive myself, the inner aspect of this outer reserve is not only indifference but more often than we are aware, it is a slight aversion, a mutual strangeness and repulsion, which will break into hatred and fight at the moment of a closer contact, however caused. The whole inner organization of such an extensive communi-cative life rests upon an extremely varied hierarchy of sympathies, indifferences and aversions of the briefest as well as of the most per-manent nature. The sphere of indifference in this hierarchy is not as large as might appear on the surface. Our psychic activity still responds to almost every impression of somebody else with a somewhat distinct feeling. The unconscious, fluid and changing character of this im-pression seems to result in a state of indifference. Actually this indiffer-ence would be just as unnatural as the diffusion of indiscriminate mutual suggestion would be unbearable. From both these typical dangers of the metropolis, indifference and indiscriminate suggest-ibility, antipathy protects us. A latent antipathy and the preparatory stage of practical antagonism effect the distances and aversions without which this mode of life could not at all be led. The extent and the mixture of this style of life, the rhythm of its emergence and disappear-ance, the forms in which it is satisfied – all these, with the unifying motives in the narrower sense, form the inseparable whole of the metropolitan style of life. What appears in the metropolitan style of life directly as dissociation is in reality only one of its elemental forms of socialization.

This reserve with its overtone of hidden aversion appears in turn as the form or the cloak of a more general mental phenomenon of the metropolis: it grants to the individual a kind and an amount of per-sonal freedom which has no analogy whatsoever under other conditions. The metropolis goes back to one of the large developmental tendencies of social life as such, to one of the few tendencies for which an approximately universal formula can be discovered. The earliest phase of social formations found in historical as well as in contemporary social structures is this: a relatively small circle firmly closed against neighbouring, strange or in some way antagonistic circles. However, this circle is closely coherent and allows its individual members only a narrow field for the development of unique qualities and free, self-responsible movements. Political and kinship groups, parties and religious associations begin in this way. The self-preservation of very young associations requires the establishment of strict boundaries and a centripetal unity. Therefore they cannot allow the individual freedom and unique inner and outer development. From this stage social development proceeds at once in two different, yet corresponding, directions. To the extent to which the group grows – numerically, spatially, in significance and in content of life – to the same degree the group's direct, inner unity loosens, and the rigidity of the original demarcation against others is softened through mutual relations and connections. At the same time, the individual gains freedom of movement, far beyond the first jealous delimitation. The individual also gains a specific individuality to which the division of labour in the enlarged group gives both occasion and necessity. The state and Christianity, guilds and political parties, and innumerable other groups have developed according to this formula, however much, of course, the special conditions and forces of the respective groups have modified the general scheme. This scheme seems to me distinctly recognizable also in the evolution of individuality within urban life. The small-town life in Antiquity and in the Middle Ages set barriers against movement and relations of the individual toward the outside, and it set up barriers against individual independence and differentiation within the individual self. These barriers were such that under them modern man could not have breathed. Even today a metropolitan man who is placed in a small town feels a restriction similar, at least, in kind. The smaller the circle which forms our milieu is, and the more restricted those relations to others are which dissolve the boundaries of the individual, the more anxiously the circle guards the achievements, the conduct of life, and the outlook of the individual, and the more readily a quantitative and qualitative specialization would break up the framework of the whole little circle. [. . .]

[. . .] Just as in the feudal age, the 'free' man was the one who stood under the law of the land, that is, under the law of the largest social orbit, and the unfree man was the one who derived his right merely from the narrow circle of a feudal association and was excluded from the larger social orbit – so today metropolitan man is 'free' in a spiritualized and refined sense, in contrast to the pettiness and prejudices which hem in the small-town man. For the reciprocal reserve and indifference and the intellectual life conditions of large circles are never felt more strongly by the individual in their impact upon his independence than in the thickest crowd of the big city. This is because the bodily proximity and narrowness of space makes the mental distance only the more visible. It is obviously only the obverse of this freedom if, under certain circumstances, one nowhere feels as lonely and lost as in the metropolitan crowd. For here as elsewhere it is by no means necessary that the freedom of man be reflected in his emotional life as comfort.

It is not only the immediate size of the area and the number of persons which, because of the universal historical correlation between the enlargement of the circle and the personal inner and outer freedom, has made the metropolis the locale of freedom. It is rather in transcending this visible expanse that any given city becomes the seat of cosmopolitanism. [...] The sphere of life of the small town is, in the main, self-contained and autarchic. For it is the decisive nature of the metropolis that its inner life overflows by waves into a far-flung national or international area. [...]

Cities are, first of all, seats of the highest economic division of labour. They produce thereby such extreme phenomena as in Paris the remunerative occupation of the *quatorzième*. They are persons who identify themselves by signs on their residences and who are ready at the dinner hour in correct attire, so that they can be quickly called upon if a dinner party should consist of thirteen persons. In the measure of its expansion, the city offers more and more the decisive conditions of the division of labour. It offers a circle which through its size can absorb a highly diverse variety of services. At the same time, the concentration of individuals and their struggle for customers compel the individual to specialize in a function from which he cannot be readily displaced by another. It is decisive that city life has transformed the struggle with nature for livelihood into an inter-human struggle for gain, which here is not granted by nature but by other men. For specialization does not flow only from the competition for gain but also from the underlying fact that the seller must always seek to call forth new and differentiated needs of the lured customer. In order to find a source of income which is not yet exhausted, and to find a function which cannot readily be displaced, it is necessary to specialize in one's services. This process promotes differentiation, refinement and the enrichment of the public's needs, which obviously must lead to growing personal differences within this public.

All this forms the transition to the individualization of mental and psychic traits which the city occasions in proportion to its size. There is a whole series of obvious causes underlying this process. First, one must meet the difficulty of asserting his own personality within the dimensions of metropolitan life. Where the quantitative increase in importance and the expense of energy reach their limits, one seizes upon qualitative differentiation in order somehow to attract the attention of the social circle by playing upon its sensitivity for differences. Finally, man is tempted to adopt the most tendentious peculiarities, that is, the specifically metropolitan extravagances of mannerism, caprice and preciousness. Now, the meaning of these extravagances does not at all lie in the contents of such behaviour, but rather in its form of 'being different', of standing out in a striking manner and thereby attracting attention. For many character types, ultimately the only means of saving for themselves some modicum of self-esteem and the sense of filling a position is indirect, through the awareness of others. In the same sense a seemingly insignificant factor is operating, the cumulative effects of which are, however, still noticeable. I refer to the brevity and scarcity of the inter-human contacts granted to the metropolitan man, as compared with social intercourse in the small town. The temptation to appear 'to the point', to appear concentrated and strikingly characteristic, lies much closer to the individual in brief metropolitan contacts than in an atmosphere in which frequent and prolonged association assures the personality of an unambiguous image of himself in the eyes of the other.

The most profound reason, however, why the metropolis conduces to the urge for the most individual personal existence – no matter whether justified and successful – appears to me to be the following: the development of modern culture is characterized by the preponderance of what one may call the 'objective spirit' over the 'subjective spirit'. This is to say, in language as well as in law, in the technique of production as well as in art, in science as well as in the objects of the domestic environment, there is embodied a sum of spirit. The individual in his intellectual development follows the growth of this spirit very imperfectly and at an ever-increasing distance. If, for instance, we view the immense culture which for the last hundred years has been embodied in things and in knowledge, in institutions and in comforts, and if we compare all this with the cultural progress of the individual during the same period – at least in high status groups – a frightful disproportion in growth between the two becomes evident. Indeed, at some points we notice a retrogression in the culture of the individual with reference to spirituality, delicacy and idealism. This discrepancy results essentially from the growing division of labour.

For the division of labour demands from the individual an ever more one-sided accomplishment, and the greatest advance in a one-sided pursuit only too frequently means dearth to the personality of the individual. In any case, he can cope less and less with the overgrowth of objective culture. The individual is reduced to a negligible quantity, perhaps less in his consciousness than in his practice and in the totality of his obscure emotional states that are derived from this practice. The individual has become a mere cog in an enormous organization of things and powers which tear from his hands all progress, spirituality, and value in order to transform them from their subjective form into the form of a purely objective life. It needs merely to be pointed out that the metropolis is the genuine arena of this culture which outgrows all personal life. Here in buildings and educational institutions, in the wonders and comforts of space-conquering technology, in the formations of community life, and in the visible institutions of the state, is offered such an overwhelming fullness of crystallized and impersonalized spirit that the personality, so to speak, cannot maintain itself under its impact. On the one hand, life is made infinitely easy for the personality in that stimulations, interests, uses of time and consciousness are offered to it from all sides. They carry the person as if in a stream, and one needs hardly to swim for oneself. On the other hand, however, life is composed more and more of these impersonal contents and offerings which tend to displace the genuine personal colourations and incomparabilities. This results in the individual's summoning the utmost in uniqueness and particularization, in order to preserve his most personal core. He has to exaggerate this personal element in order to remain audible even to himself. The atrophy of individual culture through the hypertrophy of objective culture is one reason for the bitter hatred which the preachers of the most extreme individualism, above all Nietzsche, harbour against the metropolis. But it is, indeed, also a reason why these preachers are so passionately loved in the metropolis and why they appear to the metropolitan man as the prophets and saviours of his most unsatisfied yearnings.

If one asks for the historical position of these two forms of individualism which are nourished by the quantitative relation of the metropolis, namely individual independence and the elaboration of individuality itself, then the metropolis assumes an entirely new rank order in the world history of the spirit. The eighteenth century found the individual in oppressive bonds which had become meaningless – bonds of a political, agrarian, guild and religious character. They were restraints which, so to speak, forced upon man an unnatural form and outmoded, unjust inequalities. In this situation the cry for liberty and equality arose, the belief in the individual's full freedom of movement in all social and intellectual relationships. Freedom would at once permit the noble substance common to all to come to the fore, a substance which nature had deposited in every man and which society and history had only deformed. Besides this eighteenth-century ideal of liberalism, in the nineteenth century, through Goethe and Romanticism, on the one hand, and through the economic division of labour, on the other hand, another ideal arose: individuals liberated from historical bonds now wished to distinguish themselves from one another. The carrier of man's values is no longer the 'general human being' in every individual, but rather man's qualitative uniqueness and irreplaceability. The external and internal history of our time takes its course within the struggle and in the changing entanglements of these two ways of defining the individual's role in the whole of society. It is the function of the metropolis to provide the arena for this struggle and its reconciliation. For the metropolis presents the peculiar conditions which are revealed to us as the opportunities and the stimuli for the development of both these ways of allocating roles to men. Therewith these conditions gain a unique place, pregnant with inestimable meanings for the development of psychic existence. The metropolis reveals itself as one of those great historical formations in which opposing streams which enclose life unfold, as well as join one another with equal right. However, in this process the currents of life, whether their individual phenomena touch us sympathetically or antipathetically, entirely transcend the sphere for which the judge's attitude is appropriate. Since such forces of life have grown into the roots and into the crown of the whole of the historical life in which we, in our fleeting existence, as a cell, belong only as a part, it is not our task either to accuse or to pardon, but only to understand.

7 Emile Durkheim

(a) The Division of Labour in Society

Excerpt from Emile Durkheim, *The Division of Labour in Society* (trans.
G. Simpson), Free Press, 1964, pp. 49–69. First published in French in 1893.

The word *function* is used in two quite different senses. Sometimes it suggests a system of vital movements, without reference to their consequences; at others it expresses the relation existing between these movements and corresponding needs of the organism. Thus, we speak of the function of digestion, of respiration, etc.; but we also say that digestion has as its function the incorporation into the organism of liquid or solid substances designed to replenish its losses, that respiration has for its function the introduction of necessary gases into the tissues of an animal for the sustainment of life, etc. It is in the second sense that we shall use the term. To ask what the function of the division of labour is, is to seek for the need which it supplies. When we have answered this question, we shall be able to see if this need is of the same sort as those to which other rules of conduct respond whose moral character is agreed upon.

We have chosen this term because any other would be inexact or equivocal. We cannot employ *aim* or *object* and speak of the end of the division of labour because that would presuppose that the division of labour exists *in the light of results* which we are going to determine. The terms, 'results' or 'effects', would be no more satisfactory, because they imply no idea of correspondence. On the other hand, the term 'role' or 'function', has the great advantage of implying this idea, without prejudging the question as to how this correspondence is established, whether it results from an intentional and preconceived adaptation or an aftermath adjustment. What is important for our purposes is to establish its existence and the elements of its existence; not to inquire whether there has been a prior presentiment of it, nor even if it has been sensibly felt afterwards.

Nothing seems easier to determine, at first glance, than the role of the division of labour. Are not its effects universally recognized? Since it combines both the productive power and the ability of the workman, it is the necessary condition of development in societies, both intellectual and material development. It is the source of civilization. Besides, since we quite facilely assign an absolute value to civilization, we do not bethink ourselves to seek any other function for the division of labour.

Though it may truly have this effect, there would be in that nothing to amplify through discussion. But if it had no other, and did not serve any other purpose, there would be no reason to assign it a moral character.

In short, the services that it renders are very near to being foreign to the normal life, or at least have only indirect and remote relation to it. Although it may be common enough today to reply to the polemic of Rousseau with dithyrambs of opposite meaning, nevertheless there is no proof at all that civilization is a moral fact. To meet the problem, we cannot refer to concepts which are necessarily subjective ; rather it would be necessary to employ a standard by which to measure the level of average morality, and to observe, thus, how it varies in proportion to the progress of civilization. Unfortunately, this standard of measurement is not forthcoming, but we do possess one for collective immorality. The average number of suicides, of crimes of all sorts, can effectively serve to mark the intensity of immorality in a given society. If we make this experiment it does not turn out creditably for civilization, for the number of these morbid phenomena seems to increase as the arts, sciences and industry progress. Doubtless, there would be some inadvertence in concluding from this fact that civilization is immoral, but one can at least be certain that, if it has a positive and favourable influence on the moral life, it is quite weak.

But, if we analyse this badly defined complex called civilization, we find that the elements of which it is composed are bereft of any moral character whatever.

It is particularly true of the economic activity which always accompanies civilization. Far from serving moral progress, it is in the great industrial centres that crimes and suicides are most numerous. In any event, it evidently does not present the external indices by which we recognize moral facts. We have replaced stage coaches by railroads, sailboats by transatlantic liners, small shops by manufacturing plants. All this changed activity is generally considered useful, but it contains nothing morally binding. The artisan and the private *entrepreneur* who resist this general current and obstinately pursue their modest enterprises do their duty quite as well as the great manufacturer who covers a country with machines and places a whole army of workers under his command. The moral conscience of nations is in this respect correct ; it prefers a little justice to all the industrial perfection in the world. No doubt industrial activities have a reason for existing. They respond to needs, but these needs are not moral.

The case is even stronger with art, which is absolutely refractory to all that resembles an obligation, for it is the domain of liberty. It is a luxury and an acquirement which it is perhaps lovely to possess, but which is not obligatory; what is superfluous does not impose itself. On the other hand, morality is the least indispensable, the strictly necessary, the daily bread without which societies cannot exist. Art responds to our need of pursuing an activity without end, for the pleasure of the pursuit, whereas morality compels us to follow a determinate path to a definite end. Whatever is obligatory is at the same time constraining. Thus, although art may be animated by moral ideas or find itself involved in the evolution of phenomena which, properly speaking, are moral, it is not in itself moral. It might even be contended that in the case of individuals, as in societies, an intemperant development of the aesthetic faculties is a serious sign from a moral point of view.

Of all the elements of civilization, science is the only one which, under certain conditions, presents a moral character. That is, societies are tending more and more to look upon it as a duty for the individual to develop his intelligence by learning the scientific truths which have been established. At present, there are a certain number of propositions which we must all understand. We are not forced to inject ourselves into the industrial mêlée; we do not have to be artists, but every one is now forced not to be ignorant. This obligation is, indeed, so strongly intrenched that, in certain societies, it is sanctioned not only by public opinion, but also by law. It is, moreover, not difficult to understand whence comes this special status accorded to science. Science is nothing else than conscience carried to its highest point of clarity. Thus, in order for society to live under existent conditions, the field of conscience, individual as well as social, must be extended and clarified. That is, as the environments in which they exist become more and more complex, and, consequently, more and more changeable, to endure, they must change often. On the other hand, the more obscure conscience is, the more refractory to change it is, because it does not perceive quickly enough the necessity for changing nor in what sense it must change. On the contrary, an enlightened conscience prepares itself in advance for adaptation. That is why intelligence guided by science must take a larger part in the course of collective life.

But the science which everybody is thus required to possess does not merit the name at all. It is not science; it is at most the common part and the most general. It is reduced, really, to a small number of indispensable propositions which are necessary for all to have only because they are within reach of everybody. Science, properly considered, is far above this common modicum. It does not encompass only what it is shameful not to know, but everything that it is possible to know. It does not ask of those who cultivate it only ordinary faculties that every man possesses, but special qualifications. Accordingly, being available only to an elite, it is not obligatory ; it is a useful and good thing, but it is not imperatively necessary for society to avail itself of it. It is advantageous to have ; there is nothing immoral in not having acquired it. It is a field of action which is open to the initiative of all, but where none is forced to enter. We do not have to be scholars any more than we have to be artists. Science is, then, as art and industry, outside the moral sphere.[1]

So many controversies have taken place concerning the moral charac-
ter of civilization because very often moralists have no objective criterion to distinguish moral facts from those not moral. We fall into the habit of qualifying as moral everything that has a certain nobility and some value, everything that is an object of elevated aspirations, and it is because of this over-extension of the term that we have considered civilization as moral. But the domain of ethics is not so nebulous ; it consists of all the rules of action which are imperatively imposed upon conduct, to which a sanction is attached, but no more. Consequently, since there is nothing in civilization which presents this moral criterion, civilization is morally indifferent. If then, the division of labour had no other role than to render civilization possible, it would participate in the same moral neutrality.

It is because they have not seen any further function of the division of labour that the theories that have been proposed are inconsistent on this point. In short, though there exist a zone neutral to morals, the division of labour cannot be part of it.[2] If it is not good, it is bad; if it is not moral, it is immoral. If, then, it has no other use, one falls into unresolvable antinomies, for the greater economies that it offers are offset by moral inconveniences, and since it is impossible to separate these two heterogeneous and incomparable quantities, we could not decide which prevailed over the other, nor, consequently, take a position on the matter. We would invoke the primacy of morality as a sweeping condemnation of the division of labour. However, this *ultima ratio* is arrived at through a scientific *coup d'état*, and the evident necessity for specialization makes such a position untenable.

Moreover, if the division of labour does not fill any other role, not

1. 'The essential character of good compared with true is that of being obligatory. Truth, taken by itself, does not have this character' (Janet).
2. For it is in opposition to a moral rule.

only does it not have a moral character, but it is difficult to see what reason for existence it can have. We shall see that, taken by itself, civilization has no intrinsic and absolute value ; what makes it valuable is its correspondence to certain needs. But the proposition will be demonstrated later that these needs are themselves results of the division of labour. Because the latter does not go forward without a demand for greater expenditure of energy, man is led to seek, as compensation, certain goods from civilization which, otherwise, would not interest him in the least. If, however, the division of labour replied to no other needs than these, it would have no other function than to diminish the effects which it produces itself, or to heal the wounds which it inflicts. Under these conditions, we would have to endure it, but there would be no reason for desiring it since the services it would render would reduce its function to replenishing the losses that it caused.

All this leads us to seek some other function for the division of labour. Certain current facts put us on the road to a solution.

Everybody knows that we like those who resemble us, those who think and feel as we do. But the opposite is no less true. It very often happens that we feel kindly towards those who do not resemble us, precisely because of this lack of resemblance. These facts are apparently so contradictory that moralists have always vacillated concerning the true nature of friendship and have derived it sometimes from the former, sometimes from the latter. The Greeks had long ago posed this problem.

Friendship (says Aristotle) causes much discussion. According to some people, it consists in a certain resemblance, and we like those who resemble us : whence the proverbs 'birds of a feather flock together' and 'like seeks like', and other such phrases. Others, on the contrary, say that all who are alike are opposed to one another. Again, some men push their inquiries on these points higher and reason from a consideration of nature. So Euripides says,
The earth by drought consumed doth love the rain,
And the great heaven overcharged with rain,
Doth love to fall in showers upon the earth.
Heraclitus, again, maintains that 'contrariety is expedient, and that the best agreement arises from things differing, and that all things come into being in the way of the principle of antagonism' (*Nichomachean Ethics*).

These opposing doctrines prove that both types are necessary to natural friendship. Difference, as likeness, can be a cause of mutual attraction. However, certain differences do not produce this effect. We do not find any pleasure in those completely different from us. Spendthrifts do not seek the company of misers, nor moral and honest people that of hypocrites and pretenders; sweet and gentle spirits have no taste for sour and malevolent temperaments. Only certain kinds of differences attract each other. They are those which, instead of opposing and excluding, complement each other. As Bain says, there is a type of difference which repels, another which attracts, one which leads to rivalry, another which leads to friendship. If one of two people has what the other has not, but desires, in that fact lies the point of departure for a positive attraction. Thus it is that a theorist, a subtle and reasoning individual, often has a very special sympathy for practical men, with their quick sense and rapid intuitions; the timid for the firm and resolute, the weak for the strong, and conversely. As richly endowed as we may be, we always lack something, and the best of us realize our own insufficiency. That is why we seek in our friends the qualities that we lack, since in joining with them, we participate in some measure in their nature and thus feel less incomplete. So it is that small friendly associations are formed wherein each one plays a role conformable to his character, where there is a true exchange of services. One urges on, another consoles; this one advises, that one follows the advice, and it is this apportionment of functions or, to use the usual expression, this division of labour, which determines the relations of friendship.

We are thus led to consider the division of labour in a new light. In this instance, the economic services that it can render are picayune compared to the moral effect that it produces, and its true function is to create in two or more persons a feeling of solidarity. In whatever manner the result is obtained, its aim is to cause coherence among friends and to stamp them with its seal. [. . .]

The social relations to which the division of labour gives birth have often been considered only in terms of exchange, but this misinterprets what such exchange implies and what results from it. It suggests two beings mutually dependent because they are each incomplete, and translates this mutual dependence outwardly. It is, then, only the superficial expression of an internal and very deep state. Precisely because this state is constant, it calls up a whole mechanism of images which function with a continuity that exchange does not possess. The image of the one who completes us becomes inseparable from ours, not only because it is frequently associated with ours, but particularly because it is the natural complement of it. It thus becomes an integral and permanent part of our conscience, to such a point that we can no longer separate ourselves from it and seek to increase its force. That is why we enjoy the society of the one it represents, since the presence of the object that it expresses, by making us actually perceive it, sets it off more. On the other hand, we will suffer from all circumstances which, like absence or death, may have as effect the barring of its return or the diminishing of its vivacity.

As short as this analysis is, it suffices to show that this mechanism is not identical with that which serves as a basis for sentiments of sympathy whose source is resemblance. Surely there can be no solidarity between others and us unless the image of others unites itself with ours. But when the union results from the resemblance of two images, it consists in an agglutination. The two representations become solidary because, being indistinct, totally or in part, they confound each other, and become no more than one, and they are solidary only in the measure which they confound themselves. On the contrary, in the case of the division of labour, they are outside each other and are linked only because they are distinct. Neither the sentiments nor the social relations which derive from these sentiments are the same in the two cases.

We are thus led to ask if the division of labour would not play the same role in more extensive groups, if, in contemporary societies where it has developed as we know, it would not have as its function the integration of the social body to assure unity. It is quite legitimate to suppose that the facts which we have just observed reproduce themselves here, but with greater amplitude, that great political societies can maintain themselves in equilibrium only thanks to the specialization of tasks, that the division of labour is the source, if not unique, at least principal, of social solidarity. Comte took this point of view. Of all sociologists, to our knowledge, he is the first to have recognized in the division of labour something other than a purely economic phenomenon. He saw in it 'the most essential condition of social life', provided that one conceives it 'in all its rational extent ; that is to say, that one applies it to the totality of all our diverse operations of whatever kind, instead of attributing it, as is ordinarily done, to simple material usages'. Considered in this light, he says,

'it leads immediately to regarding not only individuals and classes, but also, in many respects, different peoples, as at once participating, following a definite path in a special degree, exactly determined, in a work, immense and communal, whose inevitable gradual development links actual cooperators to their predecessors and even to their successors. It is thus the continuous repartition of different human endeavors which especially constitutes social solidarity and which becomes the elementary cause of the extension and growing complication of the social organism' (*Cours de philosophie positive*).

If this hypothesis were proved, the division of labour would play a role much more important than that which we ordinarily attribute to it. It would serve not only to raise societies to luxury, desirable perhaps, but superfluous ; it would be a condition of their existence. Through it, or at least particularly through it, their cohesion would be assured ; it would determine the essential traits of their constitution. Accordingly, although we may not yet be in position to resolve the question rigorously, we can, however, imply from it now that, if such is really the function of the division of labour, it must have a moral character, for the need of order, harmony and social solidarity is generally considered moral.

But before seeing whether this common opinion is well founded, we must verify the hypothesis that we have just given forth concerning the role of the division of labour. Let us see if, in effect, in the societies in which we live, it is from this that social solidarity essentially derives.

But how shall we proceed to such verification?

We must not simply look to see if, in these types of society, there exists a social solidarity which comes from the division of labour. That is a self-evident truism, since in such societies the division of labour is highly developed and produces solidarity. Rather we must especially determine in what degree the solidarity that it produces contributes to the general integration of society, for it is only then that we shall know how far necessary it is, whether it is an essential factor of social cohesion, or whether, on the contrary, it is only an accessory and secondary condition. To reply to this question, we must compare this social link to others in order to measure how much credit is due to it in the total effect ; and to that end, we must begin by classifying the different types of social solidarity.

But social solidarity is a completely moral phenomenon which, taken by itself, does not lend itself to exact observation nor indeed to measurement. To proceed to this classification and this comparison, we must substitute for this internal fact which escapes us an external index which symbolizes it and study the former in the light of the latter.

This visible symbol is law. In effect, despite its immaterial character, wherever social solidarity exists, it resides not in a state of pure potentiality, but manifests its presence by sensible indices. Where it is strong, it leads men strongly to one another, frequently puts them in contact, multiplies the occasions when they find themselves related. To speak correctly, considering the point our investigation has reached, it is not easy to say whether social solidarity produces these phenomena, or

Emile Durkheim 101

whether it is a result of them, whether men relate themselves because it is a driving force, or whether it is a driving force because they relate themselves. However, it is not, at the moment, necessary to decide this question; it suffices to state that the two orders of fact are linked and vary at the same time and in the same sense. The more solidary the members of a society are, the more they sustain diverse relations, one with another, or with the group taken collectively, for, if their meetings were rare, they would depend upon one another only at rare intervals, and then tenuously. Moreover, the number of these relations is necessarily proportional to that of the juridical rules which determine them. Indeed, social life, especially where it exists durably, tends inevitably to assume a definite form and to organize itself, and law is nothing else than this very organization in so far as it has greater stability and precision. The general life of society cannot extend its sway without juridical life extending its sway at the same time and in direct relation. We can thus be certain of finding reflected in law all the essential varieties of social solidarity.

The objection may be raised, it is true, that social relations can fix themselves without assuming a juridical form. Some of them do not attain this degree of consolidation and precision, but they do not remain undetermined on that account. Instead of being regulated by law, they are regulated by custom. Law, then, reflects only part of social life and furnishes us with incomplete data for the solution of the problem. Moreover, it often happens that custom is not in accord with law; we usually say that it tempers law's severity, that it corrects law's formalism, sometimes, indeed, that it is animated by a different spirit. Would it not then be true that custom manifests other sorts of solidarity than that expressed in positive law?

This opposition, however, crops up only in quite exceptional circumstances. This comes about when law no longer corresponds to the state of existing society, but maintains itself, without reason for so doing, by the force of habit. In such a case, new relations which establish themselves in spite of it are not bereft of organization, for they cannot endure without seeking consolidation. But since they are in conflict with the old existing law, they can attain only superficial organization. They do not pass beyond the stage of custom and do not enter into the juridical life proper. Thus conflict ensues. But it arises only in rare and pathological cases which cannot endure without danger. Normally, custom is not opposed to law, but is, on the contrary, its basis. It happens, in truth, that on such a basis nothing may rear its head. Social relations ensue which convey a diffuse regulation which comes from custom; but they lack importance and continuity, except in the abnormal cases of which we were just speaking. If, then, there are types of social solidarity which custom alone manifests, they are assuredly secondary; law produces those which are essential and they are the only ones we need to know.

Shall we go further and say that social solidarity does not completely manifest itself perceptibly, that these manifestations are only partial and imperfect, that behind law and custom there is an internal state whence it derives, and that in order to know it truly we must intuit it without intermediaries?—But we can know causes scientifically only by the effects that they produce, and in order to determine their nature, science chooses from these effects only the most objective and most easily measurable. Science studies heat through the variations in volume which changes in temperature produce in bodies, electricity through its physico-chemical effects, force through movement. Why should social solidarity be an exception?

What remains of it divested of social forms? What gives it its specific characters is the nature of the group whose unity it assures; that is why it varies according to social types. It is not the same in the family and in political societies; we are not attached to our country in the same fashion as the Roman was to his city or the German to his tribe. But since these differences relate themselves to social causes, we can understand them only with reference to the differences that the social effects of solidarity present. If, then, we neglect the latter, all the varieties become indiscernible and we can no longer perceive what is common to all of them, that is, the general tendency to sociability, a tendency which is always and everywhere the same and is special to no particular social type. But this residue is only an abstraction, for sociability in itself is nowhere found. What exists and really lives are the particular forms of solidarity, domestic solidarity, occupational solidarity, national solidarity, yesterday's, today's, etc. Each has its proper nature; consequently, these general remarks, in every case, give only a very incomplete explanation of a phenomenon, since they necessarily omit the concrete and the vital.

The study of solidarity thus grows out of sociology. It is a social fact we can know only through the intermediary of social effects. If so many moralists and psychologists have been able to treat the question without following this procedure, it has been by circumventing the difficulty. They have eliminated from the phenomenon all that is peculiarly social in order to retain only the psychological germ whence it developed. It is surely true that solidarity, while being a social fact of the first order, depends on the individual organism. In order to exist, it must be contained in our physical and psychic constitution. One can thus rigorously limit oneself to studying this aspect. But, in that case, one sees only the most indistinct and least special aspect. It is not even solidarity properly speaking, but rather what makes it possible.

Moreover, this abstract study would not be very fertile in results. For, in its dependence upon a state of simple disposition in our psychic nature, solidarity is much too indefinite to be comprehended easily. It is an intangible phenomenon which does not lend itself to observation. In order to assume a comprehensible form, certain social consequences must translate it overtly. Moreover, even in this indeterminate state, it depends upon social conditions which explain it and from which, consequently, it cannot be detached. That is why it is very rare that some sociological views do not find their way into these analyses of pure psychology. For example, we speak of the influence of the *gregarious state* on the formation of social sentiment in general (Bain, 1859, p. 131); or perhaps indicate in short compass the principal social relations on which sociability quite apparently depends (Spencer, 1872, pt 8, ch. 5). Without doubt, these complementary considerations, introduced helter-skelter, with examples and following chance suggestions, will not suffice to elucidate very much of the social nature of solidarity. They show, at least, that the sociological point of view is incumbent even upon psychologists.

Our method has now been fully outlined. Since law reproduces the principal forms of social solidarity, we have only to classify the different types of law to find therefrom the different types of social solidarity which correspond to it. It is now probable that there is a type which symbolizes this special solidarity of which the division of labour is the cause. That found, it will suffice, in order to measure the part of the division of labour, to compare the number of juridical rules which express it with the total volume of law.

For this task, we cannot use the distinctions utilized by the jurisconsults. Created for practical purposes, they can be very useful from this point of view, but science cannot content itself with these empirical classifications and approximations. The most accepted is that which divides law into public and private; the first is for the regulation of the relations of the individual to the State, the second, of individuals among themselves. But when we try to get closer to these terms, the line of demarcation which appeared so neat at the beginning fades away. All law is private in the sense that it is always about individuals who are present and acting; but so, too, all law is public, in the sense that it is a social function and that all individuals are, whatever their varying titles, functionaries of society. Marital functions, paternal, etc., are neither delimited nor organized in a manner different from ministerial and legislative functions, and it is not without reason that Roman law entitled tutelage *munus publicum*. What, moreover, is the State? Where does it begin and where does it end? We know how controversial the question is ; it is not scientific to make a fundamental classification repose on a notion so obscure and so badly analysed.

To proceed scientifically, we must find some characteristic which, while being essential to juridical phenomena, varies as they vary. Every precept of law can be defined as a rule of sanctioned conduct. Moreover, it is evident that sanctions change with the gravity attributed to precepts, the place they hold in the public conscience, the role they play in society. It is right, then, to classify juridical rules according to the different sanctions which are attached to them.

They are of two kinds. Some consist essentially in suffering, or at least a loss, inflicted on the agent. They make demands on his fortune, or on his honour, or on his life, or on his liberty, and deprive him of something he enjoys. We call them repressive. They constitute penal law. It is true that those which are attached to rules which are purely moral have the same character, only they are distributed in a diffuse manner, by everybody indiscriminately, whereas those in penal law are applied through the intermediary of a definite organ ; they are organized. As for the other type, it does not necessarily imply suffering for the agent, but consists only of *the return of things as they were*, in the reestablishment of troubled relations to their normal state, whether the incriminated act is restored by force to the type whence it deviated, or is annulled, that is, deprived of all social value. We must then separate juridical rules into two great classes, accordingly as they have organized repressive sanctions or only restitutive sanctions. The first comprise all penal law ; the second, civil law, commercial law, procedural law, administrative and constitutional law, after abstraction of the penal rules which may be found there.

References

BAIN, A. (1859), *The Emotions and the Will*, Longmans, Green.
SPENCER, H. (1872), *Principles of Psychology*, Williams & Norgate, 2 vols.

(b) Anomic Suicide

Excerpt from Emile Durkheim, *Suicide: A Study in Sociology* (trans. J. A. Spaulding and G. Simpson), Free Press, 1952, pp. 241–54. First published in French in 1897.

Society is not only something attracting the sentiments and activities of individuals with unequal force. It is also a power controlling them. There is a relation between the way this regulative action is performed and the social suicide-rate.

It is a well-known fact that economic crises have an aggravating effect on the suicidal tendency.

In Vienna, in 1873 a financial crisis occurred which reached its height in 1874; the number of suicides immediately rose. From 141 in 1872, they rose to 153 in 1873 and 216 in 1874. The increase in 1874 is 53 per cent [1] above 1872 and 41 per cent above 1873. What proves this catastrophe to have been the sole cause of the increase is the special prominence of the increase when the crisis was acute, or during the first four months of 1874. From 1 January to 30 April there had been 48 suicides in 1871, 44 in 1872, 43 in 1873; there were 73 in 1874. The increase is 70 per cent.[2] The same crisis occurring at the same time in Frankfurt-on-Main produced the same effects there. In the years before 1874, twenty-two suicides were committed annually on the average; in 1874 there were thirty-two, or 45 per cent more.

The famous crash is unforgotten which took place on the Paris Bourse during the winter of 1882. Its consequences were felt not only in Paris but throughout France. From 1874 to 1886 the average annual increase was only 2 per cent; in 1882 it was 7 per cent. Moreover, it was unequally distributed among the different times of year, occurring principally during the first three months or at the very time of the crash. Within these three months alone 59 per cent of the total rise occurred. So distinctly is the rise the result of unusual circumstances that it not only is not encountered in 1881 but has disappeared in 1883, although on the whole the latter year had a few more suicides than the preceding one:

1. Durkheim incorrectly gives this figure as 51 per cent. [Ed.]
2. In 1874 over 1873. [Ed.]

	1881	1882	1883
Annual total	6741	7213 (plus 7%)	7267
First three months	1589	1770 (plus 11%)	1604

This relation is found not only in some exceptional cases, but is the rule. The number of bankruptcies is a barometer of adequate sensitivity, reflecting the variations of economic life. When they increase abruptly from year to year, some serious disturbance has certainly occurred. From 1845 to 1869 there were sudden rises, symptomatic of crises, on three occasions. While the annual increase in the number of bankruptcies during this period is 3·2 per cent, it is 26 per cent in 1847, 37 per cent in 1854 and 20 per cent in 1861. At these three moments, there is also to be observed an unusually rapid rise in the number of suicides. While the average annual increase during these twenty-four years was only 2 per cent, it was 17 per cent in 1847, 8 per cent in 1854 and 9 per cent in 1861.

But to what do these crises owe their influence? Is it because they increase poverty by causing public wealth to fluctuate? Is life more readily renounced as it becomes more difficult? The explanation is seductively simple; and it agrees with the popular idea of suicide. But it is contradicted by facts.

Actually, if voluntary deaths increased because life was becoming more difficult, they should diminish perceptibly as comfort increases. Now, although when the price of the most necessary foods rises excessively, suicides generally do the same, they are not found to fall below the average in the opposite case. In Prussia, in 1850 wheat was quoted at the lowest point it reached during the entire period of 1848–81; it was at 6·91 marks per fifty kilograms; yet at this very time suicides rose from 1527 where they were in 1849 to 1736, or an increase of 13 per cent, and continued to increase during the years 1851, 1852 and 1853 although the cheap market held. In 1858–9 a new fall took place; yet suicides rose from 2038 in 1857 to 2126 in 1858 and to 2146 in 1859. From 1863 to 1866 prices which had reached 11·04 marks in 1861 fell progressively to 7·95 marks in 1864 and remained very reasonable for the whole period; suicides during the same time increased 17 per cent (2112 in 1862, 2485 in 1866). [. . .]

So far is the increase in poverty from causing the increase in suicide that even fortunate crises, the effect of which is abruptly to enhance a country's prosperity, affect suicide like economic disasters.

The conquest of Rome by Victor-Emmanuel in 1870, by definitely forming the basis of Italian unity, was the starting point for the country of a process of growth which is making it one of the great powers of Europe. Trade and industry received a sharp stimulus from it and surprisingly rapid changes took place. Whereas in 1876, 4459 steam boilers with a total of 54,000 horse-power were enough for industrial needs, the number of machines in 1887 was 9983 and their horse-power of 167,000 was threefold more. Of course the amount of production rose proportionately during the same time (di Verce, 1894, pp. 77–83). Trade followed the same rising course ; not only did the merchant marine, communications and transportation develop, but the number of persons and things transported doubled (pp. 108–17). As this generally heightened activity caused an increase in salaries (an increase of 35 per cent is estimated to have taken place from 1873 to 1889), the material comfort of workers rose, especially since the price of bread was falling at the same time (pp. 86–104). Finally, according to calculations by Bodio, private wealth rose from forty-five and a half billions on the average during the period 1875–80 to fifty-one billions during the years 1880–85 and fifty-four billions and a half in 1885–90.[8]

Now, an unusual increase in the number of suicides is observed parallel with this collective renaissance. From 1866 to 1870 they were roughly stable ; from 1871 to 1877 they increased 36 per cent. There were in

1864–70	29 suicides per million	1874	37 suicides per million
1871	31 suicides per million	1875	34 suicides per million
1872	33 suicides per million	1876	36·5 suicides per million
1873	36 suicides per million	1877	40·6 suicides per million

And since then the movement has continued. The total figure, 1139 in 1877, was 1463 in 1889, a new increase of 28 per cent. [. . .]

What proves still more conclusively that economic distress does not have the aggravating influence often attributed to it, is that it tends rather to produce the opposite effect. There is very little suicide in Ireland, where the peasantry leads so wretched a life. Poverty-stricken Calabria has almost no suicides ; Spain has a tenth as many as France. Poverty may even be considered a protection. In the various French departments the more people there are who have independent means, the more numerous are suicides.

If therefore industrial or financial crises increase suicides, this is not because they cause poverty, since crises of prosperity have the same result ; it is because they are crises, that is, disturbances of the collec-

3. The increase is less during the period 1885–90 because of a financial crisis.

Departments where, per 100,000 inhabitants, suicides were committed (1878–87)		Average number of persons of independent means per 1000 inhabitants in each group of departments (1886)
Suicides	Number of departments	
From 48 to 43	5	127
From 38 to 31	6	73
From 30 to 24	6	69
From 23 to 18	15	59
From 17 to 13	18	49
From 12 to 8	26	49
From 7 to 3	10	42

tive order.[4] Every disturbance of equilibrium, even though it achieves greater comfort and a heightening of general vitality, is an impulse to voluntary death. Whenever serious readjustments take place in the social order, whether or not due to a sudden growth or to an unexpected catastrophe, men are more inclined to self-destruction. How is this possible? How can something considered generally to improve existence serve to detach men from it?

For the answer, some preliminary considerations are required.

No living being can be happy or even exist unless his needs are sufficiently proportioned to his means. In other words, if his needs require more than can be granted, or even merely something of a different sort, they will be under continual friction and can only function painfully. Movements incapable of production without pain tend not to be reproduced. Unsatisfied tendencies atrophy, and as the impulse to live is merely the result of all the rest, it is bound to weaken as the others relax.

In the animal, at least in a normal condition, this equilibrium is established with automatic spontaneity because the animal depends on purely material conditions. All the organism needs is that the supplies of substance and energy constantly employed in the vital process should

4. To prove that an increase in prosperity diminishes suicides, the attempt has been made to show that they become less when emigration, the escape-valve of poverty, is widely practised (Legoyt, 1881, pp. 257–9). But cases are numerous where parallelism instead of inverse proportions exist between the two. In Italy from 1876 to 1890 the number of emigrants rose from 76 per 100,000 inhabitants to 335, a figure itself exceeded between 1887 and 1889. At the same time suicides did not cease to grow in numbers.

be periodically renewed by equivalent quantities; that replacement be equivalent to use. When the void created by existence in its own resources is filled, the animal, satisfied, asks nothing further. Its power of reflection is not sufficiently developed to imagine other ends than those implicit in its physical nature. On the other hand, as the work demanded of each organ itself depends on the general state of vital energy and the needs of organic equilibrium, use is regulated in turn by replacement and the balance is automatic. The limits of one are those of the other; both are fundamental to the constitution of the existence in question, which cannot exceed them.

This is not the case with man, because most of his needs are not dependent on his body or not to the same degree. Strictly speaking, we may consider that the quantity of material supplies necessary to the physical maintenance of a human life is subject to computation, though this be less exact than in the preceding case and a wider margin left for the free combinations of the will; for beyond the indispensable minimum which satisfies nature when instinctive, a more awakened reflection suggests better conditions, seemingly, desirable ends craving fulfilment. Such appetites, however, admittedly sooner or later reach a limit which they cannot pass. But how determine the quantity of well-being, comfort or luxury legitimately to be craved by a human being? Nothing appears in man's organic nor in his psychological constitution which sets a limit to such tendencies. The functioning of individual life does not require them to cease at one point rather than at another; the proof being that they have constantly increased since the beginnings of history, receiving more and more complete satisfaction, yet with no weakening of average health. Above all, how establish their proper variation with different conditions of life, occupations, relative importance of services, etc? In no society are they equally satisfied in the different stages of the social hierarchy. Yet human nature is substantially the same among all men, in its essential qualities. It is not human nature which can assign the variable limits necessary to our needs. They are thus unlimited so far as they depend on the individual alone. Irrespective of any external regulatory force, our capacity for feeling is in itself an insatiable and bottomless abyss.

But if nothing external can restrain this capacity, it can only be a source of torment to itself. Unlimited desires are insatiable by definition and insatiability is rightly considered a sign of morbidity. Being unlimited, they constantly and infinitely surpass the means at their command; they cannot be quenched. Inextinguishable thirst is constantly renewed torture. It has been claimed, indeed, that human activity naturally aspires beyond assignable limits and sets itself unattainable goals. But how can such an undetermined state be any more reconciled with the conditions of mental life than with the demands of physical life? All man's pleasure in acting, moving and exerting himself implies the sense that his efforts are not in vain and that by walking he has advanced. However, one does not advance when one walks toward no goal, or – which is the same thing – when his goal is infinity. Since the distance between us and it is always the same, whatever road we take, we might as well have made the motions without progress from the spot. Even our glances behind and our feeling of pride at the distance covered can cause only deceptive satisfaction, since the remaining distance is not proportionately reduced. To pursue a goal which is by definition unattainable is to condemn oneself to a state of perpetual unhappiness. Of course, man may hope contrary to all reason, and hope has its pleasures even when unreasonable. It may sustain him for a time ; but it cannot survive the repeated disappointments of experience indefinitely. What more can the future offer him than the past, since he can never reach a tenable condition nor even approach the glimpsed ideal? Thus, the more one has, the more one wants, since satisfactions received only stimulate instead of filling needs. Shall action as such be considered agreeable? First, only on condition of blindness to its uselessness. Secondly, for this pleasure to be felt and to temper and half veil the accompanying painful unrest, such unending motion must at least always be easy and unhampered. If it is interfered with only restlessness is left, with the lack of ease which it, itself, entails. But it would be a miracle if no insurmountable obstacle were ever encountered. Our thread of life on these conditions is pretty thin, breakable at any instant.

To achieve any other result, the passions first must be limited. Only then can they be harmonized with the faculties and satisfied. But since the individual has no way of limiting them, this must be done by some force exterior to him. A regulative force must play the same role for moral needs which the organism plays for physical needs. This means that the force can only be moral. The awakening of conscience interrupted the state of equilibrium of the animal's dormant existence ; only conscience, therefore, can furnish the means to re-establish it. Physical restraint would be ineffective ; hearts cannot be touched by physiochemical forces. So far as the appetites are not automatically restrained by physiological mechanisms, they can be halted only by a limit that they recognize as just. Men would never consent to restrict their desires if they felt justified in passing the assigned limit. But, for reasons given above, they cannot assign themselves this law of justice. So they must receive it from an authority which they respect, to which they yield spontaneously. Either directly and as a whole, or through the agency of one of its organs, society alone can play this moderating role; for it is the only moral power superior to the individual, the authority of which he accepts. It alone has the power necessary to stipulate law and to set the point beyond which the passions must not go. Finally, it alone can estimate the reward to be prospectively offered to every class of human functionary, in the name of the common interest.

As a matter of fact, at every moment of history there is a dim perception, in the moral consciousness of societies, of the respective value of different social services, the relative reward due to each, and the consequent degree of comfort appropriate on the average to workers in each occupation. The different functions are graded in public opinion and a certain coefficient of well-being assigned to each, according to its place in the hierarchy. According to accepted ideas, for example, a certain way of living is considered the upper limit to which a workman may aspire in his efforts to improve his existence, and there is another limit below which he is not willingly permitted to fall unless he has seriously demeaned himself. Both differ for city and country workers, for the domestic servant and the day-labourer, for the business clerk and the official, etc. Likewise the man of wealth is reproved if he lives the life of a poor man, but also if he seeks the refinements of luxury overmuch. Economists may protest in vain; public feeling will always be scandalized if an individual spends too much wealth for wholly superfluous use, and it even seems that this severity relaxes only in times of moral disturbance.[5] A genuine regimen exists, therefore, although not always legally formulated, which fixes with relative precision the maximum degree of ease of living to which each social class may legitimately aspire. However, there is nothing immutable about such a scale. It changes with the increase or decrease of collective revenue and the changes occurring in the moral ideas of society. Thus what appears luxury to one period no longer does so to another; and the well-being which for long periods was granted to a class only by exception and supererogation finally appears strictly necessary and equitable.

Under this pressure, each in his sphere vaguely realizes the extreme limit set to his ambitions and aspires to nothing beyond. At least if he respects regulations and is docile to collective authority, that is, has a

5. Actually, this is a purely moral reprobation and can hardly be judicially implemented. We do not consider any re-establishment of sumptuary laws desirable or even possible.

wholesome moral constitution, he feels that it is not well to ask more. Thus, an end and goal are set to the passions. Truly, there is nothing rigid nor absolute about such determination. The economic ideal assigned each class of citizens is itself confined to certain limits, within which the desires have free range. But it is not infinite. This relative limitation and the moderation it involves, make men contented with their lot while stimulating them moderately to improve it; and this average contentment causes the feeling of calm, active happiness, the pleasure in existing and living which characterizes health for societies as well as for individuals. Each person is then at least, generally speaking, in harmony with his condition, and desires only what he may legitimately hope for as the normal reward of his activity. Besides, this does not condemn man to a sort of immobility. He may seek to give beauty to his life ; but his attempts in this direction may fail without causing him to despair. For, loving what he has and not fixing his desire solely on what he lacks, his wishes and hopes may fail of what he has happened to aspire to, without his being wholly destitute. He has the essentials. The equilibrium of his happiness is secure because it is defined, and a few mishaps cannot disconcert him.

But it would be of little use for everyone to recognize the justice of the hierarchy of functions established by public opinion, if he did not also consider the distribution of these functions just. The workman is not in harmony with his social position if he is not convinced that he has his desserts. If he feels justified in occupying another, what he has would not satisfy him. So it is not enough for the average level of needs for each social condition to be regulated by public opinion, but another, more precise rule, must fix the way in which these conditions are open to individuals. There is no society in which such regulation does not exist. It varies with times and places. Once it regarded birth as the almost exclusive principle of social classification ; today it recognizes no other inherent inequality than hereditary fortune and merit. But in all these various forms its object is unchanged. It is also only possible, everywhere, as a restriction upon individuals imposed by superior authority, that is, by collective authority. For it can be established only by requiring of one or another group of men, usually of all, sacrifices and concessions in the name of the public interest.

Some, to be sure, have thought that this moral pressure would become unnecessary if men's economic circumstances were only no longer determined by heredity. If inheritance were abolished, the argument runs, if everyone began life with equal resources and if the competitive struggle were fought out on a basis of perfect equality, no one could think its results unjust. Each would instinctively feel that things are as they should be.

Truly, the nearer this ideal equality were approached, the less social restraint will be necessary. But it is only a matter of degree. One sort of heredity will always exist, that of natural talent. Intelligence, taste, scientific, artistic, literary or industrial ability, courage and manual dexterity are gifts received by each of us at birth, as the heir to wealth receives his capital or as the nobleman formerly received his title and function. A moral discipline will therefore still be required to make those less favoured by nature accept the lesser advantages which they owe to the chance of birth. Shall it be demanded that all have an equal share and that no advantage be given those more useful and deserving? But then there would have to be a discipline far stronger to make these accept a treatment merely equal to that of the mediocre and incapable.

But like the one first mentioned, this discipline can be useful only if considered just by the peoples subject to it. When it is maintained only by custom and force, peace and harmony are illusory; the spirit of unrest and discontent are latent; appetites superficially restrained are ready to revolt. This happened in Rome and Greece when the faiths underlying the old organization of the patricians and plebeians were shaken, and in our modern societies when aristocratic prejudices began to lose their old ascendancy. But this state of upheaval is exceptional; it occurs only when society is passing through some abnormal crisis. In normal conditions the collective order is regarded as just by the great majority of persons. Therefore, when we say that an authority is necessary to impose this order on individuals, we certainly do not mean that violence is the only means of establishing it. Since this regulation is meant to restrain individual passions, it must come from a power which dominates individuals; but this power must also be obeyed through respect, not fear.

It is not true, then, that human activity can be released from all restraint. Nothing in the world can enjoy such a privilege. All existence being a part of the universe is relative to the remainder; its nature and method of manifestation accordingly depend not only on itself but on other beings, who consequently restrain and regulate it. Here there are only differences of degree and form between the mineral realm and the thinking person. Man's characteristic privilege is that the bond he accepts is not physical but moral; that is, social. He is governed not by a material environment brutally imposed on him, but by a conscience superior to his own, the superiority of which he feels. Because the greater, better part of his existence transcends the body, he escapes the body's yoke, but is subject to that of society.

But when society is disturbed by some painful crisis or by beneficent but abrupt transitions, it is momentarily incapable of exercising this influence ; thence come the sudden rises in the curve of suicides which we have pointed out above.

In the case of economic disasters, indeed, something like a declassification occurs which suddenly casts certain individuals into a lower state than their previous one. Then they must reduce their requirements, restrain their needs, learn greater self-control. All the advantages of social influence are lost so far as they are concerned ; their moral education has to be recommenced. But society cannot adjust them instantaneously to this new life and teach them to practise the increased self-repression to which they are unaccustomed. So they are not adjusted to the condition forced on them, and its very prospect is intolerable ; hence the suffering which detaches them from a reduced existence even before they have made trial of it.

It is the same if the source of the crisis is an abrupt growth of power and wealth. Then, truly, as the conditions of life are changed, the standard according to which needs were regulated can no longer remain the same ; for it varies with social resources, since it largely determines the share of each class of producers. The scale is upset ; but a new scale cannot be immediately improvised. Time is required for the public conscience to reclassify men and things. So long as the social forces thus freed have not regained equilibrium, their respective values are unknown and so all regulation is lacking for a time. The limits are unknown between the possible and the impossible, what is just and what is unjust, legitimate claims and hopes and those which are immoderate. Consequently, there is no restraint upon aspirations. If the disturbance is profound, it affects even the principles controlling the distribution of men among various occupations. Since the relations between various parts of society are necessarily modified, the ideas expressing these relations must change. Some particular class especially favoured by the crisis is no longer resigned to its former lot, and, on the other hand, the example of its greater good fortune arouses all sorts of jealousy below and about it. Appetites, not being controlled by a public opinion become disoriented, no longer recognize the limits proper to them. Besides, they are at the same time seized by a sort of natural erethism simply by the greater intensity of public life. With increased prosperity desires increase. At the very moment when traditional rules have lost their authority, the richer prize offered these appetites stimulates them and makes them more exigent and impatient of control. The state of de-regulation or anomy is thus further heightened by passions being less disciplined, precisely when they need more disciplining.

But then their very demands make fulfillment impossible. Overweening ambition always exceeds the results obtained, great as they may be, since there is no warning to pause here. Nothing gives satisfaction and all this agitation is uninterruptedly maintained without appeasement. Above all, since this race for an unattainable goal can give no other pleasure but that of the race itself, if it is one, once it is interrupted the participants are left empty-handed. At the same time the struggle grows more violent and painful, both from being less controlled and because competition is greater. All classes contend among themselves because no established classification any longer exists. Effort grows, just when it becomes less productive. How could the desire to live not be weakened under such conditions?

This explanation is confirmed by the remarkable immunity of poor countries. Poverty protects against suicide because it is a restraint in itself. No matter how one acts, desires have to depend upon resources to some extent; actual possessions are partly the criterion of those aspired to. So the less one has the less he is tempted to extend the range of his needs indefinitely. Lack of power, compelling moderation, accustoms men to it, while nothing excites envy if no one has superfluity. Wealth, on the other hand, by the power it bestows, deceives us into believing that we depend on ourselves only. Reducing the resistance we encounter from objects, it suggests the possibility of unlimited success against them. The less limited one feels, the more intolerable all limitation appears. Not without reason, therefore, have so many religions dwelt on the advantages and moral value of poverty. It is actually the best school for teaching self-restraint. Forcing us to constant self-discipline, it prepares us to accept collective discipline with equanimity, while wealth, exalting the individual, may always arouse the spirit of rebellion which is the very source of immorality. This, of course, is no reason why humanity should not improve its material condition. But though the moral danger involved in every growth of prosperity is not irremediable, it should not be forgotten.

References

LEGOYT, A. (1881), *Le suictde ancien et moderne*, Paris.
VERCE, F. DI (1894), *La criminalita e le vicende economiche d'Italia*, Turin.

Part Two Interaction

Having included some of the basic ideas of sociology in the
first part, we now move on to the theme of interaction. Here the
pieces stress the centrality of the individual human actor,
interaction between human actors, and such concepts as 'self'
and 'social exchange'. Although these themes are in turn
quite varied, there is nevertheless a sharp contrast with some of
the pieces in Part One – such as Durkheim's view of Society
as an entity largely imposed upon individual actions rather than
constructed by them. Nevertheless this contrast should not be
over-emphasized. The contrast is partly to be found within the work
of a single sociologist, such as Max Weber.

Edward Sapir (Reading 8), an American cultural anthropologist,
argues that language is a deeply and subtly social phenomenon.

The next piece is from an extremely influential passage of Max
Weber's writings (Reading 9). Weber sets about defining a list of
crucial concepts. First he defines his particular kind of sociology –
interpretive sociology, or 'the interpretive understanding of
social action'. Then he moves on to define 'meaning'. Weber
stresses the *subjective* understanding of behaviour. He then clarifies
what it is that makes an action a 'social action'. For Weber
'social action' requires that 'the actor's behaviour is meaningfully
oriented to that of others'; Weber neatly illustrates his concept
by discussing an episode of two cyclists in collision. Weber then
classifies four types of social interaction and finally defines 'social
relationship'. Throughout Weber stresses the importance of
'rationality' – a concept of his we met previously (Reading 5 (b)).

G. H. Mead's analysis of the 'Self' (Reading 10) has a different
flavour from that of Weber. Mead's approach is somewhat more
philosophical. His work on the self has been a major influence in
'Symbolic interactionist' sociology.

McCall and Simmons (Reading 11) present an analysis of social
interactions – which builds on much of the recent literature in this field.

Miyamoto and Dornbusch (Reading 12) in a brief article show how the interactionist approach to the self can be empirically tested.

Goffman's article (Reading 13) shows how his symbolic inteactionist perspective can be applied to situations in mental hospitals where doctors and patients meet in circumstances of very unequal status and power.

With Robert Merton's writing on the 'role-set' (Reading 14) we return to another more conceptual piece. This passage is extracted from a much longer article on 'Reference groups' – a concept dealt with later in this volume by Runciman (Reading 21). Merton here addresses himself to the problem of the human actor involved in several different role-relationships and shows various ways in which an actor may be able to manage the conflicting pressures exerted upon him within his constellation of roles.

Peter Blau's analysis of social exchange (Reading 15) shows how deeply embedded notions of exchange are within human society; most human interaction tends to have an exchange element. Blau bases his approach upon a variety of materials – anthropological evidence, economic theory, fiction, social psychology studies of small groups – and starts to develop a general theory of social exchange.

8 Edward Sapir

Language

Excerpt from Edward Sapir, *Selected Writings in Language, Culture and Personality* (ed. David Mandelbaum), University of California Press, 1949, pp. 6–20.

Language has certain psychological qualities which make it peculiarly important for the student of social science. In the first place, language is felt to be a perfect symbolic system, in a perfectly homogeneous medium, for the handling of all references and meanings that a given culture is capable of, whether these be in the form of actual communications or in that of such ideal substitutes of communication as thinking. The content of every culture is expressible in its language and there are no linguistic materials whether as to content or form which are not felt to symbolize actual meanings, whatever may be the attitude of those who belong to other cultures. New cultural experiences frequently make it necessary to enlarge the resources of a language, but such enlargement is never an arbitrary addition to the materials and forms already present; it is merely a further application of principles already in use and in many cases little more than a metaphorical extension of old terms and meanings. It is highly important to realize that once the form of a language is established it can discover meanings for its speakers which are not simply traceable to the given quality of experience itself but must be explained to a large extent as the projection of potential meanings into the raw material of experience. If a man who has never seen more than a single elephant in the course of his life, nevertheless speaks without the slightest hesitation of ten elephants or a million elephants or a herd of elephants or of elephants walking two by two or three by three or of generations of elephants, it is obvious that language has the power to analyse experience into theoretically dissociable elements and to create that world of the potential intergrading with the actual which enables human beings to transcend the immediately given in their individual experiences and to join in a larger common understanding. This common understanding constitutes culture, which cannot be adequately defined by a description of those more colorful patterns of behavior in society which lie open to observation. Language is heuristic, not merely in the simple sense which this example suggests, but in the much more far-reaching sense that its forms predetermine for us certain modes of observation and interpretation. This means of course that as our scientific experience grows we must learn to fight the implications of language. 'The grass waves in the wind' is shown by its linguistic form to be a member of the same relational class of experiences as 'The man works in the house'. As an interim solution of the problem of expressing the experience referred to in this sentence it is clear that the language has proved useful, for it has made significant use of certain symbols of conceptual relation, such as agency and location. If we feel the sentence to be poetic or metaphorical, it is largely because other more complex types of experience with their appropriate symbolisms of reference enable us to reinterpret the situation and to say, for instance, 'The grass is waved by the wind' or 'The wind causes the grass to wave'. The point is that no matter how sophisticated our modes of interpretation become, we never really get beyond the projection and continuous transfer of relations suggested by the forms of our speech. After all, to say 'Friction causes such and such a result' is not very different from saying 'The grass waves in the wind'. Language is at one and the same time helping and retarding us in our exploration of experience, and the details of these processes of help and hindrance are deposited in the subtler meanings of different cultures.

A further psychological characteristic of language is the fact that while it may be looked upon as a symbolic system which reports or refers to or otherwise substitutes for direct experience, it does not as a matter of actual behavior stand apart from or run parallel to direct experience but completely interpenetrates with it. This is indicated by the widespread feeling, particularly among primitive people, of that virtual identity or close correspondence of word and thing which leads to the magic of spells. On our own level it is generally difficult to make a complete divorce between objective reality and our linguistic symbols of reference to it; and things, qualities and events are on the whole felt to be what they are called. For the normal person every experience, real or potential, is saturated with verbalism. This explains why so many lovers of nature, for instance, do not feel that they are truly in touch with it until they have mastered the names of a great many flowers and trees, as though the primary world of reality were a verbal one and as though one could not get close to nature unless one first mastered the terminology which somehow magically expresses it. It is this constant interplay between language and experience which removes language from the cold status of such purely and simply symbolic systems as mathematical symbolism or flag signalling. This interpenetration is not only an intimate associative fact; it is also a contextual one. It is important to realize that language may not only refer to experience or even mold, interpret and discover experience, but that it also substitutes for it in the sense that, in those sequences of interpersonal behavior which form the greater part of our daily lives, speech and action supplement each other and do each other's work in a web of unbroken pattern. If one says to me 'Lend me a dollar', I may hand over the money without a word or I may give it with an accompanying 'Here it is' or I may say 'I haven't got it' or 'I'll give it to you tomorrow'. Each of these responses is structurally equivalent, if one thinks of the larger behavior pattern. It is clear that if language is in its analysed form a symbolic system of reference, it is far from being merely that if we consider the psychological part that it plays in continuous behavior. The reason for this almost unique position of intimacy which language holds among all known symbolisms is probably the fact that it is learned in the earliest years of childhood.

It is because it is learned early and piecemeal, in constant association with the color and the requirements of actual contexts, that language, in spite of its quasi-mathematical form, is rarely a purely referential organization. It tends to be so only in scientific discourse, and even there it may be seriously doubted whether the ideal of pure reference is ever attained by language. Ordinary speech is directly expressive and the purely formal pattern of sounds, words, grammatical forms, phrases and sentences are always to be thought of as compounded by intended or unintended symbolisms of expression, if they are to be understood fully from the standpoint of behavior. The choice of words in a particular context may convey the opposite of what they mean on the surface. The same external message is differently interpreted according to whether the speaker has this or that psychological status in his personal relations, or whether such primary expressions as those of affection or anger or fear may inform the spoken words with a significance which completely transcends their normal value. On the whole, however, there is no danger that the expressive character of language will be overlooked. It is too obvious a fact to call for much emphasis. What is often overlooked and is, as a matter of fact, not altogether easy to understand is that the quasi-mathematical patterns, as we have called them, of the grammarian's language, unreal as these are in a contextual sense, have, nevertheless, a tremendous intuitive vitality; and that these patterns, never divorced in experience from the expressive ones, are nevertheless easily separated from them by the normal individual. The fact that almost any word or phrase can be made to take on an infinite variety of meanings seems to indicate that in all language behavior there are intertwined, in enormously complex patterns, isolable patterns of two distinct orders. These may be roughly defined as patterns of reference and patterns of expression.

That language is a perfect symbolism of experience, that in the actual context of behavior it cannot be divorced from action and that it is the carrier of an infinitely nuanced expressiveness are universally valid psychological facts. There is a fourth general psychological peculiarity which applies more particularly to the languages of sophisticated peoples. This is the fact that the referential form systems which are actualized in language behavior do not need speech in its literal sense in order to preserve their substantial integrity. The history of writing is in essence the long attempt to develop an independent symbolism on the basis of graphic representation, followed by the slow and begrudging realization that spoken language is a more powerful symbolism than any graphic one can possibly be and that true progress in the art of writing lay in the virtual abandonment of the principle with which it originally started. Effective systems of writing, whether alphabetic or not, are more or less exact transfers of speech. The original language system may maintain itself in other and remoter transfers, one of the best examples of these being the Morse telegraph code. It is a very interesting fact that the principle of linguistic transfer is not entirely absent even among the unlettered peoples of the world. Some at least of the drum signal and horn signal systems of the West African natives are in principle transfers of the organizations of speech, often in minute phonetic detail.

Many attempts have been made to unravel the origin of language, but most of these are hardly more than exercises of the speculative imagination. Linguists as a whole have lost interest in the problem, and this for two reasons. In the first place, it has come to be realized that we have no truly primitive languages in a psychological sense, that modern researches in archaeology have indefinitely extended the time of man's cultural past and that it is therefore vain to go much beyond the perspective opened up by the study of actual languages. In the second place, our knowledge of psychology, particularly of the symbolic processes in general, is not felt to be sound enough or far-reaching enough to help materially with the problem of the emergence of speech. It is probable that the origin of language is not a problem that can be solved out of the resources of linguistics alone but that it is essentially a particular case of a much wider problem of the genesis of symbolic behavior and of the specialization of such behavior in the laryngeal region, which may be presumed to have had only expressive functions to begin with. Perhaps a close study of the behavior of very young children under controlled conditions may provide some valuable hints, but it seems dangerous to reason from such experiments to the behavior of precultural man. It is more likely that the kinds of studies which are now in progress of the behavior of the higher apes will help to give us some idea of the genesis of speech.

The most popular earlier theories were the interjectional and onomatopoeic theories. The former derived speech from involuntary cries of an expressive nature, while the latter maintained that the words of actual language are conventionalized forms of imitation of the sounds of nature. Both of these theories suffer from two fatal defects. While it is true that both interjectional and onomatopoeic elements are found in most languages, they are always relatively unimportant and tend to contrast somewhat with the more normal materials of language. The very fact that they are constantly being formed anew seems to indicate that they belong rather to the directly expressive layer of speech which intercrosses with the main level of referential symbolism. The second difficulty is even more serious. The essential problem of the origin of speech is not to attempt to discover the kinds of vocal elements which constitute the historical nucleus of language. It is rather to point out how vocal articulations of any sort could become dissociated from their original expressive value. About all that can be said at present is that while speech as a finished organization is a distinctly human achievement, its roots probably lie in the power of the higher apes to solve specific problems by abstracting general forms or schemata from the details of given situations; that the habit of interpreting certain selected elements in a situation as signs of a desired total one gradually led in early man to a dim feeling for symbolism; and that, in the long run and for reasons which can hardly be guessed at, the elements of experience which were most often interpreted in a symbolic sense came to be the largely useless or supplementary vocal behavior that must have often attended significant action. According to this point of view language is not so much directly developed out of vocal expression as it is an actualization in terms of vocal expression of the tendency to master reality, not by direct and *ad hoc* handling of this element but by the reduction of experience to familiar form. Vocal expression is only superficially the same as language. The tendency to derive speech from emotional expression has not led to anything tangible in the way of scientific theory and the attempt must now be made to see in language the slowly evolved product of a peculiar technique or tendency which may be called the symbolic one, and to see the relatively meaningless or incomplete part as a sign of the whole. Language, then, is what it is essentially, not because of its admirable expressive power but in spite of it. Speech as behavior is a wonderfully complex blend of two pattern systems, the symbolic and the expressive, neither of which could have developed to its present perfection without the interference of the other.

It is difficult to see adequately the functions of language, because it is so deeply rooted in the whole of human behavior that it may be suspected that there is little in the functional side of our conscious behavior in which language does not play its part. The primary function of language is generally said to be communication. There can be no quarrel with this so long as it is distinctly understood that there may be effective communication without overt speech and that language is highly relevant to situations which are not obviously of a communicative sort. To say that thought, which is hardly possible in any sustained sense without the symbolic organization brought by language, is that form of communication in which the speaker and the person addressed are identified in one person is not far from begging the question. The autistic speech of children seems to show that the purely communicative aspect of language has been exaggerated. It is best to admit that language is primarily a vocal actualization of the tendency to see realities symbolically, that it is precisely this quality which renders it a fit instrument for communication and that it is in the actual give and take of social intercourse that it has been complicated and refined into the form in which it is known today. Besides the very general function which language fulfils in the spheres of thought, communication and expression which are implicit in its very nature, there may be pointed out a number of special derivatives of these which are of particular interest to students of society.

Language is a great force of socialization, probably the greatest that exists. By this is meant not merely the obvious fact that significant social intercourse is hardly possible without language but that the mere fact of a common speech serves as a peculiarly potent symbol of the social solidarity of those who speak the language. The psychological significance of this goes far beyond the association of particular languages with nationalities, political entities or smaller local groups. In between the recognized dialect or language as a whole and the individualized speech of a given individual lies a kind of linguistic unit which is not often discussed by the linguist but which is of the greatest importance to social psychology. This is the subform of a language which is current among a group of people who are held together by ties of common interest. Such a group may be a family, the undergraduates of a college, a labor union, the underworld in a large city, the members of a club, a group of four or five friends who hold together through life in spite of differences of professional interest, and untold thousands of other kinds of groups. Each of these tends to develop peculiarities of speech which have the symbolic function of somehow distinguishing the group from the larger group into which its members might be too completely absorbed. The complete absence of linguistic indices of such small groups is obscurely felt as a defect or sign of emotional poverty. Within the confines of a particular family, for instance, the name 'Georgy', having once been mispronounced 'Doody' in childhood, may take on the latter form forever after ; and this unofficial pronunciation of a familiar name as applied to a particular person becomes a very important symbol indeed of the solidarity of a particular family and of the continuance of the sentiment that keeps its members together. A stranger cannot lightly take on the privilege of saying 'Doody' if the members of the family feel that he is not entitled to go beyond the degree of familiarity symbolized by the use of 'Georgy' or 'George'. Again, no one is entitled to say 'trig' or 'math' who has not gone through such familiar and painful experiences as a high school or undergraduate student. The use of such words at once declares the speaker a member of an unorganized but psychologically real group. A self-made mathematician has hardly the right to use the word 'math' in referring to his own interests because the student overtones of the word do not properly apply to him. The extraordinary importance of minute linguistic differences for the symbolization of psychologically real as contrasted with politically or sociologically official groups is intuitively felt by most people. 'He talks like us' is equivalent to saying 'He is one of us'.

There is another important sense in which language is a socializer beyond its literal use as a means of communication. This is in the establishment of rapport between the members of a physical group, such as a house party. It is not what is said that matters so much as that something is said. Particularly where cultural understandings of an intimate sort are somewhat lacking among the members of a physical group it is felt to be important that the lack be made good by a constant supply of small talk. This caressing or reassuring quality of speech in general, even where no one has anything of moment to communicate, reminds us how much more language is than a mere technique of communication. Nothing better shows how completely the life of man as an animal made over by culture is dominated by the verbal substitutes for the physical world.

The use of language in cultural accumulation and historical transmission is obvious and important. This applies not only to sophisticated levels but to primitive ones as well. A great deal of the cultural stock in trade of a primitive society is presented in a more or less well defined linguistic form. Proverbs, medicine formulae, standardized prayers, folk tales, standardized speeches, song texts, genealogies are some of the more overt forms which language takes as a culture-preserving instrument. The pragmatic ideal of education, which aims to reduce the influence of standardized lore to a minimum and to get the individual to educate himself through as direct a contact as possible with the realities of his environment, is certainly not realized among the primitives, who are often as word-bound as the humanistic tradition itself. Few cultures perhaps have gone to the length of the classical Chinese culture or of the rabbinical Jewish culture in making the word do duty for the thing or the personal experience as the ultimate unit of reality. Modern civilization as a whole, with its schools, its libraries, and its endless stores of knowledge, opinion and sentiment stored up in verbalized form, would be unthinkable without language made eternal as document. On the whole, we probably tend to exaggerate the differences between 'high' and 'low' cultures or saturated and emergent cultures in the matter of traditionally conserved verbal authority. The enormous differences that seem to exist are rather differences in the outward form and content of the cultures themselves than in the psychological relation which obtains between the individual and his culture.

In spite of the fact that language acts as a socializing and uniformizing force, it is at the same time the most potent single known factor for the growth of individuality. The fundamental quality of one's voice, the phonetic patterns of speech, the speed and relative smoothness of articulation, the length and build of the sentences, the character and range of the vocabulary, the scholastic consistency of the words used, the readiness with which words respond to the requirements of the social environment, in particular the suitability of one's language to the language habits of the persons addressed – all these are so many complex indicators of the personality. 'Actions speak louder than words' may be an excellent maxim from the pragmatic point of view but betrays little insight into the nature of speech. The language habits of people are by no means irrelevant as unconscious indicators of the more important traits of their personalities, and the folk is psychologically wiser than the adage in paying a great deal of attention, willingly or not, to the psychological significance of a man's language. The normal person is never convinced by the mere content of speech but is very sensitive to many of the implications of language behavior, however feebly (if at all) these may have been consciously analysed. All in all, it is not too much to say that one of the really important functions of language is to be constantly declaring to society the psychological place held by all of its members.

Besides this more general type of personality expression or fulfilment there is to be kept in mind the important role which language plays as a substitutive means of expression for those individuals who have a greater than normal difficulty in adjusting to the environment in terms of primary action patterns. Even in the most primitive cultures the strategic word is likely to be more powerful than the direct blow. It is unwise to speak too blithely of 'mere' words, for to do so may be to imperil the value and perhaps the very existence of civilization and personality.

9 Max Weber

The Definitions of Sociology, Social Action and Social Relationship

Excerpt from Max Weber, *The Theory of Social and Economic Organization* (trans. A. M. Henderson and Talcott Parsons, ed. Talcott Parsons), Oxford University Press, 1964, pp. 88–120. First published in German in 1922.

Sociology (in the sense in which this highly ambiguous word is used here) is a science which attempts the interpretive understanding of social action in order thereby to arrive at a causal explanation of its course and effects. In 'action' is included all human behaviour when and in so far as the acting individual attaches a subjective meaning to it. Action in this sense may be either overt or purely inward or subjective; it may consist of positive intervention in a situation, or of deliberately refraining from such intervention or passively acquiescing in the situation. Action is social in so far as, by virtue of the subjective meaning attached to it by the acting individual (or individuals) it takes account of the behaviour of others and is thereby oriented in its course.

The methodological foundations of sociology

'Meaning' may be of two kinds. The term may refer first to the actual existing meaning in the given concrete case of a particular actor, or to the average or approximate meaning attributable to a given plurality of actors; or secondly to the theoretically conceived *pure type* of subjective meaning attributed to the hypothetical actor or actors in a given type of action. In no case does it refer to an objectively 'correct' meaning or one which is 'true' in some metaphysical sense. It is this which distinguishes the empirical sciences of action, such as sociology and history, from the dogmatic disciplines in that area, such as jurisprudence, logic, ethics and aesthetics, which seek to ascertain the 'true' and 'valid' meanings associated with the objects of their investigation.

The line between meaningful action and merely reactive behaviour to which no subjective meaning is attached, cannot be sharply drawn empirically. A very considerable part of all sociologically relevant behaviour, especially purely traditional behaviour, is marginal between the two. In the case of many psychophysical processes, meaningful, i.e. subjectively understandable, action is not to be found at all; in others it is discernible only by the expert psychologist. Many mystical experiences which cannot be adequately communicated in words are, for a person who is not susceptible to such experiences, not fully understandable. At the same time the ability to imagine oneself performing a similar action is not a necessary prerequisite to understanding; 'one need not have been Caesar in order to understand Caesar'. For the verifiable accuracy of interpretation of the meaning of a phenomenon, it is a great help to be able to put oneself imaginatively in the place of the actor and thus sympathetically to participate in his experiences, but this is not an essential condition of meaningful interpretation. Understandable and non-understandable components of a process are often intermingled and bound up together. [. . .]

For the purposes of a typological scientific analysis it is convenient to treat all irrational, affectually determined elements of behaviour as factors of deviation from a conceptually pure type of rational action. For example a panic on the stock exchange can be most conveniently analysed by attempting to determine first what the course of action would have been if it had not been influenced by irrational affects; it is then possible to introduce the irrational components as accounting for the observed deviations from this hypothetical course. Similarly, in analysing a political or military campaign it is convenient to determine in the first place what would have been a rational course, given the ends of the participants and adequate knowledge of all the circumstances. Only in this way is it possible to assess the causal significance of irrational factors as accounting for the deviations from this type. The construction of a purely rational course of action in such cases serves the sociologist as a type ('ideal type') which has the merit of clear understandability and lack of ambiguity. By comparison with this it is possible to understand the ways in which actual action is influenced by irrational factors of all sorts, such as affects and errors, in that they account for the deviation from the line of conduct which would be expected on the hypothesis that the action were purely rational. [. . .]

Understanding may be of two kinds: the first is the direct observational understanding of the subjective meaning of a given act as such, including verbal utterances. We thus understand by direct observation, in this sense, the meaning of the proposition $2 \times 2 = 4$ when we hear or read it. This is a case of the direct rational understanding of ideas. We also understand an outbreak of anger as manifested by facial expression, exclamations or irrational movements. This is direct observational understanding of irrational emotional reactions. We can understand in a similar observational way the action of a woodcutter or of somebody who reaches for the knob to shut a door or who aims a gun at an animal. This is rational observational understanding of actions.

Understanding may, however, be of another sort, namely explanatory understanding. Thus we understand in terms of *motive* the meaning an actor attaches to the proposition twice two equals four, when he states it or writes it down, in that we understand what makes him do this at precisely this moment and in these circumstances. Understanding in this sense is attained if we know that he is engaged in balancing a ledger or in making a scientific demonstration, or is engaged in some other task of which this particular act would be an appropriate part. This is rational understanding of motivation, which consists in placing the act in an intelligible and more inclusive context of meaning. Thus we understand the chopping of wood or aiming of a gun in terms of motive in addition to direct observation if we know that the wood-chopper is working for a wage or is chopping a supply of firewood for his own use or possibly is doing it for recreation. But he might also be 'working off' a fit of rage, an irrational case. Similarly we understand the motive of a person aiming a gun if we know that he has been commanded to shoot as a member of a firing squad, that he is fighting against an enemy or that he is doing it for revenge. The last is affectually determined and thus in a certain sense irrational. Finally we have a motivational understanding of the outburst of anger if we know that it has been provoked by jealousy, injured pride or an insult. The last examples are all affectually determined and hence derived from irrational motives. In all the above cases the particular act has been placed in an understandable sequence of motivation, the understanding of which can be treated as an explanation of the actual course of behaviour. Thus for a science which is concerned with the subjective meaning of action, explanation requires a grasp of the complex of meaning in which an actual course of understandable action thus interpreted belongs. In all such cases, even where the processes are largely affectual, the subjective meaning of the action, including that also of the relevant meaning complexes, will be called the 'intended' meaning. This involves a departure from ordinary usage, which speaks of intention in this sense only in the case of rationally purposive action.

In all these cases understanding involves the interpretive grasp of the meaning present in one of the following contexts: (a) as in the historical approach, the actually intended meaning for concrete individual action; or (b) as in cases of sociological mass phenomena, the average of, or an approximation to, the actually intended meaning; or (c) the meaning appropriate to a scientifically formulated pure type (an ideal type) of a common phenomenon. The concepts and 'laws' of pure economic theory are examples of this kind of ideal type. They state what course a given type of human action would take if it were strictly rational, unaffected by errors or emotional factors and if, furthermore, it were completely and unequivocally directed to a single end, the maximization of economic advantage. In reality, action takes exactly this course only in unusual cases, as sometimes on the stock exchange ; and even then there is usually only an approximation to the ideal type.

Every interpretation attempts to attain clarity and certainty, but no matter how clear an interpretation as such appears to be from the point of view of meaning, it cannot on this account alone claim to be the causally valid interpretation. On this level it must remain only a peculiarly plausible hypothesis. In the first place the 'conscious motives' may well, even to the actor himself, conceal the various 'motives' and 'repressions' which constitute the real driving force of his action. Thus in such cases even subjectively honest self-analysis has only a relative value. Then it is the task of the sociologist to be aware of this motivational situation and to describe and analyse it, even though it has not actually been concretely part of the conscious 'intention' of the actor ; possibly not at all, at least not fully. This is a borderline case of the interpretation of meaning. Secondly, processes of action which seem to an observer to be the same or similar may fit into exceedingly various complexes of motive in the case of the actual actor. Then even though the situations appear superficially to be very similar we must actually understand them or interpret them as very different, perhaps, in terms of meaning, directly opposed. Third, the actors in any given situation are often subject to opposing and conflicting impulses, all of which we are able to understand. In a large number of cases we know from experience it is not possible to arrive at even an approximate estimate of the relative strength of conflicting motives and very often we cannot be certain of our interpretation. Only the actual outcome of the conflict gives a solid basis of judgement.

More generally, verification of subjective interpretation by comparison with the concrete course of events is, as in the case of all hypotheses, indispensable. Unfortunately this type of verification is feasible with relative accuracy only in the few very special cases susceptible of psychological experimentation. The approach to a satisfactory degree of accuracy is exceedingly various, even in the limited number of cases of mass phenomena which can be statistically described and unambiguously interpreted. For the rest there remains only the possibility of comparing the largest possible number of historical or contemporary processes which, while otherwise similar, differ in the one decisive point of their relation to the particular motive or factor the role of which is being investigated. This is a fundamental task of comparative sociology. Often, unfortunately, there is available only the dangerous and uncertain procedure of the 'imaginary experiment' which consists in thinking away certain elements of a chain of motivation and working out the course of action which would then probably ensue, thus arriving at a causal judgement.

For example, the generalization called Gresham's Law is a rationally clear interpretation of human action under certain conditions and under the assumption that it will follow a purely rational course. How far any actual course of action corresponds to this can be verified only by the available statistical evidence for the actual disappearance of undervalued monetary units from circulation. In this case our information serves to demonstrate a high degree of accuracy. The facts of experience were known before the generalization, which was formulated afterwards; but without this successful interpretation our need for causal understanding would evidently be left unsatisfied. On the other hand, without the demonstration that what can here be assumed to be a theoretically adequate interpretation also in some degree relevant to an actual course of action, a 'law', no matter how fully demonstrated theoretically, would be worthless for the understanding of action in the real world. In this case the correspondence between the theoretical interpretation of motivation and its empirical verification is entirely satisfactory and the cases are numerous enough so that verification can be considered established. But to take another example, Eduard Meyer has advanced an ingenious theory of the causal significance of the battles of Marathon, Salamis and Platea for the development of the cultural peculiarities of Greek, and hence, more generally, Western, civilization. This is derived from a meaningful interpretation of certain symptomatic facts having to do with the attitudes of the Greek oracles and prophets towards the Persians. It can only be directly verified by reference to the examples of the conduct of the Persians in cases where they were victorious, as in Jerusalem, Egypt and Asia Minor, and even this verification must necessarily remain unsatisfactory in certain respects. The striking rational plausibility of the hypothesis must here necessarily be relied on as a support. In very many cases of historical interpretation which seem highly plausible, however, there is not even a possibility of the order of verification which was feasible in this case. Where this is true the interpretation must necessarily remain a hypothesis.

A motive is a complex of subjective meaning which seems to the actor himself or to the observer an adequate ground for the conduct in question. We apply the term 'adequacy on the level of meaning' to the subjective interpretation of a coherent course of conduct when and in so far as, according to our habitual modes of thought and feeling, its component parts taken in their mutual relation are recognized to constitute a 'typical' complex of meaning. It is more common to say 'correct'. The interpretation of a sequence of events will on the other hand be called *causally* adequate in so far as, according to established generalizations from experience, there is a probability that it will always actually occur in the same way. An example of adequacy on the level of meaning in this sense is what is, according to our current norms of calculation or thinking, the correct solution of an arithmetical problem. On the other hand, a causally adequate interpretation of the same phenomenon would concern the statistical probability that, according to verified generalizations from experience, there would be a correct or an erroneous solution of the same problem. This also refers to currently accepted norms but includes taking account of typical errors or of typical confusions. Thus causal explanation depends on being able to determine that there is a probability, which in the rare ideal case can be numerically stated, but is always in some sense calculable, that a given observable event (overt or subjective) will be followed or accompanied by another event.

A correct causal interpretation of a concrete course of action is arrived at when the overt action and the motives have both been correctly apprehended and at the same time their relation has become meaningfully comprehensible. A correct causal interpretation of typical action means that the process which is claimed to be typical is shown to be both adequately grasped on the level of meaning and at the same time the interpretation is to some degree causally adequate. If adequacy in respect to meaning is lacking, then no matter how high the degree of uniformity and how precisely its probability can be numerically determined, it is still an incomprehensible statistical probability, whether dealing with overt or subjective processes. On the other hand, even the most perfect adequacy on the level of meaning has causal significance from a sociological point of view only in so far as there is some kind of proof for the existence of a probability that action in fact normally takes the course which has been held to be meaningful. For this there must be some degree of determinable frequency of approximation to an average or a pure type.

Statistical uniformities constitute understandable types of action in the sense of this discussion, and thus constitute 'sociological generalizations', only when they can be regarded as manifestations of the understandable subjective meaning of a course of social action. Conversely, formulations of a rational course of subjectively understandable action constitute sociological types of empirical process only when they can be empirically observed with a significant degree of approximation. It is unfortunately by no means the case that the actual likelihood of the occurrence of a given course of overt action is always directly proportional to the clarity of subjective interpretation. There are statistics of processes devoid of meaning such as death rates, phenomena of fatigue, the production rate of machines, the amount of rainfall, in exactly the same sense as there are statistics of meaningful phenomena. But only when the phenomena are meaningful is it convenient to speak of sociological statistics. Examples are such cases as crime rates, occupational distributions, price statistics and statistics of crop acreage. Naturally there are many cases where both components are involved, as in crop statistics.

Processes and uniformities which it has here seemed convenient not to designate as (in the present case) sociological phenomena or uniformities because they are not 'understandable', are naturally not on that account any the less important. This is true even for sociology in the present sense which restricts it to subjectively understandable phenomena – a usage which there is no intention of attempting to impose on anyone else. Such phenomena, however important, are simply treated by a different method from the others ; they become conditions, stimuli, furthering or hindering circumstances of action.

Action in the sense of a subjectively understandable orientation of behaviour exists only as the behaviour of one or more *individual* human beings. For other cognitive purposes it may be convenient or necessary to consider the individual, for instance, as a collection of cells, as a complex of bio-chemical reactions, or to conceive his 'psychic' life as made up of a variety of different elements, however these may be defined. Undoubtedly such procedures yield valuable knowledge of causal relationships. But the behaviour of these elements, as expressed in such uniformities, is not subjectively understandable. This is true even of psychic elements because the more precisely they are formulated from a point of view of natural science, the less they are accessible to subjective understanding. This is never the road to interpretation in terms of subjective meaning. On the contrary, both for sociology in the present sense, and for history, the object of cognition is the subjective meaning-complex of action. The behaviour of physiological entities such as cells, or of any sort of psychic elements may at least in principle be observed and an attempt made to derive uniformities from such observations. It is further possible to attempt, with their help, to obtain a causal explanation of individual phenomena, that is, to subsume them under uniformities. But the subjective understanding of action takes the same account of this type of fact and uniformity as of any others not capable of subjective interpretation. This is true, for example, of physical, astronomical, geological, meteorological, geographical, botanical, zoological and anatomical facts and of such facts as those aspects of psycho-pathology which are devoid of subjective meaning or the facts of the natural conditions of technological processes.

For still other cognitive purposes as, for instance, juristic, or for practical ends, it may on the other hand be convenient or even indispensable to treat social collectivities, such as states, associations, business corporations, foundations, as if they were individual persons. Thus they may be treated as the subjects of rights and duties or as the performers of legally significant actions. But for the subjective interpretation of action in sociological work these collectivities must be treated as *solely* the resultants and modes of organization of the particular acts of individual persons, since these alone can be treated as agents in a course of subjectively understandable action. Nevertheless, the sociologist cannot for his purposes afford to ignore these collective concepts derived from other disciplines. For the subjective interpretation of action has at least two important relations to these concepts. In the first place it is often necessary to employ very similar collective concepts, indeed often using the same terms, in order to obtain an understandable terminology. Thus both in legal terminology and in everyday speech the term 'state' is used both for the legal concept of the state and for the phenomena of social action to which its legal rules are relevant. For sociological purposes, however, the phenomenon 'the state' does not consist necessarily or even primarily of the elements which are relevant to legal analysis ; and for sociological purposes there is no such thing as a collective personality which 'acts'. When reference is made in a sociological context to a 'state', a 'nation', a 'corporation', a 'family' or an 'army corps', or to similar collectivities, what is meant is, on the contrary, *only* a certain kind of development of actual or possible social actions of individual persons. Both because of its precision and because it is established in general usage the juristic concept is taken over, but is used in an entirely different meaning.

Secondly, the subjective interpretation of action must take account of a fundamentally important fact. These concepts of collective entities which are found both in common sense and in juristic and other technical forms of thought, have a meaning in the minds of individual persons, partly as of something actually existing, partly as something with normative authority. This is true not only of judges and officials, but of ordinary private individuals as well. Actors thus in part orient their action to them, and in this role such ideas have a powerful, often a decisive, causal influence on the course of action of real individuals. This is above all true where the ideas concern a recognized positive or negative normative pattern. Thus, for instance, one of the important aspects of the 'existence' of a modern state, precisely as a complex of social interaction of individual persons, consists in the fact that the action of various individuals is oriented to the belief that it exists or should exist, thus that its acts and laws are valid in the legal sense. This will be further discussed below. Though extremely pedantic and cumbersome it would be possible, if purposes of sociological terminology alone were involved, to eliminate such terms entirely, and substitute newly-coined words. This would be possible even though the word 'state' is used ordinarily not only to designate the legal concept but also the real process of action. But in the above important connection, at least, this would naturally be impossible.

Thirdly, it is the method of the so-called 'organic' school of sociology to attempt to understand social interaction by using as a point of departure the 'whole' within which the individual acts. His action and behaviour are then interpreted somewhat in the way that a physiologist would treat the role of an organ of the body in the 'economy' of the organism, that is from the point of view of the survival of the latter. How far in other disciplines this type of functional analysis of the relation of 'parts' to a 'whole' can be regarded as definitive, cannot be discussed here; but it is well known that the bio-chemical and bio-physical modes of analysis of the organism are on principle opposed to stopping there. For purposes of sociological analysis two things can be said. First this functional frame of reference is convenient for purposes of practical illustration and for provisional orientation. In these respects it is not only useful but indispensable. But at the same time if its cognitive value is overestimated and its concepts illegitimately 'reified', it can be highly dangerous. Secondly, in certain circumstances this is the only available way of determining just what processes of social action it is important to understand in order to explain a given phenomenon. But this is only the beginning of sociological analysis as here understood. In the case of social collectivities, precisely as distinguished from organisms, we are in a position to go beyond merely demonstrating functional relationships and uniformities. We can accomplish something which is never attainable in the natural sciences, namely the subjective understanding of the action of the component individuals. The natural sciences on the other hand cannot do this, being limited to the formulation of causal uniformities in objects and events and the explanation of individual facts by applying them. We do not 'understand' the behaviour of cells, but can only observe the relevant functional relationships and generalize on the basis of these observations. This additional achievement of explanation by interpretive understanding, as distinguished from external observation, is of course attained only at a price – the more hypothetical and fragmentary character of its results. Nevertheless, subjective understanding is the specific characteristic of sociological knowledge. [. . .]

It has continually been assumed as obvious that the science of sociology seeks to formulate type concepts and generalized uniformities of empirical process. This distinguishes it from history, which is oriented to the causal analysis and explanation of individual actions, structures and personalities possessing cultural significance. The empirical material which underlies the concepts of sociology consists to a very large extent, though by no means exclusively, of the same concrete processes of action which are dealt with by historians. Among the various bases on which its concepts are formulated and its generalizations worked out, is an attempt to justify its important claim to be able to make a contribution to the causal explanation of some historically and culturally important phenomenon. As in the case of every generalizing science the abstract character of the concepts of sociology is responsible for the fact that, compared with actual historical reality, they are relatively lacking in fullness of concrete content. To compensate for this disadvantage, sociological analysis can offer a greater precision of concepts. This precision is obtained by striving for the highest possible degree of adequacy on the level of meaning in accordance with the definition of that concept put forward alone. It has already been repeatedly stressed that this aim can be realized in a particularly high degree in the case of concepts and generalizations which formulate rational processes. But sociological investigation attempts to include in its scope various irrational phenomena, as well as prophetic, mystic and affectual modes of action, formulated in terms of theoretical concepts which are adequate on the level of meaning. In *all* cases, rational or irrational, sociological analysis both abstracts from reality and at the same time helps us to understand it, in that it shows with what degree of approximation a concrete historical phenomenon can be subsumed under one or more of these concepts. For example, the same historical phenomenon may be in one aspect 'feudal', in another 'patrimonial', in another 'bureaucratic' and in still another 'charismatic'. In order to give a precise meaning to these terms, it is necessary for the sociologist to formulate pure ideal types of the corresponding forms of action which in each case involve the highest possible degree of logical integration by virtue of their complete adequacy on the level of meaning. But precisely because this is true, it is probably seldom if ever that a real phenomenon can be found which corresponds exactly to one of these ideally constructed pure types. [. . .]

The concept of social action

Social action, which includes both failure to act and passive acquiescence, may be oriented to the past, present or expected future behaviour of others. Thus it may be motivated by revenge for a past attack, defence against present, or measures of defence against future aggression. The 'others' may be individual persons, and may be known to the actor as such, or may constitute an indefinite plurality and may be entirely unknown as individuals. Thus, 'money' is a means of exchange which the actor accepts in payment because he orients his action to the expectation that a large but unknown number of individuals he is personally unacquainted with will be ready to accept it in exchange on some future occasion.

Not every kind of action, even of overt action, is 'social' in the sense of the present discussion. Overt action is non-social if it is oriented solely to the behaviour of inanimate objects. Subjective attitudes constitute social action only so far as they are oriented to the behaviour of others. For example, religious behaviour is not social if it is simply a matter of contemplation or of solitary prayer. The economic activity of an individual is only social if, and then only in so far as, it takes account of the behaviour of someone else. Thus very generally in formal terms it becomes social in so far as the actor's actual control over economic goods is respected by others. Concretely it is social, for instance, if in relation to the actor's own consumption the future wants of others are taken into account and this becomes one consideration affecting the actor's own saving. Or, in another connection, production may be oriented to the future wants of other people.

Not every type of contact of human beings has a social character; this is rather confined to cases where the actor's behaviour is meaningfully oriented to that of others. For example, a mere collision of two cyclists may be compared to a natural event. On the other hand, their attempt to avoid hitting each other, or whatever insults, blows, or friendly discussion might follow the collision, would constitute 'social action'.

Social action is not identical either with the similar actions of many persons or with action influenced by other persons. Thus, if at the beginning of a shower a number of people on the street put up their umbrellas at the same time, this would not ordinarily be a case of action mutually oriented to that of each other, but rather of all reacting in the same way to the like need of protection from the rain. [. . .]

The types of social action

Social action, like other forms of action, may be classified in the following four types according to its mode of orientation:

1. In terms of rational orientation to a system of discrete individual ends (*Zweckrational*), that is, through expectations as to the behaviour of objects in the external situation and of other human individuals, making use of these expectations as 'conditions' or 'means' for the successful attainment of the actor's own rationally chosen ends.

2. In terms of rational orientation to an absolute value (*Wertrational*); involving a conscious belief in the absolute value of some ethical, aesthetic, religious or other form of behaviour, entirely for its own sake and independently of any prospects of external success.

3. In terms of affectual orientation, especially emotional, determined by the specific affects and states of feeling of the actor.

4. Traditionally oriented, through the habituation of long practice.

Strictly traditional behaviour, like the reactive type of imitation discussed above, lies very close to the borderline of what can justifiably be called meaningfully oriented action, and indeed often on the other side. For it is very often a matter of almost automatic reaction to habitual stimuli which guide behaviour in a course which has been repeatedly followed. The great bulk of all everyday action to which people have become habitually accustomed approaches this type. Hence, its place in a systematic classification is not merely that of a limiting case because, as will be shown later, attachment to habitual forms can be upheld with varying degrees of self-consciousness and in a variety of senses. In this case the type may shade over into number two (*Wertrationalität*).

Purely affectual behaviour also stands on the borderline of what can be considered 'meaningfully' oriented, and often it, too, goes over the line. It may, for instance, consist in an uncontrolled reaction to some exceptional stimulus. It is a case of sublimation when affectually determined action occurs in the form of conscious release of emotional tension. When this happens it is usually, though not always, well on the road to rationalization in one or the other or both of the above senses.

The orientation of action in terms of absolute value is distinguished from the affectual type by its clearly self-conscious formulation of the ultimate values governing the action and the consistently planned orientation of its detailed course to these values. At the same time the two types have a common element, namely that the meaning of the action does not lie in the achievement of a result ulterior to it, but in carrying out the specific type of action for its own sake. Examples of affectual action are the satisfaction of a direct impulse to revenge, to sensual gratification, to devote oneself to a person or ideal, to contemplate bliss or, finally, toward the working off of emotional tensions. Such impulses belong in this category regardless of how sordid or sublime they may be.

Examples of pure rational orientation to absolute values would be the action of persons who, regardless of possible cost to themselves, act to put into practice their convictions of what seems to them to be required by duty, honour, the pursuit of beauty, a religious call, personal loyalty or the importance of some 'cause' no matter in what it consists. For the purposes of this discussion, when action is oriented to absolute values, it always involves 'commands' or 'demands' to the fulfilment of which the actor feels obligated. It is only in cases where human action is motivated by the fulfilment of such unconditional demands that it will be described as oriented to absolute values. This is empirically the case in widely varying degrees, but for the most part only to a relatively slight extent. Nevertheless, it will be shown that the occurrence of this mode of action is important enough to justify its formulation as a distinct type; though it may be remarked that there is no intention here of attempting to formulate in any sense an exhaustive classification of types of action.

Action is rationally oriented to a system of discrete individual ends (*Zweckrational*) when the end, the means and the secondary results are all rationally taken into account and weighed. This involves rational consideration of alternative means to the end, of the relations of the end to other prospective results of employment of any given means, and finally of the relative importance of different possible ends. Determination of action, either in affectual or in traditional terms, is thus incompatible with this type. Choice between alternative and conflicting ends and results may well be determined by considerations of absolute value. In that case, action is rationally oriented to a system of discrete individual ends only in respect to the choice of means. On the other hand, the actor may instead of deciding between alternative and conflicting ends in terms of a rational orientation to a system of values, simply take them as given subjective wants and arrange them in a scale of consciously assessed relative urgency. He may then orient his action to this scale in such a way that they are satisfied as far as possible in order of urgency, as formulated in the principle of 'marginal utility'. The orientation of action to absolute values may thus have various different modes of relation to the other type of rational action, in terms of a system of discrete individual ends. From the latter point of view, however, absolute values are always irrational. Indeed, the more the value to which action is oriented is elevated to the status of an absolute value, the more 'irrational' in this sense the corresponding action is. For, the more unconditionally the actor devotes himself to this value for its own sake, to pure sentiment or beauty, to absolute goodness or devotion to duty, the less is he influenced by considerations of the consequences of his action. The orientation of action wholly to the rational achievement of ends without relation to fundamental values is, to be sure, essentially only a limiting case.

It would be very unusual to find concrete cases of action, especially of social action, which were oriented *only* in one or another of these ways. Furthermore, this classification of the modes of orientation of action is in no sense meant to exhaust the possibilities of the field, but only to formulate in conceptually pure form certain sociologically important types, to which actual action is more or less closely approximated or, in much the more common case, which constitute the elements combining to make it up. The usefulness of the classification for the purposes of this investigation can only be judged in terms of its results.

The concept of social relationship

The term 'social relationship' will be used to denote the behaviour of a plurality of actors in so far as, in its meaningful content, the action of each takes account of that of the others and is oriented in these terms. The social relationship thus *consists* entirely and exclusively in the existence of a *probability* that there will be, in some meaningfully understandable sense, a course of social action. For purposes of definition there is no attempt to specify the basis of this probability.

Thus, as a defining criterion, it is essential that there should be at least a minimum of mutual orientation of the action of each to that of the others. Its content may be of the most varied nature ; conflict, hostility, sexual attraction, friendship, loyalty or economic exchange. It may involve the fulfilment, the evasion or the denunciation of the terms of an agreement ; economic, erotic or some other form of 'competition' ; common membership in national or class groups or those sharing a common tradition of status. In the latter cases mere group membership may or may not extend to include social action ; this will be discussed later. The definition, furthermore, does not specify whether the relation of the actors is 'solidary' or the opposite.

The 'meaning' relevant in this context is always a case of the meaning imputed to the parties in a given concrete case, on the average or in a theoretically formulated pure type – it is never a normatively 'correct' or a metaphysically 'true' meaning. Even in cases of such forms of social organization as a state, church, association or marriage, the social relationship consists exclusively in the fact that there has existed, exists or will exist a probability of action in some definite way appropriate to this meaning. It is vital to be continually clear about this in order to avoid the 'reification' of these concepts. A 'state', for example, ceases to exist in a sociologically relevant sense whenever there is no longer a probability that certain kinds of meaningfully oriented social action will take place. This probability may be very high or it may be negligibly low. But in any case it is only in the sense and degree in which it does exist or can be estimated that the corresponding social relationship exists. It is impossible to find any other clear meaning for the statement that, for instance, a given 'state' exists or has ceased to exist.

The subjective meaning need not necessarily be the same for all the parties who are mutually oriented in a given social relationship ; there need not in this sense be 'reciprocity'. 'Friendship', 'love', loyalty', 'fidelity to contracts', 'patriotism', on one side, may well be faced with an entirely different attitude on the other. In such cases the parties associate different meanings with their actions and the social relationship is in so far objectively 'asymmetrical' from the points of view of the two parties. It may nevertheless be a case of mutual orientation in so far as, even though partly or wholly erroneously, one party presumes a particular attitude toward him on the part of the other and orients his action to this expectation. This can, and usually will, have consequences for the course of action and the form of the relationship. A relationship is objectively symmetrical only as, according to the typical expectations of the parties, the meaning for one party is the same as that for the other. Thus the actual attitude of a child to its father may be at least approximately that which the father, in the individual case, on the average or typically, has come to expect. A social relationship in which the attitudes are completely and fully corresponding is in reality a limiting case. But the absence of reciprocity will, for terminological purposes, be held to exclude the existence of a social relationship only if it actually results in the absence of a mutual orientation of the action of the parties. Here as elsewhere all sorts of transitional cases are the rule rather than the exception.

A social relationship can be of a temporary character or of varying degrees of permanence. That is, it can be of such a kind that there is a probability of the repeated recurrence of the behaviour which corresponds to its subjective meaning, behaviour which is an understandable consequence of the meaning and hence is expected. In order to avoid fallacious impressions, let it be repeated and continually kept in mind, that it is *only* the existence of the probability that, corresponding to a given subjective meaning complex, a certain type of action will take place, which constitutes the 'existence' of the social relationship. Thus that a 'friendship' or a 'state' exists or has existed means this and only this: that we, the observers, judge that there is or has been a probability that on the basis of certain kinds of known subjective attitude of certain individuals there will result in the average sense a certain specific type of action. For the purposes of legal reasoning it is essential to be able to decide whether a rule of law does or does not carry legal authority, hence whether a legal relationship does or does not 'exist'. This type of question is not, however, relevant to sociological problems.

The subjective meaning of a social relationship may change, thus a political relationship, once based on solidarity, may develop into a conflict of interests. In that case it is only a matter of terminological convenience and of the degree of continuity of the change whether we say that a new relationship has come into existence or that the old one continues but has acquired a new meaning. It is also possible for the meaning to be partly constant, partly changing.

The meaningful content which remains relatively constant in a social relationship is capable of formulation in terms of maxims which the parties concerned expect to be adhered to by their partners, on the average and approximately. The more rational in relation to values or to given ends the action is, the more is this likely to be the case. There is far less possibility of a rational formulation of subjective meaning in the case of a relation of erotic attraction or of personal loyalty or any other affectual type than, for example, in the case of a business contract.

The meaning of social relationship may be agreed upon by mutual consent. This implies that the parties make promises covering their future behaviour, whether toward each other or toward third persons. In such cases each party then normally counts, so far as he acts rationally, in some degree on the fact that the other will orient his action to the meaning of the agreement as he (the first actor) understands it. In part, they orient their action rationally to these expectations as given facts with, to be sure, varying degrees of subjectively 'loyal' intention of doing their part. But in part also they are motivated each by the value to him of his 'duty' to adhere to the agreement in the sense in which he understands it. This much may be anticipated.

10 George Herbert Mead

Self

Excerpts from George Herbert Meade, *Mind, Self and Society*, 1934,
reprinted in Anselm L. Strauss (ed.), *The Social Psychology of
George Herbert Meade*, University of Chicago Press, 1956, pp. 199–246.

The self is something which has a development; it is not initially there at birth but arises in the process of social experience and activity, that is, develops in the given individual as a result of his relations to that process as a whole and to other individuals within that process. The intelligence of the lower forms of animal life, like a great deal of human intelligence, does not involve a self. In our habitual actions, for example, in our moving about in a world that is simply there and to which we are so adjusted that no thinking is involved, there is a certain amount of sensuous experience such as persons have when they are just waking up, a bare 'thereness' of the world. Such characters about us may exist in experience without taking their place in relationship to the self. One must, of course, under those conditions, distinguish between the experience that immediately takes place and our own organization of it into the experience of the self. One says upon analysis that a certain item had its place in his experience, in the experience of his self. We inevitably do tend at a certain level of sophistication to organize all experience into that of a self. We do so intimately identify our experiences, especially our affective experiences, with the self that it takes a moment's abstraction to realize that pain and pleasure can be there without being the experience of the self. Similarly, we normally organize our memories upon the string of our self. When we date things we always date them from the point of view of our past experiences. We frequently have memories that we cannot date, that we cannot place. A picture comes before us suddenly, and we are at a loss to explain when that experience originally took place. We remember perfectly distinctly the picture, but we do not have it definitely placed, and until we can place it in terms of our past experience we are not satisfied. Nevertheless, I think it is obvious, when one comes to consider it, that the self is not necessarily involved in the life of the organism, nor involved in what we term our sensuous experience, that is, experience in a world about us for which we have habitual reactions.

We can distinguish very definitely between the self and the body.

The body can be there and can operate in a very intelligent fashion without there being a self involved in the experience. The self has the characteristic that it is an object to itself, and that characteristic distinguishes it from other objects and from the body. It is perfectly true that the eye can see the foot, but it does not see the body as a whole. We cannot see our backs; we can feel certain portions of them, if we are agile, but we cannot get an experience of our whole body. There are, of course, experiences which are somewhat vague and difficult of location, but the bodily experiences are for us organized about a self. The foot and hand belong to the self. We can see our feet, especially when we look at them from the wrong end of an opera glass, as strange things which we have difficulty in recognizing as our own. The parts of the body are quite distinguishable from the self. We can lose parts of the body without any serious invasion of the self. The mere ability to experience different parts of the body is not different from the experience of a table. The table presents a different feel from what the hand does when one hand feels another, but it is an experience of something with which we come definitely into contact. The body does not experience itself as a whole, in the sense in which the self in some way enters into the experience of the self.

It is the characteristic of the self as an object to itself that I want to bring out. This characteristic is represented in the word 'self', which is a reflexive, and indicates that which can be both subject and object. This type of object is essentially different from other objects, and in the past it has been distinguished as conscious, a term which indicates an experience with, an experience of, one's self. It was assumed that consciousness in some way carried this capacity of being an object to itself. In giving a behavioristic statement of consciousness we have to look for some sort of experience in which the physical organism can become an object to itself.

When one is running away from someone who is chasing him, he is entirely occupied in this action, and his experience may be swallowed up in the objects about him, so that he has, at the time being, no consciousness of self at all. We must be, of course, very completely occupied to have that take place, but we can, I think, recognize that sort of a possible experience in which the self does not enter. We can, perhaps, get some light on that situation through those experiences in which during very intense action there appear in the experience of the individual, back of this intense action, memories and anticipations. Tolstoy as an officer in the war gives an account of having pictures of his past experience in the midst of his most intense action. There are also the pictures that flash into a person's mind when he is drowning. In such instances there is a contrast between an experience that is absolutely wound up in outside activity in which the self as an object does not enter, and an activity of memory and imagination in which the self is the principal object. The self is then entirely distinguishable from an organism that is surrounded by things and acts with reference to things, including parts of its own body. These latter may be objects like other objects, but they are just objects out there in the field, and they do not involve a self that is an object to the organism. This is, I think, frequently overlooked. It is that fact which makes our anthropomorphic reconstructions of animal life so fallacious. How can an individual get outside himself (experientially) in such a way as to become an object to himself? This is the essential psychological problem of selfhood or of self-consciousness; and its solution is to be found by referring to the process of social conduct or activity in which the given person or individual is implicated. The apparatus of reason would not be complete unless it swept itself into its own analysis of the field of experience or unless the individual brought himself into the same experiential field as that of the other individual selves in relation to whom he acts in any given social situation. Reason cannot become impersonal unless it takes an objective, non-affective attitude toward itself; otherwise we have just consciousness, not *self*-consciousness. And it is necessary to rational conduct that the individual should thus take an objective, impersonal attitude toward himself, that he should become an object to himself. For the individual organism is obviously an essential and important fact or constituent element of the empirical situation in which it acts; and without taking objective account of itself as such, it cannot act intelligently or rationally.

The individual experiences himself as such, not directly, but only indirectly, from the particular standpoints of other individual members of the same social group or from the generalized standpoint of the social group as a whole to which he belongs. For he enters his own experience as a self or individual, not directly or immediately, not by becoming a subject to himself, but only in so far as he first becomes an object to himself just as other individuals are objects to him or are in his experience; and he becomes an object to himself only by taking the attitudes of other individuals toward himself within a social environment or context of experience and behavior in which both he and they are involved.

The importance of what we term 'communication' lies in the fact that it provides a form of behavior in which the organism or the individual may become an object to himself. It is that sort of communication which we have been discussing – not communication in the sense of the cluck of the hen to the chickens, or the bark of a wolf to the pack, or the lowing of a cow, but communication in the sense of significant symbols, communication which is directed not only to others but also to the individual himself. So far as that type of communication is a part of behavior, it at least introduces a self. Of course, one may hear without listening; one may see things that he does not realize; do things that he is not really aware of. But it is when one does respond to that which he addresses to another and when that response of his own becomes a part of his conduct, when he not only hears himself but responds to himself, talks and replies to himself as truly as the other person replies to him, that we have behavior in which the individuals become objects to themselves.

Such a self is not, I would say, primarily the physiological organism. The physiological organism is essential to it, but we are at least able to think of a self without it. Persons who believe in immortality, or believe in ghosts, or in the possibility of the self leaving the body, assume a self which is quite distinguishable from the body. How successfully they can hold these conceptions is an open question, but we do, as a fact, separate the self and the organism. It is fair to say that the beginning of the self as an object, so far as we can see, is to be found in the experiences of people that lead to the conception of a 'double'. Primitive people assume that there is a double, located presumably in the diaphragm, that leaves the body temporarily in sleep and completely in death. It can be enticed out of the body of one's enemy and perhaps killed. It is represented in infancy by the imaginary playmates which children create and through which they come to control their experiences in their play.

The self, as that which can be an object to itself, is essentially a social structure, and it arises in social experience. After a self has arisen, it in a certain sense provides for itself its social experiences, and so we can conceive of an absolutely solitary self. But it is impossible to conceive of a self arising outside of social experience. When it has arisen, we can think of a person in solitary confinement for the rest of his life, but who still has himself as a companion and is able to think and to converse with himself as he had communicated with others. That process to which I have just referred, of responding to one's self as another responds to it, taking part in one's own conversation with others, being aware of what one is saying and using that awareness of what one is saying to determine what one is going to say thereafter – that is a process with which we are all familiar. We are continually following up our own address to other persons by an understanding of what we are saying and using that understanding in the direction of our continued speech. We are finding out what we are going to say, what we are going to do, by saying and doing, and in the process we are continually controlling the process itself. In the conversation of gestures what we say calls out a certain response in another and that in turn changes our own action, so that we shift from what we started to do because of the reply the other makes. The conversation of gestures is the beginning of communication. The individual comes to carry on a conversation of gestures with himself. He says something and that calls out a certain reply in himself which makes him change what he was going to say. One starts to say something, we will presume an unpleasant something, but when he starts to say it he realizes it is cruel. The effect on himself of what he is saying checks him ; there is here a conversation of gestures between the individual and himself. By significant speech we mean that the action is one that affects the individual himself and that the effect upon the individual himself is part of the intelligent carrying-out of the conversation with others. Now we, so to speak, amputate that social phase and dispense with it for the time being, so that one is talking to one's self as one would talk to another person.

This process of abstraction cannot be carried on indefinitely. One inevitably seeks an audience, has to pour himself out to somebody. In reflective intelligence one thinks to act and to act solely so that this action remains a part of a social process. Thinking becomes preparatory to social action. The very process of thinking is, of course, simply an inner conversation that goes on, but it is a conversation of gestures which in its completion implies the expression of that which one thinks to an audience. One separates the significance of what he is saying to others from the actual speech and gets it ready before saying it. He thinks it out and perhaps writes it in the form of a book ; but it is still a part of social intercourse in which one is addressing other persons and at the same time addressing one's self, and in which one controls the address to other persons by the response made to one's own gesture. That the person should be responding to himself is necessary to the self, and it is this sort of social conduct which provides behaviour within which that self appears. I know of no other form of behavior than the linguistic in which the individual is an object to himself, and, so far as I can see, the individual is not a self in the reflective sense unless he is an object to himself. It is this fact that gives a critical importance to communication, since this is a type of behavior in which the individual does so respond to himself.

We realize in everyday conduct and experience that an individual does not mean a great deal of what he is doing and saying. We frequently say that such an individual is not himself. We come away from an interview with a realization that we have left out important things, that there are parts of the self that did not get into what was said. What determines the amount of the self that gets into communication is the social experience itself. Of course, a good deal of the self does not need to get expression. We carry on a whole series of different relationships to different people. We are one thing to one man and another thing to another. There are parts of the self which exist only for the self in relationship to itself. We divide ourselves up in all sorts of different selves with reference to our acquaintances. We discuss politics with one and religion with another. There are all sorts of different selves answering to all sorts of different social reactions. It is the social process itself that is responsible for the appearance of the self; it is not there as a self apart from this type of experience. [...]

Play, the game and the generalized other

[...] The organized community or social group which gives to the individual his unity of self can be called 'the generalized other'. The attitude of the generalized other is the attitude of the whole community. Thus, for example, in the case of such a social group as a ball team, the team is the generalized other in so far as it enters – as an organized process on social activity – into the experience of any one of the individual members. [...]

If the given human individual is to develop a self in the fullest sense, it is not sufficient for him merely to take the attitudes of other human individuals toward himself and toward one another within the human social process and to bring that social process as a whole into his individual experience merely in these terms. He must also, in the same way that he takes the attitudes of other individuals toward himself and toward one another, take their attitudes toward the various phases or aspects of the common social activity or set of social undertakings in which, as members of an organized society or social group, they are all engaged. He must then, by generalizing these individual attitudes of that organized society or social group itself as a whole, act toward different social projects which at any given time it is carrying out, or toward the various larger phases of the general social process which constitutes the group's life and of which these projects are specific manifestations. Getting these broad activities of any given social whole or organized society within the experiential field of any one of the individuals involved or included in that whole is, in other words, the essential basis and prerequisite of the fullest development of that individual's self – only in so far as he takes the attitudes of the organized social group to which he belongs toward the organized, cooperative social activity or set of such activities in which that group as such is engaged, does he develop a complete self or possess the sort of complete self he has developed. And on the other hand, the complex cooperative processes and activities and institutional functionings of organized human society are also possible only in so far as every individual involved in them or belonging to that society can take the general attitudes of all other such individuals with reference to these processes and activities and institutional functionings and to the organized social whole of experiential relations and interactions thereby constituted – and can direct his own behavior accordingly.

It is in the form of the generalized other that the social process influences the behavior of the individuals involved in it and carrying it on, that is, that the community exercises control over the conduct of its individual members ; for it is in this form that the social process or community enters as a determining factor into the individual's thinking. In abstract thought the individual takes the attitude of the generalized other toward himself, without reference to its expression in any particular other individuals ; and in concrete thought, he takes that attitude in so far as it is expressed in the attitudes toward his behavior of those other individuals with whom he is involved in the given social situation or act. But only by taking the attitude of the generalized other toward himself, in one or another of these ways, can he think at all ; for only thus can thinking – or the internalized conversation of gestures which constitutes thinking – occur. And only through the taking by individuals of the attitude or attitudes of the generalized other toward themselves is the existence of a universe of discourse, as that system of common or social meanings which thinking presupposes as its context, rendered possible.

The self-conscious human individual, then, takes or assumes the organized social attitudes of the given social group or community (or of some one section thereof) to which he belongs, toward the social problems of various kinds which confront that group or community at any given time and which arise in connection with the correspondingly different social projects or organized cooperative enterprises in which that group of community as such is engaged ; and as an individual participant in these social projects or cooperative enterprises, he governs his own conduct accordingly. In politics, for example, the individual identifies himself with an entire political party and takes the organized attitudes of that entire party toward the rest of the given social community and toward the problems which confront the party within the given social situation ; and he consequently reacts or responds in terms of the organized attitudes of the party as a whole. He thus enters into a special set of social relations with all the other individuals who belong to that political party ; and in the same way he enters into various other special sets of social relations, with various other classes of individuals respectively, the individuals of each of these classes being the other members of some one of the particular organized subgroups (determined in socially functional terms) of which he himself is a member within the entire given society, or social community. In the most highly developed, organized and complicated human social communities – those evolved by civilized man – these various socially functional classes or subgroups of individuals to which any given individual belongs (and with the other individual members of which he thus enters into a special set of social relations) are of two kinds. Some of them are concrete social classes or subgroups, such as political parties, clubs, corporations, which are all actually functional social units, in terms of which their individual members are directly related to one another. The others are abstract social classes or subgroups, such as the class of debtors and the class of creditors, in terms of which their individual members are related to one another only more or less indirectly and which only more or less indirectly function as social units, but which afford or represent unlimited possibilities for the widening and ramifying and enriching of the social relations among all the individual members of the given society as an organized and unified whole. The given individual's membership in several of these abstract social classes or subgroups makes possible his entrance into definite social relations (however indirect) with an almost infinite number of other individuals who also belong to or are included within one or another of these abstract social classes or subgroups cutting across functional lines of demarcation which divide different human social communities from one another, and including individual members from several (in some cases from all) such communities. Of these abstract social classes or subgroups of human individuals the one which is most inclusive and extensive is, of course, the one defined by the logical universe of discourse (or system of universally significant symbols) determined by the participation and communicative interaction of individuals ; for all such classes or subgroups, it is the one which claims the largest number of individual members and which enables the largest conceivable number of human individuals to enter into some sort of social relation, however indirect or abstract it may be, with one another – a relation arising from the universal functioning of gestures as significant symbols in the general human social process of communication.

I have pointed out, then, that there are two general stages in the full development of the self. At the first of these stages, the individual's self is constituted simply by an organization of the particular attitudes of other individuals toward himself and toward one another in the specific social acts in which he participates with them. But at the second stage in the full development of the individual's self, that self is constituted not only by an organization of these particular individual attitudes, but also by an organization of the social attitudes of the generalized other or the social group as a whole to which he belongs. These social or group attitudes are brought within the individual's field of direct experience and are included as elements in the structure or constitution of his self, in the same way that the attitudes of particular other individuals are ; and the individual arrives at them, or succeeds in taking them, by means of further organizing, and then generalizing, the attitudes of particular other individuals in terms of their organized social bearings and implications. So the self reaches its full development by organizing these individual attitudes of others into the organized social or group attitudes, and by thus becoming an individual reflection of the general systematic pattern of social or group behavior in which it and the others are all involved – a pattern which enters as a whole into the individual's experience in terms of these organized group attitudes which, through the mechanism of his central nervous system, he takes toward himself, just as he takes the individual attitudes of others.

The game has a logic, so that such an organization of the self is rendered possible. There is a definite end to be obtained ; the actions of the different individuals are all related to each other with reference to that end so that they do not conflict ; one is not in conflict with himself in the attitude of another man on the team. If one has the attitude of the person throwing the ball, he can also have the response of catching the ball. The two are related so that they further the purpose of the game itself. They are interrelated in a unitary, organic fashion. There is a definite unity, then, which is introduced into the organization of other selves when we reach such a stage as that of the game, as against the situation of play where there is a simple succession of one role after another, a situation which is, of course, characteristic of the child's own personality. The child is one thing at one time and another at another, and what he is at one moment does not determine what he is at another. That is both the charm of childhood as well as its inadequacy. You cannot count on the child; you cannot assume that all the things he does are going to determine what he will do at any moment. He is not organized into a whole. The child has no definite character, no definite personality.

The game is then an illustration of the situation out of which an organized personality arises. In so far as the child does take the attitude of the other and allows that attitude of the other to determine the thing he is going to do with reference to a common end, he is becoming an organic member of society. He is taking over the morale of that society and is becoming an essential member of it. He belongs to it in so far as he does allow the attitude of the other that he takes to control his own immediate expression. What is involved here is some sort of an organized process. That which is expressed in terms of the game is, of course, being continually expressed in the social life of the child, but this wider process goes beyond the immediate experience of the child himself. The importance of the game is that it lies entirely inside the child's own experience, and the importance of our modern type of education is that it is brought as far as possible within this realm. The different attitudes that a child assumes are so organized that they exercise a definite control over his response, as the attitudes in a game control his own immediate response. In the game we get an organized other, a generalized other, which is found in the nature of the child itself, and finds its expression in the immediate experience of the child. And it is that organized activity in the child's own nature controlling the particular response which gives unity, and which builds up his own self.

What goes on in the game goes on in the life of the child all the time. He is continually taking the attitudes of those about him, especially the roles of those who in some sense control him and on whom he depends. He gets the function of the process in an abstract sort of way at first. It goes over from the play into the game in a real sense. He has to play the game. The morale of the game takes hold of the child more than the larger morale of the whole community. The child passes into the game, and the game expresses a social situation in which he can completely enter; its morale may have a greater hold on him than that of the family to which he belongs or the community in which he lives. There are all sorts of social organizations, some of which are fairly lasting, some temporary, into which the child is entering, and he is playing a sort of social game in them. It is a period in which he likes 'to belong', and he gets into organizations which come into existence and pass out of existence. He becomes a something which can function in the organized whole, and thus tends to determine himself in his relationship with the group to which he belongs. That process is one which is a striking stage in the development of the child's morale. It constitutes him a self-conscious member of the community to which he belongs.

Such is the process by which a personality arises. I have spoken of this as a process in which a child takes the role of the other and said that it takes place essentially through the use of language. Language is predominantly based on the vocal gesture by means of which cooperative activities in a community are carried out. Language in its significant sense is that vocal gesture which tends to arouse in the individual the attitude which it arouses in others, and it is this perfecting of the self by the gesture which mediates the social activities that gives rise to the process of taking the role of the other. The latter phrase is a little unfortunate because it suggests an actor's attitude which is actually more sophisticated than that which is involved in our own experience. To this degree it does not correctly describe that which I have in mind. We see the process most definitely in a primitive form in those situations where the child's play takes different roles. Here the very fact that he is ready to pay money, for instance, arouses the attitude of the person who receives money, the very process is calling out in him the corresponding activities of the other person involved. The individual stimulates himself to the response which he is calling out in the other person, and then acts in some degree in response to that situation. In play the child does definitely act the role which he himself has aroused in himself. It is that which gives, as I have said, a definite content in the individual which answers to the stimulus that affects him as it affects somebody else. The content of the other that enters into one personality is the response in the individual which his gesture calls out in the other. [. . .]

I have so far emphasized what I have called the structures upon which the self is constructed, the framework of the self, as it were. Of course we are not only what is common to all : each one of the selves is different from everyone else ; but there has to be such a common structure as I have sketched in order that we may be members of a community at all. We cannot be ourselves unless we are also members in whom there is a community of attitudes which control the attitudes of all. We cannot have rights unless we have common attitudes. That which we have acquired as self-conscious persons makes us members of society and gives us selves. Selves can only exist in definite relationships to other selves. No hard-and-fast line can be drawn between our own selves and the selves of others, since our own selves exist and enter as such into our experience only in so far as the selves of others exist and enter as such into our experience also. The individual possesses a self only in relation to the selves of the other members of his social group; and the structure of his self expresses or reflects the general behavior pattern of this social group to which he belongs, just as does the structure of the self of every other individual belonging to this social group.

The self and the subjective

Emphasis should be laid on the central position of thinking when considering the nature of the self. Self-consciousness, rather than affective experience with its motor accompaniments, provides the core and primary structure of the self, which is thus essentially a cognitive rather than an emotional phenomenon. The thinking or intellectual process – internalization and inner dramatization, by the individual, of the external conversation of significant gestures which constitutes his chief mode of interaction with other individuals belonging to the same society – is the earliest experiential phase in the genesis and development of the self. Cooley and James, it is true, endeavor to find the basis of the self in reflexive affective experiences, that is, experiences involving 'self-feeling'; but the theory that the nature of the self is to be found in such experiences does not account for the origin of the self or of the self-feeling which is supposed to characterize such experiences. The individual need not take the attitudes of others toward himself in these experiences, since these experiences merely in themselves do not necessitate his doing so, and unless he does so, he cannot develop a self; and he will not do so in these experiences unless his self has already originated otherwise, namely, in the way we have been describing. The essence of the self, as we have said, is cognitive. It lies in the internalized conversation of gestures which constitutes thinking or in terms of which thought or reflection proceeds. And hence the origin and foundations of the self, like those of thinking, are social.

The 'I' and the 'me'

We have discussed at length the social foundations of the self and hinted that the self does not consist simply in the bare organization of social attitudes. We may now explicitly raise the question as to the nature of the 'I' which is aware of the social 'me'. [...]

The simplest way of handling the problem would be in terms of memory. I talk to myself, and I remember what I said and perhaps the emotional content that went with it. The 'I' of this moment is present in the 'me' of the next moment. There again I cannot turn around quick enough to catch myself. I become a 'me' in so far as I remember what I said. [...]

The 'I' is the response of the organism to the attitudes of the others; the 'me' is the organized set of attitudes of others which one himself assumes. The attitudes of the others constitute the organized 'me', and then one reacts toward that as an 'I'. [...]

A contrast of individualistic and social theories of the self

The differences between the type of social psychology which derives the selves of individuals from the social process in which they are implicated and in which they empirically interact with one another and the type of social psychology which instead derives that process from the selves of the individuals involved in it are clear. The first type assumes a social process or social order as the logical and biological precondition of the appearance of the selves of the individual organisms involved in that process or belonging to that order. The other type, on the contrary, assumes individual selves as the presuppositions, logically and biologically, of the social process or order within which they interact.

The difference between the social and the individual theories of the development of mind, self and the social process of experience or behavior is analogous to the difference between the evolutionary and the contract theories of the state as held in the past by both rationalists and empiricists. The latter theory takes individuals and their individual experiencing – individual minds and selves – as logically prior to the social process in which they are involved, and explains the existence of that social process in terms of them; whereas the former takes the social process of experience or behavior as logically prior to the individuals and their individual experiencing which are involved in it, and explains their existence in terms of that social process. But the latter type of theory cannot explain that which is taken as logically prior at all, cannot explain the existence of minds and selves; whereas the former type of theory can explain that which it takes as logically prior, namely, the existence of the social process of behavior, in terms of such fundamental biological or physiological relations and interactions as reproduction, or the cooperation of individuals for mutual protection or for the securing of food.

Our contention is that mind can never find expression, and could never have come into existence at all, except in terms of a social environment; that an organized set or pattern of social relations and interactions (especially those of communication by means of gestures functioning as significant symbols and thus creating a universe of discourse) is necessarily presupposed by it and involved in its nature. And this entirely social theory or interpretation of mind – this contention that mind develops and has its being only in and by virtue of the social process of experience and activity, which it hence presupposes, and that in no other way can it develop and have its being – must be clearly distinguished from the partially (but only partially) social view of mind. On this view, though mind can get expression only within or in terms of the environment of an organized social group, yet it is nevertheless in some sense a native endowment – a congenital or hereditary biological attribute – of the individual organism and could not otherwise exist or manifest itself in the social process at all ; so that it is not itself essentially a social phenomenon, but rather is biological both in its nature and in its origin and is social only in its characteristic manifestations or expressions. According to this latter view, moreover, the social process presupposes, and in a sense is a product of, mind ; in direct contrast is our opposite view that mind presupposes, and is a product of, the social process. The advantage of our view is that it enables us to give a detailed account and actually to explain the genesis and development of mind ; whereas the view that mind is a congenital biological endowment of the individual organism does not really enable us to explain its nature and origin at all – neither what sort of biological endowment it is, nor how organisms at a certain level of evolutionary progress come to possess it. Furthermore, the supposition that the social process presupposes, and is in some sense a product of, mind seems to be contradicted by the existence of the social communities of certain of the lower animals, especially the highly complex social organizations of bees and ants, which apparently operate on a purely instinctive or reflex basis, and do not in the least involve the existence of mind or consciousness in the individual organisms which form or constitute them. And even if this contradiction is avoided by the admission that only at its higher levels – only at the levels represented by the social relations and interactions of human beings – does the social process of experience and behavior presuppose the existence of mind or become necessarily a product of mind, still it is hardly plausible to suppose that this already ongoing and developing process should suddenly, at a particular stage in its evolution, become dependent for its further continuance upon an entirely extraneous factor, introduced into it, so to speak, from without.

The individual enters as such into his own experience only as an object, not as a subject ; and he can enter as an object only on the basis of social relations and interactions, only by means of his experiential transactions with other individuals in an organized social environment. It is true that certain contents of experience (particularly kinaesthetic) are accessible only to the given individual organism and not to any others ; and that these private or 'subjective', as opposed to public or 'objective', contents of experience are usually regarded as being peculiarly and intimately connected with the individual's self, or as being in a special sense self-experiences. But this accessibility solely to the given individual organism of certain contents of its experience does not affect, nor in any way conflict with, the theory as to the social nature and origin of the self that we are presenting. Existence of private or 'subjective' contents of experience does not alter the fact that self-consciousness involves the individual's becoming an object to himself by taking the attitudes of other individuals toward himself within an organized setting of social relationships, and that unless the individual had thus become an object to himself he would not be self-conscious or have a self at all. Apart from his social interactions with other individuals, he would not relate the private or 'subjective' contents of his experience to himself and he could not become aware of himself as such, that is, as an individual, a person, merely by means or in terms of these contents of his experience ; for in order to become aware of himself as such he must, to repeat, become an object to himself, or enter his own experience as an object, and only by social means – only by taking the attitudes of others toward himself – is he able to become an object to himself.

It is true, of course, that once mind has arisen in the social process it makes possible the development of that process into much more complex forms of social interaction among the component individuals than was possible before it had arisen. But there is nothing odd about a product of a given process contributing to, or becoming an essential factor in, the further development of that process. The social process, then, does not depend for its origin or initial existence upon the existence and interactions of selves, though it does depend upon the latter for the higher stages of complexity and organization which it reaches after selves have arisen within it.

11 George J. McCall and J. L. Simmons

The Dynamics of Interactions [1]

Excerpt from George J. McCall and J. L. Simmons, *Identities and Interactions*, Collier-Macmillan, 1966, pp. 125–66.

'Social interaction' is one of the most widely used concepts in the social sciences, yet comparatively little is actually known about the concrete processes of face-to-face interaction. We are all steeped in interaction experiences, yet this pan-human store of experience remains largely untranslated into explicit scientific knowledge.

How do persons modify their conduct when they encounter one another and go on to engage in more or less sustained interactions? Each brings a distinctive set of identities, goals and problems to an encounter ; how do they conduct themselves so that their own concerns are advanced (or at least not significantly damaged) without so jeopardizing the others' concerns that the very fabric of the interaction itself dissolves?

Man, both as animal and as dreamer, is highly dependent upon interaction with his fellows. His daily life, which takes place in the intersection of these two worlds, must be lived in consort with the other humans on the scene. Through what means does this consort take place?

Despite the centrality of this question for understanding social man and his behaviors, little is known about its answers. In this chapter, drawing upon the scattered insights of others, we shall attempt to frame a partial answer to the *how* of interaction. We must emphasize that it is only a partial answer, for face-to-face interaction is a richly faceted and multiplex phenomenon containing many simultaneous and intertwined strands. We shall be able to consider only a handful of the major processes involved: those of symbolic interaction, negotiated exchange, social influence and power, and task performance. Many others of nearly comparable importance, like social control, conflict, social integration and the like, are regrettably omitted here.

---

1. Many of the problems, concepts and propositions discussed in this chapter receive detailed amplification and elaboration in McCall and McCall (1970).

Identification and interaction

When people encounter one another, they pose problems for one another all around. Other people are always somewhat unknown quantities, for they are complex, flighty, changeable creatures of mood and impulse. A woman, to be sure, is a 'sometime thing'. And who knows for sure whether or not that nice man downstairs may someday invade one's chambers armed with an axe and bent on mayhem? It happens somewhere every day. People can never be taken quite for granted, for one never knows what they may do. Even the lowliest 'worm' may turn, and every 'dog' has her day. As a consequence, we find that we must ever be appraising anew our friends and our lovers, our parents and our children. And we, in turn, are as much enigmas to others.

We try to judge others in terms of their significances for us, their implications for our plans of action. Literally, we do not know what to do with respect to another person until we have established his meaning for us and our meanings for him. [. . .]

But we must now consider the fact that, in a concrete interaction situation, *every* person must appraise *everyone else*, and the pictures they come up with must all be at least roughly consensual, else some interactors will be acting in quite groundless fashion and at crosspurposes with the others. This latter outcome, of course, not infrequently occurs.

More important, however, it is still true that in the great majority of interactions people do manage to attain some fumbling consensus on the situations and the warm bodies within them, and they thus go on to conduct their respective businesses. It must be emphasized that such 'consensus' does not mean real agreement on all appraisals among all the actors. Rather, consensus is defined here as the lack of impeding disagreements. *All that is needed is a sufficient lack of disagreement about one another for each to proceed in some degree with his own plans of action.*

This achievement is, in itself, no mean feat, however. It is a complex and quite problematic accomplishment. In the early sections of this chapter we shall examine the processes by means of which people are able to achieve such rough and ready 'working consensuses' on the identities and meanings of the persons present. Later in the chapter we shall inquire how, social identities having been thus established, these persons carry out and mutually adjust their individual lines of action, how interactive roles are devised and performed.

Structured situations

We are all aware that things are easier to understand when they are seen in context. A deformed tree becomes understandable within the context of a wind-swept plateau, and some of the ambiguities of foreign movies disappear when we have learned something of the cultures that produced them.

The same is true when it comes to judging persons. We can usually better understand them and their behavior when we know the contexts of their actions. Behavior that seems at first glance bizarre and irrational often becomes eminently reasonable when we know the web of circumstances in which it occurred. Behavior, even extreme behavior like suicide, gang delinquency and paranoia, is 'reasonable' from the perspective – the definition of the situation – of the behaving person.

The context or *situation* within which people encounter one another often affords excellent clues to their meaning for one another's plans of action. In fact, much of socialization involves learning to define, at a glance, the more common situations of the immediate society and the limitations and opportunities they entail. For example, if we walk into a theater and find a man in non-military uniform standing expectantly at the door, we know automatically that he is a ticket-taker and that we must present to him valid tickets if we wish to continue into the theater. The ticket-taker is not so labeled, nor is his uniform particularly distinctive, yet we do not have to ask why he is blocking our entrance, because the situation itself is so standardized in our culture that it provides sufficient clues as to the mutual implications of the persons involved. This and a host of other recurring and conventional situations themselves tell the contemporary American how he must conduct himself.

But this clarity of circumstance does not obtain in every human encounter or even in the majority of them. In fact, it is most likely to occur in precisely such routine and superficial interactions as the exchange of a ticket for entrance to the theater. And even then, the interaction may 'spill over' from the specified into other exchanges and responses if the ticket-taker has a curious haircut, is an attractive girl, or is the son of one's insurance man.

Unstructured situations

In most human encounters the contexts or situations are to some degree ambiguous and unstructured; that is, the situations are not clearly defined in the eyes of the interactors. The degree of unstructuredness results either from the uncertainty of the actors about which of their identities will be involved or from ambiguities in the meanings of the situation for the identities that have already become involved (or, not uncommonly, both of these factors).

Typically, the problem in such cases is not that there are no available interpretations but rather that there are two or more *alternative* interpretations that could be placed upon the situation, each of which implies a somewhat different and perhaps conflicting meaning for the persons involved. If the alternative interpretations are held by different actors, a 'situation-defining phase' is likely to occur.

For example, the ticket-taker may also be a very close friend. The significance of this warm body, its implications for one's plans of action, is rather different if it is only that of a ticket-taker than it would be if it were only that of a close friend. In the first case, he will simply reach out for the tickets, tear them and return the stubs, perhaps throwing in a mechanical 'thank you'. In the second case, he would stop any other activities (at least momentarily) to greet one warmly, inquire into one's present health, and engage in some idle conversation.

But as he is actually both ticket-taker *and* friend, it is not clear which of these patterns one should expect. If he is a very close friend, there may even be some consideration that he should let one into the theater without demanding a ticket. Rival interpretations of the situation, as being one of an impersonal encounter between theater official and patron or as being one of an encounter between warm friends, are competing for acceptance in this concrete case.

Between the two parties, an agreement on which interpretation to accept must be worked out quickly and unobtrusively. They must decide between them which scene to stage here, the meeting of official with patron or the meeting of friend with friend. They must decide, in effect, which identities are to be honored.

This decision is, of course, seldom an either–or decision even in 'simple' situations like that described. Most often some sort of compromise interpretation is negotiated so that both sets of identities receive partial recognition in the situation without either completely prevailing to the exclusion of the other.

In the typical concrete interaction, the 'working consensus' arrived at is such that several identities of each of the interactors are involved. Usually the several identities are so blended together in the unfolding interaction that they can be separated only analytically.

The means by which these identities are 'negotiated, legislated and adjudicated' are quite complex, and we shall group them into two categories: the cognitive processes and the expressive processes.

Cognitive processes in interaction

This group of essentially covert processes has a certain logical priority in the complex flow of interaction, for these processes have to do with judging the identities that the various interactors (including oneself) are likely to claim in the situation. Working from subtle clues and faint impressions, one attempts to discern the identities relevant to each of the several participants.

Imputation of role to alter

A person's social identities are not ordinarily to be physically perceived but are to be inferred from his appearance and, especially, his actions. The man in blue uniform may not be a policeman but an actor or a bus driver; the man in shirtsleeves may not be a customer but a captain of detectives. Even sexual identification is subject to error and deception. Social identities are seldom simply read off from a person's appearance but must be inferred from visible clues and from his behaviors.

When we use a person's behaviors as the basis for our inferences about his identities, we are employing the process of *role-taking*, a process that has been very widely discussed in the social-science literature (Turner, 1956). Role-taking is but a special case of the general process of appraising persons that was discussed in the preceding chapter. The distinctiveness of role-taking as a perceptual process lies in its aim, which is to discover not the qualities of a person but the role he is performing before one and, thereby, his operative social identities.

An interactive role is, it will be remembered, the characteristic and plausible line of action that flows from, is truly expressive of, a distinctive character. The same person, of course, takes on different characters under different circumstances, and his roles, accordingly, also differ. His conduct at any moment is behavior organized under the influence of his current role, that is, the line of action that flows from and expresses his current character.

In role-taking, then, one is not trying to see through to a person's true self (his prominence hierarchy); one is merely trying to discover the contours of the role the other is currently projecting and the character (salient subset of identities) that underlies it. One is trying to see through the other's specific acts to discover the line of action that gives them direction, coherence and meaning.

Behavior is said to make sense when a series of actions is interpretable as indicating that the actor has in mind some role which guides his behavior. . . . The isolated action becomes a datum for role analysis only when it is interpreted as the manifestation of a configuration. The individual acts as if he were expressing some role through his behavior and may assign a higher degree of reality to the assumed role than to his specific actions. The role becomes the point of reference for placing interpretations on specific actions, for anticipating that one line of action will follow upon another, and for making evaluations of individual actions. For example, the lie which is an expression of the role of friend is an altogether different thing from the same lie taken as a manifestation of the role of confidence man (Turner, 1962, p. 24).

The unity of a role cannot consist simply in the bracketing of a set of specific behaviors, since the same behavior can be indicative of different roles under different circumstances. The unifying element is to be found *in some assignment of purpose or sentiment to the actor*. Various actions by an individual are classified as intentional and unintentional (relevant and irrelevant) on the basis of a role designation. . . . Role-taking involves selective perception of the actions of another and a great deal of selective emphasis, organized about some purpose or sentiment attributed to the other (p. 28).

In trying to discern alter's role, then, we impute to him certain purposes or motives in the light of which alter's actions appear coherently organized as a recognizable line of action. 'The key to person perception lies in our attention to what he is *trying to do*' (Allport, 1961, p. 520).

To understand, explain or justify specific actions, then, we impute (or avow) *motives*. If we were so crude as to grill alter about why he did a certain thing in a situation, he would try to explain his behavior, to justify his conduct, by avowing certain motives or purposes for those actions (Peters, 1958). Men, unlike other animals, are always under the scrutiny of their fellows and are potentially held accountable for their every action, as we have noted before. Consequently, they must always be prepared to avow the motives that justify their every act, past, present and future.

They do not have complete freedom of choice in this avowal, however. 'Institutionally different situations have different vocabularies of motive appropriate to their respective behaviors' (Mills, 1940). That is, there is only a finite and small number of motives recognized in the culture for avowal or imputation, and these few motives are differentially associated with certain situations and certain social positions. Therefore, a motive avowed in one type of situation may constitute a perfectly acceptable justification of one's acts, whereas the very same motive avowed in a different type of situation would not be accepted as a justification. For example, a person caught in a lie can often justify his conduct by claiming to have been trying to protect a friend's feelings, but, if he is caught in the same lie in a courtroom situation, this motive will not persuade the judge.

In our pluralistic society with its competing groups, each of which fosters its own distinctive perspectives on the world, there have developed divergent vocabularies of motive. The homosexual may be able to justify his conduct to the 'gay' world but not to the courts. A medieval monk avowed that he gave food to a poor but pretty woman because it was 'for the glory of God and the eternal salvation of his soul', but the Freudians would question this avowal and impute frankly sexual motives to him.

What is reason for one man is rationalization for another. The variable is the accepted vocabulary of motives, the ultimates of (justificatory) discourse, of each man's dominant group about whose opinion he cares (Mills, 1940).

If we are to understand a person's behavior, to discern a role through it, we must try to discover for which audience he is avowing and imputing motives, and whether or not the vocabulary in terms of which he does so is an acceptable one to that particular audience. Once we decide whom he is playing to, so to speak, we can usually discern the motives or purposes that are organizing his line of action. If we do not share the vocabulary of motives held by that particular audience, however, we may be totally unable to make sense of alter's actions.

These remarks and our daily experiences point up the fact that role-taking is at least as complex and uncertain a process as is social perception generally. A number of researches – and, again, our daily experiences – shows that people vary markedly in the 'breadth', the 'depth' and other aspects of their role-taking abilities.

A modicum of role-taking ability is widespread in every population because most interactions pertain to only a fairly small number of types of social identity, and most members of the population have had at least some experience with each. In the course of our lives, most of us experience at least something of all the fundamental human themes and relationships. Most of us have had at least fleeting experience with being leader and follower, poet and performer of repetitive routines, active manipulator and passive recipient, idealist and opportunist, success and failure. The extent and the content of experience with these archetypical identities and themes vary tremendously, of course, but some experience with the forms, at least vicariously, is probably fairly universal within a given culture.

Each individual therefore has, incorporated into his 'inner forum', a repertoire of many different perspectives and vocabularies of motives, albeit in different proportions and balances. This repertoire, and the use of analogies, enables us to take roles. The analogies, so common in literature and daily discourse, enable us to relate an initially un-fathomed human action to our own repertoire and thus to gain in-sight into it: 'Riding in a small plane is no more upsetting than riding a ferris wheel, and flying in a jetliner is like sitting in your living room – after a fast elevator ride up.'

We can take another's role, then, if some components of our own 'inner forums' are at least generally similar to the identities that are salient in his actions. We temporarily and hypothetically 'stretch' our own hierarchies of identity-perspectives until the situation is viewed from a vantage point, opportunity structure, and motivations similar to those of alter. If we and alter are 'like-minded' or 'see eye to eye', role-taking is relatively easy. But we shall never completely match alter's perspective, and the more dissimilar he is from us the more 'elastic' our own perspectives must be to catch even a glimpse of his own point of view.

It must be emphasized that 'role-taking' is a metaphor. We do not and cannot literally 'take' alter's role. When we 'project' ourselves into his situation and imagine how we would feel, we are sometimes im-pressed by the intensity and realism of our own feelings, but these feelings are *ours*, not his, and the accuracy of our role-taking remains uncertain.

The variables that determine the accuracy, breadth and depth of our role-taking abilities in interaction situations derive from the nature of the role-taking process itself (see Allport, 1961, pp. 497–548). The first and most important are the amount and breadth of our experiences. We learn role-taking not only from our own accumulated direct ex-perience with various roles but also, to a lesser extent yet more broadly, from observing the counterrole performances of those who have inter-acted with us. In this manner, for example, persons develop some insight into the perspectives of the opposite sex, and children have some glimmering of what it means to be a parent. The information accumulated from observing those who are in counterroles to our-selves is one of the major avenues of 'anticipatory' socialization more generally.

Role-taking ability can thus develop both from 'subjective' experience with similar roles and from more 'objective' experience in observing others in these roles. Professionals often develop a great deal of this 'objective' knowledge about their clients, and the latter are often sur-prised by what seems to them uncanny familiarity with their own points of view. Such knowledge on the part of the doctor, the teacher, the official points up the fact that 'empathy' must not be confused with sympathy or emotional involvement of any kind ; the professional is often quite aloof and 'clinically distant' from his client.

Role-taking ability is also affected by the conventionality of the identities and performances involved. In fact, role-taking is almost always a partial and selective process that focuses upon the more superficial and conventional aspects of the other person's identities. This incompleteness is present of necessity, as these conventional aspects are the 'common denominators' of imagery and motivation in that social grouping.

And finally, role-taking ability is subject to the degree of familiarity with the other person. This familiarity may be direct, through long interaction with the particular person, or indirect, through a good deal of interaction with other but similar persons, which is why role-taking ability tends to decrease with social distance and why interaction with foreigners poses such problems.

Role-taking is altogether, then, a variable and uncertain business, but it is a crucial aspect of negotiating interactions.

Improvisation of a role for self

Once we have discovered what we (rightly or wrongly) conceive to be alter's current interactive role, we modify our own lines of action on the basis of what we perceive alter's implications to be with respect to our manifest and latent plans of action. That is, having imputed a role to alter, we devise (or improvise) our own roles in the light of what alter's putative role means for us.

This description must not be taken to imply that alter's role (lover, for example) determines our own role in the simple sense that we are thereby led to play the corresponding counterrole (Juliet to his Romeo). Instead, we devise our roles in terms of how we can best make use of alter's line of action ; if alter's imputed role happens to be one that is unfavorable to our plans, we devise our role in terms of how we can induce alter to *change* his line of action to one more profitable to us.

In other words, the interactive role that we believe we discern in alter's behaviors is appraised in terms of the *opportunity structure* this role presents for us. Perceived opportunity structure, it will be recalled, is one of the important determinants of our own salience hierarchies or situational selves. It is in this fashion that the role we impute to alter influences the contents of our own roles, by making certain of our role-identities (those for which alter's role constitutes opportunities) more salient in the situation. We attempt to work into our situational performances, or interactive roles, those identities that are currently most salient. Given the salience hierarchies and the perceived opportunity structure, our purposes or aims in the encounter are relatively clear cut: We wish to enact certain contents of the salient identities with the aim of obtaining certain kinds and amounts of social reward – role-support and intrinsic and extrinsic gratifications. Of course, we do not necessarily expect to receive these rewards from alter himself; we may be performing toward alter but *for* such alternative audiences as bystanders and spectators or even absent third parties in terms of whose perspectives we ourselves can appraise our performances and thus receive vicarious social support.

Alter, meanwhile, must also attempt to discern these roles of ours (and, consequently, to modify his own). He must endeavor to identify which audiences, identities and vocabularies of motives are relevant to our improvised roles. Once he has imputed interactive roles to us, he can proceed to devise and revise his own role.

If the parties are to achieve any kind of rudimentary accommodation in the situation, each party's improvised role must be at least roughly in line with the role imputed to him by the other parties. In all but the most standardized situations, this rough correspondence is entirely problematic. The chances of crossing one another up are very great, especially in those cases in which one is reluctant to go along with alter's role or with the role alter imputes to one. A person's imputed and improvised roles must be somehow squared with one another, through communication with alter, who faces the same problems.

This process of communication takes place through another, more overt set of processes, the expressive processes.

Expressive processes in interaction

The imputation and improvisation of interactive roles are purely cognitive or perceptual matters, involving the identification of persons and lines of action, and are passive in nature. Even the improvisation of one's own role is purely a matter of thinking about oneself and one's course of action, a matter of identifying who one is or would like to be in the current situation. It does not involve doing anything about it.

The expressive processes to which we now turn are, on the other hand, not covert and operating upon received impressions, are not cognitive and responsive. They are instead overt processes involving expression of information in active attempts to affect situations. These processes are those employed to bring the imputations of one party into line with the improvisations of another party through the expression of images of self and other.

Presentation of self

The first of these expressive processes is the selective presentation of self, the tactics of which have been very thoroughly explored by Goffman (1957). By carefully controlling one's expressive behaviors one can convey to alter an image of the character one desires to assume in the situation. If this control is exercised skillfully, if one's performance thoroughly sustains one's role and character, alter will have little ground for denying one's claims to identity (at least in terms of the information available in the encounter itself ; if alter is able to examine one in a broader context he may, of course, be more able to expose one's claims).

In the case of such skillful performances, ego virtually constrains alter to accept ego's claim to character and to conduct himself toward ego in the fashion appropriate when in the presence of such a character. That is, when an individual 'makes an implicit or explicit claim to be a person of a particular kind, he automatically exerts a moral demand upon the others, obliging them to value and treat him in the manner that persons of his kind have a right to expect' (p. 13). In effect, then, an individual's presentation of self tends to become a self-fulfilling image. By conducting himself as if he were a certain kind of person, he exerts leverage on others to *act toward him* as if he were that kind of person and thus to support his performance and his claims. If a person claims to be a writer or an expert fisherman or a topflight golfer *and if nothing about his talk or performance enables us to dispute that claim,* we have no choice but to go along, at least publicly, with his claim to that identity, at least for the time being.

It is precisely this leverage on others that allows us to maintain our conceptions of ourselves in some degree, as long as we can avoid tripping ourselves up through our own performances. People are obliged to give us the benefit of the doubt as long as the case against our claims is not established *beyond* reasonable doubt.

Because this leverage tempts us to exploitation, however, the others tend privately to be quite skeptical and to develop subtle tactics for testing our performances for signs of deception. We, in turn, attempt to counter these tactics with dramaturgical techniques of our own, so that the most ordinary encounters come to resemble the maneuverings of highly developed intelligence and counterintelligence agencies.

None the less, until the evidence is in, each must accord the other the benefit of the doubt.

Altercasting

The second expressive process, that of altercasting (Weinstein and Deutschberger, 1964 ; 1963) resembles presentation of self in its form but differs in its point of application. Not only does our performance express an image of who *we* are, but it also simultaneously expresses an image of whom we take *alter* to be. This image, too, has a tendency to become self-fulfilling, for we act toward alter as if he were indeed the sort of person we take him to be, and we may continue to do so regardless of what alter actually does. The amorous male may treat a girl as if she were infatuated with him, and her protestations and denials may be interpreted as merely coy expressions of her infatuation, thus confirming his image of her and perpetuating his line of action toward her. And, in fact, casting her in this manner *may* actually lead her eventually to adopt the role of lover herself. Therein lies the eventual utility of this expressive process.

Yet neither presentation of self nor altercasting necessarily or automatically brings into line the roles and characters that we devise for ourselves with those imputed to us by alter. These processes only serve to express to alter the results of our cognitive processes, to express the roles we have imputed to alter and the roles we have devised for ourself. Alter may not even 'read' these expressive messages correctly, for it is a long leap from expressions sent to impressions received. Whether accurately read or not, the expressed roles for self and alter may not be acceptable to alter in terms of his own hierarchy of role-identities.

In such a case, one's expressive processes do not serve to structure the encounter but only suggest to alter the direction in which one would like to modify the roles of each party. Alter, in turn, will employ these processes to indicate to one the somewhat different direction in which he would like to modify the interactive roles. If neither party is willing to give on these issues, both will continue to talk right past each other, acting profitlessly on incompatible bases.

Typically, however, the two parties will negotiate some sort of compromise, each acceding somewhat to the other's demands, though seldom in equal degree.

The negotiation of social identities

This compromise definition of the role and character of each is not executed in a single step but is the eventual result of a complex process of negotiation or bargaining. There are essentially two stages in this bargaining: the negotiation of social identities and the negotiation of interactive roles. That is, agreement must first be reached simply on the broad outlines of who each party is in terms of social categories like doctor, lawyer and Indian chief before bargaining can begin on the specific contents of the present behavior of such characters. We shall confine ourselves to this first stage of the negotiation in this section and return in subsequent sections to the negotiation of the actual contents of interactive roles.

At both stages of the negotiation, the moves of each party are motivated by cost–reward considerations but take the form of insinuations about identities. At base, that is, the negotiation is a process of bargaining or haggling over the terms of exchange of social rewards, yet it does not assume the outward appearance of a crude naming of prices. Rather, it takes the form of an argument or debate over who each person is ; the tactics of rhetorical persuasion or dramatic arts are more evident in the process than are those of the market place. Each move is presented as a change (or a refusal to change) in the presentation of self or in altercasting. If the move is in a direction acceptable to the other party, he will alter his expressive behavior in a manner that tacitly signals his concurrence and his concession (or perhaps signals his demand for still further concessions in the same direction from his partner). If the move is not acceptable, it is countered by a studied and emphatic persistence in his line of altercasting and presentation of self. Among the socially skilled, this rhetoric has sometimes been elevated to a high art form (as in the manuals of Stephen Potter, 1955, 1954), and encounters between particularly adept performers often become legendary.

None the less, considerations of exchange underlie the process. Each person seeks to incorporate into his performance in the situation those identities that are uppermost at the moment in his salience hierarchy of role-identities. The negotiation is basically a process of settling which, how many and how much of his salient role-identities each person will be allowed to incorporate into his performance. Weinstein and Deutschberger (1964) have pointed out that there are not one but two bargains to be struck in this connection, one with oneself and one with alter.

In our terms, one must, first of all, somehow reconcile the role he improvises for himself (in response to the role imputed to alter) with the demands of his own salience hierarchy. He is seldom allowed by others to perform exactly the interactive role he would like ; he is seldom able to comply exactly with the preferences established by his own salience hierarchy but will have to settle for the most profitable compromise. (This necessity for compromising with one's own situational self is, incidentally, a prime cause of the omnipresent discrepancy between the role-support gained from a particular performance and the demands of the identities themselves.)

Second, he must also reconcile his improvised role toward alter with the demands of *alter's* salience hierarchy. The content of one or more of alter's salient role-identities may dictate that the person act toward him in an altogether different fashion than indicated by his own improvised and expressed role.

The first stage in this process, as mentioned, is to negotiate the social identities of each participant, to come to agreement simply upon the relevant social categories and social positions to which each person belongs for purposes of the present encounter. This agreement represents essentially a *working agreement* on which the parties can stand while they continue to bargain, negotiating the specifics of their inter-active roles. The form of such a working agreement is schematically represented in Figure 1.

A working agreement can be said to exist when the cognitive processes of one person, with respect to social identities, are not in gross conflict with the expressive processes of the other person. It exists, that is, when the altercasting of one party is not greatly inconsistent with the improvised role of the other party and when the presentation of self by one party is not in conflict with the role imputed him by the other, as in Figure 1.

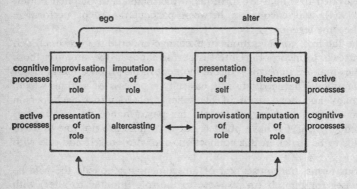

Figure 1 The working agreement

Such an agreement is problematic in its attainment and far from stable. Let us illustrate the negotiation of such an agreement with the case of a man and woman at a critical and awkward point in a relationship in which the pair is wavering between being friends and being more than friends. Many of the relevant social identities may be agreed upon, but there is lack of agreement upon the identity of 'lover'. Perhaps it is the man who first raises the issue, imputing the role of lover to the woman and devising the corresponding role for himself. By his actions he expresses these images, initiating minor but frankly sexual advances, thus presenting himself in the role of lover and simultaneously casting her in a corresponding role. It may happen that the woman is unwilling to think of herself and this man in those roles and still thinks of them as simply friends. She expresses these images by brushing off his preliminary advances and perhaps suggesting that they go out for the evening, to dinner and a concert. He may interpret this rebuff not as a rejection of the lover's role but as a coy performance of it and may cheerfully go along with her suggestion, on the premise that romantic activity is merely being conventionally deferred until after the date. At that point she may be dismayed to find him resuming his amorous advances and may have to protest explicitly that they are, after all, simply friends.

The eventual resolution of this particular difference in identification of self and other is not important for our purposes, but it is important to recognize the considerable strain the unresolved difference places upon the interaction. Until the two come to an agreement, neither can safely pursue his own course with respect to the other. Perhaps he will prove more persuasive under the circumstances, perhaps she. Or they may be forced to agree to be, not simply friends nor yet quite lovers, but some special category of very dear friends instead. Whatever the direction of the resolution, it must be attained in one of the several fashions we have portrayed.

If a pattern of interaction has been established between two particular actors – if an 'interpersonal relationship' has developed – this first phase of agreement can perhaps be assumed, but, if the relationship changes or the actors are thrown into new situations, these rudimentary interaction processes begin anew.

Such a working agreement, in which the expressive processes of one party are in rough agreement with the cognitive processes of the other and vice versa, constitutes the 'definition of the situation'. In routine and standardized encounters, this agreement is readily attained ; in the more typical situation, it must be hammered out through this process of negotiation. Despite the claims of some theorists, it must be emphasized that the attainment of such a 'definition of the situation' does not settle the matter of identities and the meaning of persons for the remainder of that encounter. On the contrary, it is only the beginning, an agreement on which the parties can stand while they continue to negotiate the finer points of their roles and characters through many more rounds of bargaining.

We must take certain exception, for example, to the views of Goffman on this point (1961). Goffman has argued that such a 'definition of the situation' serves as a set of boundary rules governing the subject matter that can be admitted to that particular encounter and that these rules must be treated with utmost gravity, for a threat to them is a threat to the structure of the entire encounter. Reaching such a working agreement is, after all, a social act, generating social objects – the consensual roles and characters of the people present. If any one person should then act out of character, the selves of all would be threatened and restorative measures required.

This analysis is certainly valid; the working agreement is assuredly a delicate balance of interactive processes and is easily tipped. What Goffman omits is that there is every pressure to continue the struggle over one's character and role, to bring them more into line with one's role-identities. As a natural consequence, someone will occasionally push too hard in this struggle and upset the working agreement, spoiling the encounter and embarrassing the character of everyone present. This risk is always present in the bargaining process, but it is one that is very often taken by at least one party to the negotiation, in the hope of winning greater opportunity to fulfil his role-identities.

If the working agreement, the definition of the situation, is upset in this fashion, it is neither the end of the world nor necessarily the end of the encounter. Very often a new agreement is negotiated, perhaps itself to be upset and superseded. A single encounter, then, often presents the appearance of successive *phases* of interaction, each marked by the negotiation of a new working agreement (Strauss, 1959).

A working agreement is so easily upset simply because it is a precarious balance of processes, the balance that has been portrayed in Figure 1. It is an agreement only as long as the expressive processes of one party roughly correspond with the cognitive processes of the other. These processes do not cease when an agreement is attained but go on as long as the parties are in contact. The persistence of the working agreement depends upon the continuing correspondence of the constituent processes. One must continually monitor the expressive implications of his behaviors so as not to contradict alter's images of him and alter, and alter must do the same. If an act should contradict one of these images, it must be successfully explained away, or the working agreement will at once collapse. We shall have more to say about this problem shortly.

Tasks and interaction

Our emphasis thus far on identities in interaction must not be allowed to obscure the obvious fact that more is involved in encounters than skirmishes over identity. After all, people do much of their work in the company of other people, and in fact an increasing proportion of jobs consists entirely of doing things to, for, with or against other people. Play, too, is typically an interactional endeavor, as are family life, politics and most of our other social institutions.

The establishment of identities within an encounter is usually little more than a necessary prerequisite to the execution of other social tasks. It is a necessary but seldom an exclusive task in face-to-face encounters. Many complex activities are carried on in the presence of other people, and in most instances these activities (rather than the establishment of identities) are the main focus of the encounter. The negotiation of identities is the *first* task of interaction, and, although it is never completely settled, it ordinarily fades into the background as a working agreement, in terms of which the interactors can turn to the main business of the encounter, can go on to build canoes, make love or eat dinner.

This task focus can assume an infinitude of forms. It may be a merely sociable conversation, it may be the negotiation of a military surrender, it may be a game of craps or it may be the purchase of a girdle. It may be entirely non-verbal, as in the case of underwater demolition experts rigging a charge, or it may consist entirely of talk, as in the case of psychiatrist and patient.

Whatever the task, *it* is ordinarily 'figure', and the negotiated identities are the 'ground' in the encounter. Occasionally, however, something may call into question this working agreement on identities, causing a figure–ground reversal, so to speak (see Vernon, 1962, pp. 40–46). If, in a team of professional carpenters, one should happen to strike his thumb rather than the nail or if a league bowler should happen to throw a gutter ball or two, these errant task performances raise to prominence the legitimacy of his claims to the identity that has previously been accepted by all present. To choose a rather different sort of example, it may develop that, in the course of buying a pair of shoes, the customer's casual remark reveals that he is the brother-in-law of the clerk's Thursday-night bridge partner; this remark then leads to a renegotiation of the identities that had underlain the encounter.

These 'figure–ground reversals' stem from the fact that the cognitive and expressive processes are carried on *throughout the encounter*, even after rough accord has been reached between them. The working agreement can be called into question whenever the expressive implications of one person's task-oriented actions come to differ from another's accepted image of him. Task performance will then be largely suspended until the working agreement can be restored (for example, through joking, disavowal, explanation or apology) or renegotiated. Far from being an unusual and destructive occurrence, such occasional oscillation between interactional concern for the task and concern for the working agreement appears to be more the norm than the exception.[2]

None the less, it remains true that this occasional shift of focus does engender a certain strain in the encounter, for the two concerns are somewhat incompatible. If attention must be diverted from the ongoing task to reconsideration of the negotiation of identities, the task performance necessarily suffers in the meantime. If the execution of the task has implications for the role of one of the participants, the performance necessarily threatens the negotiated agreement. Therefore, there is ordinarily a certain amount of strain between these two concerns in any encounter.

This strain, however, is a variable quantity, being more intense in certain types of encounter. Perhaps the polar types in this respect are a sociable party and a personal quarrel. In the case of the party, as Simmel has pointed out (1950; Watson, 1958), the task itself is essentially nothing more than identity negotiation, so that the task concern is virtually identical with the concern for the working agreement. In the personal quarrel, on the other hand, the demands of the encounter itself (to negotiate a working agreement on which to stand) run counter to the demands of the task proper, which is to deny and demolish the assumed role of the other person. The two concerns of the encounter are thus quite antithetical. Most encounters, of course, are intermediate between these two extremes in relation to the strain between the two interactional concerns. [. . .]

The individual and encounters

We have seen in this chapter the numerous constraints placed upon the individual's preferred line of action in a social encounter. Although his salience hierarchy of role-identities provides him with reasonably definite preferences as to the character and role to be assumed in the encounter, the necessity for bargaining with the other participants typically forces him to settle for something less and something else.

2. Compare, for example, with Bales's concept of the 'equilibrium problem' in the context of small-group interaction (1953).

Others seldom allow him to perform a role exactly as he would like to, thus creating (or exacerbating) a discrepancy between his performance and his conceptions of himself. There is, then, a chronic need for legitimation of these conceptions of self; few interactions are altogether satisfying in this respect.

Particular interactions are also less than satisfying in the respect that only a few of one's many role-identities can be worked into a given encounter. Large segments of one's self-structure are forced to go unhonored in any particular gathering, because they would not be particularly compatible with one's emerging role in the encounter as shaped by the negotiation process.

For these reasons, the individual cannot safely stake his self on a single encounter but must evolve means of staking it on an indeterminate *series* of encounters. [. . .]

As no single performance can satisfy all a person's needs and desires, a series of qualitatively different performances must be staged in order to cover all these needs. As they are different in content, some of these performances may be less than compatible and will at least differ in the types of audience, resources and other elements that they require for successful staging. To cope with these incompatibilities and differential requirements, the person must set up *agendas*, or schedules of performances.

These agendas (or life plans) come in all different sizes, some roughly covering the remainder of the life span, some covering only the rest of the week, and some (perhaps the most important) covering the remainder of the day. In constructing these agendas, priority is given, as far as possible, to one's more salient identities, and the others are worked into the remaining time as far as resources and the opportunity structure permit. Once the agenda is tentatively set, one moves from stage to stage according to schedule, staging *this* performance in the setting most favorable to its success and staging *that* one over there (Kuhn, 1964; Miller, Galanter and Pribram, 1960). The course of daily movement through space and time is largely determined by the dramaturgical exigencies of staging role-performances most effectively.

But of course this kind of agenda is not entirely ours to establish, for performances typically require audiences and supporting casts, which in turn implies dramaturgical discipline on all our parts to show up at the right place and time, ready for our cooperative endeavors. Agendas, like performances themselves, are interactively negotiated and not necessarily with equal voice by each participant. Duly established agendas, requiring dramaturgical discipline, are none the less often disrupted by accidents, unpredictable events and the competing demands of other encounters. In the case of such disruption of one's agenda, whether by others or by himself, his whole enterprise of identity legitimation is threatened until he can work out a new, 'next best' answer to the staging problems posed by his variety of desired role-performances. [...]

Even though a given performance is always relevant to more than one of our identities, no single performance or daily agenda of performances can serve to legitimate all our role-identities; there are simply too many of them, and they have to be tended all the time. What a moment ago was accepted as a legitimate claim to an identity may no longer be, for we recognize that people are most fickle and changeable indeed.

Identity, like freedom, must be won and rewon every day. Each identity must continually be legitimated. Legitimating one's self-structure is like dusting a huge old house: If he starts by dusting the parlor, by the time he gets to the upstairs guest room, the parlor is already badly in need of dusting again. Woman's work is never done, nor is that of maintaining the self.

Agendas, then, must be arranged in such a way as to provide continual legitimation of each of one's various role-identities.[3] Because of this constantly recurring need for legitimation, one seeks stable, dependably recurring *means* of such legitimation. Typically, such means are to be found in *interpersonal relationships*, in which at least one and usually both parties can usually be counted upon to aid in the legitimation of one or several of the other person's role-identities, on a somewhat routine basis and for a succession of interactions over a substantial period of time.

3. It should be emphasized that such legitimation can be only continual, rather than continuous, for the variegated nature of the self requires that any given role-identity be omitted from one's performance, at least on occasion, as incompatible or irrelevant.

References

ALLPORT, G. W. (1961), *Pattern and Growth in Personality*, Holt, Rinehart & Winston.

BALES, R. F. (1953), 'The equilibrium problem in small groups', in T. Parsons, R. F. Bales and E. A. Shils (eds.), *Working Papers in the Theory of Action*, Free Press.

GOFFMAN, E. (1957), *The Presentation of Self in Everyday Life*, Doubleday.

GOFFMAN, E. (1961), *Encounters*, Bobbs-Merrill.

KUHN, M. H. (1964), 'Major trends in symbolic interaction theory in the past twenty-five years', *Sociol. Q.*, vol. 5, no. 2, pp. 61–84.

McCALL, G. J., and M. M. (1970), *Social Relationships*, Aldine.

MILLER, G. A., GALANTER, E., and PRIBRAM, K. H. (1960), *Plans and the Structure of Behavior*, Holt, Rinehart & Winston.

MILLS, C. W. (1940), 'Situated actions and vocabularies of motive ', *Amer. Sociol. Rev.*, vol. 5, no. 6, pp. 904–13.

PETERS, R. S. (1958), *The Concept of Motivation*, Routledge & Kegan Paul.

POTTER, S. (1954), *The Theory and Practice of Gamesmanship*, Holt, Rinehart & Winston.

POTTER, S. (1955), *Oneupmanship*, Holt, Rinehart & Winston.

SIMMEL, G. (1950), *The Sociology of Georg Simmel*, Free Press.

STRAUSS, A. (1959), *Mirrors and Masks*, Free Press.

TURNER, R. H. (1956), 'Role taking, role standpoint and reference group behavior', *Amer. J. Soc.*, vol. 61, no. 4, pp. 316–28.

TURNER, R. H. (1962), 'Role-taking, process versus conformity,' in A. M. Rose (ed.), *Human Behavior and Social Processes*, Houghton Mifflin.

VERNON, M. D. (1962), *The Psychology of Perception*, Penguin.

WATSON, J. (1958), 'A formal analysis of sociable interaction', *Sociometry*, vol. 21, no. 4, pp. 269–80.

WEINSTEIN, E. A., and DEUTSCHBERGER, P. (1963), 'Some dimensions of altercasting', *Sociometry*, vol. 26, no. 4, pp. 454–66.

WEINSTEIN, E. A., and DEUTSCHBERGER, P. (1964), 'Tasks, bargains and identities in social interaction ', *Social Forces*, vol. 42, no. 4, pp. 451–6.

12 S. Frank Miyamoto and Sandford M. Dornbusch

A Test of Interactionist Hypotheses of Self-Conception

S. Frank Miyamoto and Sandford M. Dornbusch, 'A test of interactionist
hypotheses of self-conception', *American Journal of Sociology*, vol. 61,
1956, pp. 399–403.

The aim of this paper is an empirical study of certain basic assumptions in the interactionist view of the self and self-conception.
Essentially dynamic, the interactionist theory of the self is not easily
translated into research operations. This paper does not study the
ongoing process but concentrates instead on static consequences which
can reasonably be deduced from Mead. The method here employed is
too crude for investigating subtle aspects of Mead's theory, but
improvements and refinements of the method are possible. Moreover,
many interesting lines of inquiry into the self can be pursued with the
method, such as it is.

Our concern is three problems suggested by the interactionist view of
the self. First, a basic contribution of Mead and Cooley to the understanding of the self and self-conception lay in their emphasis upon
the influence of the responses of others in shaping self-definitions.
This principle, once recognized, may appear so self-evident as not to
require empirical confirmation. However, it seems of interest to consider any empirical test which will confirm or deny the generalization.

Second, although it is Mead's habit to speak of 'the response of
the other' as providing the key to the definition of the self (1934,
pp. 144–9), the phrase is somewhat ambiguous, for a distinction may
be drawn between (a) the actual response of the other and (b) the
subject's perception of the response of the other. Mead often does not
distinguish between these two; but it is consistent with his view that
the perception of the other's response is the critical aspect. Will an
empirical test support this assumption?

Finally, one of Mead's most illuminating analyses is his account of
how the self may take the role of the generalized other. The 'generalized other' refers to the individual's conception of the organized social
process of which he is a part (pp. 152–64). This organized social process
is composed of numerous specialized roles, and the individual identifies
his own role in it and so fulfils his part as to enable the organized
process to continue. On the other hand, individuals often enter into

social relations wherein the organization of roles is obscure or minimal. In such a case, the individual cannot take the role of the generalized other in Mead's sense; yet, for the individual to act in the situation, some conception of the generalized other may be necessary. What kind of conception of self and others may be employed under these circumstances?

In our research we used social groups whose members were, at best, loosely joined by friendship and had no definite organized group activity within which to identify their respective roles. They were engaged as individuals, at the moment, in making emphatic judgements about one another. It seemed reasonable to assume that the individual might be able to define – and would, in fact, use – a self-conception based on the *typical* attitudes of others toward him. Hence the third problem concerns the relation of self-conceptions to the perception of the typical attitudes of others toward one's self.

Method

Index of self-conception. In recent years, due mainly to the renewed interest of phychologists in the study of the self, a number of methods have been developed for getting self-evaluations from experimental subjects. In one, subjects are requested to give self-characterizations by means of one of the following devices: checking appropriate words on an adjective check list of self-descriptive terms (Sarbin, 1954), responding to a standard personality inventory or to some other form of questionnaire that yields self-revealing responses (Chertok), or writing out self-evaluative autobiographical sketches.[1] These techniques are designed to reveal the content of individual self-conceptions.

A second method requires subjects to indicate their expected score on some test prior to taking the test – usually an aptitude or attitude scale – thus providing a picture of how an individual evaluates himself (Torrance, 1954; Newcomb, 1943). Here the unique feature is the objective measure of performance or attitude against which the individual's expectation (self-conception) may be compared.

A third approach that combines features of the previous two requires subjects in a group of limited size to rate themselves on specified personal characteristics, relative to the others. For example, in a study by Calvin and Holtzman, members of fraternity groups (about twenty members each) ranked all group members, including themselves, on characteristics such as leadership, adjustment, tolerance, drive and so on (1953). Not only was it possible to use the individuals' self-rankings

1. For an interesting variation on the autobiographical method see the WAY technique of Bugenthal and Zelen (1950).

as a measure of self-concept, but, because each member was rated by all others in the group, it was also possible to derive an average of the others' ratings against which the self-concept could be compared.

For the purpose of investigating interactionist hypotheses of the self, the latter provides the most satisfactory method. In the present study the index of self-conception was derived in the course of investigating a different problem, namely, the measuring of empathic ability, by means of an adaptation of a method developed by Rosalind Dymond and Leonard Cottrell (1949). The Dymond–Cottrell method requires subjects in a group to give self-ratings as well as ratings on every other group member on a short list of specified personal characteristics.

Source of data. Our data were gathered from 195 subjects in ten groups ranging in size from eight to forty-eight persons. Four groups, totaling sixty-three subjects, consisted of volunteering members of two fraternities and two sororities. Each member had lived in his own club's house for at least three months. The other six groups, totaling 132 subjects, were classes in sociology, almost all class members of which participated in the study.

Definition of variables. For convenience of identifying the four variables in this study, labels have been adopted and given specific meanings. Our terminology implies no more than is stated in our definitions.

1. 'Self-conception': Each subject was asked to rate himself on a five-point scale for each of the following four characteristics: intelligence, self-confidence, physical attractiveness and likableness. Subjects were told that the middle of the scale should be regarded as 'average for *this* group'. The analysis for each characteristic is separate, no summing operations being performed in the four ratings.

2. 'Actual response of others': Each member of a group rated every other member of the group on the same four characteristics, using the five-point scale. The mean response to each subject was computed for each of the four characteristics.

The response of others as here defined does not correspond exactly with Mead's meaning of the term; he obviously refers to responses made in direct interpersonal relations, while our reference is to responses on a paper-and-pencil rating scale. It seems reasonable to assume, however, that the rating-scale response would tend to be a condensed symbolic version of real-life responses and that the two would correspond sufficiently for the purposes of this investigation.

Mead himself often spoke of 'the attitude of the other' interchangeably with the term 'the role of the other'.

3. 'Perceived response of others': Each member of a group predicted how every other member would rate him on the scale. The mean prediction of each subject was found for each of the four characteristics.

4. 'The generalized other': Each subject was asked to state, using the same scale, how he perceived *most* persons as viewing him. The specific question was: 'How intelligent (self-confident, physically attractive, likable) do most people think you are?'

Method of analysis. As in most studies of personal perception, good sampling was not easily achieved. Our sample was larger and more varied than those in most studies of this type, but our findings may not be reliable. Furthermore, data obtained as ours were, are not sufficiently sensitive to allow refined analyses. Because of these limitations in the design, we set restrictions upon our analysis.

First, since the groups are not a random sample from any known universe, statistical tests of significance are not employed, and the data are examined only for consistent tendencies from group to group. Second, we rely for our test upon inspection of gross differences. For each group, on each of the four characteristics, we determine whether the data support or do not support a specific hypothesis. Thus the ten groups and four characteristics yield forty results. If a hypothesis is supported forty times in the forty possible tests, we regard is as receiving perfect support; if the score is only twenty supporting tests out of the possible forty, the hypothesis is regarded as having no more than chance success.

The findings

Hypothesis 1. According to the interactionist view, the self-conceptions of most persons are likely to be determined by internalization of the

Table 1

Characteristic	Hypothesis supported	Hypothesis not supported	Tie
Intelligence	9	0	1
Self-confidence	8	2	0
Physical attractiveness	9	1	0
Likableness	9	1	0
Total	35	4	1

behavior of others toward them. If so, those accorded high esteem by others should reflect a higher self-esteem than those poorly regarded. Stating this in the form of a testable hypothesis: *The mean of the actual responses of others to the subject will be higher for those persons with a high self-rating than for those with a low self-rating*. Sorting each group into high and low self-raters and comparing the means of the 'actual responses of others' toward the subjects in each subclass, we get the results given in Table 1.

Analysis of the ten groups for all characteristics taken together shows that the hypothesis is supported ten out of ten times.

Hypothesis 2. Earlier it was suggested that it is of interest to evaluate separately the effect on self-conception of the 'actual response of others' and the 'perceived response of others'. As a first step in this analysis, the same procedure applied in the previous test to the 'actual responses' may be applied to the 'perceived responses'. Again, after the high and low self-raters have been sorted, the hypothesis now reads: *The mean of the perceived responses of others will be higher for those persons with a high self-rating than for those with a low self-rating*. The results are shown in Table 2. Ten out of ten groups showed differences in the expected direction.

Table 2

Characteristic	Hypothesis supported	Hypothesis not supported	Tie
Intelligence	10	0	0
Self-confidence	10	0	0
Physical attractiveness	10	0	0
Likableness	10	0	0
Total	40	0	0

Hypothesis 3. The next question is the relative effect on self-conception of the perceived response of others as compared to the effect of their actual responses. Social-psychological theory leads us to believe that the perceived behavior of others toward the self has a more direct influence than their actual behavior. Hence the hypothesis: *Self-conception tends to be closer to the mean perceived response of others to the subject than to the mean actual response of others*. The findings are summarized in Table 3. Of the ten groups, nine showed a tendency to support the hypothesis, with one class of eleven persons indeterminate, confirming the hypothesis for two characteristics and not confirming for the other two.

Table 3

Characteristic	Hypothesis supported	Hypothesis not supported	Tie
Intelligence	8	2	0
Self-confidence	9	0	1
Physical attractiveness	10	0	0
Likableness	7	3	0
Total	34	5	1

Hypothesis 4. It will be remembered that the index of the generalized other was determined by asking each subject, 'How intelligent (etc.) do most people think you are?' In effect, the question which was used in testing Hypothesis 2, with respect to specific individuals in a specific group, was broadened to include all other social contacts of our subjects. Hence it is reasonable to assume that the line of thinking employed in developing the earlier hypothesis should apply here. Again using high and low self-raters to provide subclasses with differential self-conception, the following hypothesis is investigated: *Those persons who have high self-ratings on a characteristic will have a higher mean perception of the generalized other than will those with low self-ratings* (Table 4). Once again, all ten groups showed differences as anticipated.

Table 4

Characteristic	Hypothesis supported	Hypothesis not supported	Tie
Intelligence	9	0	1
Self-confidence	9	1	0
Physical attractiveness	10	0	0
Likableness	10	0	0
Total	38	1	1

Hypothesis 5. In rating the 'perceived responses of others', the subjects considered only those other persons present in the test group. However, self-conception emerges from interaction in divergent groups. Therefore, it should more closely reflect the way most persons are perceived as viewing the subject than the perception of the responses of any particular group of individuals to the subject. *Accordingly,*

*self-conception should correspond more closely with the generalized
other than with the mean of the perceived responses of others.* The
results are shown in Table 5. The hypothesis is confirmed for thirty-
five out of forty comparisons. Only for self-confidence is there any
tendency to show marked deviations from the expected direction.
Analysis of the ten groups shows all ten tending to confirm the hypothesis. A deficiency of the test of Hypothesis 5 is that both self-
conception and generalized other are discrete variables, while mean
perception is continuous. Essentially, the results show that self-
conception and generalized other are usually given the identical rating.

Table 5

Characteristic	Hypothesis supported	Hypothesis not supported	Tie
Intelligence	10	0	0
Self-confidence	5	4	1
Physical attractiveness	10	0	0
Likableness	10	0	0
Total	35	4	1

Summary

The results of this research lend empirical support to the symbolic interactionist view of self-conception. Our findings indicate that the
response, or at least the attitude, of others is related to self-conception ;
but they also indicate that the subject's perception of that response is
even more closely related. We also find that an individual's self-
conception is more closely related to his estimate of the generalized
attitude toward him than to the perceived attitude of response of
members of a particular group.

These empirical findings do little more than reinforce fundamental
notions contained in the interactionist theory of self-conception.
Beyond that, however, they suggest possibilities in studying self-
conception within the symbolic interactionist framework.

References

BUGENTAL, J. F. T., and ZELEN, S. L. (1950), 'Investigation with the self-concept',
  J. Personality, vol. 18, pp. 483–98.
CALVIN, A. D., and HOLTZMAN, W. H. (1953), 'Adjustment and the discrepancy
  between self-concept and the inferred self', *J. consult. Psychol.*, vol. 17,
  pp. 39–44.

CHERTOK, E. S., Ph.D. dissertation in department of sociology, University of Washington.

DYMOND, R. F., and COTTRELL, L. (1949), 'A scale for the measurement of emphatic ability', *J. consult. Psychol.*, vol. 13, pp. 127–33.

MEAD, G. H. (1934), *Mind, Self and Society*, University of Chicago Press.

NEWCOMB, T. M. (1943), *Personality and Social Change*, Dryden Press.

SARBIN, T. R. (1954), 'Role theory', in G. Lindzey (ed.), *Handbook of Social Psychology*, Addison-Wesley.

TORRANCE, E. P. (1954), 'Rationalizations about test performance as a function of self-concepts', *J. soc. Psychol.*, vol. 34, pp. 211–17.

13 Erving Goffman

The Nature of Deference and Demeanor

Excerpts from Erving Goffman, 'The nature of deference and demeanor', *American Anthropologist*, vol. 58, 1956, pp. 47–85.

Under the influence of Durkheim and Radcliffe-Brown, some students of modern society have learned to look for the symbolic meaning of any given social practice and for the contribution of the practice to the integrity and solidarity of the group that employs it. However, in directing their attention away from the individual to the group, these students seem to have neglected a theme that is presented in Durkheim's chapter on the soul. There he suggests that the individual's personality can be seen as one apportionment of the collective *mana*, and that (as he implies in later chapters), the rites performed to representations of the social collectivity will sometimes be performed to the individual himself (Durkheim, 1954, pp. 240–72).

In this paper I want to explore some of the senses in which the person in our urban secular world is allotted to a kind of sacredness that is displayed and confirmed by symbolic acts. An attempt will be made to build a conceptual scaffold by stretching and twisting some common anthropological terms. This will be used to support two concepts which I think are central to this area: deference and demeanor. Through these reformulations I will try to show that a version of Durkheim's social psychology can be effective in modern dress.

Data for the paper are drawn chiefly from a brief observational study of mental patients in a modern research hospital.[1] I use these data on the assumption that a logical place to learn about personal proprieties is among persons who have been locked up for spectacularly failing to maintain them. Their infractions of propriety occur in the confines of a ward, but the rules broken are quite general ones, leading us outward from the ward to a general study of our Anglo-American society.

1. Within limits, it is possible to treat Ward A as an example of an orderly non-mental ward and Ward B as an example of a ward with somewhat disturbed mental patients. It should be made quite clear that only one aspect of the data will be considered, and that for every event cited additional interpretations would be in order, for instance, psychoanalytical ones.

Introduction

A rule of conduct may be defined as a guide for action, recommended not because it is pleasant, cheap or effective, but because it is suitable or just. Infractions characteristically lead to feelings of uneasiness and to negative social sanctions. Rules of conduct infuse all areas of activity and are upheld in the name and honor of almost everything. Always, however, a grouping of adherents will be involved – if not a corporate social life – providing through this a common sociological theme. Attachment to rules leads to a constancy and patterning of behavior ; while this is not the only source of regularity in human affairs it is certainly an important one. Of course, approved guides to conduct tend to be covertly broken, side-stepped or followed for unapproved reasons, but these alternatives merely add to the occasions in which rules constrain at least the surface of conduct.

Rules of conduct impinge upon the individual in two general ways: directly, as *obligations*, establishing how he is morally constrained to conduct himself ; indirectly, as *expectations*, establishing how others are morally bound to act in regard to him. A nurse, for example, has an obligation to follow medical orders in regard to her patients ; she has the expectation, on the other hand, that her patients will pliantly cooperate in allowing her to perform these actions upon them. This pliancy, in turn, can be seen as an obligation of the patients in regard to their nurse, and points up the interpersonal, actor–recipient character of many rules: what is one man's obligation will often be another's expectation.

Because obligations involve a constraint to act in a particular way, we sometimes picture them as burdensome or irksome things, to be fulfilled, if at all, by gritting one's teeth in conscious determination. In fact, most actions which are guided by rules of conduct are performed unthinkingly, the questioned actor saying he performs 'for no reason' or because he 'felt like doing so'. Only when his routines are blocked may he discover that his neutral little actions have all along been consonant with the proprieties of his group and that his failure to perform them can become a matter of shame and humiliation. Similarly, he may so take for granted his expectations regarding others that only when things go unexpectedly wrong will he suddenly discover that he has grounds for indignation.

Once it is clear that a person may meet an obligation without feeling it, we can go on to see that an obligation which *is* felt as something that *ought* to be done may strike the obligated person either as a desired thing or as an onerous one, in short, as a pleasant or unpleasant duty. In fact, the same obligation may appear to be a desirable duty at one point and an undesirable one at another, as when a nurse, obliged to administer medication to patients, may be glad of this when attempting to establish social distance from attendants (who in some sense may be considered by nurses to be not 'good enough' to engage in such activity), yet burdened by it on occasions when she finds that dosage must be determined on the basis of illegibly written medical orders. Similarly, an expectation may be perceived by the expectant person as a wanted or unwanted thing, as when one person feels he will deservedly be promoted and another feels he will deservedly be fired. In ordinary usage, a rule that strikes the actor or recipient as a personally desirable thing, apart from its propriety, is sometimes called a right or privilege, as it will be here, but these terms have additional implications, suggesting that special class of rules which an individual may invoke but is not required to do so. It should also be noted that an actor's pleasant obligation may constitute a recipient's pleasant expectation, as with the kiss a husband owes his wife when he returns from the office, but that, as the illustration suggests, all kinds of combinations are possible.

When an individual becomes involved in the maintenance of a rule, he tends also to become committed to a particular image of self. In the case of his obligations, he becomes to himself and others the sort of person who follows this particular rule, the sort of person who would naturally be expected to do so. In the case of his expectations, he becomes dependent upon the assumption that others will properly perform such of their obligations as affect him, for their treatment of him will express a conception of him. In establishing himself as the sort of person who treats others in a particular way and is treated by them in a particular way, he must make sure that it will be possible for him to act and be this kind of person. For example, with certain psychiatrists there seems to be a point where the obligation of giving psychotherapy to patients, *their* patients, is transformed into something they must do if they are to retain the image they have come to have of themselves. The effect of this transformation can be seen in the squirming some of them may do in the early phases of their careers when they may find themselves employed to do research, or administer a ward, or give therapy to those who would rather be left alone.

In general then, when a rule of conduct is broken we find that two individuals run the risk of becoming discredited: one with an obligation, who should have governed himself by the rule; the other with an expectation, who should have been treated in a particular way because of this governance. Both actor and recipient are threatened.

An act that is subject to a rule of conduct is, then, a communication, for it represents a way in which selves are confirmed – both the self for which the rule is an obligation and the self for which it is an expectation. An act that is subject to rules of conduct but does not conform to them is also a communication – often even more so – for infractions make news and often in such a way as to disconfirm the selves of the participants. Thus rules of conduct transform both action and inaction into expression, and whether the individual abides by the rules or breaks them, something significant is likely to be communicated. For example, in the wards under study, each research psychiatrist tended to expect his patients to come regularly for their therapeutic hours. When patients fulfilled this obligation, they showed that they appreciated their need for treatment and that their psychiatrist was the sort of person who could establish a 'good relation' with patients. When a patient declined to attend his therapeutic hour, others on the ward tended to feel that he was 'too sick' to know what was good for him, and that perhaps his psychiatrist was not the sort of person who was good at establishing relationships. Whether patients did or did not attend their hours, something of importance about them and their psychiatrist tended to be communicated to the staff and to other patients on the ward.

In considering the individual's participation in social action, we must understand that in a sense he does not participate as a total person but rather in terms of a special capacity or status; in short, in terms of a special self. For example, patients who happen to be female may be obliged to act shamelessly before doctors who happen to be male, since the medical relation, not the sexual one, is defined as officially relevant. In the research hospital studied, there were both patients and staff who were Negro, but this minority-group status was not one in which these individuals were officially (or even, in the main, unofficially) active. Of course, during face-to-face encounters individuals may participate officially in more than one capacity. Further, some unofficial weight is almost always given to capacities defined as officially irrelevant, and the reputation earned in one capacity will flow over and to a degree determine the reputation the individual earns in his other capacities. But these are questions for more refined analysis.

In dealing with rules of conduct it is convenient to distinguish two classes, symmetrical and asymmetrical (Thouless, 1951, pp. 272–3). A symmetrical rule is one which leads an individual to have obligations or expectations regarding others that these others have in regard to him. For example, in the two hospital wards, as in most other places in our society, there was an understanding that each individual was not to steal from any other individual, regardless of their respective statuses, and that each individual could similarly expect not to be stolen from by anyone. What we call common courtesies and rules of public order tend to be symmetrical, as are such biblical admonitions as the rule about not coveting one's neighbor's wife. An asymmetrical rule is one that leads others to treat and be treated by an individual differently from the way he treats and is treated by them. For example, doctors give medical orders to nurses, but nurses do not give medical orders to doctors. Similarly, in some hospitals in America nurses stand up when a doctor enters the room, but doctors do not ordinarily stand up when a nurse enters the room.

Students of society have distinguished in several ways among types of rules, as for example, between formal and informal rules ; for this paper, however, the important distinction is that between substance and ceremony (Durkheim, 1935, pp. 42–3; Radcliffe-Brown, 1952, pp. 143–4; Parsons, 1937, pp. 430–33).[2] A substantive rule is one which guides conduct in regard to matters felt to have significance in their own right, apart from what the infraction or maintenance of the rule expresses about the selves of the persons involved. Thus, when an individual refrains from stealing from others, he upholds a substantive rule which primarily serves to protect the property of these others and only incidentally functions to protect the image they have of themselves as persons with proprietary rights. The expressive implications of substantive rules are officially considered to be secondary ; this appearance must be maintained, even though in some special situations everyone may sense that the participants were primarily concerned with expression.

A ceremonial rule is one which guides conduct in matters felt to have secondary or even no significance in their own right, having their primary importance – officially anyway – as a conventionalized means of communication by which the individual expresses his character or conveys his appreciation of the other participants in the situation. This usage departs from the everyday one, where 'ceremony' tends to imply a highly specified, extended sequence of symbolic actions performed by august actors on solemn occasions when religious sentiments are likely to be invoked. In my attempt to stress what is common to such practices as tipping one's hat and coronations, I will perforce ignore the differences among them to an extent that many anthropologists might perhaps consider impracticable.

In all societies, rules of conduct tend to be organized into codes which guarantee that everyone acts appropriately and receives his due. In our society the code which governs substantive rules and substantive expressions comprises our law, morality and ethics, while the code which governs ceremonial rules and ceremonial expressions is incorporated in what we call etiquette. All of our institutions have both kinds of codes, but in this paper attention will be restricted to the ceremonial one.

2. Sometimes the dichotomy is phrased in terms of 'intrinsic' or 'instrumental' versus 'expressive' or 'ritual'.

The acts or events, that is, the sign-vehicles or tokens which carry ceremonial messages, are remarkably various in character. They may be linguistic, as when an individual makes a statement of praise or depreciation regarding self or other, and does so in a particular language and intonation (Garvin and Riesenberg, 1952) ; gestural, as when the physical bearing of an individual conveys insolence or obsequiousness ; spatial, as when an individual precedes another through the door, or sits on his right instead of his left ; task-embedded, as when an individual accepts a task graciously and performs it in the presence of others with aplomb and dexterity ; part of the communication structure, as when an individual speaks more frequently than the others, or receives more attentiveness than they do. The important point is that ceremonial activity, like substantive activity, is an analytical element referring to a component or function of action, not to concrete empirical action itself. While some activity that has a ceremonial component does not seem to have an appreciable substantive one, we find that all activity that is primarily substantive in significance will nevertheless carry some ceremonial meaning, provided that its performance is perceived in some way by others. The manner in which the activity is performed, or the momentary interruptions that are allowed so as to exchange minor niceties, will infuse the instrumentally orientated situation with ceremonial significance.

All of the tokens employed by a given social group for ceremonial purposes may be referred to as its ceremonial idiom. We usually distinguish societies according to the amount of ceremonial that is injected into a given period and kind of interaction, or according to the expansiveness of the forms and the minuteness of their specification ; it might be better to distinguish societies according to whether required ceremony is performed as an unpleasant duty or, spontaneously, as an unfelt or pleasant one.

Ceremonial activity seems to contain certain basic components. As suggested, a main object of this paper will be to delineate two of these components, deference and demeanor, and to clarify the distinction between them.

Deference

By deference I shall refer to that component of activity which functions as a symbolic means by which appreciation is regularly conveyed *to* a recipient *of* this recipient, or of something of which this recipient is taken as a symbol, extension or agent. These marks of devolution represent ways in which an actor celebrates and confirms his relation to a recipient. In some cases, both actor and recipient may not really be individuals at all, as when two ships greet each other with four short whistle blasts when passing. In some cases, the actor is an individual but the recipient is some object or idol, as when a sailor salutes the quarter-deck upon boarding ship, or when a Catholic genuflects to the altar. I shall only be concerned, however, with the kind of deference that occurs when both actor and recipient are individuals, whether or not they are acting on behalf of something other than themselves. Such ceremonial activity is perhaps seen most clearly in the little salutations, compliments and apologies which punctuate social intercourse, and may be referred to as 'status rituals' or 'interpersonal rituals'. I use the term 'ritual' because this activity, however informal and secular, represents a way in which the individual must guard and design the symbolic implications of his acts while in the immediate presence of an object that has a special value for him.[3] [. . .]

The individual may desire, earn and deserve deference, but by and large he is not allowed to give it to himself, being forced to seek it from others. In seeking it from others, he finds he has added reason for seeking them out, and in turn society is given added assurance that its members will enter into interaction and relationships with one another. If the individual could give himself the deference he desired there might be a tendency for society to disintegrate into islands inhabited by solitary cultish men, each in continuous worship at his own shrine.

The appreciation carried by an act of deference implies that the actor possesses a sentiment of regard for the recipient, often involving a general evaluation of the recipient. Regard is something the individual constantly has for others, and knows enough about to feign on occasions; yet in having regard for someone, the individual is unable to specify in detail what in fact he has in mind.

Those who render deference to an individual may feel, of course, that they are doing this merely because he is an instance of a category, or a representative of something, and that they are giving him his due not because of what they think of him 'personally' but in spite of it. Some organizations, such as the military, explicitly stress this sort of rationale for according deference, leading to an impersonal bestowal of something that is specifically directed toward the person. By easily showing a regard that he does not have, the actor can feel that he is preserving a kind of inner autonomy, holding off the ceremonial order by the very

3. This definition follows Radcliffe-Brown's (1952, p. 123) except that I have widened his term 'respect' to include other kinds of regard: 'There exists a ritual relation whenever a society imposes on its members a certain attitude towards an object, which attitude involves some measure of respect expressed in a traditional mode of behavior with reference to that object.'

act of upholding it. And of course in scrupulously observing the proper forms he may find that he is free to insinuate all kinds of disregard by carefully modifying intonation, pronunciation, pacing and so forth.

In thinking about deference it is common to use as a model the rituals of obeisance, submission and propitiation that someone under authority gives to someone in authority. Deference comes to be conceived as something a subordinate owes to his superordinate. This is an extremely limiting view of deference on two grounds. First, there are a great many forms of symmetrical deference which social equals owe to one another ; in some societies, Tibetan for example, salutations between high-placed equals can become prolonged displays of ritual conduct, exceeding in duration and expansiveness the kind of obeisance a subject may owe his ruler in less ritualized societies. Similarly, there are deference obligations that superordinates owe their subordinates ; high priests all over the world seem obliged to respond to offerings with some equivalent of 'Bless you, my son'. Secondly, the regard in which the actor holds the recipient need not be one of respectful awe ; there are other kinds of regard that are regularly expressed through interpersonal rituals also, such as trust, as when an individual welcomes sudden strangers into his house, or capacity-esteem, as when the individual defers to another's technical advice. A sentiment of regard that plays an important role in deference is that of affection and belongingness. We see this in the extreme in the obligation of a newly married man in our society to treat his bride with affectional deference whenever it is possible to twist ordinary behavior into a display of this kind. We find it more commonly, for example, as a component in many farewells where, as in our middle-class society, the actor will be obliged to infuse his voice with sadness and regret, paying deference in this way to the recipient's status as someone whom others can hold dearly. In 'progressive' psychiatric establishments, a deferential show of acceptance, affection and concern may form a constant and significant aspect of the stance taken by staff members when contacting patients. On Ward B, in fact, the two youngest patients seemed to have become so experienced in receiving such offerings, and so doubtful of them, that they would sometimes reply in a mocking way, apparently in an effort to re-establish the interaction on what seemed to these patients to be a more sincere level.

It appears that deference behavior on the whole tends to be honorific and politely toned, conveying appreciation of the recipient that is in many ways more complimentary to the recipient than the actor's true sentiments might warrant. The actor typically gives the recipient the benefit of the doubt, and may even conceal low regard by extra punctiliousness. Thus acts of deference often attest to ideal guide lines to which the actual activity between actor and recipient can now and then be referred. As a last resort, the recipient has a right to make a direct appeal to these honorific definitions of the situation, to press his theoretic claims, but should he be rash enough to do so, it is likely that his relationship to the actor will be modified thereafter. People sense that the recipient ought not to take the actor literally or force his hand, and ought to rest content with the show of appreciation as opposed to a more substantive expression of it. Hence one finds that many automatic acts of deference contain a vestigial meaning, having to do with activity in which no one is any longer engaged and implying an appreciation long since not expected – and yet we know these antique tributes cannot be neglected with impunity.

In addition to a sentiment of regard, acts of deference typically contain a kind of promise, expressing in truncated form the actor's avowal and pledge to treat the recipient in a particular way in the on-coming activity. The pledge affirms that the expectations and obligations of the recipient, both substantive and ceremonial, will be allowed and supported by the actor. Actors thus promise to maintain the conception of self that the recipient has built up from the rules he is involved in. (Perhaps the prototype here is the public act of allegiance by which a subject officially acknowledges his subservience in certain matters to his lord.) Deferential pledges are frequently conveyed through spoken terms of address involving status-identifiers, as when a nurse responds to a rebuke in the operating room with the phrase, 'yes, Doctor', signifying by term of address and tone of voice that the criticism has been understood and that, however unpalatable, it has not caused her to rebel. When a putative recipient fails to receive anticipated acts of deference, or when an actor makes clear that he is giving homage with bad grace, the recipient may feel that the state of affairs which he has been taking for granted has become unstable, and that an insubordinate effort may be made by the actor to reallocate tasks, relations and power. To elicit an established act of deference, even if the actor must first be reminded of his obligations and warned about the consequence of discourtesy, is evidence that if rebellion comes it will come slyly; to be pointedly refused an expected act of deference is often a way of being told that open insurrection has begun. [. . .]

Deference can take many forms, of which I shall consider only two broad groupings, avoidance rituals and presentational rituals.

Avoidance rituals, as a term, may be employed to refer to those forms of deference which lead the actor to keep at a distance from the recipient and not violate what Simmel has called the 'ideal sphere' that lies around the recipient.

Although differing in size in various directions and differing according to the person with whom one entertains relations, this sphere cannot be penetrated, unless the personality value of the individual is thereby destroyed. A sphere of this sort is placed around man by his honor. Language poignantly designates an insult to one's honor as 'coming too close', the radius of this sphere marks, as it were, the distance whose trespassing by another person insults one's honor (Simmel, 1950, p. 321).

Any society could be profitably studied as a system of deferential stand-off arrangements, and most studies give us some evidence of this. Avoidance of other's personal name is perhaps the most common example from anthropology, and should be as common in sociology.

Here, it should be said, is one of the important differences between social classes in our society: not only are some of the tokens different through which consideration for the privacy of others is expressed, but also, apparently, the higher the class the more extensive and elaborate are the taboos against contact. [. . .]

Where an actor need show no concern about penetrating the recipient's usual personal reserve, and need have no fear of contaminating him by any penetration into his privacy, we say that the actor is on terms of familiarity with the recipient. (The mother who feels at liberty to pick her child's nose is an extreme example.) Where the actor must show circumspection in his approach to the recipient, we speak of non-familiarity or respect. Rules governing conduct between two individuals may, but need not, be symmetrical in regard to either familiarity or respect.

There appear to be some typical relations between ceremonial distance and other kinds of sociological distance. Between status equals we may expect to find interaction guided by symmetrical familiarity. Between superordinate and subordinate we may expect to find asymmetrical relations, the superordinate having the right to exercise certain familiarities which the subordinate is not allowed to reciprocate. Thus, in the research hospital, doctors tended to call nurses by their first names, while nurses responded with 'polite' or 'formal' address. Similarly, in American business organizations the boss may thoughtfully ask the elevator man how his children are, but this entrance into another's life may be blocked to the elevator man, who can appreciate the concern but not return it. Perhaps the clearest form of this is found in the psychiatrist–patient relation, where the psychiatrist has a right to touch on aspects of the patient's life that the patient might not even allow himself to touch upon, while of course this privilege is not reciprocated. (There are some psycho-analysts who believe it desirable to 'analyse the counter-transference with the patient' but this or any other familiarity on the part of the patient is strongly condemned by official psychoanalytical bodies.) Patients, especially mental ones, may not even have the right to question their doctor about his opinion of their own case; for one thing, this would bring them into too intimate a contact with an area of knowledge in which doctors invest their special apartness from the lay public which they serve.

While these correlations between ceremonial distance and other kinds of distance are typical, we must be quite clear about the fact that other relationships are often found. Thus, status equals who are not well acquainted may be on terms of reciprocal respect, not familiarity. Further, there are many organizations in America where differences in rank are seen as so great a threat to the equilibrium of the system that the ceremonial aspect of behavior functions not as a way of iconically expressing these differences but as a way of carefully counterbalancing them. In the research hospital under study, psychiatrists, psychologists and sociologists were part of a single ceremonial group as regards first-naming, and this symmetrical familiarity apparently served to allay some feeling on the part of psychologists and sociologists that they were not equal members of the team, as indeed they were not. Similarly, in a study of small-business managers, the writer found that filling-station attendants had the right to interrupt their boss, slap him on the back, rib him, use his phone and take other liberties, and that this ritual license seemed to provide a way in which the manager could maintain morale and keep his employees honest. We must realize that organizations that are quite similar structurally may have quite different deference styles, and that deference patterns are partly a matter of changing fashion.

In our society, rules regarding the keeping of one's distance are multitudinous and strong. They tend to focus around certain matters, such as physical places and properties defined as the recipient's 'own', the body's sexual equipment, etc. An important focus of deferential avoidance consists in the verbal care that actors are obliged to exercise so as not to bring into discussion matters that might be painful, embarrassing or humiliating to the recipient. In Simmel's words:

The same sort of circle which surrounds man—although it is value-accentuated in a very different sense—is filled out by his affairs and by his characteristics. To penetrate this circle by taking notice, constitutes a violation of his personality. Just as material property is, so to speak, an extension of the ego, and any interference with our property is, for this reason, felt to be a violation of the person, there also is an intellectual private-property, whose violation effects a lesion of the ego in its very center.

Discretion is nothing but the feeling that there exists a right in regard to the sphere of the immediate life contents. Discretion, of course, differs in its extension with different personalities just as the positions of honor and of property have different radii with respect to 'close' individuals, and to strangers, and indifferent persons' (1950, p. 322).

[. . .] Violation of rules regarding privacy and separateness is a phenomenon that can be closely studied on mental wards because ordinarily there is so much of it done by patients and staff. Sometimes it arises from what are felt to be the substantive or instrumental requirements of the situation. When a mental patient checks into a hospital, an itemized account is usually made of every one of his belongings ; this requires his giving himself up to others in a way that he may have learned to define as a humiliation. Periodically his effects may have to be searched in a general effort to clear the ward of 'sharps', liquor, narcotics and other contraband. The presence of a microphone known to be concealed in each patient's room and connected with a speaker in the nurses' station is an additional invasion (but one provided only in the newest hospitals) ; the censoring of outgoing mail is another. Psychotherapy, especially when the patient appreciates that other staff members will learn about his progress and even receive a detailed report of the case, is another such invasion ; so too is the practice of having nurses and attendants 'chart' the course of the patient's daily feelings and activity. Efforts of staff to 'form relations' with patients, to break down periods of withdrawal in the interest of therapy, is another example. Classic forms of 'non-person treatment' are found, with staff members so little observing referential avoidance that they discuss intimacies about a patient in his presence as if he were not there at all. There will be no door to the toilet, or one that the patient cannot lock ; dormitory sleeping, especially in the case of middle-class patients, is a similar encroachment on privacy. The care that is given to 'very disturbed' patients in many large public hospitals leads in a similar direction, as with forced medication, cold packs applied to the naked body, or confinement while naked in an empty strongroom into which staff and patients may look. Another instance is forced feeding, whereby a frightened mute patient who may want to keep certain food out of his mouth is matched against an attendant who must see that patients are fed.

Invasions of privacy which have an instrumental technical rationale can be paralleled with others of a more purely ceremonial nature. Thus 'acting out' and 'psychopathic' patients are ones who can be counted on to overreach polite bounds and ask embarrassing questions of fellow-patients and staff, or proffer compliments which would not ordinarily be in their province to give, or proffer physical gestures of appreciation such as hugging or kissing, which are felt to be inappropriate. Thus, on Ward B, male staff members were plagued by such statements as 'Why did you cut yourself shaving like that', 'Why do you always wear the same pants, I'm getting sick of them', 'Look at all the dandruff you've got'. If seated by one of the patients, a male staff member might have to edge continuously away so as to keep a seemly safe distance between himself and the patient.

Some of the ways in which individuals on Ward A kept their distance were made clear in contrast to the failure of Ward B's patients to do so. On Ward A the rule that patients were to remain outside the nurses' station was observed. Patients would wait for an invitation or, as was commonly the case, stay in the doorway so that they could talk with those in the station and yet not presume upon them. It was therefore not necessary for the staff to lock the station door when a nurse was in the station. On Ward B it was not possible to keep three of the patients out of the station by request alone, and so the door had to be kept locked if privacy was to be maintained. Even then, the walls of the station were effectively battered down by continuous banging and shouting. In other words, on Ward A the protective ring that nurses and attendants drew around themselves by retreating into the station was respected by the patients, whereas on Ward B it was not. [. . .]

Avoidance rituals have been suggested as one main type of deference. A second type, termed *presentational rituals*, encompasses acts through which the individual makes specific attestations to recipients concerning how he regards them and how he will treat them in the on-coming interaction. Rules regarding these ritual practices involve specific prescriptions, not specific proscriptions; while avoidance rituals specify what is not to be done, presentational rituals specify what is to be done. Some illustrations may be taken from social life on Ward A as maintained by the group consisting of patients, attendants, and nurses. These presentational rituals will not, I think, be much different from those found in many other organizations in our society.

When members of the ward passed by each other, salutations would ordinarily be exchanged, the length of the salutation depending on the period that had elapsed since the last salutation and the period that seemed likely before the next. At table, when eyes met a brief smile of recognition would be exchanged; when someone left for the weekend, a farewell involving a pause in on-going activity and a brief exchange of words would be involved. In any case, there was the understanding that when members of the ward were in a physical position to enter into eye-to-eye contact of some kind, this contact would be effected. It seemed that anything less would not have shown proper respect for the state of relatedness that existed among the members of the ward.

Associated with salutations were practices regarding the 'noticing' of any change in appearance, status or repute, as if these changes represented a commitment on the part of the changed individual which had to be underwritten by the group. New clothes, new hairdos, occasions of being 'dressed up' would call forth a round of compliments, whatever the group felt about the improvement. Similarly, any effort on the part of a patient to make something in the occupational therapy room or to perform in other ways was likely to be commended by others. Staff members who participated in the hospital amateur theatricals were complimented, and when one of the nurses was to be married, pictures of her fiancé and his family were viewed by all and approved. In these ways a member of the ward tended to be saved from the embarrassment of presenting himself to others as someone who had risen in value, while receiving a response as someone who had declined, or remained the same. [...]

Two main types of deference have been illustrated: presentational rituals through which the actor concretely depicts his appreciation of the recipient; and avoidance rituals, taking the form of proscriptions, interdictions and taboos, which imply acts the actor must refrain from doing lest he violate the right of the recipient to keep him at a distance. We are familiar with this distinction from Durkheim's classification of ritual into positive and negative rites (1954, p. 299).

In suggesting that there are things that must be said and done to a recipient, and things that must not be said and done, it should be plain that there is an inherent opposition and conflict between these two forms of deference. To ask after an individual's health, his family's well-being or the state of his affairs, is to present him with a sign of sympathetic concern; but in a certain way to make this presentation is to invade the individual's personal reserve, as will be made clear if an actor of wrong status asks him these questions, or if a recent event has made such a question painful to answer. As Durkheim suggested, 'The human personality is a sacred thing; one dare not violate it nor infringe its bounds, while at the same time the greatest good is in communion with others' (1953, p. 37). I would like to cite two ward illustrations of this inherent opposition between the two forms of deference.

On Ward A, as in other wards in the hospital, there was a 'touch system'.[4] Certain categories of personnel had the privilege of expressing

4. The only source I know on touch systems is the very interesting work by Gross (1949) on rights regarding pinching of females of private secretarial rank in a commercial business office.

their affection and closeness to others by the ritual of bodily contact with them. The actor places his arms around the waist of the recipient, rubs a hand down the back of the recipient's neck, strokes the recipient's hair and forehead, or holds the recipient's hand. Sexual connotation is of course officially excluded. The most frequent form that the ritual took was for a nurse to extend such a touch-confirmation to a patient. None the less, attendants, patients and nurses formed one group in regard to touch rights, the rights being symmetrical. Any one of these individuals had a right to touch any member of his own category or any member of the other categories. (In fact some forms of touch, as in playful fighting or elbow-strength games, were intrinsically symmetrical.) Of course some members of the ward disliked the system, but this did not alter the rights of others to incorporate them into it. The familiarity implicit in such exchanges was affirmed in other ways, such as symmetrical first-naming. It may be added that in many mental hospitals, patients, attendants and nurses do not form one group for ceremonial purposes, and the obligation of patients to accept friendly physical contact from staff is not reciprocated.

In addition to these symmetrical touch relations on the ward, there were also asymmetrical ones. The doctors touched other ranks as a means of conveying friendly support and comfort, but other ranks tended to feel that it would be presumptuous for them to reciprocate a doctor's touch, let alone initiate such a contact with a doctor.

Now it should be plain that if a touch system is to be maintained, as it is in many hospitals in America, and if members of the ward are to receive the confirmation and support this ritual system provides, then persons other than doctors coming to live or work on the ward must make themselves intimately available to the others present. Rights of apartness and inviolability which are demanded and accorded in many other establishments in our society must here be forgone, in this particular. The touch system, in short, is only possible to the degree that individuals forego the right to keep others at a physical distance. [. . .]

Demeanor

It was suggested that the ceremonial component of concrete behavior has at least two basic elements, deference and demeanor. Deference, defined as the appreciation an individual shows of another to that other, whether through avoidance rituals or presentational rituals, has been discussed and demeanor may now be considered.

By demeanor I shall refer to that element of the individual's ceremonial behavior typically conveyed through deportment, dress and bearing, which serves to express to those in his immediate presence that he is a person of certain desirable or undesirable qualities. In our society, the 'well' or 'properly' demeaned individual displays such attributes as: discretion and sincerity; modesty in claims regarding self; sportsmanship; command of speech and physical movements; self-control over his emotions, his appetites and his desires; poise under pressure and so forth.

When we attempt to analyse the qualities conveyed through demeanor, certain themes become apparent. The well-demeaned individual possesses the attributes popularly associated with 'character training' or 'socialization', these being implanted when a neophyte of any kind is housebroken. Rightly or wrongly, others tend to use such qualities diagnostically, as evidence of what the actor is generally like at other times and as a performer of other activities. In addition, the properly demeaned individual is someone who has closed off many avenues of perception and penetration that others might take to him, and is therefore unlikely to be contaminated by them. Most importantly, perhaps, good demeanor is what is required of an actor if he is to be transformed into someone who can be relied upon to maintain himself as an interactant, poised for communication, and to act so that others do not endanger themselves by presenting themselves as interactants to him.

It should be noted once again that demeanor involves attributes derived from interpretations others make of the way in which the individual handles himself during social intercourse. The individual cannot establish these attributes for his own by verbally avowing that he possesses them, though sometimes he may rashly try to do this. (He can, however, contrive to conduct himself in such a way that others, through their interpretation of his conduct, will impute the kinds of attributes to him he would like others to see in him.) In general, then, through demeanor the individual creates an image of himself, but properly speaking this is not an image that is meant for his own eyes. Of course this should not prevent us from seeing that the individual who acts with good demeanor may do so because he places an appreciable value upon himself, and that he who fails to demean himself properly may be accused of having 'no self-respect' or of holding himself too cheaply in his own eyes.

As in the case of deference, an object in the study of demeanor is to collect all the ceremonially relevant acts that a particular individual performs in the presence of each of the several persons with whom he comes in contact, to interpret these acts for the demeanor that is symbolically expressed through them, and then to piece these meanings together into an image of the individual, an image of him in others' eyes.

Rules of demeanor, like rules of deference, can be symmetrical or asymmetrical. Between social equals, symmetrical rules of demeanor seem often to be prescribed. Between unequals many variations can be found. For example, at staff meetings on the psychiatric units of the hospital, medical doctors had the privilege of swearing, changing the topic of conversation and sitting in undignified positions; attendants, on the other hand, had the right to attend staff meetings and to ask questions during them (in line with the milieu-therapy orientation of these research units) but were implicitly expected to conduct themselves with greater circumspection than was required of doctors. (This was pointed out by a perceptive occupational therapist who claimed she was always reminded that a mild young female psychiatrist was really an M.D. by the fact that this psychiatrist exercised these prerogatives of informal demeanor.) The extreme here perhaps is the master–servant relation as seen in cases where valets and maids are required to perform in a dignified manner services of an undignified kind. Similarly, doctors had the right to saunter into the nurses' station, lounge on the station's dispensing counter, and engage in joking with the nurses; other ranks participated in this informal interaction with doctors, but only after doctors had initiated it.

On Ward A, standards of demeanor were maintained that seem to be typical in American middle-class society. The eating pace maintained at table suggested that no one present was so over-eager to eat, so little in control of impulses, so jealous of his rights, as to wolf down his food or take more than his share. At pinochle, the favorite card game, each player would coax spectators to take his hand and spectators would considerately decline the offer, expressing in this way that a passion for play had in no way overwhelmed them. Occasionally a patient appeared in the day-room or at meals with bathrobe (a practice permitted of patients throughout the hospital) but ordinarily neat street wear was maintained, illustrating that the individual was not making his appearance before others in a lax manner or presenting too much of himself too freely. Little profanity was employed and no open sexual remarks.

On Ward B, bad demeanor (by middle-class standards) was quite common. This may be illustrated from meal-time behavior. A patient would often lunge at an extra piece of food or at least eye an extra piece covetously. Even when each individual at table was allowed to receive an equal share, over-eagerness was shown by the practice of taking all of one's share at once instead of waiting until one serving had been eaten. Occasionally a patient would come to table half-dressed.

One patient frequently belched loudly at meals and was occasionally flatulent. Messy manipulation of food sometimes occurred. Swearing and cursing were common. Patients would occasionally push their chairs back from the table precipitously and bolt for another room, coming back to the table in the same violent manner. Loud sounds were sometimes made by sucking on straws in empty pop bottles. Through these activities, patients expressed to the staff and to one another that their selves were not properly demeaned ones.

These forms of misconduct are worth study because they make us aware of some aspects of good demeanor we usually take for granted; for aspects even more usually taken for granted, we must study 'back' wards in typical mental hospitals. There patients are denudative, incontinent and they openly masturbate; they scratch themselves violently; drooling occurs and a nose may run unchecked; sudden hostilities may flare up and 'paranoid' immodesties be projected; speech or motor activity may occur at a manic or depressed pace, either too fast or too slow for propriety; males and females may comport themselves as if they were of the other sex or hardly old enough to have any. Such wards are of course the classic settings of bad demeanor.

A final point about demeanor may be mentioned. Whatever his motives for making a well demeaned appearance before others, it is assumed that the individual will exert his own will to do so, or that he will pliantly cooperate should it fall to someone else's lot to help him in this matter. In our society, a man combs his own hair until it gets too long, then he goes to a barber and follows instructions while it is being cut. This voluntary submission is crucial, for personal services of such a kind are done close to the very center of the individual's inviolability and can easily result in transgressions; server and served must cooperate closely if these are not to occur. If, however, an individual fails to maintain what others see as proper personal appearance, and if he refuses to cooperate with those who are charged with maintaining it for him, then the task of making him presentable against his will is likely to cost him at the moment a great deal of dignity and deference, and this in turn may create complex feelings in those who find they must cause him to pay this price. This is one of the occupational dilemmas of those employed to make children and mental patients presentable. It is easy to order attendants to 'dress up' and shave male patients on visitors' day, and no doubt when this is done patients make a more favorable appearance, but while this appearance is in the process of being achieved – in the showers or the barbershop, for example – the patients may be subjected to extreme indignities.

Deference and demeanor

Deference and demeanor are analytical terms; empirically there is much overlapping of the activities to which they refer. An act through which the individual gives or withholds deference to others typically provides means by which he expresses the fact that he is a well or badly demeaned individual. Some aspects of this overlapping may be cited. First, in performing a given act of presentational deference, as in offering a guest a chair, the actor finds himself doing something that can be done with smoothness and aplomb, expressing self-control and poise, or with clumsiness and uncertainty, expressing an irresolute character. This is, as it were, an incidental and adventitious connection between deference and demeanor. It may be illustrated from recent material on doctor–patient relationships, where it is suggested that one complaint a doctor may have against some of his patients is that they do not bathe before coming for an examination; while bathing is a way of paying deference to the doctor it is at the same time a way for the patient to present himself as a clean, well demeaned person. A further illustration is found in acts such as loud talking, shouting or singing, for these acts encroach upon the right of others to be let alone, while at the same time they illustrate a badly demeaned lack of control over one's feelings.

The same connection between deference and demeanor has had a bearing on the ceremonial difficulties associated with intergroup interaction: the gestures of deference expected by members of one society have sometimes been incompatible with the standards of demeanor maintained by members of another. For example, during the nineteenth century, diplomatic relations between Britain and China were embarrassed by the fact that the *Kot'ow* demanded of visiting ambassadors by the Chinese Emperor was felt by some British ambassadors to be incompatible with their self-respect (Douglas, 1895, pp. 291–6).

A second connection between deference and demeanor turns upon the fact that a willingness to give others their deferential due is one of the qualities which the individual owes it to others to express through his conduct, just as a willingness to conduct oneself with good demeanor is in general a way of showing deference to those present.

In spite of these connections between deference and demeanor, the analytical relation between them is one of 'complementarity', not identity. The image the individual owes to others to maintain of himself is not the same type of image these others are obliged to maintain of him. Deference images tend to point to the wider society outside the interaction, to the place the individual has achieved in the hierarchy of this society. Demeanor images tend to point to qualities which any social position gives its incumbents a chance to display during interaction, for these qualities pertain more to the way in which the individual handles his position than to the rank and place of that position relative to those possessed by others.

Further, the image of himself the individual owes it to others to maintain through his conduct is a kind of justification and compensation for the image of him that others are obliged to express through their deference to him. Each of the two images in fact may act as a guarantee and check upon the other. In an interchange that can be found in many cultures, the individual defers to guests to show how welcome they are and how highly he regards them; they in turn decline the offering at least once, showing through their demeanor that they are not presumptuous, immodest or over-eager to receive favor. Similarly, a man starts to rise for a lady, showing respect for her sex; she interrupts and halts his gesture, showing she is not greedy of her rights in this capacity but is ready to define the situation as one between equals. In general, then, by treating others deferentially one gives them an opportunity to handle the indulgence with good demeanor. Through this differentiation in symbolizing function the world tends to be bathed in better images than anyone deserves, for it is practical to signify great appreciation of others by offering them deferential indulgences, knowing that some of these indulgences will be declined as an expression of good demeanor.

There are still other complementary relations between deference and demeanor. If an individual feels he ought to show proper demeanor in order to warrant deferential treatment, then he must be in a position to do so. He must, for example, be able to conceal from others aspects of himself which would make him unworthy in their eyes, and to conceal himself from them when he is in an undignified state, whether of dress, mind, posture or action. The avoidance rituals which others perform in regard to him give him room to maneuver, enabling him to present only a self that is worthy of deference; at the same time, this avoidance makes it easier for them to assure themselves that the deference they have to show him is warranted.

To show the difference between deference and demeanor, I have pointed out the complementary relation betwen them, but even this kind of relatedness can be overstressed. The failure of an individual to show proper deference to others does not necessarily free them from the obligation to act with good demeanor in his presence, however disgruntled they may be at having to do this. Similarly, the failure of an individual to conduct himself with proper demeanor does not always relieve those in his presence from treating him with proper deference. It is by separating deference and demeanor that we can appreciate many things about ceremonial life, such as that a group may be noted for excellence in one of these areas while having a bad reputation in the other. Hence we can find a place for arguments such as De Quincey's (1890, pp. 327–34) that an Englishman shows great self-respect but little respect for others while a Frenchman shows great respect for others but little respect for himself.

We are to see, then, that there are many occasions when it would be improper for an individual to convey about himself what others are ready to convey about him to him, since each of these two images is a warrant and justification for the other, and not a mirror image of it. The Meadian notion that the individual takes toward himself the attitude others take to him seems very much an oversimplification. Rather the individual must rely on others to complete the picture of him of which he himself is allowed to paint only certain parts. Each individual is responsible for the demeanor image of himself and the deference image of others, so that for a complete man to be expressed, individuals must hold hands in a chain of ceremony, each giving deferentially with proper demeanor to the one on the right what will be received deferentially from the one on the left. While it may be true that the individual has a unique self all his own, evidence of this possession is thoroughly a product of joint ceremonial labor, the part expressed through the individual's demeanor being no more significant than the part conveyed by others through their deferential behavior toward him. [. . .]

References

DOUGLAS, R. K. (1895), *Society in China*, Innes.
DURKHEIM, E. (1953), 'The determination of moral facts', *Sociology and Philosophy*, Free Press.
DURKHEIM, E. (1954), *The Elementary Forms*, Free Press.
GARVIN, P. L., and RIESENBERG, H. S. (1952), 'Respect behavior on Pronape: an ethnolinguistic study', *Amer Anthrop.*, vol. 54, no. 2, pp. 201–20.
GROSS, E. (1949), 'Informal relations and the social organization of work', Ph.D. dissertation, University of Chicago.
PARSONS, T. (1937), *The Structure of Social Action*, McGraw-Hill.
QUINCEY, T. DE (1890), 'French and English manners', in D. Mason (ed.), *Collected Writings of Thomas De Quincey*, Black.
RADCLIFFE-BROWN, A. R. (1952), 'Taboo', in *Structure and Function in Primitive Society*, Free Press.
SIMMEL, G. (1950), *The Sociology of Georg Simmel*, Free Press.
THOULESS, R. H. (1951), *General and Social Psychology*, University Tutorial Press.

14 Robert K. Merton

Role-Sets

Excerpt from Robert K. Merton, *Social Theory and Social Structure*,
Free Press, 1968, pp. 422–34. First published in 1957.

For some time now, at least since the influential writings of Ralph
Linton on the subject, it has been recognized that two concepts – social
status and social role – are fundamental to the description, and to the
analysis, of a social structure.[1]

By status Linton meant a position in a social system occupied by
designated individuals; by role, the behavioral enacting of the patterned
expectations attributed to that position. Status and role, in these terms,
are concepts serving to connect the culturally defined expectations with
the patterned behavior and relationships which comprise social structure.
Linton went on to observe that each person in society inevitably occupies
multiple statuses and that, for each of these statuses, there is *an* associated role (1936)[2] This proved to be a useful first approximation, as
later social research amply testifies. In this first approximation, however,
Linton assumed that each status has *its distinctive role*.[3]

Without engaging in heavier deliberation than the subject deserves, we
must note that a particular social status involves, not a single associated
role, but an array of associated roles. This is a basic characteristic of
social structure. This fact of structure can be registered by a distinctive
term, *role-set*, by which I mean that *complement of role relationships
which persons have by virtue of occupying a particular social status.*

1. To say that Linton was not 'the first' to introduce these twin concepts into
social science would be as true as it is irrelevant. For the fact is that it was only
after his famous ch. 8 (1936) that these concepts, and their implications, became
systematically incorporated into a developing theory of social structure.

2. See Linton (1945) which, it might be suggested, has apparently not been
accorded the notice it deserves.

3. As one among many instances of this conception, see Linton's observation
that 'a particular status within a social system can be occupied, and *its associated
role* known and exercised, by a number of individuals simultaneously' (1945, p.
77). On occasion, Linton did make passing mention of 'roles connected with the
. . . status', but did not work out the structural implications of multiple roles
being associated with a single status (1936, p. 127), provides one such statement.

Theodore Newcomb has clearly seen that each position in a system of roles
involves multiple role-relations. *Social Psychology*, 285–6.

As one example: the single status of medical student entails not only the role of a student in relation to his teachers, but also an array of other roles relating the occupant of that status to other students, nurses, physicians, social workers, medical technicians, etc.[4] Again: the status of a public-school teacher has its distinctive role-set, relating the teacher to his pupils, to colleagues, the school principal and superintendent, the Board of Education, and, on frequent occasion, to local patriotic organizations, to professional organizations of teachers, Parent–Teachers Associations, and the like.

It should be plain that the role-set differs from the structural pattern which has long been identified by sociologists as that of 'multiple roles'. For in the established usage, multiple roles refer to the complex of roles associated, not with a *single* social status, but with the *various* statuses (often, in differing institutional spheres) in which individuals find themselves – the roles, for example, connected with the distinct statuses of teacher, wife, mother, Catholic, Republican and so on. We designate this complement of social statuses of an individual as his *status-set*, each of the statuses in turn having its distinctive role-set.

The concepts of role-set and of status-set are structural and refer to parts of the social structure *at a particular time*. Considered as changing in the course of time, the succession of statuses occurring with sufficient frequency as to be socially patterned will be designated as a *status-sequence*, as in the case, for example, of the statuses successively occupied by a medical student, intern, resident and independent medical practitioner. In much the same sense, of course, we can observe *sequences of role-sets and status-sets*.

The patterned arrangements of role-sets, status-sets and status-sequences can be held to comprise the social structure. The concepts remind us, in the unlikely event that we need to be reminded of this insistent and obstinate fact, that even the seemingly simple social structure is extremely complex. For operating social structures must somehow manage to organize these sets and sequences of statuses and roles so that an appreciable degree of social order obtains, sufficient to enable most of the people most of the time to go about their business of social life without having to improvise adjustments anew in each newly confronted situation.

The concepts serve further to help us identify some of the substan-

4. For a preliminary analysis of the role-set of the medical student which is of direct import for reference group theory, see Huntington (1957), this being part of the studies conducted by the Columbia University Bureau of Applied Social Research under a grant from the Commonwealth Fund.

tive problems of social structure which require analysis. Which social processes tend to make for disturbance or disruption of the role-set, creating conditions of structural instability? Through which social mechanisms do the roles in the role-set become articulated so that conflict among them becomes less than it would otherwise be?

Structural sources of instability in the role-set

It would seem that the basic source of disturbance in the role-set is the structural circumstance that anyone occupying a particular status has role-partners who are differently located in the social structure. As a result, these others have, in some measure, values and moral expectations differing from those held by the occupant of the status in question. The fact, for example, that the members of a school board are often in social and economic strata quite different from that of the public-school teacher will mean that, in certain respects, their values and expectations differ from those of the teacher. The individual teacher may thus be readily subject to conflicting role-expectations among his professional colleagues and among the influential members of the school board and, at times, derivatively, of the superintendent of schools. What is an educational frill for the one may be judged as an essential of education by the other. These disparate and inconsistent evaluations complicate the task of coming to terms with them all. What holds conspicuously for the status of the teacher holds, in varying degree, for the occupants of other statuses who are structurally related, in their role-set, to others who themselves occupy diverse statuses.

As things now stand, this appears to be the major structural basis for potential disturbance of a stable role-set. The question does not arise, of course, in those special circumstances in which all those in the role-set have the same values and same role-expectations. But this is a special and, perhaps historically rare, situation. More often, it would seem, and particularly in highly differentiated societies, the role-partners are drawn from diverse social statuses with, to some degree, correspondingly different social values. To the extent that this obtains, the characteristic situation should be one of disorder, rather than of relative order. And yet, although historical societies vary in the extent to which this is true, it seems generally the case that a substantial degree of order rather than of acute disorder prevails. This, then, gives rise to the problem of identifying the social mechanisms through which some reasonable degree of articulation among the roles in role-sets is secured or, correlatively, the social mechanisms which break down so that structurally established role-sets do not remain relatively stabilized.

Social mechanisms for the articulation of roles in the role-set

Before beginning to examine some of these mechanisms, we should reiterate that it is not being assumed that, as a matter of historical fact, all role-sets do operate with substantial efficiency. We are concerned, not with a broad historical generalization that social order prevails but with the analytical problem of identifying the social mechanisms which operate to produce a greater degree of social order than would obtain, if these mechanisms were not called into play. Otherwise put, it is sociology, not history, which is of immediate interest here.

1. *The mechanism of differing intensity of role-involvement among those in the role-set.* Role-partners are variously concerned with the behavior of those in a particular social status. This means that the role-expectations of those in the role-set are not maintained with the same degree of intensity. For some, this role-relationship may be of only peripheral concern; for others, it may be central. As an hypothetical example: the parents of children in a public school may be more directly engaged in appraising and controlling the behavior of teachers than, say, the members of a local patriotic organization who have no children in the school. The values of the parents and of the patriotic organization may be at odds in numerous respects and may call for quite different behavior on the part of the teacher. But if the expectations of the one group in the role-set of the teacher are central to their concerns and interests, and the expectations of the other group only peripheral, this eases the problem of the teacher seeking to come to terms with these disparate expectations.

We have noted before, in the listing of structural properties of groups, that there is patterned variation in the scope and intensity of involvement of group members in their statuses and roles. Such variation serves to cushion the disturbance to a role-set involving conflicting expectations of the behavior of those occupying a particular status. The teacher, for whom this status holds primary significance, is in this degree better able to withstand the demands for conformity with the differing expectations of those in his role-set for whom this relationship has only peripheral significance. This is not to say, of course, that teachers are not vulnerable to these expectations which are at odds with their professional commitments. It is only to say that they are less vulnerable than they would otherwise be (or sometimes are) when the powerful members of their role-set are only little concerned with this particular relationship. [. . .]

2. *The mechanism of differences in the power of those involved in a role-set.* A second mechanism which affects the stability of a role-set is

potentially provided by the distribution of power. By power, in this connection, is meant nothing more than the observed and predictable capacity for imposing one's own will in a social action, even against the resistance of others taking part in that action.[5]

The members of a role-set are not apt to be equally powerful in shaping the behavior of occupants of a particular status. However, it does not follow that the individual group or stratum in the role-set which is *separately* most powerful uniformly succeeds in imposing its expectations upon the status-occupants – say, the teacher. This would be so only in the circumstance when the one member of the role-set has an effective monopoly of power, either to the exclusion of all others or outweighing the combined power of the others. Failing this special situation, the individuals subject to conflicting expectations among the members of their role-set can effect, deliberately or unwittingly, *coalitions of power* among them which enable these individuals to go their own way. The conflict is then not so much between the status-occupants and the diverse members of their role-set as between the members of the role-set itself. The counterpoise to any one powerful member of the role-set is at times provided by a coalition of lesser powers in combination. The familiar pattern of 'balance of power' is not confined to power struggles among nations ; in less easily visible form, it can be found in the workings of role-sets generally, as the child who succeeds in having his father's decision offset his mother's contrasting decision has ample occasion to know. When conflicting powers in the role-set neutralize one another, the status-occupant has relative freedom to proceed as he intended in the first place.

Thus, even in those potentially unstable structures in which the members of a role-set hold distinct and contrasting expectations of what the status-occupant should do, the latter is not wholly at the mercy of the most powerful among them. Moreover, a high degree of involvement in his status reinforces his relative power. For to the extent that powerful members of his role-set are not primarily concerned with this particular relationship in the same degree as the status-occupant, they will not be motivated to exercise their potential power to the full. Within wide margins of his role-activity, the status-occupant will then be free to act, uncontrolled because unnoticed.

This does not mean, of course, that the status-occupant subject to conflicting expectation among members of his role-set is in fact immune to control by them. It is only to say that the power-structure of role-sets

5. This will be recognized as Max Weber's conception of power, and one not far removed from other contemporary versions of the concept (1948, p. 180).

is often such that the status-occupant more nearly has autonomy than would be the case if this structure of competing powers did not obtain.

3. *The mechanism of insulating role-activities from observability by members of the role-set.* The occupant of a status does not engage in continuous interaction with all those in his role-set. This is not an incidental fact, but is integral to the operation of role-sets. The interaction with each member (individual or groups) of the role-set is variously limited and intermittent ; it is not equally sustained throughout the range of relationships entailed by the social status. This fundamental fact of role-structure allows for role-behavior which is at odds with the expectations of some in the role-set to proceed without undue stress. For, as we have seen at some length, effective social control presupposes an appreciable degree of *observability* of role-behavior. To the extent that the role-structure insulates the status-occupant from direct observation by some of his role-set, he is not uniformly subject to competing pressures. It should be emphasized that we are dealing here with a fact of social structure, not with individual adjustments whereby this or that person *happens* to conceal parts of his role-behavior from certain members of his role-set.

The structural fact is that social statuses differ in the extent to which some of the associated role-behavior is insulated from ready observability by all members of the role-set. Variations in this structurally imposed attribute of social statuses accordingly complicate the problem of coping with the disparate expectations of those in the role-set. Thus, occupants of all occupational statuses sometimes face difficult decisions which involve their sense of personal integrity, i.e. of living up to the norms and standards basically governing the performance of their occupational role. But these statuses differ in the extent of ready observability of occupational behavior. As Senator Kennedy notes, in that book to which we have made admiring reference, few, if any, occupations face such difficult decisions 'in the glare of the spotlight as do those in public office. Few, if any, face the same dread finality of decision that confronts a Senator facing an important call of the roll' (1955, p. 8).

In contrast, other social statuses have a functionally significant insulation from easy observability by some of those in the role-set. The status of the university teacher provides one example. The norm which holds that what is said in the classrooms of universities is privileged, in the sense of being restricted to the professor and his students, has this function of maintaining a degree of autonomy for the teacher. For if this were uniformly made available to all those comprising the role-set of the teacher, he might be driven to teach not what he knows or what the evidence leads him to believe, but what will placate the numerous and diverse expectations of all those concerned with 'the education of youth'. This would serve to lower the level of instruction to the lowest common denominator. It would be to transform teaching and place it on the plane of the television show, concerned to do whatever is needed to improve its popularity rating. It is, of course, this exemption from observability from all and sundry who may wish to impose their will upon the instructor which is an integral part of academic freedom, conceived as a functional complex of values and norms.

More broadly, the concept of privileged information and confidential communication in the professions – law and medicine, teaching and the ministry – has the same function of insulating clients from ready observability of their behavior and beliefs by others in their role-set. If the physician or priest were free to tell all they have learned about the private lives of their clients, they could not adequately discharge their functions. More, as we have seen in our review of observability, if the facts of all role-behavior and all attitudes were freely available to anyone, social structures could not operate. [. . .]

The mechanism of insulation from observability can, of course, miscarry. Were the politician or statesman fully removed from the public spotlight, social control of his behavior would be correspondingly reduced. Anonymous power anonymously exercised does not make for a stable structure of social relations meeting the values of the society, as the history of secret police amply testifies. The teacher who is fully insulated from observation by peers and superiors may fail to live up to the minimum requirements of his status. The physician in his private practice who is largely exempt from the judgement of competent colleagues may allow his role-performance to sink below tolerable standards. The secret policeman may violate the values of the society, and not be detected.

All this means that some measure of observability of role-performance by members of the role-set is required, if the indispensable social requirement of accountability is to be met. This statement obviously does not contradict earlier statements to the effect that some measure of insulation from observability is also required for the effective operation of social structures. Instead, the two statements, taken in conjunction, hold again that there is some optimum of observability, difficult as yet to identify in measurable terms and doubtless varying for different social statuses, which will simultaneously make for accountability of role-performance and for autonomy of role-performance, rather than for a frightened acquiescence with the distribution of power that happens, at a given moment, to obtain in the role-set. Varying patterns of observability can operate to enable the occupants of social statuses to cope with the conflicting expectations among members of their role-sets.

4. *The mechanism making for observability by members of the role-set of their conflicting demands upon the occupants of a social status.* This mechanism is implied by the two foregoing accounts of the power structure and pattern of insulation from observability; it therefore needs only passing comment here. As long as members of the role-set are happily ignorant that their demands upon the occupants of a status are incompatible, each member may press his own case upon the status-occupants. The pattern is then many against one. But when it is made plain that the demands of some members of the role-set are in full contradiction with the demands of other members, it becomes the task of the role-set, rather than the task of the status-occupant, to resolve these contradictions, either by a struggle for exclusive power or by some degree of compromise. As the conflict becomes abundantly manifest, the pressure upon the status-occupant becomes temporarily relieved.

In such cases, the occupant of the status subjected to conflicting demands and expectations can become cast in the role of the *tertius gaudens*, the third (or more often the *n*th) party who draws advantage from the conflict of the others (see Simmel, 1950, pp. 154–69, 232–9). The status-occupant, originally at the focus of the conflict, virtually becomes a more or less influential bystander whose function it is to highlight the conflicting demands by members of his role-set and to make it a problem for them, rather than for him, to resolve their contradictory demands. Often enough, this serves to change the structure of the situation.

This social mechanism can be thought of as working to eliminate one form of what Allport described as 'pluralistic ignorance', that is, the pattern in which individual members of a group *assume* that they are virtually alone in holding the social attitudes and expectations they do, all unknowing that others privately share them (Allport, 1924; Schank, 1932). This is a frequently observed condition of a group which is so organized that mutual observability among its members is slight. This basic notion of pluralistic ignorance can, however, be usefully enlarged to take account of a formally similar but substantively different condition. This is the condition now under review, in which the members of a role-set do not know that their expectations of the behaviour appropriate for the occupants of a particular status are *different* from those held by other members of the role-set. There are two patterns of pluralistic ignorance – the unfounded assumption that one's own attitudes and expectations are unshared and the unfounded assumption that they are uniformly shared. [. . .]

5. *The mechanism of social support by others in similar social statuses with similar difficulties of coping with an unintegrated role-set.* This mechanism presupposes the not unusual structural situation that others occupying the same social status have much the same problems of dealing with their role-sets. Whatever he may believe to the contrary, the occupant of a social status is usually not alone. The very fact that it is a *social status* means that there are others more or less like-circumstanced. The actual and potential experience of confronting conflicting role-expectations among those in one's role-set is to this extent common to occupants of the status. The individual subject to these conflicts need not, therefore, meet them as a wholly private problem which must be handled in a wholly private fashion. Such conflicts of role-expectations become patterned and shared by occupants of the same social status.

These facts of social structure afford a basis for understanding the formation of organizations and normative systems among those occupying the same social status. Occupational and professional associations, for example, constitute a structural response to the problems of coping with the power structure and (potentially or actually) conflicting demands by those in the role-set of the status. They constitute social formations designed to counter the power of the role-set ; of being, not merely amenable to these demands, but of helping to shape them. The organization of status-occupants – so familiar a part of the social landscape of differentiated societies – serves to develop a normative system which anticipates and thereby mitigates the conflicting demands made of those in this status. They provide social support to the individual status-occupant. They minimize the need for his improvising private adjustments to conflict situations.

It is this same function, it might be said, which also constitutes part of the sociological significance of the emergence of professional codes which are designed to state in advance what the socially supported behavior of the status-occupant should be. Not, of course, that such codes operate with automatic efficiency, serving to eliminate in advance those demands judged illegitimate in terms of the code and serving to indicate unequivocally which action the status-occupant should take when confronted with conflicting demands. Codification, of ethical as of cognitive matters, implies abstraction. The codes still need to be interpreted before being applied to concrete instances. Nevertheless, social support is provided by consensus among status-peers as this consensus is recorded in the code or is expressed in the judgments of status-peers oriented toward the code. The function of such codes becomes all the more significant in those cases in which status-occupants are vulnerable to pressures from their role-set precisely because they are relatively isolated from one another. Thus, thousands of librarians sparsely distributed among the towns and villages of the nation and not infrequently subject to censorial pressures received strong support from the code on censorship developed by the American Library Association in conjunction with the American Book Publishers Council (American Library Association, 1953 ; McKeon, Merton and Gellhorn, 1957). This kind of social support for conformity to the requirements of the status when confronted with pressures by the role-set to depart from these requirements serves to counteract the instability of role-performance which would otherwise develop.

6. *Abridging the role-set: disruption of role-relationships.* This is, of course, the limiting case in modes of coping with incompatible demands upon status-occupants by members of the role-set. Certain relationships are broken off, leaving a consensus of role-expectations among those that remain. But this mode of adaptation is possible only under special and limited conditions. It can be effectively utilized only in those circumstances where it is still possible for the status-occupant to perform his other roles, without the support of those with whom he has discontinued relations. Otherwise put, this requires that the remaining relationships in the role-set are not substantially damaged by this device. It presupposes that social structure provides the option to discontinue some relations in the role-set as, for example, in a network of personal friendships. By and large, however, this option is far from unlimited, since the role-set is not so much a matter of personal choice as a matter of the social structure in which the status is embedded. Under these conditions, the option is apt to be that of the status-occupant removing himself from the status rather than that of removing the role-set, or an appreciable part of it, from the status. Typically, the individual goes, and the social structure remains.

Residual conflict in the role-set

There can be little doubt but that these are only some of the mechanisms working to articulate the expectations of those in the role-set. Inquiry will uncover others, just as it will probably modify the preceding account of those we have provisionally identified. But I believe that the logical structure of this analysis may remain largely intact. This can be briefly recapitulated.

First, it is assumed that each social status has its organized complement of role-relationships which can be thought of as comprising a role-set.

Second, the relationships are not only between the occupant of the particular status and each member of the role-set but, always potentially and often actually, between members of the role-set itself.

Third, to some extent, those in the role-set and especially those occupying disparate social statuses, may have differing expectations (moral and actuarial) of the behavior of the status-occupant.

Fourth, this gives rise to the problem of their diverse expectations being sufficiently articulated for the status- and role-structure to operate with a modicum of effectiveness.

Fifth, inadequate articulation of these role-expectations tends to call one or more social mechanisms into play, which operate to reduce the amount of patterned role-conflict below that which would be involved if these mechanisms were not operating.

Sixth, finally and importantly, even when these mechanisms are at work, they may not, in particular instances, prove sufficient to reduce the conflict of expectations among those comprising the role-set below the level required for the role-system to operate with substantial efficiency. This residual conflict within the role-set may be enough to interfere materially with the effective performance of roles by the occupant of the status in question. Indeed, it will probably turn out that this condition is the most frequent – role-systems operating at considerably less than full efficiency. [...]

References

ALLPORT, F. H. (1924), *Social Psychology*, Houghton Mifflin.
AMERICAN LIBRARY ASSOCIATION (1953), *The Freedom to Read*, Chicago.
HUNTINGTON, M. J. (1957), 'The development of a professional self-image', in R. K. Merton, P. L. Kendal and G. G. Reader (eds.), *The Student Physician: Introductory Studies in the Sociology of Medical Education*, Harvard University Press.
KENNEDY, J. F. (1955), *Profiles in Courage*, Harper & Row.
LINTON, R. (1936), *The Study of Man*, Appleton-Century-Crofts.
LINTON, R. (1945), *The Cultural Background of Personality*, Appleton-Century-Crofts.
McKEON, R. P., MERTON, R. K., and GELLHORN, W. (1957), *The Freedom to Read*, Bowker.
SCHANK, R. L. (1932), 'A study of a community and its groups and institutions conceived of as behaviors of individuals', *Psychol. Monographs*, vol. 43, no. 2.
SIMMEL, G. (1950), *The Sociology of Georg Simmel*, Free Press.
WEBER, M. (1948), *From Max Weber: Essays in Sociology*, Routledge & Kegan Paul.

15 Peter M. Blau

Social Exchange

Excerpts from Peter M. Blau, *Exchange and Power in Social Life*, Wiley, 1964, pp. 88–114.

The moral type on the other hand is not based on stated terms, but the gift or other service is given as to a friend, although the giver expects to receive an equivalent or greater return, as though it had not been a free gift but a loan; and as he ends the relationship in a different spirit from that in which he began it, he will complain. The reason of this is that all men, or most men, wish what is noble but choose what is profitable; and while it is noble to render a service not with an eye to receiving one in return, it is profitable to receive one. One ought, therefore, if one can, to return the equivalent of services received, and to do so willingly. . . .
Aristotle, *The Nichomachean Ethics*

Processes of social association can be conceptualized, following Homans's lead, 'as an exchange of activity, tangible or intangible, and more or less rewarding or costly, between at least two persons' (1961, p. 31). [. . .] Neighbors exchange favors; children, toys; colleagues, assistance; acquaintances, courtesies; politicians, concessions; discussants, ideas; housewives' recipes. The pervasiveness of social exchange makes it tempting to consider all social conduct in terms of exchange, but this would deprive the concept of its distinctive meaning. People do things for fear of other men or for fear of God or for fear of their conscience, and nothing is gained by trying to force such action into a conceptual framework of exchange.

Mauss and other anthropologists have called attention to the significance and prevalence of the exchange of gifts and services in simpler societies.

In theory such gifts are voluntary but in fact they are given and repaid under obligation. . . . Further, what they exchange is not exclusively goods and wealth, real and personal property, and things of economic value. They exchange rather courtesies, entertainments, ritual, military assistance, women, children, dances and feasts; and fairs in which the market is but one element and the circulation of wealth but one part of a wide and enduring contact (1954, pp. 1, 3).

The institutionalized form the exchange of gifts frequently assumes in simpler societies highlights the two general functions of social, as distinct from strictly economic, exchange, namely, to establish bonds of friendship and to establish superordination over others. The creation of friendship bonds is typified by the ceremonial Kula exchange in the Western Pacific, where 'the Kula partnership provides every man within its ring with a few friends near at hand, and with some friendly allies in the far-away, dangerous, foreign districts' (Malinowski, 1961, p. 92). A polar example of the establishment of superordination over others is the potlatch in the American Northwest, in which 'status in associations and clans, and rank of every kind, are determined by the war of property' (Mauss, 1954, p. 35). What is most interesting, however, is that the exchanges in the same institution serve sometimes to cement peer relations and sometimes to produce differentiation of status, contradictory as these two consequences appear to be.

The basic principles underlying the conception of exchange may be briefly summarized. An individual who supplies rewarding services to another obligates him. To discharge this obligation, the second must furnish benefits to the first in turn. Concern here is with extrinsic benefits, not primarily with the rewards intrinsic to the association itself, although the significance of the social 'commodities' exchanged is never perfectly independent of the interpersonal relation between the exchange partners. If both individuals value what they receive from the other, both are prone to supply more of their own services to provide incentives for the other to increase his supply and to avoid becoming indebted to him. As both receive increasing amounts of the assistance they originally needed rather badly, however, their need for still further assistance typically declines.

'The profits from exchange decrease with the number of exchanges' (Homans, 1961, p. 70), in technical terms, the marginal utility of increasing amounts of benefits eventually diminishes. If we need help in our work, for example, five minutes of an expert's assistance are worth much to us, and another five minutes are perhaps just as valuable, but once he has aided us for half an hour another five minutes of his time are undoubtedly less significant than were the first five. Ultimately, the declining marginal utility of additional benefits is no longer worth the cost of obtaining them, and the point at which this happens for both partners, often after some adjustment in the ratio at which they exchange services, governs the level of transactions most advantageous for both at which the volume of exchange between them presumably becomes stabilized. Although personal considerations – for instance, the desire not to antagonize a colleague – modify these rational decisions, such factors also can be taken into account in more complex versions of the basic model, at least in principle.

Take the association of a new member of a profession with a respected senior colleague as an illustration of these processes. The junior is rewarded by the senior's stimulating expert discussions of professional matters and by the senior's willingness to treat him as a colleague, which symbolizes acceptance as a full-fledged professional. He reciprocates by his deferential admiration, which is rewarding for the senior. The gratification the senior derives from being listened to with great respect prompts him to devote some of his limited time to the association, but his gratification is not proportionately increased if he extends the period in which the other admires his expert opinions from half an hour every few days to several hours daily. Moreover, the more time the senior devotes to the association, the costlier it becomes for him to further restrict the time available to him for other activities. Hence, he will be inclined to limit the time he spends in discussions with the junior to the level at which the support he receives from his admiration still outweighs in significance the advantages foregone by taking time from other pursuits. At this point, however, the junior may still profit from further association with the senior. Since his admiration does not suffice to increase the association time, the junior must endeavor to furnish supplementary rewards, for example, by doing odd jobs for his senior colleague, thereby obligating him to reciprocate by devoting more time to the association than he otherwise would. Eventually, the marginal advantages for the junior of associating still more with the senior will no longer outweigh the marginal cost of providing more services for him, and the exchange will tend to level off. The assumption is not that individuals make these calculations explicitly but that such implicit calculations underlie the feelings of boredom or pressure from other work that prompt their decisions to spend only a certain amount of time together.

Unspecified obligations and trust

The concept of exchange can be circumscribed by indicating two limiting cases. An individual may give another money because the other stands in front of him with a gun in a holdup. While this could be conceptualized as an exchange of his money for his life, it seems preferable to exclude the result of physical coercion from the range of social conduct encompassed by the term 'exchange'. An individual may also give away money because his conscience demands that he help support the underprivileged and without expecting any form of gratitude from them. While this could be conceptualized as an exchange of his money for the internal approval of his superego, here again it seems preferable to exclude conformity with internalized norms from the purview of the concept of social exchange.[1] A social exchange is involved if an individual gives money to a poor man because he wants to receive the man's expressions of gratitude and deference and if he ceases to give alms to beggars who withhold such expressions.

'Social exchange', as the term is used here, refers to voluntary actions of individuals that are motivated by the returns they are expected to bring and typically do in fact bring from others. Action compelled by physical coercion is not voluntary, although compliance with other forms of power can be considered a voluntary service rendered in exchange for the benefits such compliance produces, as already indicated. Whereas conformity with internalized standards does not fall under the definition of exchange presented, conformity to social pressures tends to entail indirect exchanges. Men make charitable donations, not to earn the gratitude of the recipients, whom they never see, but to earn the approval of their peers who participate in the philanthropic campaign. Donations are exchanged for social approval, though the recipients of the donations and the suppliers of the approval are not identical, and the clarification of the connection between the two requires an analysis of the complex structures of indirect exchange. Our concern here is with the simpler direct exchanges.

The need to reciprocate for benefits received in order to continue receiving them serves as a 'starting mechanism' of social interaction and group structure, as Gouldner has pointed out (1960). When people are thrown together, and before common norms or goals or role expectations have crystallized among them, the advantages to be gained from entering into exchange relations furnish incentives for social interaction, and the exchange processes serve as mechanisms for regulating social interaction, thus fostering the development of a network of social relations and a rudimentary group structure. Eventually, group norms to regulate and limit the exchange transactions emerge, including the fundamental and ubiquitous norm of reciprocity, which makes failure to discharge obligations subject to group sanctions. In contrast to Gouldner, however, it is held here that the norm of reciprocity merely reinforces and stabilizes tendencies inherent in the character of social exchange itself and that the fundamental starting mechanism of patterned social intercourse is found in the existential conditions of exchange, not in the norm of reciprocity. It is a necessary condition of exchange that individuals, in the interest of continuing to receive needed services, discharge their obligations for having received them in the

1. Mises refers to this type as autistic exchange. 'Making one-sided presents without the aim of being rewarded by any conduct on the part of the receiver or of a third person is autistic exchange' (1949, p. 196).

past. Exchange processes utilize, as it were, the self-interests of individuals to produce a differentiated social structure within which norms tend to develop that require individuals to set aside some of their personal interests for the sake of those of the collectivity. Not all social constraints are normative constraints, and those imposed by the nature of social exchange are not, at least not originally.

Social exchange differs in important ways from strictly economic exchange. The basic and most crucial distinction is that social exchange entails *unspecified* obligations. The prototype of an economic transaction rests on a formal contract that stipulates the exact quantities to be exchanged.[2] The buyer pays $30,000 for a specific house, or he signs a contract to pay that sum plus interest over a period of years. Whether the entire transaction is consummated at a given time, in which case the contract may never be written, or not, all the transfers to be made now or in the future are agreed upon at the time of sale. Social exchange, in contrast, involves the principle that one person does another a favor, and while there is a general expectation of some future return, its exact nature is definitely *not* stipulated in advance. The distinctive implications of such unspecified obligations are brought into high relief by the institutionalized form they assume in the Kula discussed by Malinowski:

The main principle underlying the regulations of actual exchange is that the Kula consists in the bestowing of a ceremonial gift, which has to be repaid by an equivalent counter-gift after a lapse of time. . . . But it can never be exchanged from hand to hand, with the equivalence between the two objects being discussed, bargained about and computed. . . . The second very important principle is that the equivalence of the counter-gift is left to the giver, and it cannot be enforced by any kind of coercion. . . . If the article given as a counter-gift is not equivalent, the recipient will be disappointed and angry, but he has no direct means of redress, no means of coercing his partner (1961, pp. 95–6).

Social exchange, whether it is in this ceremonial form or not, involves favors that create diffuse future obligations, not precisely specified ones, and the nature of the return cannot be bargained about but must be left to the discretion of the one who makes it. Thus, if a person gives a dinner party he expects his guests to reciprocate at some future date. But he can hardly bargain with them about the kind of party to which they should invite him, although he expects them not simply to ask him

2. This is not completely correct for an employment contract or for the purchase of professional services, since the precise services the employee or professional will be obliged to perform are not specified in detail in advance. Economic transactions that involve services generally are somewhat closer to social exchange than the pure type of economic exchange of commodities or *products* of services.

for a quick lunch if he had invited them to a formal dinner. Similarly, if a person goes to some trouble on behalf of an acquaintance, he expects *some* expression of gratitude, but he can neither bargain with the other over how to reciprocate nor force him to reciprocate at all.

Since there is no way to assure an appropriate return for a favor, social exchange requires trusting others to discharge their obligations. While the banker who makes a loan to a man who buys a house does not have to trust him, although he hopes he will not have to foreclose the mortgage, the individual who gives another an expensive gift must trust him to reciprocate in proper fashion. Typically, however, exchange relations evolve in a slow process, starting with minor transactions in which little trust is required because little risk is involved. A worker may help a colleague a few times. If the colleague fails to reciprocate, the worker has lost little and can easily protect himself against further loss by ceasing to furnish assistance. If the colleague does reciprocate, perhaps excessively so out of gratitude for the volunteered help and in the hope of receiving more, he proves himself trustworthy of continued and extended favors. (Excessive reciprocation may be embarrassing, because it is a bid for a more extensive exchange relation than one may be willing to enter.) By discharging their obligations for services rendered, if only to provide inducements for the supply of more assistance, individuals demonstrate their trustworthiness, and the gradual expansion of mutual service is accompanied by a parallel growth of mutual trust. Hence, processes of social exchange, which may originate in pure self-interest, generate trust in social relations through their recurrent and gradually expanding character.

Only social exchange tends to engender feelings of personal obligation, gratitude and trust ; purely economic exchange as such does not. An individual is obligated to the banker who gives him a mortgage on his house merely in the technical sense of owing him money, but he does not feel personally obligated in the sense of experiencing a debt of gratitude to the banker, because all the banker's services, all costs and risks, are duly taken into account in and fully repaid by the interest on the loan he receives. A banker who grants a loan without adequate collateral, however, does make the recipient personally obligated for this favorable treatment, precisely because this act of trust entails a social exchange that is superimposed upon the strictly economic transaction.

In contrast to economic commodities, the benefits involved in social exchange do not have an exact price in terms of a single quantitative medium of exchange, which is another reason why social obligations are unspecific. It is essential to realize that this is a substantive fact, not simply a methodological problem. It is not just the social scientist who cannot exactly measure how much approval a given helpful action is worth ; the actors themselves cannot precisely specify the worth of approval or of help in the absence of a money price. The obligations individuals incur in social exchange, therefore, are defined only in general, somewhat diffuse terms. Furthermore, the specific benefits exchanged are sometimes primarily valued as symbols of the supportiveness and friendliness they express, and it is the exchange of the underlying mutual support that is the main concern of the participants. Occasionally, a time-consuming service of great material benefit to the recipient might be properly repaid by mere verbal expressions of deep appreciation, since these are taken to signify as much supportiveness as the material benefits (see Goffman, 1962, pp. 274–86). In the long run, however, the explicit efforts the associates in a peer relation make on one another's behalf tend to be in balance, if only because a persistent imbalance in these manifestations of good will raise questions about the reciprocity in the underlying orientations of support and congeniality.

Extrinsic benefits are, in principle, detachable from the source that supplies them, but their detachability is a matter of degree. At one extreme are economic commodities, the significance of which is quite independent of the firm that supplies them. The value of a share in a corporation is not affected by the broker from whom we buy it. At the other extreme is the diffuse social support we derive in a love relationship, the significance of which depends entirely on the individual who supplies it. The typical extrinsic benefits socially exchanged, such as advice, invitations, assistance or compliance, have a distinctive significance of their own that is independent of their supplier, yet an individual's preferences for them are also affected by his interpersonal relations with the supplier. Although the quality of advice determines its basic value for an individual, regardless of who furnishes it, he tends to prefer to consult a colleague whose friendly relations with him make it easy for him to do so rather than a more expert consultant whom he hardly knows (Blau, 1963, pp. 123–31). The ease with which he can approach a colleague, the jokes and conviviality that surround the consultation, and other rewards he obtains from the association combine with the quality of the advice itself to determine the value of the total transaction for him. Indeed, the exchange of instrumental assistance may sometimes largely serve the function for participants of providing opportunities for exchanging these other more salient rewards. Going over and helping a fellow worker with his task might simply be an excuse for chatting with him and exchanging social support.

Since social benefits have no exact price, and since the utility of a given benefit cannot be clearly separated from that of other rewards derived from a social association, it seems difficult to apply the economic principles of maximizing utilities to social exchange (Homans, 1961, p. 72). The impersonal economic market is designed to strip specific commodities of these entangling alliances with other benefits, so to speak, and thus to make possible rational choices between distinct alternatives with a fixed price. Even in economic exchange, however, the significance of each alternative is rarely confined to a single factor, which confounds rational decision-making; people's job choices are affected by working conditions as well as salaries, and their choices of merchants, by the atmosphere in a store as well as the quality of the merchandise. Although the systematic study of social exchange poses distinctive problems, the assumptions it makes about the maximization of utilities implicit in choice behavior are little different from those made by the economist in the study of consumption. [. . .]

Conditions of exchange

A variety of conditions affect processes of social exchange: the stage in the development and the character of the relationship between exchange partners, the nature of the benefits that enter into the transactions and the costs incurred in providing them, and the social context in which the exchanges take place.

The initial offer of a favor to a stranger or an acquaintance is of special significance, whether it takes the form of a few friendly words, a cigar, the first invitation to one's home or some helpful suggestions. It entails the risk of rejection of the offer itself and the risk of rejection of the overture implied by it through failure to reciprocate and enter into a friendly relationship. By taking these risks, an individual brings to an end the complete indifference between himself and another and forces on the other a choice of two alternatives, as Lévi-Strauss has noted: 'From now on it must become a relationship either of cordiality or hostility' (1957, p. 90). The offer cannot be refused without being insulting, and acceptance of it invites some friendly exchange, if only of greetings and a few cordial words. Simmel took the extreme view that the first kindness of a person can never be fully repaid, because it alone is a spontaneous gesture of good will for another, whereas any future favor is prompted by the obligation to reciprocate (1950).

The establishment of exchange relations involves making investments that constitute commitments to the other party. Since social exchange requires trusting others to reciprocate, the initial problem is to prove oneself trustworthy. We have already seen how the gradual expansion of exchange transactions promotes the trust necessary for them. As individuals regularly discharge their obligations, they prove themselves trustworthy of further credit. Moreover, the investments an individual has made by fostering a friendly relation with another, in which it is easy to exchange services of various sorts, and by neglecting to cultivate other associates, who might constitute alternative sources of such services, commit him to the relationship. His commitment, which would make it disadvantageous for him to abandon the partnership in favor of another, gives the other additional reasons to trust him not to evade his obligations in their relationship.[3] Both partners gain advantages from a stable exchange partnership, but the greater commitment of one constitutes a particular advantage for the other. [. . .]

Since trust is essential for stable social relations, and since exchange obligations promote trust, special mechanisms exist to perpetuate obligations and thus strengthen bonds of indebtedness and trust. [. . .]

Although an invitation to a party can be repaid any time, it is not proper to do so too promptly. Generally, posthaste reciprocation of favors, which implies a refusal to stay indebted for a while and hence an insistence on a more business-like relationship, is condemned as improper. 'Excessive eagerness to discharge an obligation is a form of ingratitude' (La Rochefoucauld, 1940, p. 73). Social bonds are fortified by remaining obligated to others as well as by trusting them to discharge their obligations for considerable periods.

The nature of social rewards can be distinguished along several lines. First, some social rewards cannot be bartered in exchange, notably intrinsic attraction to a person, approval of his opinions and judgements, and respect for his abilities, because their significance rests on their being spontaneous reactions rather than calculated means of pleasing him. These evaluations of a person or his attributes reward him only if he has reason to assume that they are *not* primarily motivated by the explicit intention to reward him. Rewarding actions, in contrast to evaluations, can be bartered in social exchange since the fact that they are intended as inducements does not infringe on their inherent value as rewards. Social acceptance in a group to which a person is attracted, instrumental services of various kinds, and compliance with his wishes constitute rewards for him even if he knows that they are furnished in exchange for benefits expected of him. Second, within each of these two categories, rewards that are intrinsic to the association between individuals, such as personal attraction and social acceptance, can be distinguished from extrinsic ones, such as approval of decisions or opinions

3. Commitment has been conceptionalized as a side bet that promotes trust by making it disproportionately disadvantageous for a person to violate an agreement (Schelling, 1960, ch. 2; Becker, 1960).

and instrumental services. Third, rewards that individuals may mutually supply for each other, as the four types just mentioned, can be distinguished from those that are necessarily unilateral, which are manifest in the general respect for a person that bestows superior prestige on him and in the prevailing compliance with his requests that bestows superior power on him. The six types of rewards delineated can be presented in this schema:

	Intrinsic	Extrinsic	Unilateral
Spontaneous evaluations	Personal attraction	Social approval*	Respect–prestige†
Calculated actions	Social acceptance*	Instrumental services*	Compliance–power†

* Entails investment costs for suppliers in addition to those needed to establish the social association.

† Entails the direct cost of subordination for suppliers.

The person who receives rewards from associating with another has an incentive to furnish inducements to the other to continue the association, and this is also the case if the rewards are spontaneous reactions that must not be bartered in exchange. Since it is rewarding for an individual to associate with others who accord him high respect, he is likely to provide sufficient inducements for them to continue the association unless he suspects them of simulating respect in order to obtain benefits from him. Positive evaluations of a person must not be bartered lest they cease to be accepted as genuine and thus lose their significance, but they do make social associations rewarding and worth some cost to the recipient and consequently enable the evaluator to reap some benefits from associating with him. Men sometimes take advantage of this fact and express approval of another in a calculating manner to obtain benefits from him in exchange, but this strategy of the sycophant can succeed only as long as its calculating intent remains hidden.

The cost incurred in providing social rewards in exchange for others may be thought of as 'investment cost', 'direct cost' and 'opportunity cost'. Investments in time and effort are necessary to acquire the skills required for furnishing many instrumental services, and such investments are also necessary to command respect for one's approval and thereby make it valuable for others. A group's investments that benefit its membership determine the value of social acceptance in the group and the contributions it can demand in exchange for acceptance. The supply of other social rewards usually entails no investments beyond those needed to establish the exchange relations. The most distinctive direct cost in social transactions is the subordination involved in expressing respect or manifesting compliance, that is, in rewarding another with prestige or with power. The most general cost incurred in supplying any social reward is the time required to do so in social associations. Since the significance of this time depends on the alternatives foregone by devoting it to a given exchange relation, it may be considered an opportunity cost. [. . .]

The social context in which exchange transactions take place affects them profoundly in several respects, which must be briefly adumbrated in this discussion of the conditions of exchange, although a more complete analysis of the interrelations between exchange processes and social structure is reserved for later chapters. First, even if we abstract the exchange transactions in a single pair, they are influenced by the 'role-set' of each partner, that is, by the role relations either has by virtue of occupying the social status relevant to the exchange, since these role relations govern the alternative opportunities of the two. The larger circle of acquaintances of the members of a clique who exchange invitations, for example, or the dating opportunities of two lovers, define the alternatives foregone by each and hence affect the cost each incurs in order to obtain rewards from his present association.

Second, the entire exchange transactions in a group determine a prevailing rate of exchange, and this group standard puts pressure on any partnership whose transactions deviate from it to come into line. These are not normative pressures in the sense of moral standards supported by group sanctions that enforce conformity but pressures resulting from existing opportunities. The demand for and supply of certain mechanical skills in a group of factory workers, for instance, influence how much respect and other benefits a highly skilled worker can command on the average for helping others with their tasks. Considerable departures from this average in a given exchange partnership create strong inducements for one of the partners to abandon it, inasmuch as more profitable opportunities for social interaction are elsewhere available to him. Third, potential coalitions among the weaker members of a collectivity tend to restrain its stronger members from fully exploiting their advantageous position in exchange transactions. Fourth, the differences in power to which exchange processes typically give rise in a group subsequently modify these processes, since established power enables an individual to compel others to provide services without offering a fair return, although the danger of the formation of coalitions to destroy his power may discourage its exploitative use.

Finally, the social situation exerts a subtle but important influence by making the transactions in a given exchange relation part of other exchanges that occur in the background and that may, nevertheless, be the more salient ones. A person may give a waiter a large tip to elicit the approval of his companions at the table for his generosity, not primarily to earn the waiter's gratitude. [. . .]

People want to gain approval and they want to gain advantage in their social associations, and the two desires often come into conflict, since heedless pursuit of advantage tends to elicit disapproval. The multi-group affiliations of individuals in modern societies help to resolve this conflict. [. . .]

People's positive sentiments toward and evaluations of others, such as affection, approval and respect, are rewards worth a price that enter into exchange transactions, but they must not be explicitly bartered in exchange lest their value as genuine feelings or judgements be compromised. The actions of people that benefit others, however, remain significant whatever the underlying motive ; hence their value as rewards is not jeopardized if they are explicitly used for bargaining in exchange transactions. This is particularly so for instrumental services, which constitute extrinsic rewards, including the generic instrumental service of compliance with another's wishes. But the distinction between rewards that are intrinsic to a social association and those that are extrinsic and, in principle, detachable from it is an analytical and relative one.

Social exchange always entails elements of intrinsic significance for the participants, which distinguishes it from strictly economic transactions, although its focus is on benefits of some extrinsic value and on, at least, implicit bargaining for advantage, which distinguishes it from the mutual attraction and support in profound love. The taboo on explicit bargaining in the exchange of gifts is designed to protect their significance as tokens of friendship, that is, as signs of intrinsic attraction, from being obliterated by the inherent value of the objects themselves. Social exchange, then, is an intermediate case between pure calculation of advantage and pure expression of love. However, even economic transactions and love relations rarely express the polar processes in entirely pure form, since the multiple gains and costs typically involved in any economic transaction prevent unambiguous calculation of advantage, and since extrinsic benefits are exchanged in love relations and often help to produce mutual affection. Economic institutions, such as the impersonal market and the contract that stipulates the price terms of the exchange, are designed to separate concern with distinct objects of exchange from other considerations and to specify the exact obligations incurred in a transaction, thus maximizing the possibility of rational calculation. Social exchange, in contrast, involves unspecified obligations, the fulfilment of which depends on trust because it cannot be enforced in the absence of a binding contract. But the trust required for social exchange is generated by its own gradual expansion in a self-adjusting manner.

Furnishing benefits to others may lead to the development of bonds of fellowship with them or to a position of superiority over them. A person who distributes gifts and services to others makes a claim to superior status. By reciprocating and, particularly, by making excessive returns that now obligate the first to them, others invalidate his claim and invite further transactions in expanding exchange relations of mutual trust between peers. Their failure to reciprocate, on the other hand, validates his claim to superiority, and so does their failure to accept his offer, unless their evident affluence proves that their rejection is not due to their inability to enter into egalitarian exchange relations with him but to their unwillingness to do so, in which case it is likely to produce hostility. A person can establish superiority over others by overwhelming them with benefits they cannot properly repay and thus subduing them with the weight of their obligations to him. But once superiority is firmly rooted in political or economic structures, it enables an individual to extract benefits in the form of tribute from subordinates without any peril to his continued superiority over them.

It seems to be typical of social associations that the individuals who establish them have some common and some conflicting interests. A stable social relationship requires that individuals make some investments to bring it into being and maintain it in existence, and it is to the advantage of each party to have the other or others assume a disproportionate share of the commitments that secure their continuing association. Hence the common interest of individuals in sustaining a relation between them tends to be accompanied by conflicting interests as to whose investment should contribute most to its sustenance. We have seen that the first choice of group members who are attracted to each other is typically to have their position in the group buttressed by the unilateral respect of others for them, although most of them are willing to settle for a position in which they must pay respect to others in preference to being excluded from the group. Similarly, lovers gain advantage from having the other more committed, but their interest in maintaining the love relationship often induces them to make the greater commitment if necessary. In parallel fashion, exchange partners derive most advantage from having the other make the bulk of the investment needed to stabilize their relationship, although their interest in the continuing partnership gives each of them an incentive to make the major investment himself rather than let the profitable association fall apart. In every exchange transaction, finally, each participant hopes to gain much at little cost, yet to profit at all both must come to some agreement. The coexistence of conflicting and common interests in all these social associations means that associates always have first choices that conflict but last choices that are identical, and the first choice of either is the second-last of the other, though it may still be preferable to any available alternative. These preferences, however, are continually modified in the process of maneuvering between partners and exploring alternative opportunities until stable social relations have become crystallized.

Aside from these interpersonal conflicts, there is also the intrapersonal conflict between the individual's desire to gain social approval and support and his desire to gain instrumental advantage in his social associations. This conflict is usually resolved by obtaining intrinsic support primarily from some associates and extrinsic benefits largely from others. The multi-group affiliations of individuals in modern society facilitate this solution, permitting them to pursue their advantage without regard for approval in one social context and to elicit approval and support by their generosity and supportiveness in another, for example, in their business and in their family, respectively. Social approval has less pervasive significance as a restraining force in complex societies than in simpler ones, because the multiplicity of groups and the possible mobility between them in complex societies enables deviants of nearly all sorts to escape from the impact of community disapproval by finding a subgroup of like-minded persons where they can gain approval. Impersonal restraints are, therefore, of special importance in modern societies, and a basic source of impersonal restraint is power.

References

BECKER, H. S. (1960), 'Notes on the concept of commitment', *Amer J. Sociol.*, vol. 66, no. 1, pp. 32–40.

BLAU, P. (1963), *The Dynamics of Bureaucracy*, University of Chicago Press.

GOFFMAN, E. (1962), *Asylums*, Aldine.

GOULDNER, A. W. (1960), 'The norm of reciprocity', *Amer. Sociol. Rev.*, vol. 25, no. 2, pp. 161–78.

HOMANS, G. C. (1961), *Social Behavior*, Harcourt, Brace & World.

LA ROCHEFOUCAULD, F. (1940), *The Maxims*, Oxford University Press.

LEVI-STRAUSS, C. (1957), 'The principle of reciprocity', in L. A. Coser and B. Rosenberg (eds.), *Sociological Theory*, Macmillan.

MALINOWSKI, B. (1961), *Argonauts of the Western Pacific*, Dalton.

MISES, L. VON (1949), *Human Action*, Yale University Press.

MAUSS, M. (1954), *The Gift*, Free Press.

MERTON, R. K. (1957), *Social Theory and Social Structure*, Free Press.

SCHELLING, T. C. (1960), *The Strategy of Conflict*, Harvard University Press.

SIMMEL, G. (1950), *The Sociology of Georg Simmel*, Free Press.

Part Three **Stratification**

It is impossible to progress far in any discussion of social stratification without becoming aware of the enduring influence of the work of Karl Marx. Controversy still abounds about what he 'really meant', and also about what he would have said had he lived. Two selections of his work are presented here. In the first (Reading 16(a)) together with Friedrich Engels, he outlines his basic contention concerning the nature of social stratification in industrial societies – that it is composed of two antagonistic social classes, the bourgeoisie and the proletariat.

The social class to which any one individual belongs is determined, according to Marx, by the relationship the individual has to the means of production. The conflict of interests between the social classes, Marx believed, would certainly increase as each class became more conscious of its own situation and then sought to improve its own position by political action. The difficulties associated with the working out of this process are outlined in the second selection (Reading 16(b)), where Marx is concerned with the emergence of more than two classes and the effects this has on the creation of effective class consciousness. Unfortunately Marx died before he could write a definitive statement on his theory of social class.

In 'Class, Status, Party' (Reading 17), Max Weber continues the discussion about the economic basis of class, but is also concerned to emphasize the importance of another independent principle underlying the emergence of social hierarchy; that of status stratification. Complicating his analysis further he also seeks to demonstrate the relationships which may obtain between class, status and political power. As in the case of Marx, however, Weber died before completing his final statement on this matter.

The next piece, by Talcott Parsons (Reading 18), was given as an address in 1948 on the centenary of the appearance of the Communist Manifesto. After revising Marx's conception of the nature of social class, Parsons goes on to consider the consequences this alternative interpretation has for the form and possible emergence of class conflict.

T. B. Bottomore (Reading 19) also relates his argument to the approach of Marx. In considering the use of the concepts 'ruling class' and 'power elite' in empirical research, he concludes that the more useful is 'ruling class' when it is used heuristically as an 'ideal-type' concept.

Concern with basic concepts continues in the next Reading. Here T. H. Marshall (Reading 20) discusses the term 'status' as a key concept in the analysis of social stratification.

In the next Reading W. G. Runciman (Reading 21) demonstrates the complexity of factors which need to be included in any discussion of the effects and meaning of stratification. By use of the concepts 'relative deprivation' and 'reference group' he shows how objective assessments of 'deprivation' are by no means infallible indicators of the 'deprivation' *experienced* by the individual.

The final three Readings are all concerned with broader comparative analyses of stratification systems. In the first Seymour M. Lipset (Reading 22), compares stratification in the United States and Great Britain. He seeks to show that stable forms of democratic government may rest on different kinds of stratification systems, underpinned by different values.

The second piece, by John H. Goldthorpe (Reading 23), takes as its theme the contention that the stratification patterns of the advanced industrial nations are 'converging', and presents a searching critique of the influence attributed to the 'logic of industrialism'. Concern with this problem is continued in the final Reading of this section. Here, Frank Parkin (Reading 24) examines the changing nature of stratification systems in socialist societies and presents evidence to suggest the re-appearance of social class distinctions in Eastern Europe.

16(a) Karl Marx and Friedrich Engels

Bourgeois and Proletarians [1]

The history of all hitherto existing society [2] is the history of class struggle.

Freeman and slave, patrician and plebeian, lord and serf, guild master [3] and journeyman, in a word, oppressor and oppressed, stood in constant opposition to one another, carried on an uninterrupted, now hidden, now open fight, a fight that each time ended either in a revolutionary reconstitution of society at large or in the common ruin of the contending classes.

In the earlier epochs of history we find almost everywhere a complicated arrangement of society into various orders, a manifold gradation of social rank. In ancient Rome we have patricians, knights, plebeians, slaves; in the Middle Ages, feudal lords, vassals, guild masters, journeymen, apprentices, serfs; in almost all of these classes, again, subordinate gradations.

1. By bourgeoisie is meant the class of modern capitalists, owners of the means of social production and employers of wage labour. By proletariat, the class of modern wage labourers, who having no means of production of their own are reduced to selling their labour power in order to live. [Note by Engels to the English edition of 1888.]

2. That is, all written history. In 1847 the pre-history of society, the social organization existing previous to recorded history, was all but unknown. Since then Haxthausen discovered common ownership of land in Russia. Maurer proved it to be the social formation from which all Teutonic races started in history, and by and by village communities were found to be, or to have been, the primitive form of society everywhere from India to Ireland. The inner organization of the primitive communistic society was laid bare in its typical form by Morgan's crowning discovery of the true native of the *gens* and its relation to the *tribe*. With the dissolution of these primeval communities society begins to be differentiated into separate and finally antagonistic classes. I have attempted to retrace this process of dissolution in *Der Ursprung der Familie, des Privateigenthums und des Staats* (*The Origin of the Family, Private Property and the State*; 2nd ed, Stuttgart, 1886). [Note by Engels to the English edition of 1888.]

3. Guild master, that is, a full member of a guild, a master within, not a head of a guild. [Note by Engels to the English edition of 1888.]

The modern bourgeois society that has sprouted from the ruins of feudal society has not done away with class antagonisms. It has but established new classes, new conditions of oppression, new forms of struggle in place of the old ones.

Our epoch, the epoch of the bourgeoisie, possesses, however, this distinctive feature: it has simplified the class antagonisms. Society as a whole is more and more splitting up into two great hostile camps, into two great classes directly facing each other: bourgeoisie and proletariat.

From the serfs of the Middle Ages sprang the chartered burghers of the earliest towns. From these burgesses the first elements of the bourgeoisie were developed.

The discovery of America, the rounding of the Cape opened up fresh ground for the rising bourgeoisie. The East Indian and Chinese markets, the colonization of America, trade with the colonies, the increase in the means of exchange and in commodities generally, gave to commerce, to navigation, to industry an impulse never before known, and thereby, to the revolutionary element in the tottering feudal society, a rapid development.

The feudal system of industry, under which industrial production was monopolized by closed guilds, now no longer sufficed for the growing wants of the new markets. The manufacturing system took its place. The guild masters were pushed on one side by the manufacturing middle class; division of labour between the different corporate guilds vanished in the face of division of labour in each single workshop.

Meantime the markets kept ever growing, the demand ever rising. Even manufacture no longer sufficed. Thereupon steam and machinery revolutionized industrial production. The place of manufacture was taken by the giant, modern industry, the place of the industrial middle class by industrial millionaires, the leaders of whole industrial armies, the modern bourgeois.

Modern industry has established the world market, for which the discovery of America paved the way. This market has given an immense development to commerce, to navigation, to communication by land. This development has, in its turn, reacted on the extension of industry; and in proportion as industry, commerce, navigation, railways extended, in the same proportion the bourgeoisie developed, increased its capital, and pushed into the background every class handed down from the Middle Ages.

We see, therefore, how the modern bourgeoisie is itself the product of a long course of development, of a series of revolutions in the modes of production and of exchange.

Each step in the development of the bourgeoisie was accompanied by a corresponding political advance of that class. [. . .]

The executive of the modern state is but a committee for managing the common affairs of the whole bourgeoisie.

The bourgeoisie, historically, has played a most revolutionary part.

The bourgeoisie, wherever it has got the upper hand, has put an end to all feudal, patriarchal, idyllic relations. It has pitilessly torn asunder the motley feudal ties that bound man to his 'natural superiors', and has left remaining no other nexus between man and man than naked self-interest, than callous 'cash payment'. It has drowned the most heavenly ecstasies of religious fervour, of chivalrous enthusiasm, of Philistine sentimentalism in the icy water of egotistical calculation. It has resolved personal worth into exchange value and, in place of the numberless indefeasible chartered freedoms, has set up that single, unconscionable freedom – free trade. In one word, for exploitation, veiled by religious and political illusions, it has substituted naked, shameless, direct, brutal exploitation.

The bourgeoisie has stripped of its halo every occupation hitherto honoured and looked up to with reverent awe. It has converted the physician, the lawyer, the priest, the poet, the man of science into its paid wage labourers.

The bourgeoisie has torn away from the family its sentimental veil, and has reduced the family relation to a mere money relation. [. . .]

The bourgeoisie cannot exist without constantly revolutionizing the instruments of production, and thereby the relations of production, and with them the whole relations of society. Conservation of the old modes of production in unaltered form was, on the contrary, the first condition of existence for all earlier industrial classes. Constant revolutionizing of production, uninterrupted disturbance of all social conditions, everlasting uncertainty and agitation distinguish the bourgeois epoch from all earlier ones. All fixed, fast-frozen relations, with their train of ancient and venerable prejudices and opinions, are swept away, all new-formed ones become antiquated before they can ossify. All that is solid melts into air, all that is holy is profaned, and man is at last compelled to face with sober senses his real conditions of life and his relations with his kind.

The need of a constantly expanding market for its products chases the bourgeoisie over the whole surface of the globe. It must nestle everywhere, settle everywhere, establish connections everywhere.

The bourgeoisie has through its exploitation of the world market given a cosmopolitan character to production and consumption in every country. To the great chagrin of reactionists, it has drawn from under the feet of industry the national ground on which it stood. All old-established national industries have been destroyed or are daily being destroyed. They are dislodged by new industries, whose introduction becomes a life and death question for all civilized nations, by industries that no longer work up indigenous raw material, but raw material drawn from the remotest zones; industries whose products are consumed not only at home, but in every quarter of the globe. In place of the old wants, satisfied by the productions of the country, we find new wants, requiring for their satisfaction the products of distant lands and climes. In place of the old local and national seclusion and self-sufficiency we have intercourse in every direction, universal interdependence of nations. And as in material, so also in intellectual production. The intellectual creations of individual nations become common property. National one-sidedness and narrow-mindedness become more and more impossible, and from the numerous national and local literatures there arises a world literature. [...]

The bourgeoisie keeps more and more doing away with the scattered state of the population, of the means of production and of property. It has agglomerated population, centralized means of production, and has concentrated property in a few hands. The necessary consequence of this was political centralization. Independent, or but loosely connected provinces, with separate interests, laws, governments and systems of taxation, became lumped together into one nation, with one government, one code of laws, one national class interest, one frontier and one customs tariff. [...]

We see then: the means of production and of exchange, on whose foundation the bourgeoisie built itself up, were generated in feudal society. At a certain stage in the development of these means of production and of exchange, the conditions under which feudal society produced and exchanged, the feudal organization of agriculture and manufacturing industry, in one word, the feudal relations of property, became no longer compatible with the already developed productive forces; they became so many fetters. They had to be burst asunder; they were burst asunder.

Into their place stepped free competition, accompanied by a social and political constitution adapted to it, and by the economic and political sway of the bourgeois class. [...]

In proportion as the bourgeoisie, i.e. capital, is developed, in the same proportion is the proletariat, the modern working class, developed – a class of labourers, who live only so long as they find work, and who find work only so long as their labour increases capital. These labourers, who must sell themselves piecemeal, are a commodity, like every other article of commerce, and are consequently exposed to all the vicissitudes of competition, to all the fluctuations of the market.

Owing to the extensive use of machinery and to division of labour, the work of the proletarians has lost all individual character and, consequently, all charm for the workman. He becomes an appendage of the machine, and it is only the simplest, most monotonous, and most easily acquired knack that is required of him. Hence the cost of production of a workman is restricted, almost entirely, to the means of subsistence that he requires for his maintenance and for the propagation of his race. But the price of a commodity, and therefore also of labour, is equal to its cost of production. In proportion, therefore, as the repulsiveness of the work increases, the wage decreases. Nay, more, in proportion as the use of machinery and division of labour increases, in the same proportion the burden of toil also increases, whether by prolongation of the working hours, by increase of the work exacted in a given time, or by increased speed of the machinery, etc.

Modern industry has converted the little workshop of the patriarchal master into the great factory of the industrial capitalist. Masses of labourers, crowded into the factory, are organized like soldiers. As privates of the industrial army they are placed under the command of a perfect hierarchy of officers and sergeants. Not only are they slaves of the bourgeois class, and of the bourgeois state; they are daily and hourly enslaved by the machine, by the over-looker, and, above all, by the individual bourgeois manufacturer himself. The more openly this despotism proclaims gain to be its end and aim, the more petty, the more hateful, and the more embittering it is. [. . .]

The proletariat goes through various stages of development. With its birth begins its struggle with the bourgeoisie. At first the contest is carried on by individual labourers, then by the workpeople of a factory, then by the operatives of one trade, in one locality, against the individual bourgeois who directly exploits them. They direct their attacks not against the bourgeois conditions of production, but against the instruments of production themselves; they destroy imported wares that compete with their labour, they smash to pieces machinery, they set factories ablaze, they seek to restore by force the vanished status of the workman of the Middle Ages. [. . .]

But with the development of industry the proletariat not only increases in number; it becomes concentrated in greater masses, its strength grows, and it feels that strength more. The various interests and conditions of life within the ranks of the proletariat are more and more equalized, in proportion as machinery obliterates all distinctions of labour and nearly everywhere reduces wages to the same low level. The growing competition among the bourgeois and the resulting commercial crises make the wages of the workers ever more fluctuating. The unceasing improvement of machinery, ever more rapidly developing, makes their livelihood more and more precarious; the collisions between individual workmen and individual bourgeois take more and more the character of collisions between two classes. Thereupon the workers begin to form combinations (trade unions) against the bourgeois; they club together in order to keep up the rate of wages; they found permanent associations in order to make provision beforehand for these occasional revolts. Here and there the contest breaks out into riots.

Now and then the workers are victorious, but only for a time. The real fruit of their battles lies not in the immediate result, but in the ever expanding union of the workers. This union is helped on by the improved means of communication that are created by modern industry and that place the workers of different localities in contact with one another. It was just this contact that was needed to centralize the numerous local struggles, all of the same character, into one national struggle between classes. But every class struggle is a political struggle. And that union, to attain which the burghers of the Middle Ages, with their miserable highways, required centuries, the modern proletarians, thanks to railways, achieve in a few years.

This organization of the proletarians into a class, and consequently into a political party, is continually being upset again by the competition between the workers themselves. But it ever rises up again, stronger, firmer, mightier. It compels legislative recognition of particular interests of the workers by taking advantage of the divisions among the bourgeoisie itself. Thus the ten-hour bill in England was carried.

Altogether collisions between the classes of the old society further, in many ways, the course of development of the proletariat. The bourgeoisie finds itself involved in a constant battle. At first with the aristocracy; later on, with those portions of the bourgeoisie itself whose interests have become antagonistic to the progress of industry; at all times, with the bourgeoisie of foreign countries. In all these battles it sees itself compelled to appeal to the proletariat, to ask for its help, and thus to drag it into the political arena. The bourgeoisie itself, therefore, supplies the proletariat with its own elements of political and general education: in other words, it furnishes the proletariat with weapons for fighting the bourgeoisie.

Further, as we have already seen, entire sections of the ruling classes are, by the advance of industry, precipitated into the proletariat, or are at least threatened in their conditions of existence. These also supply the proletariat with fresh elements of enlightenment and progress.

Finally, in times when the class struggle nears the decisive hour, the process of dissolution going on within the ruling class, in fact within the whole range of old society, assumes such a violent, glaring character that a small section of the ruling class cuts itself adrift and joins the revolutionary class, the class that holds the future in its hands. Just as, therefore, at an earlier period, a section of the nobility went over to the bourgeoisie, so now a portion of the bourgeoisie goes over to the proletariat, and in particular a portion of the bourgeois ideologists, who have raised themselves to the level of comprehending theoretically the historical movement as a whole. [. . .]

Hitherto every form of society has been based, as we have already seen, on the antagonism of oppressing and oppressed classes. But in order to oppress a class certain conditions must be assured to it under which it can, at least, continue its slavish existence. The serf, in the period of serfdom, raised himself to membership in the commune, just as the petty bourgeois, under the yoke of feudal absolutism, managed to develop into a bourgeois. The modern labourer, on the contrary, instead of rising with the progress of industry, sinks deeper and deeper below the conditions of existence of his own class. He becomes a pauper, and pauperism develops more rapidly than population and wealth. And here it becomes evident that the bourgeoisie is unfit any longer to be the ruling class in society, and to impose its conditions of existence upon society as an over-riding law. It is unfit to rule because it is incompetent to assure an existence to its slave within his slavery, because it cannot help letting him sink into such a state that it has to feed him instead of being fed by him. Society can no longer live under the bourgeoisie: in other words, its existence is no longer compatible with society.

The essential condition for the existence, and for the sway of the bourgeois class, is the formation and augmentation of capital; the condition for capital is wage labour. Wage labour rests exclusively on competition between the labourers. The advance of industry, whose involuntary promoter is the bourgeoisie, replaces the isolation of the labourers, due to competition, by their revolutionary combination, due to association. The development of modern industry, therefore, cuts from under its feet the very foundation on which the bourgeoisie produces and appropriates products. What the bourgeoisie, therefore, produces, above all, is its own gravediggers. Its fall and the victory of the proletariat are equally inevitable.

16(b) Karl Marx

Social Classes and Conflict

Excerpts from Karl Marx, *Capital*, vol. 3, 1893–4; 'Zur Kritik der Hegelschen Rechtsphilosophie: Einleitung', in *Deutsch-Französische Jarbücher*, 1844; *Communist Manifesto*, 1848; *The Eighteenth Brumaire of Louis Bonaparte*, 1852; *Theorien über den Mehrwert*, 1905–10. Reprinted in T. B. Bottomore and M. Rubel (eds.), *Karl Marx*, Watts, 1956; Penguin, 1963, pp. 186–98.

The owners of mere labour-power, the owners of capital and the landowners, whose respective sources of income are wages, profit and rent of land, or in other words, wage-labourers, capitalists and landowners, form the three great classes of modern society based on the capitalist mode of production.

The economic structure of modern society is indisputably most highly and classically developed in England. But even here the class structure does not appear in a pure form. Intermediate and transitional strata obscure the class boundaries even in this case, though very much less in the country than in the towns. However, this is immaterial for our analysis. We have seen that the constant tendency, the law of development of the capitalist mode of production, is to separate the means of production increasingly from labour, and to concentrate the scattered means of production more and more into large aggregates, thereby transforming labour into wage-labour and the means of production into capital. There corresponds to this tendency, in a different sphere, the independent separation of landed property from capital and labour, or the transformation of all landed property into a form which corresponds with the capitalist mode of production.

The first question to be answered is – what constitutes a class? The answer can be found by answering another question: What constitutes wage-labourers, capitalists and landlords as the three great social classes?

At first glance it might seem that the identity of revenues and of sources of revenue is responsible. The classes are three great social groups whose components, the individual members, live from wages, profit and rent respectively, that is, from the utilization of their labour power, capital and landed property.

However, from this point of view, doctors and officials would also form two distinct classes, for they belong to two different social groups, and the revenues of the members of each group come from the same source. The same would also be true of the infinite distinctions of interest and position which the social division of labour creates among workers as among capitalists and landowners; in the latter case, for instance, between owners of vineyards, farms, forests, mines and fisheries. ...

(*Manuscript ends*)

It is not a *radical* revolution, *universal human* emancipation, which is a Utopian dream for Germany, but rather a partial, *merely* political revolution which leaves the pillars of the building standing. What is the basis of a partial, merely political revolution? Simply this: *a fraction of civil society* emancipates itself and achieves a dominant position, a certain class undertakes, from its *particular situation,* a general emancipation of society. This class emanicipates society as a whole, but only on condition that the whole of society is in the same situation as this class, for example, that it possesses or can acquire money or culture.

No class in civil society can play this part unless it can arouse, in itself and in the masses, a moment of enthusiasm in which it associates and mingles with society in general, identifies itself with it, and is felt and recognized as the *general representative* of this society. Its aims and interests must genuinely be the aims and interests of society itself, of which it becomes in fact the social head and heart. It is only in the name of general interests that a particular class can claim general supremacy. In order to attain this liberating position and the political direction of all spheres of society, revolutionary energy and consciousness of its own power do not suffice. For a *popular revolution* and the *emancipation of a particular class* of civil society to coincide, for *one* class to represent the whole of society, another class must concentrate in itself all the evils of society, a particular class must embody and represent a general obstacle and limitation. A particular social sphere must be regarded as the *notorious crime* of the whole society, so that emancipation from this sphere appears as a general emancipation. For one class to be the liberating class *par excellence,* it is essential that another class should be openly the oppressing class. The negative significance of the French nobility and clergy produced the positive significance of the bourgeoisie, the class which stood next to them and opposed them.

But every class in Germany lacks the logic, insight, courage and clarity, which would make it a negative representative of society. Moreover, there is also lacking in every class the generosity of spirit which identifies itself, if only for a moment, with the popular mind, that genius which pushes material force to political power, that revolutionary daring which throws at its adversary the defiant phrase, *I am nothing and I should be everything*. The essence of German morality and honour, in classes as in individuals, is a *modest egoism* which displays, and allows others to display, its own narrowness. The relation between the different spheres of German society is therefore not dramatic, but epic. Each of these spheres begins to be aware of itself and to establish itself at the side of the others, not from the moment when it is oppressed, but from the moment that circumstances, without any action of its own, have created a new sphere which it can in turn oppress. Even *the moral sentiment of the German middle class* has no other basis than the consciousness of being the representative of the narrow and limited mediocrity of all the other classes. It is not therefore only the German kings who ascend their thrones *mal à propos*; each sphere of civil society suffers a defeat before gaining the victory ; it erects its own barrier before having destroyed the barrier which opposes it; it displays the narrowness of its views before having displayed their generosity, and thus every opportunity of playing an important role has passed before it properly existed, and each class, at the very moment when it begins its struggle against the class above it, remains involved in a struggle against the class beneath. For this reason, the princes are in conflict with the monarch, the bureaucracy with the nobility, the bourgeoisie with all of them, while the proletariat is already beginning its struggle with the bourgeoisie. The middle class hardly dares to conceive the idea of emancipation from its own point of view before the development of social conditions, and the progress of political theory, show that this point of view is already antiquated, or at least disputable.

In France it is enough to be something in order to desire to be everything. In Germany no one has the right to be anything without first renouncing everything. In France partial emancipation is a basis for complete emancipation. In Germany complete emancipation is a *conditio sine qua non* for any partial emancipation. In France it is the reality, in Germany the impossibility, of a progressive emancipation which must give birth to complete liberty. In France every class of the population is *politically idealistic* and considers itself first of all, not as a particular class, but as the representative of the general needs of society. The role of *liberator* can therefore pass successively in a dramatic movement to different classes in the population, until it finally reaches the class which achieves social freedom, no longer assuming certain conditions external to man, which are none the less created by human society, but organizing all the conditions of human life on the basis of social freedom. In Germany, on the contrary, where practical life is as little intellectual as intellectual life is practical, no class of civil society feels the need for, or the ability to achieve, general emancipation, until it is forced to it by its *immediate* situation, by *material* necessity, and by its *fetters themselves*.

Where is there, then, a *real* possibility of emancipation in Germany? This is our reply. A class must be formed which has *radical chains*, a class in civil society which is not a class of civil society, a class which is the dissolution of all classes, a sphere of society which has a universal character because its sufferings are universal, and which does not claim a *particular redress* because the wrong which is done to it is not a *particular wrong* but *wrong in general*. There must be formed a sphere of society which claims no *traditional* status but only a *human* status, a sphere which is not opposed to particular consequences but is totally opposed to the assumptions of the German political system, a sphere finally which cannot emancipate itself without emancipating itself from all the other spheres of society, without therefore emancipating all these other spheres, which is, in short, a *total loss* of humanity and which can only redeem itself by a *total redemption of humanity*. This dissolution of society, as a particular class, is the *proletariat*.

The proletariat is only beginning to form itself in Germany as a result of the industrial movement. For what constitutes the proletariat is not *naturally existing* poverty, but poverty *artificially produced*, is not the mass of people mechanically oppressed by the weight of society but the mass resulting from the *disintegration* of society, and above all from the disintegration of the middle class. Needless to say, however, the numbers of the proletariat are also increased by the victims of natural poverty and of Teutonic-Christian serfdom.

When the proletariat announces the *dissolution of the existing social order*, it only declares the *secret of its own existence*, for it constitutes the *effective* dissolution of this order. When the proletariat demands the *negation of private property* it only lays down as a *principle for society* what society has already made a principle *for the proletariat* and what the *latter* involuntarily embodies already as the negative result of society. Thus the proletarian has the same right, in relation to the new world which is coming into being, as the *German king* has in relation to the existing world when he calls the people *his* people or a horse *his* horse. In calling the people his private property, the king simply declares that the owner of private property is king.

Just as philosophy finds its *material* weapons in the proletariat, so the proletariat finds its *intellectual* weapons in philosophy. And once the lightning of thought has penetrated deeply into this virgin soil of the people, the *Germans* will emancipate themselves and become *men*.

Let us sum up these results. The emancipation of Germany is only possible *in practice* if one adopts the point of view of that theory according to which man is the highest being for man. Germany will not be able to emancipate itself from the *Middle Ages* unless it emancipates itself at the same time from the *partial* victories over the Middle Ages. In Germany *no* type of enslavement can be abolished unless *all* enslavement is destroyed. Germany, which likes to get to the bottom of things, can only make a revolution which upsets the whole order of things. The *emancipation of Germany* will be an *emancipation of man*. *Philosophy* is the *head* of this emancipation and the *proletariat* is its *heart*. Philosophy can only be realized by the abolition of the proletariat, and the proletariat can only be abolished by the realization of philosophy. [...]

The lower strata of the middle class – the small trades-people, shop-keepers and retired tradesmen generally, the handicraftsmen and peasants – all these sink gradually into the proletariat, partly because their diminutive capital does not suffice for the scale on which modern industry is carried on, and is swamped in the competition with the large capitalists, partly because their specialized skill is rendered worthless by new methods of production. Thus the proletariat is recruited from all classes of the population.

The small-holding peasants form a vast mass, the members of which live in similar conditions but without entering into manifold relations with one another. Their mode of production isolates them from one another instead of bringing them into mutual intercourse. ... In so far as millions of families live under economic conditions of existence that separate their mode of life, their interests and their culture from those of the other classes, and put them in hostile opposition to the latter, they form a class. In so far as there is merely a local inter-connection among these small-holding peasants, and the identity of their interests begets no community, no national bond and no political organization among them, they do not form a class.

What [Ricardo] forgets to mention is the continual increase in numbers of the middle classes, ... situated midway between the workers on one side and the capitalists and landowners on the other. These middle classes rest with all their weight upon the working class and at the same time increase the social security and power of the upper class.

17 Max Weber

Class, Status, Party

Excerpts from Max Weber, *Wirtschaft und Gesellschaft*, 1922, reprinted in Hans Gerth and C. Wright Mills (eds. and trans.), *From Max Weber: Essays in Sociology*, Routledge & Kegan Paul, 1948, pp. 180–95.

Economically determined power and the social order

Law exists when there is a probability that an order will be upheld by a specific staff of men who will use physical or psychical compulsion with the intention of obtaining conformity with the order, or of inflicting sanctions for infringement of it.[1] The structure of every legal order directly influences the distribution of power, economic or otherwise, within its respective community. This is true of all legal orders and not only that of the state. In general, we understand by 'power' the chance of a man or of a number of men to realize their own will in a communal action even against the resistance of others who are participating in the action.

'Economically conditioned' power is not, of course, identical with 'power' as such. On the contrary, the emergence of economic power may be the consequence of power existing on other grounds. Man does not strive for power only in order to enrich himself economically. Power, including economic power, may be valued 'for its own sake'. Very frequently the striving for power is also conditioned by the social 'honor' it entails. Not all power, however, entails social honor: the typical American Boss, as well as the typical big speculator, deliberately relinquishes social honor. Quite generally, 'mere economic' power, and especially 'naked' money power, is by no means a recognized basis of social honor. Nor is power the only basis of social honor. Indeed, social honor, or prestige, may even be the basis of political or economic power, and very frequently has been. Power, as well as honor, may be guaranteed by the legal order, but, at least normally, it is not their primary source. The legal order is rather an additional factor that enhances the chance to hold power or honor; but it cannot always secure them.

1. *Wirtschaft und Gesellschaft*, part III, chap. 4, pp. 631–40. The first sentence in paragraph one and the several definitions in this chapter which are in brackets do not appear in the original text. They have been taken from other contexts of *Wirtschaft und Gesellschaft*.

The way in which social honor is distributed in a community between typical groups participating in this distribution we may call the 'social order'. The social order and the economic order are, of course, similarly related to the 'legal order'. However, the social and the economic order are not identical. The economic order is for us merely the way in which economic goods and services are distributed and used. The social order is of course conditioned by the economic order to a high degree, and in its turn reacts upon it.

Now: 'classes', 'status groups' and 'parties' are phenomena of the distribution of power within a community.

Determination of class-situation by market-situation

In our terminology, 'classes' are not communities; they merely represent possible, and frequent, bases for communal action. We may speak of a 'class' when (a) a number of people have in common a specific causal component of their life chances, in so far as (b) this component is represented exclusively by economic interests in the possession of goods and opportunities for income, and (c) is represented under the conditions of the commodity or labor markets. [These points refer to 'class situation', which we may express more briefly as the typical chance for a supply of goods, external living conditions and personal life experiences, in so far as this chance is determined by the amount and kind of power, or lack of such, to dispose of goods or skills for the sake of income in a given economic order. The term 'class' refers to any group of people that is found in the same class situation.]

It is the most elemental economic fact that the way in which the disposition over material property is distributed among a plurality of people, meeting competitively in the market for the purpose of exchange, in itself creates specific life chances. According to the law of marginal utility this mode of distribution excludes the non-owners from competing for highly valued goods; it favors the owners and, in fact, gives to them a monopoly to acquire such goods. Other things being equal, this mode of distribution monopolizes the opportunities for profitable deals for all those who, provided with goods, do not necessarily have to exchange them. It increases, at least generally, their power in price wars with those who, being propertyless, have nothing to offer but their services in native form or goods in a form constituted through their own labor, and who above all are compelled to get rid of these products in order barely to subsist. This mode of distribution gives to the propertied a monopoly on the possibility of transferring property from the sphere of use as a 'fortune', to the sphere of 'capital goods'; that is, it gives them the entrepreneurial function and all chances to share directly or indirectly in returns on capital. All this holds true within the area in which pure market conditions prevail. 'Property' and 'lack of property' are, therefore, the basic categories of all class situations. It does not matter whether these two categories become effective in price wars or in competitive struggles.

Within these categories, however, class situations are further differentiated: on the one hand, according to the kind of property that is usable for returns; and, on the other hand, according to the kind of services that can be offered in the market. Ownership of domestic buildings; productive establishments; [. . .] disposition over products of one's own labor or of others' labor differing according to their various distances from consumability; disposition over transferable monopolies of any kind – all these distinctions differentiate the class situations of the propertied just as does the 'meaning' which they can and do give to the utilization of property, especially to property which has money equivalence. Accordingly, the propertied, for instance, may belong to the class of rentiers or to the class of entrepreneurs.

Those who have no property but who offer services are differentiated just as much according to their kinds of services as according to the way in which they make use of these services, in a continuous or discontinuous relation to a recipient. But always this is the generic connotation of the concept of class: that the kind of chance in the *market* is the decisive moment which presents a common condition for the individual's fate. 'Class situation' is, in this sense, ultimately 'market situation'. The effect of naked possession *per se,* which among cattle breeders gives the non-owning slave or serf into the power of the cattle owner, is only a fore-runner of real 'class' formation. However, in the cattle loan and in the naked severity of the law of debts in such communities, for the first time mere 'possession' as such emerges as decisive for the fate of the individual. This is very much in contrast to the agricultural communities based on labor. The creditor–debtor relation becomes the basis of 'class situations' only in those cities where a 'credit market', however primitive, with rates of interest increasing according to the extent of dearth and a factual monopolization of credits, is developed by a plutocracy. Therewith 'class struggles' begin.

Those men whose fate is not determined by the chance of using goods or services for themselves on the market, e.g. slaves, are not, however, a 'class' in the technical sense of the term. They are, rather, a 'status group'.

Communal action flowing from class interest

According to our terminology, the factor that creates 'class' is unambiguously economic interest, and indeed, only those interests involved in the existence of the 'market'. Nevertheless, the concept of 'class-interest' is an ambiguous one: even as an empirical concept it is ambiguous as soon as one understands by it something other than the factual direction of interests following with a certain probability from the class situation for a certain 'average' of those people subjected to the class situation. The class situation and other circumstances remaining the same, the direction in which the individual worker, for instance, is likely to pursue his interests may vary widely, according to whether he is constitutionally qualified for the task at hand to a high, to an average, or to a low degree. In the same way, the direction of interests may vary according to whether or not a *communal* action of a larger or smaller portion of those commonly affected by the 'class situation', or even an association among them, e.g. a 'trade union', has grown out of the class situation from which the individual may or may not expect promising results. [Communal action refers to that action which is oriented to the feeling of the actors that they belong together. Societal action, on the other hand, is oriented to a rationally motivated adjustment of interest.] The rise of societal or even of communal action from a common class situation is by no means a universal phenomenon.

The class situation may be restricted in its effects to the generation of essentially *similar* reactions, that is to say, within our terminology, of 'mass actions'. However, it may not have even this result. Furthermore, often merely an amorphous communal action emerges. For example, the 'murmuring' of the workers known in ancient oriental ethics: the moral disapproval of the work-master's conduct, which in its practical significance was probably equivalent to an increasingly typical phenomenon of precisely the latest industrial development, namely, the 'slow down' (the deliberate limiting of work effort) of laborers by virtue of tacit agreement. The degree in which 'communal action' and possibly 'societal action', emerges from the 'mass actions' of the members of a class is linked to general cultural conditions, especially to those of an intellectual sort. It is also linked to the extent of the contrasts that have already evolved, and is especially linked to the *transparency* of the connections between the causes and the consequences of the 'class situation'. For however different life chances may be, this fact in itself, according to all experience, by no means gives birth to 'class action' (communal action by the members of a class). The fact of being conditioned and the results of the class situation must be distinctly recognizable. For only then the contrast of life chances can be felt not as an absolutely given fact to be accepted, but as a resultant from either (a) the given distribution of property, or (b) the structure of the concrete economic order. It is only then that people may react against the class structure not only through acts of an intermittent and irrational protest, but in the form of rational association. There have been 'class situations' of the first category (a), of a specially naked and transparent sort, in the urban centres of Antiquity and during the Middle Ages; especially then, when great fortunes were accumulated by factually monopolized trading in industrial products of these localities or in foodstuffs. Furthermore, under certain circumstances, in the rural economy of the most diverse periods, when agriculture was increasingly exploited in a profit-making manner. The most important historical example of the second category (b) is the class situation of the modern 'proletariat'.

Types of 'class struggle'

Thus every class may be the carrier of any one of the possibly innumerable forms of 'class action', but this is not necessarily so. In any case, a class does not in itself constitute a community. To treat 'class' conceptually as having the same value as 'community' leads to distortion. That men in the same class situation regularly react in mass actions to such tangible situations as economic ones in the direction of those interests that are most adequate to their average number is an important and after all simple fact for the understanding of historical events. Above all, this fact must not lead to that kind of pseudo-scientific operation with the concepts of 'class' and 'class interests' so frequently found these days, and which has found its most classic expression in the statement of a talented author, that the individual may be in error concerning his interests but that the 'class' is 'infallible' about its interests. Yet, if classes as such are not communities, nevertheless class situations emerge only on the basis of communalization. The communal action that brings forth class situations, however, is not basically action between members of the identical class; it is an action between members of different classes. Communal actions that directly determine the class situation of the worker and the entrepreneur are: the labor market, the commodities market and the capitalistic enterprise. But, in its turn, the existence of a capitalistic enterprise presupposes that a very specific communal action exists and that it is specifically structured to protect the possession of goods *per se*, and especially the power of individuals to dispose, in principle freely, over the means of production. The existence of a capitalistic enterprise is preconditioned by a specific kind of 'legal order'. Each kind of class situation, and above all when it rests upon the power of property *per se*, will become most clearly efficacious when all other determinants of reciprocal relations are, as far as possible, eliminated in their significance. It is in this way that the utilization of the power of property in the market obtains its most sovereign importance.

Now 'status groups' hinder the strict carrying through of the sheer market principle. In the present context they are of interest to us only from this one point of view. Before we briefly consider them, note that not much of a general nature can be said about the more specific kinds of antagonism between 'classes' (in our meaning of the term). The great shift, which has been going on continuously in the past, and up to our times, may be summarized although at the cost of some precision: the struggle in which class situations are effective has progressively shifted from consumption credit toward, first, competitive struggles in the commodity market and, then, toward price wars on the labor market. The 'class struggles' of antiquity – to the extent that they were genuine class struggles and not struggles between status groups – were initially carried on by indebted peasants, and perhaps also by artisans threatened by debt bondage and struggling against urban creditors. For debt bondage is the normal result of the differentiation of wealth in commercial cities, especially in seaport cities. A similar situation has existed among cattle breeders. Debt relationships as such produced class action up to the time of Cataline. Along with this, and with an increase in provision of grain for the city by transporting it from the outside, the struggle over the means of sustenance emerged. It centred in the first place around the provision of bread and the determination of the price of bread. It lasted throughout antiquity and the entire Middle Ages. The propertyless as such flocked together against those who actually and supposedly were interested in the dearth of bread. This fight spread until it involved all those commodities essential to the way of life and to handicraft production. There were only incipient discussions of wage disputes in antiquity and in the Middle Ages. But they have been slowly increasing up into modern times. In the earlier periods they were completely secondary to slave rebellions as well as to fights in the commodity market.

The propertyless of antiquity and of the Middle Ages protested against monopolies, pre-emption, forestalling and the withholding of goods from the market in order to raise prices. Today the central issue is the determination of the price of labor.

This transition is represented by the fight for access to the market and for the determination of the price of products. Such fights went on between merchants and workers in the putting-out system of domestic handicraft during the transition to modern times. Since it is quite a general phenomenon we must mention here that the class antagonisms that are conditioned through the market situation are usually most bitter between those who actually and directly participate as opponents in price wars. It is not the rentier, the shareholder and the banker who suffer the ill will of the worker, but almost exclusively the manufacturer and the business executives who are the direct opponents of workers in price wars. This is so in spite of the fact that it is precisely the cash boxes of the rentier, the shareholder and the banker into which the more or less 'unearned' gains flow, rather than into the pockets of the manufacturers or of the business executives. This simple state of affairs has very frequently been decisive for the role the class situation has played in the formation of political parties. For example, it has made possible the varieties of patriarchal socialism and the frequent attempts – formerly, at least – of threatened status groups to form alliances with the proletariat against the 'bourgeoisie'.

Status honor

In contrast to classes, *status groups* are normally communities. They are, however, often of an amorphous kind. In contrast to the purely economically determined 'class situation' we wish to designate as 'status situation' every typical component of the life fate of men that is determined by a specific, positive or negative, social estimation of *honor*. This honor may be connected with any quality shared by a plurality, and, of course, it can be knit to a class situation: class distinctions are linked in the most varied ways with status distinctions. Property as such is not always recognized as a status qualification, but in the long run it is, and with extraordinary regularity. In the subsistence economy of the organized neighborhood, very often the richest man is simply the chieftain. However, this often means only an honorific preference. For example, in the so-called pure modern 'democracy', that is, one devoid of any expressly ordered status privileges for individuals, it may be that only the families coming under approximately the same tax class dance with one another. This example is reported of certain smaller Swiss cities. But status honor need not necessarily be linked with a class situation. On the contrary, it normally stands in sharp opposition to the pretensions of sheer property.

Both propertied and propertyless people can belong to the same status group, and frequently they do with very tangible consequences. This 'equality' of social esteem may, however, in the long run become quite precarious. The 'equality' of status among the American 'gentlemen', for instance, is expressed by the fact that outside the subordination determined by the different functions of 'business', it would be considered strictly repugnant – wherever the old tradition still prevails – if even the richest 'chief', while playing billiards or cards in his club in the evening, would not treat his 'clerk' as in every sense fully his equal in birthright. It would be repugnant if the American 'chief' would bestow upon his 'clerk' the condescending 'benevolence' marking a distinction of 'position', which the German chief can never dissever from his attitude. This is one of the most important reasons why in America the German 'clubby-ness' has never been able to attain the attraction that the American clubs have.

Guarantees of status stratification

In content, status honor is normally expressed by the fact that above all else a specific *style of life* can be expected from all those who wish to belong to the circle. Linked with this expectation are restrictions on 'social' intercourse (that is, intercourse which is not subservient to economic or any other of business's 'functional' purposes). These restrictions may confine normal marriages to within the status circle and may lead to complete endogamous closure. As soon as there is not a mere individual and socially irrelevant imitation of another style of life, but an agreed-upon communal action of this closing character, the 'status' development is under way.

In its characteristic form, stratification by 'status groups' on the basis of conventional styles of life evolves at the present time in the United States out of the traditional democracy. For example, only the resident of a certain street ('the street') is considered as belonging to 'society', is qualified for social intercourse, and is visited and invited. Above all, this differentiation evolves in such a way as to make for strict submission to the fashion that is dominant at a given time in society. This submission to fashion also exists among men in America to a degree unknown in Germany. Such submission is considered to be an indication of the fact that a given man *pretends* to qualify as a gentleman. This submission decides, at least *prima facie*, that he will be treated as such. And this recognition becomes just as important for his employment chances in 'swank' establishments, and above all, for social intercourse and marriage with 'esteemed' families, as the qualification for dueling among the Germans in the Kaiser's day. [...] The development of status is essentially a question of stratification resting upon usurpation. Such usurpation is the normal origin of almost all status honor. But the road from this purely conventional situation to legal privilege, positive or negative, is easily traveled as soon as a certain stratification of the social order has in fact been 'lived in' and has achieved stability by virtue of a stable distribution of economic power.

'Ethnic' segregation and 'caste'

Where the consequences have been realized to their full extent, the status group evolves into a closed 'caste'. Status distinctions are then guaranteed not merely by conventions and laws, but also by *rituals*. This occurs in such a way that every physical contact with a member of any caste that is considered to be 'lower' by the members of a 'higher' caste is considered as making for a ritualistic impurity and to be a stigma which must be expiated by a religious act. Individual castes develop quite distinct cults and gods.

In general, however, the status structure reaches such extreme consequences only where there are underlying differences which are held to be 'ethnic'. The 'caste' is, indeed, the normal form in which ethnic communities usually live side by side in a 'societalized' manner. These ethnic communities believe in blood relationship and exclude exogamous marriage and social intercourse. Such a caste situation is part of the phenomenon of 'pariah' peoples and is found all over the world. These people form communities, acquire specific occupational traditions of handicrafts or of other arts, and cultivate a belief in their ethnic community. They live in a 'diaspora' strictly segregated from all personal intercourse, except that of an unavoidable sort, and their situation is legally precarious. Yet, by virtue of their economic indispensability, they are tolerated, indeed, frequently privileged, and they live in interspersed political communities. The Jews are the most impressive historical example.

A 'status' segregation grown into a 'caste' differs in its structure from a mere 'ethnic' segregation: the caste structure transforms the horizontal and unconnected coexistences of ethnically segregated groups into a vertical social system of super- and subordination. Correctly formulated: a comprehensive societalization integrates the ethnically divided communities into specific political and communal action. In their consequences they differ precisely in this way: ethnic coexistences condition a mutual repulsion and disdain but allow each ethnic community to consider its own honor as the highest one ; the caste structure brings about a social subordination and an acknowledgment of 'more honor' in favour of the privileged caste and status groups. This is due to the fact that in the caste structure ethnic distinctions as such have become 'functional' distinctions within the political societalization (warriors, priests, artisans that are politically important for war and for building, and so on) But even pariah people who are most despised are usually apt to continue cultivating in some manner that which is equally peculiar to ethnic and to status communities: the belief in their own specific 'honor'. This is the case with the Jews.

Only with the negatively privileged status groups does the 'sense of dignity' take a specific deviation. A sense of dignity is the precipitation in individuals of social honor and of conventional demands which a positively privileged status group raises for the deportment of its members. The sense of dignity that characterizes positively privileged status groups is naturally related to their 'being' which does not transcend itself, that is, it is to their 'beauty and excellence' (καλο-κάφαθια). Their kingdom is 'of this world'. They live for the present and by exploiting their great past. The sense of dignity of the negatively privileged strata naturally refers to a future lying beyond the present, whether it is of this life or of another. In other words, it must be nurtured by the belief in a providential 'mission' and by a belief in a specific honour before God. The 'chosen people's' dignity is nurtured by a belief either that in the beyond 'the last will be the first', or that in this life a Messiah will appear to bring forth into the light of the world which has cast them out the hidden honor of the pariah people. [. .] But selection is far from being the only, or the predominant, way in which status groups are formed. Political membership or class situation has at all times been at least as frequently decisive. And today the class situation is by far the predominant factor, for of course the possibility of a style of life expected for members of a status group is usually conditioned economically.

Status privileges

For all practical purposes, stratification by status goes hand in hand with a monopolization of ideal and material goods or opportunities, in a manner we have come to know as typical. Besides the specific status honor, which always rests upon distance and exclusiveness, we find all sorts of material monopolies. Such honorific preferences may consist of the privilege of wearing special costumes, of eating special dishes taboo to others, of carrying arms – which is most obvious in its consequences – the right to pursue certain non-professional dilettante artistic practices, e.g. to play certain musical instruments. Of course, material monopolies provide the most effective motives for the exclusiveness of a status group; although, in themselves, they are rarely sufficient, almost always they come into play to some extent. Within a status circle there is the question of intermarriage: the interest of the families in the monopolization of potential bridegrooms is at least of equal importance and is parallel to the interest in the monopolization of daughters. The daughters of the circle must be provided for. With an increased inclosure of the status group, the conventional preferential opportunities for special employment grow into a legal monopoly of special offices for the members. Certain goods become objects for monopolization by status groups. In the typical fashion these include 'entailed estates' and frequently also the possessions of serfs or bondsmen and, finally, special trades. This monopolization occurs positively when the status group is exclusively entitled to own and to manage them; and negatively when, in order to maintain its specific way of life, the status group must *not* own and manage them.

The decisive role of a 'style of life' in status 'honor' means that status groups are the specific bearers of all 'conventions'. In whatever way it may be manifest, all 'stylization' of life either originates in status groups or is at least conserved by them. Even if the principles of status conventions differ greatly, they reveal certain typical traits, especially among those strata which are most privileged. Quite generally, among privileged status groups there is a status disqualification that operates against the performance of common physical labor. This disqualification is now 'setting in' in America against the old tradition of esteem for labor. Very frequently every rational economic pursuit, and especially 'entrepreneurial activity', is looked upon as a disqualification of status. Artistic and literary activity is also considered as degrading work as soon as it is exploited for income, or at least when it is connected with hard physical exertion. An example is the sculptor working like a mason in his dusty smock as over against the painter in his salon-like 'studio' and those forms of musical practice that are acceptable to the status group.

Economic conditions and effects of status stratification

The frequent disqualification of the gainfully employed as such is a direct result of the principle of status stratification peculiar to the social order, and of course, of this principle's opposition to a distribution of power which is regulated exclusively through the market. These two factors operate along with various individual ones, which will be touched upon below.

We have seen above that the market and its processes 'knows no personal distinctions': 'functional' interests dominate it. It knows nothing of 'honor'. The status order means precisely the reverse, viz.: stratification in terms of 'honor' and of styles of life peculiar to status groups as such. If mere economic acquisition and naked economic power still bearing the stigma of its extra-status origin could bestow upon anyone who has won it the same honor as those who are interested in status by virtue of style of life claim for themselves, the status order would be threatened at its very root. This is the more so as, given equality of status honor, property *per se* represents an addition even if it is not overtly acknowledged to be such. Yet if such economic acquisition and power gave the agent any honor at all, his wealth would result in his attaining more honor than those who successfully claim honor by virtue of style of life. Therefore all groups having interests in the status order react with special sharpness precisely against the pretensions of purely economic acquisition. In most cases they react the more vigorously the more they feel themselves threatened. Calderon's respectful treatment of the peasant, for instance, as opposed to Shakespeare's simultaneous and ostensible disdain of the *canaille* illustrates the different way in which a firmly structural status order reacts as compared with a status order that has become economically precarious. This is an example of a state of affairs that recurs everywhere. Precisely because of the rigorous reactions against the claims of property *per se*, the 'parvenu' is never accepted, personally and without reservation, by the privileged status groups, no matter how completely his style of life has been adjusted to theirs. They will only accept his descendants who have been educated in the conventions of their status group and who have never besmirched its honor by their own economic labor.

As to the general *effect* of the status order, only one consequence can be stated, but it is a very important one: the hindrance of the free development of the market occurs first for those goods which status groups directly withheld from free exchange by monopolization. This monopolization may be effected either legally or conventionally. For example, in many Hellenic cities during the epoch of status groups, and also originally in Rome, the inherited estate (as is shown by the old formula for indiction against spendthrifts) was monopolized just as were the estates of knights, peasants, priests and especially the clientele of the craft and merchant guilds. The market is restricted, and the power of naked property *per se*, which gives its stamp to 'class formation', is pushed into the background. The results of this process can be most varied. Of course, they do not necessarily weaken the contrasts in the economic situation. Frequently they strengthen these contrasts, and in any case, where stratification by status permeates a community as strongly as was the case in all political communities of antiquity and of the Middle Ages, one can never speak of a genuinely free market competition as we understand it today. There are wider effects than this direct exclusion of special goods from the market. From the contrariety between the status order and the purely economic order mentioned above, it follows that in most instances the notion of honor peculiar to status absolutely abhors that which is essential to the market: higgling. Honor abhors higgling among peers and occasionally it taboos higgling for the members of a status group in general. Therefore, everywhere some status groups, and usually the most influential, consider almost any kind of overt participation in economic acquisition as absolutely stigmatizing.

With some over-simplification, one might thus say that 'classes' are stratified according to their relations to the production and acquisition of goods; whereas 'status groups' are stratified according to the principles of their *consumption* of goods as represented by special 'styles of life'.

An 'occupational group' is also a status group. For normally, it successfully claims social honor only by virtue of the special style of life which may be determined by it. The differences between classes and status groups frequently overlap. It is precisely those status communities most strictly segregated in terms of honor (viz. the Indian castes) who today show, although within very rigid limits, a relatively high degree of indifference to pecuniary income. However, the Brahmins seek such income in many different ways.

As to the general economic conditions making for the predominance of stratification by 'status', only very little can be said. When the bases of the acquisition and distribution of goods are relatively stable, stratification by status is favored. Every technological repercussion and economic transformation threatens stratification by status and pushes the class situation into the foreground. Epochs and countries in which the naked class situation is of predominant significance are regularly the periods of technical and economic transformations. And every slowing down of the shifting of economic stratifications leads, in due course, to the growth of status structures and makes for a resuscitation of the important role of social honor.

Parties

Whereas the genuine place of 'classes' is within the economic order, the place of 'status groups' is within the social order, that is, within the sphere of the distribution of 'honor'. From within these spheres, classes and status groups influence one another and they influence the legal order and are in turn influenced by it. But 'parties' live in a house of 'power'.

Their action is oriented toward the acquisition of social 'power', that is to say, toward influencing a communal action no matter what its content may be. In principle, parties may exist in a social 'club' as well as in a 'state'. As over against the actions of classes and status groups, for which this is not necessarily the case, the communal actions of 'parties' always mean a societalization. For party actions are always directed toward a goal which is striven for in planned manner. This goal may be a 'cause' (the party may aim at realizing a program for ideal or material purposes), or the goal may be 'personal' (sinecures, power, and from these, honor for the leader and the followers of the party). Usually the party action aims at all these simultaneously. Parties are, therefore, only possible within communities that are societalized, that is, which have some rational order and a staff of persons available who are ready to enforce it. For parties aim precisely at influencing this staff, and if possible, to recruit it from party followers.

In any individual case, parties may represent interests determined through 'class situation' or 'status situation', and they may recruit their following respectively from one or the other. But they need be neither purely 'class' nor purely 'status' parties. In most cases they are partly class parties and partly status parties, but sometimes they are neither. They may represent ephemeral or enduring structures. Their means of attaining power may be quite varied, ranging from naked violence of any sort to canvassing for votes with coarse or subtle means: money, social influence, the force of speech, suggestion, clumsy hoax and so on to the rougher or more artful tactics of obstruction in parliamentary bodies.

The sociological structure of parties differs in a basic way according to the kind of communal action which they struggle to influence. Parties also differ according to whether or not the community is stratified by status or by classes. Above all else, they vary according to the structure of domination within the community. For their leaders normally deal with the conquest of a community. They are, in the general concept which is maintained here, not only products of specially modern forms of domination. We shall also designate as parties the ancient and medieval 'parties', despite the fact that their structure differs basically from the structure of modern parties. By virtue of these structural differences of domination it is impossible to say anything about the structure of parties without discussing the structural forms of social domination *per se*. Parties, which are always structures struggling for domination, are very frequently organized in a very strict 'authoritarian' fashion. ...

Concerning 'classes', 'status groups' and 'parties', it must be said in general that they necessarily presuppose a comprehensive societalization, and especially a political framework of communal action, within which they operate. This does not mean that parties would be confined by the frontiers of any individual political community. On the contrary, at all times it has been the order of the day that the societalization (even when it aims at the use of military force in common) reaches. beyond the frontiers of politics. This has been the case in the solidarity of interests among the Oligarchs and among the democrats in Hellas, among the Guelfs and among Ghibellines in the Middle Ages, and within the Calvinist party during the period of religious struggles. It has been the case up to the solidarity of the landlords (international congress of agrarian landlords), and has continued among princes (holy alliance, Karlsbad decrees), socialist workers, conservatives (the longing of Prussian conservatives for Russian intervention in 1850). But their aim is not necessarily the establishment of new international political, i.e. *territorial*, dominion. In the main they aim to influence the existing dominion.[2]

2. The posthumously published text breaks off here. We omit an incomplete sketch of types of 'warrior estates'.

18 Talcott Parsons

Social Classes and Class Conflict in the Light of Recent
Sociological Theory

Excerpts from Talcott Parsons, *Essays in Sociological Theory*, Free Press, 1964,
pp. 323–35. First published in 1948.

The Marxian view as a point of departure

Nineteen hundred and forty-eight is the centenary of the Communist
Manifesto – the first major theoretical statement of Marxism – and
some stocktaking of where Marx and Engels stood in an important
line of the development of social science rather than only as the ideological founders of 'scientific socialism' is in order. [. . .]

From my point of view, looking toward the development of modern
sociological theory, Marx represented a first major step beyond the
point at which the Utilitarian theorists, who set the frame of reference
within which the classical economics developed, stood. Marx introduced no fundamental modification of the general theory of human
social behavior in the terms which this school of thought represented.
He did, however, unlike the Utilitarians, see and emphasize the massive
fact of the structuring of interests rather than treating them as distributed at random. The structure of the productive forces which Marx
outlined for capitalist society is real and of fundamental importance.
Naturally, many refinements in the presentation of the structural facts
and their historical development have been introduced since Marx's
day, but the fundamental fact is certainly correct. The theory of class
conflict is an integral part of this. It is of great interest to sociology.

Marx, however, tended to treat the socio-economic structure of
capitalist enterprise as a single indivisible entity rather than breaking
it down analytically into a set of the distinct variables involved in it.
It is this analytical breakdown which is for present purposes the most
distinctive feature of modern sociological analysis, and which must be
done to take advantage of advances that have taken place. It results
both in a modification of the Marxian view of the system itself and
enables the establishment of relations to other aspects of the total
social system, aspects of which Marx was unaware. This change results
in an important modification of Marx's empirical perspective in relation to the class problem as in other contexts. The primary structural
emphasis no longer falls on the orientation of capitalistic enterprise to

profit and the theory of exploitation but rather on the structure of occupational roles within the system of industrial society.

Thus class conflict and its structural bases are seen in a somewhat different perspective. Conflict does not have the same order of inevitability, but is led back to the interrelations of a series of more particular factors, the combinations of which may vary. Exactly how serious the element of conflict is becomes a matter of empirical investigation. Similarly, the Marxian utopianism about the classlessness of communist society is brought into serious question. There is a sense in which the Marxian view of the inevitability of class conflict is the obverse of the utopian factor in Marxian thought.

It should, however, be clearly noted how important Marx was in the development of modern sociological thought. All three of the writers who may be regarded as its most important theoretical founders – Vilfredo Pareto, Emile Durkheim and Max Weber – were profoundly concerned with the problems raised by Marx. Each of them took the Marxian view with great seriousness as compared with its Utilitarian background, but none of them ended up as a Marxian. Each pushed on to a further development in a distinctive direction which in spite of the diversity of their backgrounds contains a striking common element. (Parsons, 1949).

The approach to the analysis of social stratification in terms of modern sociological theory

On the basis of modern sociological approach, it may perhaps be said that Marx looked at the structure of capitalistic enterprise and generalized a social system from it, including the class structure and, to him, the inevitable conflicts involved in it. Conversely, the concept of the generalized social system is the basis of modern sociological thinking. Analysed in this framework, both capitalistic enterprise and social stratification are seen in the context of their role in such a social system. The organization of production and social stratification are, of course, both variable in these terms, though also functionally related to each other. For the functional basis of the phenomena of stratification, it is necessary to analyse the problem of integrating and ordering social relationships within a social system. Some set of norms governing relations of superiority and inferiority is an inherent need of every stable social system. There will be immense variation, but this is a constant point of reference. Such a patterning or ordering is the stratification system of the society.

As with all other major structural elements of the social system, the norms governing its stratification tend to become institutionalized;

that is, moral sentiments crystallize about them and the whole system of motivational elements (including both disinterested and self-interested components) tends to be structured in support of conformity to them. There is a system of sanctions, both formal and informal, in support; so that deviant tendencies are met with varying degrees and kinds of disapproval, withdrawal of co-operation, and positive infliction of punishment. Conversely, there are rewards for conformity and institutionalized achievements (Parsons, 1954).

It follows that in relation to the problem of social class as in other fields, the general problem of economic motivation must be viewed in an institutional context. Even the system of profit seeking of modern capitalism is, there is abundant evidence, an institutionalized system. To be sure, it grew up as a result of emancipation from previous institutional controls in a pre-capitalistic order, but it could not have become established and stabilized to the extent that actually happened had it not had a positive system of moral sentiments underlying it and had it not acquired an institutional status of its own. The Marxian interpretation of this problem tends to see the structuring and control of self-interest only in terms of the realistic situation in which people are placed. Modern sociological theory accedes fully to the importance of this aspect, but insists that it must be seen in combination with a structure of institutionalized moral sentiments as well, so that conformity is determined by a system of mutually reinforcing situational pressures and subjective motivational elements, which in one sense are obverse aspects of the same process.

The fundamentals of stratification in a modern industrialized social system

The distinctive feature of this structure called 'social stratification' is that it ranks individuals in the general social hierarchy in generalized terms, not in any one specific context. For the sake of simplicity, we may first speak specifically of the importance of two such contexts in a modern industrial society and then of the articulations between them.

Looked at in the large, by far the most prominent structure of modern Western society is that organized around the 'work' people do, whether this work is in the field of economic enterprise, of governmental function, or of various other types of private non-profit activity, such as that of our own academic profession. The extremely elaborate division of labor, which permits a tremendous specialization of functions of this sort, of course necessitates an equally elaborate system of exchange, where the products of the work of specialized groups (whether they be material or immaterial) are made available to those who can utilize them, and vice versa, the specialist is enabled to live without performing innumerable functions for himself, because he has access to the results of the work of innumerable others. Similarly, there must be a property system which regulates claims to transferable entities, material or immaterial, and thereby secures rights in means of life and in the facilities which are necessary for the performance of function. This whole complex of structural elements in our society may be called 'the instrumental complex'. Its three fundamental elements – occupation, exchange and property – are all inextricably interdependent.

On a high level of the structural differentiation of a social system, the occupational system seems to be the least variable of the three and thus in a certain sense structurally the most fundamental. Elaboration of the system of exchange and its segregation from functionally irrelevant contexts are certainly essential. But there may be great variation in the extent to which the units in the exchange process enjoy autonomy in their decisions and are thus free to be oriented to their own 'profit' or act merely as agents of a more comprehensive organization. Similarly, though presumably something like the Roman-modern institution of ownership is called for, the organization units in which such rights inhere may also vary, and with them the line between property and contractual rights.

Within such ranges of variation, a highly developed system of occupational roles, with functional considerations dominating them, will tend to have certain relatively constant features. Perhaps the most important of these features, seen in comparative perspective, is its inherently 'individualistic' character. That is, the status of the individual must be determined on grounds essentially peculiar to himself, notably his own personal qualities, technical competence, and his own decisions about his occupational career and with respect to which he is not identified with any solidary group.

This is, of course, not in the least to suggest that he has complete freedom; he is subject to all manner of pressures, many of which are from various points of view 'irrational'. It is nevertheless fundamental that status and role allocation and the processes of mobility from status to status are in terms of the individual as a unit and not of solidary groups, like kinship groups, castes, village communities, etc.

There is, furthermore, an inherent hierarchical aspect to such a system. There are two fundamental functional bases on the hierarchical aspect. One is the differentiation of levels of skill and competence involved in the many different functional roles. The requirement of rare abilities on the one hand and of competence which can only be acquired by prolonged and difficult training on the other make such differentiation inherent. Secondly, organization on an ever increasing scale is a fundamental feature of such a system. Such organization naturally involves centralization and differentiation of leadership and authority ; so that those who take responsibility for coordinating the actions of many others must have a different status in important respects from those who are essentially in the role of carrying out specifications laid down by others. From a sociological point of view, one of the fundamental problems in such a system is the way in which these basic underlying differentiations get structured into institutionalized status differentiations.

The second major context of an industrialized social system which is relevant to its stratification is that of kinship. The fundamental principle of kinship relationships is that of the solidarity of the members of the kinship unit which precludes individualistic differentiation of fortune and status in the sense in which this is fundamental to the occupational system. In other societies, extended kinship units are very prominent indeed. In our society, the size of the unit has been reduced to a relative minimum – the conjugal family of parents and immature children. Only on this basis is it compatible with our occupational system at all. Nevertheless, this minimum is fundamental to our social system and differentiations of status, except those involved in age and sex roles, cannot be tolerated within it. The same individual who has a role in the occupational system is also a member of the family unit. In the latter context, his status must be shared within broad limits by the others, irrespective of their personal competence, qualities and deserts. The articulation of the two is possible only by virtue of the fact that in the type case only one member of a family unit, the husband or father, is in the fullest sense normally a functioning member of the occupational system. Important though this degree of segregation of the two is, for it to be complete would be functionally impossible.

Wives, by virtue of at least different qualities and achievements than those of their husbands, must in the relevant contexts share their status. This means that criteria and symbols of status relevant to the family must be extended to realms outside the sphere of the same order of functionally utilitarian considerations on which a woman's husband's status in his occupation is based. The style of life of a family and its implication in the realm of feminine activities, however dependent it may be on a husband's income, precludes that total status should be a simple function of the 'shop' concerns of a man's occupational world. Equally important, children must share the status of their parents if there is to be a family system at all. If the status of the parents is hierarchically differentiated, there will inevitably be an element of differential access to opportunity.

It is only in terms of the articulation of these two fundamentals, the instrumental complex and kinship, that I should speak of social class in a sociological sense. A class may then be defined as a plurality of kinship units which, in those respects where status in a hierarchical context is shared by their members, have approximately equal status. The class status of an individual, therefore, is that which he shares with the other members in an effective kinship unit. We have a class system, therefore, only in so far as the differentiations inherent in our occupational structure, with its differential relations to the exchange system and to property, remuneration, etc., has become ramified out into a system of strata, which involve differentiations of family living based partly on income, standard of life and style of life, and, of course, differential access for the younger generation to opportunity as well as different pressures to which they are subject. There is no doubt that everywhere that modern industrial society has existed there has been a class system in this sense. There are, however, considerable variations from one society to another, particularly between the European versions of industrial capitalism and the American. [. . .]

The analysis of class conflict in sociological terms

The above sociological analysis of social stratification is based heavily on the general view that stratification is to an important degree an integrating structure in the social system. The ordering of relationships in this context is necessary to stability. This is necessary precisely because of the importance of potential though often latent conflicts. Therefore, the problem of class conflict may be approached in terms of an analysis of these latent conflicts and of the ways in which the institutional integration of the system does and does not succeed in developing adequate control mechanisms. The following principal aspects of the tendency to develop class conflict in our type of social system may be mentioned.

1. There is an inherently competitive aspect of our individualistic occupational system. Because it is differentiated on a prestige scale and because there is individual choice of occupation and a measure of equality of opportunity, there will inevitably be some differentiation into winners and losers. Certain psychological consequences of such situations are known. There will be certain tendencies to arrogance on the part of some winners and to resentment and to a 'sour grapes' attitude on the part of some losers. The extent to which the system is institutionalized in terms of genuine standards of fair competition is the critical problem.

2. The role of organization means that there must be an important part played by discipline and authority. Discipline and authority do not exist on a grand scale without generating some resistance. Some form, therefore, of structuring in terms of an opposition of sentiments and interests between those in authority and those subject to it is endemic in such a system. The whole problem of the institutionalization of authority so as to insure its adequate acceptance where necessary and protect against its abuse is difficult – doubly so in such a complex system.

3. There does seem to be a general tendency for the strategically placed, the powerful, to exploit the weaker or less favorably placed. The ways in which such a tendency works out and in which it is controlled and counteracted are almost infinitely various in different societies and social situations. Among the many possibilities, Marxian theory of capitalistic exploitation selects what it claims to be an integrated combination of reinforcing factors, the principal components of which are the use of positions of authority within organizations (the capitalistic 'boss') ; the exploitation of bargaining advantage in market relations (e.g. labor market); and the use of the power of the state to the differential advantage of certain private interests ('executive committee of the *bourgeoisie*'). In my opinion, the Marxian view of this factor needs to be broken down into such components which are certainly independently variable and related to a variety of other factors which Marx did not consider. In the face of ideology and counter-ideology, this is particularly difficult but it is essential if one is to reach a basis for a scientific judgement of the Marxian doctrine of the dynamics of capitalism.

4. There seem to be inherent tendencies for those who are structurally placed at notably different points in a differentiated social structure to develop different 'cultures'. There will tend to be a differentiation of attitude systems, of ideologies, and of definitions of the situation to a greater or less degree around the structure of the occupational system and of the other components of the instrumental complex, such as the relation to markets and profits. The development of these differentiated cultures may readily impede communication across the lines of these groups. Under certain circumstances, this tendency to develop a hiatus may become cumulative unless counteracted by effective integrative mechanisms. A leading modern example is the opposing ideologies of business and labor groups in modern industrial society. Marx provided a beginning of analysis in this direction – but it did not go far enough.

5. It is precisely in the area of such a subculture, which is integrated with a structural status, that the problem of articulation with kinship becomes most important. The differences in the situation of people placed at

different points in the occupational system and of the consequences for family income and living conditions seem to lead to a notable differentiation of family type. In American urban society, a relatively clear differentiation of this kind has been shown to exist between 'middle-class' and 'lower-class' groups as they are generally called in the sociological literature. These differences are apparently such as to penetrate into the deepest psychological layers of attitude determination. There are indications from our society that the family structure of the lower groups is such as to favor attitudes which positively handicap their members in competition for status in the occupational system. The role of the integration between occupation and kinship, therefore, under certain circumstances can become an important factor in pushing towards cumulative separation of classes and potential conflict between them.

6. Absolute equality of opportunity in the occupational system, which is, in a sense, the ideal type norm for such a system, is in practice impossible. There seem to be two main types of limitation.

(a) Certain of these are, as noted above, inherent in the functional requirements of family solidarity. Children must share the status of their parents, and in so far as this is differentiated, the more favored groups will have differential access to opportunity. This seems to be counteracted by certain compensating mechanisms, such as leading some of the children of the upper groups into paths which positively handicap them in occupational competition (e.g. the playboy pattern). It may also be pointed out that a differential birth rate has a functional significance in leaving relatively more room at the top for the children of the lower groups.

(b) There are important reasons to believe that the complete institutionalization of the universalistic and functionally specific standards so prominent in our occupational world is not possible in a large-scale social system. Such problems as the difficulty in establishing comparability of different lines of achievement, the lack of complete adequacy of objective standards of judgement of them, and similar things necessitate mechanisms which avoid too direct a comparison and which favor a very rough, broad scale rather than one of elaborately precise comparison. To take just one example in the academic profession, there is a wide variation of degrees of distinction between the senior members of any large university faculty. The tendency, however, is to play down these variations in favor of a broad similarity of status; for instance, as full professor, to conceal differentiations of salary within this group from public view, and to concentrate the most highly competitive elements at certain very narrowly specified points, such as the appointment to permanent rank. Considerations such as these lead to the view that there will be elements in an occupational system which run counter to the main structural type but which have the function of cushioning the impact of the latter on certain 'human factors' and thus protect the stability of the system.

The fundamental problem then is how far factors such as these operate to produce deep-seated and chronic conflict between classes and how far they are counteracted by other factors in the social system such as the last mentioned. It should first, of course, be pointed out that these are not the only directions in which a structuring tending to conflict takes place. There is considerable evidence that in the modern Western World, national solidarity tends generally to take precedence over class solidarity and that, even more generally, the solidarity of ethnic groupings is of particularly crucial significance. One cannot help having the impression that in these matters Marx chose one among the possibilities rather than proving that there could be only one of crucial significance.

Furthermore, in Europe the precapitalistic residues of the old class structure in the ways in which they got tied in with the consequences of the developing industrial society have a great deal to do with the acuteness of class conflict. A good example of this is Germany with the continuing powerful position during the imperial and even the Weimar periods of the nobility and the old civil service and professional groups which were certainly not the product of the capitalistic process alone. The problem of the 'threat of communism' in Germany just before Hitler was certainly colored by their role. Class conflict certainly exists in the United States, but it is different from the German case and much less influenced than the latter by precapitalistic structures. Marxian theory inhibited the recognition of differences such as this – all class conflicts in a society in any sense capitalistic had to be reduced to a single pattern. Another most important set of conclusions from this type of analysis is that there must be certain elements of fundamental identity of the functional problems of social stratification and class in capitalist and socialist societies, if we have given two really fundamental elements: the large-scale organization and occupational role differentiation of industrial society and a family system. The history of Soviet Russia would seem to confirm this view. The role of the managerial and intelligentsia class, which has been progressively strengthened since the revolution, does not have a place in the Marxist utopia. In certain major respects, the role of managers and technical personnel closely resembles American society. I, for one, do not believe that there is a sharp and fundamental sociological distinction between capitalist society and all non-capitalist industrial societies. I believe that class conflict is endemic in our modern industrial type of society. I do not, however, believe that the case has been made for believing that it is the dominant feature of every such society and of its dynamic development. Its relation to other elements of tension, conflict and dynamic change is a complex matter, about which we cannot attempt the Marxian order of generalization with certainty until our science is much further developed than it is today.

It is relevant to this set of problems that since Marx wrote, our knowledge of comparative social structures has immensely broadened and deepened. Seen in the perspective of such knowledge, the sociological emphases on the interpretation of modern Western society have shifted notably. Capitalist and socialist industrialisms tend to be seen as variants of a single fundamental type, not as drastically distinct stages in a single process of dialectic evolution. Indeed, to the modern sociologist the rigid evolutionary schema of Marxian thought appears as a straightjacket rather than a genuine source of illumination of the immensely variant facts of institutional life.

Conclusion

The Marxian theory of class conflict seen as a step in the development of social science rather than as a clarion call to revolution thus represents a distinct step in advance of the utilitarian background of the predominant economic thought of a century ago. Though couched in terms of a neo-Hegelian evolutionary theory of history, it was, seen in terms of subsequent developments of social science, an advance more on the level of empirical insight and generalization from it than of the analytical treatment of dynamic factors in social process. The endless exegetical discussions of the 'relations' or 'conditions' of production and of what was meant or implied in them is an indication of this.

As a point of focus for the subsequent development of modern sociological theory, however, the Marxian ideas have had an important place, forming a point of departure for the formulation of many of the fundamentals of the theory of social institutions. The Marxian view of the importance of class structure has in a broad way been vindicated.

When the problem of the genesis and importance of social classes and their conflicts is approached in these modern sociological terms, however, considerable modifications of the Marxian position are necessitated. Systems of stratification in certain respects are seen to have positive functions in the stabilization of social systems. The institutionalization of motivation operates within the system of capitalistic profit-making. The Marxian ideal of a classless society is in all probability utopian – above all so long as a family system is maintained, but also for other reasons. The differences between capitalist and socialist societies, particularly with respect to stratification, are not as great as Marx and Engels thought.

In both types there is a variety of potential sources of class conflict centering about the structure of the productive process. Those lying within the Marxian purview are not so monolithically integrated in the process of capitalist exploitation as Marx thought, but are seen to be much more specific and in certain degrees independently variable. Some of them, like the relation to family solidarity, lay outside the Marxian focus of emphasis on the relations of production.

In so far as Marx and Engels were true social scientists, as indeed in one principal aspect of their role they were, we justly celebrate their centennial in a scientific meeting. They promulgated ideas which were a notable advance on the general state of knowledge in the field at the time. They provided a major stimulus and definition of problems for further notable advances. They formed an indispensable link in the chain of development of social science. The fact that social science in this aspect of their field has evolved beyond the level to which they brought it is a tribute to their achievement.

References

PARSONS, T. (1949), *The Structure of Social Action*, Allen & Unwin.
PARSONS, T. (1954), *Essays in Sociological Theory*, Collier-Macmillan.

From the Ruling Class to the Power Elite

Excerpts from T. B. Bottomore, *Elites and Society*, Watts, 1964; Penguin, 1966, pp. 28–47.

The value of Marx's concept of the ruling class depends upon the truth of his general social theory. If that theory is not universally valid a ruling class may be conceived as originating from military power, or in modern times from the power of a political party, just as well as from the ownership of the means of production. It may still be maintained, however, that the consolidation of a ruling class requires the concentration of the various types of power – economic, military and political – and that, as a matter of fact, in most societies the formation of this class has begun with the acquisition of economic power. But this raises a more fundamental question about the idea of a ruling class. Is it the case that in every society other than the most simple and primitive this concentration of power occurs, that a ruling class is formed? It should be said at once that the different types of society conform in varying degrees with Marx's model of a society which is clearly divided between a ruling class and subject classes. The most favourable case is probably that of European feudalism, characterized by the rule of a warrior class (Bloch, 1965, vol. 2, bk. 3, ch. 1) which had securely in its hands the ownership of land, military force and political authority, and which received the ideological support of a powerful Church. But even here, a number of qualifications are necessary. The idea of a cohesive ruling class is contradicted by the decentralization of political power which was characteristic of feudal societies (Bloch, 1965), and at the stage when this decentralization was overcome – in the absolute monarchies – the European societies were no longer ruled, in a strict sense, by a warrior nobility. Nevertheless, the nobility of the *ancien régime* does come close to the ideal type of a ruling class.

Another case which fits Marx's model well in many respects is that of the *bourgeoisie* of early capitalism. The development of the *bourgeoisie* as an important social class can well be explained by economic changes, and its rise in the economic sphere was accompanied by the acquisition of other positions of power and prestige in society – in politics, administration, the armed forces and the educational system. This conquest of power in the different spheres of society was a long and confused process, which had many local variations in the European countries, and Marx's model was an abstraction from the complex historical reality, bringing together the experiences of the revolution in France – the most violent ideological and political expression of the rise of a new class – and those of the industrial revolution in England. Nevertheless, the pattern of events does conform broadly with Marx's scheme ; in England, the Reform Act of 1832 gave political power to the *bourgeoisie*, and it produced changes in the character of legislation even if it did not, for some considerable time, change the social composition of Parliament or cabinets (Guttsman, 1963, ch. 3); the reform of the Civil Service after 1855 opened the way for upper-middle-class aspirants to the highest administrative posts (Kingsley, 1944, ch. 3) ; and the development of public schools created new opportunities for children from the newly rich industrial and commercial families to be trained for elite positions. The *bourgeosie* also gained powerful ideological support, according to Marx's account, from the political economists and the utilitarian philosophers.

Nevertheless, the *bourgeoisie* appears in several respects a less cohesive ruling class than the feudal nobility. It does not actually combine in the same persons military, political and economic power, and there arises the possibility of conflicts of interest between the different groups which *represent* (as Marx says) the *bourgeoisie*. Furthermore, capitalist society is more open and mobile than was feudal society, and in the ideological sphere especially, with the development of secular intellectual occupations, conflicting doctrines may arise. Marx expected that the polarization of the two principal classes – the *bourgeoisie* and industrial working class – would accompany the development of capitalism, and that the rule of the *bourgeoisie* would become more manifest and more onerous. But this did not happen in the advanced capitalist societies: the different spheres of power appear to have become more distinct, and the sources of power more numerous and varied ; the opposition between the 'two great classes' of Marx's theory has been modified by the growth of the new middle classes and by a much more complex differentiation of occupation and status ; and political rule has become altogether more mild and less repressive. One important element in this development has been the introduction of universal adult suffrage, which produces, in principle, a separation between economic and political power. Marx himself considered that the attainment of universal suffrage would be a *revolutionary* step, and that it would transfer political power to the working class ('The Chartists', *New York Daily Tribune*, 25 August 1852). Thus, whereas the connection between economic and political power can easily be established in the case of feudal society, or in the case of early capitalism with its limitation of political rights to property owners, it cannot be so easily established in the case of the modern capitalist democracies, and the notion of a distinct and settled ruling class becomes dubious and unclear. Marxist fundamentalists, in their attempts to preserve Marx's social theory intact, have been obliged to argue that even in political democracies the *bourgeoisie* always effectively rules through the indirect influence of wealth, but this is more easily asserted than demonstrated.

These, in brief, are some of the principal difficulties in Marx's conception of the ruling class. Its value lies in the rigorous attempt to analyse the sources of political power, and to explain major changes of political regime. With the aid of this conception Marx succeeded in expressing in a more exact form an idea which recurs continually in popular thought and in social theory: namely, that one of the principal structural features of human societies is their division into a ruling and exploiting group on one side, and subject, exploited groups on the other (Ossowski, 1963, ch. 2); in providing an explanation of the causes of this division by connecting in an impressive synthesis a mass of hitherto unrelated economic, political and cultural facts; and in accounting for changes in social structure by the rise and fall of classes. The concept of the 'governing elite' or 'political class' was proposed as an alternative, partly, as we have seen, in order to demonstrate the impossibility of attaining a classless form of society, but also to meet the theoretical difficulties which we have just considered. The concept of a governing elite avoids, in particular, the difficulty of showing that a particular class, defined in terms of its economic position, does in fact dominate all the spheres of social life; but it does so only at the cost of abandoning any attempt to explain the phenomena to which it refers. The governing elite, according to Mosca and Pareto, comprises those who occupy the recognized positions of political power in society. Thus, when we ask, who has power in a particular society, the reply is, those who have power, i.e. those who occupy the specified positions. This is scarcely illuminating; it does not tell us how these particular individuals come to occupy the positions of power. Or else it is misleading; if, for example, those who appear to have power in the formal system of government are in fact subject to the power of other individuals or groups outside this system. Nor does this idea of a governing elite provide much help in the explanation of political changes. [...]

The difficulties in the concept of a governing elite can be seen most clearly in a recent work which shows the influence of Marx on one side and of Mosca and Pareto on the other (Mills, 1956). Mills explains his preference for the term 'power elite' rather than 'ruling class' by saying:

'Ruling class' is a badly loaded phrase. 'Class' is an economic term; 'rule' a political one. The phrase 'ruling class' thus contains the theory that an economic class rules politically. That short-cut theory may or may not at times be true, but we do not want to carry that one rather simple theory about in the terms that we use to define our problems; we wish to state the theories explicitly, using terms of more precise and unilateral meaning. Specifically, the phrase 'ruling class', in its common political connotation, does not allow enough autonomy to the political order and its agents, and it says nothing about the military as such. ... We hold that such a simple view of 'economic determinism' must be elaborated by 'political determinism' and 'military determinism'; that the higher agents of each of these three domains now often have a noticeable degree of autonomy; and that only in the often intricate ways of coalition do they make up and carry through the most important decisions (1956, p. 277).

Mills defines the power elite in much the same way as Pareto defined his 'governing elite', for he says 'we may define the power elite in terms of the means of power – as those who occupy the command posts' (p. 23). But the analysis which proceeds from this definition has a number of unsatisfactory features. In the first place, Mills distinguishes three major elites in the USA – the corporation heads, the political leaders and the military chiefs – and he is obliged to go on to inquire whether these three groups together form a single power elite, and if so, what it is that binds them together. One possible answer to these questions is to say that the three groups do form a single elite because they are representatives of an upper class, which has to be regarded, consequently, as a ruling class. But Mills, although he emphasizes that most of the members of these elites are in fact drawn from a socially recognized upper class, says initially that he will leave open the question of whether or not it is such a class which rules through the elites, and when he returns to the problem it is only to reject the Marxist idea of a ruling class in the brief passage cited above. In short, the question is never seriously discussed, and this is a curious failing in the particular case which Mills is examining, and in the context of the ideas which he is expressing. He has previously rejected the view that there is popular control of the power elite through voting or other means, and has emphasized the unity of the elite, as well as the homogeneity of its social origins – all of which points to the consolidation of a ruling class. The formulation which he actually gives is vague and unconvincing: it is a reference to 'the often uneasy coincidence of economic, military and political power', a coincidence which he proposes to explain largely by the pressures of the international conflict in which America has been engaged.

These problems have frequently been raised in criticisms of Mosca and Pareto. Thus, Friedrich observed that one of the most problematical parts of all elite doctrines is the assumption that the men of power do constitute a cohesive group:

In the light of the continuous change in the composition of the majority, it is not possible to say, under conditions such as prevail in a functioning democracy, that those who play some considerable part in government constitute a cohesive group (1950, pp. 259–60).

This view of the elite in modern democracies has been widely held; it is stated boldly in the conclusions of a recent study of the upper strata of British society:

The rulers are not at all close-knit or united. They are not so much in the centre of a solar system, as in a cluster of interlocking circles, each one largely preoccupied with its own professionalism and expertise, and touching others only at one edge ... they are not a single Establishment but a ring of Establishments, with slender connections. The frictions and balances between the different circles are the supreme safeguard of democracy. No one man can stand in the centre, for there is no centre (Sampson, 1962, p. 624).

Mills rejects this fashionable liberal-minded doctrine, which he summarizes as follows:

Far from being omnipotent, the elites are thought to be so scattered as to lack any coherence as a historical force. ... Those who occupy the formal places of authority are so checkmated – by other elites exerting pressure, or by the public as an electorate, or by constitutional codes – that although there may be upper classes, there is no ruling class; although there may be men of power, there is no power elite; although there may be a system of stratification, it has no effective top (1956, pp. 16–17).

As we have seen, he insists that the three principal elites – economic, political and military – are, in fact, a cohesive group, and he supports his view by establishing the similarity of their social origins, the close personal and family relationships between those in the different elites, and the frequency of interchange of personnel between the three spheres. But since he resists the conclusion that the group is a ruling class he is unable to provide a convincing explanation, as distinct from description, of the solidarity of the power elite. Furthermore, by eliminating the idea of a ruling class, he also excludes that of classes in opposition; and so he arrives at an extremely pessimistic account of American society. The real themes of his book are, first, the transformation of a society in which numerous small and autonomous groups had an effective say in the making of political decisions, into a mass society in which the power elite decides all important issues and keeps the masses quiet by flattery, deception and entertainment; and secondly, the corruption of the power elite, itself, which he attributes primarily to a state of affairs in which it is not accountable for its decisions to any organized public, and also to the dominant value of the acquisition of wealth. Mills's account of the historical changes, which does indeed bring to light some important features of modern politics – the growing political influence of military chiefs, for example – is pessimistic in the sense that it suggests no way out of the situation which it describes and condemns. Like Pareto and Mosca, Mills seems to be saying that if we look at modern societies without illusions we shall see that, however democratic their constitutions, they are in fact ruled by an elite; and to be adding, in a devastating fashion, that even in a society so favourably placed as was the USA at its origins – without a feudal system of ranks, with every considerable equality of economic and social condition among its citizens, and with a strongly democratic ideology – the force of events has produced a governing elite of unprecedented power and unaccountability. Where Mills differs from the other Machiavellians is in condemning a state of affairs which they either praised or, in a spirit of disillusionment, accepted.

The concepts of 'ruling class' and 'governing elite' are used in descriptions and explanations of political happenings, and their value must be judged by the extent to which they make possible reasonable answers to important questions about political systems. Do the rulers of society constitute a social group? Is it a cohesive or divided, an open or closed group? How are its members selected? What is the basis of their power? Is this power unrestricted or is it limited by that of other groups in society? Are there significant and regular differences between societies in these respects, and if so, how are they to be explained?

The two concepts are alike in emphasizing the division between rulers and ruled as one of the most important facts of social structure.[1] But they state the division in different ways: the concept of a 'governing elite'

1. 'From the point of view of scientific research the real superiority of the concept of the ruling, or political, class ["political elite" in our terminology. TBB] lies in the fact that the varying structure of ruling classes has a preponderant importance in determining the political type, and also the level of civilization, of the different peoples' (Mosca, 1960, p. 51).

T. B. Bottomore 281

contrasts the organized, ruling minority with the unorganized majority, or masses, while the concept of a 'ruling class' contrasts the dominant class with subject classes, which may themselves be organized, or be creating organizations. From these different conceptions arise differences in the way of conceiving the relations between rulers and ruled. In the Marxist theory, which employs the concept of a ruling class, the conflict between classes becomes the principal force producing changes of social structure; but in the elite theories – in spite of the fact that Pareto praised highly Marx's conception of class struggle, which he described as 'profoundly true' (1902, p. 405) – the relations between the organized minority and the unorganized majority are necessarily represented as more passive, and the resulting problem of how to explain the rise and fall of ruling elites, if it is confronted at all, has to be dealt with either by postulating a recurrent decadence in the elite (Pareto) or by introducing the idea of the rise of new 'social forces' among the masses (Mosca) which brings the theory close to Marxism.

A further difference between the two concepts lies in the extent to which they make possible explanations of the cohesion of the ruling minority. The 'governing elite', defined as those who occupy the positions of command in a society, is merely assumed to be a cohesive group, unless other considerations, such as their membership of the wealthy class, or their aristocratic family origins are introduced (as they are consistently by Mosca, and occasionally by Pareto). But the 'ruling class', defined as the class which owns the major instruments of economic production in a society, is shown to be a cohesive social group; first, because its members have definite economic interests in common, and, more importantly, because it is engaged permanently in a conflict with other classes in society, through which its self-awareness and solidarity are continually enhanced. Furthermore, this concept states in a precise form what is the basis of the minority's ruling position, namely its economic dominance, while the concept of the 'governing elite' says little about the bases of the power which the elite possesses, except in so far as it incorporates elements from the Marxist theory of classes. In Mills's study of the 'power elite', there is an attempt to explain the power position of the three principal elites taken separately – that of the business executives by the growth in size and complexity of business corporations ; that of the military chiefs by the growing scale and expense of the weapons of war, determined by technology and the state of international conflict ; and that of the national political leaders, in a somewhat less satisfactory way, by the decline of the legislature, of local politics and of voluntary organizations – but the unity of the power elite as a single group, and the basis of *its* powers, are not explained. Why is there *one* power elite and not *three*?

The superiority of the concept of 'ruling class' lies in its greater fertility and suggestiveness and in its value in the construction of theories. But I have pointed out earlier some of its defects, and it is now necessary to consider whether these can be overcome. The most important step in this direction would be to give up the Marxist view of the concept as a description of a real phenomenon which is to be observed in all societies in the same general form, and to regard it instead as an 'ideal type', in the sense which Max Weber gave to this term (1950, p. 90). It we treat the concept in this way we can proceed to ask how closely the relationships in a particular society approach the ideal type of a ruling class and subject classes; and so employ the concept, properly, as a tool of thought and investigation. It is then possible to see clearly that the idea of a 'ruling class' originated in the study of a particular historical situation – the end of feudalism and the beginnings of modern capitalism [2] – and to consider how far, and in what respects, other situations diverge from this ideal type, as a result of the absence or weakness of class formation, the influence of factors other than the ownership of property in the creation of classes, and the conflict between different forms of power.

There are two sorts of situation in which we can see especially plainly a divergence from the ideal type of a ruling class. One is that in which, although there is an 'upper class' – that is to say, a clearly demarcated social group which has in its possession a large part of the property of society and receives a disproportionately large share of the national income, and which has created on the basis of these economic advantages a distinctive culture and way of life – this class does not enjoy undisputed or unrestricted political power, in the sense that it is able to maintain easily its property rights or to transmit them unimpaired from generation to generation. This kind of situation has been discerned by many observers particularly in the modern democracies, in which, as I noted earlier, there is a potential opposition between the ownership of wealth and productive resources by a small upper class, and the possession of political power, through the franchise, by the mass of the population. [. . .]

In order to determine whether in such a case there is a 'ruling class' it is necessary first to examine the degree in which the upper class has been successful in perpetuating its ownership of property. We shall have to note, on one side, that in the democratic countries during the present century a considerable number of restrictions have been placed upon the use

2. As Croce observed of the whole theory of historical materialism: 'The materialistic view of history arose out of the need to account for a definite social phenomenon, not from an abstract inquiry into the factors of historical life' (1966).

of private property, and that there has probably been some reduction in the inequalities of wealth and income, as a result of progressive taxation, and of the growth of publicly owned property and publicly administered social services. On the other side we must note that the decline in the proportion of private wealth owned by the upper class has been modest and very slow, and that the redistribution of income through taxation has not proceeded very far. The situation in Britain was very carefully examined by John Strachey, who concluded that:

Up to 1939 there had been little or no redistribution of the national income in favour of the mass of the population, either through trade union pressure or budgetary changes ... the wage earners' standard of life had risen just about in step with the rise in the total national income, their share remaining about constant ... the broad pattern of distribution which emerges ... is that at the end of the period under discussion [1939] as at the beginning [1911] some ten per cent of the population got nearly one-half of the national income and the other ninety per cent got the other half of the national income (1956, pp. 137–8; see also Seers, 1951).

In the following period, up to 1951, there was some redistribution of income which resulted in transferring some ten per cent of the total national income from property owners to wage-earners, but this trend was probably reversed again after 1951 (p. 146).[3] [. . .] The situation in the other democratic countries, with the exception of the Scandinavian countries, does not differ greatly from that in Britain; in all of them, right-wing governments have been in power during most of the present century and the redistribution of wealth and income has occurred slowly, if at all. One must be sceptical, therefore, of the view that the extension of voting rights to the mass of the population can establish at once – or has in fact established in the short period of time in which modern democracies have existed – popular rule, and eliminate the power of a ruling class. What seems to have taken place in the democratic countries up to the present time is not so much a reduction in the power of the upper class as a decline in the radicalism of the working class.

The second type of situation in which there is a divergence from the 'ruling class – subject classes' model is that in which the ruling group is not a class in Marx's sense. One instance is provided by those societies in which a stratum of intellectuals or bureaucrats may be said to wield supreme power – in China under the rule of the *literati,* or in India under the rule of the Brahmins. Another instance is to be found in the present-day Communist countries where power is concentrated in the leaders of a

3. More recently, Titmuss (1962), has undertaken the most thorough study yet made in Britain of the sources of information about the distribution of income.

political party. In these cases, however, we need to examine carefully how far the ruling stratum is clearly distinguishable from a ruling class. In India, the Brahmins, during the ages when they were most powerful, were also substantial landowners, and they were closely allied with the land-owning warrior castes in the imperial and feudal periods of India's history. [. . .]

Again, in China, the *literati* were recruited, in the feudal period, from the principal landowning families, and at other times they came in the main from wealthy families (Bottomore, 1964, p. 71); so that they were always closely linked with an upper class. There is, moreover, another important economic aspect of the rule of these groups of intellectuals and administrators to which Karl Wittfogel has drawn attention (1957). One of the principal instruments of production in China and India (and in a number of other ancient societies) (Steward, 1955) was the system of irrigation, and the *literati* and the Brahmins, without owning this pro-perty upon which agricultural production depended, still exercised a more or less complete control over its use. Consequently they possessed, in addition to their ownership of land, a vital economic power which, according to Wittfogel, was the principal support of their political dominance.

But notwithstanding these qualifications the distinction between social strata of this kind and ruling classes which base their power directly upon the legal ownership of property remains. The possession of the means of administration may be, as Max Weber argued, an alternative to the possession of means of economic production, as a basis of political power (Eisenstadt, 1969). This distinction is perhaps more obvious in the case of the present-day Communist countries, in which there is no private ownership of the means of production, and in which the officials of the ruling party and the state control the economy. Wittfogel has attempted, in a very ingenious way, to assimi-late this type of political power to the general category of 'oriental despotism' but I think the differences are too great – the existence of private ownership of land and other resources, and the intimate bonds between the officials and the property-owning classes in one case, and the specific characteristics of rule by a political party in the other (Bottomore, 1964, pp. 83–5) – for this attempt to be successful. The political system of the Communist countries seems to me to approach the pure type of a 'power elite', that is, a group which, having come to power with the support or acquiescence of particular classes in the population, maintains itself in power chiefly by virtue of being an organized minority confronting the unorganized majority ; whereas in the case of ancient China or India we have to deal with a system which combines the features of a ruling class and a power elite.

There is another element in the position of a ruling class, which has already been mentioned and which needs to be examined more fully in its bearing upon those situations in which the existence of such a class is doubtful. Since the power of a ruling class arises from its ownership of property, and since this property can easily be transmitted from generation to generation, the class has an enduring character. It is constituted by a group of families which remain as its component elements over long periods of time through the transmission of the family property. Its composition is not entirely immutable, for new families may enter it and old families may decline, but the greater part of its members continue from generation to generation. Only when there are rapid changes in the whole system of production and property ownership does the composition of the ruling class change significantly; and in that case we can say that one ruling class has been replaced by another. If, however, we were to find, in a particular society or type of society, that the movement of individuals and families between the different social levels was so continuous and so extensive that no group of families was able to maintain itself for any length of time in a situation of economic and political pre-eminence, then we should have to say that in such a society there was no ruling class. It is, in fact this 'circulation of elites' (in the terminology of the elite theorists) or 'social mobility' (in the language of more recent sociological studies) that has been fixed upon by a number of writers as a second important characteristic of modern industrial societies – the first being universal suffrage – which must qualify severely, if it does not altogether exclude, the assertion that there is a ruling class in these societies. By this means we may arrive at the view, which was formulated by Karl Mannheim among others (1940, pt 2, ch. 2), that the development of industrial societies can properly be depicted as a movement from a class system to a system of elites, from a social hierarchy based upon the inheritance of property to one based upon merit and achievement.

This confrontation between the concepts of 'ruling class' and 'political elite' shows, I think, that, while on one level they may be totally opposed, as elements in wide-ranging theories which interpret political life, and especially the future possibilities of political organization, in very different ways, on another level they may be seen as complementary concepts, which refer to different types of political system or to different aspects of the same political system. With their help we can attempt to distinguish between societies in which there is a ruling class, and at the same time elites which represent particular aspects of its interests; societies in which there is no ruling class, but a political elite which founds its power upon the control of the administration, or upon military force, rather than upon property ownership and inheritance; and societies in which there exists a multiplicity of elites among which no cohesive and enduring group of powerful individuals or families seems to be discoverable at all. In order to establish such a classification we need to examine more closely the circulation of elites, the relations between elites and classes, and the ways in which new elites and new classes are formed.

References

BLOCH, M. (1965), *Feudal Society*, Routledge & Kegan Paul.

BOTTOMORE, T. B. (1964), *Elites and Society*, Watts, 1964; Penguin, 1966.

CROCE, B. (1966), *Historical Materialism and the Economics of Karl Marx*, Cass.

EISENSTADT, S. N. (1969), *The Political Systems of Empires*, Collier-Macmillan.

FRIEDRICH, C. J. (1950), *The New Image of the Common Man*, Beacon Press, 2nd edn.

GUTTSMAN, W. L. (1963), *The British Political Elite*, MacGibbon & Kee.

KINGSLEY, J. D. (1944), *Representative Bureaucracy*, Antioch Press.

MANNHEIM, K. (1940), *Man and Society*, Routledge & Kegan Paul.

MEISEL, J. H. (1962), *The Myth of the Ruling Class*, University of Michigan Press.

MILLS, C. W. (1956), *The Power Elite*, Oxford University Press.

MOSCA, G. (1960), *The Ruling Class*, McGraw-Hill.

OSSOWSKI, S. (1963), *Class Structure in the Social Consciousness*, Routledge & Kegan Paul.

PARETO, V. (1902), *Les Systèmes Socialistes*, Marcel Girard.

SAMPSON, A. (1962), *Anatomy of Britain*, Hodder & Stoughton.

SEERS, D. (1951), *The Levelling of Incomes Since 1938*.

STEWARD, J. H. (1955), *Irrigation Civilizations: A Comparative Study*, Pan-American Union.

STRACHEY, J. (1956), *Contemporary Capitalism*, Gollancz.

TITMUSS, R. M. (1962), *Income Distribution and Social Change*, Allen & Unwin.

WEBER, M. (1950), *The Methodology of the Social Sciences*, Collier-Macmillan.

WITTFOGEL, K. (1957), *Oriental Despotism*, Yale University Press.

20 T. H. Marshall

The Nature and Determinants of Social Status

Excerpts from T. H. Marshall, *Sociology at the Crossroads*, Heinemann, 1963, pp. 181–207.

By social status, we mean a man's general standing *vis-à-vis* the other members of society or some section of it. 'General' is inserted to indicate that we refer to something more all-embracing than a specialized standing as an expert in something, such as the maintenance of motorcars, though such expertise may contribute something to social status. Secondly, social status, like stratification, carries with it the idea of superior and inferior. If we compare the social status of two people, we ask whether they are equal or unequal, and, if unequal, which is the higher and which the lower. And in such a comparison we are concerned not only with the objective facts, such as rights, wealth or education, but also with the way in which the two people regard each other, that is to say with reciprocal attitudes expressed in reciprocal behaviour. The attitudes spring from a valuation or assessment of relative positions, which is reached by valuing or assessing the relevant objective facts which are known or can be observed. Among the most relevant facts are those which we have noted in studying stratification. The relevant facts may be called the evidence, the indices or the symbols of social status, and in that sense its determinants. They are the immediate cause of the attitudes and the resultant behaviour. But behind them lie determinants in a different sense, namely the factors which determine how these relevant facts come to appear where they do. If wealth is one of the determinants in the first sense, then the forces controlling the distribution of wealth are determinants in the second. There is yet a third level which is the most difficult to explore. We may wish to discover what determines the values which society attaches to the various types of relevant fact. It is with determinants in the first sense that we are chiefly concerned in this article.

The reference to society raises an important point. Social status, we have said, is standing or position in society, and it may be misleading to describe it in terms of the relationship between two individuals. For social status rests on a collective judgement, or rather a consensus of opinion within a group. No one person can by himself confer social status on another, and if a man's social position were assessed differently by everybody he met, he would have no social status at all. In other words, social status is the position accorded in terms of the social values current in the society. It has, one might say, a conventional character. And it is a position having relevance for certain attitudes and forms of behaviour, not for all. It is so difficult as to be almost impossible to define what these are. One can only give crude examples. A doctor, for instance, may treat all his patients with equal care, regardless of social position, without inviting them all indiscriminately to dinner. Or, looking at it from another angle, the assessment of social position is not the same as the assessment of personality. Both affect reciprocal attitudes and behaviour, and it is very difficult to disentangle them. One might suggest that the best measure of social status in its pure and undiluted form is the preliminary and provisional judgement of social position based on 'paper' evidence (such as family, schooling, income, occupation) and on the impression gained by a brief contact in which such overt indices as speech and manners can be observed. On this evidence a person may be recognized as a representative of a particular group or social class. It is obvious that it is only in terms such as these that we can speak about the social status of a group, for instance of teachers. But an individual teacher may, by virtue of personality and attributes not characteristic of the group, acquire a rather different social status within a community in which he is well known. We might call the first 'positional social status' and the second 'personal social status'.

We have now identified three different levels. First, the actual social position as accorded by the attitudes and behaviour of those among whom the individual lives and moves – which we have called personal social status. Secondly, the social position accorded by the conventional values current in the society to the group or category of which the individual is representative – which we have called positional social status. And thirdly, the position in the system of stratification which is a feature of the structure of the society – which we have been rash enough to refer to as an objective fact. These three levels present us with two questions of interrelationship. First, how much freedom is there for the establishment of a personal social status differing from that indicated by positional social status? And in asking this, we must realize that, if personal social status were completely independent, positional social status would be a meaningless concept. This, it must be admitted, is a question of the greatest difficulty and complexity, and we can do little more than draw attention to the problem. Secondly, how tightly is positional social status tied to the system of stratification? It will be noticed that this question, as formulated, implies that it is bound to be tied fairly tightly but may have a certain measure of autonomy.

We need not pause long to put this question in the case of a caste system. [. . .] 'Everywhere in India', writes an Indian scholar, 'there is a definite scheme of social precedence among the castes, with the Brahmin as the head of the hierarchy.' (Ghurye, 1932, p. 6.) 'Social precedence' means the same thing as 'social status'. [. . .] We may conclude that, to all intents and purposes, social status is a mere reflection of caste membership, except, perhaps, for distinctions of personal social status within a local caste group.

The estate system deserves more attention, partly for its intrinsic interest, and partly because certain features of the estate system have survived into the age of class. [. . .]

First, where an estate was firmly entrenched, the legal rights were extended by a body of privileges so firmly rooted in social custom as to have in effect the force of law, or, one might say, to be official rather than merely conventional in character. Social status was firmly tied to estate status. The prestige of a German noble, for instance, was in all its aspects as unchallengeable as his legal rights. Secondly, we find subdivision of estates proper into sub-estates based not strictly on distinctive legal rights but on official position. Here we might instance the division in seventeenth-century France between the ancient noble families of chivalry, the *noblesse de l'épée*, and the more recent recruits to nobility by office, the *noblesse de la robe*, and further division of the latter into the *grande, moyenne* and *petite robe* (Normand, 1908). Thirdly we find, also in France, distinctions within the Third Estate which reveal what can best be described as culture groups. The urban *bourgeoisie* contained, not only oligarchies of office, but also layers united by a common economic position, that of trade as distinct from manual labour (we might call this a class within an estate), but also by a consciously cultivated culture, which in some cases, but not in all, succeeded merely in being a ridiculous imitation of the culture of the aristocracy. Such groups strove to create a social status, not based wholly on estate or class, but sustained by value judgements which they hoped would become part of the conventions of the society.

But the best example comes from England, a country in which the outlines of the estate system were generally more weakly drawn than on the Continent. As Professor Namier has said of the English class system:

Classes are the more sharply marked in England because there is no single test for them, except the final, incontestable result; and there is more snobbery than in any other country, because the gate can be entered by anyone, and yet remains, for those bent on entering it, a mysterious, awe-inspiring gate (Namier, 1961, p. 15).

The 'final, incontestable result' is acceptance or rejection by the common estimation of the group. It is 'mysterious' because it is not governed by rules, is not bound to follow the shape of any other official or objective status system, and cannot therefore be convicted of delivering a false verdict. Social status is judged in terms of social status alone.

The most perfect illustration is the peculiarly English figure of the gentleman. There is here no basis of politico-legal status ; there are no distinctive enforceable rights, no title, no office – nothing but the 'final, incontestable result' of a number of factors. The word 'gentle' and its derivatives did at one time have a certain flavour of estate about them, because they referred to those entitled to bear arms. But 'gentle' also connoted a way of life associated with ideas of chivalry. In the post-feudal age the 'gentry' were a group below the nobility but above, or at least distinct from, the *bourgeoisie*, but the word 'gentleman' could be applied to nobility and gentry combined. And this section of the population had never constituted an estate. It contained the whole of the top estate and a part of the middle one. Nor could it be wholly identified with a class, since it contained the greater and lesser landowners, the professions and some selected members of the business community. The surprising thing is, not so much that this particular social status was so autonomous and was not rigidly tied to any other system of stratification, as that the assessment was so definite and unhesitating, and that gentlemen so clearly formed a group or social class whose members enjoyed in a very real sense equality of social status, although important inequalities were super-imposed upon the fundamental equality. In nineteenth-century England one might, after hearing a long description of a man, ask: 'Yes, but is he a gentleman?' and expect, and receive, the answer yes or no. The same was true of the title 'lady', as can be seen from Trollope's description of Mrs Dale, the impoverished widow whose grandfather had been 'almost nobody'.

That she was a lady, inwards and outwards, from the crown of her head to the sole of her feet, in head, in heart and in mind, a lady by education and a lady by nature, a lady also by birth in spite of that deficiency respecting her grandfather, I hereby state as a fact – meo periculo. And the squire, though he had no special love for her, had recognized this, and in all respects treated her as his equal (Trollope, 1864, ch. 3).

The factors which figured as determinants of this social status of gentleman are easy to recognize, 'determinants' being taken to denote those attributes whose presence won recognition of the status. The most obvious necessary attributes were birth and culture. The two were easily reconciled as criteria as long as it could be maintained that the second was transmitted by the first. Transmission might be by biological heredity or family influence, and there is evidence of belief in both. But birth and family atmosphere were not enough. They required to be reinforced by education. The seventeenth-century author of *The Gentleman's Calling* went so far as to assert that men's minds are by nature of the same clay; education is the potter which moulds them into vessels of honour and dishonour (Schlatter, 1940 p. 50). This is a rather extreme view. More typical, probably, is that expressed in the opening scene of *As You Like It*. Orlando is denouncing the treatment he has received from his elder brother. At first he claims equality by birth and blood: 'I have as much of my father in me as you.' Then he says: 'My father charged you in his will to give me good education: you have trained me like a peasant, obscuring and hiding from me all gentleman-like qualities.' A gentleman was recognized, then, by his family and his education, with this difference – that a 'good' family counted even if its influence was not apparent in its product, but education (before universities and schools became a field for competitive snobbery) was judged by its results. To these we must add enough money to live the life of a gentleman and an occupation compatible with the ethos of that life, or no occupation at all.

There emerges here a point of some general importance. It might be said that, in the case of the gentleman, birth determined social status, and social status in turn determined culture; it created a right to the appropriate culture and was normally accompanied by the means with which to acquire it. But there were exceptions to this perfect correlation between birth and the appropriate way of life. The question then arises, can the reverse process take place? Can the way of life, adopted without the advantage of birth, determine social status? This question has been debated in England, often with great heat, for at least four centuries. The point at issue, however, has not been whether the simple answer should be yes or no: it must undoubtedly be yes. The argument has been rather about the time required to complete a change of status by these means – whether in one generation, or two, or more – and the degree of culture assimilation necessary to confirm it. Protests against social upstarts and their too-ready acceptance into good society were rife in Elizabethan England, as witness the well-known passage from Sir Thomas Smith:

As for gentlemen, they be made good cheap in England. For whosoever studieth the laws of the realm, who studieth in the universities, who professeth liberal sciences and, to be short, who can live idly and without manual labour and will bear the port, charge and countenance of a gentleman, he ... shall be taken for a gentleman (Rowse, 1950, ch. 6).

Satire is a favourite weapon of an aristocracy unable to stem the flood of invasion from below, and satirical attacks on the *bourgeois gentilhomme* are found in England as well as in France. The first words of Sogliardo, the *nouveau riche* in Ben Jonson's *Every Man Out of His Humour*, are: 'Nay, look you, Carlo; this is my humour now. I have land and money, my friends left me well, and I will be a gentleman whatsoever it cost me.' More subtle, perhaps, in spite of its apparent crudity, is Shakespeare's thrust in *The Winter's Tale*, which seems to strike both at ludicrous ambition and at exaggerated pride of birth. The shepherd, who fathered Perdita, and the clown, his son, have been honoured for their services and hailed as 'brother' by the king and his son: they meet Autolycus:

CLOWN: You denied to fight with me this other day, because I was no gentleman born ... give me the lie, do and try whether I am not now a gentleman born.
AUTOLYCUS: I know you are now, sir, a gentleman born.
CLOWN: Ay, and have been so any time these four hours.

Notice the test of gentle status – the right to avenge an insult. The theme can be followed right down into the nineteenth and even the twentieth century, through the fortunes of Meredith's Evan Harrington, the cultured son of a tailor, and in the pages of *Punch*, where we can laugh at the solecisms of the upstart in the hunting-field and lament over the boorish antics of the war-profiteer in his Scottish castle. The tone changes from mirth to bitterness as the defences of aristocracy fall before the invader.

This peculiar phenomenon survived into the class system of modern England, and the English gentleman has often been the object of the curious attention of foreigners. He is the symbol of English snobbery and class-consciousness. But that is not all. A similar social-status group took shape in the level next below him, the lower middle class, with its black coats and white collars, suburban villas, exclusive social circles and genteel clubs. One might be tempted to regard this as the result of imitation, were it not for the fact that something of very much the same kind appears to have happened in the United States, where the gentleman never existed at all. At one time the preoccupation with social status as something distinct from, though not independent of, position in the hierarchy of estate or class, was regarded as peculiarly English. But today this concept is being widely used in sociological investigations in America, and it is in some of the Scandinavian countries, rather than in the United States, that one will find those who look with mild surprise on the English idea of social status as a quaint anachronism. Professor Geiger, who recently studied stratification in a Danish town, held that preoccupation with hierarchy and prestige was 'an ideological vestige of estates-society, and only appropriate in a class-society in so far as this continues to manifest estate residues' (Floud, 1952). This may be true of England, but it cannot be true of the United States.

We may find the clue to this problem by looking at the earlier phase of capitalist society in America, the golden age of the independent *entrepreneurs* those sturdy individualists whose successors are today referred to as 'the old middle class'. In the last quarter of the nineteenth century they comprised about one-third of the working population, but they had a symbolic value out of proportion to their numbers. The independent *entrepreneur* was the ideal type of the American citizen in a competitive capitalist economy, holding a position to which every citizen aspired and which it was believed that every citizen worth his salt could achieve. This idealized picture of a world open to talent and enterprise was based on a belief in fundamental social equality in sharp contrast to the ethos of caste, estate or social snobbery. And social relations largely conformed to this belief. The only significant differences were those measured by success and the simple, obvious and incontrovertible fact of wealth. There was little room in such a society for an independent or autonomous set of social values to assert itself. The plain facts of economic inequality were accepted for what they were worth – but not for more ; they were not invested with any mystical meaning such as might make rich and poor appear as different species of humanity. There was no place for a snobbish preoccupation with social status.

But the situation changed. The proportion of independent *entrepreneurs* fell, the chances of achieving independence, still more of retaining it, dwindled, while the fortunes of those belonging to this sector of the economy were more and more controlled by the power and policies of the big capitalists and organized labour. But the ideal persisted, enfeebled but still alive, and we are told that today the independent *entrepreneur* 'has become the man through whom the ideology of utopian capitalism is still actively presented to many of our contemporaries' (Mills, 1951, p. 34). Meanwhile there was a steady growth of the 'new middle class', composed chiefly of the lesser professions and salaried employees, who occupied a permanent middle position in the capitalist hierarchy. It is in their ranks that we find the clearest evidence of a preoccupation with social status similar to that which had long been typical of the English.

Careful study of these two pictures, the English and the American, leads to the apparently paradoxical conclusion that preoccupation with social status may be stimulated both by fluidity and by rigidity in the social system. When a section of society is threatened by invasion from below, as the English gentlemen were in varying degrees from the sixteenth century onwards, they protect themselves by constructing barriers out of those attributes and symbols of social differences which are most difficult to acquire. Conspicuous expenditure can be copied by those who get rich quick, but correct manners, the right accent and the 'old school tie' are esoteric mysteries and jealously guarded monopolies. And it was in the nineteenth century that these symbols gained their great ascendancy in English life. Similarly, those who climb successfully from below seek by the same means to proclaim and consolidate their position, while the partially successful may devise comparable methods of identifying the half-way house which they have managed to reach.

But in America it is generally felt that social structure has become more rigid and that status consciousness in the middle ranks springs from a sense of frustration. The road upwards has been blocked, that is to say, the road that leads from one position in the economic system to another quite different one (e.g. from worker to manager), and also the road that leads up to wealth. Exaggerated importance, therefore, may attach to those minor shifts and distinctions which are still possible within the same stratum of the economic structure – such as the shift which brings the clerk within the orbit of the boss or the saleswoman in touch with higher-class customers. Thus fluidity and rigidity may have, in this respect, the same result. They may also exist together in the same social pattern – as they in fact do in contemporary society. The opportunity to move to a social level different from that into which one was born is concentrated mainly into the years of education and training. It is here that all those with just the average amount of ambition get their chance, and it is by this process that the defences of the status-conscious middle and upper layers are penetrated from below. But thereafter, once the starting-point in public life outside home and school has been found, the regular road is clearly marked ahead, it is only the exceptional who can get away from it, and its terminus is visible not very far away. A cynic might observe that modern man, having striven during childhood and youth for the realities of life, proceeds to struggle for the shadows and the symbols after he has reached years of discretion. But that would be to exaggerate the role of status consciousness in our society today.

A great many studies have recently been made, both in England and in the United States, in an attempt to discover what that role is and what contemporary man means by social class. The results are not as yet very conclusive, partly because the investigators have not always been quite certain what they were investigating. In order to avoid misunderstandings a distinction has been made between 'subjective status', a man's status as assessed by himself, and 'accorded status', or a man's status as assessed by others (Hyman, 1942). But 'subjective status' is an unfortunate term. In its original meaning status is essentially something which no man can bestow upon himself; it is always 'accorded' by the society of which he is a member. No doubt a man's estimate of his own position is an important social fact which will influence his opinions and his behaviour, but the use of the word 'status' to describe it leads to confusion. When people are questioned about 'subjective status', it is difficult to interpret their answers. Some may try to express what they believe to be their own ultimate and absolute value, judged by some personal standard of their own; others may describe the position they think they ought to have, as judged by the standards current in their society; others may say what they believe is the position they occupy in the eyes of others – they may give, as it were, the subjective view as to what is the accorded status. It is impossible wholly to disentangle these elements in the answers.

In two polls taken in the United States in 1939 and 1940, in which people were asked to assign themselves to the upper, middle or lower class, the percentages choosing the middle class were 88 and 79 (Cole, 1950). But in a subsequent inquiry in 1945, which offered the 'working class' as an additional option, the middle class percentage fell to 43, and in a follow-up study in the next year to 36 (Centers, 1949). Now it so happened that the interviews for this inquiry were taking place at the time of the British General Election, and the news of the Labour victory broke on 26 July. The percentages of those assigning themselves to the working and lower classes fluctuated according to the date of interview as follows:

Before 26 July, 51; on 26 July, 67; after 26 July, 54 (p. 139).

These figures suggest that to some people 'subjective status' is a matter of political outlook and sympathy, and their sympathies with the working class were aroused or fortified by the Labour victory. And, in fact, when people were asked what, apart from occupation, was the most important thing to know about a person in order to assign him to a social class – family, money, education or beliefs and attitudes – 47·4 per cent chose 'beliefs and attitudes' and only 29·4 per cent education, with the other criteria lagging behind (p. 91). But this may mean a number of different things. If a socialist son of a professional family assigns himself to the working class, he thereby tells us very little about his social status, either subjective or accorded.

Finally, when the outlines of social structure lack precision and when the categories to which people can most easily be assigned are not in fact homogeneous, preliminary assessments of positional social status lose much of their force and can more readily be modified by consideration of individual attributes. In other words, personal social status wins a degree of autonomy from positional social status, at least within the smaller community in which persons can be judged for what they are. There may, for example, be a rough general judgement, or common estimation, of the social status of teachers, but in a narrower circle distinctions are made between teachers of different grades and different schools ; and also between teachers of outstanding personality and culture who wield great influence within a local community, and teachers who lack the qualities necessary to rescue them from being finally classed as representatives of an occupational type.

It may be permitted to end with the observation that, when a social structure is in a state of flux, when the essentials of civilization are being more equally distributed, and when mobility of groups and individuals is increasing, it is not unnatural that there should be great preoccupation with social status, a preoccupation increased by puzzlement as to what it is all about, although the real importance of social status, and of the *mystique* of social inequality, may be steadily diminishing.

References

CENTERS, R. (1949), *The Psychology of Social Class*, Russell.
COLE, G. D. H. (1950), 'The conception of the middle class', *Brit. J. Sociol.*, vol. 1, no. 4, pp. 275–91.
FLOUD, J. (1952), 'Social stratification in Denmark', *Brit. J. Sociol.*, vol. 3, no. 2, pp. 173–8.
GHURYE, G. S. (1932), *Caste and Race in India*, Routledge & Kegan Paul.
HYMAN, H. A. (1942), 'The psychology of status', *Archives of Psychology*, no. 269.
MILLS, C. W. (1951), *White Collar*, Oxford University Press.
NAMIER, L. B. (1961), *England in the Age of the American Revolution*, Macmillan.

NORMAND, C. (1908), *La Bourgeosie française au XVI Siècle*, Alcan.
ROWSE, A. L. (1950), *The England of Elizabeth*, Macmillan.
SCHLATTER, R. B. (1940), *The Social Ideas of Religious Leaders, 1960–68*, Oxford University Press.
TROLLOPE, A. (1964), *The Small House at Allington*, Oxford University Press.

21 W. G. Runciman

Relative Deprivation and the Concept of Reference Group

Excerpts from W. G. Runciman, *Relative Deprivation and Social Justice*, Routledge & Kegan Paul, 1966, pp. 9–35.[1]

The related notions of 'relative deprivation' and 'reference group' both derive from a familiar truism: that people's attitudes, aspirations and grievances largely depend on the frame of reference within which they are conceived. Examples readily suggest themselves from everyday experience. A person's satisfactions, even at the most trivial level, are conditioned by his expectations, and the proverbial way to make oneself conscious of one's advantages is to contrast one's situation with that of others worse off than oneself. The frame of reference can work in either of two ways. On the one hand, a man who has been led to expect, shall we say, promotion in his job will be more aggrieved if he fails to achieve it than a man whose ambitions have not been similarly heightened. On the other hand, a man taken to hospital after some minor mishap will feel a good deal less sorry for himself if he is put in a bed next to the victim of a serious accident who has been permanently maimed. The same applies at the level of classes or even nations. Although at first sight a paradox, it has become a commonplace that steady poverty is the best guarantee of conservatism: if people have no reason to expect or hope for more than they can achieve, they will be less discontented with what they have, or even grateful simply to be able to hold on to it. But if, on the other hand, they have been led to see as a possible goal the relative prosperity of some more fortunate community with which they can directly compare themselves, then they will remain discontented with their lot until they have succeeded in catching up. It is this natural reaction which underlies the so-called 'revolution of rising expectations'. The usefulness of the terms 'relative deprivation' and 'reference group' is that they can help both to describe and to explain when and how these familiar psychological effects occur.

The term 'relative deprivation' was originally coined by the authors of *The American Soldier*, the large-scale social-psychological study of the American army which was carried out during the Second World War. The authors of *The American Soldier* do not give any rigorous

1. An edition of this book with a postscript qualifying some of this section will be published by Penguin (1972).

definition of relative deprivation (Stouffer, 1949), but its general sense is immediately apparent. If A, who does not have something but wants it, compares himself to B, who does have it, then A is 'relatively deprived' with reference to B. Similarly, if A's expectations are higher than B's, or if he was better off than B in the past, he may when similarly placed to B feel relatively deprived by comparison with him. A strict definition is difficult. But we can roughly say that A is relatively deprived of X when (a) he does not have X, (b) he sees some other person or persons, which may include himself at some previous or expected time, as having X (whether or not this is or will be in fact the case), (c) he wants X, and (d) he sees it as feasible that he should have X. Possession of X may, of course, mean avoidance of or exemption from Y.

The qualification of 'feasibility' is obviously imprecise, but it is necessary in order to exclude fantasy wishes. A man may say with perfect truth that he wants to be as rich as the Aga Khan, or a woman that she wants to be as beautiful as a reigning film star; but to include these under the heading of relative deprivation would rob the term of its value. Despite this restriction, however, relative deprivation retains the merit of being value-neutral as between a feeling of envy and a perception of injustice. To establish what resentment of inequality can be vindicated by an appeal to social justice will require that this distinction should somehow be made. But in determining first of all what is the empirical relation between inequality and grievance, it is important to use a term which in no way begs the distinction between 'legitimate' and 'illegitimate' grievances.

Relative deprivation may vary in magnitude, frequency or degree. The magnitude of a relative deprivation is the extent of the difference between the desired situation and that of the person desiring it (as he sees it). The frequency of a relative deprivation is the proportion of a group who feel it. The degree of a relative deprivation is the intensity with which it is felt. It is obvious that the three need not coincide. The proportion of a group feeling relatively deprived may be quite independent of either the magnitude or the intensity of the relative deprivation, and relative deprivation may be just as keenly felt when its magnitude is small as when it is large. Relative deprivation should always be understood to mean a *sense* of deprivation; a person who is 'relatively deprived' need not be 'objectively' deprived in the more usual sense that he is demonstrably lacking something. In addition, relative deprivation means that the sense of deprivation is such as to involve a comparison with the imagined situation of some other person or group. This other person or group is the 'reference group', or more accurately the 'comparative reference group'. The addition of 'comparative' is made necessary because 'reference group' can be used in two other senses which will not necessarily overlap with the comparative sense. It can not only mean the group with which a person compares himself; it can also be used to mean either the group from which he derives his standards of comparison or the group from which the comparison is extended and to which he feels that he belongs.

The term itself was first coined by Herbert Hyman (1942), but the idea behind it can be traced a good deal further back in the literature of social psychology. Like the idea behind relative deprivation, it is simple enough, but to make it more precise it is necessary to deal with a number of difficulties. Quite apart from its different possible senses, the reference 'group' need not be a group at all; it may be a single person or even an abstract idea. This initial disadvantage of the term has been recognized by Hyman himself (1942; 1960; Eisenstadt, 1954; Shibutani, 1955; Turner, 1956). But the use of it is now so well established that it does not seem worthwhile to try to replace it with a more general term. [. . .] It is groups, and particularly classes, with which the present study is mainly concerned; but it is important to emphasize that this by no means exhausts the scope of reference 'group' behaviour.

The major difficulty, however, is that reference groups may carry one or all of the three different senses, and these have not always been adequately distinguished by the writers who have adopted the term. Two of the three senses have been distinguished (Kelly, 1952) in terms of the 'comparative' and 'normative' function of the reference group. A 'comparative' reference group is the group whose situation or attributes a person contrasts with his own. A 'normative' reference group is the group from which a person takes his standards. Examples of the first might be a prosperous entrepreneur emulating the fortune of his rival, or a clerical worker trying to distinguish his manner of speech from that of manual workers, or a revolutionist trying to secure for his fellow-proletarians the goods and prerogatives of the bourgeoisie. Examples of the second might be a schoolboy imitating his classmates, or a convert to Communism adopting the political attitudes of those whom he regards as the 'true' working class.

The two may overlap, and often do. For example, a manual worker might at the same time envy the wealth of middle-class people and try to act like them, and there would be no inconsistency in this. But an important difference appears when these two functions of reference groups are connected to the idea of relative deprivation. Where a comparative reference group is 'positive' (in the sense that a person wants to share the situation of another group, not to dissociate himself from it), a relative deprivation is necessarily engendered. Where the reference group is a normative one, it may or may not be. Consider the same example of a manual worker who is very conscious of the situation of the 'middle class' (whatever he means by this). If he wants what he sees the middle class as having then he is by definition relatively deprived and one can speak of the relative deprivation as generated by his choice of reference group. But as his normative reference group, the 'middle class' carries no necessary implications for his sense of relative deprivation. If it leads him to see that he is, say, poorer than most of the normative group, then at the same time as he tries to imitate its standards of consumption a comparison may be generated which makes him feel relatively deprived of a middle-class income. But if it leads him to share the conservative politics of the middle class, it may inhibit those comparisons which a radical political viewpoint might have encouraged him to feel. Only comparative reference groups are bound up by definiton with relative deprivation. A normative reference group will generate a relative deprivation only if it embodies an unfavourable comparison at the same time as it sets a standard or imposes an outlook.

The third sense of 'reference group' is the particular role a person has in mind in the context of the inequality which he feels – proletarian, a corporal, a Negro, a student and so on. This group may or may not be the source of his norms; but whether or not it fulfils the additional function of the normative reference group, it is the basis of the comparison which he makes. Everyone is, of course, in some sense a member of an almost infinite multiplicity of groups, for every attribute which a person shares with others makes him by definition the joint member, with them, of at least this one group. But most of these are irrelevant to any feelings of inequality. The 'membership reference group' is, as it were, the starting-line for the inequality with the comparative reference group by which a feeling of relative deprivation is engendered.

The membership reference group does, however, have to be further distinguished from the common attribute which is shared by both the membership and comparative reference groups and which thereby furnishes the basis for the claim that the inequality should be redressed. A man who says, 'As a skilled worker I am entitled to better pay' may mean either that as a skilled worker he should have the pay to which all skilled workers are entitled, or that as a skilled worker he shares the attribute of better-paid workers which entitles them to their better pay. In the first case, skilled workers are not his membership reference group but the justifying criterion for his feeling of relative deprivation; his membership reference group is only the set of underpaid skilled workers. These may share some further attribute – for example, the lack of an apprenticeship qualification – which gives rise to the inequality between one skilled worker and another; but they may equally well have nothing else in common beyond their occupation, and be paid less than other skilled workers for a variety of separate and extraneous reasons. In the second case, on the other hand, the man believes that as a skilled worker he either is or does something – for example, exercises an uncommon talent or contributes to national productivity – to the same degree as those who are better paid. His membership reference group, therefore, is the class of skilled workers, of whom he feels that some or perhaps all are underpaid, and his justifying criterion is talent or productivity.

There may still appear to be some ambiguity in the notion of the membership reference group, since some inequalities are such that for a person to move to a position of equality with his comparative reference group means ceasing to be what he was, while others are such that he cannot cease to be what he was. A bricklayer who becomes the equal in income of an executive may well do so by ceasing to be a bricklayer; but a Negro bricklayer who becomes the equal in status of white bricklayers does not do so by ceasing to be a Negro. Once again, however, the confusion only arises if the membership group, comparative group and what one could call the justifying group or category are not sufficiently clearly distinguished. The distinction between inequality within and inequality between groups is purely a matter of definition ; any inequality can be described as either, according to how one chooses to delimit the boundaries between groups. If relative deprivation is to be precisely described, all inequalites which give rise to feelings of relative deprivation must be treated as inequalities between and only between the membership reference group and comparative reference group. [. . .]

The readiest illustration of an advance towards equality leading to an increase in relative deprivation is the common observation that revolutions are apt to occur at times of rising prosperity. Although no one would suggest that this is more than a part of the explanation of any particular revolution, historians of various times and places, including eighteenth-century France and twentieth-century Russia, have noticed the tendency for overt discontent to be relatively rare in stable hardship and to rise alike in frequency, magnitude and intensity as opportunity is seen to increase. The argument is stated at its most succinct by Tocqueville in discussing the French Revolution:

Thus it was precisely in those parts of France where there had been most improvement that popular discontent ran highest. ... Patiently endured so long as it seemed beyond redress, a grievance comes to appear intolerable once the possibility of removing it crosses men's minds. ... At the height of its power feudalism did not inspire so much hatred as it did on the eve of its eclipse (Tocqueville, 1955, pp. 176–7).

To take an example closer to the present study, it has been emphasized by Henry Pelling in his account of the origins of the Labour Party that in late nineteenth-century Britain

the immediate onset of what economic historians now call the 'Great Depression', so far from encouraging Socialism and the break-up of the Liberal Party, actually discouraged working class militancy and destroyed the 'advanced' elements then in existence. [Furthermore] the period of [the workers'] greatest political and industrial advance (1888 to 1891) was a period of comparative prosperity (Pelling, 1953, pp. 6, 8).

Such a tendency can perhaps be explained by the cautious pessimism which hardship inevitably breeds. But this, in effect, is to say that in hard times comparative reference groups will be more restricted than in good, which is a part of the generalization being put forward. The same point that is made by Pelling was made in more general terms by Masterman in 1909:

Socialism amongst the working peoples propagates and triumphs in times of plenty, withers up and vanishes in times of depression. This is exactly the reverse of the accepted belief, which thought that the poor are stung into Socialism by suffering, as poets are stung into poetry by wrong (Masterman, 1909, pp. 150–51).

This does not mean, however, that if times get sharply worse the frequency and intensity of relative deprivation may not be heightened. It is only poverty which seems irremediable that is likely to keep relative deprivation low. Marx and Engels were not foolish to hope for economic crises as the catalysts of revolution, for when a stable expectation is suddenly disappointed this is at least as likely to promote relative deprivation as when an expectation is suddenly heightened. What is common to both situations is that people are made aware of not having what they have been brought to think it feasible or proper or necessary that they should have. The upsetting of expectations provokes the sense of relative deprivation which may in turn provide the impetus for drastic change. Where apparently stable expectations are disappointed, the comparative reference group is likely to be the previous situation of the membership reference group. But when expectations are rising faster than the likelihood of their fulfilment, it is both more interesting and also more difficult to ascertain what has determined the choice of reference group by which the feeling of relative deprivation has been engendered.

Very violent changes can produce what since Durkheim we speak of as 'anomie' – the vacuum of standards which results from the dislocation of a stable social context. Where this occurs, there is danger of confusion and violence precisely because people do not know where to look for their reference groups, whether comparative or normative, and thereby become prone to exaggerated hopes or fears. But it is not always a sudden change by which reference groups are upset. If the poor begin to compare themselves directly to the rich, it may be a result of the storming of the Bastille or of a century of ideological change. [. . .]

The likelihood of a rise in dissatisfaction accompanying an advance towards equality will of course vary greatly from one topic to another. My own argument, indeed, will be that for British manual workers and their families during the present century it has operated very differently in the different dimensions of social inequality. But the important conclusion which follows from the discussion so far is that there is no stronger initial reason to expect the resentment of inequality to correlate with relative hardship than with relative good fortune. [. . .] In the absence of an external stimulus, the limited reference groups by which relative deprivation is kept low [. . .] tend to be self-perpetuating. This feedback effect generated by modest comparisons underlies many familiar generalizations about the hold of habit, the correlation between poverty and conservatism, or the unambitiousness of the underprivileged. Once the vicious circle has been broken, this may set off a rising spiral of expectations and comparisons which will continue until a new equilibrium is reached. But some external influence is needed. The interesting question, therefore, will always be what first broke the equilibrium at the lower level and so gave rise to the change of reference groups.

One of the most obvious of such external influences is war. It is often said that war is the most effective impetus behind social change, and although it is not always clear what is meant by this, a part of the process supposed to occur is the dislocation of familiar standards of reference. Expectations are first of all heightened by the feeling that some tangible rewards will result from victory. But as well as this, new comparisons are generated in two different ways. First, the underprivileged strata who are seen to have shared the exertions and sufferings of war in equal measure with their social superiors are encouraged to feel a common aspiration with their superiors for a joint share in a better world. Second, the purely physical disturbances of war bring the members of different classes into more immediate contact with each other than is ever likely to occur in peacetime. The result is that the magnitude, frequency and intensity of relative deprivation are all markedly heightened among people whose previous reference groups had been much closer to their own immediate situation.

War, however, is not the only disturbance by which reference groups may be upset. It is one of the biggest; but disturbances can often be brought about simply by the receipt of news. Orwell, in *The Road to Wigan Pier,* describes a man saying to him that there was no housing problem until people were told about it; or in other words, a sense of relative deprivation was aroused as soon as a different standard was introduced from outside. For people to be told that their economic or social situation is bad may be enough to convince them that it is, even if they had not been thinking so before. The proverbial stirring-up of discontent performed by revolutionaries and agitators depends precisely on their persuading people to judge their situation in terms of comparisons which it had not previously occurred to them to make. In the same way, education can upset traditional reference groups and heighten the general level of aspiration; better close the schools, as Ernest Bevin said in 1920, than create aspirations and then deny them. Conversely, religion can sometimes restrict aspirations; if it teaches that the existing order is just, it can inhibit those comparisons between one stratum and the next which might lead to the system's overthrow. The subversive potentialities of knowledge derive from its capacity to act as an independent influence on reference groups and thereby create relative deprivations where they did not exist before.

A third disrupter of reference groups is economic change. Prosperity can break the vicious circle between poverty and conservatism by making people aware of the possibility of a higher standard than it would previously have occurred to them to hope for. Conversely, a decline in prosperity, if not too violent, can restrict the sense of relative deprivation by inhibiting comparisons with more fortunate groups. There may at the same time be an influence the other way round – prosperity may, for example, result in turn from the urge to realize higher aspirations, as in Schumpeter's theory of the entrepreneur. But for the mass of the population, war, or education, or economic change are external influences by which their attitudes and expectations are altered. If it is true that the sense of inequality in society depends on the choice of reference groups, then the influences behind reference group choices will be the determinants of the relation between grievance and inequality. In particular, they will explain this relation when it is most discrepant – that is, when those at the bottom seem least discontented with the system which places them there.

Political theorists of many different persuasions have wondered at the acquiescence of the underprivileged in the inequalities to which they are subjected, and have explained this acquiescence in terms of ignorance, or habit, or traditionally restricted expectations. If the least fortunate strata of society – Saint-Simon's *classe la plus nombreuse et la plus pauvre*' – were fully aware of how unequally they were being treated, would not all societies break out into revolution? 'What is needed', said Durkheim, 'if social order is to reign is that the mass of men be content with their lot. But what is needed for them to be content, is not that they have more or less but that they be convinced that they have no right to more' (1959, p. 200). In stable societies with a long and unbroken history of customary inequalities, it is not difficult to see how the aspirations of the underprivileged could be kept low enough for the pattern to remain undisturbed. But once the possibility of improvement has been disclosed, it becomes more remarkable that inequalities should continue to be passively accepted by the great majority of those at the lower levels of society. We must beware of confusing acquiescence with contentment: the impossibility of remedy can inhibit action without inhibiting the sense of grievance. But even in societies which are no longer 'traditional', it is only rarely that egalitarian resentments are as militant or as widespread as the actual structure of inequalities would suggest to be plausible. The United States affords the most striking example. Indeed, there is a twofold interest in contrasting it with Britain, since the United States has always appeared to European observers to foreshadow the changes which their own societies would in due course undergo. In the United States, the belief in equality is more strongly entrenched and more widely held than in any other country in the world, yet this belief is not borne out by the actual structure and workings of the American system. How is it, therefore, that inequality can be so disproportionate to grievance even where equality is believed to be feasible?

One suggested answer is that the social discontents of Americans are kept low because they continue to believe, however erroneously, that the rags-to-riches myth is true (Lipset and Bendix, 1959, p. 81).

A man who believes that he is shortly to rise to great heights will not resent a brief position of inferiority. The captain who knows he will succeed the colonel does not mind saluting him, for he looks forward to being saluted in his turn. The foreman who expects to become a manager is unlikely to be a militant trade unionist. But this is not a sufficient explanation of the American case. Many manual workers in the United States may hope to rise into management or to establish a business of their own, but they are more realistic when directly asked about their expectations. An altogether different answer to the question is suggested by Hyman (1953, pp. 426–42), who has shown in a reanalysis of opinion poll results how the aspirations of less fortunate Americans are modified in accordance with their position. On Hyman's analysis, the aims of the less fortunate are channelled towards positions which are likely to be feasible for them rather than positions which will only be attained by those whose starting-point was much higher. This same conclusion is suggested by a similar study which was carried out in France in 1951 and is, as far as I know, the only other survey evidence published on this topic. In this study, by Stern and Keller (1953), the respondents in a small national sample were asked what they would consider a satisfactory standard of living for 'people like themselves'. When the investigators analysed the spontaneous reference groups given, they found little comparison with 'out-groups' and little evidence of class resentment. Their results therefore bear out Hyman's. Although the United States has a much more egalitarian ideology than France, the magnitude and frequency of relative deprivation seem to be similar: in both countries, although people may be anxious to improve their position in terms of where they actually stand, they seldom feel relatively deprived by reference to members of more fortunate groups with whom they have no reason to compare themselves.

It is dangerous to generalize too freely from this into talking about the 'unambitiousness' of the underprivileged, since the distance between a person's situation and his reference group may be equally large whether he is a labourer's son who wants to be a craftsman or a solicitor's son who wants to be a high court judge (Empey, 1956; Keller and Zavalloni, 1962, p. 2). It may well be that the magnitude of the relative deprivations which are felt by the underprivileged is no greater than the magnitude of those felt by the very prosperous. The point is rather that whatever the relative magnitudes of relative deprivation, those near the bottom are likely, even in a society with an egalitarian ideology, to choose reference groups nearer the bottom than self-conscious egalitarianism would imply. Or to phrase it more carefully, they are likely to modify their reference groups in such a way that their aspirations are diverted from those goals which the rags-to-riches myth misleadingly holds out for them.

This more circumspect phrasing is made necessary by the alternative implication suggested by Merton. In a paper entitled 'Social structure and anomie' (1957), Merton has argued that those who find themselves denied the positions which the egalitarian myth has led them to believe are open to them may be driven to adopt high but 'deviant' ambitions. In the American culture, success is mandatory; those to whom conventional success is denied because of their inferior position will therefore tend to seek success of a less conventional or even legitimate kind. Merton advances this argument without recourse to the notion of reference groups – which is surprising, in view of their relevance to it and Merton's own discussion of reference group theory. But if we translate his argument into these terms, it can be summarized by saying that the American ideology encourages the underprivileged to make extravagant reference group comparisons; but since the relative deprivations to which these give rise are demonstrably unlikely to be satisfied, the original reference groups may be modified by the adoption as goals of more feasible but less respectable positions of wealth and influence. The result is that 'deviant' ambitions are chosen by members of the underprivileged strata more frequently than would occur in the absence of the cultural norm of success for all. The ideology of egalitarianism influences reference group choices which in turn help to promote 'deviant' behaviour.

This argument might seem to be incompatible with Hyman's. Merton suggests that an egalitarian ideology promotes large ambitions among the underprivileged, while Hyman emphasizes rather their adjustment to the depressing realities of inequality. If, however, we keep in mind the caveat about 'unambitiousness', it is clear that the two amount to the same. Even in a society where the ideology of egalitarianism is most powerful, those at the bottom modify their ambitions in accordance with the facts of their situation. They may, it is true, continue to feel relatively deprived of wealth and success to a greater extent than they would in a society where equality was held neither desirable nor possible. But their reference groups will not be those implied by a literal adoption of the belief that there is a place at the top for everyone. Even where equality is an article of faith, the facts of inequality tend to restrict those feelings of relative deprivation which they might be thought to stimulate. The 'normal' situation, where inequality is not seen to be markedly diminishing, is for reference groups to be close to home. [. . .]

What happens when people make comparisons in more than one of their various capacities, and these capacities have different rankings in the hierarchy of the society to which they belong? Suppose, for example, that we are talking to a Negro businessman in the United States about equality of opportunity. As a Negro comparing himself with white businessmen, he is likely to feel relatively deprived; as a businessman comparing himself with unskilled Negroes, he is likely to feel relatively gratified. In his answers to questions about social equality he may feel aware of either or both comparisons with equal intensity. How, therefore, should his attitude be described?

The problem has received some attention among American social psychologists under the headings of 'status-consistency' and 'status-crystallization' (Lenski, 1954). Given people who belong at the same time to social categories which are differently ranked, the problem is to discover how far their attitudes or behaviour are influenced by their awareness of the discrepancies in the status of their differently ranked roles. It has been suggested, for example, that such people are likelier than others to adopt liberal political attitudes. But attempts to generalize along these lines have been subjected to some effective criticism, and no very illuminating conclusions have emerged from the studies so far carried out. It seems agreed that it is a mistake to look at status as though it were unidimensional, and that 'all forms of status inconsistency are psychologically disturbing' (Jackson, 1962), but this hardly needs saying. The significance of status inconsistency for the relation between inequality and grievance is intuitively obvious. A person who occupies two different roles or categories may well be driven by his awareness of the discrepancy betwen them into a resentment of the status accorded to him in his lower-ranked role. A university graduate who works under a man who is much better paid but has no formal qualifications may well feel that his qualifications are insufficiently rewarded; the Negro businessman may well feel more keenly aware of discrimination against Negroes than the Negro labourer. Such discrepancies will not always have the same effect. But they furnish another possible influence on the nature and frequency of feelings of relative deprivation. When, for example, manual workers achieve a greater equality of reward, but not of status, with workers who used to be above them in both, then it is probable that their frequency of relative deprivation of status will rise in proportion as their relative deprivation of income is appeased.

There is, however, yet another possible difference in the nature of the relative deprivation which they will feel. This is the difference which I briefly mentioned earlier. The manual worker whose prosperity has heightened his relative deprivation of status may have come to feel that his occupation as a whole is insufficiently esteemed (Dennis, Henriques and Slaughter, 1956, p. 70). But suppose that his prosperity rather leads him to identify with those in other occupations whose level of reward is the same. If his disparate statuses (in the sense of high reward but low esteem) influence his attitudes in this rather different way, then he will not so much wish to rise in social prestige with his membership reference group as out of it.

This is the one final distinction in types of relative deprivation which is relevant to the relation between inequality and grievance. A person's sense of relative deprivation will be affected not only by which of several membership reference groups is the basis for his chosen comparison; it will also be affected by what he feels about its relation to his comparative group. The two will, of course, share at least the common attribute without which a sense of relative deprivation could not be engendered at all. But suppose a person succeeds in reaching a position of equality with his comparative group. Did he want to rise out of his membership group, or with it? If the first, then he was dissatisfied with his position as a member of what he saw as his group; if the second, then he was dissatisfied with the position of what he saw as his group relative to other groups in the larger system. The difference between the two is obvious, but important. It is also closely bound up with the person's choice of normative reference group.

The distinction can easily be illustrated by hypothetical examples. A junior business executive balked of promotion is continuously and resentfully aware of the senior directors of his firm; he compares his position with theirs, he aspires to become one of them, and he sees this prospect as a perfectly feasible one in terms of his expectations or demands. He has no feeling that the social categories either of junor executives or of businessmen in general are lower in rewards, or esteem, or influence than they should be, nor does he feel himself a member of any other group which is ill-treated by his society as a whole. But he feels intensely deprived relative to the position of other people whom he regards as deserving no greater recognition than himself. He is, therefore, relatively deprived only in terms of his personal situation; there may be others in the same situation with whom he shares some kind of fellow-feeling, but his achievement of what would assuage his feeling of relative deprivation is in no way bound up with theirs.

Consider, by contrast, a factory worker who feels that he is grossly underpaid. He is conscious, and even militantly conscious, of belonging to the working class. He has no ambition to rise above his fellows. But he feels that he and all those like him are insufficiently rewarded both in money and status by the society to whose welfare they are contributing by their work. He feels relatively deprived as one of a class whose members all share the same conditions of life and employment. His comparative reference group might even be the same as that of the junior executive who feels he should have a higher salary ; both may feel relatively deprived by reference to what they picture as the unjustified perquisites of the chairman's nephew who holds an executive position. But there is an important difference between them when it comes to their own half, as it were, of the comparison which they are making. The factory worker comparing himself with those whom he sees as better rewarded feels relatively deprived as a factory worker – the chairman's nephew, he feels, should be no better rewarded than 'people like us'. The junior executive balked of promotion feels relatively deprived because he thinks he is more talented than other junior executives – the chairman's nephew, he feels, should be no better rewarded than 'people like me'.

The distinction can be conveniently represented in the form of a fourfold table.

	Relatively deprived because of own position as member of group	
	Satisfied	Dissatisfied
Relatively deprived because of group's position in society Satisfied	A	B
Dissatisfied	C	D

It would, of course, be unwarrantable to assume that any single person, who may occupy a variety of roles and hold a variety of attitudes to them, can arbitrarily be assigned to one or another of these four categories. If nothing else, a consistent distinction must be made between relative deprivation in the three different dimensions of social inequality which are discussed in the following chapter. But as long as it is clear that the four categories are no more than ideal types, then it may be useful to describe them in a little more detail.

Type A could perhaps be labelled 'orthodox', since it covers anyone who is neither ambitious within his group nor resentful on its behalf.

It is, however, perfectly possible for a person to be anxious to change the structure of his society without himself feeling relatively deprived. Type A, therefore, will not only include the studious conformist or the successful social climber ; it will also include the prosperous altruist who is not himself relatively deprived, but is at the same time driven by guilt or conviction into radical attitudes. In addition, Type A will include those who are low in the social hierarchy but who, for whatever reasons, are not in fact resentful of their position. It is the members of Type A who show how Durkheim's problem comes to be solved – how, that is, people who do not have very much become comfortably convinced that they have no right to more – and who exemplify all the most glaring disparities between inequality and grievance.

Type B, by contrast, covers the sort of 'striver' who is dissatisfied with his present situation, but not in a way that gives him common cause with others like him. A hypothetical example of Type B has been described already in the junior executive balked of promotion. He can be presented in such a way that he appears a rather greedy and unpleasant sort of person, but this may be unfair. He might, for example, be a poor but talented artist who feels that his merits are unrecognized, or an intelligent adolescent denied a university scholarship, or an unemployed man refused the scale of benefit to which he is entitled under the regulations in force.

Type C also has been described already. It includes all the exemplars of the strong lateral solidarity traditionally found within the working class. But members of Type C need not belong only to a group which resents the inequalities to which it is subjected in the hierarchy of economic class. The member of a religious movement or a minority race may equally feel only a collective relative deprivation, and have no wish to improve his personal position in relation to any of the social categories to which he feels that he belongs. In general, the relative deprivations of Type C are those which play the largest part in the transformation of an existing structure of social inequalities.

Type D, finally, consists of those most relatively deprived of all, who are dissatisfied both with the position of their group and also with their membership of it. Their ideal type will be the tribune of the plebs – the man who not only feels the deprivations and injustices imposed on his class but who explicitly aspires to lead or even ultimately to rule his class in the course of securing redress on their behalf. Individual examples of Type D have had striking effects on the course of history. But for the purposes of the present study the two most interesting types are B and C. In order to refer to them and to the two types of relative deprivation which they exemplify, I shall use the terms 'egoists' (for Type B) and 'fraternalist' (for Type C).

Neither term is entirely satisfactory, but it is better to use existing words in a specialized sense than to have recourse to neologisms. Although 'fraternalistic' relative deprivations are more naturally suggestive of a working-class person and 'egoistic' of a middle-class person, this need not be so by definition. There is nothing to prevent a working-class person feeling relatively deprived within but not on behalf of his class, and, as we shall see, middle-class people are very capable of fraternalistic relative deprivation. There is, however, a significance in the fact that 'fraternalism' is traditionally characteristic of the working, and 'egoism' of the middle class ; and a part of the answer to the relation between inequality and grievance might lie in the circumstances by which the working class has been influenced in the direction of egoistic rather than fraternalistic relative deprivations. The difference between the two, indeed, can be redefined in terms of normative reference groups. Consider once again the example of a working-class person whose comparative reference group is the middle class, or a section of it. If his normative reference group is the working class, then his relative deprivations will in principle be fraternalistic ; if it is the middle class, they will be egoistic.

The distinction cannot in practice be applied quite as easily as this suggests. Not only can the notion of a normative reference group not be rigorously defined, but it need never imply any one particular comparison out of the range of relevant inequalities. A manual worker may well think of himself as belonging to the 'middle class' (whatever this means to him), and whether or not he feels relatively deprived will depend on the comparisons which he makes as a self-styled middle-class person. Furthermore, his assessment of others in what he sees as his class will in turn affect whether his relative deprivation, if he feels one, is of a fraternalistic or an egoistic kind. But once the answers to these more detailed questions can be ascertained, or at least inferred, then the relative deprivation which he feels – with whatever intensity – can in principle be fully described.

It will be clear from the account I have given that none of these terms lend themselves to completely strict definition ; but they do provide a framework within which the relation of inequality to grievance can be discussed with reasonable precision. Whatever term is used for it, relative deprivation lies at the heart of this relation. The way in which comparative reference groups are chosen, the membership reference group which gives the comparison its basis and the normative reference group which either exacerbates or mitigates the perception of inequality contain between them the answer to why inequalities are or are not regarded with a resentment proportionate to their magnitude.

References

DENNIS, N., HENRIQUES, F., and SLAUGHTER, C. (1956), *Coal is Our Life*, Eyre & Spottiswoode.

DURKHEIM, E. (1959), *Socialism and Saint-Simon*, ed. A. W. Gouldner, Routledge & Kegan Paul.

EISENSTADT, S. N. (1954), 'Studies in reference group behavior, I: norms and the social structure', *Human Relations*, vol. 7, no. 2, pp. 191-217.

EMPEY, L. T. (1956), 'Social class and occupational aspiration: a comparison of absolute and relative measurement', *Amer. Sociol. Rev.*, vol. 21, no. 6, pp. 703-9.

HYMAN, H. H. (1942), 'The psychology of status', *Archives of Psychology*, no. 269.

HYMAN, H. H. (1953), 'The value systems of different classes', in R. Bendix and S. M. Lipset (eds.), *Class, Status and Power*, Routledge & Kegan Paul.

HYMAN, H. H. (1960), 'Reflection in reference groups', *Public Opinion Q.*, vol. 24, no. 3, pp. 383-97.

JACKSON, E. F. (1962), 'Status inconsistency and symptoms of stress', *Amer. Sociol. Rev.*, vol. 27, no. 4, pp. 469-80.

KELLER, S., and ZAVALLONI, M. (1962), 'Classe sociale, ambition et réussite', *Sociologie du Travail*, vol. 4.

KELLY, H. H. (1952), 'Two functions of reference groups', G. H. Swanson (ed.), *Readings in Social Psychology*, Holt, Rinehart & Winston.

LENSKI, G. E. (1954), 'Status crystallization: a non-vertical dimension of social status', *Amer. Sociol. Rev.*, vol. 19, no. 4, pp. 405-13.

LIPSET, S. M., and BENDIX, R. (1959), *Social Mobility in Industrial Society*, University of California Press.

MASTERMAN, C. F. G. (1909), *The Condition of England*, Methuen.

MERTON, R. K. (1957), *Social Theory and Social Structure*, Free Press.

PELLING, H. (1953), *The Origins of the Labour Party, 1880-1900*, Macmillan.

SHIBUTANI, T. (1955), 'Reference groups as perspectives', *Amer. J. Sociol.*, vol. 60, no. 6, pp. 562-9.

STERN, E., and KELLER, S. (1953), 'Spontaneous group references in France', *Public Opinion Q.*, vol. 17, no. 2, pp. 208-17.

STOUFFER, S. A. (1949), *The American Soldier, I: Adjustment during Army Life*, Princeton University Press.

TOCQUEVILLE, A. DE (1955), *The Old Regime and the French Revolution*, Doubleday.

TURNER, R. H. (1956), 'Role-taking, role standpoint and reference group behavior', *Amer. J. Sociol.*, vol. 61, no. 4, pp. 316-28.

22 Seymour Martin Lipset

Value Patterns, Class and the Democratic Polity: The United States and Great Britain

Excerpt from R. Bendix and S. M. Lipset (eds.), *Class, Status and Power*, Routledge & Kegan Paul, 1967, pp. 161–70. First published in 1963.

To compare national value systems, we must be able to classify them and distinguish among them. Talcott Parsons has provided a useful tool for this purpose in his concept of 'pattern variables'. These were originally developed by Parsons as an extension of the classic distinction by Ferdinand Tönnies between 'community' and 'society' – between those systems which emphasized *Gemeinschaft* (primary, small, traditional, integrated) values, and those which stressed *Gesellschaft* (impersonal, secondary, large, socially differentiated) values (Tönnies, 1957). The pattern variables to be used in the following analysis are achievement-ascription, universalism-particularism and specificity-diffuseness. According to the achievement-ascription distinction, a society's value system may emphasize individual ability or performance or it may emphasize ascribed or inherited qualities (such as race or high birth) in judging individuals and placing them in various roles. According to the universalism-particularism distinction, it may emphasize that all people shall be treated according to the same standard (e.g. equality before the law), or that individuals shall be treated differently according to their personal qualities or their particular membership in a class or group. Specificity-diffuseness refers to the difference between treating individuals in terms of the specific positions which they happen to occupy, rather than diffusely as individual members of the collectivity.[1] [. . .] For instance, they make it possible for us to establish differences in value structures between two nations that are at the same end of the *Gemeinschaft-Gesellschaft* continuum, or are at similar levels of economic development or social complexity. They are also useful for describing differences within a society. Thus the family

1. Parsons has two other pattern variables which I ignore here, largely for reasons of parsimony; affectivity-affective neurality, and the instrumental-consummatory distinction. For a detailed presentation of the pattern variables see Parsons (1951, pp. 58–67). For Parsons's most recent elaboration of the relationship of pattern variable analysis to other elements in his conceptual framework see (1960; 1961, pp. 319–20, 329–36).

is inherently ascriptive and particularistic while the market is universalistic and achievement oriented – the weaker the kinship ties in a given society, the greater the national emphasis on achievement is likely to be.

The manner in which any set of values is introduced will obviously affect the way the values are incorporated into a nation's institutions. In France, for instance, where the values of universalism, achievement, and specificity were introduced primarily through a political revolution, we would expect to find them most prominent in the political institutions; in Germany, where they have been introduced primarily through industrialization, we would expect to find them most prominent in its economic institutions. The American example suggests that for democratic values to become legitimate in a post-revolutionary polity the norms of universalism, achievement and specificity must be introduced into its economic institutions as well. This fosters rapid economic development, and encourages the underprivileged to believe that they as individuals may personally improve their status (Deutsch *et al.*, 1957).

I shall add the equalitarian-elitist distinction to the pattern variables just outlined. According to this, a society's values may stress that all persons must be given respect simply because they are human beings, or it may stress the general superiority of those who hold positions of power and privilege. In an equalitarian society, the differences between low status and high status people are not stressed in social relationships and do not convey to the high status person a general claim to social deference. In contrast, in an elitist society, those who hold high positions in any structure, whether it be in business, in intellectual activities, or in government, are thought to deserve, and are actually given, general respect and deference.[2] All ascriptively oriented societies are necessarily also elitist in this use of the term. On the other hand, achievement orientation and egalitarianism are not necessarily highly correlated, since a stress on achievement is not incompatible with giving generalized deference to all who have achieved their elite positions. [. . .]

2. Although all four polarity distinctions are important to the analysis of the political system, ascription-achievement and universalism-particularism seem more important than the other two. As Parsons has suggested, these are the variables which have the most reference to the total social system, rather than to subparts or to the motivation of individuals. 'They are concerned . . . with the type of value-norms which enter into the structure of the social system.' Combinations of these pairs are also most useful to help account for 'structural differentiation and variability of social systems' (Parsons, 1951, p. 106). The other two pairs, specificity-diffuseness and equalitarianism-elitism, are to a considerable degree dependent on the particular combinations of the first two.

In actual fact, *no society is ever fully explicable by these analytic concepts, nor does the theory even contemplate the possible existence of such a society.*[3] [. . .] We may, however, differentiate among social structures by the extent to which they emphasize one or another of these polarities[4]. It should be added that classifications of the relative emphases among nations with respect to certain value polarities do not imply that such values are either prescriptive or descriptive of actual behaviour. Rather, they are intended to provide base lines for comparative analysis.

I have chosen to discuss the United States and Great Britain to illustrate the relationship between values and the stability of democratic political systems (Lipset, 1963, pp. 224–39).

Though the United States and Great Britain are both urbanized, industrialized and have stable, democratic political systems, they are integrated around different values and class relations. Tocqueville's *Democracy in America* and Bagehot's *The English Constitution* accurately specified these different organizing principles. According to Tocqueville, American democratic society was equalitarian and competitive (achievement oriented); according to Bagehot, Britain was deferential (elitist) and ascriptive. As both Tocqueville and Bagehot indicated, a society in which the historic ties of traditional legitimacy had been forcibly broken could sustain a stable democratic polity only if it emphasized equality and if it contained strong, independent and competitive institutions. Conversely, if the privileged classes persisted and continued to expect ascriptive (aristocratic) and elitist rights, a society could have a stable democratic system only if the lower classes accepted the status system. A stable democracy can result from different combinations of pattern variables.

The United States, more than any other modern non-Communist industrial nation, emphasizes achievement, equalitarianism, universalism and specificity (Williams, 1951, pp. 372–442). These four tend to be

3. As Parsons has put it: 'In a very broad way the differentiations between types of social systems do correspond to this order of cultural value pattern differentiation, but *only* in a very broad way. Actual social structures are not value-pattern types, but *resultants* of the integration of value-patterns with the other components of the system' (1951, p. 112).

4. It is important to note also that the pattern variables can be and have been, used to distinguish among and within different orders of social systems or structures. Thus we may characterize total epochs (feudalism compared to capitalism), whole nations (the United States compared to Britain), subsystems within nations that logically may operate with different combinations of the variables (the state or industry), subsystems within nations that logically must follow a specific set of pattern variables (the family), and subsystems within which there is conflict between different pattern variables (e.g. the French business system, to be discussed later).

mutually supportive. This does not mean that other stable combinations are not possible or that the 'American' combination does not exhibit tensions. From the perspective of the polity, however, this combination of variables does encourage stable democracy. The upper classes can accept improvements in the status and power of the lower strata *without feeling morally offended*. [. . .]

Similarly, the emphasis on equalitarianism, universalism, and specificity means that men can expect – and within limits do receive – fair treatment according to the merits of the case or their ability. Lower-class individuals and groups which desire to change their social position *need not be revolutionary*. [. . .] There is little class consciousness on their part, since this consciousness is in part an adaptation to the behaviour of the upper class in those societies characterized by ascription, elitism, particularism and diffuseness. [. . .]

The above comments are, of course, an oversimplification. In fact, American society does display ascriptive, elitist, particularistic and diffuse culture traits. These are not completely dysfunctional, as will be shown. They do create frictions (see the analyses of McCarthyism as a reaction to 'status-panic') (Bell, 1963), but in general, with the exception of race and ethnic relations, these have not affected the basic stability of the polity.

The American South, which has stressed ascriptive-elitist-particularistic-diffuse values in race relations and to some extent in its social system, has constituted a major source of instability in the American polity. It was retained in the nation only by force, and down to the present it does not have a stable, democratic polity. [. . .]

Britain has come to accept the values of achievement in its economic and educational system, and to some extent in its political system, but retains a substantial degree of elitism (the assumption that those who hold high position be given generalized deference) and ascription (that those born to high place should retain it).[5] Tocqueville described the British class system as an 'open aristocracy', which can be entered by achievement but which confers on new entrants many of the diffuse perquisites of rank enjoyed by those whose membership stems from

5. The general concept of elitism explicitly affects the training given to prospective members of the British upper class. Thus a description of the English public schools (private in the American sense) reports that 'learning and getting-fit are represented as part of the "training for leadership" which many public-schoolmasters see as their social role. . . . It infects the whole set-up with a certain smugness and a certain frightening *elite* concept. The word "breeding" is often on their lips. . . . Many of these boys go around looking for people to lead: they actually say at the University interviews that they feel they have been trained to lead . . .' (Vaizey, 1959, pp. 28–9).

their social background (1958, pp. 59–60, 67, 70–71). Thus Britain differs from the United States in having, in terms of pattern variables, a strong emphasis on ascriptive, elitist, particularistic, and diffuse values.

In the nineteenth century the British business classes challenged the traditional pre-industrial value integration (see Bendix, 1956, pp. 100–116). But the British upper class (in contrast to most Continental aristocracies) did not strongly resist the claims of the new business classes, and later those of the workers, to take part in politics. [. . .] If communication between the different strata in Britain had been blocked by jealously guarded privileges – as it had been in France – conflicts over the suffrage might have become more divisive. As Robert Michels once pointed out, the presence of upper-class leaders in a working-class party serves to reduce conservatives' hostility toward it. [. . .] It is worth noting that, unlike the British Labour Party, the German socialists have recruited few, if any, leaders from the old upper classes.

Thus the *economy* and *polity* in Britain have been characterized by achievement, elitism, universalism and diffuseness. The *social class* system, however, retains many elements of ascription, elitism, particularism and diffuseness. The traditional upper classes and their institutions – the public schools, the ancient universities and the titled aristocracy – remain at the summit of the social structure (Crosland, 1956, pp. 232–7; Williams, 1961, pp. 318–21, Sampson, 1962, pp. 160–217). At the same time, achievers in job and school are not barred from securing diffuse elite status, and the lower classes feel that the political institutions operate for their benefit. [. . .]

Having been allowed into the political club almost as soon as British labor developed organizations of its own, working-class leaders have supported the rules of the parliamentary game. Unlike many early Continental socialist parties, they were willing, while a small minority party, to cooperate with one of the older parties. And currently they remain the only socialist party whose policies 'sustain' the legitimacy of aristocracy; their leaders, like other members of the Establishment, willingly accept aristocratic titles and other honors from the Crown (Shils and Young, 1961, p. 221). [. . .]

The British upper class has long shown a high level of sophistication in handling the admission of new strata to the 'club'. Thus in 1923, as Labour was about to form its first government, the *Sunday Times* printed a manifesto by Richard Haldane (Viscount of Cloan) urging that the two old parties give Labour a fair chance at government. [. . .]

Shils (1956) seeks to account for the great emphasis on publicity concerning political matters in the United States, e.g. congressional investigations, as contrasted with the stress on privacy and secrecy in Britain. His explanation hinges on the fact that Britain is still a deferential society as compared with the United States:

The United States has been committed to the principle of publicity since its origin. The atmosphere of distrust of aristocracy and of pretensions to aristocracy in which the American Republic spent its formative years has persisted in many forms. Repugnance for governmental secretiveness was an offspring of the distrust of aristocracy.

In the United States, the political elite could never claim the immunities and privileges of the rulers of an aristocratic society. . . .

American culture is a populistic culture. As such, it seeks publicity as a good in itself. Extremely suspicious of anything which smacks of 'holding back', it appreciates publicity, not merely as a curb on the arrogance of rulers but as a condition in which the members of society are brought into a maximum of contact with each other.

. . . Great Britain is a modern, large-scale society with a politicized population, a tradition of institutionalized pluralism, a system of representative institutions and great freedom of inquiry, discussion and reporting. . . . British political life is strikingly quiet and confined. Modern publicity is hemmed about by a generally well-respected privacy. . . .

Although democratic and pluralistic, British society is not populist. Great Britain is a hierarchical country. Even when it is distrusted, the Government instead of being looked down upon, as it often is in the United States, is, as such, the object of deference because the Government is still diffused with the symbolism of a monarchical and aristocratic society. The British Government, of course, is no longer aristocratic . . . [But it] enjoys the deference which is aroused in the breast of Englishmen by the symbols of hierarchy which find their highest expression in the Monarchy. . . .

The acceptance of hierarchy in British society permits the Government to retain its secrets, with little challenge or resentment. . . . The deferential attitude of the working and middle classes is matched by the uncommunicativeness of the upper-middle classes and of those who govern. . . . The traditional sense of the privacy of executive deliberations characteristic of the ruling classes of Great Britain has imposed itself on the rest of the society and has established a barrier beyond which publicity may not justifiably penetrate (pp. 37–51, see also pp. 220–33).

The protection from populist criticism which an elitist system gives to all who possess the diffuse status of 'leaders' extends not only to the political and intellectual elites but to school teachers and the school system as well. A study of the comparative position of teachers in England and America points this out well:

Conservative, Labour and Liberal parties alike have consistently held to the view that the content of education and methods of instruction are not matters for popular debate and decision, but should be left in the hands of teachers themselves and of other professional educators. This being so, individuals or groups seeking to 'use' the schools for their own purposes are confronted, not by the hastily constructed defenses of the teacher or of a single school or school board, as in America, but by the massive disregard of experienced politicians and administrators. This willing delegation of educational issues to educators is possible because the latter form a coherent and predictable element in the authority structure that molds society. . . .

The relation between the school and the family also differs in the two countries. In America, for the most part, the parents hand over their child to the school system, but maintain a continuous scrutiny over progress. In England, 'interference' by the parents in the school is resisted both by teachers and by educational administrators. Parents' associations and parent-teacher associations are becoming increasingly common, but they limit their activities to social functions and to meetings at which school policy is explained but not debated (Baron and Tropp, 1956, p. 548).

Ralph Turner also shows how variations in the basic values of the two societies impinge on their educational systems. American education reflects the norms of *contest mobility*,

a system in which elite status is the prize in an open contest and is taken by the aspirants' own efforts. . . . Since the 'prize' of successful upward mobility is not in the hands of the established elite to give out, the latter are not in a position to determine who shall attain it and who shall not.

Conversely, British education reflects the norms of *sponsored mobility*, in which 'elite recruits are chosen by the established elite or their agents, and elite status is *given* on the basis of some criterion of supposed merit and cannot be *taken* by any amount of effort or strategy. Upward mobility is like entry into a private club, where each candidate must be "sponsored" by one or more of the members'.

The American system, with its emphasis on the common school and opportunities for further education at every level, encourages all to advance themselves through their own efforts. 'Every individual is encouraged to think of himself as competing for an elite position, so that in preparation his cultivates loyalty to the system and conventional attitudes' (Turner, 1961, pp. 122, 125). Conversely, the British system has always selected the minority who will go ahead in the educational system at a relatively early age. Those not selected, the large bulk of the population, are taught to 'regard themselves as relatively incompetent to manage society. . . . The earlier that selection of the elite recruits can be made, the sooner the masses can be taught to accept their inferiority and to make "realistic" rather than phantasy plans' (p. 126). Those selected for the elite, on the other hand, are removed from competition and admitted to a school, either public or grammar, in which there is great emphasis on absorbing the elite's aesthetic culture, manners and sense of paternalism toward the non-elite. Unlike the situation in America, where in the absence of a sense of a special elite culture the masses retain their right and ability to determine taste, English society operates on the assumption that only the elite may determine what is high or low quality (Lipset, 1960, pp. 326-8).

In his discussion of the sources of stability of English democracy, Harry Eckstein observes that authority patterns vary among the classes – authoritarian relations increase as one moves down the social ladder. Within the British elite, he suggests, social relations

tend to be quite surprisingly democratic, or at least consultative and comradely; here . . . we might note the ubiquity of committees at every conceivable level in the higher civil service, the unusual use of staff committees in the military services, and the easy relations among officers of all ranks in military regiments, especially in elitist regiments like the Guards, . . . while behaviour among pupils [in upper-class public schools] is modelled to a remarkable extent on the political system.

[Conversely, where hierarchial relations are involved, as] between members of the Administrative Class [of the Civil Service] and their underlings, officers and their men, managers, and their help, relations are highly non-consultative and certainly not comradely . . . (1961, pp. 15-16).

The United States and Great Britain differ, of course, not only in these patterns, but in the extent to which the same value orientations dominate the key status, economic and political subsystems of the society. Presumably, Eckstein would relate the stability of American populist democracy to the fact that there are egalitarian social relations within all levels. American society has more homogeneity of values than the British. On the other hand, the particular distribution of different value orientations in Britain would also seem to be congruent with the stability of an industrialized democracy, since it legitimates open participation by all groups in the economy and polity, while the diffuse elitism rewards all with a claim to high position.

Some quantitative indicators for the value differences between the United States and Great Britain particularly as it pertains to achievement, may be deduced from variations in the numbers securing higher education. [. . .] In the United States, the strong and successful efforts to extend the opportunities to attend colleges and universities have, to some considerable degree, reflected both pressures by those in lower status positions to secure the means to succeed, and recognition on the part of the privileged that American values of equality and achievement require giving the means to take part in the 'race for success' to all those who are qualified.

Thus if we relate the number enrolled in institutions of higher learning to the size of the age cohort twenty to twenty-four, we find that almost seven times as large a group was attending such schools in 1956–7 in the United States as in England and Wales[6]. Some proof that these differences reflect variation in values, and not simply differences in wealth or occupational structures, may be deduced from the fact that the one major former American colony, the Philippines, has a much larger proportion enrolled in colleges and universities than any country in Europe or the British Commonwealth, a phenomenon which seemingly reflects the successful effort of Americans to export their belief that 'everyone' should be given a chance at college education [. . .] Thus Jamaica, like many other former British colonies in Africa and Asia, has a higher education system which seems premised on the belief that only a tiny elite should receive such training; while the system in Puerto Rico, like the one in the Philippines, clearly reflects the continued impact of American assumptions concerning widespread educational opportunity. [. . .]

Table 1 Students Enrolled in Institutions of Higher Learning as Per Cent of Age Group 20–24, by Country, about 1956

Country	
United States	27·2
Australia	12·05*
Canada	8·0
England and Wales	3·7*
Scotland	5·1*
Philippines	14·5
Jamaica	0·7
Puerto Rico	11·9
Western Europe	4·5
Denmark	6·6
France	5·8
Germany (West)	4·1
USSR	11·1

Source: The educational data for the first eight countries and the USSR are calculated from materials in UNESCO (1959). and the Statistical Office of the United Nations (1960). The data for the Western European countries other than Britain are taken from Dewhurst (1961, p. 315).

6. The number attending institutions of higher learning (post-high school) has been related to the four-year age category 20–24, since in most countries the bulk of such students are in this age group. The best category for such analysis would probably be 18–21, but the more or less standardized census categories are 15–19 and 20–24. Since these two groups are about the same size, using the category 20–24 probably gives as good an estimate as is needed of the national variations in the proportion of the relevant age cohort attending schools of higher education.

The greater difference between Britain and the United States, in the extent to which populist explosions and threats to sytematic due process occur, is reflected to some degree in their attitudes toward law and order. The latter is more willing to tolerate lawlessness. The reason for this may be that the absence of traditional mechanisms of social control in the United States has weakened the pressure to conform without coercion. [. . .]

One indicator of the relative strength of the informal normative mechanisms of social control as compared with the restrictive emphases of legal sanctions seems to be the extent to which given nations need lawyers. Among the English-speaking democracies, the United States and Britain stand at polar extremes. As of 1955, the United States had 241,514 lawyers 'of whom approximately 190,000 were engaged in private practice. This means there was one lawyer in private practice per 868 of population. . . . [T]he total English legal profession seems to number about 25,000, and those in private practice can hardly be more than 20,000 or one lawyer per 2222 population' (Gower and Price, 1957, p. 317).

The emphasis on populist values derivative from equalitarianism in the United States as contrasted with the very different value emphasis in Britain is reflected in the differential status and role of judge and jury in the two countries. The American system has stressed the notion of the judge as a neutral 'umpire', in a contest which is decided by a jury drawn from the population, while the British have placed more stress on the positive role of the judge and less on the role of the jury. [. . .]

Values and the democratic process

While the stability of a democracy demands that the values of universalism and achievement be dominant in both the economic and political spheres, it does not require them to be dominant in the status hierarchies. That is, the status hierarchy may lean toward elitism, as it does in Britain, or toward equalitarianism, as in the United States, yet both of these nations are stable democracies.

However, these differences do have their effects on the ways in which the political system functions, particularly in the viability of the 'rules of the game', and in such matters as the tolerance of opposition and nonconformity and in the respect shown for the due process of the law.

Although popular agreement about the importance of such rules would seem an important requisite for their effectiveness, the empirical data do not clearly sustain this expectation. The less educated and the lower strata in most countries do not accept the need for tolerance of what they consider to be 'error' or 'wickedness', that is, opposition to what is 'clearly right'. Conversely, the 'rules of the game' are most respected where they are most significant, that is, among the various politically relevant and involved elites (Lipset, 1960, pp. 101–5, 109–14). Perhaps the highest degree of tolerance for political deviance is found, therefore, in democratic systems which are most strongly characterized by the values of elitism and diffuseness. Diffuse elitism of the variety which exists in most of the democratic monarchies of Europe tends to place a buffer between the elites and the population. The generalized deference which the latter give to the former means that even if the bulk of the electorate do not understand or support the 'rules', they accept the leadership of those who do. It is deferential respect for the elite rather than tolerant popular opinion which underlies the vaunted freedom of dissent in countries like Britain and Sweden. [. . .] In these societies, the elites, whether those of the intellect, of business, of politics or of mass organizations, are both protected and controlled by their membership in the 'club'.

The seemingly lesser respect for civil liberties and minority rights in the more equalitarian democracy such as the United States may be viewed as a consequence of a social system in which elite status is more specific, so that contending elites do not receive diffuse respect and feel less acutely the need to conform to an appropriate set of rules when in conflict with one another. They do not see themselves as part of the same club, as members of 'an establishment'. Hence disagreement about *the rules*, as well as over policies, are thrown to the broader public for settlement. And this entails appealing in some degree to a mass electorate to adjudicate on rules whose utility, in some measure, they cannot be expected to understand; appreciation of the necessity for such rules often involves a long-term socialization to the nature of the political and juridical process, secured primarily through education and/or participation. Thus, though civil liberties will be stronger in elitist democracies than in equalitarian ones, the latter may be regarded as more 'democratic' in the sense that the electorate has more access to or power over the elite.

Another of Parsons's pattern variables not discussed earlier suggests specific sources of political strain in contemporary American society. His distinction between self-orientation and collectivity-orientation stresses the extent to which values emphasize that a collectivity has a claim on the individual units within it to conform to the defined interests of the larger group, as contrasted to a stress on actions predominantly reflecting the perceived needs of the units. An emphasis on particularism tends to be linked to collectivity-orientation. Moreover, the *noblesse oblige* morality inherent in aristocracy is an aspect of collectivity-orientation. Traditionally, Britain appears to have stressed collectivity obligations more than has the United States. Consequently, the rise of socialist and welfare-state concepts have placed less of a strain on British values than on American. Although modern industrial society, including the United States, appears to be moving generally toward a greater acceptance of collectivity-orientations, the American values' emphasis on self-orientation results in a stronger resistance to accepting the new community welfare concepts than occurs elsewhere. In discussing the rise of right-wing extremism in American society, Parsons has argued that they are the most self-oriented segments of the American population which currently find the greatest need for political scapegoats and which strongly resist political changes which are accepted by the upper classes in such countries as Britain and Sweden (Parsons, 1963, pp. 183–4). Thus, the values of elitism and ascription may protect an operating democracy from the excesses of populism and may facilitate the acceptance by the privileged strata of the welfare planning state, whereas emphases on self-orientation and anti-elitism may be conducive to right-wing populism.

Elitism in the status hierarchy has major dysfunctions which should be noted here (Crosland, 1956, pp. 227–37). A system of differential status rankings requires that a large proportion of the population accept a negative conception of their own worth as compared with others in more privileged positions. To be socially defined as being low according to a system of values which one respects, must mean that, to some unspecified degree, such low status is experienced as 'punishment' in a psychological sense. This felt sense of deprivation or punishment is often manifested in 'self-hatred', a phenomenon which, when perceived as characteristic of inferior ascriptive racial or ethnic status, has often been deplored. The features of such self-hatred are: rejection of behaviour patterns associated with one's own group as uncouth, negative judgements concerning the value of occupational roles characteristic of one's own group, and the desire to leave one's own group and 'pass' into a dominant group. It is universally recognized that such feelings on the part of a Negro or a Jew are indicators of psychic punishment; yet the same reactions among the lower class are often not perceived in the same way.

To a considerable degree, the social mechanisms which operate to legitimate an existing distribution of status inequalities succeed in repressing such discontent, sometimes by structuring perceptions so that even low status individuals may view themselves as higher and therefore 'better' than some others, or by creating bonds of vicarious identification with those in higher positions. The latter mechanism is particularly prevalent in systems which emphasize ascriptive and elitist values. However, it is doubtful that such mechanisms alone are a sufficient solution for the problem of social rejection and psychological self-punishment inherent in low status.

There are different adaptive mechanisms which have emerged to reconcile low status individuals to their positions and thus contribute to the stability and legitimacy of the larger system. The three most common appear to be:

1. *Religion.* Belief in a religion with a transvaluational theology, one which emphasizes the possibility or even the probability that the poor on earth will enjoy higher status in heaven or in a reincarnation, operates to adjust them to their station, and motivates those in low positions to carry out their role requirements.[7]

2. *Social mobility.* The belief that achievement is possible and that virtue will be rewarded by success for oneself or one's children provides stabilizing functions comparable to those suggested for religion.

3. *Political action.* Participation in or support for political movements which aim to raise the position of depressed groups, and which in their ideology contain transvaluational elements – the assumption that the lower strata are morally better than the upper classes – also helps to adjust the deprived groups to their situation.

Since the three mechanisms may be regarded as functional alternatives to one another, that is, as satisfying similar needs, it may be posited that where one or more is weakly present, the other(s) will be strongly in evidence. Specifically, for example, where belief in religion or social mobility is weak, the lower strata should be especially receptive to radical transvaluational political or economic appeals.[8] Social systems undergoing major institutional changes, which weaken faith in traditional religion and which do not replace this lost faith by the value system of an open, achievement-oriented society, have experienced major extremist political movements. It has been argued by some that one of the factors sustaining the bases for Communist and anarchist movements in countries like Spain, France and Italy has been the perpetuation in society of strong ascriptive and elitist value elements together with a 'dechristianized' lower stratum.[9]

7. Religious movements may also, of course, constitute a major element in secular political protest. This is the case today among American Negroes. Lower-class churches and their ministers may directly or indirectly help form class-based political movements. And, of course, sectarian groupings have often expressed the hostility of the depressed strata to the privileged order and their religion. But such forms of institutionalized protest, like radical political movements, themselves serve as means of defining lower status in forms which are palatable to those occupying lower status positions.

8. The thesis that revolutionary socialism and transvaluational religion have served similar functions for oppressed groups was elaborated by Engels (1957, pp. 312–20).

A strong societal emphasis on achievement and equalitarianism (which in part may be perceived as a secular transvaluational ideology) combined with strong religious belief, particularly among the lower strata, should maximize the legitimacy of the existing distribution of privilege, and thus minimize the conditions for extremist protest. This is, of course, the situation in the United States. The strong emphasis in American culture on the need to 'get ahead', to be successful, seems to be accompanied by powerful transvaluational religions among those who have the least access to the approved means of success.

9. In France, for example, ecological studies which contrast degree of religious practice with Communist strength show that the Communists are most successful in regions in which the 'anti-clerical' wave had previously suppressed much of the traditional fidelity to Catholicism (LeBras, 1949; Goguel, 1951, pp. 134–5).

References

BARON, G., and TROPP (1956), 'Teachers in England and America', in E. A. Shils (ed.), *The Torment of Secrecy*, Free Press.

BELL, D. (ed.) (1963), *The Radical Right*, Doubleday.

BENDIX, R. (1956), *Work and Authority in Industry*, Wiley.

CROSLAND, C. A. R. (1956), *The Future of Socialism*, Cape.

DEWHURST, J. F. (1961), *Europe's Needs and Resources*, Twentieth-Century Fund.

DEUTSCH, K. W., BURRELL, S. A., KANN, R. A., LEE, M., LICHTERMAN, M., LINDGREN, R. E., LOEWENHEIM, F. L., and VAN WAGEREN, R. W. (1957), *Political Community and the North Atlantic Area*, Princeton University Press.

ECKSTEIN, H. (1961), *A Theory of Stable Democracy*, Centre for International Studies, Princeton University.

ENGELS, F. (1957), 'On the early history of Christianity', in K. Marx and F. Engels, *On Religion*, Moscow Foreign Language Publishing House.

GOGUEL, F. (1951), *Géographie des elections Françaises de 1870 à 1941*, Cahiers de la fondation nationale des sciences politiques, Armand Colin.

GOWER, L. C. B., and PRICE, L. (1957), 'The profession and practice of law in England and America', *Mod. Law Rev.*, vol. 20.

LEBRAS, G. (1949), 'Géographie electorale et géographie religieuse', in *Etudes de Sociologie Electorale*, Cahiers de la fondation nationale des sciences politiques, Armand Colin.

LIPSET, S. M. (1960), *Political Man: The Social Bases of Politics*, Doubleday.

LIPSET, S. M. (1963), *The First New Nation*, Basic Books.

PARSONS, T. (1951), *The Social System*, Free Press.

PARSONS, T. (1960), 'Pattern variables revisited', *Amer. Sociol. Rev.*, vol. 25, no. 4, pp. 467–83.

PARSONS, T. (1961), 'The point of view of the author', in M. Black (ed.), *The Social Theories of Talcott Parsons*, Prentice-Hall.

PARSONS, T. (1963), 'Social strains in America', in D. Bell (ed.), *The Radical Right*, Doubleday.

SAMPSON, A. (1962), *Anatomy of Britain*, Hodder & Stoughton.

SHILS, E. (1956), *The Torment of Secrecy*, Free Press.

SHILS, E., and YOUNG, M. (1961), 'The meaning of the coronation', in S. M. Lipset and N. Smelser (eds.), *Sociology: The Progress of Decade*, Prentice-Hall.

Statistical Office of the United Nations (1960), *Demographic Yearbook, 1960*, New York.

TOCQUEVILLE, A. DE (1958), *Journeys to England and Ireland*, Yale University Press.

TÖNNIES, F. (1957), *Community and Society, Gemeinschaft und Gesellschaft*, Michigan State University Press.

TURNER, R. (1961), 'Modes of social ascent through education: sponsored and contest mobility', in A. H. Halsey, J. Floud and C. A. Anderson (eds.), *Education, Economy and Society*, Collier-Macmillan.

VAIZEY, J. (1959), 'The public schools', in H. Thomas (ed.), *The Establishment*, Clarkson Potter.

WILLIAMS, R. M. (1951), *American Society*, Knopf.

WILLIAMS, R. (1961), *The Long Revolution*, Columbia University Press.

23 John H. Goldthorpe

Social Stratification in Industrial Society

Excerpts from J. H. Goldthorpe, 'Social stratification in industrial society', in R. Bendix and S. M. Lipset (eds.), *Class, Status and Power*, Routledge & Kegan Paul, 1967.

For a decade or so now, a growing interest has been apparent, chiefly among American sociologists, in the pattern of long-term social change within relatively mature industrial societies. This interest appears to derive from two main sources.

In the first place, it can be seen as resulting from broadly based studies of the sociology of industrialization, concentrating originally on the underdeveloped or developing countries of the world. For example, the theoretical statement on the 'logic' of industrialism attempted by Kerr, Dunlop, Harbison and Myers (1960). Secondly, this interest has undoubtedly been stimulated by the revival in comparative studies of social structure and social processes in economically advanced countries. [. . .]

However, it is notable that in spite of possibly different origins, current American interpretations of the development of industrial societies often reveal marked similarities. Basically, it may be said, they tend to be alike in stressing the standardizing effects upon social structures of the exigencies of modern technology and of an advanced economy. [. . .] In brief, a *convergent* pattern of development is hypothesized.

Kerr and his associates have been the most explicit in this connection – and also in the manner of specifying the type of society on which the process of convergence is focussed. In their conception, 'the road ahead' for all advanced societies leads in the direction of what they call 'pluralistic' industrialism. By this they mean a form of industrial society in which the distribution of power is neither 'atomistic' nor 'monistic', nor yet radically disputed by warring classes ; but rather a social order in which an 'omnipresent State' regulates competition and conflict between a multiplicity of interest groups on the basis of an accepted 'web of rules', and at the same time provides the means through which a degree of democratic control can be exercised over the working of the economy and over other key social processes such as the provision of welfare and public services, education and so on (1960, chs. 1 and 2). [. . .] In general, the 'logic' of industrialism has been regarded as powerfully encouraging, even if not compelling, the emergence of a new type of society from out of former 'class' and 'mass' societies alike.[1] [. . .]

The arguments concerning the development of social stratification which form a core element in American interpretations of industrialism can be usefully stated under three main heads: differentiation, consistency and mobility (Kerr *et al.*, 1960; Inkeles, 1960; Hoselitz and Moore, 1963, pp. 318–22, 353–9).[2]

Differentiation

In regard to differentiation, the major proposition that is put forward is that, in course of industrial advance, there is a decrease in the degree of differentiation in all stratification subsystems or orders. [. . .] As a result of this process, a marked increase occurs within each stratification order in the proportion of the total population falling into the middle ranges of the distribution. The 'shape' of the stratification hierarchy thus ceases to be pyramidal and approximates, rather, to that of a pentagon or even of a diamond.

This trend is related to the 'logic' of industrialism in several different ways. But, primarily, the connection is seen as being through the changing division of labour. An advancing technology and economy continually repattern the occupational structure, and in ways which progressively increase the number of higher level occupational roles; that is to say, roles requiring relatively high standards of education and training and at the same time commanding relatively high economic rewards and social status. Thus, the middle of the stratification hierarchy becomes considerably expanded.

So far as Western societies are concerned, a further factor in this homogenizing process is also recognized in the growing intervention of the state in economic affairs; particularly in governmental policies which lead to the redistribution and control of economic power. For example, it is observed that policies of progressive taxation and of social welfare in various ways modify for the benefit of the less privileged the division of income and balance of social advantage which would have resulted from

1. The issue on which, of course, there has been greatest doubt and discussion is that of whether totalitarian regimes will *inevitably* become less 'monistic' with continuing industrial advance.

2. It is, however, important to note the very marked differences in tone and style between these contributions. Kerr and his colleagues are most dogmatic and 'prophetic', but also the most diffuse in their arguments; Inkeles, on the other hand, is the most explicit yet is clearly writing, as he says, 'not to settle a point but to open a discussion'; while Moore, aiming at the summing-up of a body of research data, puts forward by far the most cautious and qualified statements.

the free operation of market mechanisms. [. . .] The state, it is argued, *must* be the key regulatory organization in any advanced society: the complexity of its technology and economy demand this. At minimum, the state must be responsible for the general rate of economic progress, and thus ultimately, for the overall allocation of resources between uses and individuals, for the quality of the national labour force, for the economic and social security of individuals and so on (Kerr *et al*., 1960, pp. 31, 40–41, 273–4, 290–92; Hoselitz and Moore, 1963, pp. 357–9).

In other words, even where greater social equality results directly from the purposive action of governments, the tendency is to see behind this action not a particular complex of socio-political beliefs, values or interests but rather the inherent compulsions of 'industrialism' itself.[3] [. . .]

Furthermore, one should note, a similar viewpoint is taken in arguing that greater equality in political power – in the form of a pluralistic system – will tend to emerge in societies which now have totalitarian (or autocratic) regimes. In the first place, it is held, the production technology of an industrial society is such that any regime must become increasingly interested in the consent of the mass of the labour force; for the efficient use of this technology requires responsible initiative and freely given co-operation on the part of those who operate it. Secondly, the growing complexity of technical problems arising in the process of government itself necessitates the greater involvement in decision-making of experts and professionals, and in this way the latter come to acquire some independent authority. Thus, a monolithic structure gives way to one in which there are a number of 'strategic' elites and of different foci of power. In brief, industrialism is regarded as being ultimately inimical to any form of monistic political order (Kerr *et al,* 1960, pp. 274–6, 288–90).

Consistency

In this respect, the central argument is that as societies become increasingly industrial, there is a growing tendency within the stratification system towards what Inkeles terms 'equilibration'; that is, a tendency for the relative position of an individual or group in any one stratification order to be the same as, or similar to, their position in other orders.[4] [. . .] With industrialism, the occupational structure takes on overwhelming primacy. The occupational role of the individual is in general in close

3. For a discussion of the strengths and weaknesses of attempts to apply this approach to the explanation of the development of social policy in nineteenth century England, see Goldthorpe (1964).

4. Inkeles's 'equilibration' (following Benoit-Smullyan, 1944) thus largely corresponds to what Lenski (1954) and Landecker (1963) have referred to as 'crystallization' and Adams (1954) and Homans (1962) as 'Congruence'. Moore refers simply to 'consistency' or 'coalescence'.

correlation with most other of his attributes which are relevant to his position in the stratification hierarchy as a whole: his economic situation, his educational level, his prestige in the local community and so on (Kerr, *et al*, 1960, pp. 272–3, 284, 292–3; Inkeles, 1960, pp. 341–2; Hoselitz and Moore, 1963, pp. 356–7). [. . .] In industrial society, it is argued, the distribution of both economic rewards and prestige must come into a close relationship with occupational performance since this type of society in fact presupposes an overriding emphasis upon achievement, as opposed to ascription, as the basis of social position – and specifically upon achievement in the sphere of production. At the same time, though, as a result of technological progress, occupational achievement becomes increasingly dependent upon education, and in this way closer ties are formed between economic standing on the one hand and life-styles and subculture on the other. In other words, the argument is that inevitably in modern societies, the various determinants of an individual's placing in the overall stratification hierarchy come to form a tight nexus; and that in this nexus occupation can be regarded as the central element – providing as it does the main link between the 'objective' and 'subjective' aspects of social inequality.

Implicit, then, in this interpretation is the view that in industrial societies stratification systems tend to become relatively highly integrated, in the sense that specifically class differences (i.e. those stemming from inequalities in the economic order) are generally paralleled by status differences (i.e. those based on inequalities in social evaluation); and, thus, that changes in the pattern of the former will automatically result in changes in the pattern of the latter. [. . .]

Mobility

In regard to mobility, the central proposition that is made is one which complements the previous arguments concerning differentiation and consistency. It is that once societies have reached a certain level of industrialization, their overall rates of social mobility tend to become relatively high – higher that is, than is typical in pre-industrial or traditional societies. The increasing number of intermediate positions in the stratification hierarchy widens the opportunity for movement upward from the lower levels, while the emphasis upon occupational achievement rather than on the ascription of social positions means that intergenerationally the talented will tend to rise at the expense of those whose talent is unequal to their birth. In this respect, the educational system is seen as the crucial allocative mechanism, sieving ability and matching capacity to the demands and responsibilities of occupational roles (Kerr *et al.*, 1960,

In this approach, thus, there is little room for consideration of institutional variations or of value differences between industrial societies which might be associated with *differing* patterns of mobility. It is taken that the overall similarities in this respect are, or at any rate are certainly becoming, the feature of major significance. I would now like to turn to what I have to say by way of criticism of these arguments. [. . .]

On the question of reduced differentiation – or greater equality – in stratification systems, my remarks at this stage will be largely confined to the economic order. [. . .]

At the outset it may be said that, although the evidence is often very patchy, a broad trend towards greater economic equality *does* seem to be discernible in the case of all those societies which have so far progressed from a traditional to an industrial form.

But there are no grounds at all, in my view, for regarding the regularity in question as manifesting the operation of some process inherent in industrialism – of some general economic law – which will necessarily persist in the future and ensure a continuing egalitarian trend. Rather, the possibility must be left quite open that where such a trend exists, it may at some point be checked – and at a point, moreover, at which considerable economic *in*equality remains. [. . .]

For the distributions of income and wealth alike, it is true that figures exist to show a movement towards greater equality in most western industrial societies over the years for which adequate time-series are available; that is, from the late inter-war or early post-war period onwards (see, e.g. United Nations, 1957; Solow, 1960; Lydall, 1959; Lydall and Tipping, 1961). However, it is now becoming increasingly clear that these figures, which are largely based on tax returns, are not always to be taken at their face value. [. . .] Such conclusions have been suggested for the United Kingdom, for example, in Professor Titmuss's recent study (1962). It must, of course, be admitted that the whole matter remains a highly controversial one (Prest and Titmuss, 1963), and it is not possible here to enter into all its complexities. But what is, I think, justified [. . .] is Titmuss's contention that

we should be much more hesitant in suggesting that any equalizing forces at work in Britain since 1938 can be promoted to the status of a 'natural law' and projected into the future. . . . There are other forces, deeply rooted in the

5. Inkeles does not include the factor of increased mobility as a separate element in his model of the 'modernization' of stratification systems. It is, however, incorporated in his discussion of both decreasing differentiation and growing consistency. e.g. in modern societies, 'Movement from one to another position on the scale . . . will not be sharply proscribed. Fluidity will characterize the [stratification] system as a whole . . . (1960, p. 341).

social structure and fed by many complex institutional factors inherent in large-scale economies, operating in reverse directions (1962, p. 198).[6]

A similar point of view is maintained, with reference to the United States, in Kolko's somewhat neglected book (1962). . . . Kolko suggests that over as long a period as 1910 to 1959 there has been no significant *general* trend in the USA towards greater income equality (ch. 1).[7]

Kolko's study prompts one to note the often overlooked point that simply because there may be some levelling of incomes going on in *certain ranges* of the total income distribution, this does not necessarily mean that *overall* equality is increasing; for in other ranges inegalitarian trends may simultaneously be operating. For example, there may be a tendency towards greater equality in that the number of middle-range incomes is growing; but at the same time the position of the lower income groups, relative to the upper and middle groups alike, may be worsening. [. . .]

Gunnar Myrdal, for example, has argued in his book (1963) that while many Americans in the intermediate social strata may well be benefiting from a levelling upwards of living standards, at the base of the stratification hierarchy there is increasing inequality, manifested in the emergence of an 'underclass' of unemployed and unemployable persons and families. In other words, the middle ranks of the income distribution may be swelling, but the gap between the bottom and the higher levels is, if anything, tending to widen (ch. 3).

Moreover, what is also significant in Myrdal's study for present purposes is the way in which he brings out the *political* aspects of the problem. Myrdal observes that structural unemployment, resulting from technological innovation in industry, is a basic, and increasingly serious, cause of poverty in America, whereas, in a country like Sweden, in which technological advance is also proceeding rapidly, full employment has been steadily maintained. Again, he notes the relative failure of the United States, compared with most western European countries, to stabilize aggregrate demand in its economy on a high and rising level (pp. 13–15, 27–30). The explanation of these differences, Myrdal then argues, while not of course entirely political, must none the less be regarded as being significantly so. In particular, he stresses

6. In this connection it should also be remembered that certain major developments which have made for greater equality in incomes in the recent past are of a non-repeatable kind – notably, the ending of large-scale unemployment and the considerable expansion in the number of working-class wives in gainful employment.

7. The data in question refer to pre-tax incomes, but Kolko is prepared to argue (ch. 2) that 'Taxation has not mitigated the fundamentally unequal distribution of income.'

the inadequate achievement of government in America in long-range economic planning, in redistributional reforms and in the provision of public services and advanced social welfare schemes. And the sources of this governmental inadequacy he traces back to certain basic American socio-political dispositions and also to a relative lack of 'democratic balance' in the institutional infrastructure of the American policy. On the one hand, Myrdal claims, there is among the powerful business community and within government itself a reluctance to take the long view and to envisage more central direction and control of the economy; also 'a serious and irrational bias against public investment and consumption'. On the other hand, among the lower strata of American society there is an unusual degree of political apathy and passivity which is most clearly seen in the general failure of the poorer sections of the population to organize themselves effectively and to press for the fundamental social reforms that would be in their interest. In this way an imbalance in organized power is brought about within the 'plural society' which makes the need for initiative on the part of government all the more pressing – at the same time as it seems to paralyse this (chs. 4, 6, 7; Harrington, 1962; Rousseas and Farganis, 1963). [. . .] It follows that we should look somewhat doubtfully on arguments about a new equality which 'has nothing to do with ideology' but which is the direct outcome of technological and economic advance. Such new equality there may be for some. But for those at the base of stratification hierarchies at least – how 'equal' they are likely to become seems to have a good deal to do with ideology, or at any rate with purposive social action, or lack of this, stemming from specific social values and political creeds as well as from interests.[8] And differences between some industrial societies in these respects may well be giving rise to divergent, rather than convergent, patterns of change in their stratification systems.

On the second set of arguments – those concerning growing consistency between different stratification orders – I shall have relatively little to say for the good reason that there is little empirical data which directly bears on the crucial issue here; that is, the issue of whether there really is a *continuing* increase in the degree of integration of the stratification system of *advanced* societies. [. . .]

My main comment is that such evidence as does appear relevant to this issue indicates that in some industrial societies, at least, on-going economic progress is resulting in stratification systems becoming, if any-

8. See Harrington's emphasis on the fact that 'If there is to be a way out (of poverty) it will come from human action, from political change, not from automatic processes' (p. 162).

thing, somewhat *less* well integrated in certain respects. This evidence refers to what has become known as the 'new working class'. It suggests that the appreciable gains in income and in general living standards recently achieved by certain sections of the manual labour force have not for the most part been accompanied by changes in their life-styles of such a kind that their *status* position has been enhanced commensurately with their *economic* position. In other words, there is evidence of cultural and, in particular, of 'social' barriers still widely existing between 'working class' and 'middle class' even in cases where immediate material differences have now disappeared (Goldthorpe and Lockwood, 1963; Berger, 1960; Andrieux and Lignon, 1960).[9] Thus it seems that contrary to the expectations of Kerr and his associates, 'middle incomes' have not resulted, as yet at least, in the generalization of 'middle-class' ways of life or of 'middle-class' status. [. . .]

As Kerr himself recognizes, there will still exist in the forseeable future in such societies a division between 'managers' and 'managed' – between those who are in some way associated with the exercise of authority in productive and administrative organizations and those who are not. And this division, one would suggest, will remain associated with differences in prestige, as well as in power, while at the same time managers and managed overlap to some extent in terms of living standards. One would agree that in an economically advanced society a broad stratum of workers, performing skilled or, one would add, particularly arduous or irksome jobs, are likely to earn middle-range incomes. But there are no grounds for automatically assuming that they will thereby become socially accepted and assimilated into even the lower levels of what Renner has usefully termed the 'service class' (1953).

In sum, one might suggest that the 'increasing consistency' argument is flawed because it fails to take into account first, that occupational roles with similar economic rewards may in some instances be quite differently related to the exercise of authority; and secondly, that relatively high income may serve as recompense for work of otherwise high 'disutility' to the operative as well as for work involving expertise and responsibility.

Lastly, then, we come to the matter of social mobility. In this case, the first question which arises is that of whether it is in fact valid to regard industrial societies as having regularly higher rates of mobility than pre-industrial societies. [. . .] To the extent that education becomes a key determinant of occupational achievement, the chances of 'getting

9. In all these contributions a common emphasis is that on the growing *disparity* between the situation of the manual worker as *producer* and *consumer*.

ahead' for those who start in a lowly position are inevitably diminished. This fact is most clearly demonstrated in recent studies of the recruitment of industrial managers. [. . .] Thus, for that large proportion of the population at least, with rank-and-file jobs and 'ordinary' educational qualifications, industrial society appears to be growing significantly *less* 'open' than it once was.

However, other, and perhaps more basic, issues arise from the arguments concerning mobility which I earlier outlined; in particular issues relating to the determinants of mobility patterns and rates. What are the grounds, one might ask, for believing that in advanced societies the crucial factor here is the occupational distribution, and thus that from one such society to another social mobility will tend to be much the same? Support for this view can be found in the well-known Lipset and Zetterberg study which led, in fact, to the conclusion that Western industrial societies have broadly similar rates of intergenerational mobility, and which produced no evidence to suggest that factors other than the 'standardizing' one of the occupational structure were of major significance (1956). [. . .] But it has to be noted that, as Lipset and Zetterberg themselves make quite clear, their findings in this respect refer only to 'mass' mobility; that is, simply to movements across the manual-non-manual line. And indeed they point out that the investigation of some aspects of 'elite' mobility – for example, the recruitment of higher civil servants – has indicated some important national variations (Lipset and Bendix, 1959, pp. 38–42).

Moreover, we have more recently the outstanding study of comparative social mobility made by Miller (1960). This covers a still greater amount of data than Lipset and Zetterberg's work and demonstrates fairly conclusively that when *range* as well as frequency of mobility is taken into consideration, industrial societies do reveal quite sizeable differences in their mobility patterns. Such differences tend to be most evident in the case of long-range mobility. This is generally low – another reason for querying just how 'open' and 'meritocratic' industrial societies have so far become – but certain countries, the USA and USSR, for example, appear to have attained quite significantly higher rates of 'elite' mobility than do others, such as many in Western Europe. Further, though, Miller shows that countries with low long-range mobility may still have relatively high short-range mobility – as, for instance, does Great Britain: there is no correlation between rates of mobility of differing distance. Thus, industrial societies have quite various 'mobility profiles'; the overall similarity indicated by the study of 'mass' mobility turns out to be somewhat spurious.

On this basis, then, Miller is able to argue very strongly that patterns of social mobility in advanced societies cannot be understood *simply* in terms of occupational structure – or, one would add, in terms of any 'inherent' features of industrialism. Their diversity precludes this. It appears necessary, rather, to consider also the effects on mobility of other, and more variable, aspects of social structure – educational institutions, for example, and their articulation with the stratification hierarchy itself – and further, possibly, *pace* Lipset and Zetterberg, the part played by cultural values (Turner, 1961). As Miller points out, what is perhaps most surprising about his data is the *lack* of convergence in mobility patterns that is indicated between societies at broadly comparable levels of economic development. The 'logic' of industrialism, it appears, is often confused by 'extraneous' factors. [. . .]

In conclusion of this paper, I would like to make a more basic objection which relates to the theoretical position underlying these arguments. Specifically, I would like to question the idea that the stratification systems of all industrial societies are *ipso facto* of the same generic type, and thus that they may in principle be expected to follow convergent or parallel lines of development. Against this view, I would like to suggest that social stratification in the advanced societies of the Communist world – or at any rate in the USSR and its closer satellites – is *not* of the same generic type as in the West and that, because of this, the hypotheses earlier discussed cannot in this case really apply.

Soviet society is, of course, stratified ; and, furthermore, it is true that in spite of the absence of private property in production, it appears to be stratified on an often similar pattern to the capitalist or post-capitalist societies of the West. [. . .]

But, I would argue, this similarity is only of a phenotypical kind : genotypically, stratification in Soviet society is significantly different from stratification in the West.

Primarily, it may be said, this difference derives from the simple fact that in Soviet society the economy operates within a 'monistic', or totalitarian, political order and is, in principle at least, totally planned, whereas in advanced Western societies political power is significantly less concentrated and the economy is planned in a far less centralized and detailed way. From this it results that in the West economic, and specifically market forces act as the crucial stratifying agency within society. They are, one could say, the major source of social inequality. And consequently, the *class* situation of individuals and groups, understood in terms of their economic power and resources, tends to be the most important single determinant of their general life-chances. This is why we can usefully speak of Western industrial society as being 'class' stratified. However, in the case of Soviet society, market forces cannot be held to play a comparable role in the stratification process. These forces operate, of course, and differences in economic power and resources between individuals and groups have, as in the West, far reaching social and human consequences. But one would argue, to a significantly greater extent than in the West, stratification in Soviet society is subjected to *political* regulation; market forces are not permitted to have the primacy or the degree of autonomy in this respect that they have even in a 'managed' capitalist society. Undoubtedly, the functional requirements of the economy exert pressures upon the system of stratification, and these pressures may in some cases prove to be imperative. But the nature of the political order means that far more than with Western democracy, the pattern of social inequality can be shaped through the purposive action of the ruling party, and still more so, of course, the 'life-fates' of particular persons.[10]

For example, during the years of Stalin's rule, economic inequality in the USSR generally increased. Numerous writers have in fact commented upon the progressive abandonment over this period of the egalitarian aspects of Marxist-Leninist ideology and of post-revolutionary attempts to operate egalitarian economic and social policies (Moore, 1950). From the early 1930s differential rewards in relation to skill, effort and responsibility were introduced into industry and administration, and thus from this point the range of wages and salaries tended to widen. Further, changes in the 1940s in the income tax and inheritance laws were conducive to greater inequalities in incomes and personal wealth alike. Then again, high ranking officials and other favoured persons appear to have received increasingly important non-monetary rewards in the form of cars, apartments, villas, free holidays and so on. By the end of the war decade, these developments had led to a degree of inequality in Soviet society which, in the view of many commentators, was greater than that which was generally to be found in the industrial societies of the West (Inkeles, 1950).[11] However, in more recent years it has become clear that contrary to most expectations, this inegalitarian trend in the USSR has been checked and, moreover, that in certain respects at least it has even been reversed. Minimum wages in industry have been increased several times since the late 1950s and the incomes of the *kolkhozy* have for the most part risen quite considerably. This latter development has had the effect of closing somewhat the income gap between industrial and agricultural workers and has also been associated with a reduction

10. Also relevant here, of course, is a further distinctive feature of a totalitarian political system – the absence of a 'rule of law'.
11. This paper contains an excellent factual account of the ways through which both economic and status inequality was increased during the Stalin era.

in differentials in the earnings of the *kolkhoz* peasants themselves. At the same time, there is evidence of limitations being placed on the more excessive salaries of higher officials and of more stringent measures being taken against the abuse of privileges. Finally, tax changes in the past few years have tended to favour the poorer against the richer groups, and various kinds of welfare provision have been substantially improved. In these ways, then, economic differences between the manual and non-manual categories overall have almost certainly been reduced to some extent, as well as differences within these categories (Feldmesser, 1967; Nove, 1961).

Now these changes can, of course, be rightly regarded as being in some degree economically conditioned. Clearly, for instance, the increased differentiation in wages and salaries in the Stalin era must in part be understood in terms of the exigencies and consequences of rapid industrialization. But, I would argue, there can be little question that at the same time these changes were the outcome of political decisions. [. . .] Moreover, the wide social distance which was in this way created between the top and bottom of the stratification hierarchy had the manifest function of insulating the 'elite' from the masses and from their needs and wishes. And thus, as Professor Feldmesser has pointed out, those in high positions were helped to learn 'that success was to be had by winning the favour not of those below them but of those above them, which was exactly what Stalin wanted them to learn' (p. 579) [12].

Similarly, the more recent move towards reducing inequalities have again fairly evident political aims, even though in some cases, they may also have been economically required.[13] On the one hand, it seems clear that the present Soviet leadership is working towards a future Communist society which will be characterized by a high level of social welfare, and indeed eventually by private affluence, while still remaining under the undisputed dominance of the Party. [. . .]

On the other hand, the security of the regime also requires that the bureaucratic and managerial 'elite' does not become so well established as to gain some measure of independence from the Party chiefs. Thus, Krushchev has been concerned to show the members of this group that they remain the creatures of the Party and that their privileges are not permanent but still rest upon their obedience and service to the

12. This political subordination of members of the 'elite', concomitant with their economic and status elevation, is the reason for using inverted commas. As Feldmesser notes, the 'elite' created by Stalin is surely distinctive by virtue of its general lack of autonomy.

13. As, e.g. in the case of the increase in peasant incomes which was essential if genuine incentives to improve production were to be offered in agriculture (see Bialer, 1960).

Party. Those whom Djilas has referred to as the 'new class' in Communist society (1957) cannot in fact be allowed by the Party leadership to become a class – in the sense of a collectivity which is capable of maintaining its position in society (and that of its children) through its own social power, and which possesses some degree of group consciousness and cohesion. For the emergence of such a class would constitute a serious threat to the Party's totalitarian rule, different only in degree from the threat that would be posed by the emergence of an independent trade union, professional body or political organization. [. . .] As Feldmesser notes, if a 'new class' – a 'state bourgeoisie' – were in fact in existence in the USSR, then exactly the reverse of this might have been expected; that is, a move to make access to these scarce facilities *more,* rather than less, dependent upon the ability to pay (Feldmesser, 1967, pp. 576–8).

It is then not too much to say that in Soviet society hierarchical differentiation is an instrument of the regime. To a significant degree stratification is *organized* in order to suit the political needs of the regime; and, as these needs change, so too may the particular structure of inequality. In other words, the Soviet system of stratification is characterized by an important element of 'deliberateness', and it is this which basically distinguishes it from the Western system, in spite of the many apparent similarities. In the industrial societies of the West, one could say, the action of the state sets limits to the extent of social inequalities which derive basically from the operation of a market economy. [. . .] For this reason, one may conclude, Soviet society is not, in the same way as Western society, *class* stratified. As Raymond Aron has observed, class stratification and a monistic political system are to be regarded as incompatibles (1950).

If, then, the foregoing analysis is accepted, it follows that the arguments I earlier outlined on the development of stratification systems can have no general validity. Their underlying rationale, in terms of the exigencies of an advanced industrial technology and economy, is destroyed. The experience of Soviet society can be taken as indicating that the structural and functional imperatives of an industrial order are not so stringent as to prevent quite wide variations in patterns of social stratification, nor to prohibit the systematic manipulation of social inequalities by a regime commanding modern administrative resources and under no constraints from an organized opposition or the rule of law.

The crucial point, in fact, at which the rationale breaks down is in the supposition that industrialism and totalitarianism cannot 'in the long run' coexist; that is, in the idea that with industrial advance a progressive diffusion of political power must of necessity occur. Were this idea valid, then it would become difficult to maintain the claim that differences between the stratification systems of the Western and Communist worlds are of a generic kind. [. . .] The regime may be compelled to give more consideration to the effect of its decisions on popular morale and to rely increasingly on the expertise of scientists, technicians and professionals of various kinds; it may also find it desirable to decentralize administration and to encourage a high degree of participation in the conduct of public affairs at a local level. But the important point is that all these things can be done, and in recent years *have* been done, without the Party leadership in any way yielding up its position of ultimate authority and control. Indeed, it is far more arguable that since the end of the period of 'collective' rule, the power of the Party leadership has become still more absolute and unrivalled. This situation, one would suggest, has been brought about as a result of Krushchev's success in reducing the power and independence, relative to the Party machine, of the other major bureaucratic structures within Soviet society – those of the political police, of the military and of government and industry. In some cases, it might be noted, the changes involved here can be seen as aspects of 'de-Stalinization' – for example, the mitigation of the terror or the dissolution of a large part of the central state apparatus. Yet at the same time these changes have had the effect of accentuating still further the totalitarian nature of Party rule. [. . .]

It is, I think, significant that Inkeles himself sees the weakest spot in the entire thesis of 'declining differentiation' as being in the application of this to the 'realm of power' within Communist society. He acknowledges the distinct possibility that here his model of stratification change may have to be revised and the prediction of increased homogenization restricted to realms other than that of power (1960, pp. 345–7). Moreover, Inkeles has elsewhere stated quite explicitly that

there is no necessary, or even compelling, force in the modern industrial social order which clearly makes it incompatible with totalitarianism.

and again that

the modern industrial order appears to be compatible with either democratic or totalitarian political and social forms (Inkeles and Bauer, 1959, p. 390).

What one would wish to stress, then, is that if such views as these are sound (as I believe they are), it becomes difficult to see how one can formulate *any* general and comprehensive propositions concerning stratification change as part of a 'logic' of industrial development. For the essential assumption involved in such propositions – that of some necessary 'primacy' of the economic system over the political – is no longer a reliable one. It has to be recognized, rather, that stratification systems are not to be understood as mere 'reflections' of a certain level of technology and industrial organization but are shaped by a range of other factors, important among which may be that of purposive political action; and further, that the importance of this latter factor in societies in which political power is highly concentrated is such as to create a distinctive type of stratification which is difficult even to discuss in terms of concepts developed in a Western, capitalist context.[14]

To end with, it might be observed that the arguments pursued in the latter part of this paper have negative implications not only for the model of stratification change with which I have been specifically concerned, but also for the kind of general theory of industrialism with which this model may be associated. The rejection of the particular hypotheses on stratification on the grounds that have been suggested obviously entail a rejection too of the idea of the convergent development of advanced societies focused on 'pluralistic industrialism', and equally of the key notion of a rigorous 'logic' of industrialism which is the engine of such development.

At least as expressed in the somewhat brash manner of Kerr and his colleagues, these ideas would seem to amount to little more than what might be called an evolutionary para-Marxism; and, as such, one would say, they share certain major flaws with the developmental theories of Marx and of the social evolutionists alike. In the first place, there is the exaggeration of the degree of determinism which is exercised upon social structures by 'material' exigencies, and, concomitantly with this, the underestimation of the extent to which a social order may be shaped through purposive action within the limits of such exigencies. Secondly, and relatedly, there is the further underestimation of the diversity of values and ideologies which may underlie purposive action; and thus, from these two things together, there results the tendency to envisage a future in which the complex patterns of past development will become increasingly orderly and aligned – the tendency, in fact, to think in terms of 'the road ahead' rather than in terms of a variety of

14. As Feldmesser has indicated, the argument that Soviet society is not 'class' stratified in the manner of Western industrial societies can also be supported from the 'subjective' point of view (1960, pp. 235–52). The available evidence suggests that Soviet citizens exhibit a relatively low level of class consciousness in the sense that their class situation is not of fundamental importance in patterning their dominant modes of thought and action. Members of different social strata in Soviet society seem more alike in their social ideologies and attitudes than their counterparts in the West, while the feature of the social structure which is most strongly reflected in their social consciousness at all levels is that of the division between 'Party people' and 'non-Party people'. On this latter point see Inkeles and Bauer (1959, ch. 13).

roads.[15] And then finally, and perhaps most culpably, there is the ethnocentric bias ; that failure of the imagination which leads the sociologist to accept his own form of society, or rather some idealized version of this, as the goal towards which all humanity is moving.

15. More radically, it may be objected that, if a long-run view is to be taken, the very concept of 'industrial society' will eventually cease to be useful. As the Spanish social scientist, Luis Diez del Corral, has pointed out, the concept remains of some significance while societies exist in which highest priority is assigned to industrial and economic values generally. During this phase, 'this secularization and concentration of values helps explain the lessening of ideological conflicts . . .' But, del Corral goes on, 'This élan will only be temporary, and this standardization, this secularization of values which results in economic growth will one day enable all values to flower, all constraints to be forgotten, unless it ends in the apocalyptic destruction of mankind. These two possibilities underline both the grandeur and the misery of our destiny' (see Aron (ed.) 1950, p. 68).

References

ADAMS, S. (1954), 'Social climate and productivity in small military groups', *Amer. Sociol. Rev.*, vol. 19, no. 4, pp. 421–5.

ANDRIEUX, A., and LIGNON, J. (1960), *L'Ouvrier d'Aujourd'hui*, Recherches de Sociologie du travail, no. 6.

ARON, R. (1950), 'Social structure and the ruling class', *Brit. J. Sociol.*, vol. 1, no. 1, pp. 1–17.

BENOIT-SMULLYAN, E. (1944), 'Status types and status interrelations', *Amer. Sociol. Rev.*, vol. 9, no. 2, pp. 151-61.

BERGER, B. (1960), *Working-Class Suburb: A Study of Auto-Workers in Suburbia*, University of California Press.

BIALER, S. (1960), 'But some are more equal than others', *Problems of Communism*, vol. 9, no. 2.

DJILAS, M. (1957), *The New Class*, Allen & Unwin.

FELDMESSER, R. A. (1960), 'Social classes and the political structure', in C. E. Black (ed.), *The Transformation of Russian Society*, Harvard University Press.

FELDMESSER, R. A. (1967), 'Towards a classless society' in R. Bendix and S. M. Lipset (eds.), *Class, Status and Power*, Routledge & Kegan Paul.

GOLDTHORPE, J. H. (1964), 'The development of political sociology in England from 1800 to 1914', *Transactions of the Fifth World Conference on Sociology*, vol. 4.

GOLDTHORPE, J. H., and LOCKWOOD, D. (1963), 'Affluence and the British class structure', *Sociol. Rev.*, vol. 11, no. 2, pp. 133–63.

HARRINGTON, M. (1962), *The Other America*, Collier-Macmillan.

HOMANS, G. C. (1962), 'Status congruence', in *Sentiments and Activities*, Routledge & Kegan Paul.

HOSELITZ, B. F., and MOORE, W. E. (eds.) (1963), *Industrialization and Society*, Humanities Press.

INKELES, A. (1950), 'Social stratification and mobility in the Soviet Union: 1940–50', *Amer. Sociol. Rev.*, vol. 15, no. 4, pp. 465–79.

INKELES, A. (1960), 'Social stratification in the modernization of Russia', in C. E. Black (ed.), *The Transformation of Russian Society*, Harvard University Press.

INKELES, A. (1967), 'Social stratification and mobility in the Soviet Union', in R. Bendix and S. M. Lipset (eds.), *Class, Status and Power*, Routledge & Kegan Paul.

INKELES, A., and BAUER, R. A. (1959), *The Soviet Citizen*, Oxford University Press.

KERR, C., DUNLOP, J. T., HARBISON, F. H., and MYERS, C. A. (1960), *Industrialism and Industrial Man*, Oxford University Press.

KOLKO, G. (1962), *Wealth and Power in America*, Praeger.

LANDECKER, W. S. (1963), 'Class crystallization and class consciousness', *Amer. Sociol. Rev.*, vol. 28, no. 2, pp. 219–29.

LENSKI, G. H. (1954), 'Status crystallization: a non-vertical dimension of social status', *Amer. Sociol. Rev.*, vol. 19, no. 4, pp. 405–13.

LIPSET, S. M., and BENDIX, R. (1959), *Social Mobility in Industrial Society*, University of California Press.

LIPSET, S. M., and ZETTERBERG, H. L. (1956), 'A theory of social mobility', *Transactions of the Third World Conference of Sociology*, vol. 3.

LYDALL, H. F. (1959), 'The long-term trend in the size distribution of income', *J. Roy. Stats. Soc.*, vol. 122, pt 1.

LYDALL, H. F., and TIPPING, D. L. (1961), 'The distribution of personal wealth in Britain, *Oxford Inst. Stats. Bull.*, vol. 23.

MILLER, S. M. (1960), 'Comparative social mobility', *Current Sociol.*, vol. 9, no. 1.

MOORE, B. (1950), *Soviet Politics: the Dilemma of Power*, Harper & Row.

MYRDAL, G. (1963), *Challenge to Affluence*, Gollancz.

NOVE, A. (1961), 'Is the Soviet Union a welfare state?', in A. Inkeles and K. Geiger (eds.), *Soviet Society*, Constable.

PREST, A. R., and TITMUSS, R. (1963), Critical review and reply on 'Income Distribution and Social Change', *British Tax Rev.* March–April.

RENNER, K. (1953), *Wardlungen der modernen Gesellschaft: zwei Abhandlingen über die Probleme der Nachkriezzeit*, Wiener volkbuchhandlung.

ROUSSEAS, S. W., and FARGANIS, J. (1963), 'American politics and the end of ideology', *Brit. J. Sociol.*, vol. 14, no. 4, pp. 347–63.

SOLOW, R. M. (1960), 'Income inequality since the war', in R. E. Freeman (ed.), *Postwar Economic Trends in the United States*, Harper & Row.

TITMUSS, R. (1962), *Income Distribution and Social Change*, Allen & Unwin.

TURNER, R. H. (1961), 'Modes of social ascent through education: sponsored and contest mobility', in A. H. Halsey, J. Floud and C. A. Anderson (eds.), *Education Economy and Society*, Collier-Macmillan.

UNITED NATIONS (1957), *Economic Survey of Europe in 1950*, Geneva.

24 Frank Parkin

Class Stratification in Socialist Societies [1]

Excerpts from Frank Parkin, 'Class stratification in socialist societies'.
British Journal of Sociology, vol. 20, 1969, pp. 355–74.

One of the most sociologically intriguing issues highlighted by the recent debate on the 'convergence' of industrial societies is that concerning differences in the class system of socialist and capitalist countries. Goldthorpe, in a celebrated paper, has summarized a number of arguments in support of the view that class stratification in totalitarian systems of the communist variety is fundamentally different from that typically found in modern Western capitalist societies (1964). [. . .] One of the most important [being] that the major social cleavage in this kind of system occurs between Party and non-Party personnel. Because of the coercive nature of the police state, differences in income or occupation or social background do not give rise to sentiments and behaviour of a class kind amongst non-Party members of the population. [. . .] Different sectors of the population would exhibit no sharp variations in values and outlook such as we typically find between the classes in Western capitalist society (Feldmesser, 1960, p. 248). Class formation would, it is argued, be deliberately discouraged by the state apparatus, since any independent grouping outside the orbit of the Party would threaten its monopoly of social control. Under these conditions, what we have is a society divided between Party elites and non-Party masses, with no intermediate groups or classes between the two. [. . .]

This view of the 'classless' socialist society does serve as a useful corrective to some of the more extravagant claims put forward by proponents of the convergence thesis, not least of all by its recognition of ideology as a possible variable in stratification systems. Clearly, the classlessness model is based very heavily on material relating to the Soviet Union, rather than other European socialist states. [. . .] In more recent years, however, many of these societies have undergone a number of

1. Although this article was prepared before the recent invasion of Czechoslovakia by Soviet forces its main argument is not really affected by that event. I have, however, inserted one or two minor alterations to make it clear that all references to the class structure in Czechoslovakia refer to the situation prior to the invasion.

important changes, both in their relation to the Soviet Union and in their internal structures. As a result, it is doubtful whether the model of a stratification order split mainly between a unified elite and a mass population lacking internal class differentiation of the Western kind is any longer appropriate. [. . .]

It may be suggested that the class system of European socialist states is best understood in terms of two contrasting ideal types. The first corresponds to the classlessness model outlined above, and the second corresponds more closely to the class system of modern Western capitalism. The central proposition of this paper is that the former ideal type is appropriate mainly to the early phase of 'socialist reconstruction', while the latter more accurately reflects the condition of socialist states entering the phase of modern industrialization. Further, it is suggested that many of the internal tensions present in East European societies may be understood as a result of their transition towards a system of class stratification not unlike the Western capitalist type. Of particular relevance here is the relationship between the middle class and the working class in socialist society. This relationship is more problematic than it is in capitalist society because socialist ideology singles out the proletariat as occupying a specially privileged place in the social order, while the occupational system of modern industrialization tends to place responsibility and authority in the hands of professional employees and white-collar experts. Thus one of the problems inherent in socialism is that of reconciling the ideologically high status of the industrial working class with their low position in the hierarchy of expertise and functional authority stemming from the technological order. Seen from the other angle, the problem can be posed by asking how far ideological imperatives can succeed in relegating the middle class to an inferior political and social status, given their command over the skills and knowledge essential to industrial progress. It can be shown that socialist societies did in fact bring about a reversal of the usual pattern of class privilege and rewards in accordance with ideological demands. This occurred during the immediate post-capitalist phase, and gave rise to a stratification order fundamentally different from that of any Western society, and one which had many of the elements of classlessness noted by the writer mentioned above. [. . .]

Classlessness and socialist reconstruction

One of the major problems facing the new rulers of any society undergoing radical structural change is that of political stabilization following the redistribution of power and privilege among different social strata. In the transformation from capitalism to socialism this is exemplified in the displacement of the bourgeoisie and its political representatives by a previously subordinate social class, the proletariat and its political leaders. This general elevation in the political, social and economic status of the industrial working class, and the corresponding demotion of formerly privileged groups, was brought about in East Europe in a various number of ways. One of the more important of these was through recruitment of Party personnel, often men of lowly social origin, to leading positions of authority and responsibility, despite their relative lack of formal qualifications and education. The fact that the Party provided an avenue to social promotion for low status individuals arose as much from strategic as from ideological reasons. [...] It was generally the case that those best technically qualified for managerial, administrative and similar posts would be members of the old middle class, and therefore politically suspect. [...]

The recruitment of former workers and peasants into elite positions by way of the Party undoubtedly helped to ensure that the proletarian bias in socialist ideology was reflected in government policies. The material condition of the formerly underprivileged improved considerably throughout East Europe with the introduction of free medical and welfare services, sweeping reforms in taxation and incomes, greater security of employment, rapid expansion of educational facilities, and the like. It would of course be true to say that the material position of workers in most Western capitalist societies also improved in the postwar years following the introduction of comprehensive welfare services and enlightened state intervention in the industrial field. [...] In socialist Europe [...] the policies of the new regimes were designed not simply to alleviate the condition of the working class but to alter the balance of advantages absolutely in their favour. One step in this direction was the marked shift towards an egalitarian incomes structure. [...] In Czechoslovakia, for example, qualified engineers and technologists earned only about 20 per cent more than manual workers, while administrative and clerical workers earned on average 20 per cent *less* than manual workers (Kubat, 1963). In Poland the ratio of white collar to blue collar incomes was 2·80 to 1·0 in 1938; under the socialist government it fell to 1·18 to 1·0 (Matejko, 1966). There was a similar trend in Yugoslavia (Sefer, 1968). Egalitarian incomes policies were often supplemented by a variety of special allowances and subsidies, as for example in housing, which again operated to the advantage of workers. [...] The system of 'positive discrimination' in favour of the working class was particularly important in the field of education. In all East European societies there was a rapid increase in the number of students in full-time higher education compared with the pre-war years. But more significant than the actual growth of the student population was the change in its social composition. Almost all the new socialist states exercised some form of discrimination against the children of the middle class in the field of higher education, either by imposing a quota system or by other selection procedures. [. . .] Thus, in Hungary, 66 per cent of the university population in 1949–50 were from working class and peasant families, compared with 11 per cent in the pre-socialist period (Murray, 1960). [. . .]

In Poland, a 1961 survey showed that more than 48 per cent of university and college students were of peasant and proletarian origin (Szczepanski, 1964, p. 259); comparable changes also occurred in Czechoslovakia (Taborsky, 1961). Thus, by an ideologically motivated selection and scholarship system East European countries succeeded in altering the social composition of the university population far more radically than any Western society had done, including those which had experienced Labour or Social Democratic governments. Because of the crucial role of education in determining an individual's occupational placement and material and social rewards, reforms in this particular field were among the most important of all the improvements in the situation of the working class. The extent to which the avenues of social mobility were opened up to former low status groups provided perhaps one of the more dramatic contrasts in the opportunity structures of the working class in socialist and capitalist societies.

These changes in the class distribution of material advantages were accompanied, it would seem, by corresponding changes in the status system. Sarapata and Wesolowski, in one of the earliest reported studies of stratification in East Europe, showed that occupational prestige in Poland in the 1950s differed in certain important respects from that commonly found in Western industrial society. Positions associated with the ownership of private property and commerce were accorded much less social honour than they generally command in capitalist society, while skilled industrial workers were given higher ranking than all other occupational groups except the intellectuals (1961). The authors of the study suggested that the reversal of the blue-collar – white-collar rank order usually found in the West was partly to be explained in terms of the impact of socialist ideology and the positive emphasis on direct productive work. [. . .] Aleksander Matejko . . . noted that a 'search for status and a feeling of instability regarding its social position' was characteristic of the Polish white collar intelligentsia (1966). [. . .]

It would again be true to say that certain sections of the middle class in post-war capitalist societies also experienced a fall in material and social status relative to manual workers. But it could hardly be claimed that their position was as embattled and precarious as that of their counterparts in the East European states. Socialist ideology and institutions had there created a political climate in which the established middle class were defined as potential opponents of the new social order. [. . .]

All these features characteristic of the socialist reconstruction period serve to demonstrate the formative role of ideology in giving rise to a stratification system fundamentally at variance with that of Western capitalism. For a number of reasons it would be possible to regard this type of system as having much in common with the model of the classless society referred to above. To begin with, a marked feature of the socialist state during this early period was the relative weakness or absence of stable grouping and institutions. [. . .] During this re-stratification process there would also be a somewhat uncertain situation in the sphere of values as the old normative order gradually gave way to the new. Under these anomic conditions clear differences in patterns of behaviour and outlook such as we find in a stable class system could not readily be expected to emerge. The social structure would in other words take on many of the characteristics typical of a 'mass' situation, with all that this implies in the way of a socially fragmented and disorganized population. One of the few stable and unified groups would be the Party apparatus, a factor which would complete the picture of a classless society split between a ruling elite and an unstructured, atomized mass.

The system of rewards in socialist society during this formative, relatively classless phase stems largely from the need of the new ruling elite to consolidate its power and to resist opposition from the potential 'class enemy'. [. . .] The emphasis upon egalitarianism and similar policies designed to favour the working class at the expense of the middle class is quite compatible with a system whose dominant concern is not the rational allocation of human and material resources with the aim of maximizing efficiency. Under these conditions the overall demotion of the middle class and the elevation of the proletariat is perfectly feasible. However, [. . .] when industrial efficiency becomes a major preoccupation, the socialist stratification order appears to come under increasing strains. This occurs largely because of the tension between the system of rewards prescribed by the formal ideology and that associated with economic rationality and technological efficiency. [. . .] The evidence from East Europe strongly suggests that in the drive towards a modern industrial system these contradictions are resolved by restoring the middle class to a more favourable position in the scale of rewards at the expense of the proletariat. The emergent emphasis upon economic rationality and the allocation of men to elite positions on the basis of meritocratic criteria leads to the erosion of traditional socialist ideology and paves the way to a form of class stratification that has much more in common with that of Western capitalism. Many East European societies have now entered this phase and for them the model of classlessness is no longer applicable.

Modern industrialism and the socialist class system

Throughout the better part of the 1960s a number of East European states have succeeded in implementing a variety of economic and industrial reforms of a far-reaching kind. [...] This was to introduce for the first time on any large scale the concept of the market into economic strategy by allowing supply and demand mechanisms more play in the formation of prices and wages (see Gamarinkow, 1964; Miller, 1963; Felker, 1966; Pejovich, 1966; Sik, 1965). [...] These reforms were initiated as part of the drive to increase economic and industrial efficiency and as a means of overcoming certain of the problems posed by excessive bureaucratic control. The general tendency has been to grant industrial enterprises more local autonomy and to judge their success or failure more in terms of certain criteria of 'profitability' than of plan fulfilment. [...] Critics have expressed concern about the effect of the new reforms on the wages structure, and particularly the tendency for increased differentials to follow in their wake. In Yugoslavia, for example, where the economy was overhauled in the direction of greater market freedom earlier and more radically than elsewhere in East Europe, a widening of income differentials between the skilled and unskilled was observed to be an immediate consequence. Paul Landy in his 1961 review of these early Yugoslav reforms, noted that, 'The most recent statistics substantiate earlier worries that "the rich will become richer and the poor will be poorer" (1961)'. [...] In 1968, following the most recent economic innovations it was reported that

Every factory now pays its workers what it can afford to pay. Enterprises which carry on a lively and profitable trade with foreign countries pay their workers (particularly the skilled ones) wages on a par with those paid in the most advanced West European countries, while enterprises that barely make ends meet pay subsistence wages. As a result, wage differentials between individual factories have become absurdly great, and they are growing (Pospielovsky, 1968). [...]

Advantages have begun to accrue not simply to skilled manual workers, but also to white-collar experts of various kinds. Following the 1966 reforms in Czechoslovakia, the average salaries of engineers and technicians increased by 5·2 per cent and those of administrative personnel by 6·2 per cent, whereas manual workers' wages have risen by only 1·4 per cent (Taborsky, 1968). Similar selective wage increases have been reported for Poland (Rawin, 1965).[2] More recently manual workers, especially the unskilled, have come to be disadvantaged in another important way as a result of the economic reforms – by rising unemployment. Unemployment had traditionally been viewed as the hallmark of a capitalist economic order, and its occurrence under socialism was hardly conceived of as a possibility. [. . .] With the new emphasis on cost-consciousness and profitability, industrial enterprises have increasingly been encouraged to shake out surplus or inefficient labour, so creating the kind of unemployment problems long familiar in the capitalist West. In Yugoslavia there are over a quarter of a million unemployed, mainly unskilled workers, and the number is expected to increase (*Politika*, 24 September 1967; Livingston, 1964). Heavy unemployment has been anticipated by the Hungarian government as a result of the recent reforms, and arrangements have been made for the migration of 100,000 workers to replenish the depleted labour force of East Germany (Solyom-Fekete, 1968). [. . .]

The new economic measures taken by European socialist states have tended to accelerate the departure from egalitarian policies of the reconstruction period. [. . .] In fact the steady shift away from an egalitarian incomes structure to one based on widening differentials is very similar to the pattern followed in the Soviet Union. [. . .]

The campaign against 'equality-mongering' [. . .] throughout the 1930s was justified in terms of the need to provide material incentives for skilled personnel essential to the crash programme of industrialization. Although the range of inequalities in East European societies is not yet as great as that found in the Soviet Union, the arguments against egalitarianism are similar to those advanced by the Russians (as well as by proponents of the functionalist theory of stratification). Professor Ota Sik, an economist who played a leading role in bringing about the Czech reforms, had complained of the fact that

---

2. Of course, not all these changes in income differentials are directly attributable to market forces. State control of wages and salaries has by no means been abandoned, although incomes policies are becoming more responsive to the market than in the past. Clearly, a command economy is as capable of creating inequalities as a market economy.

greater restrictions were placed on the factors needed to ensure desired growth in the salaries of technical, educational, scientific ... personnel than on workers' wages. ... Thus, over the years, and particularly since 1959, there occurred an increasingly damaging levelling of wages, which in turn had a harmful effect on progress in science and technology (1965, p. 22).

A number of Western scholars have also drawn attention to the apparently deleterious effect that egalitarian policies had had on the Czech economy prior to the reforms. Thus, Holesovsky states that wage equalization had been carried to such an extreme that it was not uncommon for university graduates to prefer well-paid manual work to the professional occupations they had been trained for (1968). [. . .]

At the same time, the Czech economy which was the most advanced in pre-war Eastern Europe had reached a state of acute decline by the early 1960s.[3] Although the reformers did not attribute the economic crisis solely to equalization policies, it was clear that the introduction of wider differentials – particularly between blue-collar and white-collar workers – was an important part of their solution to the problem. [. . .]

The growing preoccupation with the rational and efficient organization of industry in socialist societies appears to be shifting the balance of material and social advantages steadily away from the working class and towards the middle class. It seems that the special skills and expertise commanded by white-collar and professional groups become more highly valued and rewarded once the initial problems of political stabilization and control give way to those associated with economic and technological progress. [. . .] The long run tendency seems to have been for the proletariat to relinquish many of the advantages which accrued to it in the early period of socialist rule. This is illustrated not only by changes which have taken place in income distribution but also by educational reforms and in the changing social composition of political and secular elites. For example, membership of the Communist Party (often an important avenue to social and material advancement) has shown a marked increase in middle-class representation in all East European countries for which evidence is available. In a recent analysis of the Communist Party of the Soviet Union, Schwarz calculated that one in every three white-collar 'specialists' with higher education is now a Party member, whereas among manual workers only one in twenty-two is a Party member (1967). [. . .]

3. The United Nations Economic Commission for Europe reported a 4 per cent drop in national income for Czechoslovakia in 1963, after only 1 per cent increase in the previous year (Schaffer, 1964).

Schwarz's conclusion that workers are being 'steadily thrust into the background within the Communist Party' would seem to apply equally to the newer European socialist states. In Yugoslavia, workers and peasants comprised about 79 per cent of the membership of the League of Communists in 1948; by 1957 they made up less than half the membership (Avakumovic, 1959). [. . .]

The increase in non-manual membership was shown to have come about not simply by differential class recruitment, but also by the pattern of resignations and expulsions. In 1966, alone, of the 13,488 members purged by the Party more than 52 per cent were industrial workers, while of members who resigned voluntarily more than 54 per cent were workers. [. . .]

The situation in Poland is similar. [. . .] Concerning Czechoslovakia, Taborsky states that in the early period of socialist rule about 60 per cent of Party members were manual workers, but by 1956 this figure had already fallen to about 36 per cent (1961, pp. 32–7). [. . .]

This progressive 'de-proletarianization' of the Communist Parties in Eastern Europe is symptomatic of the general decline in the position of the working class and the trend towards secularization in many institutional spheres. [. . .] With the emergent emphasis on industrial efficiency the tendency has been to appoint men to positions of authority and responsibility more on the basis of their formal quali-fications than simply as a reward for political loyalty. The combination of a Party card and high qualifications would appear to be the best guarantee of social advancement, and possession of the former is coming to rely more and more on prior possession of the latter. [. . .] Undoubtedly quite sharp antagonisms have arisen between the younger generation of graduates and technocrats on the one hand, and the older Party veterans and partisans on the other. Bauman suggests that in Poland the former are more able to hold on to their positions in the less economically developed regions where their lack of technical skills does not put them at much of a disadvantage. In the more advanced regions, however, they are less able to compete with the new experts and are rapidly being replaced by them (1964). A similar pro-cess appears to be occurring in Yugoslavia. [. . .] The poorly developed system of stipends for needy students, the ability of many middle-class parents to pay for private coaching for their children, and the difficulty of attempting to combine studies with paid labour, all ensure that the student of working-class parents (especially the unskilled) is at a serious disadvantage in the ever-increasing competition for acade-mic honours. It is not therefore surprising that social classes in the Soviet Union show a high degree of self-recruitment. Surveys of industrial enterprises in Sverdlovsk and Leningrad have demonstrated that the great majority of workers are themselves the offspring of workers, and very few are downwardly mobile from the middle class (Utechin, 1953). [. . .]

There is some indication here that the Soviet educational system operates not so much to block upward mobility of lower status youths (as some writers have suggested) but rather that it restricts downward mobility among the offspring of higher status groups. In other words the latter groups are more self-recruiting than the former. This is because the expansion of white collar occupations is still sufficient not merely to absorb the offspring of the present middle class but also to provide places for a minority of children of working class background. S. M. Miller has suggested that rates of downward mobility are probably a better index of the openness of a class system than rates of upward mobility, and on this score the Soviet system, and that of other European socialist states, shows some signs of ossification.[4] The opportunities for a lowly born child to improve his lot in socialist society by way of higher education are still considerably better than they are for his equivalent in capitalist society. But they are not quite so favourable as they were when the middle class was less integrated into the political and social order than it has now become.

The relative decline in the material and social standing of the proletariat and the corresponding advancement of the new white collar professions has resulted in a class stratification system which is now in many ways more similar to that of Western capitalism than to the stratification order prevailing in the period of socialist reconstruction. [. . .] Of particular relevance here is the distinction between manual and non-manual occupations, which East European sociologists have also found to be a key source of variation in social outlook and activities. Polish scholars, for example, have demonstrated that blue-collar workers' perceptions of the social order closely follow the classic power or conflict model of a society divided between 'them' and 'us', while white-collar workers are much more likely to perceive it in terms of the familiar status or consensual model of an open opportunity structure (Nowak, 1964; Riddell, 1968). [. . .]

Thus, manual workers tend to display a greater belief in the principles of egalitarianism than do white-collar workers; the former understand equality to mean 'to each according to his needs', whereas the latter understand it to mean equality of opportunity to succeed in a

4. For data on class differences in educational achievement in Czechoslovakia, see Kubat (1963).

system of unequal rewards (Meister, 1964; Nowak 1964). Again, studies of the workplace have reported that men on the shop floor evaluate the rewards of work differently from the white-collar employees, stressing in particular the material satisfactions of pay and security, rather than rewards of an intrinsic nature. [...]

There are, too, certain differences in the market situation of manual and non-manual workers in socialist countries. Workers are generally paid wages which are calculated on the basis of physical output, as in the piece-rate system, whereas the white-collar employees are usually paid fixed monthly salaries, often supplemented by various bonuses. In Poland, salaried staff are entitled to three months' notice of dismissal, as against the customary two weeks' notice for manual workers (Rawin, 1965). Also, the opportunities for promotion within industry tend to be more restricted for shop-floor workers than for administrative employees, particularly in view of the increasing importance of paper qualifications. Now that unemployment has become much more of a threat in socialist states than in the past, the relative market disadvantages of manual work are likely to become even more pronounced, especially for the unskilled. [...] In Czechoslovakia, too, opposition to the economic reforms came from factory managers whose appointment owed more to their politics and proletarian origins than to their technical abilities. [...] A similar kind of resistance to economic and industrial modernization occurred in Hungary. [...]

As the white-collar intelligentsia gradually take over elite positions in politics and industry it could be predicted that social policies designed specifically to further working-class interests are less likely to be initiated. [...] In some respects in fact the conflicts generated by the new reforms could be said to have taken on a definite class character. In Czechoslovakia, for example, Novotny's opposition to changes in industry and the economy was based partly on the argument that these would disadvantage the industrial workers, as indeed appears to have been the case. It is significant that in his unsuccessful attempt to retain the Party leadership in 1968 he and his followers turned to the industrial workers for support against the white collar intelligentsia. [...]

The struggle between various class-interest groups in modernizing socialist states has rarely erupted into the kind of open conflict manifested in Czechoslovakia. But the same overall shift in the balance of advantages in favour of white-collar groups has occurred, if less dramatically. [...] The re-integration of the middle class into society has come about not simply as a result of their key role in the drive to industrial efficiency, although this is clearly an important factor. No less important is the fact that the new middle class is different in a number of ways from the bourgeoisie of the capitalist period. To begin with, its social and material privileges rest almost wholly upon the educational and occupational achievements of its members, and not upon inherited property or private wealth. Again, most of its members are young enough to have been socialized into the political values of the new order, by way of the schools and the mass media, so that unlike their predecessors they are not automatically defined as potential opponents of socialism. Many will have been upwardly mobile from the working class – beneficiaries of the early educational reforms – and their own success within the system would be liable to give it an extra patina of legitimacy in their eyes. This combination of factors tends to make for the emergence of a stable and increasingly privileged middle class owing the same kind of allegiance to their social order as the Western middle classes show towards theirs. [. . .]

Now that institutes of higher learning rarely discriminate against the sons and daughters of non-manual parents, there is a greater likelihood that middle-class elites will be more self-recruiting than in the past. [. . .] The evidence from socialist states confirms the Western experience that children from manual backgrounds have higher dropout rates and poorer academic records than those from non-manual homes. Thus, if the latter's motivational and material advantages are not offset by some form of positive discrimination in favour of working class offspring, the educational system is almost bound to consolidate the middle-class position and lead to a greater degree of class crystallization. It is at any rate significant that some such tailing off in rates of upward mobility has been reported for the Soviet Union. [. . .] S. V. Utechin drew attention in 1953 to the slowing down of vertical mobility in the Soviet Union, and this claim has been substantiated by a number of more recent accounts of Russian higher education (1953). [. . .]

The differences in patterns of behaviour and outlook between these two broad occupational categories, as well as underlying differences in their material and social advantages, are probably not as great as those found between comparable categories in capitalist society. Nevertheless, they would seem to be sufficiently marked to throw into serious doubt all claims about the inability of formal class structures to develop in Soviet-type political systems. The, admittedly fragmentary, evidence drawn together here suggests not simply that European socialist societies have a fairly clearly defined class system, but also that it is one having much in common with the class system typical of Western capitalism. The main reason for this is that the rewards structure of both types of society is based upon an occupational order moulded by the requirements of modern industry and technology. Non-work sources of income and status are unavailable to the majority of the population in either type of society, so that similarities in occupational structure account for many of the similarities in their class systems. At the same time, it would be a mistake not to recognize certain important differences between the two systems. A distinctive feature of the capitalist class structure, for example, is the role played by private property and inherited wealth. Rights in property confer material and social advantages which are functionally distinct from those stemming from the occupational order, and are a key factor in the consolidation of privilege and status over time. It is certainly true that members of the top stratum of the political bureaucracy in socialist societies also enjoy great privileges as a result of their control over state property and services. But it may be disputed whether their class position is analogous to that of a propertied bourgeoisie (as Djilas and others have argued) if only because their lack of title to state property prevents them passing it down to their heirs. [. . .] Hence the opportunities for the Party apparatus to reproduce itself from its own offspring are much more limited than those of a propertied bourgeoisie. Again, despite the abandonment of strict egalitarianism in Eastern Europe, [. . .] ideology has played a more formative role in shaping the class system than that allowed for it by the 'logic of industrialism' thesis. Of course, whether or not these differences could usefully be said to constitute two fundamentally distinct class systems would depend on the relative weighting of criteria.[5]

5. For Goldthorpe, the crucial distinction between capitalist and socialist class systems lies in the *source* of their inequaliy and stratification. Classes in capitalist society are generated largely by the market in a more or less unplanned way, with the state playing only a mediating role. In socialist society, by contrast, classes are deliberately created to a formula drawn up by the state, and the role of the market is peripheral. Such resemblances as there are between the two systems are thus seen as 'phenotypic' rather than 'genotypic' in character (Goldthorpe, 1964). For Bottomore, on the other hand, it is the final *outcome*, rather than the source of stratification, which provides the major point of comparison. Therefore, because features such as rates of social mobility, the range of material inequalities, the composition of elites, etc., are class factors which vary *within* capitalist and socialist type societies, as well as between them, there tends to be 'a continuum of differences rather than an abrupt break between the two types' (Bottomore, 1965, p. 54).

References

AVAKUMOVIC, I. (1959), 'The Communist League of Yugoslavia in figures', *J. Central Europ. Aff.*, vol. 19.

BAUMAN, Z. (1964), 'Economic growth, social structure, elite formation', *Int. Soc. Sci. J.*, vol. 16, no. 2, p. 214.

BOTTOMORE, T. B. (1965), *Classes in Modern Society*, Allen & Unwin.

FELDMESSER, R. A. (1960), 'Social classes and the political structure', in C. E. Black (ed.), *The Transformation of Russian Society*, Harvard University Press.

FELKER, J. L. (1966), *Soviet Economic Controversies: The Emerging Marketing Concept and Changes in Planning, 1960–65*, MIT Press.

GAMARINKOW, M. (1964), 'The growth of economic revisionism', *East Europe*, vol. 13.

GOLDTHORPE, J H. (1964), 'Social stratification in industrial society', *Sociol. Rev.*, no. 8, pp. 97–122.

HOLESOVSKY, V. (1968), 'Czechoslovakia's labour pains', *East Europe*, May.

KUBAT, D. (1963), 'Social mobility in Czechoslovakia', *Amer. Sociol. Rev.*, vol. 28, no. 2, pp. 203–12.

LANDY, P. (1961), 'Reforms in Yugoslavia', *Problems of Communism*, November–December.

LIVINGSTON, R. G. (1963), 'Yugoslavian unemployment trends', *Monthly Lab. Rev.*, vol. 87.

MATEJKO, A. (1966), 'Status incongruence in the Polish intelligentsia', *Sociol. Res.*, vol. 33, no. 4, pp. 611–39.

MEISTER, A. (1964), *Socialisme et autogestion: l'experience Yugoslave*, Paris.

MILLER, M. (ed.) (1963), *Communist Economy under Change*, Institute of Economic Affairs.

MURRAY, E. (1960), 'Higher education in Communist Hungary', *Slav and East Europ. Rev.*, vol. 19.

NOWAK, S. (1964), 'Changes of social structure in social consciousness', *Polish Soc. Bull.*, no. 2.

PEJOVICH, S. (1966), *The Market Planned Economy of Yugoslavia*, Minnesota University Press.

POSPIELOVSKY, D. (1968), 'Dogmas under attack', *Problems of Communism*, March–April.

RAWIN, S. J. (1965), 'Changes in social structure in Poland under conditions of industrialization', unpublished Ph.D. thesis, University of London.

RIDDELL, D. S. (1968), 'Social self-government: the background of theory and practice in Yugoslavia', *Brit. J. Sociol.*, vol. 19, no. 1, pp. 47–75.

SARAPATA, A., and WESOLOWSKI, W. (1961), 'The evaluation of occupations by Warsaw inhabitants', *Amer. J. Sociol.*, vol. 66, no. 6, pp. 581–91.

SCHAFFER, H. G. (1964), 'New tasks for the enterprise director', *East Europe*, August.

SCHWARZ, S. M. (1967), 'Education and the working class', *Survey*, October.

SEFER, B. (1968), Income distribution in Yugoslavia, *Int. Lab. Rev.*, vol. 97, no. 4, pp. 371–89.

SIK, O. (1965), 'Czechoslovakia's new system of economic planning and management', *East Europ. Econ.*, Fall.

SOLYOM-FEKETE, W. (1968), 'Hungary's new labour code', *East Europe*, March.

SZCZEPARSKI, J. (1964), 'Sociological aspects of higher education in Poland', in S. Ehrlich (ed.), *Social and Political Transformation in Poland*, Warsaw.

TABORSKY, E. (1961), *Communism in Czechoslovakia, 1948–60*, Princeton University Press.

TABORSKY, E. (1968), 'Czechoslovakia's economy reform', *East Europe*, April.

UTECHIN, S. V. (1953), 'Social stratification and mobility in the Soviet Union, *Transactions of the Second World Congress of Sociology*, vol. 2.

Part Four **Belief**

Sociology has always had a strong interest in analysing the nature of those shared beliefs to which men attach some kind of priority or sacredness, and which provide the basic perspectives around which groups of individuals organize their life. Religious beliefs have often occupied this position and so the sociology of religion has always been close to the mainstream of sociological theory. Three persistent themes have been the relationship between social stratification and religious movements (especially sects) ; the question of whether beliefs are merely determined by economic factors (as Marx suggested) or whether they can be a major factor in shaping even the economy (as Weber believed) ; and finally, the question whether the functions that religion served are now either redundant in modern society or are served by secular substitutes.

The first step in answering all these questions has to be to get straight what is meant by religion. Roland Robertson (Reading 25) shows that different answers to this question can radically affect our approaches to the other issues, especially the last issue – the process of secularization.

Ernst Troeltsch (Reading 26) provides the classic discussion of the distinction between church and sect types of religious organization. The church is an integral part of the existing social order and stabilizes it, whilst sects are formed by dissenting minorities.

J. Milton Yinger in Reading 27 elaborates the church-sect distinction into a more complex typology.

The concept of sect was used originally by Troeltsch to illuminate the religious response of economically deprived groups. Charles Glock and Rodney Stark in Reading 28 relate the typology of religious groups to a typology of deprivation on the assumption that religion compensates people for deprivations which cannot be resolved by direct means.

Max Weber set out to show that religion was not just a by-product of other social structures such as the economy. He contended that the development of Western capitalism was facilitated by some aspects of Protestant belief (Reading 29 (a)).

The Protestant Ethic thesis has continued to generate both research and controversy. Ephraim Fischoff (Reading 30) clarified the main theoretical issues in the debate.

Robert N. Bellah shows how Weber's hypothesis has stimulated research into the association between beliefs and economic activity in Asia (Reading 31).

The question of whether religion's part in society is destined to decline is treated in a variety of ways by Marx (Reading 32), Durkheim (Reading 33), Berger (Reading 34) and Shiner (Reading 35).

25 Roland Robertson

Basic Problems of Definition

Excerpt from Roland Robertson, *The Sociological Interpretation of Religion*, Basil Blackwell, 1970, pp. 34–47.

It has often been argued that it is fruitless to delve very deeply into problems of definition and conceptualization in the sociology of religion. The authority of Max Weber may be invoked in support of such a contention:

To define 'religion', to say what it *is*, is not possible at the start of a presentation. . . . Definition can be attempted, if at all, only at the conclusion of the study. The essence of religion is not even our concern, as we make it our task to study the conditions and effects of a particular type of social behaviour.

The external courses of religious behaviour are so diverse that an understanding of this behaviour can only be achieved from the viewpoint of the subjective experiences, ideas, and purposes of the individuals concerned – in short, from the viewpoint of the religious behaviour's 'meaning' (*Sinn*) (1963, p. 1).

Three points should be noted about this passage. First, Weber claims that in so far as definition is possible it can be accomplished only after empirical inquiry and discussion. But, we may ask, inquiry into and discussion about *what*? Second, he speaks of the *essence* of religion. But is this what is required of a definition of religion? Third, Weber refers to religious behaviour. But on what grounds can he logically make such reference since he has declined to define it? Our objections to Weber's position are basically that it is impossible to analyse something without having criteria for the identification of that something; and that it is not the essence of religion which we are after, as if there were something 'out there' to be apprehended as 'religious', but rather a sociological definition which will enable us to analyse in a rigorous and consistent manner. Now it should be emphasized in all fairness to Weber himself that he did quite obviously have criteria as to what constituted the sphere of his inquiry into religion. In his case it was a concern with what Parsons calls 'the grounds of meaning', or the basic perspectives around which a group or society of individuals 'organize' their life – their basic orientations to human and social life, conceptions of time, the meaning of death ; in fact the basic cosmological conceptions in relation to human existence. Thus this was Weber's primary point of reference, not 'religion' itself. On the other hand, this point of reference came very close to being what Western scholars usually meant by the term religion – since the grounds of meaning have entailed in practically all, if not entirely all, societies a subscription to beliefs in supernatural entities or forces. More generally these were beliefs which, in Pareto's term, 'surpass experience' (see Parsons, 1949; 1954). Thus although Weber was reluctant to define religion for sociological purposes he did have a fairly clear-cut conception of the boundaries of the problem-area he was discussing; and these boundaries coincided fairly well with what was widely understood at that time as constituting religion.

Weber did not arrive at a conclusive definition of the religious phenomenon. And yet in his work we can see that it is unlikely that he could really have considered the definitional problem an unimportant one. One major clue to this diagnosis is Weber's frequent emphasis upon rationality as the increasingly dominant mode of cognition and evaluation in early twentieth-century societies. He thought that modern industrial societies were characterized by the tendency for individuals to be guided in their actions by consideration of the most appropriate logical means to specific ends. Moreover the ends themselves were regarded as being of a secular kind – prestige, wealth, particular forms of social organization and so on. The important point to note here is that in spite of tending to equate inquiry into 'the grounds of meaning' with the sociology of religion, Weber did not in the final analysis regard as religious the basic 'ground of meaning' which he considered to be characteristic of modern society. Unlike some later sociologists, Weber did not regard the most general cultural orientations of modern society as being by definition 'religious' (1961, p. 270).

The value of sociological definitions, classifications and conceptualizations is to be seen in their fruitfulness in theorizing about and explaining social phenomena. There is necessarily an element of arbitrariness in sociological definitions ; but we may distinguish basically between types of definition which are in one sense extremely arbitrary, so-called *nominal* definitions, and those which are formulated in reference to empirical phenomena and in the course of an attempt to grapple with the diversity and uniqueness of those phenomena, so-called real definitions (Spiro, 1966; Berger, 1969; Goody, 1961; Horton, 1960). Whereas a nominal definition is attractive because it can be fitted into an already adumbrated conceptual scheme, more or less regardless of particular empirical problems ; a real definition is used in a very different way – namely, in the statement of a proposition about the empirical world. The proposition tends to be *constrained*, as a matter of degree, by previously explicated conceptual and theoretical schemes.[1] Thus it should be clear that the definitional problem is not a trivially scholastic one. Its solution is indeed closely bound up with the capacity to arrive at satisfactory accounts of religious phenomena. A definition which is very general and 'fuzzy' does not lend itself easily to systematic analysis.

It will probably be illuminating to consider Durkheim's approach to the problem of definition, classification and analytic isolation (1961). In his definition of religion Durkheim immediately faced the problem of the relationship between his own sociological predilections and commonsense, intuitive definitions of religion. One of his foremost concerns was that if he were to adopt a supernaturalistic conception of religion he would thereby rule Buddhism out of analytic court. As Spiro points out, this was an unwarranted worry on Durkheim's part, since Durkheim wrongly assumed that there were no supernatural conceptions in Buddhist religions (1961, p. 88).[2] (Durkheim's mistake in this respect was the rather common one of focusing upon the philosophical dimension of religious culture and paying insufficient attention to the operative beliefs of 'ordinary' individuals.) Durkheim obviously wanted to incorporate all religions (as intuitively recognized) within his purview, but to avoid the inconsistency manifested in any approach which made beliefs in a god (or gods) a defining characteristic of religion and which, at the same time, called primitive, nontheistic belief systems religious. Hence Durkheim's definition of religion as 'a unified system of beliefs and practices relative to sacred things, that is to say, things set apart and forbidden – beliefs and practices which unite into one single moral community called a Church, all those who adhere to them (1961, p. 62).[3] We have already indicated in the first

1. Thus the use of the term 'real' has here *nothing* to do with 'essence' – as it has in the work of some philosophers.
2. Spiro's argument points up the dangers of the sociologist relying too heavily on the most visible doctrinal expressions of major religious traditions and thereby ignoring the 'popular' manifestations of such traditions (see Leach, 1968).
3. Durkheim's influence in the matter of definition has been considerable. There is, however, a rather different tradition which has emphasized the property of sacredness. This stems from Otto (1929). Peter Berger thus proposes as a viable definition: 'religion is the human attitude toward a sacred order that includes

chapter the kind of difficulty to which such a general and vague specification of religion leads. Not only does such a definition 'let in' many phenomena which it is almost impossible to analyse in terms that are applicable to conventionally understood religion ; but it is also extremely difficult to handle. The latter deficiency hinges on the point that sacredness is surely a matter of degree. Are we to define as religious all those beliefs and values which are sacredly fundamental to a society – for example, belief in the virtue of worldly success? (see Luckmann and Berger, 1964).

Inclusive, broad definitions of religion appear to spring from two sources. First, they have been proposed by those whose conception of a social system emphasizes the need for individuals to be controlled by some overriding loyalty to a central set of beliefs and values. Second, they have been proposed, somewhat negatively, by sociologists who are concerned with more detailed and closely circumscribed problems, such as the study of particular religious organizations. Since basic definitional problems do not impinge directly on their work there is little intellectual incentive to use precise definitions. The pressure to employ more restrictive and exclusive, narrow definitions also arises in connection with particular intellectual stances. First, there are those sociologists who do not see social systems as necessarily held together by homogeneous commitments to a central set of precious values and beliefs. These frequently emphasize the greater importance of power and force. The restrictive or exclusive definition is attractive to some of these because they find that the claim that certain phenomena are religious is a case of special pleading for religiosity, a manifestation of an anxiety about an areligious world. Second, those who wish to assess the extent to which societies operate in terms of religious commitments, or to examine the tensions between religious and non-religious conceptions of the social order, are more likely to prefer exclusive definitions of religion. (As with the two variants of the first category of preferences, these two variants of exclusivism may be held simultaneously by the same sociologist.[4]) These two opposing sets of views and interests confront each other mainly in reference to a number

within it all being – human or otherwise. In other words, religion is the belief in a cosmos, the meaning of which both transcends and includes man' (Berger, 1967, p. 338). The accusation that sacredness is a matter of degree does not apply so easily to Berger's definition. The worry is that, at least as he states if informally it lacks specificity.

4. Furthermore, extra- or pre-sociological commitments and preferences are at work on both sides of 'the fence'. This point crops up again at various points in the book. One of the most important of these is that in some intellectual circles 'religion' tends to be used *pejoratively*.

of major changes which have taken place in industrial societies during the twentieth century. In brief the *inclusivist* will see such belief systems as Communism as of the same sociological species as religion, whereas the *exclusivist* will not. The latter will be interested, to continue with the example, in a system which, like Communism, makes an explicit claim to reject all religious commitments as such. The real problem, perhaps, is whether strong commitment to ideals, particularly those which entail an element of sacredness and preciousness and operate as basic premises on which people act or claim to act, should be considered as religious commitments. An associated problem is whether commitment to participation in the affairs of organizations and collectivities that proclaim themselves to be religious should always be regarded as religious commitment. We will deal with each of these problems in turn.

Although Communism is perhaps the most outstanding example, there are a number of 'isms' which the inclusivist tends to regard as religions. Not only political ideologies, such as nationalism and Fascism, but also other belief systems, such as secularism, humanism, psychoanalysis 'as a way of life', and so on, are regarded by the inclusivist as religions – although it is important to note that exceedingly few studies of such phenomena have been undertaken within the framework of the sociology of religion.[5] We are confronted in relation to this problem by a distinction which will recur in this analysis – between, on the one hand, definitions which are *functional,* and, on the other hand, definitions which are *substantive.* This is not the same as the distinction between nominal and real definitions – although there is a close proximity, since functional definitions tend in practice to be nominal definitions and substantive definitions tend to be real definitions. A functional definition is one which uses as the criteria for identifying and classifying a phenomenon the functions which that phenomenon performs: the functions which a system requires are stipulated and then observed social and cultural phenomena are classified and identified on the basis of the functions which they perform (Goldschmidt, 1966). From such a perspective, phenomena such as Communism may become identified as religious in a strong sense – when it is said that Communism *is* a religion, because of the function it fulfils – or in a weak sense – when it is said that Communism is a *functional equivalent* to religion. By this term is meant that Communism performs functions – has social consequences for the system

5. But see Luckmann (1967, chs. 6 and 7) and the references cited in those chapters. A number of people have pointed up the allegedly religious character of communism (see MacRae, 1954).

in which it is present – similar to those of conventionally and intuitively understood religion in non-Communist societies. The functional-equivalent thesis is important because it combines an element of substantive definition with the functional definition. That is, Communism is functionally equivalent to religion, *as substantively defined*.

Commitments to, say, humanism or 'psychoanalyticism' pose greater problems that Communism. It is much easier to see features analogous to self-declared, organized religion in Communism than in such orientations and yet some humanist movements have calculatedly espoused a religious style. Many of the recruits to such 'isms' have previously been highly committed to some obviously-religious movement and their new involvement constitutes what we will here call *surrogate religiosity* (see Weber, 1961).

The phenomenon which we have labelled surrogate religiosity bears directly on the present attempt to isolate and define the religious phenomenon. For much of the difficulty in demarcating the boundaries of religion pertains to the kinds of commitment into which people in contemporary industrial societies enter in search of an alternative to a religious adherence which no longer satisfies them. It is basically in the face of this that the present analysis tends strongly towards the exclusivist type of definitional approach. For one of the most interesting and significant characteristics of modern societies would be lost to the sociological perspective if the various 'isms' of which we have spoken were regarded as fundamentally religious for sociological purposes ; since their adherents have in many, if not all, cases chosen to renounce contact with the supernatural or spiritual, and the explicit, official values of such groups also obviously deny their reality.[6]

A number of functional definitions are employed within the sociology of religion. First, and least satisfactory, there is that functional approach which defines religion in terms of its concern with 'ultimate problems' – on the assumption that all societies or most individuals in all societies have ultimate problems.[7] In one sense this emphasis

6. Self-conscious surrogate religiosity is particularly manifest in some of the humanist societies which have developed in Britain during the past one hundred years. The National Secular Society, for example, exhibits a functional kind of 'religious' opposition to religion (see Budd, 1968).

7. This concern with 'ultimacy' is so widespread in the orthodox literature that any single citation or series of citations of its usage would be very misleading – so common has been its invocation. The really important point to note is that it derives from the work of a theologian, Paul Tillich. The attractiveness of such a definitional approach inheres in its generality and, one suspects, the fact that it has been religiously legitimated. One should note, with emphasis, that whereas sociologists seek to use the 'ultimacy' definition in a neutral, analytic sense, Tillich's formulation is *religiously prescriptive*. In any case sociologists utilizing

may be made into a substantive definition. Yinger has recently suggested that sociologists might attempt to tap the religiosity of individuals by asking them questions about themes sociologically adjudged to be within the domain of 'ultimacy' (1967). In other words, whilst that which sought to solve ultimate problems was regarded as religion – a functional definition of religion – in order to use the concept of ultimacy in empirical inquiry, religion or ultimacy be defined in something approaching substantive terms. The substance of religion therefore consists in beliefs and values relating directly to so-called ultimacy. Aside from the very formidable problem of delineating in a non-arbitrary way what the sociologist is to include and exclude from this domain, one has also to question seriously the sociological validity of research which proceeds by asking people whether they are concerned with ultimate problems, so allowing *respondents* to interpret 'ultimacy'.

Second, another functional approach, most closely linked to the work of Parsons and Bellah, specifies religion as the 'highest' and most general 'level' of culture. In practice, this closely coalesces with the ultimacy approach. But formally the argument is that in any system of human action individuals are 'controlled' by the norms of inter-action prescribed by the social system, and that in turn the social system is 'controlled' by the cultural system of beliefs, values and symbols. The cultural system performs the function of providing the general guidelines for human action ; at the most general level of the cultural system itself are 'the grounds of meaning' and these are typically identified as the sphere of religious beliefs and values. In this sense, it is said, all societies manifest religious beliefs and values (Bellah, 1965; Parsons, 1965, pp. 963–93; Geertz, 1966; Nettl and Robertson, 1968, pp. 152–6). This is the epitome of the nominal, functional approach to definition. On the other hand it is not an approach which is sustained rigorously by its proponents. They frequently speak in an ambiguous way of the differentiation of the religious sphere from other spheres – suggesting on the one hand that religion in modern societies is still of *fundamental* culture significance, and yet at the same time arguing, in reference to the *empirical* evidence, that religion has become differentiated from other spheres of socio-cultural life in such a way as to make it at best one of a series of interrelated social sectors with no significant degree of autonomy (Parsons, 1966; 1951,

Tillich's approach have yet to come to terms with his conception of God or such statements as: there is 'no place *beside* the divine ... no possible atheism ... no wall between the religious and the non-religious. ... The holy embraces both itself and the secular' (1957; Bellah, 1966).

ch. 8). In effect, these theorists cling to a purely functional and nominal definition when speaking in very abstract terms of the systems of action. But, when confronted with concrete cases, they veer, inconsistently, towards a commonsense definition based on conventional, everyday usage. This inconsistency and the intellectual strains arising from it are undoubtedly associated with the acceptability to these theorists of such notions as 'the religion of Americanism', 'secular religion' and 'civic religion'. These notions do *not* conform to the spirit of conventional definitions – which emphasize beliefs about a transcendent or superempirical reality ; rather, they overarch and 'contain' religious beliefs and values as normally understood. In this way Parsons and Bellah are able to have the best of both worlds and so maintain some semblance of consistency. A variant of this functional approach, employed most frequently by Parsons, approaches religion in terms of its significance in the social sphere alone. Parsons conceives this sphere in terms of regularized patterns of human interaction – the most salient sociological category being that of values. Committed to the view that in ongoing systems of social interaction values are the dominant factors in guiding and constraining social action, Parsons also sees religion, therefore, in terms of values when he is speaking of the social system. Numerous difficulties arise in this connection – notably the virtual impossibility of deciding whether any particular value, such as democracy or the rule of law, is in any useful sense 'religious' (Parsons, 1963, pp. 33–70).

Third, there is the functional approach proposed by Luckmann. Luckmann's definition owes nothing specifically to modern trends in functional analysis ; but is an extension of Durkheim's approach to the problem. For Luckmann everything human is also religious, religion being the capacity of the human organism to transcend its biological nature through the construction of objective, morally binding and all-embracing universes of meaning (1967, ch. 3). This, although in one sense specific, is also the most inclusive of all functional definitions. And the questions which it raises have mainly to do with the boundaries of the sociology of religion and, indeed, the whole issue of the division of labour within sociology. Basically, Luckmann and Berger (although the latter operates with a much narrower, exclusive definition of religion) see the study of religion as part of the more fundamental enterprise of the sociology of *knowledge*. The pressure towards such an inclusive definition of religion, i.e. that religion is an anthropologically distinctive attribute of the socio-cultural condition, derives from Luckmann's negative estimate of the typical sociologist's focus on institutional religion. He argues against the focus on 'objective' and 'visible' manifestations of religiosity and seeks to rest his own sociology of religion on the 'subjective' and relatively invisible aspects of religiosity (1967, p. 25). But it does not follow that one has to go as far in the direction of the 'invisible' as Luckmann does in order to bypass the traps and deficiencies of the first approach. The difficulties in Luckmann's stance are highlighted by the distinction he is forced to make between 'the world view' as 'an elementary social form of religion' (p. 53) – a 'non-specific form' (p. 78) – and 'the configuration of religious representations that form a sacred universe ..., a *specific historical social form of religion*' (p. 61). The point of stressing the first seems to be lost once the second is introduced (which it will be noticed must be *substantive*, as opposed to purely functional).

The course suggested in this book is in the direction of a definition which is substantive and real, and also as a corollary it will be exclusive rather than inclusive. One of the most common arguments for this approach is the simple one that it conforms to everyday, intuitive conceptions of religion. But a much more compelling case would rest on other considerations. First, there is the phenomenon which we have already mentioned – that of surrogate religiosity (Robertson, 1970, p. 39). Second, there is the point that unless we have a fairly tightly circumscribed conception of the religious phenomenon (or phenomena) we cannot, without extreme difficulty, engage in consistent, systematic analyses and focus on cause and effect relationships; for such exercises necessitate our being able to discriminate between religious variables and non-religious variables. Third, is it not of great sociological significance to inquire into the factors effecting changes in systems of belief and value which are explicitly super-empirical or transcendental in their reference; since nobody could conceivably deny that significant proportions of the individuals in contemporary industrial societies have either given up or come seriously to doubt the validity of such orientations? Implementation of the view propounded by Berger and Luckmann that the study of religious beliefs be located within the wider frame of reference of the sociology of knowledge would indeed enable us to examine shifts from superempirical to empirical referents (and vice versa); but the attractiveness of this approach is considerably mitigated by Luckmann's insistence that we define religion in the very broad terms already indicated.

The category 'religion' is one which has *arisen* in socio-cultural contexts where the Judeo-Christian tradition has predominated. A great analytic difficulty in the sociology of religion is the extent to which our basic conceptual apparatus is derived from the doctrines of Christian religions. The church-sect distinction developed initially in a sociological context by Weber and Troeltsch is the outstanding *specific* example of such a 'Christian' conception (Robertson, 1970, p. 14 ; Troeltsch, 1931). The ideas of religion and religiosity are products of basically Christian thinking because of the tensions expressed in Christian doctrine as between, on the one hand, social and terrestrial reality and, on the other, transcendent spiritual reality ; and, more important, the prescription either that the affairs of the former should be brought into line with the latter or that the former constitutes some God-given testing ground, to be lived through, confronted and not eschewed.[8] As Weber put it so often, Christianity is basically an inner-worldly religious orientation. To be religious therefore 'makes sense' in Christianity in a way which is, strictly speaking, alien to other 'religions' – the contrast appearing most sharply as between Christianity on the one hand and Buddhism on the other. The category 'religion' thus arises in a situation in which there is a particular type of ambivalence as to the relationship between this, material world and another 'world'. In different forms the Buddhist orientations and the Hindu orientation are other-worldly, seeking an escape from this world. Christianity, most markedly in its Protestant variations, perpetuates the category 'religion' precisely because it has images of how the world ought to be.

In these terms two basic problems of analysis arise. The first of these relates to Christianity ; the second to Eastern religions. Christianity, it may be argued, is in a sense a self-destroying system (Berger, 1969 ; Troeltsch, 1912; Robertson, 1970, pp. 169–81). Weber's interpretation of the development of Christianity from its earliest to its modern Protestant forms emphasizes the historical trend towards an ever-increasing inner-worldliness. The culmination of this process, as Weber saw it, was the way in which Protestantism promoted economic rationality, a rationality which eventually became autonomous and self-sustaining. Parsons in elaboration and modification of the Weber thesis has tried to demonstrate how, through the successive stages of what are called respectively the 'medieval synthesis', the 'reformation phase' and the 'denominational phase', Christian religious values have become increasingly embedded in the social structure of Western societies (notably, with respect to the modern period, the United States) ; at the same time religious organizations and religious action became more differentiated from other spheres of social activity (Parsons, 1963). As Parsons develops his thesis the problem is posed

8. This statement is only intended as a brief indication of the major socio-cultural characteristics of Christianity.

very acutely as to what we mean by 'religious' and religiosity. Parsons rightly maintains that it would be wrong to equate religiosity in a simple way with other-worldliness in the Weberian sense. On such an interpretation Protestantism would be the least religious of all religions (Robertson, 1970, pp. 89–95). How then do we define the sphere of religion in predominantly Christian societies, when the Christian is enjoined to preoccupy himself, and historically has preoccupied himself, with the attempt to Christianize society and in so doing has made religion a differentiated sphere of activity? By Christianization of society Parsons means basically that the social values implicated in Christian culture have become institutionalized in secular society ; that is, they have become 'part and parcel' of the everyday operation of social life. Thus we may note an important difference between Parsons and Weber. Whereas Weber appears to say that Protestantism promoted its own eventual destruction by its emphasis on individualism and social involvement (Robertson, 1970, pp. 169–81). Parsons maintains that such involvement is from the sociologist's standpoint the type-case of the social grounding of religion.[9] Religious values have become more, not less, the keynote of the value systems of modern Western societies. And yet Parsons in the same analysis remains well aware of the kind of problem which has been raised in this chapter:

Values – i.e. moral orientations towards the problems of life in this world – are never the whole of religion, if indeed its most central aspect. My suggestion is that the principal roots of the present religious concern do not lie in *relative* moral decline or inadequacy (relative, that is, to other periods in our society's history) but rather in problems in the other areas of religion, problems of the bases of faith and the definitions of the ultimate problems of meaning (Parsons, 1963).[10]

In the light of these observations on the relation of the category of religion to Christian doctrine and the history of Christianity, we may crystallize the major problem as having to do with the attempt to delineate sociologically the category of religion *bearing in mind its Christian basis*. In Christian terms, as O'Dea has put it, 'religion both needs most and suffers most from institutionalization' (1963). How can we know when religion has been institutionalized? If we know, can we still say that it is religion? [. . .]

9. Parsons's view might be best expressed by the aesthetically unattractive neologism, *social religionization* (Bellah, 1964).

10. Parsons's emphasis here upon morals and the normative significance of religion, whilst conforming to many interpretations of what 'religion ought to do', runs against the grain of analyses which have stressed its 'meaning' or *cognitive* significance. For an earlier, more systematic and satisfactory attempt to deliniate religious beliefs analytically, see Parsons (1951).

Primitive societies do not of course face problems of this kind. Both because they are culturally inhibitive of and relatively well insulated from a situational religion/non-religion distinction and because they are almost by definition removed from the political exigencies of having to face the problem, we do not find obvious parallels or analogies to the situation obtained in the industrialized or industrializing societies of the world. But it is precisely because the distinction arises neither in an intrinsic cultural respect nor in an instrumental political respect that the sociologist is burdened with analytical perplexities. We shall have cause to look at the primitive societal problems at a later stage. Suffice to point out here that indigenous *conceptions* of super-empirical and transcendental realms are often only of minor significance in the thought patterns of primitive societies. And yet of course beliefs in the spiritual and extra- or superhuman qualities of inanimate and non-human animate objects are manifold. In this respect crucial decisions have to be taken about the inclusion or exclusion of the latter from the sphere of religion.[11]

The category 'religion' is historically, then, a societal category. It is only, like many other sociological concepts and categories, by derivation a sociological category or concept.[12] Bearing this in mind we must ask: What adequate case can be made for extending or violating its usage? To modify it along the lines suggested by some functional sociologists is both to miss the really interesting and demanding *sociological* problems *and at the same time to go beyond the role of the sociologist into the role of the theologian or religious intellectual.*

That we have argued here for a conformity to the ordinary cultural connotations of 'religion' does *not* mean that we can be content with using the term loosely as in everyday discourse. There has to be some degree of 'tightening' and analytic shaping. The definitions proposed here rest upon the substantive, cultural content of religious phenomena. In these terms we define, first, *religious culture. Religious culture is that set of beliefs and symbols (and values deriving directly therefrom) pertaining to a distinction between an empirical and a super-empirical, transcendent reality; the affairs of the empirical being subordinated in significance to the non-empirical.* Second, we define *religious action* simply as: *action shaped by an acknowledgment of the empirical/super-*

11. The attention of the uninitiated reader should be drawn to the fact that the discussion is proceeding at two levels: not only at the sociological interpretation of religion, but also at the way in which sociologists have interpreted it. In spite of much recent philosophical debate of these problems sociologists and anthropologists have paid far too little attention to them.

12. This is in line with Schutz's distinction between first-order, commonsense concepts and second-order, scientific concepts (1954).

empirical distinction. These definitions constitute merely an analytic base-line.

References

BELLAH, R. (1966), 'Words for Paul Tillich', *Harvard Divinity Bull.*, vol. 30, pp. 15–16.

BELLAH, R. (1964), 'Religious evolution', *Amer. Social. Rev.*, vol. 29, pp. 358–9.

BELLAH, R. (1965), *Religion and Progress in Modern Asia*, Free Press.

BERGER, P. (1969), *The Social Reality of Religion*, Faber.

BERGER, P. (1967), 'Religious institutions', in N. J. Smelser (ed.), *Sociology: An Introduction*, Wiley.

BUDD, S. (1968), 'The humanist societies: the consequences of a diffuse belief system', in B. R. Wilson (ed.), *Patterns of Sectarianism*, Heinemann.

DURKHEIM, E. (1961), *The Elementary Forms of the Religious Life*, Allen & Unwin.

GEERTZ, C. (1966), 'Religion as a cultural system', in M. Banton (ed.), *Anthropological Approaches to the Study of Religion*, Tavistock.

GOLDSCHMIDT, W. (1966), *Comparative Functionalism*, Cambridge University Press.

GOODY, J. (1961), 'Religion and ritual: the definitional problem', *Brit. J. Sociol.*, vol. 12, pp. 142–64.

HORTON, R. (1960), 'A definition of religion and its uses', *J. Royal Anthropol. Inst.*, *vol.* 90, pp. 201–26.

LEACH, E. R. (1968), *Dialectic in Practical Religion*, Cambridge University Press.

LUCKMANN, T. (1967), *The Invisible Religion*, Macmillan.

LUCKMANN, T., and BERGER, P. (1964), 'Social mobility and personal identity', *Europ. J. Sociol.*, vol. 5, pp. 331–44.

MACRAE, D. G. (1954), 'The Bolshevik ideology', *Cambridge J.*, vol. 3, pp. 164–77.

NETTL, J. P. and ROBERTSON, R. (1968), *International Systems and the Modernization of Societies*, Faber.

O'DEA, T. F. (1963), 'Sociological dilemmas: five paradoxes of institutionalization', in E. A. Tiryakian (ed.) *Sociological Theory, Values and Sociocultural Change*, Free Press.

OTTO, R. (1929), *The Idea of the Holy*, Oxford University Press.

PARSONS, T. (1949), *The Structure of Social Action*, Allen & Unwin.

PARSONS, T. (1951), *The Social System*, Free Press.

PARSONS, T. (1954), 'The theoretical development of the sociology of religion', in *Essays in Sociological Theory*, Free Press.

PARSONS, T. (1963), 'Christianity and modern industrial society', in E. A. Tiryakian (ed.), *Sociological Theory, Values and Sociocultural Change*, Free Press.

PARSONS, T. (1965), *Theories of Society*, Free Press.

PARSONS, T. (1966), 'Religion in a modern pluralistic society', *Rev. Religious Res.*, vol. 7, pp. 125–46.

ROBERTSON, R. (1970), *The Sociological Interpretation of Religion*, Blackwell.

SCHUTZ, A. (1954), 'Concept and theory formation in the social sciences', *J. Phil.*, vol. 51, pp. 272–3.

SPIRO, M. E. (1966), in M. Barton (ed.), *Anthropological Approaches to the Study of Religion*, Tavistock.

TILLICH, P. (1957), *The Protestant Era*, University of Chicago Press.

TROELTSCH, E. (1912), *Protestantism and Progress*, Putman.

TROELTSCH, E. (1931), *The Social Teaching of the Christian Churches*, Allen & Unwin.

WEBER, M. (1961), *General Economic History*, Collier-Macmillan.

WEBER, M. (1963), *The Sociology of Religion*, Beacon.

YINGER, J. M. (1967), 'Pluralism, religion and secularism', *J. Sci. Stud. Relig.*, vol. 6, no. 1, pp. 17–28.

26 Ernst Troeltsch

Sect-Type and Church-Type

Excerpts from Ernst Troeltsch, *The Social Teaching of the Christian Churches*, 2 vols., Allen & Unwin, 1931, vol. 1, pp. 331–3, 338–41.

At the outset the actual differences are quite clear. The Church is that type of organization which is overwhelmingly conservative, which to a certain extent accepts the secular order, and dominates the masses; in principle, therefore, it is universal, i.e. it desires to cover the whole life of humanity. The sects, on the other hand, are comparatively small groups; they aspire after personal inward perfection, and they aim at a direct personal fellowship between the members of each group. From the very beginning, therefore, they are forced to organize themselves in small groups, and to renounce the idea of dominating the world. Their attitude towards the world, the state and society may be indifferent, tolerant or hostile, since they have no desire to control and incorporate these forms of social life; on the contrary, they tend to avoid them; their aim is usually either to tolerate their presence alongside of their own body, or even to replace these social institutions by their own society.

Further, both types are in close connection with the actual situation and with the development of Society. The fully developed Church, however, utilizes the State and the ruling classes, and weaves these elements into her own life; she then becomes an integral part of the existing social order; from this standpoint, then, the Church both stabilizes and determines the social order; in so doing, however, she becomes dependent upon the upper classes, and upon their development. The sects, on the other hand, are connected with the lower classes, or at least with those elements in Society which are opposed to the State and to Society; they work upwards from below, and not downwards from above.

Finally, too, both types vary a good deal in their attitude towards the supernatural and transcendent element in Christianity, and also in their view of its system of asceticism. The Church relates the whole of the secular order as a means and a preparation to the supernatural aim of life, and it incorporates genuine asceticism into its structure as one element in this preparation, all under the very definite direction of the

Church. The sects refer their members directly to the supernatural aim of life, and in them the individualistic, directly religious character of asceticism, as a means of union with God, is developed more strongly and fully; the attitude of opposition to the world and its powers, to which the secularized Church now also belongs, tends to develop a theoretical and general asceticism. It must, however, be admitted that asceticism in the Church, and in ecclesiastical monasticism, has a different meaning from that of the renunciation of or hostility to the world which characterizes the asceticism of the sects.

The asceticism of the Church is a method of acquiring virtue, and a special high watermark of religious achievement, connected chiefly with the repression of the senses, or expressing itself in special achievements of a peculiar character; otherwise, however, it presupposes the life of the world as the general background, and the contrast of an average morality which is on relatively good terms with the world. Along these lines, therefore, ecclesiastical asceticism is connected with the asceticism of the redemption cults of late antiquity, and with the detachment required for the contemplative life; in any case, it is connected with a moral dualism.

The asceticism of the sects, on the other hand, is merely the simple principle of detachment from the world, and is expressed in the refusal to use the law, to swear in a court of justice, to own property, to exercise dominion over others, or to take part in war. The sects take the Sermon on the Mount as their ideal; they lay stress on the simple but radical opposition of the Kingdom of God to all secular interests and institutions. They practise renunciation only as a means of charity, as the basis of a thoroughgoing communism of love, and, since their rules are equally binding upon all, they do not encourage extravagant and heroic deeds, nor the vicarious heroism of some to make up for the worldliness and average morality of others. The ascetic ideal of the sects consists simply in opposition to the world and to its social institutions, but it is not opposition to the sense-life, nor to the average life of humanity. It is therefore only related with the asceticism of monasticism in so far as the latter also creates special conditions, within which it is possible to lead a life according to the Sermon on the Mount, and in harmony with the ideal of the communism of love. In the main, however, the ascetic ideal of the sects is fundamentally different from that of monasticism, in so far as the latter implies emphasis upon the mortification of the senses, and upon works of supererogation in poverty and obedience for their own sake. In all things the ideal of the sects is essentially not one which aims at the destruction of the sense-life and of natural self-feeling, but a union in love which is not affected by the social inequalities and struggles of the world. [. . .]

The essence of the Church is its objective institutional character. The individual is born into it, and through infant baptism he comes under its miraculous influence. The priesthood and the hierarchy, which hold the keys to the tradition of the Church, to sacramental grace and ecclesiastical jurisdiction, represent the objective treasury of grace, even when the individual priest may happen to be unworthy; this Divine treasure only needs to be set always upon the lampstand and made effective through the sacraments, and it will inevitably do its work by virtue of the miraculous power which the Church contains. The Church means the eternal existence of the God-Man; it is the extension of the Incarnation, the objective organization of miraculous power, from which, by means of the Divine Providential government of the world, subjective results will appear quite naturally. From this point of view compromise with the world, and the connection with the preparatory stages and dispositions which it contained, was possible, for in spite of all individual inadequacy the institution remains holy and Divine, and it contains the promise of its capacity to overcome the world by means of the miraculous power which dwells within it. Universalism, however, also only becomes possible on the basis of this compromise; it means an actual domination of the institution as such, and a believing confidence in its invincible power of inward influence. Personal effort and service, however fully they may be emphasized, even when they go to the limits of extreme legalism, are still only secondary; the main thing is the objective possession of grace and its universally recognized dominion; to everything else these words apply: *et cetera adjicientur vobis*. The one vitally important thing is that every individual should come within the range of the influence of these saving energies of grace; hence the Church is forced to dominate Society, compelling all the members of Society to come under its sphere and influence; but, on the other hand, her stability is entirely unaffected by the fact of the extent to which her influence over all individuals is actually attained. The Church is the great educator of the nations, and like all educators she knows how to allow for various degrees of capacity and maturity, and how to attain her end only by a process of adaptation and compromise.

Compared with this institutional principle of an objective organism, however, the sect is a voluntary community whose members join it of their own free will. The very life of the sect, therefore, depends on actual personal service and cooperation; as an independent member each individual has his part within the fellowship; the bond of union has not been indirectly imparted through the common possession of Divine grace, but it is directly realized in the personal relationships of life. An individual is not born into a sect; he enters it on the basis of conscious conversion; infant baptism, which, indeed, was only introduced at a later date, is almost always a stumbling-block. In the sect spiritual progress does not depend upon the objective impartation of Grace through the Sacrament, but upon individual personal effort; sooner or later, therefore, the sect always criticizes the sacramental idea. This does not mean that the spirit of fellowship is weakened by individualism; indeed, it is strengthened, since each individual proves that he is entitled to membership by the very fact of his services to the fellowship. It is, however, naturally a somewhat limited form of fellowship, and the expenditure of so much effort in the maintenance and exercise of this particular kind of fellowship produces a certain indifference towards other forms of fellowship which are based upon secular interests; on the other hand, all secular interests are drawn into the narrow framework of the sect and tested by its standards, in so far as the sect is able to assimilate these interests at all. Whatever cannot be related to the group of interests controlled by the sect, and by the Scriptural ideal, is rejected and avoided. The sect, therefore, does not educate nations in the mass, but it gathers a select group of the elect, and places it in sharp opposition to the world. In so far as the sect-type maintains Christian universalism at all, like the Gospel, the only form it knows is that of eschatology; this is the reason why it always finally revives the eschatology of the Bible. That also naturally explains the greater tendency of the sect towards 'ascetic' life and thought, even though the original ideal of the New Testament had not pointed in that direction. The final activity of the group and of the individual consists precisely in the practical austerity of a purely religious attitude towards life which is not affected by cultural influences. That is, however, a different kind of asceticism, and this is the reason for that difference between it and the asceticism of the Church-type which has already been stated. It is not the heroic special achievement of a special class, restricted by its very nature to particular instances, nor the mortification of the senses in order to further the higher religious life; it is simply detachment from the world, the reduction of worldly pleasure to a minimum, and the highest possible development of fellowship in love; all this is interpreted in the old Scriptural sense. Since the sect-type is rooted in the teaching of Jesus, its asceticism also is that of primitive Christianity and of the Sermon on the Mount, not that of the Church and of the contemplative life; it is narrower and more scrupulous than that of Jesus, but, literally understood, it is still the continuation of the attitude of Jesus towards the world. The concentration on personal effort, and the sociological connection with a practical ideal, makes an extremely exacting claim on individual effort, and avoidance of all other forms of human association. The asceticism of the sect is not an attempt to popularize and universalize an ideal which the Church had prescribed only for special classes and in special circumstances. The Church ideal of asceticism can never be conceived as a universal ethic; it is essentially unique and heroic. The ascetic ideal of the sect, on the contrary, is, as a matter of course, an ideal which is possible to all, and appointed for all, which, according to its conception, united the fellowship instead of dividing it, and according to its content is also capable of a general realization in so far as the circle of the elect is concerned.

Thus, in reality we are faced with two different sociological types. This is true in spite of the fact (which is quite immaterial) that incidentally in actual practice they may often impinge upon one another. If objections are raised to the terms 'Church' and 'Sect', and if all sociological groups which are based on and inspired by monotheistic, universalized, religious motives are described (in terminology which is in itself quite appropriate) as 'Churches', we would then have to make the distinction between institutional churches and voluntary churches. It does not really matter which expression is used. The all-important point is this: that both types are a logical result of the Gospel, and only conjointly do they exhaust the whole range of its sociological influence, and thus also indirectly of its social results, which are always connected with the religious organization.

27 J. Milton Yinger

Types of Religious Organizations

Excerpt from J. Milton Yinger, *Religion, Society and the Individual*,
Macmillan Co., 1957, pp. 147–55.

Refinements of the typology

Although the church-sect dichotomy can be a highly informative concept, it is not adequate to describe the full range of the data. On the basis of two criteria – the degree of inclusiveness of the members of a society and the degree of attention to the function of social integration as contrasted with the function of personal need – a six-step classification can be described that may prove to be helpful.

The universal church

This is a religious structure that is relatively successful in supporting the integration of a society, while at the same time satisfying, by its pattern of beliefs and observances, many of the personality needs of individuals on all levels of the society. It combines both church and sect tendencies in a systematic and effective way. It is thus universal both in the sense that it includes all the members of a society and in the fact that the two major functions of religion are closely interrelated. In heterogeneous societies, this balance is likely to be achieved only very rarely and is not likely to be maintained very long: the lack of flexibility of the system itself, the insistent demands of the ruling groups that the order favorable to them be maintained without the adjustments that are inevitable in a changing society, the variations in personality needs – these all lead to the tendency toward schism' so common in the religions of complex societies. The Catholic Church of the thirteenth century is perhaps the best illustration of a universal church in Western civilization. It was relatively successful in finding a place (primarily the monastries) for the individualizing tendencies in Christianity, its system of beliefs and rites was satisfactory to large numbers of people on all levels, and it reflected and helped to maintain a fairly well-integrated social structure. Even the most thoroughly universal church, however, can be described only as relatively capable of fulfilling these various functions, for the intense problem of order, the continuing intrusions of man's selfish tendencies, the pervasiveness of the problems of suffering are not difficulties easily to be solved.

One needs to be aware, moreover, of the continuing possibility of dysfunctions. In this regard it is perhaps well to indicate again that a judgement concerning the church's ability to maintain itself as a 'moving equilibrium' and to hold the allegiance of most of the members of a society is not at the same time a value judgement – a distinction that is difficult to maintain in functional analysis.

The ecclesia

We have borrowed here a term from Howard Becker's adaptation of the systematic work of Wiese. Like the universal church, the ecclesia reaches out to the boundaries of the society; formal identification with the group is found on all levels of society. But the ecclesia is less successful than the universal church in incorporating the sect tendencies. It has become so well adjusted to the dominant elements that the needs of many of its adherents, particularly from the lower classes, are frustrated. It is more successful in reinforcing the existing pattern of social integration than in fulfilling the many personality functions of religion. There tend, therefore, to be widespread indifference, sectarian protests, and secular opposition. The ecclesia, as we are using the term, might be called a universal church in a state of rigidification. Established national churches tend toward the ecclesiastical type, although they vary widely in the degree to which they incorporate sectarian elements. (Compare the contemporary state churches in the Scandinavian countries, which are in the direction of the universal type, with the Russian Orthodox Church of 1915, which, when confronted with both religious and secular 'schism' only embraced the established order the more closely. This suggests again the close relationship between type of religion and type of society.) Becker describes the ecclesia in these terms:

The social structure known as the ecclesia is a predominantly conservative body, not in open conflict with the secular aspects of social life, and professedly universal in its aims. . . . The fully developed ecclesia attempts to amalgamate with the state and the dominant classes, and strives to exercise control over every person in the population. Members are *born into* the ecclesia, they do not have to *join* it. It is therefore a social structure somewhat akin to the nation or the state, and is in no sense elective. . . . The ecclesia naturally attaches a high importance to the means of grace which it administers, to the system of doctrine which it has formulated, and to the official administration of sacraments and teaching by official clergy. . . . The ecclesia as an inclusive social structure is closely allied with national and economic interests; as a plurality pattern its very nature commits it to adjustment of its ethics to the ethics of the secular world; it must represent the morality of the respectable majority (Von Wiese and Becker, 1932, pp. 624–5; Pfautz, 1955).

The class church or denomination

This religious-group type is still less successful in achieving universality than the ecclesia, because it not only minimizes the sectarian tendency to criticize or withdraw from the social order, but it is also limited by class, racial and sometimes regional boundaries. It may still be called a church, because it is in substantial – not perfect – harmony with the secular power structure. Few churches are of a 'pure' type – there are sectarian elements in all of them and all class levels tend to be represented in their membership (although unequally, and to a lesser degree in positions of leadership). This is partly due to the fact that many denominations started out as sects and have not completely escaped their origins. One must also note the range within this type, in American society, for example, from Congregationalism, with fairly persistent sectarian tendencies, to Lutheranism, which is more thoroughly accommodated to the secular powers. In general, however, the denomination is conventional and respectable; it has gone rather far along the road of compromise. This is partly due to the fact that in a society of religious divisions, in contrast with the relative unity of the Middle Ages, the sect elements are much more likely to form their own institutions, instead of being incorporated into a universal church. Even during the Middle Ages, of course, sectarian and theological protests signified the pressures toward religious diversity.

The established sect

The next three types ought, perhaps, to be read in reverse order, for the established sect is an outgrowth of the fifth and sixth types. They are written in this order to maintain the continuum relative to the two criteria, the degree of universality and degree of emphasis on social integration as compared with personal needs, that we indicated above. The small, uncompromising religious groups that we have described as sects are, by their very nature, unstable. Either the group disintegrates when the members die, or it has been molded into a more formal structure with techniques for admitting new members and preserving their common interests. Professional leaders emerge, because the intense enthusiasm of the first generation which sustained the lay character of the movement tends to decline. The needs of 'birthright' members are frequently different and their class status may be improved. Direct challenge or opposition to the social order subsides. Nevertheless, the full transition into a class or national church may not take place. Certainly one cannot fully equate Methodism and Quakerism today, although both started out as sectarian protests and both have changed a great deal through the generations. Methodism has evolved into a denomination, as we have defined it, while Quakerism has developed into an established sect. An adequate theory must account for the difference. It does not seem that differences in status improvement can explain the contrast, because both Methodists and Quakers moved up the class ladder. Quakers were much more vigorously opposed and persecuted, developing in them a stronger feeling of isolation and more intense group morale. But this, in part, is only a proximate cause. Why were they more strongly persecuted? This seems to lead back to the nature of the sect in terms of its original protests. Those sects will tend to develop into denominations which, in the first instance, emphasized problems of individual anxiety and sin, those that are primarily efforts to reduce burdens of confusion and guilt. Middle-class sectarian developments usually fall into this group. They develop rather quickly into denominations. On the other hand, sects will tend to develop into established sects whose original concern was predominantly with the evils of society. Such groups make demands for social justice and reform, as did the Anabaptists and Levellers and to a lesser degree the Quakers; or they withdraw from the society by refusing certain obligations or by establishing isolated communities. The contrast between the two types of sects is well described by Niebuhr:

Methodism was far removed in its moral temper from the churches of the disinherited in the sixteenth and seventeenth century. Briefly, the difference lay in the substitution of individual ethics and philanthropism for social ethics and millenarianism. . . . The Methodist movement remained throughout its history in the control of men who had been born and bred in the middle class and who were impressed not so much by the social evils from which the poor suffered as by the vices to which they had succumbed (1954, pp. 65–7).

Niebuhr suggests that leaderships is an important variable in setting the direction of a movement. One must add to that the process of selectivity that takes place in membership of different sects, as a result of varying emphases. Individuals who believe that the reform of the evils of a society are the primary problems will be drawn into the ethical-protest sects. Those who feel most strongly the burden of individual doubt and suffering will be drawn into sects that emphasize individual regeneration. This selectivity will, in turn, condition the development of doctrine.

Actual religious organizations seldom correspond precisely to the types we are defining, but the type pictures should make comparison more accurate. Certainly there are many denominational elements in contemporary Quakerism: its opposition to the state has strongly subsided, professional leadership is common among some branches, most members have been 'born into' the group. Methodism is also a mixed case, as it has been from the beginning, for, despite the middle-class and educated status of its top leaders, it was predominantly a lower-class movement with substantial lay leadership. Sectarian elements remain: pacifism among a small, but significant, minority; and a persistent interest in social reform. Yet the two must still be differentiated in terms of the degree of their accommodation to the secular world.

A sharper contrast can be drawn between a strictly middle-class sect that rapidly became a denomination and a sectarian movement that was even more pessimistic than the Quakers in their view of the world, that, even after three centuries, has not developed into a denomination. We refer to Christian Science on the one hand and the Mennonites, an outgrowth of the Anabaptists, on the other. The difficulties which are expressed in the emergence of a middle-class sect are not primarily economic hardship or a sense of injustice in the secular world. They are more likely to be a feeling of inadequacy, confusion of standards in a highly mobile world, guilt and physical pain. A religious movement that attempts to meet these difficulties has no need to make a sharp challenge to the society and the established churches; the pendulum swing away from them is much shorter and the return much quicker. This kind of sect represents a protest against the lack of attention to these needs in the churches; but since the churches can begin to pay more attention to these needs without raising any serious questions about the structure of society, without any need for a basic reorganization of their views of the world, they can quickly absorb these new emphases from the sect. Thus churches 'steal the thunder' of such sects very easily. This is part of the meaning of the development of 'pastoral psychology', of attention to 'peace of soul', of advice on 'confident living'. This too is christian science if not Christian Science. The sect, in its turn, goes through the familiar process of institutionalization. We may say, then, that a sect will become a denomination instead of an established sect if the protest it represents can readily be absorbed into the dominant religious stream without a serious challenge to the secular social structure and without the necessity for a reorganization of the religious pattern.

The challenge of the Anabaptists was sharp: the society which makes us suffer and the churches which sanctify it are evil. Bear no arms, swear no oaths, accept the religious fellowship only of those who have proved themselves. Such doctrines set a group on a different road from that traveled by the less uncompromising sects. Once set in motion, these influences may resist for many generations the disintegrating effects of improved economic status, mobility, persecution and education.

The Sect

After this lengthy discussion of the established sect as a type and some of the processes by which it emerges, we need say little more about the sect.

It can be described substantially in Troeltsch's terms, given in the basic dichotomy with which we started. We need only make more explicit the sub-divisions of this type that result from the differences in need from which they spring and the differences in response. This can be done in terms of the three possible responses to an undesired situation: One can accept it, one can aggresively oppose it, or one can seek ways to avoid it. All three of these responses are usually found in a sect movement, but one is likely to predominate.

Acceptance. Middle-class sects are likely to accept the social pattern without much challenge. Although the members feel confronted with serious problems which the dominant churches are not helping them to solve, they do not interpret these in social terms. Society, on the whole, has been good to them and those with whom they associate. The key difficulties, they believe, are lack of faith, selfishness and isolation, not an evil society. Therefore, have faith, show the hand of friendship, come together in a congenial group. The Oxford Group Movement illustrates this type of sect.

Aggression. As we have seen, some lower-class sects express most strongly the problems of poverty and powerlessness. In Christianity, they interpret the teachings of Jesus in radical-ethical terms: His was a program of social reform. Society which treats us so badly is evil and true religion, therefore, must reorganize the social order. Such a group runs into strong opposition and, it would seem, pretty certain failure. It is likely, as a result, to disappear or to be transformed into the third type. Again we may cite the Anabaptists as illustrative of this type.

Avoidance. If one cannot accept society with the first type or have hope of reforming it with the second, one can devalue the significance of this life, project one's hopes into the supernatural world, and meanwhile reduce one's problems by forming into a communion of likeminded fellows. This is the most common sectarian protest, particularly in the contemporary world where aggressive protests are more likely to be secular than religious in nature. It faces the hard facts of life for the lower classes, as the first type does not (poverty and suffering and injustice and powerlessness are persistent); it cannot so easily be broken by failure as can the second type, for who can prove, to those who believe, that another life will not redress the ills of this world; it grows easily out of the church which, for all its failure to adjust to new problems as they emerge, has never been able to disregard the problem of evil. The avoidance reaction is similar to what Clark calls the pessimistic or adventist sects. They have reached a final despair of satisfying their needs in society.

They see no good in the world and no hope of improvement, it is rushing speedily to hell, according to the will and plan of God. The adherents of such sects magnify millenarianism and see the imminent end of the present world-order by means of a cosmic catastrophe. They have turned on the world, and they seek escape through a cataclysm which will cast down those who have been elevated, and secure to the faithful important places in a new temporal kingdom as well as eternal bliss in heaven (1949, p. 22).

This type of sect, like the first, is more likely to develop into a deno-mination than into an established sect, for it is less in conflict with society than indifferent to it, so that accommodation to its major patterns is fairly easy. The various 'holiness' groups in the United States represent the 'avoidance' response. We shall explore some of their functions in our discussion of 'class and religion' in the next chapter.

There are, of course, other ways to classify sects (Niebuhr, 1949, vol. 2, pp. 169–80). Clark, whom we have cited above, divides the small sects of America into seven classes, primarily on the basis of cultural differences – variations in beliefs, rituals, taboos, etc. – although some functional elements intrude into his principle of classification. Important questions concerning cultural systems and personality systems arise from his typology. Persons with what kinds of tendencies, in what kinds of cultural contexts will, for example, build their religious adjustment primarily out of the belief in the second-coming of Christ as compared with those who are primarily concerned with trances, visions, 'speaking with tongues', and the 'spirit of prophecy' (the charis-matic or pentecostal sects, in Clark's terminology)? To whom is per-fectionism likely to appeal as the right way to meet the problems of human existence? There has as yet been little study to help us answer questions of this kind, so that 'cultural' classifications have been largely on the descriptive level. For our purposes, the adventist, pentecostal, and to a lesser degree the perfectionist sects can be classified together as 'avoidance' groups, and their varying beliefs and practices can be understood in terms of a common function – to struggle with life's problems by transforming the meaning of life, by substituting 'religious status for social status', in Liston Pope's meaningful phrase.

The cult

The term cult is used in many different ways, usually with the con-notations of small size, search for a mystical experience, lack of an organizational structure and presence of a charismatic leader. Some of these criteria (mysticism, for example) emphasize cultural characteristics that are inappropriate in our classification scheme; yet there seems to be the need for a term that will describe groups that are similar to sects, but represent a sharper break, in religious terms, from the dominant religious tradition of a society. By a cult, therefore, we will mean a group that is at the farthest extreme from the 'universal church' with which we started. It is small, short-lived, often local, frequently built around a dominant leader (as compared with the greater tendency toward widespread lay participation in the sect). Both because its beliefs and rites deviate quite widely from those that are traditional in a society (there is less of a tendency to appeal to 'primitive Christianity', for example) and because the problems of succession following the death of a charismatic leader are often difficult, the cult tends to be small, to break up easily, and is relatively unlikely to develop into an established sect or a denomination. The cult is concerned almost wholly with problems of the individual, with little regard for questions of social order; the implications for anarchy are even stronger than in the case of the sect, which is led by its interest in 'right behavior' (whether the avoidance of individual sin or the establishment of social justice) back to the problem of social integration. The cults are religious 'mutants', extreme variations on the dominant themes by means of which men try to solve their problems. Pure type cults are not common in Western society; most groups that might be called cults are fairly close to the sect type. Perhaps the best examples are the various Spiritualist groups and some of the 'Moslem' groups among American Negroes.

References

CLARK, E. T. (1949), *The Small Sects in America*, Peter Smith.
NIEBUHR, R. (1949), *The Nature and Destiny of Man*, Scribner.
NIEBUHR, H. R. (1954), *The Social Sources of Denominationalism*, Shoestring Press.
PFAUTZ, H. W. (1955), 'The sociology of secularization: religious groups', *Amer. J. Sociol.*, vol. 61, pp. 121–8.
VON WIESE, L., and BECKER, H. (1932), *Systematic Sociology*, Wiley.

28 Charles Y. Glock and R. Stark

On the Origins and Evolution of Religious Groups

Excerpt from Charles Y. Glock and R. Stark, *Religion and Society in Tension,*
Rand McNally, 1965, pp. 242–59.

During the nineteenth century the impact of Darwinian biology on social thought led to a scholarly preoccupation with the origins and evolution of social institutions. Consequently, an enormous amount of work in the sociology of religion sought to establish how it was that religious ideas and traditions sprang up in human societies. But, as social Darwinism passed out of vogue, it was recognized that the question of how men first came to be religious is shrouded in the unknowable past, and is badly put in any event (Davis, 1949, ch. 19). Nevertheless it has remained relevant and seemingly fruitful to ask about a process of religious innovation and development that is still with us: What accounts for the rise and evolution of new religious groups in society?

This question remains generally unanswered although it has received more attention than any other problem in the sociology of religion. In this chapter we shall review the current state of social-science knowledge on the origins of new religious groups, particularly those theories which attribute these innovations to class conflicts. Then we shall propose the outlines for a more general theory which seems to overcome the limitations of existing theories, and suggest how this broader conception can also help account for the directions in which religious groups evolve.

Current thinking about the origin and development of religious groups in Western society has been largely informed by so-called 'sect-church' theory. The distinction between church and sect, as formulated in the work of Max Weber (1948) and his contemporary, Ernst Troeltsch (1949, vol. 1, pp. 331–43), was initially an attempt to distinguish types of religious groups and not an effort to discover the conditions under which religious groups originate. Sects were characterized, for example, as being in tension with the world, as having a converted rather than an inherited membership, and as being highly emotional in character. Churches, in contrast, were seen as compromising with the world, as having a predominantly inherited membership, and as restrained and ritualistic in their services.

The sect-church distinction was later refined by H. Richard Niebuhr who postulated a dynamic interrelationship between the two types and saw in this interrelationship a way to help account for the development of new religious groups (1929). Briefly, the compromising tendencies of the church lead some of its members to feel that the church is no longer faithful to its religious traditions. These dissenting members then break away to form new religious groups. At the outset, these new groups take on a highly sect-like character, eschewing the dominant characteristics of the church they have rejected. They assume an uncompromising posture toward the world, they gainsay a professional clergy, they insist on a conversion experience as a condition for membership, and they adopt a strict and literalistic theology.

Over time, however, the conditions which gave rise to the sect change, and a process begins which leads the sect slowly to take on the church-like qualities which it had originally denied. Once it has made the transition from sect to church, the religious group then becomes the breeding ground for new sects which proceed anew through the same process.

New sects, according to sect-church theory, recruit their membership primarily from the economically deprived, or as Niebuhr calls them, 'the disinherited' classes of society. Their emergence, therefore, is to be understood as a result not only of religious dissent but of social unrest as well. The theological dissent masks an underlying social protest. However, the new sect functions to contain the incipient social protest, and later, to help eliminate the conditions which produced it.

The containment is accomplished through a process of derailment. The sects provide a channel through which their members come to transcend their feelings of deprivation by replacing them with feelings of religious privilege. Sect members no longer compare themselves to others in terms of their relatively lower economic position, but in terms of their superior religious status.

Built into the sect ideology, however, is a puritanical ethic which stresses self-discipline. Thrift, frugality, industry are highly valued. Over time, their ideology helps to elevate sect members to middle-class statuses which in turn socialize them to middle-class values. Because the economic deprivation itself has been eliminated, feelings of economic deprivation no longer need to be assuaged. As the sect members become accommodated to the larger society, their religious movement proceeds to accommodate itself too. In so doing, it makes the transition from sect to church.

This is an admittedly brief and simplified account of sect-church theory and omits the many refinements that have been made in it over the last decades (Yinger, 1946; Wilson, 1959; Von Wiese and Becker, 1932). However, for our purposes, it conveys the essential points of traditional theory, namely, that new religious movements begin by being sect-like in character, that they arise by breaking off from church-type bodies, that they are rooted in economic deprivation, and that they gradually transform themselves into churches.

This theory is valid for many cases. Nevertheless, in a number of ways it falls short of being a general theory of the origin and evolution of religious groups. Overlooked is the fact that not all religious groups emerge as sects. Some are churches in their original form. This was true of Reform Judaism in Europe and of Conservative Judaism in America. Most Protestant groups were from their beginnings more like churches than like sects.

Not only may new religious groups emerge in other than sect form, they need not, contrary to the theory, draw their membership primarily from the lower class. The American Ethical Union was clearly a middle-class movement from its inception, as were Unity and, probably, Christian Science.

The theory also does not take account of cults. These are religious movements which draw their inspiration from other than the primary religion of the culture, and which are not schismatic movements in the same sense as sects, whose concern is with preserving a purer form of the traditional faith. Thus, while the theory may be adequate to explain the Pentecostal movement or the evolution of such religious groups as the Disciples of Christ (The Christian Church) and the Church of God in Jesus Christ, it does not provide a way to account for Theosophy, or the I AM movement, or the Black Muslims. Nor does the theory account for religious movements which show no signs of evolving toward the church form. Finally, the theory ignores the question of the conditions which produce a secular rather than a religious response to economic deprivation.

As may be clear, our quarrel with sect-church theory is not over what it does, but what it fails to do – too many innovating religious movements fall beyond the present scope of the theory. Consequently, in attempting to formulate the elements of a more satisfactory theory of religious origins we shall not discard sect-church theory so much as try to generalize and extend it. We shall continue to regard deprivation as a necessary condition for the rise of new religious movements. However, the concept of deprivation seems due for a general extension and restatement (Merton, 1957).

Sect-church theory conceives of deprivation almost entirely in economic terms. To be sure, in every society there are individuals and groups which are economically underprivileged relative to others, and some are always at the very bottom of the economic hierarchy. However, there are forms of deprivation other than economic ones, and these too, we suggest, have implications for the development of religious and, as we shall see, secular movements as well.

Deprivation, as we conceive it, refers to *any and all of the ways that an individual or group may be, or feel disadvantaged in comparison either to other individuals or groups or to an internalized set of standards.* The experience of deprivation may be conscious, in which case the individual or group may be aware of its causes. It may also be experienced as something other than deprivation, in which case its causes will be unknown to the individual or the group. But, whether directly or indirectly experienced, whether its causes are known or unknown, deprivation tends to be accompanied by a desire to overcome it.[1] Efforts to deal with deprivation will differ, however, according to the degree to which its nature is correctly perceived and individuals and groups are in a position to eliminate its cause.

Types of deprivation

There are five kinds of deprivation to which individuals or groups may be subject relative to others in society. We shall call these five: economic, social, organismic, ethical and psychic. The types are not pure; any one individual or group may experience more than one kind of deprivation. However, we can distinguish among them not only analytically, but empirically, since one type of deprivation is likely to be dominant for particular individuals and groups in particular situations.

Economic deprivation has its source in the differential distribution of income in societies and in the limited access of some individuals to the necessities and luxuries of life. Economic deprivation may be judged on objective or on subjective criteria. The person who appears economically privileged on objective criteria might nevertheless perceive himself as economically deprived. For our purposes the subjective assessment is likely to be the more important.

Social deprivation, our second type, is based on society's propensity to value some attributes of individuals and groups more highly than others and to distribute such social rewards as prestige, power, status and

1. This is not the case, however, where the value system of the society warrants deprivation, for example, the Hindu Caste System.

opportunities for social participation accordingly. Social deprivation, then, arises out of the differential distribution of highly regarded attributes. The grounds for such differentiation are virtually endless. In our society, for example, we regard youth more highly than old age, greater rewards tend to go to men rather than to women, and the 'gifted' person is given privileges denied the mediocre.

Social deprivation is additive in the sense that the fewer the number of desirable attributes the individual possesses, the lower his relative status, and the reverse is also true. In our society, it is in general 'better' to be educated than uneducated. But one's status is further enhanced if one is white rather than Negro, Protestant rather than Catholic, youthful rather than old.

The distinction between economic and social deprivation is akin to the distinction sociologists make between social class and social status. Designations of social class tend to be made on economic criteria. Social status distinctions, on the other hand, give greater attention to considerations of prestige and acceptance. While the two tend to go together, the correlation is not perfect. For our present purposes, we will consider social deprivation to be limited to situations in which it exists independently of economic deprivation.

Organismic deprivation comprises ways in which persons are disadvantaged relative to others through physical or mental deformities, ill health, or other such stigmatizing or disabling traits. Within this class of deprivations would be persons suffering from neuroses and psychoses or who are feeble minded. On the physiological side, it would include the blind, the deaf, the dumb, the crippled, the chronically ill, in short all who suffer physical impairment.

Ethical deprivation refers to value conflicts between the ideals of society and those of individuals or groups. Such conflicts seemingly may stem from many sources. They can occur because some persons perceive incompatibilities in the values of the society, or detect negative latent functions of rules and standards, or even because they are struck by discrepancies between ideals and realities. Often such value conflicts occur because of contradictions in social organization. For example, some persons may find themselves embedded in situations conducive to the development and maintenance of values not held by the greater society, and, indeed, that conflict with general societal values. A classic example of ethical deprivation of this sort is provided in Veblen's analysis of the role strain on engineers who are torn between their own attachment to efficiency and excellence as standards for judging their own products, and the value of maximum profits imposed on them by management (Veblen, 1943).

The celebrated conflicts of the intellectuals to 'sell out' their own criteria of excellence in art, journalism and the like, because their standards are not shared by the public, have been used to explain the propensity of these objectively privileged groups for radical politics (Lipset, 1960, pp. 318–19). Such conceptions fit well with current theories of revolution which specify that there must be a defection from the ranks of the elite in order that direction and leadership be provided for lower class discontent, if revolution is to occur.

Ethical deprivation, then, is basically philosophical. Many great religious innovators, such as Luther and Wesley, as well as political innovators such as Marx, seem to have been motivated primarily by a sense of deprivation stemming from their ethical conflicts with society – an inability to lead their lives according to their own lights.

Psychic deprivation occurs, not in the face of value conflicts, but when persons find themselves without a meaningful system of values by which to interpret and organize their lives. Such a condition is primarily the result of severe and unresolved social deprivations which, by denying access to rewards, cause men to lose any stake in, and commitment to, existing values.

A likely response to psychic deprivation is the search for new values, a new faith, a quest for meaning and purpose. The vulnerability of the deprived to new ideologies reflects their psychic deprivation. In contrast, the ethically deprived have a firm commitment to values, albeit values that conflict with prevailing conditions. Thus, psychic deprivation can be thought of primarily as an intervening variable, state of despair, estrangement, or anomie stemming from objective deprivations (social, economic, or organismic) that leads to actions to relieve these deprivations.[2]

We suggest that a necessary precondition for the rise of any organized social movement, whether it be religious or secular, is a situation of felt deprivation. However, while a necessary condition, deprivation is not, in itself, a sufficient condition. Also required are the additional conditions that the deprivation be shared, that no alternative institutional arrangements for its resolution are perceived, and that a leadership emerge with an innovating idea for building a movement out of the existing deprivation.

Where these conditions exist, the organizational effort to overcome deprivation may be religious, or it may be secular. In the case of economic,

2. Despite the enormous amount of work done on various forms of this concept under a variety of names, it has been primarily treated as an outcome of economic deprivation or as a cause of political extremism, and too few attempts have been made to place it in a context of deprivation plus action.

social and organismic deprivation – the three characterized by deprivation relative to others – religious resolutions are more likely to occur where the nature of the deprivation is inaccurately perceived or those experiencing the deprivation are not in a position to work directly at eliminating the causes. The resolution is likely to be secular under the opposite conditions – where the nature of the deprivation is correctly assessed by those experiencing it and they have, or feel they have, the power, or feel they can gain the power, to deal with it directly. Religious resolutions, then, are likely to compensate for feelings of deprivation rather than to eliminate its causes. Secular resolutions, where they are successful, are more likely to eliminate the causes, and therefore, also the feelings.

These tendencies do not hold for ethical and psychic deprivation. In the case of ethical and psychic deprivation, as we shall see, a religious resolution may be as efficacious as a secular one in overcoming the deprivation directly. In America, resolutions to psychic deprivation usually tend to be religious, defined in the broad sense of invoking some supernatural authority. However, radical political movements may be the outcome of psychic deprivation combined with economic deprivation.

Both religious and secular resolutions, then, may follow from each kind of deprivation. However, whether religious or secular, the resolution will be different in character according to which type stimulates it.

Organizational resolutions of deprivations

Economic deprivation, once it becomes intense, has in it the seed of revolution. And indeed, where the movements which it stimulates are secular, they are likely to be revolutionary. However, to be successful, revolutions require a degree of power which the deprived group is unlikely to be able to muster. Consequently, even when it is intense, economic deprivation seldom leads to revolution.

Religious resolutions to economic deprivation, while not literally revolutionary, are symbolically so. The latent resentment against society tends to be expressed in an ideology which rejects and radically devalues the society. Thus, for those in the movement, the society is symbolically transformed while actually, of course, it is left relatively untouched.

This is characteristically what sects do, and it is this form of religious organization which is likely to arise out of economic deprivation. This is in accord with what we have said earlier in our discussion of sect-church theory, and we need not elaborate further on the way in which sect members compensate for economic disadvantage by substituting religious privilege in its place. We would add, however, that the religious movement which grows out of economic deprivation need not have its theological base in the traditional religion of the society. The Black Muslim movement, for example, borrows heavily from an 'alien' religious doctrine. Yet, in its strong tone of social protest and its doctrine of Negro superiority, it exemplifies the kind of religious movement which grows out of economic deprivation (with, of course, its accompanying social deprivation).

Social deprivation, where it exists without a strong economic component, ordinarily does not require a complete transformation of society, either literally or symbolically, to produce relief. What is at fault is not the basic organization of society, but one or several of its parts. Consequently, efforts at resolution are likely to be directed at the parts, without questioning the whole. As with economic deprivation, however, resolutions are not always possible. Once again, responses to the deprivation are most likely to be secular where its cause can be attacked more or less directly.

Many secular movements with roots in one or another kind of social deprivation have arisen in America over the last century. The woman's suffrage movement, the Townsend movement, the NAACP, and various professional organizations such as those for druggists and beauticians, all represent movements whose purpose has been to eliminate the social deprivation of some particular group by raising its status.

Other semi-secular groups have attempted to compensate for lack of status by supplying an alternative status system. In particular, fraternal clubs and lodges have played such a role, especially for disadvantaged racial and ethnic groups. A man may amount to little all week long, but on Friday nights he can become the Most Venerated, Consecrated and All-Powerful Poobah of the Grand Lodge of Water Buffalo, dress in a gaudy costume, and whisper secret rites.

Social deprivations may be directly connected with religious status and hence generate religious innovations. Such groups as the African Methodist Episcopal Church and the ethnic subdenominations of Lutheranism were organized because the existing religious structure was incapable of meeting the status needs of the groups involved. While overtly a means to overcome religious disadvantages, these organizations also served to overcome sources of social deprivation.

Classic instances are provided by the Jewish Reform movement and the founding of Conservative Judaism. Both movements were launched as an effort to provide Jews with a religious connection with their heritage while allowing them to dispense with those aspects of Orthodoxy, particularly customs of dress and food, which interfered with their attaining status in secular society (Steinberg, 1965).

The organizational form of religious groups which emerge out of social deprivation tends to be church-like rather than sect-like. This is because the basic interest of the socially deprived is to accommodate themselves to the larger society rather than to escape from it or, alternatively, to completely transform it. Consequently, they also tend to adopt those institutional arrangements with which the larger society is most comfortable.

The psychoanalytic movement, group dynamics and Alcoholics Anonymous are examples of a secular response to organismic deprivation where the mental component of this form of deprivation is dominant. In turn, the Society for the Blind, the Society for Crippled Children and the myriad formal and informal social groups constructed around an ailment exemplify secular efforts toward resolution where the physiological element is primary. However successful or unsuccessful are these movements, they all represent attempts to deal with a problem directly. They are revolutionary in that they seek to transform the individual either mentally or physiologically. However, they do not question the value system of the society *per se*.

There have been religious movements – healing cults, for example – which are organized primarily as resolutions to organismic deprivation. More often, however, we find that religious responses to this form of deprivation are not the entire *raison d'être* of a religious movement, but are included as one aspect of it. We may note that a faith healing movement has been organized within the Episcopal Church. Many sects – Father Divine, for example – include a healing element as do cults such as Christian Science and Unity. Thus, religious responses seem not to be identified with any particular organizational form. We suspect, however, that where healing is the exclusive concern of the religious movement, it is more likely to be cult-like in character, such as early Christian Science, than to be a sect or a church.

Responses to ethical deprivations are more typically reformist than revolutionary, and, we suspect, more likely to be religious or secular depending on the prevailing ethos of the time in which they occur. Reformers in medieval times sought to enforce or establish religious values, while since the Enlightenment a great deal of ethical deprivation has been expressed in humanistic terms. In our own time both kinds of response flourish.

Secular movements based on ethical deprivations sometimes lead to revolution, particularly when an ethically deprived elite enlists the support of economically deprived masses. But more often ethical deprivations lead to reform movements aimed at enforcing some neglected value or changing some portion of the prevailing value system without abandoning a commitment to the general outlines of existing social organization. The American Civil Liberties Union illustrates one secular response to ethical deprivation. This group is concerned with enforcing the ideals expressed in the Bill of Rights upon day-to-day realities. Similarly the American Planned Parenthood League derives from ethical deprivation, but is concerned with establishing a general value concerning family planning, and with altering religious prohibitions against birth control. Political reform groups, both of the left and right often are motivated by a sense of ethical deprivation. Indeed, the current right-wing activity in American politics seems to stem to a great extent from the perceptions of small town and rural Americans that their traditional values are no longer predominant in American society.

Religious movements growing out of ethical deprivations can lead to religious revolutions, as in the case of the Lutherans, when the movement is both powerful and powerfully opposed. But it must be recalled that Luther did not intend to found a new faith or lead a revolution, rather he hoped to reform the Church to make it more closely correspond to its avowed ideals. More commonly religious movements based on ethical deprivations do not lead to religious revolutions, but to reform movements. The Prohibition movement in the early part of this century is a classic example, while the participation of white religious leaders in the current civil-rights movement is another.[3] Other examples are the Ethical Culture Union and Unitarianism, both of which seem to have been produced as a solution to the conflict felt by some persons between traditional religious orthodoxy and scientific discovery. Secular counterparts may be seen in the beatnik and existentialist movements.

Ethical deprivations may well be typically limited to members of society's elites, or at least to the middle classes or above. The notion of value conflicts presupposes a certain intellectualism, such as that required in theological or philosophical disputation, which is commonly regarded as an idiosyncracy of the leisured and learned classes.

Whether the movement is secular or religious, responses to psychic deprivation are generally extreme because it constitutes a rejection of the prevailing value orientation of the society. When persons have become psychically deprived in response to economic deprivations they may adopt a new ideology that embodies a revolutionary political program (whether on the left or the right). When they take up a religious solution it will typically be of the cult variety. Recent research among

3. The involvement of Negroes in the civil-rights movement obviously is based on their economic and social deprivation. However, white clergymen do not share the Negroes' deprived lot, but instead are responding to the discrepancies between Christian and social ideals of equality and the actual denial of equality to Negroes.

members of a millenarian religious group showed that all had passed through a period of 'church-hopping', ultimately rejected all available religious perspectives, and passed through a period of religious despair before being converted to the new movement (Lofland, 1966). The entire occult milieu is made up of persons afflicted with psychic deprivations. Movements born in this setting, such as Theosophy, Vedanta, the I AM or the various Flying Saucer groups, are essentially religious innovations that reject dominant American religious traditions, and are classified as cults.

Deprivation need not be immediately present to stimulate an organizational response. The prospect of deprivation may produce a similar effect. The White Citizens' Councils in the South, for example, can be conceived of as organizations growing out of anticipated economic and social deprivation. The John Birch Society is a response to anticipated social deprivation. Protestants and Other Americans United is an example of a religious movement organized around anticipated ethical and social deprivation.

In sum, deprivation – present or anticipated – would appear to be a central factor in the rise of new movements. The organizational response to deprivation may be either religious or secular. In the case of economic, social, and organismic deprivation, religious responses tend to function as compensations for the deprivation, secular ones as means to overcome it. The type of deprivation around which a movement arises is influential in shaping its character in all cases except those of organismic and ethical deprivation. Generally speaking, religious movements emerge as sects where they are stimulated by economic deprivation, as churches where the deprivation is social, and as cults where it is psychic.

Deprivation and organizational evolution

Deprivation is important not only to the rise of new movements but to the path of their development and their potential for survival. Movements may evolve in a myriad of ways, and we have no intention of trying to cope with all of their variety. We would suggest, however, that movements tend to follow one of three basic patterns. They may flower briefly and then die. They may survive indefinitely in substantially their original form. Or, they may survive but in a form radically different from their original one. How movements develop, and whether or not they survive, is influenced by the type of deprivation which stimulated them, how they deal with this deprivation, and the degree to which the deprivation persists in the society and, therefore, provides a continuing source of new recruits.

Movements arising out of economic deprivation tend to follow a pattern of either disappearing relatively quickly or of having to change their organizational form to survive. They seldom survive indefinitely in their original form. This is because the deprivation they respond to may itself be short-lived or because they themselves help to overcome the deprivation of their adherents.

Few sects survive as sects. They either disappear or evolve from a sect into a church. Where they follow the former course, it is likely that their source of recruitment suddenly withers because of conditions over which they have no control. Thus, depression-born sects tend to have a low survival rate, lasting only as long as the depression itself. Sects also have the tendency, noted earlier, to socialize their members to higher economic status. In the process, their organizational form is transformed to conform to the changing status of their membership.

Secular responses to economic deprivation follow a similar pattern. Depression-born movements – technocracy, for example – tend to flower briefly and then die. More fundamental movements, such as revolutions, tend, where they are successful, to lose their revolutionary character and to survive as movements functioning to maintain the advantages which have been gained.

Organizational responses to social deprivation may also follow a pattern of disappearing quickly, but where they survive, they are likely to do so without radical alteration of their original form. Which of these paths is followed is largely dependent on the persistence of the deprivation which gave rise to the movement. Successful elimination of the experienced deprivation – for example, the successful attempt to gain women the right to vote – is likely to produce an early end to the movement.

It is characteristic of many kinds of social deprivation to persist over extended periods of time and to continue from generation to generation. This is because the value systems of societies tend to change slowly, and the differential social rewards and punishments of one era are not likely, in the natural course of events, to be radically altered in the next.

The ability of churches to survive in basically unchanged form is, in substantial part, a consequence of the persistence of social deprivation. Participation in a church, we would suggest, functions to provide individuals with a source of gratification which they cannot find in the society-at-large. Since there are always individuals who are socially deprived in this sense, there exists a continuing source of new recruits to the church. Furthermore, church participation only compensates for the deprivation; it does not eliminate it. Thus, in contrast with the sect, the primary reasons for the existence of the church are not likely to be dissipated over time.

The contention that a major function of church participation is to relieve members' feelings of social deprivation is made here primarily on theoretical grounds. What little empirical evidence there is, however, suggests that churches tend to gain their greatest commitment from individuals who are most deprived of the rewards of the larger society. Thus, it is the less gifted intellectually, the aged, women and those without normal family lives who are most often actively involved in the church.

Organismic deprivation produces movements whose evolution is likely to be influenced by the development of new knowledge about the causes and treatment of mental and physical disorders. Existing movements can expect to thrive only so long as the therapies they provide are subjectively perceived as efficacious and superior to prevailing alternatives. However, the survival of these movements is constantly threatened by innovations in therapy or treatment which eliminate their *raison d'être*. Under such conditions, they may simply disband – like the Sister Kenny Foundation, for example – or they may elect to chart their course along a different path, like the National Foundation.

Religious movements or submovements which are sustained by organismic deprivation may, of course, survive for a very long time, and indeed recruit new members from those who cannot find relief through secular sources. However, in the long run they too are likely to fall victim to innovations in medical knowledge. For, as Malinowski reported of the Trobriand Islanders, people do not resort to magic when they have more effective means of control.

Many movements which arise out of ethical deprivation, we suggest, have a propensity to be short-lived. This is not because ethical deprivation is not a persistent element in society; there are always likely to be individuals who feel that some portion of the dominant value system ought to be changed or reapplied. However, the ethically deprived are likely to generate strong opposition to their efforts to reform or change society and, furthermore, resolutions that seem appropriate at one time are not likely to be so at another. Consequently, ethical deprivation tends to be subject to fads, and while responses to ethical deprivations may capture attention for the movement, they tend to be quickly replaced by new solutions. The various beatnik and bohemian movements are cases in point.

The exceptions – the movements of this kind which survive – do so because they provide solutions which have relevance to long-term trends in society. Such trends function to provide these movements with a continuing source of new recruits. For example, the long-term trend toward secularization in American life is, we suspect, a major factor in the survival and recent acceleration in growth of the Unitarian movement. In general, ethical deprivation characterizes only a small minority of a population at a given time and movements which respond to such deprivation are likely — whether they survive or not — always to be minority movements.

Movements based on psychic deprivations typically follow one of two courses. Either they rise to power and transform societies, and are then themselves transformed, or they die out quickly. Since movements stemming from psychic deprivations taken on value orientations incompatible with those prevalent in a society, they engender strong opposition and must either succeed or be crushed. When they take a religious form they are usually defined as cults and subject to public definitions of 'evil', 'demented', 'dangerous' and 'subversive'. We have elsewhere sketched the degree to which cults are the object of public harassment and even persecution (Glock and Stark, 1966). However, cult movements may also succeed (for example, Christianity was a cult viewed from the standpoint of traditional Roman religions), and by success find themselves faced with problems similar to those of the religion they replaced. That is, once in power a new religion is not in a much better position to resolve the endemic basis for economic, social, organismic and even ethical deprivation than the religious institution that it replaced. Thus, while new religious movements like I AM, Theosophy, Mankind United or Understanding, Inc., may initially provide a new meaning system to their converts, they are not able to overcome the social sources of deprivation which initially produced psychic deprivation, or despair. These are left to produce a new clientele for new movements, or to at least form a festering sore in the integration of any society.

Similarly the extremist secular movements that spring up in response to psychic deprivations are faced with massive opposition. If they succeed in overcoming such opposition, they too face the problem of being transformed by their responsibilities so they may no longer provide a suitable outlet for the psychically deprived.

Conclusions

Our aim in this chapter has been to assess some implications of an extension of the concept of deprivation for the origin and evolution of social movements, particularly religious movements. Our specula-

tions have been informed by the assumption that religion functions
to compensate persons for deprivations for which direct means of
resolution are not available.

We have tried to show that the original form and subsequent development of religious movements may be largely determined by the
variety of deprivation which provided them with an available clientele.
A summary of our suggestions appear in Table 1.

Table 1 Origins, Forms and Development of Religious Groups

Type of deprivation	Form of religious group	Success expectations
Economic	Sect	Extinction or trans-formation
Social	Church	Retain original form
Organismic	Healing movement	Becomes cult-like or is destroyed by medical discoveries
Ethical	Reform movement	Early extinction due to success, opposition or becoming irrelevant
Psychic	Cult	Total success resulting in extinction through transformation, or failure due to extreme opposition

We must, of course, acknowledge the fact that our observations on
the relationship between kinds of deprivations and types of religious
groups are imprecise and very provisional. This is necessarily the case
since these suggested extensions of existing theory have not yet been
subjected to empirical testing. Nevertheless, no matter how greatly
our notions may be altered by future analysis, it seems likely that
some theoretical extension along these lines will be necessary if we are
to achieve any precise understanding of the forces which give birth to
and shape new religious and secular groups.

References

DAVIS, K. (1949), *Human Society*, Macmillan Co.
GLOCK, C. Y., and STARK, R. (1966), *Christian Beliefs and Anti-Semitism*,
Harper & Row.
LIPSET, S. M. (1960), *Political Man*, Doubleday.
LOFLAND, J. (1966), *Doomsday Cult*, Prentice-Hall.
MERTON, R. K. (1957), 'Social structure and anomie', in *Social Theory and Social
Structure*, Free Press.

NIEBUHR, H. R. (1929), *The Social Sources of Denominationalism*, Holt, Rinehart & Winston.

STEINBERG, S. (1965), 'Reform Judaism: the origin and evolution of a church movement', *J. Sci. Stud. Religion*, vol. 5, no. 1, pp. 117–29.

TROELTSCH, E. (1949), *Social Teachings of the Christian Churches*, Macmillan Co.

VEBLEN, T. (1943), *The Instincts of Workmanship and the State of Industrial Arts*, Viking Press.

VON WIESE, L., and BECKER, H. (1932), *Systematic Sociology*, Wiley.

WEBER, M. (1948), 'The social psychology of the world's religions', in H. Gerth and C. W. Mills (eds.), *From Max Weber: Essays in Sociology*, Routledge & Kegan Paul.

WILSON, B. (1959), 'An analysis of sect development', *Amer. Sociol. Rev.*, vol. 24, no. 1, pp. 3–15.

YINGER, J. M. (1946), *Religion in the Struggle for Power*, Duke University Press.

29 Max Weber

(a) The Protestant Ethic

Excerpt from S. M. Miller (ed.), *Max Weber*, Crowell, 1963, pp. 32–41.
Originally published in English in Max Weber, *The Protestant Ethic and the Spirit of Capitalism* (trans. Talcott Parsons), Allen & Unwin, 1930.
First published in German in 1904.

The impulse to acquisition, pursuit of gain, of money, of the greatest possible amount of money, has in itself nothing to do with capitalism. This impulse exists and has existed among waiters, physicians, coachmen, artists, prostitutes, dishonest officials, soldiers, nobles, crusaders, gamblers and beggars. One may say that it has been common to all sorts and conditions of men at all times and in all countries of the earth, wherever the objective possibility of it is or has been given. It should be taught in the kindergarten of cultural history that this naïve idea of capitalism must be given up once and for all. Unlimited greed for gain is not in the least identical with capitalism, and is still less its spirit. Capitalism *may* even be identical with the restraint, or at least a rational tempering, of this irrational impulse. But capitalism is identical with the pursuit of profit, and forever *renewed* profit, by means of continuous, rational, capitalistic enterprise. For it must be so: in a wholly capitalistic order of society, an individual capitalistic enterprise which did not take advantage of its opportunities for profit-making would be doomed to extinction.

Hence in a universal history of culture the central problem for us is not, in the last analysis, even from a purely economic view-point, the development of capitalistic activity as such, differing in different cultures only in form: the adventurer type, or capitalism in trade, war, politics or administration as sources of gain. It is rather the origin of this sober bourgeois capitalism with its rational organization of free labour. Or in terms of cultural history, the problem is that of the origin of the Western bourgeois class and of its peculiarities, a problem which is certainly closely connected with that of the origin of the capitalistic organization of labour, but is not quite the same thing. For the bourgeois as a class existed prior to the development of the peculiar modern form of capitalism, though, it is true, only in the Western hemisphere.

[. . .] it is a question of the specific and peculiar rationalism of Western culture. Now by this term very different things may be understood, as the following discussion will repeatedly show. There is, for example, rationalization of mystical contemplation, that is of an attitude which, viewed from other departments of life, is specifically irrational, just as much as there are rationalizations of economic life, of technique, of scientific research, of military training, of law and administration. Furthermore, each one of these fields may be rationalized in terms of very different ultimate values and ends, and what is rational from one point of view may well be irrational from another. Hence rationalizations of the most varied character have existed in various departments of life and in all areas of culture. To characterize their differences from the viewpoint of cultural history it is necessary to know what departments are rationalized, and in what direction. It is hence our first concern to work out and to explain genetically the special peculiarity of Occidental rationalism, and within this field that of the modern Occidental form. Every such attempt at explanation must, recognizing the fundamental importance of the economic factor, above all take account of the economic conditions. But at the same time the opposite correlation must not be left out of consideration. For though the development of economic rationalism is partly dependent on rational technique and law, it is at the same time determined by the ability and disposition of men to adopt certain types of practical rational conduct. When these types have been obstructed by spiritual obstacles, the development of rational economic conduct has also met serious inner resistance. The magical and religious forces, and the ethical ideas of duty based upon them, have in the past always been among the most important formative influences on conduct. In the studies collected here we shall be concerned with these forces.

The most important opponent with which the spirit of capitalism, in the sense of a definite standard of life claiming ethical sanction, has had to struggle, was that type of attitude and reaction to new situations which we may designate as traditionalism.

[...] we provisionally use the expression spirit of (modern) capitalism to describe that attitude which seeks profit rationally and systematically in the manner which we have illustrated by the example of Benjamin Franklin. This, however, is justified by the historical fact that that attitude of mind has on the one hand found its most suitable expression in capitalistic enterprise, while on the other the enterprise has derived its most suitable motive force from the spirit of capitalism.
The ideal type of the capitalistic entrepreneur [...] has no relation to

[. . .] [social] climbers. He avoids ostentation and unnecessary expenditure, as well as conscious enjoyment of his power, and is embarrassed by the outward signs of the social recognition which he receives. His manner of life is, in other words, often, and we shall have to investigate the historical significance of just this important fact, distinguished by a certain ascetic tendency, as appears clearly enough in the sermon of Franklin which we have quoted. It is, namely, by no means exceptional, but rather the rule, for him to have a sort of modesty which is essentially more honest than the reserve which Franklin so shewdly recommends. He gets nothing out of his wealth for himself, except the irrational sense of having done his job well.

But it is just that which seems to the pre-capitalistic man so incomprehensible and mysterious, so unworthy and contemptible. That anyone should be able to make it the sole purpose of his life-work, to sink into the grave weighed down with a great material load of money and goods, seems to him explicable only as the product of a perverse instinct, the *auri sacra fames*.

Now, how could activity, which was at best ethically tolerated, turn into a calling in the sense of Benjamin Franklin? The fact to be explained historically is that in the most highly capitalistic centre of that time, in Florence of the fourteenth and fifteenth centuries, the money and capital market of all the great political Powers, this attitude was considered ethically unjustifiable, or at best to be tolerated. But in the backwoods small bourgeois circumstances of Pennsylvania in the eighteenth century, where business threatened for simple lack of money to fall back into barter, where there was hardly a sign of large enterprise, where only the earliest beginnings of banking were to be found, the same thing was considered the essence of moral conduct, even commanded in the name of duty. To speak here of a reflection of material conditions in the ideal superstructure would be patent nonsense. What was the background of ideas which could account for the sort of activity apparently directed towards profit alone as a calling toward which the individual feels himself to have an ethical obligation? For it was this idea which gave the way of life of the new entrepreneur its ethical foundation and justification.

The religious believer can make himself sure of his state of grace either in that he feels himself to be the vessel of the Holy Spirit or the tool of the divine will. In the former case his religious life tends to mysticism and emotionalism, in the latter to ascetic action; Luther stood close to the former type, Calvinism belonged definitely to the latter. The Calvinist also wanted to be saved *sola fide*. But since Calvin viewed all pure feelings and emotions, no matter how exalted they might seem to be, with suspicion, faith had to be proved by its objective results in order to provide a firm foundation for the *certitudo salutis*. It must be a *fides efficax*, the call to salvation an effectual calling (expression used in Savoy Declaration).

If we now ask further, by what fruits the Calvinist thought himself able to identify true faith? the answer is: by a type of Christian conduct which served to increase the glory of God. Just what does so serve is to be seen in his own will as revealed either directly through the Bible or indirectly through the purposeful order of the world which he has created (*lex naturae*). Especially by comparing the condition of one's own soul with that of the elect, for instance the patriarchs, according to the Bible, could the state of one's own grace be known. Only one of the elect really has the *fides efficax*, only he is able by virtue of his rebirth (*regeneratio*) and the resulting sanctification (*sanctificatio*) of his whole life, to augment the glory of God by real, and not merely apparent, good works. It was through the consciousness that his conduct, at least in its fundamental character and constant ideal (*propositum oboedientiae*), rested on a power within himself working for the glory of God ; that it is not only willed of God but rather done by God that he attained the highest good towards which this religion strove, the certainty of salvation. That it was attainable was proved by 2 Cor. xiii. 5. Thus, however useless good works might be as a means of attaining salvation, for even the elect remain beings of the flesh, and everything they do falls infinitely short of divine standards, nevertheless, they are indispensable as a sign of election. They are the technical means, not of purchasing salvation, but of getting rid of the fear of damnation. In this sense they are occasionally referred to as *directly* necessary for salvation or the *possessio salutis* is made conditional on them.

In practice this means that God helps those who help themselves. Thus the Calvinist, as it is sometimes put, himself creates his own salvation, or, as would be more correct, the conviction of it. But this creation cannot, as in Catholicism, consist in a gradual accumulation of individual good works to one's credit, but rather in a systematic self-control which at every moment stands before the inexorable alternative, chosen or damned.

The God of Calvinism demanded of His believers not single good works, but a life of good works combined into a unified system. There was no place for the very human Catholic cycle of sin, repentance, atonement, release, followed by renewed sin. Nor was there any balance of merit for a life as a whole which could be adjusted by temporal punishments or the Churches' means of grace.

The moral conduct of the average man was thus deprived of its planless and unsystematic character and subjected to a consistent method for conduct as a whole. It is no accident that the name of Methodists stuck to the participants in the last great revival of Puritan ideas in the eighteenth century just as the term Precisians, which has the same meaning, was applied to their spiritual ancestors in the seventeenth cenutry. For only by a fundamental change in the whole meaning of life at every moment and in every action could the effects of grace transforming a man from the *status naturae* be proved.

[. . .] In the course of its development Calvinism added [. . .] the idea of the necessity of proving one's faith in worldly activity. Therein it gave the broader groups of religiously inclined people a positive incentive to asceticism. By founding its ethic in the doctrine of predestination, it substituted for the spiritual aristocracy of monks outside of and above the world the spiritual aristocracy of the predestined saints of God within the world. It was an aristocracy which, with its *character indelebilis*, was divided from the eternally damned remainder of humanity by a more impassable and in its invisibility more terrifying gulf, than separated the monk of the Middle Ages from the rest of the world about him, a gulf which penetrated all social relations with its sharp brutality. This consciousness of divine grace of the elect and holy was accompanied by an attitude toward the sin of one's neighbour, not of sympathetic understanding based on consciousness of one's own weakness, but of hatred and contempt for him as an enemy of God bearing the signs of eternal damnation. This sort of feeling was capable of such intensity that it sometimes resulted in the formation of sects. This was the case when, as in the Independent movement of the seventeenth century, the genuine Calvinist doctrine that the glory of God required the Church to bring the damned under the law, was outweighed by the conviction that it was an insult to God if an unregenerate soul should be admitted to His house and partake in the sacraments, or even, as a minister, administer them.

As he observed his own conduct, the later Puritan also observed that of God and saw His finger in all the details of life. And, contrary to the strict doctrine of Calvin, he always knew why God took this or that measure. The process of sanctifying life could thus almost take on the character of a business enterprise. A thoroughgoing Christianization of the whole of life was the consequence of this methodical quality of ethical conduct into which Calvinism as distinct from Lutheranism forced men. That this rationality was decisive in its influence on practical life must always be borne in mind in order rightly to understand the influence of Calvinism. On the one hand we can see that it took this element to exercise such an influence at all. But other faiths as well necessarily had a similar influence when their ethical motives were the same in this decisive point, the doctrine of proof.

The fact is that Lutheranism, on account of its doctrine of grace, lacked a psychological sanction of systematic conduct to compel the methodical rationalization of life.

This sanction, which conditions the ascetic character of religion, could doubtless in itself have been furnished by various different religious motives, as we shall soon see. The Calvinistic doctrine of predestination was only one of several possibilities. But nevertheless we have become convinced that in its way it had not only a quite unique consistency, but that its psychological effect was extraordinarily powerful. In comparison with it the non-Calvinistic ascetic movements, considered purely from the viewpoint of the religious motivation of asceticism, form an attenuation of the inner consistency and power of Calvinism.

One of the fundamental elements of the spirit of modern capitalism, and not only of that but of all modern culture: rational conduct on the basis of the idea of the calling, was born – that is what this discussion has sought to demonstrate – from the spirit of Christian asceticism. One has only to re-read [...] [Benjamin] Franklin [...] in order to see that the essential elements of the attitude which was there called the spirit of capitalism are the same as [...] the content of the Puritan worldly asceticism, only without the religious basis, which by Franklin's time had died away.

[...] Protestant Asceticism was in turn influenced in its development and its character by the totality of social conditions, especially economic. The modern man is in general, even with the best will, unable to give religious ideas a significance for culture and national character which they deserve. But it is, of course, not my aim to substitute for a one-sided materialistic an equally one-sided spiritualistic causal interpretation of culture and of history. Each is equally possible, but each, if it does not serve as the preparation, but as the conclusion of an investigation, accomplishes equally little in the interest of historical truth.

(b) Confucianism and Puritanism

Excerpt from Max Weber, *The Religion of China* (trans. Hans Gerth), Free Press, 1951, pp. 247–9. First published in German in 1924.

The typical Confucian used his own and his family's savings in order to acquire a literary education and to have himself trained for the examinations. Thus he gained the basis for a cultured status position. The typical Puritan earned plenty, spent little and reinvested his income as capital in rational capitalist enterprise out of an asceticist compulsion to save. 'Rationalism' – and this is our second lesson – was embodied in the spirit of both ethics. But only the Puritan rational ethic with its supra-mundane orientation brought economic rationalism to its consistent conclusion. This happened merely because nothing was further from the conscious Puritan intention. It happened because inner-worldly work was simply expressive of the striving for a transcendental goal. The world, as promised, fell to Puritanism because the Puritans alone 'had striven for God and his justice'. In this is vested the basic difference between the two kinds of rationalism. Confucian rationalism meant rational adjustment to the world; Puritan rationalism meant rational mastery of the world. Both the Puritan and the Confucian were 'sober men'. But the rational sobriety of the Puritan was founded in a mighty enthusiasm which the Confucian lacked completely; it was the same enthusiasm which inspired the monk of the Occident. The rejection of the world by occidental asceticism was insolubly linked to its opposite, namely, its eagerness to dominate the world. In the name of a supra-mundane God the imperatives of asceticism were issued to the monk and, in variant and softened form, to the world. Nothing conflicted more with the Confucian ideal of gentility than the idea of a 'vocation'. The 'princely' man was an aesthetic value; he was not a tool of a god. But the true Christian, the other-worldly and inner-worldly asceticist, wished to be nothing more than a tool of his God; in this he sought his dignity. Since this is what he wished to be he was a useful instrument for rationally transforming and mastering the world.

The Chinese in all probability would be quite capable, probably more capable than the Japanese, of assimilating capitalism which has technically and economically been fully developed in the modern culture area. It is obviously not a question of deeming the Chinese 'naturally ungifted' for the demands of capitalism. But compared to the Occident, the varied conditions which externally favoured the origin of capitalism in China did not suffice to create it. Likewise capitalism did not originate in occidental or oriental Antiquity, or in India, or where Islamism held sway. Yet in each of these areas different and favourable circumstances seemed to facilitate its rise. Many of the circumstances which could or had to hinder capitalism in China similarly existed in the Occident and assumed definite shape in the period of modern capitalism. Thus, there were the patrimonial traits of occidental rulers, their bureaucracy, and the fact that the money economy was unsettled and undeveloped. The money economy of Ptolemaic Egypt was carried through much more thoroughly than it was in fifteenth- or sixteenth-century Europe. Circumstances which are usually considered to have been obstacles to capitalist development in the Occident had not existed for thousands of years in China. Such circumstances as the fetters of feudalism, landlordism and, in part also, the guild system were lacking there. Besides, a considerable part of the various trade-restricting monopolies which were characteristic of the Occident did not apparently exist in China. Also, in the past, China knew time and again the political conditions arising out of preparation for war and warfare between competing states. In ancient Babylon and in Antiquity, there were conditions conducive to the rise of political capitalism which the modern period also shares with the past. It might be thought that modern capitalism, interested in free-trading opportunity, could have gained ground once the accumulation of wealth and profit from political sources became impossible. This is perhaps comparable to the way in which, in recent times, North America has offered the freest space for the development of high capitalism in the almost complete absence of organization for war.

Political capitalism was common to occidental Antiquity until the time of the Roman emperors, to the Middle Ages and to the Orient. The pacification of the Empire explains, at least indirectly, the non-existence of political capitalism but it does not explain the non-existence of modern capitalism in China. To be sure the basic characteristics of the 'mentality', in this case the practical attitudes toward the world, were deeply co-determined by political and economic destinies. Yet, in view of their autonomous laws, one can hardly fail to ascribe to these attitudes effects strongly counteractive to capitalist development.

(c) Judaism, Christianity and the Socio-Economic Order

Excerpt from Max Weber, *The Sociology of Religion* (trans. E. Fischoff), Methuen, 1965, pp. 251–3. First published in German in 1922.

Let us summarize the respective situations in which Catholics, Jews and Protestants found themselves in regard to economic enterprises. The devout Catholic, as he went about his economic affairs, found himself continually behaving – or on the verge of behaving – in a manner that transgressed papal injunctions. His economic behavior could be ignored in the confessional only on the principle of *rebus sic stantibus*, and it could be permissible only on the basic of a lax, probabilistic morality. To a certain extent, therefore, the life of business itself had to be regarded as reprehensible or, at best, as not positively favourable to God. The inevitable result of this Catholic situation was that pious Jews were encouraged to perform economic activities among Christians which if performed among Jews would have been regarded by the Jewish community as unequivocally contrary to the law or at least as suspect from the point of view of Jewish tradition. At best these transactions were permissible on the basis of a lax interpretation of the Judaic religious code, and then only in economic relations with strangers. Never were they infused with positive ethical value. Thus, the Jew's economic conduct appeared to be permitted by God, in the absence of any formal contradiction with the religious law of the Jews, but ethically indifferent, in view of such conduct's correspondence with the average evils in the society's economy. This is the basic of whatever factual truth there was in the observations concerning the inferior standard of economic legality among Jews. That God crowned such economic activity with success could be a sign to the Jewish businessman that he had done nothing clearly objectionable or prohibited in this area and that indeed he had held fast to God's commandments in other areas. But it would still have been difficult for the Jew to demonstrate his ethical merit by means of characteristically modern business behaviour.

But this was precisely the case with the pious Puritan. He could demonstrate his religious merit through his economic activity because he did nothing ethically reprehensible, he did not resort to any lax interpretations of religious codes or to systems of double moralities, and he did not act in a manner that could be indifferent or even reprehensible in the general realm of ethical validity. On the contrary, the Puritan could demonstrate his religious merit precisely in his economic activity. He acted in business with the best possible conscience, since through his rationalistic and legal behaviour in his business activity he was factually objectifying the rational methodology of his total life pattern. He legitimated his ethical pattern in his own eyes, and indeed within the circle of his community, by the extent to which the absolute – not relativized – unassailability of his economic conduct remained beyond question. No really pious Puritan – and this is the crucial point – could have regarded as pleasing to God any profit derived from usury, exploitation of another's mistake (which was permissible to the Jew), haggling and sharp dealing, or participation in political or colonial exploitation. Quakers and Baptists believed their religious merit to be certified before all mankind by such practices as their fixed prices and their absolutely reliable business relationships with everyone, unconditionally legal and devoid of cupidity. Precisely such practices promoted the irreligious to trade with them rather than with their own kind, and to entrust their money to the trust companies or limited liability enterprises of the religious sectarians rather than those of their own people – all of which made the religious sectarians wealthy, even as their business practices certified them before their God.

30 Ephraim Fischoff

The Protestant Ethic and the Spirit of Capitalism: The History of a Controversy

Ephraim Fischoff, 'The Protestant ethic and the spirit of capitalism: the history of a controversy', *Social Research*, vol. 11, 1944, pp. 61–71.

Weber's original intention in *The Protestant Ethic* must be seen against the background of his time. An heir of the historical school (he regarded himself as one of the epigoni of Schmoller[1]) and of the Marxist tradition, both of which had combated the isolative treatment of the economic process and the *homo economicus* by abstract classical economics, he probed the history of culture to determine the decisive interconnections of economics with the totality of culture. The whole historical work of Weber has ultimately one primary object, the understanding of contemporary European culture, especially modern capitalism.[2] It presses forward to the underlying morale (*Geist*) of capitalism and its pervasive attitudes to life; and beyond this to modern Occidental rationalism as such, which he came to regard as the crucial characteristic of the modern world.

The discussion of problems raised by Marx, who gave the subject of capitalism its large importance in modern social theory, resulted in a great literature on this theme. Certain German scholars had already begun to assimilate Marx's theoretical work into the conceptual framework developed by the German historical school, among them some of the *Kathedersozialisten*, principally Tönnies and Sombart. These bourgeois economists and social theorists were much concerned with the problem of the psychological foundations of capitalism, and suggested certain corrections of the Marxist hypotheses under the general rubric of 'the spirit of capitalism'. Weber paid the highest tribute to Marx's genius and recognized the enormous usefulness of the materialistic method as a

1. See the address delivered by Weber on the anniversary of Schmoller's achievement (Brinkman, 1937, p. 8). See also Weber (1922) where he avows his membership of the historical school, though noting his deviation in the direction of a Kantian view of science.

2. In Weber's essay on assuming the editorship of the *Archiv* in 1904, he set forth the leading principle that social science research must be oriented to the understanding of the modern world, and declared that because of its crucial importance the unbiased investigation of capitalism was an imperative task for the social sciences (1922, pp. 162, 170; Marianne Weber, 1926, p. 290).

heuristic device,[3] but he resisted all efforts to absolutize it into the sole method of social science, much less into a *Weltanschauung*. The true value of this method, as indeed of all intellectual schemata, he regarded as only 'ideal-typical'. As against the Marxian doctrine of the economic determination of social change, Weber propounded a pluralistic interactional theory.

It is necessary to be clear as to the limited character of Weber's goal and the cautious manner of his procedure in this essay. In this first work inquiring into the influence of religious doctrines on economic behavior he had not the slightest intention of producing a complete theory of capitalism, a social theory of religion, or even a complete treatment of the relation between religion and the rise of capitalism. The essay was intended as a tentative effort at understanding one of the basic and distinctive aspects of the modern ethos, its professional, specialized character and its sense of calling or vocation. Already he was impressed by the dominantly rational character of modern life; and he was concerned to demonstrate that there were various types of rationalization, a fact generally overlooked by technological theories of history.

Defining capitalism from his historistic view as a unique system[4] characterized by the general trends of antitraditionalism, dynamism, rationalism and calculated long-range industrial production, he was principally concerned to analyse and trace the genesis of the character-structure adequate to and congruent with it. In his view, modern capitalism was not the automatic product of technological development but of many objective factors, including climate – which influences the conduct of life and labor costs – and many social-political factors, such as the character of the mediaeval inland city and its citizenry. But he insisted that there was one factor which could not be ignored: the emergence of a rational, antitraditional spirit in the human agents involved. The two main aspects of this are the evolution of modern science and its com-

3. Weber indicated an interest in reestablishing the value of the method of historical materialism, but only in the functional sense. Yet he added significantly that to derive capitalism from religious ideas would be quite inadequate (1922, p. 169).

4. It was Weber's contention that in the economic history of the world there was a whole scale of capitalisms, adventurous, piratical, usurious, speculative, financial, etc., and that modern rational industrial capitalism, idiosyncratic of our Occidental culture complex, was distinctively different from these earlier forms. The nub of Weber's argument is that for the emergence of our type of capitalism there was required a combination of factors: the full development of certain economic tendencies, the beginnings of which had been apparent in the culture area but which had been impeded for various historical reasons; and the emergence of a 'capitalistic spirit', a morale or set of attitudes growing out of the various great historical forces which crystallized our distinctive *Lebensform*.

paratively modern relationship to economics, and the growth of the modern organization of individual life (*Lebensführung*), particularly in its practical consequences for economic activity (1910). Weber's limited thesis was merely that in the formation of this pattern of rationally ordered life, with its energetic and unremitting pursuit of a goal and eschewal of all magical escapes, the religious component must be considered as an important factor.[5] How important he was unable to say, and indeed he felt that in historical imputation such quantification is impossible (1910, p. 598). Consequently his view was that no one can tell how the capitalist economic system would have evolved had the specifically modern elements of the capitalistic spirit been lacking (1910, p. 597).

In tracing the affinity between the bourgeois life pattern and certain components of the religious stylization of life, as shown most consistently by ascetic Protestantism, Weber emphasized the gradual genesis of a psychological habit which enabled men to meet the requirements of early modern capitalism. That is, instead of the entrepreneur feeling that his gaining of wealth was at best tolerated by God, or that his *usuraria pravitas* had to be atoned for (as did the native Hindu trader), he went about his business with sturdy confidence that Providence purposely enabled him to prosper for God's glory, that this success was construable as a visible sign of God and, when achieved by legal means, as a measure of his value before God as well as man. On the other hand, the handworker or laborer, with his willingness to work, derived his sense of a religious state of grace from his conscientiousness in his calling. Finally, because of the abomination of the generic sin of idolatry or apotheosis of created things (*Kreaturvergötterung*), as manifested in hoarding possessions, indulgence and frivolous consumption, the money accumulated in the exercise of a calling was turned back into the business enterprise, or saved.

Weber strongly emphasized the importance to bourgeois accumulation of planned this-worldly asceticism (*innerweltliche Askese*), as distinguished from other-worldly asceticism, and of the emotional type of pietism. He insisted that Protestant sects, especially the Quakers and Baptists, engendered a methodical regulation of life, in striking contrast to Catholicism, Lutheranism and Anglicanism. His crucial point was that ascetic Protestantism (1910)[6] created for capitalism the appropriate

5. See Weber (1908) for a clear statement that his intention was only to trace the characterological effects of different types of piety, not to discover any predominant factors in the historical occurrences of any particular epoch or any general or universal dynamic forces in the historical process; for him there were no such 'ghosts' in history.

6. Weber firmly rejected the contention of Fischer that the spirit of the methodical conduct of life had appeared before Puritanism.

spirit, so that the vocational man (*Berufsmenschen*) in his acquisition of wealth no longer suffered from the deep inner lesions characteristic of the more earnest individuals of an earlier day, no matter what their apparent solidity and exemplary power. One example of this inner uncertainty regarding economic activity was the practice of restoring at death goods obtained by usury; another was the establishment of religious institutions to atone for financial success. There were innumerable theoretical and practical compromises between conscience and economic activity, between the ideal of *Deo placere non potest*, accepted even by Luther, and the acquisitive careers entered into by many earnest Catholics. In Weber's view the noteworthy degree of congruence or affinity between the modern capitalistic system and the set of attitudes toward it made for a high inner integration, which was of great importance for the subsequent development of capitalism. It was this integration which was the central concern of his essay.

Weber made it clear that it was his intention to analyse just one component of the generic *Lebensstil* of our rationalized civilization, among the many which stood at the cradle of modern capitalism, and to trace its changes and its ultimate disappearance. He warned against exclusive concentration on the religious factor, as exerted through the inner psychological motivations and the powerful educational force and discipline provided by the Protestant sects. It was, he insisted, only one factor, and he rejected all attempts to identify it with the spirit of capitalism, or to derive capitalism from it. Taking the religious ethic of Protestantism as a constant, and assuming temporarily that it was predominantly a religious product, he proposed to trace the congruence between it and the characterological type requisite for capitalism. It was his intention, however, to return to the problem and investigate the nonreligious components of the religious ethic.

As to the insistence by some of his critics, such as Fischer and Rachfahl, that the problem required a statistical-historical approach, Weber recognized the need of research on the development of particular areas in order to determine the numbers and strength of the various religious groups involved, and the importance of the vocational ethics in comparison with other factors.[7] But he insisted that his was a study in the sociology of cultures, investigating the convergence of religious and eco-

7. His acceptance of empirical research of the quantitative type in the social sciences was, however, rather limited. In his essay on Roscher (1922, p. 37), written before *The Protestant Ethic*, he appears to affirm Roscher's attitude that only limited use should be made of figures by the healthy sense of the empirical investigator who wishes to understand reality, not dissipate it. Indeed, he thought it nonsensical to expect a statistical study of ultimate value attitudes.

nomic factors in the production of modern 'rational' man, and that for his type of study the statistical method was not indicated. His concern was to ascertain the specific direction in which a given religion might operate, the diverse effects of a specific system of religious ethics on the style of life. This problem, he felt, could be approached only by the 'understanding' method of motivational analysis which he employed. In this first essay, therefore, he concentrated on tracing the complex ramifications leading from articles of faith to practical conduct, in an acute and learned examination of the psychological motivations issuing out of Reformed Protestantism and leading to methodical rationalization of activity and the consequent encouragement of capitalist behavior and attitudes.[8] This thesis is carried through all the varieties of Reformed Christianity with a subtle and insightful *dogmengeschichtliche* analysis.

The Protestant essay was not regarded by Weber as a final or dogmatic formulation of a theory of the genesis or evolution of the Reformation, but as a preliminary investigation of the influence of certain religious ideas on the development of an economic spirit or the ethos of an economic system. He was not producing an idealistic (or as he preferred to term it, a spiritual) interpretation of capitalism, deriving it from religious factors. Much nonsense has been written on this point because of his alleged rejection of Marxism. Actually, he was an admirer of the Marxian hypothesis, only objecting that it should not be made absolute and universal, a summary philosophy; but then he rejected all absolutes and all monisms. Hence he rejected at least as forcibly any idealistic monism, and in the essay and its supplements he explicitly disavowed the foolish attribution to him of any spiritualistic hypothesis.

He sought no 'psychological determination of economic events', but rather emphasized the 'fundamental importance of the economic factor'. He recognized clearly that economic changes arise in response to economic needs, and are conditioned by a wide variety of factors, including the demogogic, geographic, technological and monetary (1930, 161, p. 354; 1922b, p. 808). He recognized that capitalism would have arisen without Protestantism, in fact that it had done so in many culture complexes; and that it would not and did not come about where the objective conditions were not ripe for it. He admitted that several other systems of religious ethics had developed approaches to the religious ethic of Reformed Protestantism, but he insisted that the psychological motivations involved were necessarily different; what was decisive was the ethos engendered,

8. The decisive matter for him was the unbroken unity of the vocation with the inner ethical core of the personality. He admitted that there were numerous approaches to practical vocational ethics of this sort in the Middle Ages, but insisted that the spiritual bond was lacking.

not preachments or theological compendia, and this, he argued, was unique in Reformed Protestantism for a variety of reasons. He recognized that there are constant functional interactions between the realms of religion and economics, but in this study he concentrated on the influences emanating from the side of religion. He not only indicated his awareness of the other side, but demonstrated how by an irony of fate the very fulfilment of religious injunctions had induced changes in the economic structure, which in turn engendered the massive irreligion of a capitalist order. He admitted that the religious ethic itself is not determined exclusively by religion, and he clearly urged the necessity of investigating the influence of the social milieu, especially economic conditions, upon the character and development of religious attitudes (1930, p. 183).

Yet he held that the religious revelation of the founder of a sect is an autonomous experience and not a mere reflection of accommodation to economic or other needs. It was his feeling that it is no solution to the problem of the distinctiveness of the Calvinist religious form to say that it is an adjustment to capitalistic practices already in existence; the question then arises as to why Catholicism did not show the same results after making the accommodation. But when a religious revelation has become a social phenomenon and has given rise to a community, a process of social selection sets in and class stratification supervenes in the originally homogeneous religious group, causing the formation of distinctive, socially determined differences within the religion. Weber was going to study this side of the problem, but he never returned to the task. In *The Protestant Ethic* he concentrated on the religious factor alone, considering it as though it were exclusively a religious entity. He was, however, well aware of the tentative nature of his contribution, and he sketched the mammoth and indeed unrealizable program of studies necessary before the project could be regarded as complete.

By no means all the criticisms leveled against Weber were due to bias or failure to heed his cautions regarding the intention of his essay. First, there is the indubitable fact that as the essay stands it has certain elementary defects of structure, particularly because of the incompleteness which exposes it to misunderstandings by a careless reader, although Weber protested that an academic critic should never be guilty of such malfeasance. Writing in the *Archiv* in 1908, Weber explained again the reasons for the non-completion of the essay – partly personal factors, partly the pressure of other work and partly the fact that Troeltsch had begun to treat in the 'most felicitous manner a whole series of problems that lay on Weber's route', which the latter was loath to duplicate; and he expressed the hope that in the coming year he might work on the essay and issue it separately. He admitted that critics had a right to charge that the original essay was incomplete, and he recognized the danger that the hasty reader might overlook this fact, but he insisted that it could scarcely be construed as an idealistic construction of history.

Replying to Fischer's criticism, Weber insisted that in the Protestant essay he had expressed himself with utter clarity on the relationship between religion and economics generally, but he none the less admitted that misunderstanding might possibly have arisen from certain turns of phrase. Accordingly he promised to remove in a future reissue all expressions which seemed to suggest the derivation of institutions from religious motives, and he expressed his intention of clarifying the fact that it was the spirit of a 'methodical' *Lebensführung* which he was deriving from Protestant asceticism, and which is related to economic forms only through congruence (*Adäquanz*). In a later anticritical article, adverting with regret to the incompleteness of the essay, Weber suggests ironically that had he completed it as promised by tracing the influence of economic conditions on the formation of reformed Protestantism, he would probably have been accused of having capitulated to historical materialism, even as he was now charged with an overemphasis on the religious or ideological factor. Hence, he insisted, his essay should properly be regarded only as a fraction of an investigation into the history of the development of the idea of vocation and its infusion into certain callings.

Apart from its incompleteness this essay betrays the other faults so characteristic of most of Weber's writing – a great carelessness of the reader's requirements, evinced in the plethora of detail in the text and above all in the ocean of footnotes, inundating the reader and frequently sweeping him far from the mainland. His wife speaks of 'die montströse Form dieser Abhandlung', which was aggravated in the second edition when the 'Fussnotengeschwulst' increased enormously. She sought, however, to justify this flood by pointing out that since Weber was using 'careful causal imputation of intuitively apprehended connections', he wished to provide all possible proof in this extensive scholarly apparatus, and 'to guard himself against any misunderstanding of his cautious relativizations'.

The essay may be justly criticized for various errors of fact and interpretation. Weber himself later corrected some erroneous statements appearing in the original essay, as by indicating that when he had said that Calvinism shows the juxtaposition of intensive piety and capitalism, wherever found, he had meant only Diaspora Calvinism.

Another justifiable line of attack on Weber's thesis is based on concrete researches into the economic history of the continent, principally Holland and the Rhineland. Both Weber and Troeltsch had based their work on inadequate study of sources, and had quoted Anglo-Saxon writers to demonstrate the effect of German and Netherland Calvinists on the economic development of the Rhineland. On the basis of investigations into the history of Holland – and it must be recalled that this republic was probably the first country in which capitalism developed on a large scale – recent Netherland historians like DeJong, Knappert and de Pater find no proof to sustain such a theory of a connection between Calvinism and capitalism among the Netherlanders. Further, Beins's researches into the economic ethic of the Calvinist church in the Netherlands between 1565 and 1650 lead him to raise serious objections to Weber's thesis. A similar view is expressed in the important economic history of the Netherlands by Baasch, who stresses the secular factors in the evolution of capitalism in Holland which made the Netherlanders the chief bankers of the seventeenth century and by the end of the eighteenth made the colony of Jews in Amsterdam the largest in Europe. The same adverse conclusion is reached by Koch's investigation of the economic development of the lower Rhine area and Andrew Sayous's study of the Genevans; Hashagen's essay on the relation between Calvinism and capitalism in the German Rhineland comes to similar conclusions. Evidence has also accumulated that Calvinism did not have any necessary effect on the rise of capitalism in Hungary, Scotland or France.

These researches militate against Weber's hypothesis that the Calvinist belief buttressed capitalism or even favored its emergence. But this line of criticism readily degenerates into the oversimplification referred to above, that Weber was intent on establishing the causal primacy of the Protestant ethic in the genesis of capitalism and the necessary determination of the latter by the former wherever it appeared. The tendency toward such an oversimplification vitiates most of the arguments of Robertson and of Hyma, who closely follows him. In so far as all these writers, among whom may be included Brentano, Sée, Pirenne, Brodnitz and von Schulze-Gävernitz, construe Weber's thesis as implying a necessary causal influence exerted by Calvinism on the evolution of capitalism, they have misread Weber.

Most animadversions on his thesis, even in works composed during the last decade, spring from a misunderstanding or oversimplification of his theory, for which he is only slightly to blame. Surely Weber, one of the foremost historians of jurisprudence and economics in his generation, needed no reminder that the origins of capitalism are complex and diverse, and are due to changes in economic process as well as in spiritual outlook.[9] By and large most of his critics have simply not perceived the direction of his interest, the moderation of his purpose and the caution of his procedure.

Only a very few of his critics rose to the level of his argument and recognized that his errors or shortcomings were inherent in his particular method. And the handful who did attack Weber's method such as Sée, Robertson, Walker and Borkenau, did so in ignorance of his writings on the nature of social science and the method appropriate to it. Weber's shortcomings were not due to ignorance, naïvete or partisanship; on the contrary, he had a considered and subtle approach. An acquaintance with Weber's views as to the nature and goal of the social sciences – his view of theory as only ideal-typical, and his peculiar method of historical research committed to the interpretative understanding of historical atoms, of particular emergents chosen on the basis of their cultural significance and understood by means of a controlled intuitive method – might have clarified the reason for a whole range of errors or inadequacies in his *Protestant Ethic*. Certainly no validation of his method is here projected: clearly it has shortcomings; its usefulness has very plain limitations; and its employment is fraught with particular occupational hazards. But any essay avowedly composed under that method should be evaluated on its own terms, as an essay in interpretative understanding. From this view not a few of the strictures here listed would lose their point, or would at least appear in their proper perspective as the inevitable consequences of Weber's atomistic method.

His employment of the ideal-type method leads to various distortions, as in his overemphasis of the concepts of vocation (Hyma, 1937, pp. 4,

9. Thus, in accounting for the non-appearance of a positive dynamic attitude toward capitalism in antiquity, despite the presence of 'capitalist' activities, Weber remarks that the causes are essentially political, the requirement of *Staatsräson* and the autarchy of the polis. He held that the bias of ancient political theory against the gaining of wealth was not primarily ethical, at least was far less so than that of the medieval church, which was antipathetic to purely commercial relations because of their impersonal character. But he insisted that one could not leave out of consideration the psychological factor of the antipathy to work and productive activity in general, including business, which was the dominant attitude of the ruling class. There was no ethical idealization of vocational activity (*Erwerbsarbeit*); and only among the cynics and Hellenistic-Oriental petty bourgeoisie are there even slight traces of such activity. Thus the 'economic man' of antiquity lacked the support for the rationalization of economic life which his counterpart found at the beginning of the modern period in the vocational ethic, largely a product of religious motivation. The lack of integration in men's attitudes to economic activity must therefore be accounted as one of the reasons for the non-appearance in antiquity of the modern type of capitalism (1909, vol. 1, p. 66).

125; Fanfani, 1935, p. 204; Robertson, 1933, pp. 6, 8, 28, 202) and pre-destination. Here a bias in the choice of the historical atom to be inter-preted and in the definition of its character and influence makes itself strongly felt. The oversimplification induced by the method also extends to his construction of the Protestant ethic as a component of Calvinism, Puritanism, Pietism, Methodism and the Anabaptist sects (Hall, 1930, p. 210), and to his treatment of Puritanism (1930, pp. 6–11). Another instance is his definition of modern capitalism, accentuating its novelty, rationality and ascetic character. Once he had so defined it he did not have much difficulty in discovering elements of congruity with the schematic construction of the Protestant ethic slanted in the same direction. To the empirical historian the whole procedure necessarily appears suffused by a tendency to idealization, with a comparative neglect of secular factors, economic, political and technological.

Weber's method of atomistic isolation necessarily leads to oversimpli-fication of a complex historical entity through the accentuation and iso-lation of a particular component factor regarded as significant from a certain point of view; its tracing of alleged influences on the further course of historical evolution; and its tendency toward reifying the par-ticular component factors of a given historical entity. In the nature of the case this method cannot serve for the illumination of a total historical problem, or the interpretation of a whole epoch or movement.

His pluralistic agnosticism, manifested in his refusal to pledge allegi-ance to any exclusive viewpoint lest it do injustice to the unique individu-ality of historical entities and the perpetual shift of cultural horizons, was laudable in intention. It seemed to be pointing the way to the func-tionalization of research and interpretation in the social sciences. Actu-ally, however, Weber's isolative treatment led to inevitable distortions. His method entailed the breakdown of any complex phenomenon into its components, and then choosing each one seriatim as a constant, trac-ing its effects on the other variables. At the end of the process, he indi-cated, there would have to be a return to assess the varying force of each component in the actual historical composite, and to determine how closely the empirical phenomena approached the ideal types he had for-mulated. This he had planned to do for his problem of the relationship between the Protestant ethic and the spirit of capitalism, but he must have felt the infinite and impossible nature of the task. Moreover, his approach offers no method for determining the interrelation of factors, the degree of influence pertaining to each, or their temporal variations, thereby leaving room for the play of personal evaluation in the choice and characterization of the particular historical atoms.

For the historian concerned with determining the causes of a particular historical datum, the problem of timing historical phenomena and tracing temporal variations is one of the crucial difficulties arising out of the impossibility, inherent in Weber's method, of determining the degree of influence to be assigned to the various factors involved. The ideal-type method neglects the time coefficient, or at any rate impairs the possibility of establishing time sequences, because it involves a telescoping of data. Granted, for instance, that Weber's interpretation of Calvinist theology is correct and that it was of the type that would result in activism, dynamism, industry, etc., the question still remains whether these influences did not begin to exert a significant effect only after capitalism had already reached a dominant position.

Consequently, while there is readiness enough to accept the congruity between Calvinism and capitalism, it has been suggested that a consideration of the crucial question of timing will show that Calvinism emerged later than capitalism where the latter became decisively powerful. Hence the conclusion that Calvinism could not have causally influenced capitalism, and that its subsequent favorable disposition to capitalist practice and ethics is rather to be construed as an adaptation (Tawney, 1926, Robertson, 1933, Laski, 1936, p. 34; Hyma, 1937, pp. 126, 161).

The development of the Weberian thesis by Troeltsch, and his American disciple, Reinhold Niebuhr, meets this criticism by tracing the modifications induced in later Calvinism by the various social factors impinging upon it after the first appearance of the original doctrine, such as religious wars, political pressures and the exigencies of acquisitive life. His rich analysis reveals how the social ethic was the net result of the particular religious and ethical peculiarities of Calvinism, which showed a marked individuality in its doctrine of predestination, its activism and its ethic, aiming at achieving what was possible and practical. On the other hand Troeltsch emphasizes the importance in the evolution of the ethic of the republican tendency in politics, the capitalistic tendency in economics and the diplomatic and militaristic tendencies in international affairs. All these tendencies radiated from Geneva, at first in a very limited way; then they united with similar elements within the Calvinist religion and ethic, and in this union they became stronger and stronger, until in connection with the political, social and ecclesiastical history of individual countries they received that particular character of the religious morality of the middle classes (or bourgeois world) which differs from the early Calvinism of Geneva and France (Troeltsch, 1931, vol. 2, pp. 519, 645, 818, 894, 911).

In the light of all this, Weber's thesis must be construed not according to the usual interpretation, as an effort to trace the causative influence of the Protestant ethic upon the emergence of capitalism, but as an exposition of the rich congruency of such diverse aspects of a culture as religion and economics. The essay should be considered as a stimulating project of hermeneutics, a demonstration of interesting correlations between diverse cultural factors. Although at the time of the republication of the essay Weber insisted that he had not changed his views on this matter at all, the whole intent of his later work does show an implicit shift of view, or at any rate of emphasis. No longer laying the basic stress on the causal factors in the economic ethic of radical Protestantism as related to the capitalist spirit, his later researches, culminating in the systematic sociology of religion, accepted rather the congruency of these diverse aspects of our culture, and their subsumption under the comprehensive process of rationalization. It is important to emphasize that some of the distortions involved in Weber's ideal-type method are neutralized in his later sociological studies of the non-Christian religions, to which all too little attention has been paid. In these mighty studies, which are cultural sociologies of the *Weltreligionen*, Weber traces the influence of material, geographic and economic circumstances on the religious and ethical ideas of different cultures. Yet though he treated religious norms, institutions and practices with cold detachment, he never denied the historical reality and power of the religious complex. His general view remained that human affairs are infinitely complicated, with numerous elements interacting; and it was his unshakable conviction that to attribute causal primacy is to be guilty of oversimplification.

In view of Weber's limited intention and the cautious demarcation of his task (including the frequently expressed indication of its incompleteness), his idiosyncratic method which would not permit statistical proof or disproof, and his later supplementation of the original effort by systematic studies in the sociology of religion, it must be concluded that his task was justified by its results. Although the discussion of his problem has not in itself promoted our knowledge of past economic life in proportion to the considerable effort it has evoked, it has greatly sharpened our appreciation of Catholic and Protestant doctrinal history; and it has also paved the way for the formulation of an adequate social theory of religion. Weber's essay on *The Protestant Ethic* is also in a peculiar sense an introduction to his massive system of sociology and his philosophy of history, and exemplifies in striking fashion the anfractuosities of his intellect and temper. As an illuminating tentative[10] approach to a great problem, as an introduction to the domain of the sociology of religion

10. A poignant expression of Weber's feeling concerning the tentativeness of science and the fateful transiency of the achievements of the scientist, who must none the less accept this tragic fact as his destiny and persevere in his calling, is his eloquent essay 'Wissenchaft als Beruf' (Weber, 1922a).

which it served to stake out, as the stimulus to a generation of researchers in this new discipline, and finally, as the precursor of functional analysis in culture history, Weber's essay deserves a better fate than it has thus far enjoyed.

References

BRINKMAN, C. (1937), *Gustav Schmoller und die Volkswirtschaftslehre*, Stuttgart.

FANFANI, A. (1935), *Catholicism, Protestantism and Capitalism*, Sheed & Ward.

HALL, T. C. (1930), *Religious Background of American Culture*, Little Brown.

HYMA, A. (1937), *Christianity, Capitalism and Communism*, University of Michigan Press.

LASKI, H. (1936), *The Rise of European Liberalism*, Allen & Unwin.

ROBERTSON, H. M. (1933), *Aspects of the Rise of Economic Individualism*, Cambridge University Press.

TAWNEY, R. H. (1926), *Religion and the Rise of Capitalism*, Harcourt, Brace & World.

TROELTSCH, E. (1931), *Social Teachings of the Christian Churches*, Allen & Unwin.

WEBER, MARIANNE (1926), *Max Weber*, Tübingen.

WEBER, M. (1908), *Archiv*, vol. 26.

WEBER, M. (1909), 'Agrarverhältnisse in Altertum, in *Handwörterbüch der Staatwissenschaften*, Tübingen.

WEBER, M. (1910), 'Antikritisches Schlusswortzun Geist des Kapitalismus', *Archiv für Sozialwisserschaft und Sozialpolitick*, vol. 31, pp. 554–99.

WEBER, M. (1922a), *Gesammelte Aufsätze zur Wissenschaftslehre*, Tübingen.

WEBER, M. (1922b), *Wirtschaft und Gesellschaft*, Tübingen.

WEBER, M. (1930), *The Protestant Ethic*, Allen & Unwin.

WEBER, M. (1961), *General Economic History*, Collier-Macmillan.

31 Robert N. Bellah

Reflections on the Protestant Ethic Analogy in Asia

Robert N. Bellah, 'Reflections on the Protestant ethic analogy in Asia',
Journal of Social Issues, vol. 19, 1963, pp. 52–60.

The work of Weber, especially the so-called 'Protestant Ethic hypothesis', continues to exercise an impressive influence on current research
in the social sciences, as a glance at recent journals and monographs
will quickly show (Lenski, 1961, McClelland, 1961). The great bulk of
this research is concerned with refining the Weberian thesis about the
differential effects of Protestant compared with Catholic religious
orientations in the sphere of economic activity. In recent years, however,
there have been increasing though still scattered attempts to apply
Weber's argument to material drawn from various parts of Asia. The
present paper will not undertake to review these attempts with any
completeness. Rather it will be devoted to a selective consideration of
several different approaches to the problem with a view to determining
some of their possibilities and limitations.

Perhaps the commonest approach has been to interpret the Weber
hypothesis in terms of the economists' emphasis on the importance of
entrepreneurship in the process of economic development. Weber's
'Protestant Ethic' is seen as an ideological orientation tending to lead
those who hold it into an entrepreneurial role where they then contribute to economic growth. We will consider shortly how seriously this
oversimplification of Weber's view distorts his intention. At any rate
those who have taken this interpretation have proceeded to analyse
various Asian religious groups to see whether examples of this-worldly
asceticism, the religious significance of work in a calling and so forth
have been associated with successful economic activity. Cases in which
the association has been claimed include in Japan, Zen Buddhists and
Jodo (McClelland, 1961, pp. 369–70), the Hotoku and Shingaku movements (Bellah, 1957, ch. 5); in Java the Santri Muslims (Geertz, 1960;
1956); in India the Jains, Parsis and various business or merchant
castes and so forth. McClelland has recently subsumed a number of
such examples under the general rubric of 'Positive Mysticism' within
which he finds Weber's Protestant example to be merely a special case.

Whether or not the claim to have discovered a religious ethic analogous to Weber's type case can be substantiated in all of these Asian examples, this general approach has much to recommend it. For one thing it calls attention to the motivational factor which historians, economists and sociologists have often overlooked. For another it calls attention to subtle and non-obvious connections between cultural and religious beliefs and behavioral outcomes. This latter point is one which some readers of Weber have consistently failed to understand, Samuelson being merely one of the more recent examples. The latter claims in refutation of Weber that since the puritan fathers did not espouse a materialistic dog-eat-dog capitalism their theology could not possibly have led to its development. Milton Singer on the other hand proves himself a more discerning pupil of Weber when he argues that economic development is not supported merely by 'materialistic' values but may be advanced by an 'ethic of austerity' based perhaps in the case of India on the tradition of religious asceticism (1958).

But the application of the 'entrepreneurship model' or motivational approach to Weber's thesis has, I believe, certain grave limitations. Some of the difficulty lies in the original essay itself when it is not grasped in its proper relation to the whole of Weber's work. One of the most serious of these limitations is emphasis on the importance of the motivational factor at the expense of the historical and institutional setting.

However important motivational factors may be they have proven time and again to be highly sensitive to shifts in institutional arrangements. The consequences for economic development depend as much on the institutional channeling of motivation as on the presence or absence of certain kinds of motivation. For example the entrepreneurial potential of the Japanese samurai, who from at least the sixteenth century comprised what most observers would agree was the most achievement oriented group in Japan, could not be realized until the Meiji period when legal restraints on their entering trade were abolished and their political responsibilities eliminated. Chinese merchants who made an indifferent showing within the institutional limitations of imperial China turned into a vigorous capitalist class under more favorable conditions in South-East Asia. Geertz has shown how the Muslim Santri group in Java, characterized by a long merchant tradition and a favorable religious ethic, began to burgeon into entrepreneurship under favorable economic conditions early in this century only to wither on the vine when economic conditions worsened markedly during the great depression (1956). Papanek in a recent paper has indicated how several relatively small 'communities' (quasi-castes) of traditional traders were able to spearhead Pakistan's remarkable industrial growth in recent years by taking advantage of highly favorable economic conditions which had not previously existed (1962). On the basis of such examples one might argue that there exists in most Asian countries a small but significant minority which has the motivation necessary for entrepreneurial activity. If this is the case, then, it would be advisable to consider motivation in close connection with institutional structure and its historical development.

In *The Protestant Ethic and the Spirit of Capitalism*, Weber himself seems to lean rather heavily on the motivational variable and this may be what has led some of his readers astray. In the later comparative studies in the sociology of religion, however, we get a much more balanced view and an implicit correction of emphasis in the earlier work. Following Weber's comparative studies a number of students have undertaken what might be called an 'institutional approach', attempting to discern institutional factors favorable or unfavorable to economic development. Examples of this kind of study are Feuerwerker (1958), Bellah (1957), about the inadequacies of which I will speak in a moment, Elder's dissertation on India (1959), and perhaps the most comprehensive in scope and historical coverage, Geertz's work on Java contained in a number of published and unpublished writings (1956). In all of these studies Weber's emphasis on the religious ethic continues to receive a central focus. It is seen, however, not simply in relation to personal motivation but also as embodied in or related to a wide range of institutional structures. Feuerwerker writes, '... one institutional breakthrough is worth a dozen textile mills or shipping companies established within the framework of the traditional society and its system of values' (1958, p. 242). And Geertz says in a similar vein:

The extent and excellence of a nation's resources, the size and skill of its labor force, the scope and complexity of its productive 'plant', and the distribution and value of entrepreneurial abilities among its population are only one element in the assessment of its capacity for economic growth; the institutional arrangements by means of which these various factors can be brought to bear on any particular economic goal is another. . . . It is for this reason that economic development in 'underdeveloped' areas implies much more than capital transfers, technical aid and ideological exhortation: it demands a deep going transformation of the basic structure of society and, beyond that, perhaps even in the underlying value-system in terms of which that structure operates (1956, pp. 105–6).

My study of Tokugawa Japan taking a somewhat more optimistic approach to traditional society, stressed the extent to which traditional Japanese institutions were or could under certain circumstances be made to be favorable to economic development. In so doing I drew a number of parallels between certain aspects of 'rationalization' in Japan and the rationalization Weber was talking about in the West. It was precisely on this point that Maruyama Masao's review in *Kokka Gakkai Zasshi* was sharply critical (1958). Without denying that a number of the mechanisms I discussed, for example the concentration of loyalty in the emperor, may have been effective in bringing about certain social changes contributing to economic growth, he points out that they were far from rational in Weber's sense and indeed had profoundly irrational consequences in subsequent Japanese development, not the least of which were important economic inefficiencies.

With Maruyama's strictures in mind one is perhaps better able to deal with some remarks of Singer near the end of his sensitive and illuminating review article on Weber's *Religion of India.*:

To evaluate Weber's conclusions is not easy. In view of the complexity of Hinduism, and of Asian religions generally, any characterization of them or any comparison of them with Western religion is going to involve large simplifications. Certainly Weber has brilliantly constructed a characterization based on an impressive knowledge of both textual and contextual studies. But one may wonder whether the construction does justice to elements of Asian religions. Some of these are: a strand of this-worldly asceticism; the economic rationality of merchants, craftsmen, and peasants; the logically-consistent system of impersonal determinism in Vedánta and Buddhism, with direct consequences for a secular ethic; the development of 'rational empirical' science; religious individualism and personal monotheism. Weber is certainly aware of all these elements and discusses them in his study. ... But in the construction of the 'Spirit' he does not give very much weight to these elements. With the evidence today before us of politically independent Asian states actively planning their social, economic and scientific and technical development, we would attach a good deal more importance to these elements and see less conflict between them and the religious 'spirit' (1961).

For Maruyama the mere *presence* of rational elements for which I argued in the Japanese case along lines quite parallel to those of Yinger is simply not enough if they exist passively side by side with irrational elements (as they do in both Japanese and Indian cases) and are not pushed through 'methodically and systematically' to their conclusion as they were in Weber's paradigmatic case of Protestantism. If Maruyama is right, and I am coming increasingly to believe that he is, then it becomes necessary to press beyond both the motivational and the institutional approaches and to view matters in an even broader perspective as the above quote from Geertz already hinted,

Concretely, this means that we are forced to take seriously Weber's argument for the special significance of Protestantism. The search through Asia for religious movements which here and there have motivational or institutional components analogous to the Protestant Ethic ultimately proves inadequate. The Protestant Reformation is not after all some mere special case of a more general category. It stands in Weber's whole work, not in the *Protestant Ethic* essay alone, as the symbolic representation of a fundamental change in social and cultural structure with the most radical and far-reaching consequences. The proper analogy in Asia then turns out to be, not this or that motivational or institutional component, but reformation itself. What we need to discern is the 'transformation of the basic structure of society' and its 'underlying value-system', to use Geertz's language. Before trying to discover some examples of this structural approach to the Protestant Ethic analogy in Asia it is necessary to note briefly that we see here an example of what must occur in any really serious confrontation with Asian examples: we are forced back to a reconsideration of the European case which provides us so many of the conscious and unconscious categories of our investigation.

The first consideration is that the development in Europe is neither even nor uniform. Developments in different countries and at different times have very different significance. As Bendix has so clearly indicated it was Weber's growing discernment of the failure of structural transformation in important sectors of German society which led him to the Protestant Ethic problem (1960, ch. 2). As every reader of the famous essay knows the material is derived from England primarily, and not from Germany where the Reformation remained abortive in important respects and its structural consequences stunted. This is indeed the background for Weber's profound cultural pessimism. Interestingly enough one of the first Japanese to penetrate deeply into the structure of Western culture, Uchimura, made a similar diagnosis. Writing in 1898 he said:

One of the many foolish and deplorable mistakes which the Satsuma-Chōshū Government have committed in their having selected Germany as the example to be followed in their administrative policy. Because its military organization is well-nigh perfect, and its imperialism a gift of its army, therefore they thought that it ought to be taken as the pattern of our own Empire. . . .

Germany certainly is a great nation, but it is not the greatest, neither is it the most advanced. It is often said that Art, Science and Philosophy have their homes in Germany, that Thought has its primal spring there. But it is not in Germany that Thought is realized to the fullest extent. Thought may originate in Germany, but it is actualized somewhere else. The Lutheran Reformation bore its best fruit in England and America (1933, vol. 16, pp. 361–2).

These suggestions about European developments, which must in the present brief paper remain without adequate elaboration, have a further important implication. Germany is certainly one of the most economically developed nations in the world, yet it lagged, according to Weber, in some of the structural transformations which he discovered to be crucial in the development of modern society. Once the crucial breakthroughs have been accomplished it becomes possible for other nations to take some of them over piecemeal without the total structure being transformed. Possible, but at great cost, as the German case indicates.

These considerations bring us back to Maruyama's criticism of my work and the criticism of a number of Japanese intellectuals of American analyses of Japan in general. Japan, too, comparatively speaking, is one of the world's most economically advanced nations. Looking at economic growth as our sole criterion, we are inclined to consider Japan as a rather unambiguous success story. But to Japanese intellectuals who feel as acutely as Weber did the failure of modern Japan to carry through certain critical structural transformations which are associated with modern society, the evaluation of Japan's modern history is much more problematic. It would be convenient for social scientists and policy makers if economic growth were an automatic index to successful structural transformation. This does not, however, seem to be the case. Indeed where economic growth is rapid and structural change is blocked, or as in the Communist cases distorted, social instabilities result which under present world conditions are serious enough to have potentially fatal consequences for us all. A broader perspective than has often been taken would seem then to be in order.

As examples of the structural approach, which I believe to be the most adequate application of the Weberian problem to Asia, I may cite again the work of Geertz on Indonesia and especially a very suggestive recent article on Bali, together with a highly interesting study of recent religious and social developments in Ceylon by Ames (1963). In the Balinese case only the beginnings of the questioning of traditional assumptions are evident and the degree to which rationalization at the value level will have social consequence is not yet clear. In Ceylon Ames documents the existence of movements of religious reform which have gone far in changing some of the most fundamental assumptions of traditional Buddhism and replacing them with orientations supporting social reform. The degree to which the structural reform itself has gotten under way is not as yet clear. In Japan a century of ideological ferment has given rise to a number of tendencies and potentialities which need much more clarification, a problem on which the writer is currently working.

There are indications from a number of Asian countries that traditional elements are being reformulated as part of new nationalist ideologies. Elder has presented some evidence that the Indian caste ethic is being transformed into a universalistic ethic of occupational responsibility detached from its earlier anchorage in the hereditary caste structure. Such examples would seem to support Singer's argument as quoted above, as indeed in a sense they do. But it should not be forgotten that these reformulations have occurred under Western impact (not infrequently under Protestant Christian impact as Ames shows in Ceylon) and involve fundamental alterations in pattern even when based on traditional material, making them often formally similar to Western paradigms. This is not to imply that Asian cultures are inherently imitative but rather that modern Western societies are not fortuitous cultural sports. Since they represent the earliest versions of a specific structural type of society it is inevitable that Asian societies should in some patterned way come to resemble them as they shift toward that type. Another set of problems arising from the structural approach have to do with the extent to which nationalism or communism can supply the ideological underpinning, the cultural Reformation if you like, for the necessary structural transformations. It is not possible to review here all the work done on these topics, some of which is certainly relevant to the present problem concern.

In conclusion let me say that the whole range of problems having to do with social change in Asia would be greatly illuminated if we had a comprehensive social taxonomy based on evolutionary principles of the sort that Durkheim called for in 1895 (1950, ch. 4). Among recent sociologists I can think only of Eisenstadt as having made significant contributions to this end (1956; 1963). With such a taxonomy in hand we would be in a much stronger position to interpret the meaning of the results obtained by those currently concentrating on motivational and institutional research. We might also be in a better position to clear up profound problems both of science and policy which hover around the definition of the concept of modernization.

References

AMES, M. (1963), 'An outline of recent social and religious changes in Ceylon', *Human Organization*, vol. 22, no. 1, pp. 45–53.

BELLAH, R. N. (1957), *Tokugawa Religion*, Free Press.

BELLAH, R. N. (1953), Ph.D. dissertation, department of social relations, Harvard University.

BENDIX, R. (1960), *Max Weber: An Intellectual Portrait*, Doubleday.

DURKHEIM, E. (1950), *The Rules of Sociological Method*, Free Press.

EISENSTADT, S. N. (1956), *From Generation to Generation*, Free Press.

EISENSTADT, S. N. (1963), *The Political Systems of Empires*, Free Press.

ELDER, J. (1959), *Industrialism in Hindu Society: A Case Study in Social Change*, Ph.D. Dissertation, Harvard University.

FEUERWERKER, A. (1958), *Chinese Early Industrialization*, Harvard University Press.

GEERTZ, C. (1954), 'The development of the Javanese economy: a socio-cultural approach', Center for International Studies, MIT.

GEERTZ, C. (1956a), 'Religious belief and economic behaviour in a central Javanese town: some preliminary considerations', *Economic Development and Cultural Change*, vol. 4, no. 2, pp. 134–58.

GEERTZ, C. (1956b), 'The social context of economic change: an Indonesian case study', Center for International Studies, MIT.

GEERTZ, C. (1960), *The Religion in Java*, Free Press.

LENSKI, G. (1961), *The Religious Factor*, Doubleday.

MCCLELLAND, D. C. (1961), *The Achieving Society*, Princeton University Press.

MARUYAMA, M. (1958), 'Kokka gakkai zasshi', *J. Assoc. Polit. Soc., Sci.*, vol. 72, no 4.

PAPANEK, G. (1962), 'The development of entrepreneurship', *Amer. Econ. Rev.*, vol. 52, no. 2.

SINGER, M. (1961), Review article, *Amer. Anthropol*, vol. 63, no. 1, p. 150.

SINGER, M. (1958), 'India's cultural values and economic development: a discussion', *Economic Development and Cultural Change*, vol. 7, no. 1, pp. 1–12.

UCHIMURA, K. (1933), *Uchimura Kanzo Zenshū*, Iwanami Shoten.

32 Karl Marx

On the Future of Religion

From Karl Marx and Friedrich Engels, *On Religion*, Moscow Foreign
Languages Publishing House, 1955, pp. 41–2. First published in 1844.

For Germany the *criticism of religion* is in the main complete, and
criticism of religion is the premise of all criticism.

The *profane* existence of error is discredited after its *heavenly
oratio pro aris et focis*[1] has been rejected. Man, who looked for a
superman in the fantastic reality of heaven and found nothing there
but the *reflection* of himself, will no longer be disposed to find but
the *semblance* of himself, the non-human [*Unmensch*] where he seeks
and must seek his true reality.

The basis of irreligious criticism is: *Man makes religion*, religion
does not make man. In other words, religion is the self-consciousness
and self-feeling of man who has either not yet found himself or has
already lost himself again. But *man* is no abstract being squatting
outside the world. Man is *the world of man*, the state, society. This
state, this society, produce religion, *a reversed world-consciousness*,
because they are a *reversed world*. Religion is the general theory of
that world, its encyclopedic compendium, its logic in a popular form,
its spiritualistic *point d'honneur*, its enthusiasm, its moral sanction, its
solemn completion, its universal ground for consolation and justification. It is *the fantastic realization* of the human essence because the
human essence has no true reality. The struggle against religion is
therefore mediately the fight against *the other world*, of which religion
is the spiritual *aroma*.

Religious distress is at the same time the *expression* of real distress
and the *protest* against real distress. Religion is the sigh of the oppressed creature, the heart of a heartless world, just as it is the spirit
of a spiritless situation. It is the *opium* of the people.

The abolition of religion as the *illusory* happiness of the people is
required for their *real* happiness. The demand to give up the illusions
about its condition is the *demand to give up a condition which needs
illusions*. The criticism of religion is therefore *in embryo the criticism
of the vale of woe*, the *halo* of which is religion.

1. Speech for the altars and hearths. [Ed.]

Criticism has plucked the imaginary flowers from the chain not so that man will wear the chain without any fantasy or consolation but so that he will shake off the chain and cull the living flower. The criticism of religion disillusions man to make him think and act and shape his reality like a man who has been disillusioned and has come to reason, so that he will revolve round himself and therefore round his true sun. Religion is only the illusory sun which revolves round man as long as he does not revolve round himself.

The task of history, therefore, once the *world beyond the truth* has disappeared, is to establish the *truth of this world*. The immediate *task of philosophy*, which is at the service of history, once the *saintly form* of human self-alienation has been unmasked, is to unmask self-alienation in its *unholy forms*. Thus the criticism of heaven turns into the criticism of the earth, the *criticism of religion* into the *criticism of right* and the *criticism of theology* into the *criticism of politics*.

33 Emile Durkheim

On the Future of Religion

Excerpts from Emile Durkheim, *The Elementary Forms of the Religious Life*
(trans. J. W. Swain), Collier-Macmillan, 1961, pp. 474–9.
First published in French in 1912.

Thus there is something eternal in religion which is destined to survive
all the particular symbols in which religious thought has successively
enveloped itself. There can be no society which does not feel the need
of upholding and reaffirming at regular intervals the collective sentiments and the collective ideas which make its unity and its personality.
Now this moral remaking cannot be achieved except by the means of
reunions, assemblies and meetings where the individuals, being closely
united to one another, reaffirm in common their common sentiments;
hence come ceremonies which do not differ from regular religious
ceremonies, either in their object, the results which they produce, or
the processes employed to attain these results. What essential difference
is there between an assembly of Christians celebrating the principal
dates of the life of Christ, or of Jews remembering the exodus from
Egypt or the promulgation of the decalogue, and a reunion of citizens
commemorating the promulgation of a new moral or legal system
or some great event in the national life?

If we find a little difficulty today in imagining what these feasts and
ceremonies of the future could consist in, it is because we are going
through a stage of transition and moral mediocrity. The great things
of the past which filled our fathers with enthusiasm do not excite
the same ardour in us, either because they have come into common
usage to such an extent that we are unconscious of them, or else
because they no longer answer to our actual aspirations; but as yet
there is nothing to replace them. We can no longer impassionate ourselves for the principles in the name of which Christianity recommended to masters that they treat their slaves humanely, and, on the
other hand, the idea which it has formed of human equality and
fraternity seems to us today to leave too large a place for unjust
inequalities. Its pity for the outcast seems to us too Platonic; we desire
another which would be more practicable; but as yet we cannot
clearly see what it should be nor how it could be realized in facts.
In a word, the old gods are growing old or already dead, and others

are not yet born. This is what rendered vain the attempt of Comte with the old historic souvenirs artificially revived: it is life itself, and not a dead past which can produce a living cult. But this state of incertitude and confused agitation cannot last for ever. A day will come when our societies will know again those hours of creative effervescence, in the course of which new ideas arise and new formulae are found which serve for a while as a guide to humanity; and when these hours shall have been passed through once, men will spontaneously feel the need of reliving them from time to time in thought, that is to say, of keeping alive their memory by means of celebrations which regularly reproduce their fruits. We have already seen how the French Revolution established a whole cycle of holidays to keep the principles with which it was inspired in a state of perpetual youth. If this institution quickly fell away, it was because the revolutionary faith lasted but a moment, and deceptions and discouragements rapidly succeeded the first moments of enthusiasm. But though the work may have miscarried, it enables us to imagine what might have happened in other conditions; and everything leads us to believe that it will be taken up again sooner or later. There are no gospels which are immortal, but neither is there any reason for believing that humanity is incapable of inventing new ones. As to the question of what symbols this new faith will express itself with, whether they will resemble those of the past or not, and whether or not they will be more adequate for the reality which they seek to translate, that is something which surpasses the human faculty of foresight and which does not appertain to the principal question.

But feasts and rites, in a word, the cult, are not the whole religion. This is not merely a system of practices, but also a system of ideas whose object is to explain the world; we have seen that even the humblest have their cosmology. Whatever connection there may be between these two elements of the religious life, they are still quite different. The one is turned towards action, which it demands and regulates; the other is turned towards thought, which it enriches and organizes. Then they do not depend upon the same conditions, and consequently it may be asked if the second answers to necessities as universal and as permanent as the first.

When specific characteristics are attributed to religious thought, and when it is believed that its function is to express, by means peculiar to itself, an aspect of reality which evades ordinary knowledge as well as science, one naturally refuses to admit that religion can ever abandon its speculative role. But our analysis of the facts does not seem to have shown this specific quality of religion. The religion which we have just studied is one of those whose symbols are the most disconcerting for the reason. There all appears mysterious. These beings which belong to the most heterogeneous groups at the same time, who multiply without ceasing to be one, who divide without diminishing, all seem, at first view, to belong to an entirely different world from the one where we live; some have even gone so far as to say that the mind which constructed them ignored the laws of logic completely. Perhaps the contrast between reason and faith has never been more thorough. Then if there has ever been a moment in history when their heterogeneousness should have stood out clearly, it is here. But contrary to all appearances, as we have pointed out, the realities to which religious speculation is then applied are the same as those which later serve as the subject of reflection for philosophers: they are nature, man, society. The mystery which appears to surround them is wholly superficial and disappears before a more pains-taking observation: it is enough merely to set aside the veil with which mythological imagination has covered them for them to appear such as they really are. Religion sets itself to translate these realities into an intelligible language which does not differ in nature from that employed by science; the attempt is made by both to connect things with each other, to establish internal relations between them, to classify them and to systematize them. We have even seen that the essential ideas of scientific logic are of religious origin. It is true that in order to utilize them, science gives them a new elaboration; it purges them of all accidental elements; in a general way, it brings a spirit of criticism into all its doings, which religion ignores; it surrounds itself with precautions to 'escape precipitation and bias', and to hold aside the passions, prejudices and all subjective influences. But these perfectionings of method are not enough to differentiate it from religion. In this regard, both pursue the same end; scientific thought is only a more perfect form of religious thought. Thus it seems natural that the second should progressively retire before the first, as this becomes better fitted to perform the task.

And there is no doubt that this regression has taken place in the course of history. Having left religion, science tends to substitute itself for this latter in all that which concerns the cognitive and intellectual functions. Christianity has already definitely consecrated this substitution in the order of material things. Seeing in matter that which is profane before all else, it readily left the knowledge of this to another discipline, *tradidit mundum hominum disputationi*, 'He gave the world over to the disputes of men'; it is thus that the natural sciences have been able to establish themselves and make their authority recognized without very great difficulty. But it could not give up the world of souls so easily; for it is before all other souls that the god of the Christians aspires to reign. That is why the idea of submitting the psychic life to science produced the effect of a sort of profanation for a long time; even today it is repugnant to many minds. However, experimental and comparative psychology is founded and today we must reckon with it. But the world of the religious and moral life is still forbidden. The great majority of men continue to believe that here there is an order of things which the mind cannot penetrate except by very special ways. Hence comes the active resistance which is met with every time that someone tries to treat religious and moral phenomena scientifically. But in spite of these oppositions, these attempts are constantly repeated and this persistence even allows us to foresee that this final barrier will finally give way and that science will establish herself as mistress even in this reserved region.

That is what the conflict between science and religion really amounts to. It is said that science denies religion in principle. But religion exists; it is a system of given facts; in a word, it is a reality. How could science deny this reality? Also, in so far as religion is action, and in so far as it is a means of making men live, science could not take its place, for even if this expresses life, it does not create it; it may well seek to explain the faith, but by that very act it presupposes it. Thus there is no conflict except upon one limited point. Of the two functions which religion originally fulfilled, there is one, and only one, which tends to escape it more and more: that is its speculative function. That which science refuses to grant to religion is not its right to exist, but its right to dogmatize upon the nature of things and the special competence which it claims for itself for knowing man and the world. As a matter of fact, it does not know itself. It does not even know what it is made of, nor to what need it answers. It is itself a subject for science, so far is it from being able to make the law for science! And from another point of view, since there is no proper subject for religious speculation outside that reality to which scientific reflection is applied, it is evident that this former cannot play the same role in the future that it has played in the past.

However, it seems destined to transform itself rather than to disappear.

We have said that there is something eternal in religion, it is the cult and the faith. Men cannot celebrate ceremonies for which they see no reason, nor can they accept a faith which they in no way understand. To spread itself or merely to maintain itself, it must be justified, that is to say, a theory must be made of it. A theory of this sort must undoubtedly be founded upon the different sciences, from the moment when these exist; first of all, upon the social sciences, for religious faith has its origin in society; then upon psychology, for society is a synthesis of human consciousnesses ; and finally upon the sciences of nature, for man and society are a part of the universe and can be abstracted from it only artificially. But howsoever important these facts taken from the constituted sciences may be, they are not enough; for faith is before all else an impetus to action, while science, no matter how far it may be pushed, always remains at a distance from this. Science is fragmentary and incomplete ; it advances but slowly and is never finished; but life canot wait. The theories which are destined to make men live and act are therefore obliged to pass science and complete it prematurely. They are possible only when the practical exigencies and the vital necessities which we feel without distinctly conceiving them push thought in advance, beyond that which science permits us to affirm. Thus religions, even the most rational and laicized, cannot and never will be able to dispense with a particular form of speculation which, though having the same subjects as science itself, cannot be really scientific: the obscure intuitions of sensation and sentiment too often take the place of logical reasons. On one side, this speculation resembles that which we meet with in the religions of the past; but on another, it is different. While claiming and exercising the right of going beyond science, it must commence by knowing this and by inspiring itself with it. Ever since the authority of science was established, it must be reckoned with; one can go farther than it under the pressure of necessity, but he must take his direction from it. He can affirm nothing that it denies, deny nothing that it affirms, and establish nothing that is not directly or indirectly founded upon principles taken from it. From now on, the faith no longer exercises the same hegemony as formerly over the system of ideas that we may continue to call religion. A rival power rises up before it which, being born of it, ever after submits it to its criticism and control. And everything makes us foresee that this control will constantly become more extended and efficient, while no limit can be assigned to its future influence.

34 Peter L. Berger

Secularization and the Problem of Plausibility

Excerpts from Peter L. Berger, *The Social Reality of Religion*, Faber & Faber, 1969, pp. 106–9, 126–34, 150–53. First published in the United States as *The Sacred Canopy* in 1967

The term 'secularization' has had a somewhat adventurous history (Luebbe, 1965). It was originally employed in the wake of the Wars of Religion to denote the removal of territory or property from the control of ecclesiastical authorities. In Roman canon law the same term has come to denote the return to the 'world' of a person in orders. In both these usages, whatever the disputes in particular instances, the term could be used in a purely descriptive and non-evaluative way. This, of course, has not been the case in the usage of more recent times. The term 'secularization', and even more its derivative 'secularism', has been employed as an ideological concept highly charged with evaluative connotations, sometimes positive and sometimes negative (Luebbe, 1965). In anti-clerical and 'progressive' circles it has come to stand for the liberation of modern man from religious tutelage, while in circles connected with the traditional church it has been attacked as 'de-Christianization', 'paganization' and the like. Both these ideologically charged perspectives, within which the same empirical phenomena appear with opposite value indices, can be rather entertainingly observed in the work of sociologists of religion inspired, respectively, by Marxist and Christian viewpoints (Klohr, 1966; Acquaviva, 1961). The situation has not been clarified by the fact that since the Second World War a number of theologians, namely Protestants taking up certain strands in the later thought of Bonhoeffer, have reversed the previous Christian evaluation of 'secularization' and hailed it as a realization of crucial motifs of Christianity itself (Bethge, 1955; Loen, 1965; Cox, 1965; Von Oppen, 1960). Not surprisingly, the position has been advanced that, in view of this ideological furor, the term should be abandoned as confusing if not downright meaningless (Matthes, 1964; Rendtorff and Martin, 1966).

We would not agree with this position, despite the justification of the ideological analysis on which it is based. The term 'secularization' refers to empirically available processes of great importance in modern Western history. Whether these processes are to be deplored or welcomed is, of course, irrelevant within the universe of discourse of the historian or the sociologist. It is possible, actually without too great an effort, to describe the empirical phenomenon without taking up an evaluative stance. It is also possible to inquire into its historical origins, *including* its historical connection with Christianity, without asserting that this represents either a fulfillment or a degeneration of the latter. This point should be particularly stressed in view of the current discussion among theologians. It is one thing to maintain that there is a relationship of historical causality between Christianity and certain features of the modern world. It is an altogether different matter to say that, 'therefore', the modern world, including its secular character, must be seen as some sort of logical realization of Christianity. A salutary thing to remember in this connection is that most historical relationships are ironical in character, or, to put it differently, that the course of history has little to do with the intrinsic logic of ideas that served as causal factors in it.[1]

It is not difficult to put forth a simple definition of secularization for the purpose at hand. By secularization we mean the process by which sectors of society and culture are removed from the domination of religious institutions and symbols. When we speak of society and institutions in modern Western history, of course, secularization manifests itself in the evacuation by the Christian church of areas previously under their control or influence – as in the separation of church and state, or in the expropriation of church lands, or in the emancipation of education from ecclesiastical authority. When we speak of culture and symbols, however, we imply that secularization is more than a social-structural process. It affects the totality of cultural life and of ideation, and may be observed in the decline of religious contents in the arts, in philosophy, in literature and, most important of all, in the rise of science as an autonomous, thoroughly secular perspective on the world. Moreover, it is implied here that the process of secularization has a subjective side as well. As there is a secularization of society and culture, so is there a secularization of consciousness. Put simply, this means that the modern West has produced an increasing number of individuals who look upon the world and their own lives without the benefit of religious interpretations.

While secularization may be viewed as a global phenomenon of modern societies, it is not uniformly distributed within them. Different

1. This point gains poignancy if one reflects on the prominence of Weber's work in this discussion. Anyone who cites Weber in this context should certainly recall his understanding of the ironic relationship between human intentions and the historical consequences!

groups of the population have been affected by it differently (LeBras, 1955; Pin, 1956; Isambert, 1961; Fichter, 1951). Thus it has been found that the impact of secularization has tended to be stronger on men than on women, on people in the middle age range than on the very young and the old, in the cities than in the country, on classes directly connected with modern industrial production (particularly the working class) than on those of more traditional occupations (such as artisans or small shopkeepers), on Protestants and Jews than on Catholics, and the like. At least as far as Europe is concerned, it is possible to say with some confidence, on the basis of these data, that church-related religiosity is strongest (and thus, at any rate, social-structural secularization least) on the margins of modern industrial society, both in terms of marginal classes (such as the remnants of old petty bourgeoisies) and marginal individuals (such as those eliminated from the work process) (Luckmann, 1967). The situation is different in America, where the churches still occupy a more central symbolic position, but it may be argued that they have succeeded in keeping this position only by becoming highly secularized themselves, so that the European and American cases represent two variations on the same underlying theme of global secularization (Luckmann, 1967; Herberg, 1955; Berger, 1961). What is more, it appears that the same secularizing forces have now become worldwide in the course of Westernization and modernization (Lerner, 1958; Bellah, 1965; Smith, 1966). Most of the available data, to be sure, pertain to the social-structural manifestations of secularization rather than to the secularization of consciousness, but we have enough data to indicate the massive presence of the latter in the contemporary West.[2] We cannot here pursue the interesting question of the extent to which there may be, so to speak, asymmetry between these two dimensions of secularization, so that there may not only be secularization of consciousness within the traditional religious institutions but also a continuation of more or less traditional motifs of religious consciousness outside their previous institutional contexts (Stammler, 1960).

If for heuristic purposes, we were to take an epidemiological viewpoint with regard to secularization, it would be natural to ask what are its 'carriers'.[3] In other words, what socio-cultural processes and

2. While the material accumulated by Catholic sociologists mainly concerns the institutional aspects of secularization (particularly as expressed in the externals of religious practice), a good many data on the subjective correlates of this may also be found there (Acquaviva, 1961; Carrier, 1960; Allport, 1951; Woelber, 1959; Goldsen, 1960).

3. The term 'carrier' is used here in a Weberian sense.

groups serve as vehicles or mediators of secularization? Viewed from outside Western civilization (say, by a concerned Hindu traditionalist), the answer is obviously that it is that civilization as a whole in its spread around the world (and it need hardly be emphasized that, from that viewpoint, Communism and modern nationalism are just as much manifestations of Westernization as their 'imperialist' predecessors). Viewed from inside Western civilization (say, by a worried Spanish country priest), the original 'carrier' of secularization is the modern economic process, that is, the dynamic of industrial capitalism. To be sure, it may be 'secondary' effects of this dynamic that constitute the immediate problem (for example, the secularizing contents of modern mass media or the influences of a heterogeneous mass of tourists brought in by modern means of transportation). But it does not take long to trace these 'secondary' effects back to their original source in the expanding capitalist-industrial economy. In those parts of the Western world where industrialism has taken socialist forms of organization, closeness to the processes of industrial production and its concomitant styles of life continues to be the principal determinant of secularization (Klohr, 1966 ; Bayés, 1965). Today, it would seem, it is industrial society in itself that is secularizing, with its divergent ideological legitimations serving merely as modifications of the global secularization process. [. . .] One of the most obvious ways in which secularization has affected the man in the street is as a 'crisis of credibility' in religion. Put differently, secularization has resulted in a widespread collapse of the plausibility of traditional religious definitions of reality. This manifestation of secularization on the level of consciousness ('subjective secularization', if one wishes) has its correlate on the social-structural level (as 'objective secularization'). Subjectively, the man in the street tends to be uncertain about religious matters. Objectively, the man in the street is confronted with a wide variety of religious and other reality defining agencies that compete for his allegiance or at least attention, and none of which is in a position to coerce him into allegiance. In other words, the phenomenon called 'pluralism' is a social-structural correlate of the secularization of consciousness. This relationship invites sociological analysis (Berger and Luckmann, 1966; Berger, 1963; Luckmann, 1967).

Such analysis affords a very nice opportunity to show *in concreto* the dialectical relationship between religion and its infrastructure that has previously been developed theoretically. It is possible to analyse secularization in such a way that it appears as a 'reflection' of concrete infrastructural processes in modern society. This is all the more convincing because secularization appears to be a 'negative' phenomenon, that is, it seems to be without causal efficacy of its own and continually dependent upon processes other than itself. Such an analysis, however, remains convincing only if the contemporary situation is viewed in isolation from its historical background. Religion under the impact of secularization can, indeed, be analysed convincingly as a 'dependent variable' *today*. As soon, though, as one asks about the historical origins of secularization the problem poses itself in quite different terms. As we have tried to indicate, one is then led to consider specific elements of the religious tradition of Western culture precisely as historical forces, that is, as 'independent variables'.

The dialectical relationship between religion and society thus precludes the doctrinaire approaches of either 'idealism' or 'materialism'. It is possible to show in concrete instances how religious 'ideas', even very abstruse ones, led to empirically available changes in the social structure. In other instances, it is possible to show how empirically available structural changes had effects on the level of religious consciousness and ideation. Only a dialectical understanding of these relationships avoids the distortions of the one-sidedly 'idealist' and 'materialist' interpretations. Such a dialectical understanding will insist upon the rootage of all consciousness, religious or other, in the world of everyday *praxis,* but it will be very careful not to conceive of this rootage in terms of mechanistic causality.[4]

A quite different matter is the potency of religion to 'act back' upon its infrastructure in specific historical situations. On this it is possible to say that such potency varies greatly in different situations. Thus religion might appear as a formative force in one situation and as a dependent formation in the situation following historically.[5] One may describe such change as a 'reversal' in the 'direction' of causal efficacy as between religion and its respective infrastructures. The phenomenon under consideration here is a case in point. Religious developments originating in the Biblical tradition may be seen as causal factors in the formation of the modern secularized world. Once formed, however, this world precisely precludes the continuing efficacy of religion as a formative force. We would contend that here lies the great historical irony in the relation between religion and secularization, an irony that can be graphically put by saying that, historically speaking, Christianity has been its own gravedigger. In look-

4. It is in this way that the Marxian and Weberian conceptions of religion can be integrated theoretically, at least on the level of general theory (that is, bracketing specific contradictions of historical interpretation) and provided one differentiates between Marx and doctrinaire Marxism.

5. Weber's theory of charisma and the routinization of charisma provides a model for this kind of differentiated analysis (Berger, 1954).

ing at the collapse of plausibility suffered by religion in the contemporary situation, *hic et nunc*, it is logical to begin with social structure and to go on to consciousness and ideation, rather than the reverse. Quite apart from its theoretical justification, this procedure will avoid the pitfall (to which religiously inclined observers are particularly prone) of ascribing secularization to some mysterious spiritual and intellectual fall from grace. Rather it will show the rootage of this fall from grace (the term is descriptively useful) in empirically available social-structural processes.

The original 'locale' of secularization, as we have indicated, was in the economic area, specifically, in those sectors of the economy being formed by the capitalistic and industrial processes. Consequently, different strata of modern society have been affected by secularization differentially in terms of their closeness to or distance from these processes. Highly secularized strata emerged in the immediate proximity of these same processes. In other words, modern industrial society has produced a centrally 'located' sector that is something like a 'liberated territory' with respect to religion. Secularization has moved 'outwards' from this sector into other areas of society. One interesting consequence of this has been a tendency for religion to be 'polarized' between the most public and the most private sectors of the institutional order, specifically between the institutions of the state and the family. Even at a point of far-reaching secularization of everyday life as lived at work and in the relationships that surround work one may still find religious symbols attached to the institutions of state and family. For instance, at a point where everyone takes it for granted that 'religion stops at the factory gate', it may nevertheless be also taken for granted that one does not inaugurate either a war or a marriage without the traditional religious symbolizations (Berger, 1961).

A way of putting this in terms of common sociological parlance is to say that there has been a 'cultural lag' between the secularization of the economy on the one hand and that of the state and the family on the other. As far as the state is concerned, this has meant the continuation in several countries of traditional religious legitimations of the political order at a time when those countries were already well on the way toward becoming modern industrial societies. This was certainly the case with England, the first country to embark on this journey. On the other hand, secularizing political forces have been at work in countries that still lagged behind in terms of capitalistic-industrial development, as in France in the late eighteenth century and in many of the underdeveloped countries today. The relationship between socio-economic modernization and political secularization, therefore, is not a simple one. Nevertheless we would contend that there is a tendency toward the secularization of the political order that goes naturally with the development of modern industrialism. Specifically, there is a tendency toward the institutional separation between the state and religion. Whether this is a practical matter originally unconnected with ideological anti-clericalism, as in America, or is linked to an anti-clerical or even anti-religious '*laïcisme*', as in France, is dependent upon peculiar historical factors at work in different national societies. The global tendency seems to be in all cases the emergence of a state emancipated from the sway of either religious institutions or religious rationales of political action. This is also true in those 'antiquarian' cases in which the same political secularization continues to be decorated with the traditional symbols of religio-political unity, as in England or Sweden. Indeed, the anachronism of the traditional symbols in these cases only serves to underline the actuality of the secularization that has taken place despite them.

One of the most important consequences of this is that the state no longer serves as an enforcement agency on behalf of the previously dominant religious institution. Indeed, this is one of the major tenets in the political doctrine of the separation of state and church, both in its American and French versions (whatever their other differences may be), and it is equally strongly expressed in the various doctrines of religious toleration and liberty even where these are not legitimated in terms of the separation of state and church, as in England, Germany or the Scandinavian countries. The state now takes on a role *vis-à-vis* the competing religious groups that is strikingly reminiscent of its role in *laissez-faire* capitalism – basically, that of impartial guardian of order between independent and uncoerced competitors. As we shall see in a moment, this analogy between economic and religious 'free enterprise' is far from accidental.

Of course, there are differences in the specific attitude taken by the state toward religion in different national societies. But if one keeps in mind the basic similarity of the cessation of coercion these differences appear as less than decisive. Thus there are obvious differences between the American situation, in which the state is most benign to religion and in which the different religious groups profit equally from the fiscal bonanza guaranteed to them by the tax exemption laws, and the situation in Communist Europe, in which the state, for its own ideological reasons, is hostile to religion in both theory and practice. It is important to keep in mind, though, that both these situations, if they are compared with traditional 'Christian societies', are similar to the extent that the churches can no longer call upon the political arm to enforce their claims of allegiance. In both these situations the churches are 'on their own' in having to enlist the voluntary adherence of their respective clienteles, though of course the American state facilitates their endeavor in the same measure as the Communist state tries to hinder them. Equally interesting is the failure of attempts to replicate the traditional coercive support of religion by the state under conditions of modernization. Contemporary Spain and Israel serve as interesting examples of such attempts, it being safe to say that in both cases the attempts are in process of failing. We would argue that the only chance of success in these countries would lie in the reversal of the modernization process, which would entail their remaking into preindustrial societies – a goal as close to the impossible as anything in the realm of history.

The dynamics behind this are far from mysterious. Their roots are in the processes of rationalization released by modernization (that is, by the establishment of, first, a capitalist, then an industrial socio-economic order) in society at large and in the political institutions in particular.[6] The afore-mentioned 'liberated territory' of secularized sectors of society is so centrally 'located', in and around the capitalistic-industrial economy, that any attempt to 'reconquer' it in the name of religio-political traditionalism endangers the continued functioning of this economy. A modern industrial society requires the presence of large cadres of scientific and technological personnel, whose training and ongoing social organization presupposes a high degree of rationalization, not only on the level of infrastructure but also on that of consciousness. Any attempts at traditionalistic *reconquista* thus threaten to dismantle the rational foundations of modern society. Furthermore, the secularizing potency of capitalistic-industrial rationalization is not only self-perpetuating but self-aggrandizing. As the capitalistic-industrial complex expands, so do the social strata dominated by its rationales, and it becomes ever more difficult to establish traditional controls over them. Since the expansion of the same complex is international (today just about worldwide), it becomes increasingly difficult to isolate any particular national society from its rationalizing effects without at the same time keeping that society in a condition of economic backwardness. The impact of modern mass communications and mass transportation (both nicely concentrated in the phenomenon of tourism) on contemporary Spain may serve as an illustration. As the modern state is increasingly occupied with the political and legal requirements of the gigantic economic machinery of industrial production, it must gear its own structure and ideology to this end. On the level of structure, this means above all the establishment of highly rational bureaucracies; on the level of ideology, it means the maintenance of legitimations that are adequate for such bureaucracies. Thus,

6. The category of rationalization is, again, aplied here in a Weberian sense.

inevitably, there develops an affinity, both in structure and in 'spirit', between the economic and the political spheres. Secularization then passes from the economic to the political sphere in a near-inexorable process of 'diffusion'. The religious legitimations of the state are then either liquidated altogether, or remain as rhetorical ornamentations devoid of social reality. It may be added that, given an advanced state of industrialization, it seems of little consequence *in this respect* whether the rationalization of the political order takes place under capitalist or socialist, democratic or authoritarian auspices. The decisive variable for secularization does not seem to be the institutionalization of particular property relations, nor the specifics of different constitutional systems, but rather the process of rationalization that is the prerequisite for *any* industrial society of the modern type.

While the presence of religion within modern political institutions is, typically, a matter of ideological rhetorics, this cannot be said about the opposite 'pole'. In the sphere of the family and of social relationships closely linked to it, religion continues to have considerable 'reality' potential, that is, continues to be relevant in terms of the motives and self-interpretations of people in this sphere of everyday social activity. The symbolic liaison between religion and the family is, of course, of ancient lineage indeed, grounded in the very antiquity of kinship institutions as such. The continuation of this liaison may then, in certain cases, be simply looked upon as an institutional 'survival'. More interesting, though, is the reappearance of the religious legitimation of the family even in highly secularized strata, as for instance in the contemporary American middle classes (Nash and Berger, 1962). In these instances religion manifests itself in its peculiarly modern form, that is, as a legitimating complex voluntarily adopted by an uncoerced clientele. As such, it is located in the private sphere of everyday social life and is marked by the very peculiar traits of this sphere in modern society (Gehlen, 1957; Luckmann, 1967; Habermas, 1962). One of the essential traits is that of 'individualization'. This means that privatized religion is a matter of the 'choice' or 'preference' of the individual or the nuclear family, *ipso facto* lacking in common, binding quality. Such private religiosity, however 'real' it may be to the individuals who adopt it, cannot any longer fulfil the classical task of religion, that of constructing a common world within which all of social life receives ultimate meaning binding on everybody. Instead, this religiosity is limited to specific enclaves of social life that may be effectively segregated from the secularized sectors of modern society. The values pertaining to private religiosity are, typically, irrelevant to institutional contexts other than the private sphere. For example, a businessman or politician may faithfully adhere to the religiously legitimated norms of family life, while at the same time conducting his activities in the public sphere without any reference to religious values of any kind. It is not difficult to see that such segregation of religion within the private sphere is quite 'functional' for the maintenance of the highly rationalized order of modern economic and political institutions. The fact that this privatization of the religious tradition poses a problem for the theoreticians of the institutions embodying this tradition need not concern us at the moment.

The overall effect of the afore-mentioned 'polarization' is very curious. Religion manifests itself as public rhetoric and private virtue. In other words, in so far as religion is common it lacks 'reality', and in so far as it is 'real' it lacks commonality. This situation represents a severe rupture of the traditional task of religion, which was precisely the establishment of an integrated set of definitions of reality that could serve as a common universe of meaning for the members of a society. The world-building potency of religion is thus restricted to the construction of sub-worlds, of fragmented universes of meaning, the plausibility structure of which may in some cases be no larger than the nuclear family. Since the modern family is notoriously fragile as an institution (a trait it shares with all other formations of the private sphere), this means that religion resting on this kind of plausibility structure is of necessity a tenuous construction. Put simply, a 'religious preference' can be abandoned as readily as it was first adopted. This tenuousness can (indeed must) be mitigated by seeking more broadly based plausibility structures. Typically, these are the churches or other wider religious groupings. By the very nature of their social character as voluntary associations 'located' primarily in the private sphere, however, such churches can only augment the strength and durability of the required plausibility structures to a limited extent.

The 'polarization' of religion brought about by secularization and the concomitant loss of commonality and/or 'reality', can also be described by saying that secularization *ipso facto* leads to a pluralistic situation. The term 'pluralism', to be sure, has usually been applied only to those cases (of which the American one is prototypical) in which different religious groups are tolerated by the state and engage in free competition with each other. There is little point to arguments over terminology and there is nothing wrong with this limited use of the term. If, however, one looks at the underlying social forces producing even this limited kind of pluralism, the deeper linkage between secularization and pluralism becomes apparent. One may then say that, as we have seen, secularization brings about a demonopolization of religious traditions and thus, *ipso facto*, leads to a pluralistic situation.

Through most of human history religious establishments have existed as monopolies in society – monopolies, that is, in the ultimate legitimation of individual and collective life. Religious institutions really were *institutions* properly speaking, that is, regulatory agencies for both thought and action. The world as defined by the religious institution in question was *the* world, maintained not just by the mundane powers of the society and their instruments of social control, but much more fundamentally maintained by the 'common sense' of the members of that society. To step outside the world as religiously defined was to step into a chaotic darkness, into anomy, possibly into madness. [. . .]

As we have seen, the two global processes of pluralization and secularization are closely linked. However, there would also be a crisis in credibility brought on by pluralism as a *social-structural* phenomenon, quite apart from its linkage with the 'carriers' of secularization. The pluralistic situation, in demonopolizing religion, makes it ever more difficult to maintain or to construct anew viable plausibility structures for religion. The plausibility structures lose massivity because they can no longer enlist the society as a whole to serve for the purpose of social confirmation. Put simply, there are always 'all those others' that refuse to confirm the religious world in question. Put simply in a different way, it becomes increasingly difficult for the 'inhabitants' of any particular religious world to remain *entre nous* in contemporary society. Disconfirming others (not just individuals, but entire strata) can no longer be safely kept away from 'one's own'. Furthermore, the plausibility structures lose the appearance of durability as a result of the afore-mentioned dynamics of consumer culture. As religious contents become susceptible to 'fashion' it becomes increasingly difficult to maintain them as unchangeable verities. These processes, to repeat, are not understood if one views them only as phenomena of consciousness – rather, they must be understood as grounded in the specific infrastructure established by modern industrial society. One may say, with only some exaggeration, that economic data on industrial productivity or capital expansion can predict the religious crisis of credibility in a particular society more easily than data derived from the 'history of ideas' of that society.

The pluralistic situation multiplies the number of plausibility structures competing with each other. *Ipso facto,* it relativizes their religious contents. More specifically, the religious contents are 'de-objectivated', that is, deprived of their status as taken-for-granted, objective reality in consciousness. They become 'subjectivized' in a double sense: their 'reality' becomes a 'private' affair of individuals, that is, loses the quality of self-evident intersubjective plausibility – thus one 'cannot really talk' about religion any more. And their 'reality', in so far as it is still maintained by the individual, is apprehended as being rooted within the consciousness of the individual rather than in any facticities of the external world – religion no longer refers to the cosmos or to history, but to individual *Existenz* or psychology.

On the level of theorizing, this phenomenon serves to explain the current linkage of theology with the conceptual machineries of existentialism and psychologism. These conceptual machineries are, indeed, 'empirically adequate' to the extent that they accurately reflect the 'location' of religion in contemporary consciousness, which they merely serve to legitimate theoretically. It is important to understand that these legitimations are grounded in pretheoretical phenomena of consciousness, which are grounded in turn in the infrastructure of contemporary society. The individual in fact 'discovers' religion within his own subjective consciousness, somewhere 'deep down' within himself – the existentialist or Freudian theoretician then merely explicates this 'discovery' on the level of theory. Once more, we would contend, we may predict these phenomena more accurately by means of economic data than by any 'data' on, say, the workings of the 'unconscious'. Indeed, the emergence of the 'unconscious' itself may be analysed in terms of specific structural developments of modern industrial society (Berger, 1965).

In this way the demonopolization of religion is a social-structural as well as a social-psychological process. Religion no longer legitimates 'the world'. Rather, different religious groups seek, by different means, to maintain their particular subworlds in the face of a plurality of competing subworlds. Concomitantly, this plurality of religious legitimations is internalized in consciousness as a plurality of possibilities between which one may choose. *Ipso facto*, any particular choice is relativized and less than certain. What certainty there is must be dredged up from within the subjective consciousness of the individual, since it can no longer be derived from the external, socially shared and taken-for-granted world. This 'dredging up' can then be legitimated as a 'discovery' of some alleged existential or psychological data. The religious traditions have lost their character as overarching symbols for the society at large, which must find its integrating symbolism elsewhere. Those who continue to adhere to the world as defined by the religious traditions then find themselves in the position of cognitive minorities – a status that has social-psychological as well as theoretical problems.

The pluralistic situation presents the religious institutions with two ideal-typical options. They can either accommodate themselves to the situation, play the pluralistic game of religious free enterprise, and come to terms as best they can with the plausibility problem by modifying their product in accordance with consumer demands. Or they can refuse to accommodate themselves, entrench themselves behind whatever socio-religious structures they can maintain or construct, and continue to profess the old objectivities as much as possible as if nothing had happened. Obviously there are various intermediate possibilities between these two ideal-typical options, with varying degrees of accommodation and intransigence. Both ideal-typical options have problems on the level of theory as well as on the level of 'social engineering'. These problems *together* constitute the 'crisis of theology' and the 'crisis of the church' in contemporary society.

References

ACQUAVIVA, G. (1961), *L'eclissi del sacro nella civiltà industriale*, Communità.

ALLPORT, G. (1951), *The Individual and his Religion*, Constable.

BAYÉS, R. (1963), *Los ingenieros, la sociedad y la religión*, Fontanella.

BELLAH, R. N. (ed.) (1965), *Religion and Progress in Modern Asia*, Free Press.

BERGER, P. (1954), 'The sociological study of sectarianism', *Sociol. Res.*, vol. 21, no. 4, pp. 467–85.

BERGER, P. (1961), *The Noise of Silent Assemblies*, Doubleday.

BERGER, P. (1963), 'A market model for the analysis of ecumenity', *Sociol. Res.*, vol. 30, no. 1, pp. 77–93.

BERGER, P. (1965), 'Towards a sociological understanding of psychoanalysis', *Sociol. Res.*, vol. 32, no. 1, pp. 26–41.

BERGER, P., and LUCKMANN, T. (1966), 'Secularization and pluralism', in *International Yearbook of the Sociology of Religion*, Westdeutscher Verlag.

BETHGE, E. (ed.) (1955), *Die muendige welt*, Kaiser.

CARRIER, H. (1960), *Psychosociologie de l'appartenance religieuse*, Presses de l'Université Grégorienne.

COX, H. (1965), *The Secular City*, SCM Press.

FICHTER, J. (1951), *Southern Parish*, Chicago University Press.

GEHLEN, A. (1957), *Die Seele in technischen Zeitalter*, Rowohlt.

GOLDSEN, R. (1960), *What College Students Think*, Van Nostrand.

HABERMAS, J. (1962), *Strukturwandel der Oeffentlichkeit*, Luchterhard,

HERBERG, W. (1955), *Protestant–Catholic–Jew*, Doubleday.

ISAMBERT, F. A. (1961), *Christianisme et Classe Ouvrière*, Casterman.

KLOHR, O. (ed.) (1966), *Religion und Atheismus Heute*, Deutscher Verlag.

LEBRAS, G. (1955), *Etudes de sociologie religieuse*, Presses Universitaires de France.

LERNER, D. (1958), *The Passing of Traditional Society*, Free Press.

LOEN, A. (1965), *Säckularisation*, Kaiser.

LUCKMANN, T. (1967), *The Invisible Religion*, Macmillan Co.

LEUBBE, H. (1965), *Säckularisierung: Geschichte eines ideenpolitischen Begriffs*, Alber.

MATTHES, J. (1964), *Die Emigration der Kirche aus der Gesellschaft*, Furche.

NASH, D., and BERGER, P. (1962), 'The child, the family and the religious revival in suburbia', *J. Sci. Stud. Relig.*, vol. 1, no. 1, p. 85.

PIN, E. (1956), *Pratique religieuse et classes sociales*, Spes.

RENDTORFF, T., and MARTIN, D. (1966), *International Yearbook for the Sociology of Religion*, vol. 2, Westdeutscher Verlag.

SMITH, D. (ed.) (1966), *South Asian Politics and Religion*, Princeton University Press.

STAMMLER, E. (1960), *Protestanten ohne Kirche*, Kreuz.

VON, OPPEN, D. (1960), *Das personale Zeitalter*, Kreuz.

WOELBER, H. O. (1959), *Religion ohne Entscheidung*, Vandenhoeck & Ruprecht.

35 Larry Shiner

The Concept of Secularization in Empirical Research

Larry Shiner, 'The concept of secularization in empirical research',
Journal for the Scientific Study of Religion, vol. 6, 1967, pp. 207–20.

Secularization, once branded *the* enemy, has suddenly become the darling of Protestant theology, and there are strong indications that some Roman Catholic theologians are softening. But why should such theological conundrums as 'the secular meaning of the Gospel' or 'secular Christianity' be relevant to the scientific analysis of religion? At the least, this recent theological attack on the received interpretation of secularization should inspire the analyst to reconsider the customary definitions and measures used in research. What *is* an index of secularization? Is it church attendance? Belief in immortality? The amount of private prayer? The number of scientists who believe in God? Or could it be that the indicators are more subtle, so much so that secularization could even permeate what on the surface appears to be religious fervor? Is secularization a low score on a conventional index of religiosity? Or is it another form of religiosity? Or is it an independent process quite uncorrelated with religiosity? In both the empirical and interpretive work on secularization today, the lack of agreement on what secularization is and how to measure it stands out above everything else.

The following analysis is an attempt to bring the concept of secularization at least partially into focus by considering its history, its current definitions, its use in empirical research and its weakness as an analytical tool and some possible alternatives. [. . .]

Types of secularization concept

If we put aside the special usage of economics and the legal definition derived from Westphalia, there appear to be six types of secularization concept in use today. Since what we are about to delineate are *types*, most of the actual definitions or usages one encounters in the literature will deviate to some degree or else represent combinations. Each is presented in terms of a brief definition which describes the kind of process involved and its theoretical culmination. Then a few examples are given before a critical assessment is attempted.

Decline of religion

The previously accepted symbols, doctrines and institutions lose their prestige and influence. The culmination of secularization would be a religionless society. Yinger, for example, terms secularization the process 'in which traditional religious symbols and forms have lost force and appeal' (1957, p. 119).

Examples in research. One of the most significant general studies of American religion in the last few years by Glock and Stark (1965), makes use of a doctrinal version of the decline theory. The authors accept a definition of secularization as the replacement of 'mystical and supernatural elements of traditional Christianity' by a 'demythologized, ethical rather than theological religion' (p. 116). They claim that some denominations are becoming relatively secularized in terms of the substantial percentage of members who either deny or are doubtful about many elements of their Church's historic creed (p. 116–20). Other studies have measured the decrease in clerical prestige, the number of marriages before clergymen, the amount of prayer or Church attendance, or the number of paintings with 'religious' as opposed to 'secular' themes (Lynd and Lynd, 1929). Some like Sorokin, have put together a collection of such variables relating to belief and practice and developed a general theory of decline (1966).

Assessment. There are two major difficulties with the decline thesis. One is the problem of determining when and where we are to find the supposedly 'religious' age from which decline has commenced. Martin has noted that even secularists tend to take a utopian view of medieval religious life (1966, p. 92). And as LeBras says of the term 'dechristianization' which is widely used in France, such language presupposes a 'christianized' France which never was. Moreover, although there has been a decrease in conventional forms of religious practice in France, LeBras points out that there were in former times built-in premiums and liabilities relating to practice which may have produced large scale conventional acceptance of Christianity but little depth. LeBras argues that in 'dechristianized' France today there are, among practising Catholics, probably more who participate voluntarily, faithfully and with an understanding of what they are doing than there were before 1789 (1963).

LeBras's suggestion regarding the seriousness of contemporary religious practice points to the other problems with the decline thesis: the ambiguity of most measures which are used. The easily measurable variables – church attendance, replies to belief questionnaires, proportion of contributions – are notoriously difficult to assess. Although the Glock and Stark study was a considerable improvement over past measures of belief, and although the refinements developed by Fichter, Lenski and Fukuyama have contributed much, the problem of the norm for doctrinal or practical deviation remains, as well as the question of whether such deviation from tradition is necessarily a decline.

Glock and Stark seem to accept the religious conservative's tendency to make 'liberal theologically' the equivalent of 'secularized'. But is 'liberal' theology really an adulteration of the historical faith? Or may it not be, as the best liberal theologians have always insisted, an interpretation of the essence of the tradition in the thought forms and language of today? Bultmann and others have even suggested that to repeat the old language and thought forms actually points men away from the genuine core of faith to peripheral matters and may demand an entirely unnecessary *sacrificium intellectus*. Moreover, far from being a mere capitulation or conformity to the reigning opinion of 'this world', such an approach is viewed by its creators as the *only* way to face men with the real stumbling block of Christianity (Bultmann, 1953, pp. 1–6, 120–23). What can be the social scientist's justification for calling this effort to make a religious tradition more vital a 'secularization' in the sense of a decline or subversion?

It is evident that part of the difficulty in measuring the decline of religion is the definition of religion itself (Tillich, 1956, pp. 133–8). As we proceed to examine other types of the secularization concept, the issue of the nature of religion will come up again and will finally have to be dealt with explicitly.

Conformity with 'this world'

The religious group or the religiously informed society turns its attention from the supernatural and becomes more and more interested in 'this world'. In ethics there is a corresponding tendency away from an ethic motivated by the desire to prepare for the future life or to conform to the group's ethical tradition toward an ethic adapted to the present exigencies of the surrounding society. *The culmination of secularization would be a society totally absorbed with the pragmatic tasks of the present and a religious group indistinguishable from the rest of society.* Pfautz has defined secularization as 'the tendency of sectarian religious movements to become both part of and like "the world"' (1956).

Examples in research. The classic statement of this position is Harnack's characterization of the early Church's growth in numbers and wealth, its emerging hierarchical organization, and its involvement with Greek thought as a 'secularization' (1901, p. 112). Pfautz's analysis of Christian Science measures conformity to the world in terms of an 'increasing traditional and purposeful-rational motivation, and decreasing affectual motivation' (p. 247). In an important study of the general sect-church spectrum, Pfautz develops a more complex set of variables for measuring secularization in terms of demography, ecology, associational character, structural differentiation and social-psychological texture. The movement across this typology is termed a 'secularization' because it involves a constant increase in size, complexity and rationalization of structures and modes of participation (1955).

By far the most provocative investigation of this type of secularization in America has been Herberg (1955). In his more recent Harlan Paul Douglas lectures he distinguishes between *conventional* religions (e.g. Judaism, Islam, Protestant denominations) and the *operative* religion of a society which actually provides its own 'ultimate context of meaning and value' (1961). Then he defines a secularized culture as one in which 'conventional religion is no longer the operative religion in the sociological sense'. In his earlier book Herberg measured secularization by the degree to which nominal believers who belong to conventional religions actually reflect the outlook of the operative religion of American society (1955, pp. 74–9, 82–3). In the second of his Douglas lectures, he modified Pfautz's typology of religious groups and concluded: 'The series can now be completed: *Cult – sect – denomination – socio-religious community – tri-faith system.* Beyond this, secularization cannot go' (1962).

Assessment. As in the case of the decline thesis, the main difficulty with the idea of secularization as conformity to the world is the ambiguity of the measures applied. Moreover, simply by employing the Church/world or 'this world/other world' dichotomy, the social scientist has taken over a particular theological framework as his own. In any given case we must ask whether something *integral* to a religious tradition is being surrendered in favor of 'this world' or whether the change which is taking place may not be quite compatible with the main stream of the tradition. Is it a subversion of Islam or Christianity that one becomes increasingly concerned with the good life in 'this world', or is it perhaps as much a shift of emphasis from certain elements in these traditions to other elements no less integral? And may not an apparent compromise with the world on the part of a religious group be part of a necessary differentiation within the group which leaves behind the affectional relationships of the 'good old days' without breaking down the core of the tradition?

These observations are not meant to depreciate the usefulness of Pfautz's typology, but rather to question the value of terming the process one of 'increasing secularization' when this implies a deviation or subversion from a more genuinely religious position. A similar objection may be made to Herberg's thesis, since what looks like secularization to Herberg appears to some religious liberals as the triumph of the 'common faith' of America. The latter may be in some respects false or shallow, but it is a misleading (if not simply pejorative) use of the word to term the one religion 'secularized' and treat the other as 'authentic'.

Although the three types of concept we will consider next have not been used as widely in empirical research as the two above, they are worth delineating in equal detail since they are more descriptive and also more suggestive in terms of the relationship between religious change and other variables.

Disengagement of society from religion

Society separates itself from the religious understanding which has previously informed it in order to constitute itself as an autonomous reality and consequently to limit religion to the sphere of private life. The culmination of this kind of secularization would be a religion of a purely inward character, influencing neither institutions nor corporate action, and a society in which religion made no appearance outside the sphere of the religious group. Arendt defines secularization in one place as 'first of all simply the separation of religion and politics' (1963, p. 69). The French thelogian and social analyst Mehl has described secularization as the 'historical process which tends to contest the public role of religion, to substitute other forms of authority for religious authority, and finally to relegate religion to the private sector of human existence' (1966, p. 70).

Examples in research. This understanding of secularization has been extensively investigated by historians, who see it as taking two forms, one intellectual-existential, the other institutional-social. Institutional secularization is usually traced in terms of the rise of the 'secular' state and its gradual assumption of the educational and welfare functions once performed by the churches. A recent non-Western example of this is given in Smith (1963), where it is argued that the Indian government has been secularized in the sense that it has adopted an attitude of neutrality toward both individual and group religious belief and practice. The social transformation which usually accompanies the secularization of the state has been analysed in a variety of ways and has produced studies of the secularization of work, welfare, family life, etc. The intellectual-existential aspect of disengagement has probably been as extensively explored as any phenomenon of secularization. Grotheuysen aptly describes the process as 'the attempt to establish an autonomous sphere of knowledge purged of supernatural, fideistic presuppositions' (1934, vol. 13, p. 631). Concretely, one speaks of the secularization of science or ethics or art in so far as they are separated from ecclesiastical control or from the context of a particular version of the Christian world view.

Assessment. Although more specific than the thesis of decline or conformity with the world, the concept of secularization as disengagement suffers from parallel handicaps. Smith's argument that the Indian state is secularized because it is neutral on religious beliefs and practices has been criticized as overlooking the fact that the Hindu and Islamic faiths have never been a matter of purely private beliefs and practices. Smith's critics suggest that Indian secularity involves a strong dose of secularism, by which they mean a commitment to an ideology which seeks to embrace the whole of life and to replace the role once held by the religious communities (Galanter, 1965). A number of Christian thinkers have made a similar distinction between 'secularization' or 'secularity', which they take as signifying the rejection of religious or ecclesiastical tutelage of society, and 'secularism' as signifying an all-embracing ideology which seeks to deny religious institutions or viewpoints any formative role in society. In reply, Smith acknowledges that the same sort of distinction is actually accepted by many Hindus and Moslems who find the relative restriction of their religious life to the private sphere fully consonant with the integrity of the faith (1965).

By its careful attention to the conceptual problem, Smith's work illustrates the pitfalls of defining secularization as disengagement. His work has also clearly raised the important question of how one decides when secularization in this sense has taken place and when we should speak rather of an internal adjustment within the religious tradition, or even of the triumph of one religion or religiously colored ideology over another.

One way of remedying the defects in the disengagement thesis is to substitute the more descriptive and neutral concept of *'differentiation'* that has been developed by Parsons and Bellah.

Parsons proposes 'differentiation' as an alternative to the interpretation of modern society as undergoing a process of secularization in the sense of a 'decline' of religion (1963, pp. 33–70). In an argument strikingly similar to that proposed by Gogarten, he points out that Christianity contains within itself the principle of differentiation between the community of faith and the social community as well as the differentiation within the religious community between faith and ethics. Similarly, in speaking of the Reformation's extension of the autonomy of the social and economic community and the Reformers' religious enfranchisement of the individual, Parsons notes that the Lutheran concept of the calling could be termed a secularization, but he prefers to see it as the 'endowment of secular life with a new order of religious legitimation' (p. 50). It is indeed true that many of the functions performed by the Churches and religious communities and many of the values of the Christian ethical tradition have been taken over by society at large and generalized. But this is not a sign that the Western religious tradition has collapsed; it is, rather, that the religious community plays an altered role in keeping with the general differentiation of society. Parsons is quite aware, of course, that Christianity has been facing a serious challenge to its understanding of man and the world (p. 69).

Bellah's version of the concept is intended as an overall framework for understanding religious evolution in general. He makes use of Voegelin's notion of the movement from compact to differentiated symbols, as well as describing differentiation within religious groups and between religion and other facets of society (1964). He refuses to consider even the rejection of the natural-supernatural schema and the gradual loss of concern for doctrinal orthodoxy a sign of 'indifference or secularization', seeing it as simply a reflection of a new way of conceiving and practising religion. In this he would be supported by a good number of contemporary theologians. At the least, the concept of differentiation suggests that the idea of secularization as a disengagement of society from religion which reduces religion to insignificance may be a somewhat crude and value-charged designation of a much more complex and subtle phenomenon.

Transposition of religious beliefs and institutions

Knowledge, patterns of behavior and institutional arrangements which were once understood as grounded in divine power are transformed into phenomena of purely human creation and responsibility. In the case of disengagement, the institutions or social arrangements which are secularized are seen as something which did not necessarily belong to the sphere of religion, whereas in the case of transposition it is aspects of religious belief or experience themselves which are shifted from their sacral context to a purely human context. *The culmination of this kind of secularization process would be a totally anthropologized religion and a society which had taken over all the functions previously accruing to the religious institutions.* Writing of the secularization of historical interpretation, Klempt speaks of secularization as the 'transformation of conceptions and modes of thought which were originally developed by the Christian salvation belief and its theology into ones of a world-based outlook' (1960, p. 7).

Examples in research. Although it is difficult to find examples of 'pure' transpositions with no admixture of other ideas or experience, some well-known theses have proposed the 'spirit of capitalism' as a secularization of the Calvinist ethic, the Marxist version of the consumation of the revolution as coming from Jewish–Christian eschatology, phychotherapy as a secular outgrowth of confession and the cure of souls, etc. The classical treatment of transposition comes from Troeltsch, who spoke, for example, of 'the complete severance of sexual feelings from the thought of original sin' which has been effected 'by modern art and poetry' as 'nothing else than the secularization of the intense religious emotions' (1958, p. 96). In another work he writes of the belief in progress as a 'secularization of Christian eschatology' (1922, p. 57).

Assessment. The difficulty with the transposition thesis, of course, is the problem of identifying survivals or transmigrations. Is a supposed transposition really a Jewish or Christian belief or practice now appearing under the guise of a more generalized rationale, or is it something of separate origin and conception which has taken over some of the functions of the former religious phenomenon? We need only call to mind the sharp debate over the Weber thesis to envisage the kind of disagreements which can beset any particular thesis regarding a transposition. The widespread view that Marxism contains a transposition of some Jewish–Christian elements has also come under heavy attack (Wittram, 1965; Desroche, 1962).

The German philosopher Blumenberg has offered what is perhaps the most complete and also the most perceptive critique of the concept of secularization as transposition. Using as his test case the theory that the idea of progress is a secularization of Christian eschatology, he points out that neither is there proof of causal dependence, nor are the two ideas really the same in content; the parallel, rather, is one of function (1964, pp. 249–50).

Another fallacy implicit in the transposition thesis derives from its origin in the use of the term 'secularization' for the transfer of ecclesiastical possessions from the Church to the princes. Is the vision of an ultimate consumation of history, for example, really the 'possession' of Judaism or Christianity so that its later use by other movements must be regarded as a usurpation? (pp. 247–8). Blumenberg goes so far as to suggest that this way of conceiving secularization functions simply as a weapon of the theologians in their attack on the legitimacy of the modern world, and that its use by historians and sociologists reflects a fundamental uncertainty on their part as to the rightful place of the modern outlook. Whether or not one is willing to go that far, it must be admitted that Blumenberg has given us grounds for demanding that any reputed transposition theory pass strict methodological criteria.

Desacralization of the world

The world is gradually deprived of its sacral character as man and nature become the object of rational–causal explanation and manipulation. The culmination of secularization would be a completely 'rational' world society in which the phenomenon of the supernatural or even of 'mystery' would play no part. Historian Kahler writes that secularization means 'that man became independent of religion and lived by reason, face to face with objectified, physical nature' (1943, p. 333).

Examples in research. The classical statement of this view is Weber's concept of 'disenchantment' (*Entzauberung*) which signifies an irreversible trend of rationalization leading to a view of the world as a self-contained causal nexus (Weber, 1948, p. 139). Among contemporary writers, Eliade has given us the most sensitive evocation of the loss (or suppression) of the sense of the sacred. Eliade too finds the root of desacralization in science, which has so neutralized nature and human life that no point can have 'a unique ontological status' which integrates the whole (1961, p. 17).

The proponents of the desacralization thesis do not agree as to how far this process can go. Some apparently feel that it will one day complete itself and religion, in so far as it is bound to an acknowledgement of the 'sacred' or 'holy', will disappear. Others hold that man is 'incurably religious' and believe either that the sense of the sacred has been pushed into the unconscious for the time being or that it is in the process of finding new forms of expression.

Assessment. Although less global and simplistic than the decline thesis, the desacralization concept bears certain similarities to it. The inherent problem with the desacralization view is its assumption that religion is inextricably bound up with an understanding of the world as permeated by sacred powers. There is in the Hebraic faith, however, a definite desacralization of the world through the radical transcendence of the Creator, who alone is eminently holy and who has, moreover, given the world over to the dominion of man (Gen. 1, xxiv). In Christianity the process is carried further through the separation of religion and politics and the notion of sonship through Christ in which man is free from the elemental spirits of the universe (Mark 12; xvii and Gal. 4). This phenomenon of a religious tradition which itself desacralizes the world suggests that the desacralization view of secularization is not applicable to at least the Western tradition without qualification.

Movement from a 'sacred' to a 'secular' society

This is a general concept of *social change*, emphasizing multiple variables through several stages. According to Becker, its chief developer, the main variable is resistance or openness to change. Accordingly, *the culmination of secularization would be a society in which all decisions are based on rational and utilitarian considerations and there is complete acceptance of change* (1957, pp. 133–86; 1964, pp. 613, 626). A theological version of this type of secularization concept has been developed by Meland, who defines secularization as 'the movement away from traditionally accepted norms and sensibilities in the life interests and habits of a people' (1966, p. 3). Since Meland means by sensibilities a capacity to 'respond appreciatively and with restraint to accepted ways of feeling or behavior', secularization does not refer merely to religious phenomena but to any traditional norms and perceptions (p. 8). Since this type of secularization concept is a general theory of social change rather than a theory of specifically religious change, it would take us well beyond the limits of the present inquiry if we were to examine the vast empirical literature that has grown out of it.

The secular—religious polarity

Criticism of 'religion' concept

Because the concept of secularization usually refers back to a secular—religious or sacred–profane polarity, our critique of it has often implied a parallel critique in certain definitions of 'religion'. It is evident that the criticisms made above were aimed at a view of religious phenomena which narrowly restricts them to certain external elements in the Western tradition, e.g. church attendance and financial support, conventional forms of public and private devotional practice, belief scales based on traditional creeds. The suggestion was also made that belief in the supernatural or in sacral powers pervading man and nature is not essential to all the kinds of phenomena we characterize as religious. My reasons for refusing to restrict the understanding of religion in any of these ways is twofold.

In the first place, the range of phenomena which have been considered religious is so varied that no single definition of the 'essence' of religion can embrace them all. Consequently, it would be extremely difficult to discover a list of measurable indices of decline, subversion, transposition or other radical shift away from the 'religious' toward the 'secular'. After examining some of the various ways of defining the polarity, Martin concludes that it is impossible to develop criteria for distinguishing between the religious and the secular since it would be 'an obvious absurdity' to combine 'the metaphysical and mythopoetic modes of thought, the acceptance of miracle, belief in historical purpose, rejection of material benefits, and lack of confidence towards the world under the common rubric of religion' (1965, p. 173).

Secondly, most definitions of the essence of religion, even when they have not been crude combinations of practice and belief, have assumed that there exists an *entity* called 'religion'. This reification, as Smith has pointed out, is of recent origin even in the West, and many of its current connotations represent a polemical situation growing out of the Enlightenment (1964, p. 43). This is perhaps why we not only have numerous Christian theologians denying that Christian faith is a religion (although Christianity may be), but we also have Jewish, Buddhist, Hindu and Muslim thinkers who refuse to consider their faith one of the 'religions'.

Tillich has even suggested that the existence of a religious as opposed to a secular realm in human experience is an expression of 'the tragic estrangement of man's spiritual life from its own ground and depth' (1959, p. 8). Thus, the notion of a religion as a separate part of culture presupposes an advanced stage of differentiation and reflects an attitude contrary to the way at least some of the adherents understand their own tradition. Therefore, I can sympathize with Smith's suggestion that we drop the substantive form 'religion' altogether and use the concepts 'faith' and 'tradition' to convey respectively the interior and external aspects of what have been called 'the religions' (1964, pp. 139–81). This does not mean, of course, that we should give up the attempt to describe the quality or qualities which may be designated 'religious', e.g. 'ultimate concern', 'openness for mystery', 'apprehension of harmony', 'commitment to creativity'. But unfortunately, even the term 'religious' continues to retain many connotations which would lead sensitive persons to hesitate to apply it to themselves or to their tradition.

Criticism of polarity

Before leaving the problem of the definition of 'religion' and the 'religious' one further critical question needs to be raised. Must we think in polar terms at all? There are three disadvantages to a polar concept of the secular-religious type.

First, it tends to deceive us into taking a particular form of differentiation in the West as normative. Berkes has pointed out that the usual dichotomy is based on the Western model of 'church' and 'state', which presupposes an institutionalized religion distinct from the political order. When we apply this 'spiritual-temporal' polarity to non-Western situations where such differentiations did not originally exist, we falsify the data (1963).

Second, the secular–religious polarity easily encourages the assumption that an increase of activity in the so-called secular sphere must mean a corresponding decline in the religious area. But, as Hexter has remarked of this particular intellectual trap, there is considerable evidence that in some periods of history—the sixteenth century is one—*both* aspects of society rose to higher levels of intensity (1961, pp. 40–3).

Finally, the secular–religious polarity simply compounds the deception in the idea that religion is an entity of some kind. For if one does not begin by defining religion or the religious in terms of institutional or behavioral traits there will be no need to find a polar opposite. When 'religious' is used to designate a certain quality of life or dimension of individual and social experience which concerns the whole man and the whole of society, this dimension may be as much in play in certain activities conventionally labeled 'secular' as it is not in play in some that are conventionally labeled 'religious.'

Conclusion

During its long development the term 'secularization' has often served the partisans of controversy and has constantly taken on new meanings without completely losing old ones. As a result it is swollen with overtones and implications, especially those associated with indifference or hostility to whatever is considered 'religious'.

On one hand, Martin has gone so far as to suggest that it has been a 'tool of counter-religious ideologies', which define the 'real' basis of religion and claim that religion so defined is in a process of irreversible decline. Martin believes the motives behind this are partly 'the aesthetic satisfactions found in such notions and partly as a psychological boost to the movements with which they are associated' (1965, p. 176).

At the other end of the spectrum are the all too familiar clerical lamentations over the increase of 'secularism'. Blumenberg, as we have seen, even suggests that the concept of secularization has been a tool of those theologians and clerics who want to impugn the legitimacy of the modern world.

As if the conceptual situation were not confusing enough, the current enthusiasm in theology for styling one's version of Christianity 'secular' muddies the conceptual waters almost to the point of hopelessness. As noted above, behind the present secular theology fad lies the work of several more sober theologians (Bonhoeffer, Gogarten, Michalson) who have worked out a sophisticated defence of secularization conceived in terms of man's coming into responsibility for his own destiny. To them, what Herberg calls a secularization of society is actually the triumph of 'religion', whereas the legitimate outcome of faith would be the secularization of society in the sense of neutralizing conventional religiosity. Although Bonhoeffer and Gogarten do not style themselves 'secular' theologians, the recent rash of books proclaiming 'the secular meaning of the Gospel' or a 'secular Christianity', or praising the 'secular city' as the solely authentic place of Christian existence have made 'secularization' once again an ecclesiastical battle slogan by stinging traditionalists and conservatives into a counter attack on this 'secularization of Christianity' (Mascall, 1965; Van Buren, 1963; Smith, 1966; Cox, 1965).

This accumulation of contradictory connotations would be enough of a handicap, but there is an even more serious one in the fact that so many different processes and phenomena are designated by the term 'secularization'. Often the same writer will use it in two or more senses without acknowledging the shift of meaning. Thus Weber could employ it not only for 'disenchantment' but also for transpositions (spirit of capitalism), and at times even in the sense of becoming 'worldly', as when he speaks of the 'secularizing influence of wealth' on monasticism (1930, p. 174).

The appropriate conclusion to draw from the confusing connotations and the multitude of phenomena covered by the term secularization would seem to be that we drop the word entirely and employ instead terms such as 'transposition' or 'differentiation' which are both more descriptive and neutral.

Since a moratorium on any widely used term is unlikely to be effected, however, there are two ways of salvaging 'secularization' as a useful concept in empirical research. One, of course, is for everyone who employs it to state carefully his intended meaning and to stick to it.

The other is for researchers to agree on the term as a general designation or large-scale concept covering certain subsumed aspects of religious change.

Three of the processes discussed above could be embraced significantly by the term 'secularization' since they are not contradictory but complementary: desacralization, differentiation and transposition. To a certain degree they can also be seen as representing successive and overlapping emphases in Western religious history. Although the desacralization of nature and history, for example, seems to have generally preceded political and social differentiation, the former was not accomplished all at once. And it is evident that transposition cannot take place without the prior or concomitant occurrence of differentiation. To work out the exact bearing of and the measurement criteria for these sub-concepts is a task that still requires considerable reflection. I am afraid, however, that the careless and partisan use of 'secularization' is so general that its polemical connotations will continue to cling to it despite the social scientist's efforts to neutralize it.

References

ARENDT, H. (1963), *Between Past and Future*, Meridian Books.

BECKER, H. (1957), 'The current secular-sacred theory and its development', in H. Becker and A. Boskoff (eds.), *Modern Sociological Theory in Continuity and Change*, Holt, Rinehart & Winston.

BECKER, H. (1964), 'Sacred society and secular society', in J. Gould and W. L. Kolb (eds.), *A Dictionary of the Social Sciences*, Free Press.

BELLAH, R. N. (1964), 'Religious evolution', *Amer. Sociol. Rev.*, vol. 29, no. 3, pp. 358–74.

BERKES, N. (1963), 'Religious and secular institutions in comparative perspective', *Archives de Sociologie des Religions*, vol. 8, no. 16, pp. 65–72.

BLUMENBERG, H. (1964), 'Säkularisation: Kritik einer Kategorie Historischer Illegitimität', in H. Kuhn and F. Wiedmann (eds.), *Die Philosophie und die Frage nach den Fortschritt*, Pustet.

BULTMANN, R. (1953), 'The New Testament and mythology', in H. W. Bartsch (ed.), *Kerygma and Myth*, SPCK.

COX, H. (1965), *The Secular City*, Macmillan.

DESROCHE, H. (1962), *Marxisme et Religions*, Presses Universitaires de France.

ELIADE, M. (1961), *The Sacred and the Profane*, Harper & Row.

GALANTER, M. (1965), 'Secularism, east and west, *Comparative Studies in Society and History*, vol. 7, no. 1, pp. 148–53.

GLOCK, C. Y., and STARK, R. (1965), *Religion and Society in Tension*, Rand McNally.

GROTHEUYSEN, B. (1934), 'Secularism', *Encyclopaedia of Social Sciences*.

HARNACK, A. (1901), *Monasticism: Its Ideals and History*, Williams Norgate.

HERBERG, W. (1955), *Protestant–Catholic–Jew*, Doubleday.

HERBERG, W. (1961), 'Religion in a secularized society: the new shape of religion in America', *Rev. relig. Res.*, vol. 3, no. 1, pp. 145–58.

HERBERG, W. (1962), 'The new shape of American religion: some aspects of America's three-religion pluralism', *Rev. relig. Res.*, vol. 4, no. 3, pp. 33–45.

HEXTER, J. H. (1961), *Reappraisals in History*, Harper & Row.

KAHLER, E. (1943), *Man the Measure*, Random House.

KLEMPT, A. (1960), *Die Säckularisieung der Universalhistorischen*, Auffassung, Musterschmidt.

LEBRAS, G. (1963), 'Déchristianisation: mot fallacieux', *Social Compass*, vol. 10, pp. 448–51.

LYND, R. S., and H. M. (1929), *Middletown*, Harcourt, Brace & World.

MARTIN, D. (1965), 'Towards eliminating the concept of secularization', in J. Gould (ed.), *Penguin Survey of the Social Sciences*, Penguin.

MARTIN, D. (1966). 'Utopian aspects of the concept of secularization', *International Yearbook for the Sociology of Religion*, Westdeutscher Verlag.

MASCALL, E. L. (1965), *The Secularization of Christianity*, Longman.

MEHL, R. (1966), 'De la sécularisation à l'athéisme, *Foi et Vie*, vol. 65.

MELAND, B. E. (1966), *The Secularization of Modern Cultures*, Oxford University Press.

PARSONS, T. (1963), 'Christianity and modern industrial society', in E. A. Tiryakian (ed.), *Sociological Theory, Values and Socio-Cultural Change*, Free Press.

PFAUTZ, H. (1955), 'The sociology of secularization: religious groups', *Amer. J. Sociol.*, vol. 61, no. 5, pp. 121–8.

PFAUTZ, H. (1956), 'Christian Science: a case study of the social psychological aspect of secularization', *Social Forces*, vol. 34, no. 4, pp. 121–8.

SMITH, D. E. (1963), *India as a Secular State*, Princeton University Press.

SMITH, D. E. (1965), 'Secularism in India', *Comparative Studies in Society and History*, vol. 7, pp. 169–70.

SMITH, R. G. (1966), *Secular Christianity*, Harper & Row.

SMITH, W. C. (1964), *The Meaning and End of Religion*, New American Library.

SOROKIN, P. A. (1966), 'The Western religion and morality of today', *International Yearbook of the Sociology of Religion*, Westdeutscher Verlag.

TILLICH, P. (1956), 'Existentialist aspects of modern art', in C. Michalson (ed.), *Christianity and the Existentialists*, Scribner.

TILLICH, P. (1959), *Theology of Culture*, Oxford University Press.

TROELTSCH, E. (1922), *Der Historismus und seine Probleme*, Mohr.

TROELTSCH, E. (1958), *Protestantism and Progress*, Beacon Press.

VAN BUREN, P. M. (1963), *The Secular Meaning of the Gospel*, S C M Press.

WEBER, M. (1930), *The Protestant Ethic and the Spirit of Capitalism*, Allen & Unwin.

WEBER, M. (1948), 'Science as a vocation', in H. Gerth and C. W. Mills (eds.), *From Max Weber: Essays in Sociology*, Routledge & Kegan Paul.

WITTRAM, R. (1965), 'Möglichkeiten und Grenzen der Geschichtswissenschaft in der Gegenwart', *Zeitschrift für Theologie und Kirche*, vol. 62, pp. 430–57.

YINGER, J. M. (1957), *Religion, Society and the Individual*, Macmillan.

Part Five **Sociological Perspectives**

The first part of this book dealt with the emergence of sociology
as a new and distinct perspective. But it was explicitly stated by
Gouldner, and also implied by some of the other writers, that sociology's
vision of man and society contained a variety of assumptions – some
of them contradictory. There were also problems in developing
a methodology that did justice to the unique character of
human life whilst at the same time observing the rigorous requirements
for scientific explanation.

The final part of the book will deal with some of those problems
and will provide material on the basis of which the reader can
form an opinion as to whether there is in fact one sociological
perspective or many.

In Reading 36 Robert Nisbet makes a strong case for seeing
sociology as a combination of science and art.

Ernest Nagel (Reading 37) and Alfred Schutz (Reading 38)
debate the question as to whether the character of social
phenomena is such as to require a special type of explanation
not found in the rest of science. Specifically, they discuss whether
Max Weber's claim that the social sciences should seek to
'understand' social phenomena in terms of 'meaningful' categories
of human experience entails a rejection of the kind of causal
explanation employed by the natural sciences.

Harold Fallding (Reading 39) throws some light on the problem
by showing that ideal types and models, such as Weber's
ideal type bureaucracy and Spencer's analogy of the social system
as an organism, are not in themselves explanatory theories. However,
they are useful in suggesting hypotheses that can then be tested
and so lead to an explanatory theory.

The piece by Jack Douglas (Reading 40) on the social meanings
of suicide brings out some of the difficulties faced by sociology
when it seeks to penetrate below the surface of events in its
explanations. Although suicides are external events which can be

statistically correlated with other aggregates such as particular groups, the meaning of suicide may vary from group to group and between individuals.

Johan Galtung (Reading 41) explores some of these same problems in the context of discussing the relative merits of different methods of data collection.

The article by Alan Dawe (Reading 42) takes us back to the issue raised at the beginning of the book by Gouldner: Are there in fact two radically opposed views within sociology with regard to the relationship between society and the individual? Dawe maintains that there are, and that conflict between the 'system' approach and the 'action' approach existed in the work of all the founding fathers of the classic tradition in sociology and still continues.

Peter Berger and Thomas Luckmann (Reading 43) discuss to what extent the two views of the relation between the individual and society are complementary or in conflict, in view of the fact that society seems to exist as both objective and subjective reality. In other words: Do the two approaches of social systems and social action theory simply correspond to our own ambivalent experience of society as something that constrains us and yet also something that we ourselves construct? Berger and Luckmann think that their own brand of action theory can deal with both experiences.

David Silverman (Reading 44) continues the argument and opts for the view that the two approaches offer conflicting rather than complementary frames of reference.

36 Robert A. Nisbet

Sociology as an Art Form

Excerpts from Robert A. Nisbet, *Tradition and Revolt*,
Random House, 1968, pp. 143–62. First published in the
Pacific Sociological Review, 1962.

I admit readily that both by temperament and academic background I have always been more interested in the non-uses of our discipline than the uses. I admit further to believing that theories should be tested as much by their reach as their grasp, their importance as their validity, and their elegance as their congruence with such facts as may be at hand. It is my major contention that the science of sociology makes its most significant intellectual advances under the spur of stimuli and through processes that it largely shares with art; that whatever the differences between science and art, it is what they have in common that matters most in discovery and creativeness.

Nothing I say is intended to imply that sociology is not a science. I am quite willing, for the present purposes, to put sociology on the same line with physics and biology, applying to each of these the essence of what I say about sociology. Each is indeed a science, but each is a form of art, and if we forget this we run the risk of losing the science, finding ourselves with a sandheap empiricism or methodological narcissism, each as far from science as art is from billboard advertisements.

My interest in sociology as an art form was stimulated recently by some reflections on ideas that are by common assent among the most distinctive that sociology has contributed to modern thought. Let me mention these: *mass society, alienation, anomie, rationalization, community, disorganization*. I will have more to say about these ideas and their contexts a little later. Here it suffices to note that all of them have had lasting effect upon both the theoretical and empirical character of sociology. And all have exerted notable influence on other fields of thought, scientific and humanistic.

It occurred to me that not one of these ideas is historically the result of the application of what we are today pleased to call scientific method. If there is evidence that any one of these ideas as first set forth in the writings of such men as Tocqueville, Weber, Simmel and Durkheim, is the result of problem-solving thought, proceeding rigorously and self-consciously from question to hypothesis to verified conclusion, I have been unable to discover it. On the contrary, each of these profound and seminal ideas would appear to be the consequence of intellectual processes bearing much more relation to the artist than the scientist, as the latter tends to be conceived by most of us. Apart from processes of intuition, impressionism, iconic imagination (the phrase is Sir Herbert Read's), and even objectification, it seems unlikely that any one of these ideas would have come into being to influence generations of subsequent thought and teaching. [...]

It is time to return to the ideas in sociology I referred to at the outset of my paper. Let me describe them briefly again, for they are indubitably the most distinctive and illuminating contributions of sociology to the study of culture and society. There is, first, the view of human association as containing endemic processes of disorganization, dysfunction, call them what we will. Second, there is the view of the individual as alienated and anomic. Third, there is the perspective of community – in contrast to rationalistic and contractual forms of relationship – involving the key concepts of hierarchy and status. Fourth, we have the great theme of rationalization as a process in history and in the whole structure of modern society.

We know where these ideas came from: from the writings of four or five remarkable minds in the late nineteenth century: Tocqueville, Weber, Simmel, Tönnies and Durkheim. I need not enlarge upon their formulations of the ideas. I am more interested in the processes by which the ideas came into being: that is, the contexts in which the ideas were uttered, the traditions they came out of, and, if it were possible, the mental states behind the ideas. Obviously, we are limited in what we can say positively, but I believe certain points are clear.

There is, first, the manifest discontinuity of these ideas in the history of modern social thought. Not one of them could have been deduced from the propositions of rationalism on human behavior that flourished in the Enlightenment. The true heritage of the Enlightenment is to be found, not in sociology, but in classical economics, individual psychology and utilitarian political science. What we find in sociology – that is, in its distinctive currents – is a revolt against the rationalist view of man and society.

The second point is this. Not only are the key ideas of sociology unrelated to prior 'scientific' ideas; they have their closest affinity with an art movement, Romanticism. In the same way that the Renaissance image of man proceeded from prior currents in art, so, I argue, the sociological image arises in the first instance from visions which had their earliest and most far reaching appeal in Romantic art.

Weber has somewhere likened his own concept of rationalization to the poet Schiller's earlier view of the 'disenchantment of the world'. He was candid and accurate. Tocqueville, Simmel and Durkheim might well have done likewise. From the first burst of the Romantic spirit in the late eighteenth century – rising to do battle with the classicist–rationalist view – we find luminously revealed two central visions:

1. The estrangement of the individual from a growingly impersonal and disorganized society (and the consequent spiritual inaccessibility of modern institutions – city, factory, mass society).

2. A celebration of status and community – whether rural, religious or moral – in contrast to the individualistic and contractural society of the *philosophes*.

Third, and most important, even if most elusive, are the psychological affinities between the Romantic artists and the sociologists. It is impossible, as I have already suggested, to entertain seriously the thought that these major ideas were arrived at in a manner comparable to what we think of as scientific methodology. Can you imagine what would have happened had any one of them been subjected, at the moment following its inception, to a rigorous design analysis? Can anyone believe that Weber's vision of rationalization in history, Simmel's vision of metropolis or Durkheim's vision of *anomie*, came from logico-empirical analysis as this is understood today? Merely to ask the question is to know the answer. Plainly, these men were not working with finite and ordered problems in front of them. They were not problem-solving at all. Each was, with deep intuition, with profound imaginative grasp, reacting to the world around him, even as does the artist, and, also like the artist, objectifying internal and only partly conscious, states of mind.

Consider one example: the view of society and man that underlies Durkheim's great study of suicide. Basically, it is the view of the artist as much as that of the scientist. Background, detail and characterization blend into something that is iconic in its grasp of an entire social order. How did Durkheim get his controlling idea? We may be sure of one thing: he did not get it, as the stork story of science might have it, from a preliminary examination of the vital registers of Europe, any more than Darwin got the idea of natural selection from his observations during the voyage of the *Beagle*. The idea, the plot and the conclusion of *Suicide* were well in his mind before he examined the registers. Where, then, did he get the idea?

We can only speculate. He might have got it from reading Tocqueville who could certainly have got it from Lamennais who could have got it from Bonald or Chateaubriand. Or, it could have come from personal experience – from a remembered fragment of the Talmud, from an intuition born of personal loneliness and marginality, a scrap of experience in Paris. Who can be sure? But one thing is certain. The creative blend of ideas behind *Suicide* – a blend from which we still draw in our scientific labors – was reached in ways more akin to those of the artist than to those of the data processor, the logician, or the technologist.

It is not different with the ideas and perspectives of Simmel – in many ways the most imaginative and intuitive of all the great sociologists. His treatment of fear, love, conventionality, power and friendship show the mind of the artist–essayist, and it is no distortion of values to place him with such masters as Montaigne and Bacon. Remove the artist's vision from the treatments of the stranger, the dyad and the role of secrecy, and you have removed all that gives life. In Simmel there is that wonderful tension between the esthetically concrete and the philosophically general that always lies in greatness. It is the esthetic element in Simmel's work that makes impossible the full absorption of his sociological substance by anonymous, systematic theory. One must go back to Simmel himself for the real insight. As with Darwin and Freud, it will always be possible to derive something of importance from the man directly that cannot be gleaned from impersonal statements in social theory.

This leads to another important fact. Our dependence upon these ideas and their makers is akin to the artist's dependence upon the artists who precede him. In the same way that the novelist will always be able to learn from a study and re-study of Dostoyevsky or James – to learn a sense of development and form, as well as to draw inspiration from the creative source – so the sociologist can forever learn from a re-reading of such men as Weber and Simmel.

It is this element that separates sociology from some of the physical sciences. There is, after all, a limit to what the young physicist can learn from even a Newton. Having once grasped the fundamental points of the *Principia*, he is not likely to draw very much as a physicist from re-readings (though he could as a historian of science). How different is the relation of the sociologist to a Simmel or Durkheim. Always there will be something to be gained from a direct reading; something that is informative, enlarging and creative. This is precisely like the contemporary artist's return to the study of medieval architecture, the Elizabethan sonnet or the paintings of

Matisse. This is the essence of the history of art, and why the history of sociology is so different from the history of science.

That such men as Weber, Durkheim and Simmel fall in the scientific tradition is unquestioned. Their works, for all the deep artistic sensitivity and intuition, no more belong in the history of art than the works of Balzac or Dickens do in the history of social science. The conclusion we draw is not that science and art are without differences. There are real differences, as there are among the arts and among the sciences.[1] No one asks a Picasso to verify one of his visions by repeating the process; and, conversely, we properly give short shrift to ideas in science that no one but the author can find supported by experience. The ideas of Durkheim may, as I have suggested, be dependent upon thought-processes like those of the artist, but none of them would have survived in sociology or become fruitful for others were it not for criteria and modes of communication that differ from those in art.

The conclusion, then, is not that science and art are, or should be, alike. It is the simpler but more fundamental conclusion that in both art and science the same type of creative imagination works. And everything that impedes or frustrates this imagination strikes at the source of the discipline itself.

1. Charles Morris, the philosopher, has suggested that the major difference is this: although both science and art communicate by the use of ideas and representations not completely describable in terms of sense experience, science typically seeks to make its communications capable of identification or verification by the largest number of individuals, whereas art tends to insist that each individual translate the original vision into something peculiarly his own creation.

37 Ernest Nagel

Problems of Concept and Theory Formation in the
Social Sciences

Excerpt from Ernest Nagel, 'Problems of concept and theory formation in the
social sciences', in M. Natanson (ed.), *Philosophy of the Social Sciences*,
Random House, 1963, pp. 189–209. First published in *Science,
Language and Human Rights*, 1952.

In the study of biological functions the imputation of motives,
attitudes and purposes to organic systems, or their parts, is strictly
irrelevant. In the study of social phenomena such imputation is highly
pertinent. What is the significance of this fact for the objectives and
the methods of the social sciences?

According to an influential school of functionalists, all socially
significant human behavior is an expression of motivated psychic
states, so that the 'dynamism' of social processes is identified with the
'value-oriented' behavior of human individuals. An inquiry that is
properly a *social* study has been therefore said to begin only with the
question: 'What motives determine and lead the individual members
and participants in [a given] community to behave in such a way that
the community comes into being in the first place and that it continues
to exist?' (Weber, 1964, p. 107). In consequence, the social scientist
cannot be satisfied with viewing social processes simply as the
sequential concatenations of 'externally related' events; and the establishment of correlations, or even of universal relations of concomitance, cannot be his ultimate goal. For he must not ignore the fact
that every social change involves the assessment and readjustment of
human activities relating means to ends (or 'values'). On the contrary,
he must construct 'ideal types' or 'models of motivation', in terms of
which he seeks to 'understand' overt social behavior by imputing
springs of action to the actors involved in it. But these springs of action
are not accessible to sensory observation; and the social scientist who
wishes to understand social phenomena must imaginatively identify
himself with its participants, and view the situation which they face
as the actors themselves view it. Social phenomena are indeed not
generally the *intended* resultants of individual actions; nevertheless
the central task of social science is the explanation of phenomena as
the unintended outcome of springs of action – of psychic states which
are familiar to us solely from our own 'subjective' experiences as
volitional agents.

In consequence, there is said to be a radical difference between explanations in the social and in the natural sciences. In the latter we allegedly understand the 'causal nexus' of events only in an external manner; in the former we can grasp the peculiar unity of social processes, since these involve a dynamic synthesis of subjective urges, values and goals, on the one hand, and the external environment on the other. A purely 'objective' or 'behavioristic' social science is thus declared to be a vain hope. For in the words of one recent writer, proponents of behaviorism in social science

fail to perceive the essential difference from the standpoint of causation, between a paper flying before the wind and a man flying from a pursuing crowd. The paper knows no fear and the wind no hate, but without fear and hate the man would not fly nor the crowd pursue. If we try to reduce it to its bodily concomitants we merely substitute the concomitants for the reality expressed as fear. We denude the word of meanings for the sake of a theory, itself a false meaning which deprives us of all the rest. We can interpret experience only on the level of experience (MacIver, 1931, p. 530).

In short, since social science seeks to establish 'meaningful' connections and not merely relations of concomitance, its goal and method are fundamentally different from those of natural science.

I will not take time to comment here at length on the psychological preconceptions underlying this rejection of behaviorism, nor on the adequacy with which behaviorism is portrayed. Only one point requires brief mention in this connection. It is surely not the case that we must ourselves undergo (whether actually or in imagination) other men's psychic experiences in order to know that they have them, or in order to predict their overt behaviors. But if this is so, the alleged 'privacy' or 'subjectivity' of mental states has no bearing on the acquisition of knowledge concerning the character, the determinants and the consequences of other men's dispositions and actions. A historian does not have to be Hitler, or even be capable of reenacting in imagination Hitler's frenzied hatreds, to write competently of Hitler's career and historical significance. For knowledge is not a matter of having images, whether faint or vivid; it is not a reduplication of, or a substitute for, what is claimed to be known. Knowledge involves the discovery through processes of controlled inference that something is a sign of something else; it is statable in propositional form; and it is capable of being verified through sensory observation by anyone who is prepared to make the effort to do so. It is therefore just as possible to know that a man is in a state of fear or that a crowd is animated by hatred, without recreating in imagination such fears and hatreds, as it is to know that a man is running away or that a crowd is pursuing him without an imaginary exercise of one's legs. It is possible to discover and know these things on the evidence supplied by the overt behaviors of men and crowds, just as it is possible to discover and know the atomic constitution of water on the evidence supplied by the physical and chemical behavior of that substance.

But I must consider at greater length the claim that since the social sciences seek to 'understand' social phenomena in terms of 'meaningful' categories of human experience, the 'causal-functional' approach of the natural sciences is not applicable in social inquiry. The abstract pattern of such 'meaningful' explanations appears to be as follows. Let A be some complex set of conditions (e.g. membership in certain religious groups) under which a phenomenon B occurs (e.g. the development of modern forms of capitalistic enterprise). The social agents involved in A and B are then assumed to possess certain feelings, beliefs, etc.: A^1 (e.g. belief in the sacredness of a worldly calling) and B^1 (e.g. prizing of honesty, orderliness and abstemious labor), respectively. Here A^1 and B^1 are supposedly 'meaningfully' related, because of our familiarity with motivational patterns in our own experience; and the relations between A and A^1, as well as between B and B^1, are also of the same alleged kind. Accordingly, the 'external' connection between A and B is 'meaningfully' explained, when each is 'interpreted' as an expression of certain 'motivational' states A^1 and B^1 respectively, where the connection between the latter is 'understood' in a peculiarly intimate way.

But do such explanations require a special kind of logic, distinctive of the social sciences? At the risk of belaboring the obvious, I must state the grounds for maintaining that the answer is negative. The imputation of emotions, attitudes and purposes as an explanation of overt behavior is a twofold hypothesis; it is not a self-certifying one, and evidence for it must be supplied in accordance with customary canons of empirical inquiry. The hypothesis is twofold: for on the one hand, it assumes that the agents participating in some social phenomenon are in certain psychological states; and on the other hand, it also assumes definite relations of concomitance between such states, and between such states and certain overt behaviors. But as the more responsible exponents of 'meaningful' explanations themselves emphasize, it is not easy to obtain competent evidence for either assumption. We may identify ourselves in imagination with a trader in grain, and conjecture what course of action we would take were we confronted with the problems of a fluctuating market. But conjecture is not fact, however necessary conjecture may be as part of the process of discovering what is fact. None of the psychological states which we imagine the subjects of our study to possess may in reality be theirs; and even if our imputations should be correct, none of the overt actions which allegedly issue from those states may appear to us as 'understandable' or 'reasonable' in the light of our own experiences. If the history of anthropological research proves anything, it surely testifies to the errors students commit when they interpret the actions of men in unfamiliar cultures in terms of categories drawn uncritically from their limited personal lives.

Moreover, do we 'understand' the nature and operation of human motives and their issuance in overt behavior more adequately and with greater certitude than we do the occurrences studied in the natural sciences? Do we understand more clearly and know with greater certainty why an insult tends to produce anger than why a rainbow is produced when the sun's rays strike raindrops at a certain angle? The question is rhetorical, for the obvious answer is 'no'. We may feel assured that if an illiterate and impoverished people revolts against its masters, it does so not because of adherence to some political doctrine but because of economic ills. But this assurance may only be the product of familiarity and a limited imagination; and the sense of penetrating comprehension that we may associate with the assertion, instead of guaranteeing its universal truth, may be only a sign of our provincialism. The contrast that is drawn between 'understanding' in terms of 'meaningful' categories and the merely 'external' knowledge of causal relations which the natural sciences are alleged to provide is indeed far from clear. When we 'meaningfully' explain the flight of a man from an angry crowd by imputing to him a fear of physical violence, we surely do not postulate in him a special agency called 'fear' which impels him to run; nor do we intend by such an imputation that a certain immediate quality of the man's experience is the determinant of his action. What I think we are asserting is that his action is an instance of a *pattern of behavior* which human beings exhibit under a varity of circumstances, and that since some of the relevant circumstances are realized in the given situation the person can be expected to manifest a certain particular form of that pattern. But if something like this is the content of explanations in terms of 'meaningful' categories, there is no sharp gulf separating them from explanations that involve merely 'external' knowledge of causal connections.

One final comment in this connection. While the 'dynamism' of social processes is in general identified by many functionalists with the 'motivational' character of human action, some of them have maintained that all social change must be understood in terms of those particular variations in motivation that are called 'values'. Thus, it has been argued that if we wish to ascertain why there has been a pronounced increase in the divorce rate in the US during the past fifty years, a satisfactory explanation must be of the type which stipulates

a change in valuation affecting the status of the family. The general indication is that divorce is more prevalent in those areas where the continuity of the family through several generations has less significance in the schema of cultural values than formerly or elsewhere.

More generally, the claim has been made that 'In so far as we are able to discover the changes of the evaluative schema of social groups we can attain, and thus only, a unified explanation of social change' (MacIver, 1965, pp. 338, 374).

It is not my concern to take sides in an issue of material fact, and in any case I am not qualified to do so in this particular one. But it is relevant to ask how an assumed alteration in a schema of cultural values can be established. The obvious procedure would be to take as evidence for such a change the explicit statements of the persons involved, whether these statements take the form of personal confessions, public speeches or the like. However, explicit statements of the kind required are not generally available ; and even when they are, they cannot always be taken at their face value. For there is often a great disparity between what men verbally profess and what they actually practise, and individuals may continue their verbal allegiance to a set of ideals even though their mode of living has been radically transformed. Students of human affairs are thus compelled to base their conclusions as to what are the operative evaluative schemas in a given society on evidence that is largely drawn from the overt behavior of men – from their conduct of business affairs, their mode of recreation, their domestic arrangements and so on.

There is in fact a risk that explanations of social change in terms of alterations in value-schemas collapse into tautologies, which simply restate in different language what is presumably explained. For example, if a change in the divorce rate is the sole evidence for the assumption that there has been a shift in the value associated with the continuity of the family, a proposed explanation of the former change by the latter is a spurious one. It does not follow that all explanations in terms of variations in evaluative schemas are necessarily sterile. It does follow, however, that if such sterility is to be avoided, the concept of a value-schema must be construed as a highly compact formulation of various regularities (most of which are perhaps never explicitly codified, or codified only in vague terms) between types of human behavior.

The point I wish to make is that in imputing a certain schema of values to a community, one is imputing to its members certain attitudes. But an attitude is not something that can be established by introspection, whether in the case of our own persons or of others. An attitude is a dispositional or latent trait ; and it is comparable in its *theoretical* status with viscosity or electrical resistance in physics, even if, unlike the latter, it can be usefully defined for socio-psychological purposes only in statistical terms. In any event, the concept is cognitively valuable only in so far as it effects a systematic organization of manifest data obtained from overt human responses to a variety of conditions, and only in so far as it makes possible the formulation of regularities in such responses. Whether, in point of fact, explanations of social changes in terms of variations in attitudes have a greater systematizing and predictive power than explanations employing different substantive concepts, is not the point at issue, and it cannot be settled by dogmatic *a priori* claims. But if these comments are well taken, there is nothing in such explanations which differentiates them in principle from explanations in the natural sciences, or which requires for their validation a distinctive logic of inquiry.

References

MacIver, R. M. (1931), *Society: A Textbook of Sociology*, Holt, Rinehart & Winston.
MacIver, R. M. (1965), *Social Causation*, Harper & Row.
Weber, M. (1964), *The Theory of Social and Economic Organization*, Collier-Macmillan.

38 Alfred Schutz

Concept and Theory Formation in the Social Sciences

Excerpt from Alfred Schutz, 'Concept and theory formation in the social sciences', *Journal of Philosophy*, vol. 51, 1954, pp. 257–73. Reprinted with corrections in M. Natanson (ed.), *Alfred Schutz: Collected Papers I: The Problem of Social Reality*, 3 vols Martinhus Nijhoff, 1962, pp. 48–66.

I shall here concentrate on Nagel's criticism of the claim made by Weber and his school that the social sciences seek to 'understand' social phenomena in terms of 'meaningful' categories of human experience and that, therefore, the 'causal–functional' approach of the natural sciences is not applicable in social inquiry. This school, as Nagel sees it, maintains that all socially significant human behavior is an expression of motivated psychic states, that in consequence the social scientist cannot be satisfied with viewing social processes simply as concatenations of 'externally related' events, and that the establishment of correlations or even of universal relations of concomitance cannot be his ultimate goal. On the contrary, he must construct 'ideal types' or 'models of motivations' in terms of which he seeks to 'understand' overt social behavior by imputing springs of action to the actors involved in it. If I understand Nagel's criticism correctly, he maintains:

1. That these springs of action are not accessible to sensory observation. It follows and has frequently been stated that the social scientist must imaginatively identify himself with the participants and view the situation which they face as the actors themselves view it. Surely, however, we need not undergo other men's psychic experiences in order to know that they have them or in order to predict their overt behavior.

2. That the imputation of emotions, attitudes and purposes as an explanation of overt behavior is a twofold hypothesis: it assumes that the agents participating in some social phenomenon are in certain psychological states; and it assumes also definite relations of concomitance between such states, and between such states and overt behavior. Yet none of the psychological states which we imagine the subjects of our study to possess may in reality be theirs, and even if our imputations should be correct none of the overt actions which allegedly issue from those states may appear to us understandable or reasonable.

3. That we do not 'understand' the nature and operations of human

motives and their issuance in overt behavior more adequately than the 'external' causal relations. If by meaningful explanation we assert merely that a particular action is an instance of a pattern of behavior which human beings exhibit under a variety of circumstances and that, since some of the relevant circumstances are realized in the given situation, a person can be expected to manifest a certain form of that pattern, then there is no sharp gulf separating such explanations from those involving merely 'external' knowledge of causal connections. It is possible to gain knowledge of the actions of men on the evidence supplied by their overt behavior just as it is possible to discover and know the atomic constitution of water on the evidence supplied by the physical and chemical behavior of that substance. Hence the rejection of a purely 'objective' or 'behavioristic' social science by the proponents of 'meaningful connections' as the goal of social sciences is unwarranted.

Since I shall have to disagree with Nagel's and Hempel's findings on several questions of a fundamental nature, I might be permitted to start with a brief summary of the no less important points on which I find myself happily in full agreement with them. I agree with Nagel that all empirical knowledge involves discovery through processes of controlled inference, and that it must be stateable in propositional form and capable of being verified by anyone who is prepared to make the effort to do so through observation – although I do not believe, as Nagel does, that this observation has to be sensory in the precise meaning of this term. Moreover, I agree with him that 'theory' means in all empirical sciences the explicit formulation of determinate relations between a set of variables in terms of which a fairly extensive class of empirically ascertainable regularities can be explained. Furthermore, I agree wholeheartedly with his statement that neither the fact that these regularities have in the social sciences a rather narrowly restricted universality, nor the fact that they permit prediction only to a rather limited extent, constitutes a basic difference between the social and the natural sciences, since many branches of the latter show the same features. As I shall try to show later on, it seems to me that Nagel misunderstands Weber's postulate of subjective interpretation. Nevertheless, he is right in stating that a method which would require that the individual scientific observer identify himself with the social agent observed in order to understand the motives of the latter, or a method which would refer the selection of the facts observed and their interpretation to the private value system of the particular observer, would merely lead to an uncontrollable private and subjective image in the mind of this particular student of human affairs, but never to a scientific theory. But I do not know of any social scientist of stature who ever advocated such a concept of subjectivity as that criticized by Nagel. Most certainly this was not the position of Weber.

I also think that our authors are prevented from grasping the point of vital concern to social scientists by their basic philosophy of sensationalistic empiricism or logical positivism, which identifies experience with sensory observation and which assumes that the only alternative to controllable and, therefore, objective sensory observation is that of subjective and, therefore, uncontrollable and unverifiable introspection. This is certainly not the place to renew the age-old controversy relating to the hidden presuppositions and implied metaphysical assumptions of this basic philosophy. On the other hand, in order to account for my own position, I should have to treat at length certain principles of phenomenology. Instead of doing so, I propose to defend a few rather simple propositions:

1. The primary goal of the social sciences is to obtain organized knowledge of social reality. By the term 'social reality' I wish to be understood the sum total of objects and occurrences within the social cultural world as experienced by the common-sense thinking of men living their daily lives among their fellow-men, connected with them in manifold relations of interaction. It is the world of cultural objects and social institutions into which we all are born, within which we have to find our bearings, and with which we have to come to terms. From the outset, we, the actors on the social scene, experience the world we live in as a world both of nature and of culture, not as a private but as an intersubjective one, that is, as a world common to all of us, either actually given or potentially accessible to everyone; and this involves intercommunication and language.

2. All forms of naturalism and logical empiricism simply take for granted this social reality, which is the proper object of the social sciences. Intersubjectivity, interaction, intercommunication and language are simply presupposed as the unclarified foundation of these theories. They assume, as it were, that the social scientist has already solved his fundamental problem, before scientific inquiry starts. To be sure, Dewey emphasized, with a clarity worthy of this eminent philosopher, that all inquiry starts and ends within the social cultural matrix; to be sure, Nagel is fully aware of the fact that science and its self-correcting process is a social enterprise. But the postulate of describing and explaining human behavior in terms of controllable sensory observation stops short before the description and explanation of the process by which scientist B controls and verifies the observational findings of scientist A and the conclusions drawn by him. In order to do so, B has to know what A has ob-

served, what the goal of his inquiry is, why he thought the observed fact worthy of being observed, i.e. relevant to the scientific problem at hand, etc. The knowledge is commonly called understanding. The explanation of how such a mutual understanding of human beings might occur is apparently left to the social scientist. But whatever his explanation might be, one thing is sure, namely, that such an intersubjective understanding between scientist B and scientist A occurs neither by scientist B's observations of scientist A's overt behavior, nor by introspection performed by B, nor by identification of B with A. To translate this argument into the language dear to logical positivism, this means, as Kaufmann (1944, p. 126), has shown, that so-called protocol propositions about the physical world are of an entirely different kind than protocol propositions about the psycho-physical world.

3. The identification of experience with sensory observation in general and of the experience of overt action in particular (and that is what Nagel proposes) excludes several dimensions of social reality from all possible inquiry.

(a) Even an ideally refined behaviorism can, as has been pointed out for instance by Mead (1934), merely explain the behavior of the observed, not of the observing behaviorist.

(b) The same overt behavior (say a tribal pageant as it can be captured by the movie camera) may have an entirely different meaning to the performers. What interests the social scientist is merely whether it is a war dance, a barter trade, the reception of a friendly ambassador or something else of this sort.

(c) Moreover, the concept of human action in terms of common-sense thinking and of the social sciences includes what may be called 'negative actions', i.e. intentional refraining from acting (Weber, 1964, p. 88), which, of course, escapes sensory observation. Not to sell certain merchandise at a given price is doubtless as economic an action as to sell it.

(d) Furthermore, as Thomas has shown (1951, p. 81), social reality contains elements of beliefs and convictions which are real because they are so defined by the participants and which escape sensory observation. To the inhabitants of Salem in the seventeenth century, witchcraft was not a delusion but an element of their social reality and is as such open to investigation by the social scientists.

(e) Finally, and this is the most important point, the postulate of sensory observation of overt human behavior takes as a model a particular and relatively small sector of the social world, namely, situations in which the acting individual is given to the observer in what is commonly called a face-to-face relationship. But there are many other dimensions of the social world in which situations of this kind do not prevail. If we put a letter in the mailbox we assume that anonymous fellow-men, called post-men, will perform a series of manipulations, unknown and unobservable to us, with the effect that the addressee, possibly also unknown to us, will receive the message and react in a way which also escapes our sensory observation ; and the result of all this is that we receive the book we have ordered. Or if I read an editorial stating that France fears the rearm-ament of Germany, I know perfectly well what this statement means without knowing the editorialist and even without knowing a French-man or a German, let alone without observing their overt behavior.

In terms of common-sense thinking in everyday life men have know-ledge of these various dimensions of the social world in which they live. To be sure, this knowledge is not only fragmentary since it is restricted principally to certain sectors of this world, it is also frequently inconsis-tent in itself and shows all degrees of clarity and distinctness from full insight or 'knowledge-about', as James (1890, p. 221) called it, through 'knowledge of acquaintance' or mere familiarity, to blind belief in things just taken for granted. In this respect there are considerable differences from individual to individual and from social group to social group. Yet, in spite of all these inadequacies, common-sense knowledge of everyday life is sufficient for coming to terms with fellow-men, cultural objects, social institutions – in brief, with social reality. This is so, because the world (the natural and the social one) is from the outset an intersubjective world and because, as shall be pointed out later on, our knowledge of it is in various ways socialized. Moreover, the social world is experienced from the outset as a meaningful one. The Other's body is not experienced as an organism but as a fellow-man, its overt behavior not as an occur-rence in the space-time of the outer world, but as our fellow-man's action. We normally 'know' what the Other does, for what reason he does it, why he does it at this particular time and in these particular circumstances. That means that we experience our fellow-man's action in terms of his motives and goals. And in the same way, we experience cultural objects in terms of the human action of which they are the result. A tool, for example, is not experienced as a thing in the outer world (which of course it is also) but in terms of the purpose for which it was designed by more or less anonymous fellow-men and its possible use by others.

The fact that in common-sense thinking we take for granted our actual or potential knowledge of the meaning of human actions and their pro-ducts, is, I suggest, precisely what social scientists want to express if they speak of understanding or *Verstehen* as a technique of dealing with human affairs. *Verstehen* is, thus, primarily not a method used by the social scientist, but the particular experiential form in which common-sense thinking takes cognizance of the social cultural world. It has nothing to do with introspection; it is a result of processes of learning or acculturation in the same way as the common-sense experience of the so-called natural world. *Verstehen* is, moreover, by no means a private affair of the observer which cannot be controlled by the experiences of other observers. It is controllable at least to the same extent to which the private sensory perceptions of an individual are controllable by any other individual under certain conditions. You have just to think of the discussion by a trial jury of whether the defendant has shown 'pre-meditated malice' or 'intent' in killing a person, whether he was capable of knowing the consequences of his deed, etc. Here we even have certain 'rules of procedure' furnished by the 'rules of evidence' in the juridical sense and a kind of verification of the findings resulting from processes of *Verstehen* by the Appellate Court, etc. Moreover, predictions based on *Verstehen* are continuously made in common-sense thinking with high success. There is more than a fair chance that a duly stamped and addressed letter put in a New York mailbox will reach the addressee in Chicago.

Nevertheless, both defenders and critics of the process of *Verstehen* maintain, and with good reason, that *Verstehen* is 'subjective'. Unfortunately, however, this term is used by each party in a different sense. The critics of understanding call it subjective, because they hold that understanding the motives of another man's action depends upon the private, uncontrollable and unverifiable intuition of the observer or refers to his private value system. The social scientists, such as Weber, however, call *Verstehen* subjective because its goal is to find out what the actor 'means' in his action, in contrast to the meaning which this action has for the actor's partner or a neutral observer. This is the origin of Weber's famous postulate of subjective interpretation, of which more will have to be said in what follows. The whole discussion suffers from the failure to distinguish clearly between *Verstehen* (a) as the experiential form of common-sense knowledge of human affairs, (b) as an epistemological problem, and (c) as a method peculiar to the social sciences.

So far we have concentrated on *Verstehen* as the way in which common-sense thinking finds its bearing within the social world and comes to terms with it. As to the epistemological question: 'How is such understanding or *Verstehen* possible?' Alluding to a statement Kant made in another context, I suggest that it is a 'scandal of philosophy' that so far a satisfactory solution to the problem of our knowledge of other minds and, in connection therewith, of the intersubjectivity of our experience of the natural as well as the socio-cultural world has not been found and that, until rather recent times, this problem has even escaped the attention of philosophers. But the solution of this most difficult problem of philosophical interpretation is one of the first things taken for granted in our common-sense thinking and practically solved without any difficulty in each of our everyday actions. And since human beings are born of mothers and not concocted in retorts, the experience of the existence of other human beings and of the meaning of their actions is certainly the first and most original empirical observation man makes.

On the other hand, philosophers as different as James, Bergson, Dewey, Husserl and Whitehead agree that the common-sense knowledge of everyday life is the unquestioned but always questionable background within which inquiry starts and within which alone it can be carried out. It is this *Lebenswelt*, as Husserl calls it, within which, according to him, all scientific and even logical concepts originate ; it is the social matrix within which, according to Dewey, unclarified situations emerge, which have to be transformed by the process of inquiry into warranted assertibility; and Whitehead has pointed out that it is the aim of science to produce a theory which agrees with experience by explaining the thought objects constructed by common sense through the mental constructs or thought objects of science. For all these thinkers agree that any knowledge of the world, in common-sense thinking as well as in science, involves mental constructs, syntheses, generalizations, formalizations, idealizations specific to the respective level of thought organization. The concept of Nature, for instance, with which the natural sciences have to deal is, as Husserl has shown, an idealizing abstraction from the *Lebenswelt*, an abstraction which, on principle and of course legitimately, excludes persons with their personal life and all objects of culture which originate as such in practical human activity. Exactly this layer of the *Lebenswelt*, however, from which the natural sciences have to abstract, is the social reality which the social sciences have to investigate.

This insight sheds a light on certain methodological problems peculiar to the social sciences. To begin with, it appears that the assumption that the strict adoption of the principles of concept and theory formation prevailing in the natural sciences will lead to reliable knowledge of social reality is inconsistent in itself. If a theory can be developed on such principles, say in the form of an ideally refined behaviorism – and it is certainly possible to imagine this – then it will not tell us anything about social reality as experienced by men in everyday life. As Nagel himself admits, it will be highly abstract, and its concepts will apparently be remote from the obvious and familiar traits found in any society. On the other hand, a theory which aims at explaining social reality has to develop particular devices foreign to the natural sciences in order to agree with the common-sense experience of the social world. This is indeed what all theoretical sciences of human affairs – economics, sociology, the sciences of law, linguistics, cultural anthropology, etc. – have done.

This state of affairs is founded on the fact that there is an essential difference in the structure of the thought objects or mental constructs formed by the social sciences and those formed by the natural sciences. It is up to the natural scientist and to him alone to define, in accordance with the procedural rules of his science, his observational field, and to determine the facts, data and events within it which are relevant for his problem or scientific purpose at hand. Neither are those facts and events pre-selected, nor is the observational field pre-interpreted. The world of nature, as explored by the natural scientists, does not 'mean' anything to molecules, atoms and electrons. But the observational field of the social scientist – social reality – has a specific meaning and relevance structure for the human beings living, acting and thinking within it. By a series of common-sense constructs they have pre-selected and pre-interpreted this world which they experience as the reality of their daily lives. It is these thought objects of theirs which determine their behavior by motivating it. The thought objects constructed by the social scientists, in order to grasp this social reality, have to be founded upon the thought objects constructed by the common-sense thinking of men, living their daily life within their social world. Thus, the constructs of the social sciences are, so to speak, constructs of the second degree, that is, constructs of the constructs made by the actors on the social scene, whose behavior the social scientist has to observe and to explain in accordance with the procedural rules of his science.

Thus, the exploration of the general principles according to which man in daily life organizes his experiences, and especially those of the social world, is the first task of the methodology of the social sciences. This is not the place to outline the procedures of a phenomenological analysis of the so-called natural attitude by which this can be done. We shall briefly mention only a few problems involved.

The world, as has been shown by Husserl, is from the outset experienced in the pre-scientific thinking of everyday life in the mode of typicality. The unique objects and events given to us in a unique aspect are unique within a horizon of typical familiarity and pre-acquaintanceship. There are mountains, trees, animals, dogs – in particular Irish setters and among them my Irish setter, Rover. Now I may look at Rover either as this unique individual, my irreplaceable friend and comrade or just as a typical example of 'Irish setter', 'dog', 'mammal', 'animals', 'organism' or 'object of the outer world'. Starting from here, it can be shown that whether I do one or the other, and also which traits or qualities of a given object or event I consider as individually unique and which as typical, depends upon my actual interest and the system of relevances involved – briefly, upon my practical or theoretical 'problem at hand'. This 'problem at hand', in turn, originates in the circumstances within which I find myself at any moment of my daily life and which I propose to call my biographically determined situation. Thus, typification depends upon my problem at hand for the definition and solution of which the type has been formed. It can be further shown that at least one aspect of the biographically and situationally determined systems of interests and relevances is subjectively experienced in the thinking of everyday life as systems of motives for action, of choices to be made, of projects to be carried out, of goals to be reached. It is this insight of the actor into the dependencies of the motives and goals of his actions upon his biographically determined situation which social scientists have in view when speaking of the subjective meaning which the actor 'bestows upon' or 'connects with' his action. This implies that, strictly speaking, the actor and he alone knows what he does, why he does it, and when and where his action starts and ends.

But the world of everyday life is from the outset also a social cultural world in which I am interrelated in manifold ways of interaction with fellow-men known to me in varying degrees of intimacy and anonymity. To a certain extent, sufficient for many practical purposes, I understand their behavior, if I understand their motives, goals, choices and plans originating in *their* biographically determined circumstances. Yet only in particular situations, and then only fragmentarily, can I experience the Others' motives, goals, etc. – briefly, the subjective meanings they bestow upon their actions, in their uniqueness. I can, however, experience them in their typicality. In order to do so I construct typical patterns of the actors' motives and ends, even of their attitudes and personalities, of which their actual conduct is just an instance or example. These typified patterns of the Others' behavior become in turn motives of my own actions, and this leads to the phenomenon of self-typification well known to social scientists under various names.

Here, I submit, in the common-sense thinking of everyday life, is the origin of the so-called constructive or ideal types, a concept which as a tool of the social sciences has been analysed by Hempel in such a lucid way. But at least at the common-sense level the formation of these types involves neither intuition nor a theory, if we understand these terms in the sense of Hempel's statements (1952). As we shall see, there are also other kinds of ideal or constructive types, those formed by the social scientist, which are of a quite different structure and indeed involve theory. But Hempel has not distinguished between the two.

Next we have to consider that the common-sense knowledge of everyday life is from the outset socialized in many respects.

It is first, structurally socialized, since it is based on the fundamental idealization that if I were to change places with my fellow-man I would experience the same sector of the world in substantially the same perspectives as he does, our particular biographical circumstances becoming for all practical purposes at hand irrelevant. I propose to call this idealization that of the reciprocity of perspectives.

It is, second, genetically socialized, because the greater part of our knowledge, as to its content and the particuar forms of typification under which it is organized, is socially derived and this in socially approved terms.

It is, third, socialized in the sense of social distribution of knowledge, each individual knowing merely a sector of the world and common knowledge of the same sector varying individually as to its degree of distinctness, clarity, acquaintanceship or mere belief.

These principles of socialization of common-sense knowledge, and especially that of the social distribution of knowledge, explain at least partially what the social scientist has in mind in speaking of the functional structural approach to studies of human affairs. The concept of functionalism – at least in the modern social sciences – is not derived from the biological concept of the functioning of an organism, as Nagel holds. It refers to the socially distributed constructs of patterns of typical motives, goals, attitudes, personalities, which are supposed to be invariant and are then interpreted as the function or structure of the social system itself. The more these interlocked behavior patterns are standardized and institutionalized, that is, the more their typicality is socially approved by laws, folkways, mores and habits, the greater is their usefulness in common-sense and scientific thinking as a scheme of interpretation of human behavior.

These are, very roughly, the outlines of a few major features of the constructs involved in common-sense experience of the intersubjective world in daily life, which is called *Verstehen*. As explained before, they are the first level constructs upon which the second level constructs of the social sciences have to be erected. But here a major problem emerges. On the one hand, it has been shown that the constructs on the first level, the common-sense constructs, refer to subjective elements, namely the *Verstehen* of the actor's action from his, the actor's, point of view. Consequently, if the social sciences aim indeed at explaining social reality, then the scientific constructs on the second level, too, must include a reference to the subjective meaning an action has for the actor. This is, I think, what Weber understood by his famous postulate of subjective interpretation, which has, indeed, been observed so far in the theory formation of all social sciences. The postulate of subjective interpretation has to be understood in the sense that all scientific explanations of the social world *can*, and for certain purposes *must*, refer to the subjective meaning of the actions of human beings from which social reality originates.

On the other hand, I agreed with Nagel's statement that the social sciences, like all empirical sciences, have to be objective in the sense that their propositions are subjected to controlled verification and must not refer to private uncontrollable experience.

How is it possible to reconcile these seemingly contradictory principals? Indeed, the most serious question which the methodology of the social sciences has to answer is : How is it possible to form objective concepts and an objectively verifiable theory of subjective meaning-structures? The basic insight that the concepts formed by the social scientist are constructs of the constructs formed in common-sense thinking by the actors on the social scene offers an answer. The scientific constructs formed on the second level, in accordance with the procedural rules valid for all empirical sciences, are objective ideal typical constructs and, as such, of a different kind from those developed on the first level of common-sense thinking which they have to supersede. They are theoretical systems embodying testable general hypotheses in the sense of Hempel's definition. This device has been used by social scientists concerned with theory long before this concept was formulated by Weber and developed by his school.

Before describing a few features of these scientific constructs, let us briefly consider the particular attitude of the theoretical social scientist to the social world, in contradistinction to that of the actor on the social scene. The theoretical scientist – qua scientist, not qua human being (which he is, too) – is not involved in the observed situation, which is to him not of practical but merely of cognitive interest. The system or relevances governing common-sense interpretation in daily life originates in the biographical situation of the observer. By making up his mind to become a scientist, the social scientist has replaced his personal biographical situation by what I shall call, following Kaufmann (1944, pp. 52, 251), a scientific situation. The problems with which he has to deal might be quite unproblematic for the human being within the world and vice versa. Any scientific problem is determined by the actual state of the respective science, and its solution has to be achieved in accordance with the procedural rules governing this science, which among other things warrant the control and verification of the solution offered. The scientific problem, once established, alone determines what is relevant for the scientist as well as the conceptual frame of reference to be used by him. This and nothing else, it seems to me, is what Weber means when he postulates the objectivity of the social sciences, their detachment from the value patterns which govern or might govern the behavior of the actors on the social scene.

How does the social scientist proceed? He observes certain facts and events within social reality which refer to human action and he constructs typical behavior or course-of-action patterns from what he has observed. Thereupon he coordinates to these typical course-of-action patterns models of an ideal actor or actors, whom he imagines as being gifted with consciousness. Yet it is a consciousness restricted so as to contain nothing but the elements relevant to the performing of the course-of-action patterns observed. He thus ascribes to this fictitious consciousness a set of typical notions, purposes, goals, which are assumed to be invariant in the specious consciousness of the imaginary actor-model. This homunculus or puppet is supposed to be interrelated in interaction patterns to other homunculi or puppets constructed in a similar way. Among these homunculi with which the social scientist populates his model of the social world of everyday life, sets of motives, goals, roles – in general, systems of relevances – are distributed in such a way as the scientific problems under scrutiny require. Yet – and this is the main point – these constructs are by no means arbitrary. They are subject to the postulate of logical consistency and to the postulate of adequacy. The latter means that each term in such a scientific model of human action must be constructed in such way that a human act performed within the real world by an individual actor as indicated by the typical construct would be understandable to the actor himself as well as to his fellow-men in terms of common-sense interpretation of everyday life. Compliance with the postulate of logical consistency warrants the objective validity of the thought objects constructed by the social scientist; compliance with the postulate of adequacy warrants their compatibility with the constructs of everyday life.

As the next step, the circumstances within which such a model operates may be varied, that is, the situation which the homunculi have to meet may be imagined as changed, but not the set of motives and relevances assumed to be the sole content of their consciousness. I may, for example, construct a model of a producer acting under conditions of unregulated competition, and another of a producer acting under cartel restrictions, and then compare the output of the same commodity of the same firm in the two models (Machlup, 1952, p. 9). In this way, it is possible to predict how such a puppet or system of puppets might behave under certain conditions and to discover certain 'determinate relations between a set of variables, in terms of which . . . empirically ascertainable regularities . . . can be explained'. This, however, is Nagel's definition of a theory. It can easily be seen that each step involved in the construction and use of the scientific model can be verified by empirical observation, provided that we do not restrict this term to sensory perceptions of objects and events in the outer world but include the experimental form, by which common-sense thinking in everyday life understands human actions and their outcome in terms of their underlying motives and goals.

References

HEMPEL, C. G. (1952), 'Symposium: problems of concept and theory formation in the social sciences', *Science, Language and Human Rights*, University of Pennsylvania Press, vol. 1, pp. 65–86.

JAMES, W. (1890), *Principles of Psychology*, 2 vols., Henry Holt.

KAUFMANN, F. (1944), *Methodology of the Social Sciences*, Humanities Press.

MACHLUP, F. (1952), *The Economics of Seller's Competition*, Johns Hopkins University Press.

MEAD, G. H. (1934), *Mind, Self and Society*, University of Chicago Press.

THOMAS, W. I. (1951), *Social Behaviour and Personality* (ed. E. H. Volkart), Social Science Research.

WEBER, M. (1964), *The Theory of Social and Economic Organization*, Collier-Macmillan.

39 Harold Fallding

Explanatory Theory, Analytical Theory and the Ideal Type

Excerpt from Harold Fallding, *The Sociological Task*,
Prentice-Hall, 1968, pp. 24–34.

To have a *theory* about anything is to have an explanation for it. To achieve that is the goal of science, and a discipline has no *theory* until it has a coherent explanation for the things it studies. Yet other more modest theoretical components come into one's work in the course of the search. Although these are by no means 'theories' they are part of one's theoretical armamentarium. It is important that we give recognition to them and know where they fit. We are somewhat at a loss to designate them, though, once we decide not to call them *theories*. For they express theoretical rather than empirical concerns. Essentially, their work is to sort out our world by developing concepts. Perhaps the way out of the difficulty is to call this whole area of operations *analytical* theory. This would distinguish it from *explanatory theory*, and it is of the utmost importance that we remember the definite dividing line between these. Needless confusion and recrimination have invaded sociological discussion through forgetting it. A common mistake is to think that assembling analytical concepts is tantamount to having a *theory* in the explanatory meaning of the word. When anyone who has come under this illusion learns his mistake it is even possible that he will blame the subject instead of himself. For instance, the work of Parsons has been overwhelmingly in the domain of analytical theory. It does not have the power to explain social phenomena and does not purport to do so. Its great virtue is to make us vividly aware of what is meant by *the social* and to name some of the components of it. Although this is not the end of a science, it is its quite indispensable beginning. It seems utterly obtuse, then, for anyone to blame Parsons for not having brought us to El Dorado in a day, when he has done so valiantly to get us launched. You cannot cook the goose until it is dressed.

Actually, the 'theoretical' accomplishments of sociology so far have been preponderantly at this level. There is a considerable wealth yet to be countered in concept formation in the discipline. A major project for 'theoretical' work in sociology still is to take stock of its concepts, refine their definitions, and link them up together. Without apology, I envisage the present work as a contribution to this important task. It involves no contradiction, surely, to acknowledge that explanatory theory is the ultimate goal of our science and to insist that we come to it by stages, each of which must be vigorous in itself. It is also necessary that we find the route whereby we pass from conceptual to explanatory theory. This could prove quite a delicate maneuver. Before naming our sociological concepts, then, we will give some attention to the way they operate in our exploration of the actual world and and in generating the terms for an explanatory theory of it. This brings us to a fresh assessment of the importance of heuristics and of the ideal type in particular.

A heuristic is the first match struck in the darkness. *Heuristics* refers to the processes of finding out, to search procedure, or, as it has also been expressed, to progressive thinking. It is not the window-dressing of the published report, but our fumbling and blundering – and self-correction. Possibly the heart of it is our sensitizing to relevant differentiation: in a hitherto grey world what is it that begins to stand out as significantly distinct? We attempt to give it a face.

Max Weber recommended the *ideal type* as a heuristic for adoption in sociology (1949). This is a notion that has never been entirely clear, and Weber's interpreters have scarcely succeeded in making it clearer. Every field of study probably generates its own kind of heuristic in response to the phenomena in it. What Weber proposed for sociology reflects his profoundly voluntaristic view of social action. In his view, social structures are what men make them: they are the products of purposive choices and actions. The ideal type of social activity, then, is the drawing out of the implications for action of a particular commitment, were the commitment to be followed consistently toward its logical conclusion. Weber appreciated that when a group decides that something is worth accomplishing a whole *set* of activities has to be started in order to accomplish it. These diverse activities have to elbow their way in, competing with other things for time and support, and so on. They therefore may or may not come to their full unfolding. Whether they do will depend on a variety of things: the strength of dedication of the people concerned, the strength of their competing aims, their knowledge, their resources, any outside opposition to what they are trying to do and so on. But it is not difficult to imagine what the full unfolding of their position would be, if its growth were unimpeded. And this precisely is the ideal type of it. It is the utopia of the undertaking. In the course of a few pages, Weber describes the ideal type as a 'utopia' a number of times. This is an appropriate way of summing up what he was aiming to convey and it possibly contains the whole clue to his meaning. It should have received more attention.

The ideal type is a utopia in this sense: it is what the sociologist believes the people under study would be striving for, were they unfettered by the compromises of life. It is quite likely they will never have conceptualized a utopia for themselves, but that would not prevent his imputing one to them. On the other hand, it is just as likely they will have defined their own utopia. For often a group will have its constitution or charter, policy, program or official statement of aims. These are just the kinds of tendencies Weber recognized to inhere in social action, and the sociologist makes use of them in fashioning his ideal type. The ideal type may sometimes resemble these tendencies very closely, although it remains the sociologist's construction in the end. It should be made clear, of course, that the ideal type is not the sociologist's ideal *for* anyone, and it is not something he wants to enjoin on anyone. It is closer to his ideal *of* them. That is, it is his most sympathetic picture of them according to his understanding of what they want for themselves. It is in this sense that their actions, attitudes, etc., are *idealized*.

In everyday life we continually use such ideal types to guide our thinking and action. Why, for instance, do we so often express astonishment at what people do? It is because we feel it is inconsistent with the commitment we understand them to have made. 'Fancy you missing the biggest match of the year, I thought you were a real sporting man!' 'Fancy you joining the Army, I thought you were a Quaker!' 'Fancy you not drinking tea, I thought you were an Australian!' What is being outraged in all three instances is our ideal type. We sometimes allude despairingly to this as using 'stereotypes'. Yet they are indispensable to us. The stereotype of life and ideal type of sociology are very close to one another. Rightly used they are of advantage to us: it is only the abuse of them we have to avoid. We misuse them if we forget that individual cases will diverge from type, or if we refuse to modify the type when there is mounting evidence that it is a false image. Our approach to people and situations is insightful in so far as our store of accurate stereotypes is rich. It is by the use of the same insightful procedure that Weber himself has given us ideal types of bureaucracy, feudalism, patrimony, asceticism, mysticism, charismatic leadership and other things besides.

Weber's pure type of bureaucracy will serve to illustrate his procedure (1949, pp. 196–244). It itemizes a set of characteristics. Weber believed that in committing themselves to the bureaucratic form of centralized administration, people would strive to implement certain practices. There would be a definite hierarchy of officials. Their jurisdictional areas would be strictly defined by rule. There would be a large staff of clerks to deal with records. Systematic training would be provided for the holders of executive offices. The official would regard his role as a calling that might oblige him to surrender all his working capacity to it, even though his obligatory time in the bureau may be delimited. The whole system would be run by stable rules that could be learned by those involved in it. Complexes of behavior that exhibit all these features measure up to the ideal type, those that deviate in any way are impure.

But if the ideal type is a fiction not necessarily found in life, how do we decide what to include and exclude in compiling it? It is clear that we take our cue from real life in the first instance, yet probably not so much from what is being done as from what is being aimed for. Weber says the ideal type is an '*accentuation* of one or more points of view' (1949, p. 90). I hardly think we should accept this if it meant a falsification through exaggeration. We could scarcely entertain a caricature. Nor could I concur if it meant the observer placing the accent according to his selective interest in the subject: there could be no end to the diversity and arbitrariness such an approach would license. Rather, we should try to discern what the *people observed* are accenting, where *they* are 'putting their emphasis', as we say. It is this that gives distinctive direction and character to their striving and entitles us to name it. Thus we come to adopt terms like *Methodism*, or *reaction*, or *socialism*, or *university*. Starting with that observation, we observe further what array of practices is gathered up in the train of different cases where the same end is pursued. This observation may indeed be impressionistic and intuitive, yet it is still empirical observation. We compile our ideal type from this composite image. We keep the elements that are common to all cases except that we reject any that are inconsistent with the aim, and we may add others of our own imagining that would be consistent and swell the complement. Yet this ideal type is nothing in itself. Sometimes it seems to be assumed that this is the whole end of sociological investigation – to get some ideal types – and that law-finding or theory-building have no place. But this is a grave misunderstanding, for developing an ideal type is simply part of a heuristic procedure, a stage on life's way. Weber defined its function picturesquely: 'It serves as a harbor until one has learned to navigate safely in the vast sea of empirical facts' (p. 104).

Built up in the way I have described, the ideal type is a rational construct and Weber stressed this. We keep in it or put into it actions that are rationally required by the end in view. We think it sensible to do so because experience convinces us that rationality is one of the conditions of successful social action. Although the ideal type is a fiction, then, it is not idealized in any purely arbitary way. It is commended to us as a measuring rod for actual cases. But there would be no virtue in measuring a case's deviance from a purely arbitrary norm. The ideal type is a relevant standard for measuring social phenomena because it measures a case's degree of self-realization. It is measured against what it might be and would need to be if it is to be of maximum effect.

If I am representing it correctly, then, the ideal type is nothing more than a collection of traits that we expect could occur together. We so expect partly because we have found empirically that some of them do, but partly also because we have a general theoretical expectation that other rationally linked traits will be joined with them, the goal in view being what it is. So we expect, shall we say, that A, B, C, D, E, F, G and H will occur together. Yet it is scarcely correct to call this our hypothesis: it is really never correct to equate ideal type and hypothesis. For when I say we measure actual cases against this, what we do is to see how many and which of these traits occur together in fact. We use the ideal type to ask this further question: How far have the exigencies of reality allowed this principle to unfold – this principle of feudalism, communism, democracy or whatever it may be. We will doubtless find that in fact it has been hemmed in, compromised, cut off in mid-career, got so entangled with other principles as to be obscured, perhaps riddled with inconsistencies. Yet if such imperfections occur not randomly but systematically our ideal type will have led to a hypothesis. If the same blemishes begin to recur quite regularly on the pure type we will begin to suspect that is the shape of reality. We will come to assume that these are the things which probably do occur together, irrational though some of it may be. Of the traits above, perhaps only A, B, D and H are found together and, although we had hardly expected it, X and Y besides. Once we are convinced of this pattern we adopt it for our hypothesis and can throw the ideal type away. It was meant to be expendable. We may leave the harbor now, for we have learned to navigate in the sea of empirical facts. We have not yet proven anything, but we are launched with a hypothesis.

There seems to be a pathetic lack of fulfilment about the ideal types of sociological literature. They have been too readily accepted as the end of the search instead of the means of searching. We still look back to Weber's ideal types of bureaucracy, charisma, religious rejections of the world and so on, as though we had graphic pictures of phenomena. We consider them somewhat idealized for artistic effect, but graphic pictures nevertheless. Yet Weber never intended ideal types to be regarded that way. He meant us rather to ask, concerning them: Are the real cases altogether like this, or are they quite systematically otherwise? Like the grain of wheat that falls into the ground and may die, an ideal type only bears fruit if it yields a hypothetical type. Very likely it will yield several. We then think it worthwhile to test for the existence of these hypothetical types. If, after testing, we establish them (or something like them) as factual, we may have arrived at an empirical generalization or explanation schema. For now we may demonstrate a constant relation between a single event or set of events and their causes. This will be possible if one or more traits make their appearance in advance of the others. The passage from analytical theory to explanatory theory will have been made. It is imperative that we take note that in making this passage the definition of our terms has almost certainly undergone a change; at least we will have to be sure whether that has happened or not. If we go on to crown the conjunction of empirical elements with a nonempirical explanatory variable, this variable will take its definition from its empirical matrix. *Reaction* as a general exploratory concept is an ideal type; *reaction* as a nonempirical explanatory variable intervening between empirical observations is not an ideal type and has probably changed its meaning. In any case it is *reaction* as it is defined by reference to things observed. The whole entanglement at the theory–research junction may be a reflection of neglecting to realize this. Yet Winch drew attention to the importance of recognizing the distinction between heuristic and empirical typologies (1947).

The fulcrum of the argument of this book is that the meaning of a given term used in explanatory theory is not the same as the meaning of the same term used in analytical theory. Hence the terms of analytical theory cannot enter into explanatory statements, as such; they must be transformed. Even if the collections of traits for the ideal type and empirical type are ultimately identical, the latter represents a configuration found in the real world. This cannot be guaranteed of the former (and is not in fact asked of it).

An instance of radical revision of the ideal type to make it applicable to empirical data is Johnson's revision of the Troeltsch–Weber church-sect typology (1963). In Johnson's opinion, the original typology is 'applicable only to a specific historical context' and 'encompasses a variety of elements which tend to vary independently'. Through using the typology he becomes convinced that reality diverges from it systematically. For an empirical classification of 'most groups in the Jewish, Christian and Islamic tradition' and of the 'major religious groups of the United States', Johnson consequently resorts to something that salvages only one basic distinction in the previous typology. 'A church,' he proposes, 'is a religious group that accepts the social environment in which it exists.' Actually, in spite of the explicit disavowal, Johnson appears still to assume that there are *some* constant organizational features distinguishing the sect from the church. If this were not the case, his one-factor typology would have little point. What he seems to want to imply, at the explanatory level, is that acceptance or rejection of the social environment gives rise to distinct forms of religious expression. Now there is nothing in this denouement of Johnson's thinking to bring Weber's types under a cloud. *They were ideal*. It is an index of their fruitfulness that they helped Johnson to form a conclusion about actual cases.

Another instance of revision of the ideal type that might be given is the author's modification of Zimmerman's familistic–atomistic typology for the family (Fallding, 1957 ; Zimmerman, 1947). Zimmerman imputed six main characteristics to the familistic family:

Its features were (a) a large number of children; (b) close solidarity with kinsfolk and neighbourhood, with a resulting acknowledgement of the right of kin and community to prescribe what constitutes proper family conduct; (c) the transmission between generations of a traditional concept of family roles and of one's place in society; (d) strong ties of dependence between family members because of the family's multiform functions (including the maintenance of its own property, the family estate); (e) members' acceptance of family control over their behaviour and of authority within it, and (f) a high valuation on family life and unity. In the atomistic family of the modern city, in which members are considered to be mainly bent upon egoistic satisfactions, these *structural* aspects are said to be no longer strong (Fallding, 1957, p. 55).

An empirical investigation of urban families suggested that the first four of these factors may be tied together without the last two being necessarily tied with them. The last two may occur both in the presence and absence of the first four. The implication, at the explanatory level, is that urban living had caused a weakening in the first four factors, whereas the last two were independent of it. What this finding does, in effect, is supplant a six-factor ideal type by a four-factor empirical one. But the ideal type guided the inquiry.

Finally, we may, by way of contrast, take note of a radical denouement where the empirical testing of an ideal type leads not to a modified empirical type but to abandonment of the scientific stance altogether. Studying Tepoztlan seventeen years after Redfield's investigation, Lewis sought to discover whether changes in that period conformed to the folk-urban typology of social change that Redfield had introduced (Redfield, 1930, 1941; Lewis, 1953). According to this type, any increasing urban influence on a village community is accompanied by increasing disorganization, secularization and individualization. Lewis did not consider that this constant combination of factors was confirmed. As a consequence, he abandons the attempt to characterize village community change in terms of *any* constant combination of factors, falling back on a method that takes fuller recognition of the unique features of different historical periods. To anyone committed to a science of society this is disappointing, for it amounts to something like an admission of failure. Historical data are as good for sociology as any other sort of data, but the use made of them is almost opposite the historian's. We know that historical periods exhibit different phenomena but we would still like to know whether they have features in common – and if they do, what those features are. Our disappointment is increased by Lewis's suggestion that he need not have been so radical in dismissing the method of searching for types. Perhaps he could have settled for an empirical type through modification of the ideal type in the manner I have been advocating. For in one place he states,

On the whole, many of our findings for Tepoztlan might be interpreted as confirming Redfield's more general finding for Yucatan, particularly with regard to the trend towards secularization and individualization, perhaps less so with regard to disorganization.

We should not assume that ideal types are always present or necessary in sociological inquiry. We may simply compare one case with another to find out what they have in common. Becker did this, for instance, in his 'constructed typology' of a marginal trading people (1950, pp. 93–127). In his study diverse peoples were shown to exhibit three traits in common: expedient rationality, emotional aloofness from out-groups and economic internationalism. These were exhibited by the Jews, Armenians, Parsees, some Chinese in the Dutch East Indies, some Greeks in Egypt and certain lowland-border Scots. This cluster of three traits is a hypothetical type arrived at directly by comparison, without the mediation of any ideal type at all. Becker is virtually suggesting, then, that we test for a constant association between these factors because they have already been found to occur together in some actual cases. He stresses that the constructed type occurs nowhere in actuality – and yet this triad does. What he probably means is that the triad does not occur bare, without other trappings attached, and that these trappings may be different for different cases. That is, it is *abstracted* from reality as all the generalizing concepts of science are; but it is not idealized. Yet it is a pity that Becker failed to distinguish his constructed type from the ideal type more deliberately than he has. They have often been taken for the same. In a footnote, Becker even says his constructed type is an ideal type, similar to but not identical with Weber's. Yet his reason for avoiding the term *ideal type* is not because he wishes to differentiate his notion from Weber's, but because of the misunderstandings that can attach to the word *ideal*. As if to further confuse us, in the same essay Becker reproduces his typology of religious organizations: ecclesia, sect, denomination and cult – all ideal types in the Weberian sense. He goes on to suggest that you can propose and test hypotheses about these types: for example, that the cult is transformed into the sect. But we cannot do that until we have given these terms an empirical definition. The only immediate thing we *can* do is ask how far actual cases correspond to or diverge from the type.

Becker's discussion of the generation of types is illustrative of the prevailing lack of clarity on the subject. Two recent commentaries on the practice show the same thing. They appear to be in direct contradiction with one another, the latter written actually claiming that is the case. McKinney uses the term '*constructed type*' and acknowledges what I have said to be the case – that this type is the potential basis of an explanatory schema (1957, pp. 186–235). If he intends to exclude all reference to the ideal type, what he says is unexceptionable, but it is doubtful that he means to do this. Martindale maintains that if McKinney is referring to the ideal type he has misunderstood it (1959, pp. 57–91).

All in all, the ideal type has been exposed to more than its share of misunderstanding. Perhaps this is because it occupies a place in a line of succession. It is a heuristic that abdicates at the appointed time in favor of a hypothetical type, which in turn abdicates in favor of an actual type – and this last may constitute an explanation. If we lose sight of this denouement, and fail to know where we stand at any point, we can misjudge the ideal type because we have first misrepresented it. Yet, rightly understood and handled, the progression from the ideal type to the actually demonstrated type is one of the most rewarding avenues that can be followed in sociological research. It is a research design that is born of insight and has theory as its goal. To negotiate the passage, however, requires a great deal of painstaking and wisely planned empirical work, and it may take generations – even centuries – to do so. Have not sociologists in general expected to come into their inheritance far too quickly, even with magical speed? As a science, sociology is still more a proposal than an achievement. Notions like Parsons's pattern variables (1952, pp. 65–112) and Merton's modes of adaptations (1961, pp. 131–60), for instance, are ideal types that imply a program of long-continuing work. Whole generations may have to work in the field before they wring hypotheses from them. And explanatory theory about these matters lies beyond that again.

The ideal type, as a case of the heuristic, resembles what is now called a *model*. That term has been variously employed, of course, much to the confusion of us all. Brodbeck has reviewed its different uses by sociologists, but makes no useful recommendation about a desirable restriction of use (1959, pp. 313–403). Nagel's usage is one of the most precise, and yet it seems narrower than that which has useful currency now (1961, pp. 106–17). He makes *model* refer simply to the mental imagery with which we clothe our theoretical entities in order to have some pictorial grasp of them: we say the molecule is like a ball, the social system like an organism. In regarding new and strange phenomena we believe we see a patterning similar to old, familiar ones. These are essentially analogies, yet they do more than help us visualize; they help our thinking to unfold by taking it in new directions. For them to be useful it is not necessary to believe that the molecule *is* a ball or that society *is* an organism. Nor need our suppositions from them involve the logical fallacies or argument by analogy. Furthermore, our theoretical entities are ultimately defined abstractly by the relations in which they stand to one another – so once we have used a model to imagine them the model is expendable. The model is, at is were, a scaffold for concept-building, but no integral part of conceptualization. Nagel points out that electromagnetic theory, which led to the positing of an 'ether', satisfactorily explained many experimental laws and predicted many phenomena. But even the nineteenth-century physicists who used the theory never imagined that it implied the real existence of 'ether'.

But *model* now seems to be used in a broader sense than this. It is taken to mean a system of concepts that is useful in mapping the variables in a field under investigation. It may be a corner of the field or the whole field of the subject: a model may be of bureaucracy, for instance, or of society in general. In the latter case, the system of concepts in its entirety makes a heuristic for the deductive theory in its entirety that we hope to achieve in the end. For in scientific work we do not start out with an empty mind, nor even with isolated hypotheses. We start with a guess about the whole structure of our universe of discourse. The coherence that goes into this system of concepts, a coherence whereby each concept is defined by the relationship in which it stands to the others, is analogous to explanation but is not explanation in fact. For it is not an account of reality as it has been experienced. Something like this is what has now come to be called a model, although it has also been common to call it a conceptual scheme. Recently in sociology it has fallen from favor.

References

BECKER, H. (1950), 'Constructive typology in the social sciences', in *Through Values to Social Interpretation*, Duke University Press.

BRODBECK, M. (1959), 'Models, meanings and theories', in L. Gross (ed.), *Symposium on Sociological Theory*, Harper & Row.

FALLDING, H. (1957), 'Inside the Australian family', in A. P. Elkin (ed.), *Marriage and the Family in Australia*, Angus & Robertson.

JOHNSON, B. (1963), 'On church and sect', *Amer. Sociol. Rev.*, vol. 28, no. 4, pp. 539–49.

LEWIS, O. (1953), 'Tepoztlan restudied: a critique of the folk-urban conceptualization of social change', *Rural Sociol.*, vol. 18, pp. 121–37.

MCKINNEY, J. C. (1957), 'Methodology, procedures and techniques in sociology', in H. Becker and A. Boskoff (eds.), *Modern Sociological Theory in Continuity and Change*, Holt, Rinehart & Winston.

MARTINDALE, D. (1959), 'Sociological theory and the ideal type', in L .Gross (ed.), *Symposium on Sociological Theory*, Harper & Row.

MERTON, R. K. (1961), 'Social structure and anomie', *Social Theory and Social Structure*, Free Press.

NAGEL, E. (1961), *The Structure of Science: Problems in the Logic of Scientific Explanation*, Harcourt, Brace & World.

PARSONS, T. (1952), *The Social System*, Tavistock.

REDFIELD, R. (1930), *Tepoztlán: A Mexican Village*, University of Chicago Press.

REDFIELD, R. (1941), *The Folk Culture of Yucatan*, University of Chicago Press.

WEBER, M. (1948), *From Max Weber: Essays in Sociology*, Routledge & Kegan Paul.

WEBER, M. (1949), *The Methodology of the Social Sciences*, Free Press.

WINCH, R. (1947), 'Heuristic and empirical types: a job for factor analysis', *Amer. Sociol. Rev.*, vol. 12, pp. 68–75.

ZIMMERMAN, C. C. (1947), *Family and Civilization*, Harper & Row.

40 Jack D. Douglas

The Social Meanings of Suicide

Excerpt from Jack D. Douglas, *The Social Meanings of Suicide*,
Princeton University Press, 1967, pp. 247–54.

A generally shared principle in the study of the meanings of actions (or of any meanings) is that one can safely assume a direct relation between the patterning of language and the patterning of meanings. One of the implications of this is that the more the shared linguistic terminology for dealing with some social actions, the more the shared meanings of such phenomena. (Leo Spitzer quoted the following to illustrate the principle: 'Wortwandel ist Kulturwandel'.) Though we have previously observed the invalidity of this representational interpretation as a general principle, still it is a useful tool when one has little other empirical data than the linguistic categories themselves; and we shall at this point make some use of it.

In the Western world there has clearly been an increase in the last few centuries in the degree of shared language for treating suicidal phenomena. (The very word 'suicide' and its closely related equivalents in the non-English languages is an example.) There are also many shared, associated terms: despair, unhappiness, life is not worthwhile, escape from the harsh realities, etc. And there do seem to be certain basic dimensions of meaning for which these are slightly variant means of expression. But these terms are also clearly not *sui generis* to the phenomena themselves. On the contrary, they are terms from many other areas of experience. They are terms adopted from various spheres of experience for the purposes of *constructing meanings* for these suicidal phenomena. (The line of influence is similar to that found in much of the language of rocketry today. Rockets are called birds but birds are not yet called rockets.) Moreover, there seems to be no very clear set of rules either for *ordering* the linguistic terms or *applying* them to specific phenomena: i.e. *there is variability, ambiguity and conflict in the imputations of the linguistic categories, including the fundamental category of 'suicide' (or 'suicidal') itself.*

The implication of this ambiguity in the language of 'suicidal' phenomena is simply that there is a high degree of ambiguity in the *meanings* of suicidal phenomena to the social actors within Western culture. Such phenomena, then, are not very clearly defined for the social actors *in the concrete situation*. There is also some further linguistic evidence to suggest this is the case. The linguistic expressions are not very *detailed*. On the contrary, they are generally abstract, common-sense theoretical terms. Since specific actions are not based on abstract theories, even those of a common-sense nature, the common language of suicidal phenomena (and, inferentially, the common, culturally shared meanings) cannot provide a base for interpreting specific, concrete suicidal phenomena that one is involved in (at least as long as one is involved in them – one might well become abstract in retrospect).

There is, of course, far more evidence than simply the linguistic that the *concrete, situated meanings* of suicidal phenomena are *not* very detailed or well ordered – i.e. not very *adequately defined in everyday meanings*, in spite of the adequacy of definitions in abstract, non-situated communications. Of the greatest importance is the evidence from the statements and actions of the actors and the members of the audience (the involved, significant others). First, the significant others who get involved in the suicidal phenomena by having suicidal threats made against them, or by having suicidal actions committed in such a way that they are socially defined as implicated in some other way, are frequently confused and helpless. They frequently express feelings of inadequacy in dealing with the whole matter, feelings of being at a total loss as to what to make of these actions, feelings that this just can't be 'real', can't be happening to them, etc. And they often take the action defined as appropriate for dealing with something that one cannot adequately deal with: i.e. they turn the 'problem' over to those socially defined as the experts or specialists in dealing with such 'abnormal' phenomena. Even the definitions of these statements and actions as those calling for specialist treatment may come about only after a long, complex sequence of events and feelings of uneasiness, 'despair', etc. In some cases one can even find a 'crescendo of suicidal acts' leading up to the definition of this as something requiring specialist care (Stengel and Cook, 1958, p. 77).

The specialists themselves are under great pressure to make some standardized, meaningful whole out of suicidal phenomena: it is their social responsibility to do so. But they also frequently find it extremely difficult to know what to make of suicidal phenomena. Even with a general tendency to impose categories of sickness, Freudian theories and so on, upon such phenomena, they still frequently express the belief that the whole thing is not very clearly defined or understood. For example, in the case of Virginia Arlington, reported by Kobler and Stotland, there are many instances of statements by various 'specialists' that the whole thing was not very clearly defined. After a suicidal attempt by the patient one of the psychiatrists said that it was a 'messed up picture' (1964, p. 171); a member of the ward staff believed that the ward staff was generally 'confused about whether she was sick or not, suicidal or not' (p. 195); a member of the ward staff reported that after a sequence of events involving suicidal threats the ward staff was 'thrown off balance' (p. 201); and, as a good indication of the conflict over how the patient should be defined the director of nurses stated that 'the whole time I had the feeling that nobody really knew how sick this woman was' (p. 195).

Finally, suicidal phenomena often are not generally clearly defined for the individuals who are initiating them. There are many instances of suicidal action in which the individuals seem quite 'sincerely' (to the interviewers) unable to understand what they did or why they did it; they do not seem able to make any particular 'sense' of it – i.e. to give an 'adequate' meaning from their own standpoint. (This inability to understand is, quite likely, the fundamental reason for their common inability to communicate some adequate meaning of the act to others, such as the specialists to whom they have gone for help.[1]) This lack of clear, shared meaning is very likely a general cause of the feeling of 'losing control', 'losing contact with reality', 'going out of my mind', etc., that one finds in individuals with suicidal tendencies (as well as with non-suicidal, 'schizophrenic' individuals): *if one cannot determine the meaning of something, then he does not feel that he can control it.* In the case of Virginia Arlington, for example, this theme of not understanding herself and not being able to control herself ran through her communications with others for weeks or even months and seemed to increase towards the end of her life (ended by suicide in a mental institution). The case of Virgina Arlington also shows the interdependent nature of meaningfulness and meaninglessness (in the particular sense in which we are considering 'meaning' here): as others came to consider her statements and actions to be inadequately defined, except in so far as they could be defined as lacking any adequate meaning in everyday terms – i.e. as 'insanity' or 'sickness', – so she came increasingly to see her statements and actions as lacking any adequate meaning in everyday terms:

'It doesn't seem like my behavior makes any difference to you people. When I do something or say something, do you regard it or do you just say to yourselves, she's sick.' ['Our business is to regard patient's behavior.'] 'Well, why don't you respond; like when I'm angry, have you ever tried

1. Kobler and Stotland reported that 'Mrs Clift and Dr Lyle both felt strongly at that time that Mrs Arlington's inability to communicate what was wrong to Mrs Clift was frightening her further, aggravating the anxiety and the "shattering" ' (p. 157).

to get angry with a brick wall?' ['Because we don't say anything does not mean we don't regard it.'] She continued by talking in her hopeless fashion, sàying that if she was going to be the worst one here, why didn't they strap her down and be done with it. She was desperate inside, etc. Some of it had a threatening quality (toward hospital)[2] (p. 179).

All of this does not, of course, mean that suicidal actions do not have specific meanings to the individual committing them or to the significant others involved. In many instances suicidal actions seem clearly to have very specific and certain meanings for the individual and for the others involved.[3] These instances seem to be a minority of the cases of suicidal actions, but they do exist and are by no means rare. In most instances of suicidal actions several meanings are imputed to the actions by the several people involved. Sometimes there is simply a disagreement among those involved about what the action means, so that any ambiguity of meaning would have to be considered to exist only *as a whole* (or on the average). Rarely is there one meaning imputed to suicidal actions by each person involved. There are, presumably, a number of reasons for this, one probably being the relatively unusual nature of the phenomena and the recency with which men in the Western world have seen them as worthy of serious study. But the most important reason is very likely an intrinsic ambiguity, one resulting from the conflicting meanings in Western culture of two fundamental dimensions of the meanings of such actions. As I shall argue in the next chapter, suicidal actions almost always mean something fundamental both about the person and about the situation of the person: each of these is seen as a 'cause' of the suicidal action. This means that on the most fundamental level it is always possible to argue that the action is either the result of the situation of the individual or, from the opposite side, to argue that the action is the result of something inside (something 'wrong with', etc.) the individual; and, of course, one could also argue that it is the result of some interaction of these two things.[4]

2. This quote was taken from a statement made by some member of the ward staff; but Kobler and Stotland did not give details on how the conversation was reconstructed. As noted in our later consideration of psychiatric case reports, this is one of the frequent problems in dealing with such reports.

Goffman has described many of the specific patterns of behaviour that seem to have this effect of destroying the feeling of *adequate meaning*, but has not dealt with it in these terms (1961).

3. The examples in the section below on 'revenge' suicidal actions are sometimes very specific and certain in their meanings for those involved.

4. Burke presented just such an analysis of the *ambiguities of suicide motives* in Western literature; and it was this beautiful analysis which was so important in leading this author to see the relevance of rhetoric to all suicidal actions (Burke, 1962, pp. 527–37).

Now, we have said that it is 'always possible' to argue either or both ways. This is true as long as one is considering suicidal actions in the abstract; but it is clear as soon as one considers actual cases that, though in any given case there might actually be someone who, for some reason or other, does argue either side of the case, there is generally one side of the argument that seems to most of those involved to be more likely (more plausible) than the other. This is not simply the result of chance. Rather, the particular events, previous imputations of selves to the person who commits the action, and many other aspects of the particular case are the fundamental determinants of what the meanings will be to those involved. *In very general terms we could say that the meanings of this particular event (or a sequence of events coming in one time and situation, as seen by those involved) are determined by their* contextual relations *with many other meanings.*[5]

Now, a *social constructionist theory of meanings* clearly differs from the usual building-block approach in its emphasis on the fundamental significance of the ways in which specific events, symbols, etc., are *related* by individuals to each other to determine the meanings of something to those individuals. But such a formulation leaves open as a possible interpretation the usual *mechanistic approach* to interpreting the meaning of specific things in terms of a number of 'building blocks' such as values. In terms of this interpretation the specific meanings of specific events is supposed to be given in some unspecified manner by the *structure* of meanings shared by the members of the culture being considered.

I would argue, on the contrary, that such an approach can work only on some sociologistic level at which one does not have to show how the specific meanings of specific events come about: one could only talk about non-observable 'average meanings' which can not in any specific way be shown to be derived from observable phenomena. One would have to do as Durkheim did: that is, show that there exists some statistical correlation between the official suicide rates and some type of group and then simply impute some meanings to that group so that the relative rate of suicide appropriate (in terms of one's theory) to that group will be seen to be the one found.

5. Alternatively, one could say that meanings are *functionally* determined. The use of functional in this sense has some clear precedent in the study of language (see, for example, Martinet, 1962). But there does exist an obvious, superficial similarity between our approach to meanings and the functionalist approach to the analysis of 'systems of social roles', as first clearly developed by Radcliffe-Brown. To avoid any unfounded arguments about these being 'really' the same theories, the approach to meanings used here shall be called the *social constructionist theory of meanings*.

As soon as one looks at the specific meanings imputed by those involved in suicidal phenomena, one can see that, though there is a great complexity to the various considerations made by the social actors and no specific structure inherent in some patterns of meanings, still there is some agreement on the specific meanings of these specific events. I would argue that the structure one finds in the meanings of specific suicidal phenomena is not given by the transmitted culture, though some of the specific meanings and criteria that make this structure possible are so given, but that the individuals involved *construct this structure of meanings*. Though the possible (or plausible) meanings of these phenomena are primarily determined by the *shared, cultural meanings* which are culturally defined as relevant to these phenomena (including the criteria of various sorts) and by the *shared context of meanings given to the individuals involved by their past interactions*, the specific, actualized meanings of these phenomena will be in large measure determined by the intentional actions of the individuals involved. Moreover, I would argue that the only way one can go about scientifically studying the meanings of suicidal phenomena (or any other social phenomena) is by studying the specific meanings of real-world phenomena of this socially defined type as the individuals involved construct them: we must work from the clearly observable, concrete phenomena upward to abstractions about meanings in any culture (though, I would argue, it is generally necessary to see the whole in some way in order to know how one should go about studying the particulars and abstracting from them); and the abstractions must be the results of comparisons made by sociologists of the concrete meanings of these phenomena defined as *similar* by the members of the culture. It need hardly be added that the meanings being compared must be those constructed by the actors involved in their 'natural cultural habitat' rather than those constructed by the actors in response to some 'unnatural' instrument with its own implicit assumptions about the structure of meanings being studied.

References

BURKE, K. (1962), *A Rhetoric of Motives*, World Publishing Co.
GOFFMAN, E. (1961), *Asylums*, Aldine.
KOBLER, A. L., and STOTLAND, E. (1964), *The End of Hope: A Social-Clinical Theory of Suicide*, Macmillan.
MARTINET, A. (1962), *A Functional View of Languages*, Clarendon Press.
STENGEL, E., and COOK, N. G. (1958), *Attempted Suicide: Its Social Significance and Effects*, Oxford University Press.

41 Johan Galtung

Data Collection

Excerpts from Johan Galtung, *Theory and Methods of Social Research*, Allen & Unwin, 1967, pp. 109–28.

The main forms of data-collection

We now turn to the main problem, how to obtain data. The scheme below does not apply to all kinds of units or elements of analysis, however. Instead, it is geared towards the needs of data-collection where the unit is a person who is exposed to *stimuli* and yields *responses*, these terms taken in the broader sense. But this covers a very broad class of cases of social science data collection.

By *systematic stimuli* we mean stimuli that are kept constant when the objects are changed, in the sense that *all* units are exposed to the same stimuli, systematically. If this is not the case, we shall say that the stimuli are *unsystematic*, as in more casual interviews where the interview objects are asked the questions *they* are most likely to find meaningful. In this case, a data matrix cannot be constructed on the basis of the data.

By *systematic responses* we do not mean that the responses are kept constant; that would, of course, be meaningless, since it would yield no information. What is kept constant are the response *categories*, so that the responses of the objects to stimulus Sj are recorded on a predetermined set of responses, Rj.

If this is not the case, we shall say that the responses are *unsystematic*, as in interviews where the answer is taken down, verbatim, with due regard to all possible individual variations.

These simple concepts yield a fourfold table:

Table 1 The Main Settings for Data-Collection

	Unsystematic stimuli	Systematic stimuli
Unsystematic responses	informal	formal, unstructured
Systematic responses	impossible	formal, structured

Clearly, if the stimuli are not kept constant, constancy in response categories would be rather meaningless, as the constancy would at most be extensional, never intensional. A 'strongly disagree' is not the same response if it is not a possible response to the same item. As to the other three cells, terms have been chosen that are widespread in the literature, and given a definition through their place in Table 1.

Hence, three settings for the collection of data are defined: the informal, and the two forms of formal data-collection. We now turn to the aspects of the person-unit to which these settings can be applied.

By a response we mean, as mentioned, a state of the object. It should be emphasized that a state does not necessarily imply that any kind of *change* has taken place. Inaction or continued silence may be a very important response, more revealing than many responses involving change in the state of the object. Typically, however, we assume that all responses can be classified as *acts* (with inaction as a limiting case). For 'acts' we use the simple dichotomy into *non-verbal* and *verbal*, with the latter dichotomized into *oral* and *written*. By oral acts, then, we do not refer to all acts where the mouth is the executing organ – kissing and humming are excluded possibilities. The verbal acts are acts where verbal symbols are used to communicate, whereas nodding, shrugging of shoulders, etc. are regarded as non-verbal acts.

If we now combine the three settings for data-collection with the three kinds of manifest responses, we get a ninefold table containing most known forms of data-collection in the social sciences. We could actually use the word 'all' instead of 'most', since we are dealing with two trichotomies. Another thing is that the categories certainly are not sufficiently refined to register the many variations known in the methodological literature.

Table 2 The Main Forms of Data-Collection

Responses			
Stimuli	*Non-verbal acts*	*Oral, verbal acts*	*Written, verbal acts*
informal settings	(participant) observation	conversations, use of informants	letters, articles biographies
formal, un-structured settings	systematic observation	interviews, open-ended	questionnaire, open-ended
formal, structured settings	experimental techniques	interviews, precoded	questionnaire, structured

In the cells, the most commonly used techniques corresponding to the headings are listed. However, the cells are thought of as expressing very general ideas that may also be used to generate other techniques.

The advantage of the scheme lies in its generality. If we are able to present the pros and cons for the various headings, the arguments for the singular method follow, once we know in what cell it can be properly classified. Actually, the two trichotomies used as headings in Table 2 both stem from 2×2 tables (both with an empty cell), so that the arguments may be given relative to the four dichotomies non-verbal–verbal, oral–written, informal–formal and unstructured–structured. The most important arguments will be given in the following sections.

Non-verbal *v.* verbal responses

Human beings are restricted to non-verbal acts for the first one or two years of their existence; then include oral, verbal acts if the external circumstances permit them to do so; and may later be able to include written, verbal acts in their repertoire if the social system in which they live permits this. This simple genetic sequence which it seems difficult to change may serve as a basis for explaining rankings of the three forms of acts.

From the point of view of cultural importance, the acts are probably ranked by most people in inverse order of their appearance in human life. As most social scientists should be regarded as cultured people, one should infer a certain preference for this ordering. They are mostly used to handling written, verbal acts, and this training may lead them to prefer data consisting of such acts. These acts have two very obvious advantages: they can yield an almost infinite variety of meaningful information, and they can easily be stored. In our culture, more differentiating capacity seems to be attributed to verbal than to non-verbal acts: we have no grammar or dictionary for the latter, even the rules of style are not many and not often codified – and do not even yield a good and fairly consensual typology for common use when data are collected.

There is an opposite ranking, however, of no less methodological importance: a ranking following the genetic order. Somehow, a tendency is often found in the literature to attribute more importance to the non-verbal than to the verbal. There is an asymmetry in the relationship: one thing is what a person *says* or *writes*, another thing is what he *does*. Probably linked to the genetic priority of the non-verbal act is the assumption that non-verbal acts in a sense are more *real*, more primordial, whereas the verbal acts are more to be regarded as epiphenomenal. If there is a discrepancy between what a person does and what he says he does, the interpretation is rather that the actor lies with his words than with his deeds.

In order to discuss this, let us first leave out the question of inference from past and present verbal acts to future non-verbal acts, as in the almost proverbial election prediction studies. That these inferences often are tenuous is true, but it is also true that we have little reason to believe in the complete impossibility of finding a set of verbal responses from which a satisfactory prediction of a future act can be made. This inference-problem, however, is not necessarily related to the problem of what kind of acts has the greatest share in 'reality'.

Let us further disregard a possible partial explanation of why social scientists may have come to regard verbal acts as somehow inferior: when sociologists, as the academic men and women they are, walk out of academic circles, perhaps they discover that non-verbal behavior plays a relatively much larger role – as anthropologists may do when working in the field. From this perception of differential relative presence may grow a feeling of differential importance, especially if illiterate peoples, and classes of non-professional people in literate societies are regarded consciously or unconsciously as incarnations of society in more 'pure' forms. We know of no empirical data to test this hypothesis, nor would it be of any relevance to the validity of the asymmetric argument.

What remains is first of all the undeniable statement that verbal reality and non-verbal reality are two different things, with no evaluation of relative importance. If a verbal stimulus elicits a certain verbal response, this is always of interest, as it may serve as a basis for the inference of, *at least, future verbal behavior.* If verbal behavior occupies a large proportion of total behavior, this is in itself no small gain. Without at all accepting that inference from verbal to non-verbal acts is not only difficult and tenuous but almost impossible, what we have so far said leaves us with the conclusion that verbal responses may be used and should be used for inferences about 'verbal reality', and non-verbal responses about 'non-verbal reality'.

Are non-verbal acts more consequential than verbal acts, and hence, do they constitute a more important part of the total social reality? It may be argued that since only non-verbal acts directly have physical consequences, they are more consequential. One can kill with a non-verbal act, but hardly with a verbal one. However, it may also be argued that verbal acts often precede or accompany dramatic non-verbal acts, so that a correspondence may be established between the two kinds of realities.

It may also be argued that verbal methods may be used to get at what people think, or at least what they think they think, but not at what they actually express in social situations. This is a methodological problem of constructing the data-collection situation so that valid information may be obtained. This methodological difficulty is not inescapable, at least not on technical grounds, but the researcher may certainly stumble on ethical problems if he tries to construct real-life situations.

Another problem lies in what one considers the subject matter of, for instance, sociology. It may be said that verbal responses are excellent if one is interested in ideology studies, as one may say that respondents can express their professed convictions better through verbal acts than through non-verbal acts. But the method may also be said to break down if one is interested in, for instance, communicative acts that are verbal acts but at the same time only parts of an interaction process. If sociology is considered as the science of inter*action*, this argument should be taken very seriously. However true a picture one may get of the ideology, the perceptions, cognitions and evaluations of the respondent, this may simply be said to be irrelevant to the field of sociology proper – and hence of value only if some solution is found to the inference problem.

Can a person lie with acts? It all depends on the definition of a lie. If we mean that there is an inconsistency between what the person knows and inferences people may legitimately draw from his overt behavior, then 'lie' applies equally well to the non-verbal sphere of human life. A may hate B, he may hypocritically affirm that he is fond of B (which probably is a lie), but he may also hypocritically act in what the culture defines as a way inconsistent with hatred. So what is the ultimate criterion?

We feel prone to say that the asymmetric conception of non-verbal as prior to verbal should yield to a symmetric conception of the two as manifest data in social research – to be used relatively safely for inferences within their own sphere, and with care for cross-sphere inferences.

Let us now approach this theme in more concrete terms, as a list of arguments for or against the two approaches.

1. *Universality*. By and large, observation is more applicable: observing somebody presupposes less in terms of interaction than interviewing him, not to mention asking him to fill in a questionnaire. But precisely this argument may also be turned against observation, not for methodological but for ethical reasons. One may observe a person without his knowing it; it is more difficult to approach him verbally without his consent. Particularly important here have been the techniques of participant observation where insights have been bought at the expense of morality. If techniques of observation that do not presuppose the open or tacit consent of the observed are excluded, then

observation becomes less universal and more similar to the other techniques.

2. *Specificity*. One advantage of the verbal approach lies in the specificity of the verbal expressions mentioned above.[1] The number of words, ways of combining them into sentences, and ways of combining these into human discourse is tremendous, especially in comparison with the crude distinctions we make for non-verbal behavior. Even if human non-verbal behavior has an infinite variety, in principle, our poor level of theoretization so far commands us to express this variety in words ; and since we use only a small part of our vocabulary for this purpose, the variety will have to be smaller. If behavioral science were like physical science we would measure non-verbal behavior, smiles would be expressed in curvature of the lips and gesture in kinematical terms – and we would restore the variety. But so far no meaningful system of this kind has been developed.

3. *Naturalness* v. *artificiality*. As we have discussed this at some length above, there is no need to repeat the argument here. We shall only stress the importance of a symmetric point of view. However, there is little doubt that observation would be most 'natural' in many situations. One such class of situations can be characterized as follows: many, perhaps most, actions human beings carry out are not easily verbalized, but easily observed. Hence, one can get meaningful data through observation only, when to press for verbalization would be painful and artificial. Thus, through observation a social process may be followed as it develops. Verbal techniques may give valuable reports, but *post hoc*, unless one is dealing with rather unusual respondents capable of acting and being interviewed at the same time. One can get at processes through observation, not only at the invariant structures that the individual can report on verbally because they have crystallized in his mind and are easily translated into linguistic structures.

4. *Expense*. Which approach is more expensive, in terms of money, manpower, administration, etc.? It is difficult to tell, but verbal interaction seems to produce a large quantity of data elements per unit cost, so the discussion would have to introduce the problem of quality if one should decide in favor of observation. In general, however, verbal data will probably be cheaper, especially if the relative ease with which they can be processed and analysed is considered.

1. Of particular importance here has been the discussion of the technique used by Festinger and his colleagues (1956), where social scientists disguised themselves as sect members waiting for doomsday to come, to record the reaction when doomsday did not materialize.

5. *Reliability*. It is customary to use this argument in favor of verbal techniques, and in general with good reason. The specificity of verbal categories, and particularly the possibility of varying the degree of specificity up and down as one wants, contribute to reliability. But this can also be obtained for non-verbal techniques, provided the setting for the data-collection is sufficiently formal and structured (Borgatta and Bales, 1953; Davis and Hagedorn, 1954). So far, however, there are few examples where this has been done successfully.

6. *Validity*. This problem will be treated in a more general way below. In general, no answer can be given to the problem of which approach is more valid. It depends on the possibility of verbalization the respondents have. We have mentioned social processes, especially ongoing processes as more amenable to observation. Much emphasis should be put on the simple social fact that ability to verbalize varies strongly with social position ; observation may be better at the social periphery, verbal approaches in the social center (that would also protest violently at the idea of being 'observed'). Also, in most cultures it is probably easier 'to lie with words' than 'to lie with acts', and this would turn the argument in favor of observation.[2]

In general, this leaves us with the conclusion 'it depends'. But the analysis also opens up the perspective of combining the two, to pool the strengths and avoid the weaknesses of either. Since these refer to different spheres of human activity we cannot solve the dilemma by a formula used later in this chapter: 'one of them for insight and interpretation, the other one for verification'. Rather, the two approaches should be seen as collateral and should be used for replication purposes.

Verbal responses: oral *v.* written
Much is known in pedagogical theory about types of perception, visual *v.* auditive for instance, but little seems to be known about types of expression in the terms above: oral *v.* written. However, much can be said in a list of arguments for or against the two forms of responses, since both of them imply certain social settings that a social scientist should be able to say something sensible about.

A word of caution should be inserted here. 'Oral *v.* written responses' is not exactly the same as 'interview *v.* questionnaire'. For instance, one could well imagine oral responses to written stimuli, when the responses

2. One way of examining the problem of validity, according to some authors, is to compare the results obtained by recording non-verbal and verbal data (one may object: 'what if they make the same mistake?'). This was done in Campbell (1955), where the morale of ten submarine crews was assessed in three different ways: by informants, by officers and by means of a thirty-item morale questionnaire. The rank correlation between the first and the third method was 0·9.

stimulus that is kept constant, then the questionnaire method is an example; a printed or mimeographed questionnaire is as constant as anything can be. But if it is a stimulus that has a comparable effect, there are more possibilities with interviews. The questions can be adjusted to changing social position, levels of knowledge, frames of reference, etc. The dangers of too much flexibility are just as obvious as the truth in the argument that to give to everybody shoes of size 8 is to give the same thing to everybody, yet with different effect. However, with relatively homogeneous samples, arguments in favor of the standardization offered by questionnaires are strong.

3. *Follow-up.* This is a very strong argument in favor of interviewing. The questionnaire can contain all kinds of follow-ups too, there may be filter-questions, one after the other (if your answer was 'yes' above, proceed to Question 25: if it was 'no', to Question 26, etc.) – but with two shortcomings: (a) all these follow-ups have to be made *a priori*, and (b) they are the same for all respondents, or for all in a certain class. In the interviewing process, follow-ups can be improvised and adjusted to each individual respondent so as to get out of him all that is relevant. The questionnaire may be made quite sensitive, but never so sensitive as the human instruments of empathy and projection used in a good interview. Thus, the interviewer has a unique chance of correcting misunderstandings. And he can get much more out of the interview by recording the whole setting, including subtleties, non-verbal acts, etc.

4. *Control of the setting.* The interviewer can control that nobody else is present to influence the respondent and that the work is done seriously. The respondent who receives his questionnaire through the mail or otherwise can fill it in by himself, but he can also make a good joke out of it in a circle of friends. This kind of excessive abuse is avoided with an interviewer present, it is also avoided if the questionnaire is filled in class or in the club or some other place where moderate supervision can be imposed.

But however well the interviewer is trained, there is one person's influence he cannot do much about: his own. There is an overwhelming literature on interviewer effect [4] that can only be controlled by

4. Some examples of this literature: In one of the major works on interviewing, Hyman (1954), there is an extensive discussion of the problem. Data on the impact of the ideology of the interviewers are contradictory: in some cases there is no effect, in other cases there is (pp. 129–34). A study by Rice (1929), where two thousand 'destitute' men were interviewed, shows a tendency for prohibitionists to report alcohol as the cause of the misery, whereas socialists would blame the economic conditions.

the three classical methods of keeping him *constant* (same interviewer, which is impossible even for what would today be moderate samples), making him *irrelevant* (i.e. substituting for him a questionnaire), and *randomization* (random matching of interviewers with respondents). This last method is satisfactory from the point of view of control, but not from other points of view.

5. *Temporal sequence.* In an interview the stimuli are presented in time, one after another like music ; in a questionnaire the stimuli appear as in a painting, in space. Of course, the respondent may only read one question at the time but when he has done so, the stimuli exist simultaneously for him, he can choose where to start and where to be impressed by the stimuli.

This may be advantageous in some situations, disadvantageous in others. Thus, one may want the respondent to react to all stimuli in their context, so as to avoid what often happens in interviews: the frame of reference is changed by a question that comes later on and the respondent may want to change his response. Thus, the questionnaire permits simultaneous evaluation of the stimuli, and without any hurry since there is nobody present to ask for speedy reactions. But there are also situations where one may want an answer before the next stimulus is presented – in that case the interview is preferable, or questionnaires with as little as one stimulus on each page and instructions not to turn the page before it is completed (this presupposes some kind of supervision).

6. *Naturalness* v. *artificiality.* Neither method is natural, since most stimuli ask the respondent to telescope his existence, to issue general statements about actions and attitudes. Thus, in real life he may be exposed at a certain point in space and time to the choice between the completion of some work and arriving in time for a party – but stimuli are more general: 'what do you think you would do' – and then follows a general description of the dilemma. The respondent is supposed to look at some role-behavior he has, with all its irregularities, and communicate some general policy statement. The problem is which is more natural, oral or written communication.

Obviously, this depends, but in general a strong argument in favor of interviewing is that it is reminiscent of something in social life, i.e. conversations. Thus, to the extent that one records verbal behavior in order to predict verbal behavior, interviews seem to be better, unless one is doing research on people particularly devoted to written expression.

7. *Expense*. There is little doubt that questionnaires are rather inexpensive and for that reason quite attractive. This is not merely a question of saving money, but also of saving administrative time and talent, e.g. by using the mail system instead of a costly *ad hoc* staff of interviewers. The condition is that such a mail system exists, as it does almost everywhere where such research methods would be considered at all. One special advantage lies in the simultaneity ; if it is important to reach all respondents at the same time this is probably easier by means of questionnaires than interviews unless the ratio of interviewers to interviewees is close to one. On the other hand, a skilled interviewer can always get the refusal rate down ; in general he will have more persuasive power than the letter accompanying questionnaires, even including the follow-up letters.

8. *Reliability*. In general, it is difficult to say. The interviewer is better trained to record than the respondent, but the respondent knows himself what he wants to answer and will get an immediate reinforcement and check when he circles or underlines an alternative. Thus, one extra human and fallible link is cut out, but even more important, we think, is the visual check provided by the manual operation with the questionnaire. There is nothing quite corresponding to this in interviewing. The interviewer may read aloud what he has written ; but that will probably only lead to a lengthy argument, since the respondent did not possess the answer alternatives in advance, as he does for the questionnaire.[5]

9. *Validity*. Again, it is difficult to say because of the problems mentioned under (2) above. The literature seems to favor questionnaires for many reasons, but the authors do not agree between themselves. Thus, there is argument to the effect that the flexibility provided by the interviewing permits more refinement, more nuances and thus more validity, and there is the argument that the skilled interviewer will have a number of soothing techniques for 'the embarrassing question' that can never quite be imitated in the questionnaire. We are inclined to

5. Nevertheless, there is much research to indicate that repeated surveys based on interviews give very similar results. Cantril (1945) compares different polls where the same question has been asked, altogether 99 comparisons, and finds an average percentage difference of 3·25 per cent. The difference depends on *time* (3·05 per cent when the questions were asked with an interval of less than ten days, 3·41 per cent when the interval was from eleven to seventy days), and on *content* (3·15 per cent for political questions, 3·45 per cent for unpolitical questions – probably because the former are more crystallized and anchored in ideological and other systems). Cantril concludes that the differences are not 'unduly high', and Stephan and McCarthy agree (1958).

say that 'it depends' but that in general questionnaires seem to be more valid.[6]

But this vague answer does not imply that the researcher is completely without a guide in the choice between the two methods, for it is rather obvious that the one does not exclude the other. Glancing through this list, we can easily muster arguments for a division in time, using the flexibility of the interview method in the beginning of a project and at the end, to get insight both for hypotheses and for interpretation ; and using the standardization of the questionnaire technique in the middle phase for confirmation purposes. This is yet an example of the importance in social research of not being invidious, but rather finding the adequate method for the problem at hand or restructuring the problem so that methods can be fully exploited for their strong aspects.

Informal v. formal settings

The two main dimensions of argumentation here are rather well known:

1. *Naturalness* v. *artificiality*. The formal setting involves systematic stimuli, i.e. many units are exposed to the same stimulus. There is no reason why this should imply artificiality. Both nature and society very often expose individuals (or higher level units) to the same stimulus, such as earthquakes, wars, social policies, elections, etc. These natural experiments can be exploited, as they have been. But their occurrence does not necessarily coincide with research projects ; sociologists often let obvious chances pass by because the structure of academic life and research grants, and a certain mental inertia, force them out of habits of improvisation. Besides, 'neutral' experiments may provide for a common stimulus but not for control of relevant factors. Thus, a certain amount of artificiality is called for, and one can imagine a continuum where more and more of the setting is provided for by the social

6. Barton (1958) mentions eight techniques that can be used for the really difficult question: the casual approach, the numbered card, the 'everybody' approach, the 'other people' approach, the sealed ballot technique, the projective technique, the Kinsey technique and putting the question at the end of the interview. Some of these require interviews, some are better with questionnaires. Nevertheless, Hyman (1954, pp. 139–49) gives a number of examples where questionnaires prove to be superior. In a study of 'love relationships', interviews were compared with questionnaires ; and less acceptable emotions (jealousy, sadism, masochism, aggression, very strong sexuality) appeared in the latter. On p. 144 is shown that this also applies to ordinary census questions. Also compare Stöuffer (1950, vol. 4, pp. 718–99 ; Stephan and McCarthy, 1958, p. 365).

scientist and less and less by other parts of the environment of the respondent.[7]

There have been many misunderstandings in this debate because of a confusion between the two goals of *prediction* and *explanation* in social science. It may well be that the 'natural', unmanipulated, setting is better for prediction studies and the manipulated, formal setting better for explanatory studies. A partial reason for this is that systematic variation of stimuli may permit the researcher to see his unit from many angles and not only under the limited range of variation provided by the natural setting. The physicist does this, but also one thing more to learn more about his material: *expose it to the extremes of the range of variation*. The structure of a compound is revealed by such methods as extreme pressure, temperature, bombardment by various particles, etc. A car is tested not under natural conditions but under extreme and artificial conditions. Correspondingly, the social scientist can learn more about the structure of a society, its strong and weak points, by observing it under crisis. And here the systematic stimuli of the formal setting enter: they can be regarded as some kind of bombardment to make the individuals reveal what is ordinarily not revealed.

2. *Comparability*. With more than one unit one can compare the units and use dispersion and covariation measures as analytical tools. There is little more to be said about that; the advantage of the formal setting is here rather undisputable, by definition. Actually, both the historian and the anthropologist, however anti-nomothetic and ideographic their ideology, use contrasts as their analytical tool, only that the contrasting cases are more likely to be mental constructs, and less likely to be systematic.

Again, the conclusion should never exclude one in favor of the other. Rather, the two combine dynamically into a combination that has proved to be very powerful in the research process. Most research will start at the informal end of the spectrum, during hypothesis-formation, then move towards the formal end in the phase of verification, and then again take excursions into the informal region during interpretation.

Formal settings: unstructured *v.* structured

In this section, systematic stimuli are assumed. In practical terms we are either dealing with systematic observations or questionnaires/schedules where the responses are extracted orally or in writing. The

7. No doubt social scientists could use more imagination in creating artificially 'natural' settings. Thus Stanton, Back and Litwak (1956) report on three studies where role-playing has been used to get survey-type data reliably, quickly and, perhaps, with more validity.

problem is whether we should operate with pre-fixed categories of response or not. For the observations this would mean that a set of categories for recording behavior is made up prior to the observation, and that the observations are squeezed into these categories – the most famous example being the Bales system of observation. For written questionnaires it means that the response variable is spelt out for the respondent, so that all he has to do is to choose the value that comes closest to his response. This is the 'closed question', a misnomer since it is really a 'closed answer'.

For interviews, a distinction can be made between closed questions and closed answers. In the former, the respondent is given, orally, the answer alternatives: 'Which candidate do you favor, Allende, Frei or Durán?', which means that the response variable is spelt out for him as in the questionnaire. In the latter he is asked 'Which candidate do you favor?' The question is open, but the interviewer may have closed the answers by a precoding in his schedule. This, however, is only known to him and not to the respondent, and hence serves only administrative purposes like facilitation of coding. It does not structure the mind of the respondent. We can have closed answers without closing the question, but the closed question implies closed answers. This is the case we are most interested in. The problem is what we obtain and what we lose by structuring the mind of the respondent, but we shall also mention what we obtain and what we lose by structuring the mind of the social scientist. Some of the main dimensions of discussion are as follows.

1. *Comparability*. The main advantage of the structured response is to facilitate comparability. The structured response, one hopes, will create a common frame of reference and by definition a common response variable, and hence complete comparability. Even if it is only structured for the social scientist as in the 'open question, closed answer' or systematic observation cases, the result will be at least formal comparability. Only in this case will the model of the data matrix which we have used extensively apply. 'Which car do you prefer?' may elicit two answers, one in terms of craftsmanship – but the question 'Which car do you prefer, speedy but not so solid, or solid but not so speedy?' makes for a more precise, and *known*, frame of reference. Thus, we get standardization, but possibly at the expense of

2. *Flexibility*. One major advantage of the unstructured response is the freedom it permits. The respondent may choose his frame of reference himself and one may get at the context of the answers, extra perceptions or motivations, etc. On the other hand, comparability can be obtained to a certain extent by means of content analyses of the open

answers, coding and checks for reliability of the coding. The advantage of structured responses is that they yield precise versions of the question; the advantage of the unstructured response is to be imprecise, that they permit the unexpected response.

3. *Naturalness* v. *artificiality*. Again, the argument seems to favor the unstructured technique, for the same reason as it favors the informal setting. But this presupposes that one is interested in prediction rather than explanation, and wants to infer from one 'natural setting' to another one. Explanatory studies can probably benefit by using techniques that permit more refined kinds of analyses.

4. *Expense*. Anyone who has carried out research of both kinds will know how much this argument favors the structured technique. The amount of work put into structuring the answers for the respondent and pre-coding them for the analyst is little compared with the job of doing all of it *a posteriori*. This applies to all phases of the project: structuring facilitates the data-collection enormously for both parties involved, it facilitates the data-processing and the analysis because of the comparability involved. In terms of money, administration time and manpower, this may mean considerable savings particularly appreciable in low-budget centers of research.

5. *Reliability*. The technique of structured responses permits a very high degree of reliability, whereas the differences in frames of reference and linguistic habits, etc., will make for lower reliability when the responses are unstructured. By this we do not mean 'constancy', i.e. the property of the *respondent* to give the same response when exposed to the same stimulus (very often confused with reliability in the literature); but *intra-subjectivity* (i.e. that the same social scientist codes the same response the same way) and *inter-subjectivity* (that various social scientists code the same response the same way). As to constancy, it is well known that a respondent can vary his response to the same stimulus even over rather short time intervals, for which reason it is so important to present him with a set of stimuli and combine the responses into indices in such a way that the index value is not sensitive to unsystematic variations in the responses to the individual stimuli.[8]

8. A good example of an investigation of the problem of constancy (unfortunately called 'reliability' in the title of the article and 'consistency' in the article) is Mouton, Blake and Fruchter (1955). The article surveys eight test–retest sociometric studies and finds constancy of choices to vary between 27 per cent and 77 per cent. Constancy is seen to depend on time interval (negatively), age (positively), relevance of sociometric criterion (positively), number of values in the variable (our r) (positively, the more discriminations that can be made, the more constant the choice or rather, the higher the test–retest correlation).

6. *Validity*. As usual, the requirement of reliability may conflict with the requirement of validity. The major accusation against the technique of structured responses would be that it makes for a certain quasi-validity: it looks as if the respondents are answering the same question because of the precise formulations provided by the structuring of the response, but there is always a good possibility of misinterpretation, misunderstanding, response-set, etc. The theory is often that less structuring will bring this out; but that is, of course, wrong, unless a considerable amount of probing is done that will almost by definition exclude the questionnaire as an instrument. Moreover, empirical research seems to favor structuring.[9]

Again, the arguments make for no clear picture, and for the trivial conclusion of using both. But in which order? It is rather obvious, since the structuring of responses will have to come from somewhere, and if it shall not simply be decided upon by the researcher it will have to come from using unstructured techniques first. Hence: unstructured techniques for development of hypotheses and possibly for interpretation; structured techniques for verification.

The problem of validity

This is to a considerable extent an epistemological and philosophical problem, not simply a question of measurement. It has to do with the general problem discussed in this chapter: whether some forms of data-collection (referring to Table 2) give more valid information than others. The focus on validity presupposes an asymmetric perception of the forms of data-collection – if not, validity is reduced to a question of correlation (for instance, between verbal and non-verbal behavior).

But validity is more than a question of comparing cells in the table, using one cell as a criterion for the other. With regard to verbal data (oral or written), there is a particular skepticism which seems to have three dimensions:

1. *Latent* v. *manifest*: to what extent can we infer from the verbal expressions to a person's 'true' position on a dimension that gives his attitude?

2. *Expressions* v. *thoughts*: to what extent can we infer from what a person says to what he thinks?

9. Hyman (1954, pp. 190–201), gives data that show higher percentage of errors, both 'bias' and 'non-bias', and more technical errors for unstructured than for structured interview-guides. For another point of view see Achal (1958). It was concluded that the choice of the respondents was biased by the alternatives presented, and that this effect is offset by age and education (Stephan and McCarthy, 1958, p. 365).

3. *Expressions* v. *behavior:* to what extent can we infer from verbal expressions to a person's behavior?

As it is formulated here it appears as if we accept these requirements, i.e. that there should be an unambiguous relation connecting thoughts, expressions, and behavior, so that each such chain can be mapped on a latent dimension. However, we do not necessarily accept such a view.

Let us start with the problem of the latent v. the manifest. Broadly speaking, we feel the problem cannot be attacked in terms of *one* observation variable. The problem is solved by n manifest indicators rather than one, seeing to it that these n indicators are somehow sampled from a reasonably well defined set of possible indicators, and combining these indicators into a summary measure by some kind of index formation, *or* using all of them separately (but never relying on only one, except when there is long experience supporting the belief in exactly that indicator). Following this procedure, the 'manifest v. latent' is not a problem of validity, for the latent dimension is a construct that is given content by the manifest indicators. It is in no sense an independently existing dimension that can be used as a control of the manifest indicators. The 'validity' of the manifest indicators depends on how they correlate with other variables – as will be developed later.

The problem of expressions v. thoughts is more interesting. Do people speak (or write) the truth when they are approached by interviewing or questionnaire procedures? If the 'truth' is defined as what they have in mind, obviously no absolute answer can be given. The degree of correspondence between a person's private thoughts and what he chooses to express depends on a cultural component and an individual component. We have not seen good data on this, but all experience seems to indicate that 'veracity' in the sense of thought–speech correspondence is to a considerable extent a product of culture and *socialization*. No social scientist working in former colonial nations (whether they were or are political, economic or cultural colonies) will have failed to get this 'advice' from residing *colons*: 'Do not trust what people say in interviews. They only say what they think you want to hear, not what they think themselves.' It is difficult to evaluate the degree of truth in a statement of this kind. It probably describes relatively well the kind of relationship that prevailed and prevails between the upper class (foreign or indigenous) in these parts of the world and their servants (whether working in their masters' houses or in restaurants, bars, as shoe-shiners, taxi-drivers, or in other service-positions). In a culture of servility and strong competition, there is a clear incentive for very scarce position with access to the ruling class to please the master. One way of so advancing is obviously to have a rather pragmatic view on truth.

This does not mean that the same phenomenon automatically obtains in interviews – although it is likely to be true, the more similar the interview situation is to the master–servant situation. Thus, interviewing should probably be done by natives, not by the foreign social scientist (who should, however, carry out some interviews to get first-hand insight in how the process functions). Nevertheless, the problem will remain. The researcher may reduce it by maximizing trust in the interview situation; by asking so many questions so quickly that it becomes too complicated for the interviewee to work out a system of systematic distortion; by having a number of questions that refer to facts, to past and present actions, or pure knowledge, so as to induce in the interviewee a pattern of speaking the truth (especially if some of the facts are very easily verifiable), in the hope that there may be a carry-over effect from the factual part of the questionnaire to the value part. By such techniques the discrepancy can no doubt be reduced, if not cut down to zero.

However, it will always be difficult to confirm this: confirmation would lead to the famous problem of distortion hierarchies. To measure discrepancy between expressions and thoughts, we have to use other indicators of thoughts – since our ability to read thoughts directly is at best somewhat underdeveloped. Other indicators could be obtained by a new interview – and there is again the same problem. Or, they could be obtained by observing behavior or reading letters or diaries – and there is the problem, important for historical research, of whether there is any reason at all to believe more in behavior or written documents than spoken words as expression of thoughts. We have seen no theory or evidence to support this hypothesis, and would even be inclined to believe just as much the opposite.

But we can also approach this problem from a quite different angle, asking: is the correspondence between thoughts and words really important? Or is this just a transfer of a moral problem ('Thou shalt speak the truth and nothing but the truth') to the realm of methodology without a real analysis of the implications? For we may also reason as follows: in surveys, e.g. of how people react to certain policy measures, it may be socially much more important how people say they would react than how they 'really' (meaning when they are alone with themselves) do react. If the ordinary Frenchman polled says he is in favor of the *force de frappe*, then this is more important than his inner reservations. They may be important for a personal analysis, not for an analysis of attitudes here and now. The spoken word is a social act, the inner thought is not, and the sociologist has good reasons to be most interested and concerned with the former, the psychologist perhaps with the latter. But this only transforms the problem from the problem of correspondence between words and thoughts to the problem of how representative the interview situation is as social intercourse. Thus, the idea would be that the sociologist wants to know what kind of verbal expression the respondent, given certain stimuli, would present to others – and the interview should then be a copy of such situations rather than deep, fast and probing. For this purpose, interviewing in groups may quite possibly be better, since it may give a social setting more true to life. On the other hand, it also seems obvious that interviewing that aims more at inner psychological dynamics should give data closer to the mental pre-image of the person and be less concerned with what he chooses to present to others. In short: the problem of expressions *v.* thoughts depends very much on the analytical purpose of the interviewing.

Then there is a third way of looking at the problem, which we shall just barely touch on: why presuppose a mental pre-image at all? Many questions fall on virgin soil, but that does not mean that they fall on barren soil. They are stimuli that create mental images and start mental processes, they do not tap pre-existing ideas. Hence, the idea of correspondence would be meaningless – unless we interpreted it as correspondence between words and mental *post*-images.

We turn to the basic problem of correspondence between words and deeds, between expressions and behavior. We have done some reasoning in favor of a symmetric point of view: that verbal and non-verbal data represent different spheres of behavior, and that data may be valid in their own right. Here we shall make some reflections on the relation between them.

First of all: there is also here the danger of a moralistic argument, that there shall be consistency between words and deeds. The degree of consistency will depend on a general cultural and a more specific individual component; there will be cultures inculcating norms about consistency and there are probably cultures that are more lenient in this respect, just as individuals differ. This is not simply a question of speaking the truth or not, but of conceiving of the two spheres as tightly coupled or not. Whereas to some people it seems obvious that if one expresses democratic values then one should also behave democratically in some specified way, to others this is less obvious. Words may be defined as being epiphenomenal, as belonging to a sphere of the ideal, whereas deeds are reality; and the two may belong to different regimes, so to speak ('Regimenten' in Luther's sense).

Secondly: we do not accept the idea that actions should always serve as a basis for validating words, we prefer a symmetric perspective. One may use words to validate actions as one does very often, for instance when one contrasts a person's happy-go-lucky face with his sad verbal reports about the poor health of some of his close relatives. In some cases we would say that he is lying with words ('he is not really concerned, as evidenced by the way he looks'), in other cases that he is lying with his non-verbal behavior ('he pretends he does not care', or 'he is taking it extremely well'). Which interpretation to choose depends on what other information we have; this should also be the case in social analysis, with no sweeping assumption as to what can be used as a criterion and what should be validated against that criterion.

Thirdly: whether we should require consistency or not depends, of course, on what expressions and what actions we have. Three important dimensions here are:

1. *Descriptive* v. *normative*, i.e. what did the person do, what is he doing, what is he going to do – as against what does he think he should do.

2. *Specific* v. *general*, i.e. what did you do yesterday at noon, as against what do you generally do in the middle of the day; what should one do when one's best friend spreads gossip behind one's back as against 'what do you think of gossip'.

3. *The temporally close* v. *the temporally distant*, i.e. 'what are you doing now' as against 'what did you do ten years ago' or 'what will you do in ten years'.

If a person describes his own behavior in specific terms, and the reference is to the present, or very recent past or close future, we should have good reasons to expect consistency. But if he expresses values in general terms, applying to the distant past or remote future, there are so many very acceptable reasons for inconsistency that a process of validation on that basis would be out of place. Surveys may be criticized if they do not predict correctly elections one week or one month prior to the event (provided, of course, that the sampling is adequate, that the results are not published so as to interfere with the events, and that no important external event appears on the scene in the meantime). But they should not be criticized if they refer to general values applying to choices that will be made some time in the future, and the 'predictions' do not come true. There simply is no reason to suppose consistency in this case, except as a moral dogma or an unwarranted methodological postulate.

Then, of course, it may be objected: what is the value of analyzing complex value-patterns if they do not serve as predictors of overt behavior? We have three answers to this important question.

1. They may predict *verbal* behavior, i.e. future value-assertions, quite well, as shown by the relatively high degree of consistency over time in panel analyses (except when external events have changed the perceptual field of the respondent drastically).

2. They serve as signals from the depths of the person, giving us a synchronic cut in time both in the life of the person and the life of the system, valuable for the analysis of both (if not for the prediction) up till the date of the data-collection.

3. Even if the value-patterns do not predict behavior or outcomes in a general sense, this only serves to indicate that a simplified model of consistency fails, and should lead to an analysis of *why*, not to mention to the collection of behavioral data.

Thus, imagine two different villages are presented with the same stimulus to social change, e.g. in the form of a technical assistance project. Generally, economic development may be said to depend on three kinds of factors: material and capital resources (the approach often favored by economists), social structure (the approach often favored by anthropologists), and value patterns (the approach often favored by sociologists and psychologists). Let us assume the villages are equivalent on the first dimension, and get the same input from the technical assistance project; further, that village A has values that should favor utilization of the new resources more than village B, and that village B has an organizational structure that should favor acceptance more than village A. Which factor will dominate may be very difficult to predict, but let us imagine that the structural factor dominates. This does not mean that the value factor is not consistent with behavior, only that it has been overridden by another factor that works in the opposite direction. Nor does it mean in general that social structure is a better predictor than value patterns, for this is a question of degrees. Only one thing is obvious: if village A is favored both by value patterns and by social structure, then we would be rather surprised if our prediction did not come true.[10]

In short: the question of validity is complicated. There are clear norms of how data-collection should be carried out, so as not to distort

10. This reasoning is basic to an anthropological/sociological research project on the effect of technical assistance on two villages in southern India, carried out by Arne Martin Klausen and Johan Galtung at the International Peace Research Institute, Oslo.

what is already there. But: (a) the social scientist should rather be pleased by the variety of techniques at his disposal and try to enlarge the number than try to reduce some of them to others that are seen as 'more basic', (b) he should use a variety of techniques to get data of different kinds rather than rely on one of them alone, and (c) 'the proof of the pudding is in the eating', i.e. what can be explained and predicted from the data collected is the important thing, not how much 'consistency' there is between forms of data-collection with perhaps no theoretical reason for consistency at all between them.

Finally, let us make some comments on the literature in this field. While there is a vast general literature on the problems of reliability and validity (Lindquist, 1951, chs. 15, 16; Guilford, 1954, ch. 14; Green, 1954, pp. 338–41; Stevens, 1951), we are concerned with more specific findings. Most of this literature goes to show that what people say is not what people do, and it is rather important for the social scientist to be well informed about this. We shall give some examples:

1. Mosteller, Hyman, McCarthy, Marks and Truman (1949) discuss the polls prior to the election of 1948 in the United States with a total sample of 14,696 persons. 65 per cent said they would vote, but the participation in the election was actually only 52 per cent. However, many discrepancies between forecasts and voting are explained by use of quota-samples, error in estimating who is really going to vote, erroneous treatment of people who had not yet made up their minds, and last-minute change of mind. Besides, there is the famous factor of self-denying prophecy, of people who stay at home because they feel confident after hearing the forecasts (in the famous words attributed to Elmor Roper: 'It was not the polls that went to the dogs, but the dogs that did not go to the polls').

2. Parry and Crossley (1950) discuss an experiment carried out in Denver by the Opinion Research Center. Data about how people said they had voted in 1944 were compared with election data. It appeared that 23 per cent of the respondents said they had voted, but had not voted at all. Answers about 'Community Chest contributions' were also very inaccurate, but data about whether one had a valid library card, a driver's licence, telephone, car, etc. were more accurate, but still with 5 per cent to 15 per cent of invalid answers (some of it due to the interviewers).

3. Katona (1951) compares income distributions obtained from surveys and from the income tax authorities and finds considerable discrepancies – but here the truth is likely to be located inbetween.

4. Riddle (1953) reports a study of readership. People known to read a certain magazine were asked which magazines they read, only 47·3 per cent mentioned spontaneously the magazine. However, when the remaining 52·7 per cent were asked directly whether they read the magazine, 91 per cent said that they did so. This is indicative of the importance of structured answers for increased validity, but also that 'readership studies are largely measurements of mental images and impressions'.

5. Cohen and Lipstein (1954) in a study conclude differently; they find it quite possible to collect wage statistics validly and reliably by mail questionnaire. Again, this may be an argument for questionnaires as opposed to interviews.[11]

6. Larsen and De Fleur (1955) report from one of their leaflet studies where people were asked to mail a postage-paid reply card in response to a leaflet drop. 98 per cent of those who said they had not mailed any card in fact had not done so, but only 53 per cent of those who said they had done so were verified. People with valid verbal behavior differed from the others on age.

Many more examples could be given but we do not need more to make the basic point already made above: validity varies with the technique chosen, and by and large seems to increase when we move from the upper left corner in Table 2 to the lower right corner. At the same time, this transition is the transition from exploratory to confirmatory phases of a research project, which is fortunate.

11. There is an interesting literature on how to improve the technique of mail questionnaires, which undeniably is a very attractive method since it leaves so much of the work to an outside bureaucracy, the mail system, at a moderate cost. In Bradt (1955) the idea is presented of asking mail questionnaire respondents to return a pre-paid card when they have returned the questionnaire – but separately so that anonymity is preserved. This gives a rapid check of the representativeness of the return, and also information about where to insist. After two mailings and fourteen weeks a return of 80 per cent of a sample of 5356 persons was obtained; without such techniques a 20 per cent return is not uncommon (but, of course, unacceptable).

References

ACHAL, A. P. (1958), 'Relative value of poll-end and open-end questions in search for reasons of a problem', *Educ. and Psychol.*, pp. 55–60.
BARTON, A. H. (1958), 'Asking the embarrasing question', *Public Opinion Q.*, vol. 22, no. 1, pp. 67–8.
BIRMINGHAM, W. B., and JAHODA, G. (1955), 'A pre-election survey in a semi-literate society', *Public Opinion Q.*, vol. 19, no. 2, pp. 140–52.

BORGATTA, E. F. and BALES, R. F. (1953), 'The consistency of subject behavior and the reliability of scoring in interaction process analysis', *Amer. Sociol. Rev.*, vol. 18, no. 5, pp. 556–8.

BRADT, K. (1955), 'The usefullness of a postcard technique in a mail questionnaire study', *Public Opinion Q.*, vol. 19, no. 2, pp. 218–22.

CAMPBELL, D. T. (1955), 'The informant in quantitative research', *Amer. J. Sociol.*, vol. 60, no. 4, pp. 339–42.

CANTRIL, H. (1945), 'Do different polls get the same results?', *Public Opinion Q.*, vol. 9, no. 1, pp. 61–9.

COHEN, S. E., and LIPSTEIN, B. (1954), 'Response errors in the collection of wage statistics by mail questionnaire', *J. Amer. Stats. Assoc.*, vol. 49, no. 266, pp. 240–53.

DAVIS, F. J., and HAGEDORN, R. (1954), 'Testing the reliability of systematic field observations', *Amer. Sociol. Rev.*, vol. 17, pp. 345–8.

FESTINGER, L. (1956), *When Prophecy Fails*, University of Minnesota Press.

GREEN, B. F. (1954), 'Attitude measurement', in G. Lindzey (ed.), *Handbook of Social Psychology*, Addison-Wesley.

GUILFORD, J. P. (1954), *Psychometric Methods*, McGraw-Hill.

HYMAN, H. (1954), *Interviewing in Social Research*, University of Chicago Press.

KATONA, G. (1951), *Psychological Analysis of Economic Behavior*, McGraw-Hill.

LARSEN, O. N., and DE FLEUR, M. (1955), 'Validity and reliability in measurements of message diffusion', *Proceedings of Pacific Sociological Society*, pp. 110–20.

LINDQUIST, E. F. (1951), *Educational Measurement*, American Council on Education.

MOUTON, J. S., BLAKE, R. R., and FRUCHTER, B. (1955), 'The reliability of sociometric measures', *Sociometry*, vol. 18, no. 1, pp. 7–48.

MOSTELLER, C. F., HYMAN, H. and MCCARTHY, P. J. (1949), *The Pre-election Polls of 1948*, Social Science Research Council.

PARRY, H. J., and CROSSLEY, H. M. (1950), 'Validity of responses to survey questions', *Public Opinion Q.*, vol. 14, no. 1, pp. 61–80.

RIDDLE, G. W. N. (1953), 'Validity of readership studies', *J. Marketing*, vol. 18, no. 1, pp. 26–32.

RICE, S. S. (1929), 'Contagious bias in the interview', *Amer. J. Sociol.*,

STANTON, H., BACK, K. W., and LITWAK, E. (1956), 'Role playing in social research', *Amer. J. Sociol.*, vol. 62, no. 2, pp. 172–6.

STEPHAN, F. F., and MCCARTHY, P. J. (1958), *Sampling Opinions*, Wiley.

STEVENS, S. S. (1951), *Handbook of Experimental Psychology*, Wiley.

STOUFFER, S. A. (1950), *The American Soldier*, vol. 4, Princeton University Press.

The Two Sociologies

Alan Dawe, 'The two sociologies', *British Journal of Sociology*,
vol. 21, 1970, pp. 207–18.

The thesis that sociology is centrally concerned with the problem of
social order has become one of the discipline's few orthodoxies. It is
common as a basic premise to many accounts of sociological theory,
which otherwise differ considerably in purpose and perspective
(Parsons, 1949; Nisbet, 1967; Bramson, 1961; Cohen, 1968; Aron,
1968). Essentially, the argument is that sociology was shaped by the
nineteenth-century conservative reaction to the Enlightenment, the
French Revolution and the Industrial Revolution. In opposition to what
was seen as the subversive rationalism of the first, the traumatic disorder of the second and the destructive egoism of the third, the conservative reaction sought the restoration of a supra-individual hegemony. In so doing, it created a language which, at once, defined the
solution to the problem of order and the sociological perspective ; hence
the centrality of such concepts as authority, the group, the sacred and,
above all, the organic community.

The essence of this language lies in its dependence upon notions of
externality and constraint, for the problem of order is defined in
Hobbesian terms. Indeed, the historical movements which led to the
conservative reaction could be seen as confirmation of the Hobbesian
view of human nature. It is central to this view that, in the absence of
external constraint, the pursuit of private interests and desires leads
inevitably to both social and individual disintegration. For nineteenth-
century Hobbesian revisionists, therefore, society became the new *deus
ex machina*.

In this perspective, the development of sociological thought appears
as a series of mutations in the notion of external constraint. Externality
becomes internalization, constraint becomes a moral imperative, the
individual becomes the social self, and society as a *deus ex machina*
becomes society as a reality *sui generis*. In Weber's typification of
bureaucratic order, in Durkheim's abiding concern with moral solidarity
and, latterly, in the conceptual web woven by Parsons around the

of functionally specific norms, structure roles and institutional sub-systems into the total system by defining the network of functional activities necessary for the latter's survival. When survival is threatened, from whichever environmental source, the system adjusts in such a way as to restore equilibrium. Moreover, it generates its own dynamic of change through the process of structural differentiation, in which concept the idea of the system's self-production receives its clearest expression.

Here, though, it may seem that the argument jumps too large a gap between the origins of the social-system perspective in the classic Hobbesian problem and its latest manifestation in structural-functionalism. In particular, it may be objected that successive attempts to account for the subjective dimension of action have led to the conceptual substitution of internalization for externality. The position taken here, however, is that this change has not altered the basic logic of the social-system perspective. For it boils down, in that perspective, to the concept of socialization. And this, whilst it may refine the description of how constraint is achieved, does not alter the way in which the source of constraint is conceptually located. From the point of view of the actor in the social-system framework, that source still has the attribute of externality. To put it crudely, the actor is still on the receiving-end of the system.

To amplify, the argument here is that subjective meanings are, through the postulate of consensus, ultimately derived from the central value system and are thus, at root, external conditions of the actor's situation; essentially, objects of the environment. The important, if paradoxical, consequence of this is that, once objective meaning is incorporated into the social-system perspective, it *reinforces* the latter's basic dependence on the notion of external constraint and, therefore, its link with the problem of order. For, given the view of the relationship between the social and the individual inherent in that problem, meaning can only be conceptualized by postulating social norms as being constitutive, *rather than merely regulative*, of the self. That is, the problem of order can only be solved by conceiving of the actor as a reflex of the social system and meaning as a reflex of the cultural system. Far from disappearing, constraint becomes total through internalization. No matter how many qualifying clauses may be introduced, it remains decisive because it is basic to the logic of the social-system perspective. Hence the inevitability of 'the oversocialized conception of man' (Wrong, 1961). It merely remains to utilize whatever conceptual tools may be to hand – such as Freudian notions, suitably amended – to justify it.

This argument has a further consequence. If subjective meaning is derivable, through the postulate of consensus, from a prior characterization of the central value system, then it does not have to be treated as a significant variable (Gross, Mason and McEachern, 1958). All that has to be explained is the process of internalization. In short, its treatment of the subjective dimension of action is basic to the metatheoretical, as well as the substantive position of the social-system perspective. The former position, as Scott has pointed out, is behaviourist (1963); the methodological corollary of viewing subjective meanings as, at root, external conditions of the actor's situation and thus as objects of the environment. As such, they become amenable to the methods of the natural sciences, upon whose logic sociological inquiry can therefore be modelled. Thus social systems can be conceptualized in terms of convenient analogies with natural-scientific system constructs. And, of course, given the view of society central to the social-system perspective, the convenient analogy is the organic. The logical progression is complete: the substantive and metatheoretical positions in question are defined and indissolubly linked by the doctrine of order.

It follows from the argument so far that if the problem of order is *the* central problem for sociology, then the social-system perspective must be *the* sociological perspective. This, indeed, is not an uncommon claim, nor one which cannot find support in the literature of the discipline. Certainly, there appears to be a widely accepted sociological language which is comprised of social-system concepts, in the meaning they derive from that perspective. And this language is by no means confined to 'grand theory'. Irrespective of the extent to which the assumptions behind it are made explicit, it has become common currency at virtually every level in sociology, from the basic text to the specialist sub-discipline. An obvious example here is provided by the universality of the language of role, the crucial bridging concept between the social and the individual in the social-system perspective (Dahrendorf, 1968).

At this point, however, a question arises. Throughout the history of sociology, there has also been a manifest conflict between two types of social analysis; namely the conflict variously labelled as being between the mechanistic and organismic approaches, between atomism and holism, methodological individualism and collectivism, and so on. How does the pre-eminence of the social-system perspective, which appears to opt for one side of the debate, square with the latter's persistence in sociological thought? Here, the considerable claim is made that it resolves the issue. It is said – to translate the conflict into the relevant terms – to bring together the social-system and social-action approaches to sociological analysis in one coherent, comprehensive schema. But does this synthesis work? It has, after all, been attempted many times; yet the conflict seems to endure. For example, Finlay Scott has pointed to its persistence in the powerful attempt at synthesis by Parsons (1963).

The first point to be made about this concerns the languages of the two approaches. As it has been developed in sociology (Parsons, 1949), the language of social action begins with the subjective dimension of action; conceptualizes it as the definition of the situation; spells this out in terms of actors defining situations on the basis of ends, means and conditions; and posits action as a process over time, i.e. as history. It is at this point, however, that the language of social action is absorbed by that of social system. By a combination of the principle of emergence and the postulate of consensus, unit acts are systematized in terms of central values. In the consequent synthesis, actors derive their definitions of situations from the central value system, through their internalization of the social roles ultimately defined by that system.

From the earlier argument, it will be evident that there is a conflict of meaning between the two languages. The point is that, as soon as definitions of the situation become properties of the central value system – that is, as soon as the elements of action are, in effect, reduced to the single element of situational conditions – then, *in terms of its initial premises of subjectivity and historicity*, action disappears. In short, the attempted synthesis subordinates action to system concepts in such a way as to remove the concept of action altogether. Perpetual 'orientation' takes its place.

On the analytic level, therefore the synthesis fails. But behind this failure lies a second, more fundamental point. If that synthesis is attempted on the basis of the language of consensus, central value system and internalization, it is clearly dependent upon the 'problem-of-order' thesis. And the fact is that attempts at synthesis have always rested upon precisely this foundation (Parsons, 1949; Cohen, 1968; Berger and Luckmann, 1967). A sociological language which cannot be reconciled with the social-system perspective without losing its meaning must, therefore, derive that meaning from some other source than the concern with the problem of order. The conclusion has to be that, whilst that problem has undoubtedly been central to much of sociology, it has not been the *only* central problem; from which it follows that the conservative reaction was not the only source of inspiration for the development of sociological thought.

For the location of a second source of inspiration, Nisbet's characterization of 'the age of Enlightenment' is suggestive.

The dominant objectives of the whole age . . . were those of release: release of the individual from ancient social ties and of the mind from fettering traditions (1967, p. 8).

This interpretation sums up the essential character of the Enlightenment more accurately than those, common to most historians of sociology, which emphasize its rationalism and empiricism.[1] Whilst it is dangerous to attribute an obvious intellectual coherence to that movement, Nisbet's summary points to one general aim the *philosophes* did have in common: that of human liberation. For them, the application of reason and the scientific method to social analysis was merely a means to the solution of the problem which constituted the whole point and purpose of their thought. This was the problem of how human beings could regain *control* over essentially man-made institutions and historical situations.

The movement was, of course, historically specific. Its attack was upon a specific set of hitherto-inviolable institutions and relationships sanctioned by the belief in divine authority.[2] Divinely ordered, universal situations became man-made, historical situations. Social institutions became the subject and object of social action. In a word, the Enlightenment postulated the human, as opposed to a divine construction of the ideal. It fashioned the logical gap between the 'is' and the 'ought' into a weapon of social criticism, transforming it into the gap between the actual and the ideal, in which the attainment of the ideal entailed the creative imposition of a human, as opposed to a supra-human meaning upon the actual. In such a perspective, action constitutes an unceasing attempt to exert control over existing situations, relationships and institutions in such a way as to bring them into line with human constructions of their ideal meanings.

1. See, for example, Zeitlin (1968) in which he characterizes the influence of the Enlightenment on sociology in precisely these terms. True, he is aware of the 'critical-revolutionary tendency' of the Enlightenment, but he becomes too immersed in a prolonged celebration of Marx to develop the point.

2. The stress on reason has to be understood in the light of the attack upon what the *philosophes* saw as the major characteristic of religion: its unreason. This did not mean that they wished to posit reason as the sole characteristic of man. Rather, autonomous man was whole man, in whom neither reason nor feeling were subordinated to the other. On this, see especially Gay (1964, 1966).

In sum, the suggestion here is that the Enlightenment generated what it is proposed to call, for obvious reasons, *the problem of control*. And this leads to a further proposition, to the effect that sociology has been concerned, not with one central problem, but with two. It is not difficult to see the connection between the problem of control and the language of social action. The basic point is that the initial premises of subjectivity and historicity, in which that language is grounded, are implicit in the gap between the actual and the ideal; for the attempt to transcend that gap is essentially an attempt to impose ideal meanings on existing situations. Hence the linking concepts of meaning and action ; the concepts of ends as desired future states, and of the existing situation as providing conditions to be transcended or overcome and means to be utilized; and the notion of actors defining their own situations and attempting to control them in terms of their definitions.

If these were the only points of connection, however, they would not be sufficient to establish the problem of control as having a centrality in sociology equal to, and distinct from, that of the problem of order. For the language of social action does not, as it stands, comprise a complete sociological perspective. If, for the reasons given, it cannot be genuinely reconciled with the social-system perspective, then it requires new emergent concepts ; without them, it is open to the damaging charge of individualism or atomism (Lukes, 1968). By the same token, the problem of control could not be counted as a doctrine in the same sense as the problem of order.

In point of fact, it is here that the real significance of the problem of control as a second major concern in sociology becomes clear. For it generates two emergent concepts through which, like the problem of order, it penetrates and shapes a distinctive sociology at both the substantive and metatheoretical levels. The first concept, emerging from the transcendental relation of meaning to actual historical situations, integrates unit courses of action into meaning-systems. The attempt to impose ideal meanings upon actuality can be conceptualized as an attempt by the actor to make sense of his situations in terms of some overarching meaning. Thus definitions of the different situations of everyday life – work situation, family situation, political situation and so on – can be understood by means of a concept of *central meaning*.[3] It should be clear that this notion is diametrically opposed to that of central value, since its basic reference is not to the social system, but to the social actor. The latter is conceptualized as integrating his

3. A notion which has appeared in many guises in sociology. However, since it has generally been translated into that of central value, it has not become a key concept in a distinct sociology of social action.

different situations and biographical episodes in terms of an overall life-meaning, from which he derives his situationally specific goals and definitions.[4]

It is at this point that the notion of *control* enters the action framework as an analytic concept, in the same logical progression whereby the notion of order enters the social-system framework. In the first place, it adds the dimension of action to that of meaning: to control a situation is to impose meaning upon it by acting upon it. Secondly, it adds the dimension of interaction, or relationship between actors: to control a situation is to impose one's definition upon the other actors in that situation. The concept of control refers essentially to social relationships whose properties cannot be reduced to the individual definitions and courses of action from which they emerge; it integrates actors into interaction systems.[5]

The properties of these systems, however, are not prejudged. There is no postulate of consensus or, for that matter, of cooperation, conflict or constraint. The extent to which a concrete interaction situation turns on any or all of these becomes the empirical question it really is. Nor are prior assumptions made about the extent of control itself, for it is clear that the capacity for control will, in the typical case, be differentially distributed. It depends partly on the nature and scope of situational definitions; partly on the relationship, in terms of projected outcomes, between the consequent courses of action; and partly on differential access to facilities and subjection to limiting conditions. By the same token, the relative significance of evaluation and cognitive elements in interaction, and the extent to which control depends upon normative, calculative and/or coercive mechanisms become empirical questions.[6]

Together, the concepts of central meaning and control produce the social action view of the nature of society. Social systems are conceptualized as the *outcome* of a continuous process of interaction, which turns on the 'projects' and differential capacities for control of the

4. Subjective meaning is, of course, a complex construct derived from a combination of observers' and participants' definitions and purposes. Thus the sociologist himself becomes a variable in the interaction he studies (Cicourel, 1964).

5. As it is used here, the notion or control refers neither to notions about controlling the environment (especially technology (see Etzioni, 1968)), nor to the structural-functionalist concept of social control. Clearly, it is close to notions of power and authority.

6. It is important to stress that the distinction between the social system and social action perspectives is not synonymous with the distinction and the dispute between consensus and conflict theories. In so far as the latter both rest on *postulate* of consensus and conflict, and locate them as properties of the social system, they fall within the social-system perspective.

participants. Institutions and roles are thus conceptualized at two emergent levels.[7] At the level of the social actor, they are linked by their relationship to a central meaning and by the attempt to activate that meaning across the institutional board. At the social-system level, they are linked by relationships of control and by the purposes which emerge as the result of interaction. Typically, these will be the purposes of no single actor to the extent that they will embody elements of compromise and, more important, in that they will involve unforeseen consequences. This is not, however, to divorce them from the reference to subjective meaning, for systems as unintended consequences are always referred back to the interaction from which they emerge. A social action approach always and necessarily 'demystifies' them by revealing their roots in human action. Again, the link with the problem of control is obvious.

It is also obvious at the metatheoretical level. Since the base unit of analysis is the social actor, the notion of subjective meaning is again decisive. The human capacity for the construction of meaning is taken as differentiating the subject-matter and, so, the logic of sociological enquiry from that of the natural sciences. Hence the *verstehen* view of the nature of sociology.[8]

There are, then, two sociologies: a sociology of social system and a sociology of social action. They are grounded in the diametrically opposed concerns with two central problems, those of order and control.

7. It is important to note here the way in which Parsons uses the principle of emergence in his early work, where he demonstrates it by means of the example of economic rationality, which refers to the process whereby an actor balances choices so as to achieve optimum satisfaction; i.e. the reference is to the integration of choices *by the actor*. By an intellectual sleight-of-hand, a principle referring to a system of meaning produced by the actor is then transferred to a system of meaning derived from central values. There is no logical connection between the two, and it can be argued that this is the source of later reification in Parsons.

8. The schema does not imply an assumption of rationality as the basis for explanation. A major feature of the concept of central meaning is that it overcomes the unnecessary and damaging distinction between rational and other types of action which, in particular, has made it impossible for sociology to deal adequately with affective meaning. The layers of expressive content in many 'rational' means–end relationships cannot be grasped by what is basically a distinction between reason and feeling, in which feeling is merely a residual category. In sociology, nothing more need be meant by 'rational' than that which is comprehensible in terms of participant views of the situation. There is nothing inherently rationalistic in a language of goals, means and conditions. It only becomes so through association with a nineteenth-century economic model of man. In short, change the historical context and you change the meaning of the language (Jarvie, 1964.)

And, at every level, they are in conflict. They posit antithetical views of human nature, of society and of the relationship between the social and the individual. The first asserts the paramount necessity, for societal and individual well-being, of external constraint; hence the notion of a social system ontologically and methodologically prior to its participants. The key notion of the second is that of autonomous man, able to realize his full potential and to create a truly human social order only when freed from external constraint.[9] Society is thus the creation of its members; the product of their construction of meaning, and of the action and relationships through which they attempt to impose that meaning on their historical situations (Berger and Luckmann, 1967).[10]

In summary, one views action as the derivative of system, whilst the other views system as the derivative of action.[11] And the contention here is that sociology has developed on the basis of the conflict between them. Hence the conflicts in 'the classic tradition'; for example, the obvious conflict in Durkheim's ideal of 'a sociology justifying rationalist individualism but also preaching respect for collectivist norms' (Aron, 1968, p. 97), and the consequent ambiguities in his view of the relationship between the social and the individual and of moral consensus. There is a similar conflict in the Marxian dialectic between the notion of socially creative man and the essentially Hobbesian view of nineteenth-century capitalist man. And in Weber, too: the pessimistic chronicler of the 'supreme mastery of the bureaucratic way of life' is clearly concerned with the problem of control and begins with a sociology based upon the subjective dimension of action. But, partly

9. The contrast between these postulates is pointed by the opposition between the concepts of anomie and alienation (Horton, 1964).

10. They reconcile the perspectives in terms of a dialectic which, in fact, seems to be a simple juxtaposition. Institutions are, by definition, objectified, and once objectification occurs, the analysis depends on the concepts of socialization and internalization; it is thus essentially a social-system analysis. What seems to happen is that the concepts of meaning and action are divorced, for the latter only appears in terms of an a-historical, dyadic situation. Once the dyad becomes both historical and more than dyadic, meaning is objectified and action becomes a derivative of system.

11. Obviously, the social-action perspective in no way rules out the notion of system. In this context, the logical version of the 'problem of order' thesis proposes that the question of order is logically prior to all other questions. If we are not to confuse the analytic and the concrete, this can mean nothing more startling than that we impose a conceptual order on empirical reality. On this level, order is axiomatic rather than problematic in the same sense that 'man is social' is a *conceptual* precondition for the existence of sociologyy. From this, the real question is, what kind of conceptual order? Other questions about the nature and extent of order are essentially empirical.

because of his pessimism and partly because the sociologist of the *machstaat* and of religion is also concerned with the problem of order, he finishes with a sociology in which the bureaucratic system is totally compulsive from the point of view of its participants. The obvious example in American sociology is provided by the change from the 'creative relation of men to norms' in the early work of Parsons to the 'passive, adaptive' relation in his later work (1949, pp. 396–7).

Once again, however, the conflict is not confined to the abstract realms of theory, nor indeed, to the classic tradition in general. For it seems to have spread from the latter to the modern research specialism, with the result that the issues discussed here have a contemporary relevance. It has certainly spread to a field noted earlier as comprising an archetypal example of the social-system perspective ; that of role analysis. Here, the removal of the postulate of consensus, on the grounds that it stands in the way of research, casts severe doubt on the whole social system approach and provides pointers towards a social action conception of role analysis (Gross, Mason and McEachern, 1958 ; Preiss and Ehrlich, 1966 ; Kahn, 1964). In the sociology of deviance, the work of Douglas on suicide stands in the opposition suggested here to the Durkheimian tradition (1967), whilst the work of Cicourel has given the concept of meaning a new centrality (1968). In industrial sociology, there is currently a debate about the relative merits of the socio-technical systems model and the action approach (Goldthorpe, Lockwood, Bechhofer and Platt, 1968; Goldthorpe, 1966; Silverman, 1968). In the study of social class, the role of consciousness has been of increasing concern since the *embourgeoisement* thesis and, in significant ways, the response to that thesis has led social class analysis away from its exclusive preoccupation with structural conditions (Goldthorpe *et al.*, 1968).[12] And, in general, the emergence of neo-phenomenological social analysis reflects a revived interest in the *verstehen* view of the nature of sociology.[13] In that all these areas manifest a preoccupation with the imperatives of research, one criterion of choice between the two approaches is clearly that of research utility.

It is not, however, the ultimate criterion. For it is a major conse-

12. In their notion of a group defined in terms of family-centredness, one can begin to see a central meaning, in terms of which different institutional situations link at the level of the actor and the system. Attitudes to work and relationships with workmates, which have consequences at both levels, are defined by the primary value placed upon family relationships. On the concern with the role of consciousness in general, see Runciman (1966), Lockwood (1958), Zweig (1961).

13. This I take to be a major point of Cicourel's critique of quantitative methods (1964).

quence of the whole argument that sociology is ultimately defined by its historical contexts. It is from those contexts that the problems of order and control, and so the concepts and propositions to which they lead, derive their meaning. They are generalized expressions of the human, social and moral concerns of their time and place.[14] In other words, the problems of order and control are problems of value and, to the extent that they penetrate sociology in the logical progression suggested here, it follows that values shape the discipline from beginning to end.[15] This is not to say that ethical arguments about those values can be settled within sociology itself; this would be circular.[16] But it is to say that values play a much more pervasive role in sociology than is allowed by the conventional wisdom of value-neutrality. In a very significant sense, both sociologies propose utopias. And it is from those utopias that they derive their meaning and their use; they are, indeed, doctrines.

14. In generalized form, however, they transfer, within broad cultural traditions, from one historical context to another. In Europe, from their origins as consequences of and reactions to the Enlightenment and the French Revolution, the two central problems came to represent, above all, conflicting responses to the overwhelming experience of nineteenth-century industrialism. In America, sociology developed as a response to the rampant economic individualism of the postbellum period and to the cultural diversity created by the great migrations; hence the problem of order. But it was also affected by that part of American liberal ideology which stresses grass-roots participation and which was used to legitimate the Populism and the Progressive movement, which coincided with the early years of American sociology; hence the problem of control. It can be speculated that current movements in both Europe and America, focused on the theme of participation, might have something to do with a revived concern for the problem of control in sociology.

15. The two problems do not only create sociological languages. Similar oppositions can be seen in many areas; in psychology, psychoanalysis, literature and, obviously, political thought. They, and sociology, are all creatures of the same context and thus share the same concerns. The point may seem obvious, but it is implicitly denied whenever sociologists arrogate to themselves, through claims to detachment and scientific objectivity, the capacity to stand above their own socio-historical contexts.

16. Nor is it to deny the need for increasingly sophisticated methods of social inquiry. After all, it is a requisite of all good argument that it should have recourse to accepted criteria whereby its empirical propositions can be justified.

References

ARON, R. (1968), *Main Currents in Sociological Thought*, Weidenfeld & Nicolson.
BERGER, P. L., and LUCKMANN, T. (1967), *The Social Construction of Reality*, Allen Lane, The Penguin Press.
BRAMSON, L. (1961), *The Political Content of Sociology*, Princeton University Press.

CICOUREL, A. V. (1964), *Methods and Measurement in Sociology*, Free Press.

CICOUREL, A. V. (1968), *The Social Organization of Juvenile Justice*, Wiley.

COHEN, P. S. (1968), *Modern Social Theory*, Heinemann.

DAHRENDORF, R. (1968), *Essays on the Theory of Society*, Routledge & Kegan Paul.

DOUGLAS, J. D. (1967), *The Social Meanings of Suicide*, Princeton University Press.

ETZIONI, A. (1968), *The Active Society*, Free Press.

GAY, P. (1964), *The Party of Humanity*, Weidenfeld & Nicolson.

GAY, P. (1966), *The Enlightenment: An Interpretation*, Weidenfeld & Nicolson.

GOLDTHORPE, J. H. (1966), 'Attitudes and behaviour of car-assembly workers', *Brit. J. Sociol.*, vol. 17, pp. 277–44.

GOLDTHORPE, J. H., LOCKWOOD, D., BECHHOFER, F., and PLATT, J. (1968), *The Affluent Worker: Industrial Attitudes and Behaviour*, Cambridge University Press.

GROSS, N., MASON, W. S., and MCEACHERN, A. W. (1958), *Explorations in Role Analysis*, Wiley.

HORTON, J. (1964), 'The dehumanization of alienation and anomie', *Brit. J. Sociol.*, vol. 15, no. 4, pp. 283–300.

JARVIE, I. C. (1964), *The Revolution in Anthropology*, Routledge & Kegan Paul.

KAHN, R. L. (1964), *Organizational Stress*, Wiley.

LOCKWOOD, D. (1958), *The Black-Coated Worker*, Allen & Unwin.

LUKES, S. (1968), 'Methodological individualism reconsidered', *Brit. J. Sociol.*, vol. 19, pp. 119–29.

NISBET, R. A. (1967), *The Sociological Tradition*, Heinemann.

PARSONS, T. (1949), *The Structure of Social Action*, Free Press.

PREISS, J. J., and EHRLICH, H. J. (1966), *An Examination of Role Theory*, Nebraska University Press.

RUNCIMAN, W. G. (1966), *Relative Deprivation and Social Justice*, Routledge & Kegan Paul.

SCOTT, J. F. (1963), 'The changing foundations of the Parsonian action scheme', *Amer. Sociol. Rev.*, vol. 28, no. 5, pp. 716–35.

SILVERMAN, D. (1968), 'Formal organizations of industrial sociology', *Sociology*, vol. 2, no. 2, pp. 221–88.

WRONG, D. S. (1961), 'The oversocialized conception of man in modern society', *Amer. Sociol. Rev.*, vol. 26, pp. 184–93.

ZEITLIN, I. M. (1968), *Ideology and the Development of Sociological Theory*, Prentice-Hall.

ZWEIG, F. (1961), *The Worker in an Affluent Society*, Heinemann.

43 Peter L. Berger and Thomas Luckmann

The Social Construction of Reality

Excerpts from Peter L. Berger and Thomas Luckmann, *The Social Construction of Reality*, Allen Lane The Penguin Press, 1967, pp. 77–80; 149–50; 183–4; 187; 191–3.

An institutional world is experienced as an objective reality. It has a history that antedates the individual's birth and is not accessible to his biographical recollection. It was there before he was born, and it will be there after his death. This history itself, as the tradition of the existing institutions, has the character of objectivity. The individual's biography is apprehended as an episode located within the objective history of the society. The institutions, as historical and objective facticities, confront the individual as undeniable facts. The institutions are *there*, external to him, persistent in their reality, whether he likes it or not. He cannot wish them away. They resist his attempts to change or evade them. They have coercive power over him, both in themselves, by the sheer force of their facticity, and through the control mechanisms that are usually attached to the most important of them. The objective reality of institutions is not diminished if the individual does not understand their purpose or their mode of operation. He may experience large sectors of the social world as incomprehensible, perhaps oppressive in their opaqueness, but real none the less. Since institutions exist as external reality, the individual cannot understand them by introspection. He must 'go out' and learn about them, just as he must to learn about nature. This remains true even though the social world, as a humanly produced reality, is potentially understandable in a way not possible in the case of the natural world.[1]

It is important to keep in mind that the objectivity of the institutional world, however massive it may appear to the individual, is a humanly produced, constructed objectivity. The process by which the externalized products of human activity attain the character of objectivity is

1. The preceding description closely follows Durkheim's analysis of social reality. This does *not* contradict the Weberian conception of the meaningful character of society. Since social reality always originates in meaningful human actions, it continues to carry meaning even if it is opaque to the individual at a given time. The original may be *reconstructed*, precisely by means of what Weber called *Verstehen*.

objectivation.[2] The institutional world is objectivated human activity, and so is every single institution. In other words, despite the objectivity that marks the social world in human experience, it does not thereby acquire an ontological status apart from the human activity that produced it. The paradox that man is capable of producing a world that he then experiences as something other than a human product will concern us later on. At the moment, it is important to emphasize that the relationship between man, the producer and the social world, his product, is and remains a dialectical one. That is, man (not, of course, in isolation but in his collectivities) and his social world interact with each other. The product acts back upon the producer. Externalization and objectivation are moments in a continuing dialectical process. The third moment in this process, which is internalization (by which the objectivated social world is retrojected into consciousness in the course of socialization), will occupy us in considerable detail later on. It is already possible, however, to see the fundamental relationship of these three dialectical moments in social reality. Each of them corresponds to an essential characterization of the social world. *Society is a human product. Society is an objective reality. Man is a social product.* It may also already be evident that an analysis of the social world that leaves out any one of these three moments will be distortive.[3] One may further add that only with the transmission of the social world to a new generation (that is, internalization as effectuated in socialization) does the fundamental social dialectic appear in its totality. To repeat, only with the appearance of a new generation can one properly speak of a social world.

At the same point, the institutional world requires legitimation, that is, ways by which it can be 'explained' and justified. This not because it appears less real. As we have seen, the reality of the social world gains in massivity in the course of its transmission. This reality, however, is a historical one, which comes to the new generation as a tradition rather than as a biographical memory. In our paradigmatic example, A and B, the original creators of the social world, can always reconstruct the circumstances under which their world and any part of it was

2. The term 'objectivation' is derived from the Hegelian/Marxian *Versachlichung*.

3. Contemporary American sociology tends towards leaving out the first moment. Its perspective on society thus tends to be what Marx called a reification (*Verdinglichung*), that is, an undialectical distortion of social reality that obscures the latter's character as an ongoing human production, viewing it instead in thing-like categories appropriate only to the world of nature. That the dehumanization implicit in this is mitigated by values deriving from the larger tradition of the society is, presumably, morally fortunate, but is irrelevant theoretically.

established. That is, they can arrive at the meaning of an institution by exercising their powers of recollection. A's and B's children are in an altogether different situation. Their knowledge of the institutional history is by way of 'hearsay'. The original meaning of the institutions is inaccessible to them in terms of memory. It, therefore, becomes necessary to interpret this meaning to them in various legitimating formulas. These will have to be consistent and comprehensive in terms of the institutional order, if they are to carry conviction to the new generation. The same story, so to speak, must be told to all the children. It follows that the expanding institutional order develops a corresponding canopy of legitimations, stretching over it a protective cover of both cognitive and normative interpretation. These legitimations are learned by the new generation during the same process that socializes them into the institutional order.

The development of specific mechanisms of social controls also becomes necessary with the historicization and objectivation of institutions. Deviance from the institutionally 'programmed' courses of action becomes likely once the institutions have become realities divorced from their original relevance in the concrete social processes from which they arose. To put this more simply, it is more likely that one will deviate from programmes set up for one by others than from programmes that one has helped establish oneself. The new generation posits a problem of compliance, and its socialization into the institutional order requires the establishment of sanctions. The institutions must and do claim authority over the individual, independently of the subjective meanings he may attach to any particular situation. The priority of the institutional definitions of situations must be consistently maintained over individual temptations at redefinition. The children must be 'taught to behave' and, once taught, must be 'kept in line'. So, of course, must the adults. The more conduct is institutionalized, the more predictable and thus the more controlled it becomes. If socialization into the institutions has been effective, outright coercive measures can be applied economically and selectively. Most of the time, conduct will occur 'spontaneously' within the institutionally set channels. The more, on the level of meaning, conduct is taken for granted, the more possible alternatives to the institutional 'programmes' will recede, and the more predictable and controlled conduct will be. [. . .]

Internalization of reality

Since society exists as both objective and subjective reality, any adequate theoretical understanding of it must comprehend both these aspects. As we have already argued, these aspects receive their proper recognition if society is understood in terms of an ongoing dialectical process composed of the three moments of externalization, objectivation and internalization. As far as the societal phenomenon is concerned, these moments are *not* to be thought of as occurring in a temporal sequence. Rather society and each part of it are simultaneously characterized by these three moments, so that any analysis in terms of only one or two of them falls short. The same is true of the individual member of society, who simultaneously externalizes his own being into the social world and internalizes it as an objective reality. In other words, to be in society is to participate in its dialectic.

The individual, however, is not born a member of society. He is born with a predisposition towards sociality, and he becomes a member of society. In the life of every individual, therefore, there *is* a temporal sequence, in the course of which he is inducted into participation in the societal dialectic. The beginning point of this process is internalization: the immediate apprehension or interpretation of an objective event as expressing meaning, that is, as a manifestation of another's subjective processes which thereby becomes subjectively meaningful to myself. This does not mean that I understand the other adequately. I may indeed misunderstand him: he is laughing in a fit of hysteria, but I understand his laughter as expressing mirth. But his subjectivity is nevertheless objectively available to me and becomes meaningful to me, whether or not there is congruence between his and my subjective process. Full congruence between the two subjective meanings, and reciprocal knowledge of the congruence, presupposes signification, as previously discussed. However, internalization in the general sense used here underlies both signification and its own more complex forms. More precisely, internalization in this general sense is the basis, first, for an understanding of one's fellowmen and, second, for the apprehension of the world as a meaningful and social reality.

This apprehension does not result from autonomous creations of meaning by isolated individuals, but begins with the individual 'taking over' the world in which others already live. To be sure, the 'taking over' is in itself, in a sense, an original process for every human organism, and the world, once 'taken over', *may* be creatively modified or (less likely) even re-created. In any case, in the complex form of internalization, I not only 'understand' the other's momentary subjective processes, I 'understand' the world in which he lives, and that world becomes my own. This presupposes that he and I share time in a more than ephemeral way and a comprehensive perspective, which links sequences of situations together intersubjectively. We now not only understand each other's definitions of shared situations, we define them reciprocally. A nexus of motivations is established between us and extends into the future. Most importantly, there is now an ongoing mutual identification between us. We not only live in the same world, we participate in each other's being.

Only when he has achieved this degree of internalization is an individual a member of society. The ontogenetic process by which this is brought about is socialization, which may thus be defined as the comprehensive and consistent induction of an individual into the objective world of a society or a sector of it. Primary socialization is the first socialization an individual undergoes in childhood, through which he becomes a member of society. Secondary socialization is any subsequent process that inducts an already socialized individual into new sectors of the objective world of his society. [. . .]

Socialization always takes place in the context of a specific social structure. Not only its contents but also its measures of 'success' have social-structural conditions and social-structural consequences. In other words, the micro-sociological or social-psychological analysis of phenomena of internalization must always have as its background a macro-sociological understanding of their structural aspects.

On the level of theoretical analysis attempted here we cannot enter into a detailed discussion of the different empirical relationships between the contents of socialization and social-structural configurations. Some general observations may, however, be made on the social-structural aspects of the 'success' of socialization. By 'successful socialization' we mean the establishment of a high degree of symmetry between objective and subjective reality (as well as identity, of course). Conversely, 'unsuccessful socialization' is to be understood in terms of asymmetry between objective and subjective reality. As we have seen, totally successful socialization is anthropologically impossible. Totally unsuccessful socialization is, at the very least, extremely rare, limited to cases of individuals with whom even minimal socialization fails because of extreme organic pathology. Our analysis must, therefore, be concerned with gradations on a continuum whose extreme poles are empirically unavailable. Such analysis is useful because it permits some general statements about the conditions and consequences of successful socialization.

Maximal success in socialization is likely to occur in societies with very simple division of labour and minimal distribution of knowledge. Socialization under such conditions produces identities that are socially predefined and profiled to a high degree. Since every individual is confronted with essentially the same institutional programme for his life in the society, the total force of the institutional order is brought to bear with more or less equal weight on each individual, producing a compelling massivity for the objective reality to be internalized. Identity then is highly profiled in the sense of representing fully the objective reality within which it is located. Put simply, everyone pretty much *is* what he is supposed to be. In such a society identities are easily recognizable, objectively and subjectively. Everybody knows who everybody else is and who he is himself. A knight *is* a knight and a peasant *is* a peasant, to others as well as to themselves. There is, therefore, no *problem* of identity. The question, 'Who am I?' is unlikely to arise in consciousness, since the socially predefined answer is massively real subjectively and consistently confirmed in all significant social interaction. [. . .]

Once there is a more complex distribution of knowledge in a society, unsuccessful socialization may be the result of different significant others mediating different objective realities to the individual. Put differently, unsuccessful socialization may be the result of heterogeneity in the socializing personnel. This may occur in a number of ways. There may be situations in which all the significant others of primary socialization mediate a common reality, but from considerably different perspectives. To a degree, of course, every significant other has a different perspective on the common reality simply by virtue of being a specific individual with a specific biography. But the consequences we have in mind here occur only when the differences between the significant others pertain to their social types rather than their individual idiosyncrasies. [. . .]

If discrepant worlds appear in primary socialization, the individual has the option of identifying with one of them as against the others, a process that, because it occurs in primary socialization, will be affectively charged to a high degree. Identification, disidentification and alternation will all be accompanied by affective crises, since they will invariably depend upon the mediation of significant others. The appresentation of discrepant worlds in secondary socialization produces an entirely different configuration. In secondary socialization, internalization need *not* be accompanied by affectively charged identification with significant others ; the individual may internalize different realities *without* identifying with them. Therefore, if an alternative world appears in secondary socialization, the individual may opt for it in a manipulative manner. One could speak here of 'cool' alternation. The individual internalizes the new reality, but instead of its being *his* reality, it is a reality to be used by him for specific purposes. In so far as this involves the performance of certain roles, he retains subjective detachment *vis-à-vis* them – he 'puts them on' deliberately and purposefully. If this phenomenon becomes widely distributed, the institutional order as a whole begins to take on the character of a network of reciprocal manipulations.

A society in which discrepant worlds are generally available on a market basis entails specific constellations of subjective reality and identity. There will be an increasingly general consciousness of the relativity of *all* worlds, including one's own, which is now subjectively apprehended as '*a* world', rather than '*the* world'. It follows that one's own institutionalized conduct may be apprehended as 'a role' from which one may detach oneself in one's own consciousness, and which one may 'act out' with manipulative control. For example, the aristocrat no longer simply *is* an aristocrat, but he *plays at being* an aristocrat, and so forth. The situation, then, has a much more far-reaching consequence than the possibility of individuals playing at being what they are *not* supposed to be. They also play at being what they *are* supposed to be – a quite different matter. This situation is increasingly typical of contemporary industrial society, but it would obviously transcend the scope of our present considerations to enter further into a sociology-of-knowledge and social-psychological analysis of this constellation. What should be stressed is that such a situation cannot be understood unless it is ongoingly related to its social-structural context, which follows logically from the necessary relationship between the social division of labour (with its consequences for social structure) and the social distribution of knowledge (with its consequences for the social objectivation of reality). In the contemporary situation this entails the analysis of both reality and identity pluralism with reference to the structural dynamics of industrialism, particularly the dynamics of the social stratification patterns produced by industrialism.

44 David Silverman

The Action Frame of Reference

Excerpt from David Silverman, *The Theory of Organization*,
Heinemann, 1970, pp. 126–46.

Many writers have made use of an Action approach and the works
that are discussed here include Weber (1964), Schutz (1964), Berger
(1966), Berger and Luckmann (1967), Berger and Pullberg (1966), Rose
(1962), Goffman (1959), Cicourel (1964) and Cohen (1968). Instead of
providing a summary, at this point, of these various views, I shall try to
present an ideal-typical action theory. This will fail to do justice to the
separate arguments of each author, but it will have the advantage of
presenting clearly the essential features of the perspective.

Seven propositions are presented below and the rest of the chapter
will be devoted to a discussion of them.

1. The social sciences and the natural sciences deal with entirely different orders of subject-matter. While the canons of rigour and
scepticism apply to both, one should not expect their perspective to be
the same.

2. Sociology is concerned with understanding action rather than with
observing behaviour. Action arises out of meanings which define social
reality.

3. Meanings are given to men by their society. Shared orientations
become institutionalized and are experienced by later generations as
social facts.

4. While society defines man, man in turn defines society. Particular
constellations of meaning are only sustained by continual reaffirmation
in everyday actions.

5. Through their interaction men also modify, change and transform
social meanings.

6. It follows that explanations of human actions must take account of
the meanings which those concerned assign to their acts ; the manner
in which the everyday world is socially constructed yet perceived as
real and routine becomes a crucial concern of sociological analysis.

7. Positivistic explanations, which assert that action is determined by external and constraining social or non-social forces, are inadmissible.

The distinction between the social and natural sciences. The view that the natural sciences provide the most appropriate model for the study of social life has a long and distinguished history in sociology. It suffers, however, from the fatal defect that it fails to take into account whether social and natural phenomena are the same in kind. The behaviour of matter may be regarded as a necessary reaction to a stimulus. Matter itself does not understand its own behaviour. It is literally meaningless until the scientist imposes his frame of reference upon it. There is no possibility of apprehending its subjective intentions and the logic of its behaviour may be understood solely by observation of the behaviour itself. The action of men, on the other hand, is meaningful to them. While the observer perceives water boiling when it has reached a certain temperature, men themselves define their situation and act in certain ways in order to attain certain ends. In doing so, they construct a social world. Social life, therefore, has an internal logic which must be understood by the sociologist; the natural scientist imposes an external logic on his data. As Weber (1964) and Schutz (1964) have observed, this situation is both a source of problems *and* a distinct help to the social scientist.

If social action derives from the meanings which those concerned attribute to their social world, the observer is limited by his inability to experience the experience of another. Schutz points out that the scientist's individual biography and view of society may make him perceive what is going on in a way which distorts its meanings to those involved.[1] His best defence is to develop a 'scientific' frame of reference, for the distinction between the natural and social sciences does not affect the common rules of procedure which they share (rigour, scepticism and so on). But this is very little use if the observer fails to come to grips with the problem of the subjective meanings that the actors themselves attach to their acts. Fortunately, the social scientist has one distinct advantage. He is not limited merely to the observation of uniformities of behaviour: 'In the case of social collectivities', Weber suggests, 'we

1. The problems to which this gives rise have been vividly expressed by Laing: 'If, however, experience is evidence, how can one ever study the experience *of the other*? For the experience of the other is not evident to me, as it is not and never can be an experience of mine. . . . Since your and their experience is invisible to me as mine is to you and them, I seek to make evident to the others, through their experience of my behaviour, what I infer of your experience, through my experience of your behaviour. This is the crux of social phenomenology' (1967, pp. 16–17).

can accomplish something which is never attainable in the natural sciences, namely the subjective understanding of the action of the component individuals' (1964, p. 103).

The generalizations which the social sciences develop are also fundamentally different from the laws of the natural sciences. The former are based on the probability that actors will act in terms of certain typical motives or intentions, the latter on the necessary reaction of matter to a stimulus (providing other stimuli are controlled for). Both the data and the form of explanation of the two types of science are thus fundamentally different: they share only a commitment to a systematic and rigorous analysis of their material.[2]

Action not behaviour. According to one view, observable patterns of behaviour provide the social scientist with his most reliable source of data. While what goes on in the minds of people is difficult to assess, their behaviour is concrete, quantifiable and easily susceptible to scientific analysis. Such a position has been taken by behaviourists generally, and is also favoured by those who take the Interactionist view of organizations which, while taking account of attitudes, concentrate mainly on interpersonal contacts ('interaction') and work tasks ('activities') (Whyte, 1959).

However, the mere observation of behaviour has its own set of difficulties. In order to make sense of an act, the observer must place it within a category which he can comprehend. He might distinguish, for instance, between an act associated with work and, say, an act of friendship. At the same time, however, the act will have a certain meaning to the person who carries it out and to the people at whom it is directed. What the observer takes to be merely the repetition of the same physical action may imply totally different meanings to those concerned according to the way in which they define each situation. By concentrating on the behaviour itself, it is possible to miss totally its significance to the people involved and, therefore, to be unable to predict with any accuracy the way in which those at whom it is directed will react to it. This difficulty has made itself felt most strongly among anthropologists who have to come to terms with a culture very different from their own, in which the subjective significance of actions is difficult

2. Laing has also pointed out the error of attempting to follow blindly the approach of the natural sciences in the study of the social world: 'The error fundamentally', he suggests, 'is the failure to realize that there is an ontological discontinuity between human beings and it-beings. . . . Persons are distinguished from things in that persons experience the world, whereas things behave in the world' (1967, p. 53).

to grasp. Even in his own society, however, the observer is still frequently an untutored outsider unable, without further knowledge of the commonsense assumptions being used, to comprehend the implications of the behaviour he is observing.

As has already been suggested, problems of this nature are specific to the social sciences. Matter, on the other hand, does not act, it 'behaves'. Moreover, the logic of its behaviour may be understood through an observation of the behaviour itself. The action of men, however, stems from a network of meanings which they themselves construct and of which they are conscious.[3] Weber put the relationship between social science and action clearly when he argued that sociology is concerned with: 'The interpretation of action in terms of its subjective meaning' (1964, p. 94), where action is 'all human behaviour when and in so far as the acting individual attaches a subjective meaning to it' (p. 88).

Action arises from meanings. Behaviourists argue that behaviour can be broadly explained as a response to a stimulus whose objective characteristics are perceived by the scientist. The reaction of subjects to this stimulus (e.g. 'expressive' supervision) may thus be observed and laws formulated which relate the observed response to the stimulus (e.g. expressive supervision tends to be associated with a high level of morale among those who are exposed to it).

This fails to take account, however, of the 'internal' logic of the situation. People assign meanings to situations and to the actions of others and react in terms of the interpretation suggested by these meanings.[4] Thus they may respond differently to the same objectively defined stimulus: the same supervisory behaviour may be interpreted as a friendly act by one group of workers (who, because they also desire supervision of this nature, react in a favourable way), or as an illegitimate attempt to win their sympathy in order to accomplish objectives opposed to their own. The same individual even may, at

3. Schutz (1964) notes that: 'The distinguishing characteristic of action is precisely that it is determined by a project which precedes it in time. Action then is behaviour in accordance with a plan of projected behaviour: and the project is neither more nor less than the action itself conceived and decided upon in the future perfect sense' (vol. 2, p. 11).

4. Rose (1962) points out that: 'All social objects of study . . . are "interpreted" by the individual and have social meaning. That is, they are never seen as physical "stimuli" but as "definitions of the situation"' (p. x). Similarly, Cicourel (1964) argues that 'the actor's awareness and experience of an object are determined not only by the physical object as it is . . . given, but also by the imputations he assigns to it' (p. 220).

different times or in different situations, assign varying meanings to what appears to an observer to be the same act.

Action occurs, therefore, not as a response to an observable stimulus but as a product of what Parsons (1951) has called a 'system of expectations' arising out of the actor's past experiences and defining his perception of the probable reaction of others to his act. At the level of cognition,[5] the actor defines his situation in this way and becomes aware of alternative courses of possible action. Since action is goal-oriented, that is concerned with the attainment of certain subjectively perceived ends, the actor chooses, from among the means of which he is aware, the action that seems most likely to produce what he would regard as a satisfactory outcome. At this analytical level, to use Parsons's term, he is concerned with 'evaluation'. Any instance of action (a unit act) thus stems from the ends that the actor is concerned to attain, his definition of the situation, including the range of alternative actions that he perceives to be available to him, and his choice of a means which is likely to be effective, bearing in mind the likely reaction of others to his act.

Meanings as social facts. Since action stems from meanings, it is legitimate to pose the question – 'from where do these meanings arise?' One valid answer would be that meanings are given to men by their society and the past societies that preceded it. Such a reply would draw heavily on the perspective of Durkheim, who argued that men are constrained by social facts which determine their actions and consciousness. The suicide rate, to take Durkheim's favourite example, is separate from the intentions of individual men. It is a social fact which stems from the organization of society and is thus both external and constraining to individual actors.

If we follow Durkheim, it seems clear enough that meanings reside in social institutions. Society is composed of an interrelated series of institutional orders each of which is composed of a hierarchy of status positions to which are attached rights and obligations. This hierarchy usually persists even though the occupants of offices change. Meanings are, therefore, associated with an institution itself, both in terms of the general areas within which its members are supposed to act (e.g. the economy, the law) and of the specialized expectations attached to each office. Individuals are thus located on a particular social map. They live in a particular society and play roles in some at least of its

5. This discussion is not concerned with 'cathection' – or reaction in terms of innate personality drives – which Parsons takes as another level of human response.

component institutional orders. By participating in society they are given expectations about the appropriate acts of themselves and of others when in various status positions. They are able to apprehend the meanings associated with the actions of other people and to form a view of self based on the responses of others.

The question that now arises is why people should meet the expectations of others; one comprehensive answer to this has been offered by Parsons. According to Parsons (1951), society motivates its members, while respecting their personalities and biological needs; by this means it is able to prevent too much deviance from expected ways of behaving. People *learn* the expectations contained in different social roles through the process of socialization. They *conform* to them because these expectations become part of their definitions of themselves (or are 'internalized', as Parsons put it) and because they want to retain the good opinion of those around them. Conformity thus expresses a set of shared values which is central to the existence of any society. While Parsons acknowledges that people can engage in interaction for their own private purposes, he holds that, unless one is prepared to be led 'straight to the Hobbesian thesis [of a war of all against all]', common values must predominate if the system is to survive.[6] Action thus necessarily derives not only from shared expectations or norms, but also from shared values. 'Considering that we are talking about the conditions of relatively stable interaction in social systems,' he writes, 'it follows from this that the value-standards which define institutionalized role-expectations assume to a greater or less degree a *moral* significance' (Parsons, 1951, p. 41, my italics).

The meaning of the social world is given to us by the past history and present structure of our society. Social reality is 'pre-defined' in the very language in which we are socialized. Language provides us with categories which define as well as distinguish our experiences. Language allows us to define the typical features of the social world and the typical acts of typical actors – it gives us a set of what Schutz (1964) calls 'typifications'. Typifications deal with symbols, highly abstracted from everyday experience (e.g. art, religion, science); with categories of people and the implied pattern of behaviour in which each may legitimately indulges (e.g. policeman, friend, neighbour); and with particular people with whom one has had the opportunity to

6. Parsons acknowledges that an actor's sentiments may not be involved in his action: 'But, in a general sense in social situations, the circumstances of socialization preclude that this should be the predominant situation in permanent social systems which involve the major motivational interests of the participant actors' (1951, p. 40).

interact face-to-face (e.g. a helpful policeman, a reliable friend, an unpleasant neighbour). These typifications may be viewed as composing a set of concentric circles of knowledge which vary in diameter according to our degree of familiarity with the person or object involved. Typifications provide the individual with a frame of reference which he can use to shape his own actions and to make sense of the acts of others.

Meanings are socially sustained. It is true that society constrains us; it is also true that society provides us with the belief that, rather than bowing to constraints, we are acting in a manner which expresses what common sense suggests'. Even in our routine compliance with role-expectations, we believe we are acting 'naturally' in the only way which it is possible to act. Society, as Berger (1966) has pictured it, is both a prison and a puppet-theatre, in which we are manipulated while maintaining that we are doing 'what any reasonable man would expect'.

In viewing society as a social fact, sociologists reflect the common-sense view of members. Man experiences the social world as an external and unquestioned reality. People have always acted in a certain way, they will go on acting in that way because it is 'natural' that they should do so, and an individual's wants and intentions are as nothing before 'what has to be'. Society is perceived to be something out there and we believe we have no choice but to meet its requirements. The social world is a taken-for-granted world governed by what we understand as 'the laws of nature'. 'We experience the objects of our experience', Laing puts it, 'as *there* in the outside world. The source of our experience seems to be outside ourselves' (1967, p. 33).

We can best apprehend the limitations of the common-sense view of the nature of society by asking how it is that members come to perceive the social world as an external, routine, non-problematic facticity.

To answer this question we need to take account of two phenomena: men 'know' the social world through a shared stock of knowledge and the 'correctness' of this knowledge is continually made apparent in the actions of other men. The social stock of knowledge is a series of assumptions about appropriate behaviour in different contexts. I know how I ought to behave as a teacher and I know how my students ought to behave towards me. I know what purposes may underlie their actions and I know how my purposes may appear to them. Moreover, my view is usually confirmed by the everyday actions of others which appear to stem from the same set of assumptions. I do not doubt that I am a teacher and that this man is a student because he continues to act as I imagine a student should and, by responding to my actions in the way that I expect, he confirms my impression of myself. As such reciprocal typifications develop out of interaction, expectations become institutionalized and social roles are objectified or made part of the 'natural order of things'. In this way, it becomes thought necessary, proper and natural that the roles of student and teacher should be defined in a particular manner; it is no longer noticed when subsequent generations of actors continue to meet these assumptions – after all, what other way could they behave?

This glimpse at an aspect of the everyday world, while it stresses the routine nature of interaction, paradoxically makes social order seem more problematic. To be believable, the reality of the world-taken-for-granted must be continually reaffirmed in the actions of men. Meanings are not only given, they are socially sustained. 'The realization of the drama', as Berger and Luckmann point out, 'depends upon the reiterated performance of its prescribed roles by living actors. The actors embody the roles and actualize the drama by presenting it on the given stage. Neither drama nor institution exist empirically apart from this recurrent realization' (1967, p. 75).

Social order depends upon the cooperative acts of men in sustaining a particular version of the truth. In conversation, for instance, we find it convenient to accept the prevailing definition of reality within a group and not to question the major aspects of the views of self which are being presented. When actors act in unexpected ways, however, or when, as Goffman (1959) shows, events occur which cast doubt upon an agreed definition of a situation, that part of the social order is, for the time being, no more.[7] The fact that the stock of knowledge upon which action is based tends to change rather slowly reflects the vested interest that we all have in avoiding anomie by maintaining a system of meanings which daily confirms the non-problematic nature of our definitions of ourselves.

Man makes the social world. The existence of society depends upon it being continuously confirmed in the actions of its members. Social structure, therefore, 'has no reality except a human one. It is not characterizable as being a thing able to stand on its own ... [and] exists

7. Goffman considers the definition of the situation which the actors project in face-to-face interaction. He goes on: 'we can assume that events may occur within the interaction which contradict, discredit, or otherwise throw doubt upon this projection. When these disruptive events occur, the interaction itself may come to a confused and embarrassed halt. Some of the assumptions upon which the responses of the participants had been predicated become untenable, and the participants find themselves lodged in an interaction for which the situation has been wrongly defined and is now *no longer defined*' (Goffman, 1959, p. 12, my italics).

only in so far and as long as human beings realize it as part of their world' (Berger and Pullberg, 1966, p. 63). We reify society if we regard it as having an existence which is separate from and above the actions of men: social roles and institutions exist only as an expression of the meanings which men attach to their world – they have no 'ontological status', as Berger and Pullberg put it (p. 67).

The phenomenological position adopted by Berger, Luckmann and Pullberg has clear parallels with the view of social relationships presented by the Symbolic Interactionists. If, as Rose (1962) notes, Man lives in a 'symbolic environment' and acts in terms of the social meanings that he ascribes to the world around him, then roles are merely 'clusters of related meanings' perceived to be appropriate to certain social settings (Rose, p. 10); structure, once more, refers only to meanings, in this case the meanings that define the social setting itself and the appropriate relationships between the role-players that are expected to be part of it. Both roles and structure merely provide a framework for action; they do not determine it. Both 'are the product of the activity of acting units and not of "forces" which leave such acting units out of account' (Blumer, 1962, p. 189). Industrialization, to take one example, does not determine the family form. This will, as Blumer points out, depend on the interpretations which the actors concerned place on the industrialization process.

If society is socially constructed, then the logic behind some sociological investigations becomes highly questionable. For to relate one structural variable to another, for instance organizational form and economic environment, may fail to take account of the orientations of the people involved and the meanings which they attach to 'efficiency', 'the economy' and so on. It is out of factors like these that action is generated: to pay insufficient attention to them can involve the sociologist in an empty determinism in which things happen and processes occur apparently without the direct intervention of human purposes. Indeed, what has already been said should indicate a need to extend what have been regarded as the canons of satisfactory explanation of social phenomena; a need, as Berger and Luckmann argue, for 'more than the casual obeisance that might be paid to the "human factor" behind the uncovered structural data'. Instead, we must be concerned with a 'systematic accounting of the dialectical relation between the structural realities and the human enterprise of constructing reality – in history' (1967, p. 170).

Meanings are socially changed. If the reality of the social world is socially sustained, then it follows that reality is also socially changed –

which men learn. Even if social norms are internalized, one ought not necessarily to expect them to be expressed in behaviour. Men can act in a certain way and feel guilty about offending their conscience only retrospectively. At the same time, there may be internal conflicts in the values that men learn in society. While men may generally seek approval, they may also be more concerned with the approval of certain types of men than of others and be prepared to offend the latter in the hope of satisfying the former. In doing so they continually re-define social reality as experienced by themselves and others. Parsons may, therefore, be criticized for having adopted an 'over-socialized conception of man' which overlooks the fact that role-expectations are not just given by society but arise from and depend upon on-going human interaction. Social order is, therefore, problematic. A more complete analysis would need to take account of the range of motives underlying conformity to the expectations of others, and to pay attention to the possible role of coercion in *imposing* a normative definition of the situation on others.

Weber had already noted, many years previously, that in social relationships the parties may (and to some extent always do) attach different meanings to their interaction. It is certainly true that interaction may involve shared values (Weber gives the example of a father–child relationship) but very frequently the meanings involved may not be shared and the relationship will then be, as he puts it, 'asymmetrical'.[8] What is to the shop steward, for instance, a means of 'delivering the goods' to the workers he represents, may be regarded by the manager as a necessary relationship in order to settle disputes with the minimum interruption to production. The shop steward and the manager come together not because they have the same values (indeed, each may hope one day to overturn the authority of the other) but because, for a while at least, their differing ends may be served by the same means.

Social relationships, then, need only involve the ability of the actors to predict the likely actions of others by means of the common stock of knowledge which they share. At the same time, there always exist

8. 'The subjective meaning', he notes, 'need not necessarily be the same for all the parties who are mutually oriented in a given social relationship. . . . "Friendship", "love", "loyalty", "fidelity to contracts", "patriotism", on one side, may well be faced with an entirely different attitude on the other. In such cases the parties associate different meanings with their actions and the social relationship is in so far objectively "asymmetrical" from the points of view of the two parties. . . . A social relationship in which the attitudes are completely and fully corresponding is in reality a limiting case' (Weber, 1964, p. 119). The appeal of the 'non-routine', in the form of a charismatic leader, was also a central concern of Weber's sociology.

which Schutz calls 'finite provinces of meaning', sets of orientations which govern the nature of the involvement in any particular social relationship and derive from the various experiences of different actors (their 'individual biographies', to use Schutz's term). Moreover, if conformity to the expectations of other partners in this relationship is not generated by shared values then analysis of its origins may reveal that it derives from the attempts of certain actors to attain their own personal ends and is merely tolerated by others. To take an extreme example, the relationship between the slave and master in a plantation society, while occurring on the basis of common expectations of the likely behaviour of the other, may originate in the ability of the master to impose his definition of the situation upon the slave. It need not, therefore, involve shared values, while the degree of attachment to it (and hence the measure of commitment to its continuation) may vary considerably between the participants. It becomes necessary to examine, in a similar manner, the processes through which any body of knowledge comes to be socially established as reality (i.e. institutionalized) and to take account, as Berger and Luckmann (1966) put it, of the fact that: 'He who has the bigger stick has the better chance of imposing his definitions' (p. 101).[9]

The existence of different definitions of situations indicates the advantages of an action perspective and reveals certain limitations of analysis from the point of view of the system. As Berger (1966) has noted, in an extremely useful little introduction to sociology, the System approach tends to be concerned with analysis from the viewpoint of the authorities and is primarily concerned with the problems involved in the management of social systems. However, what is a problem to one actor is often a more or less efficient means to an end from the point of view of another.[10] A situation may, therefore, be usefully examined from the vantage points of 'competing systems of interpretation', and this will provide important clues as to how it arose, why it continues in its present form, and what circumstances may make it change.

It is important to recognize that the social order is threatened not only by particular circumstances, such as revolutionary change, culture contact or marginal groups (Berger and Pullberg), but by its very

9. What the 'stick' actually consists of will vary according to the meanings attached to various sanctions by the actors' stock of knowledge. Excommunication, for instance, is at certain times a far more significant threat than more material 'sticks'.

10. 'Organizations', as Touraine puts it, 'can be thought of as social systems, but also as means limiting or providing the opportunity for the actor to attain his ends' (1964, p. 7).

David Silverman 573

nature. '*All* social reality is precarious', as Berger and Luckmann put it, '*All* societies are constructions in the face of chaos' (1966, p. 96). While people take everyday life as non-problematic, as reality, they continually step into situations that create problems which have not yet become routinized. Our normal reaction is to seek to integrate the problematic sector of reality into what is already unproblematic: we look around for an already learned definition of the situation to apply to the 'new' reality. However, this is not always possible: 'certain problems "transcend" the boundaries of everyday life and point to an altogether different reality' (p. 24).

Explanations in terms of meanings. The form of explanation which the foregoing analysis suggests is concerned with *Verstehen*, that is, it begins with 'the observation and theoretical interpretation of the subjective "states of mind" of actors'.[11] This may take the form of 'the actually intended meaning for concrete individual action ... [or] the average of, or an approximation to, the actually intended meaning' (Weber, 1964, p. 96). More usually, however, explanations are in terms of ideal-typical actors whom we take to be pursuing certain ends by choosing appropriate means on the basis of a subjective definition of the situation. 'It is not even necessary', Schutz argues 'to reduce human acts to a more or less well known individual actor. To understand them it is sufficient to find typical motives of typical actors which explain the act as a typical one arising out of a typical situation' (1964, vol. 2, p. 13). He goes on to suggest how the acts of priests, soldiers and so on, may be explained in this way.

Ideal-typical explanations, according to Weber, must be adequate on the level of meaning and also causally adequate. They must make use of what is known about the actor's definition of the situation and his ends. They must show that the action to be explained is in practice related to these meanings: that is, where the act is present, so must be the meaning. Ideal-typical explanations usually involve the assumption of rational action or the continuous weighing by the actors of means, ends and the secondary consequences of their actions (Weber calls this type of action '*zweckrational*'). It then becomes possible to examine the non-rational elements in actual behaviour – the extent to which those concerned diverge in practice from such a weighing process. As Schutz notes, it is easiest to come to grips with the subjective meanings of actors where their behaviour is most rational and, therefore, most standardized and anonymous.

Action explanations make a great deal of what Schutz calls 'in order to' motives. An action is explained when the meaning which the typical

11. Parsons, introduction to Weber (1964, p. 87, footnote 2).

actor attributes to it has been demonstrated. At the same time, action is motivated on the basis of the actor's background and environment: this is its 'because' motive. I act in a certain way, therefore, not only in order to attain certain desired ends but also because I see myself as the sort of person who engages in acts of this nature. However, it is illegitimate to say that my action is *caused* by certain characteristics of mine which only the observer perceives. 'One reifies action', as Berger and Pullberg put it, 'by claiming that it is performed *because* [. . .] the actor is an X-type person' (1966, p. 66). This is to detach an act from its performer, who is viewed merely as a collection of roles. In the same way, 'roles are reified by detaching them from human intentionality and expressivity, and transforming them into an inevitable destiny for their bearers' (p. 67).

The rejection of positivism. In equating the methods of studying social and natural reality, positivism may take any one of three approaches. It may try to explain human behaviour in terms of universal psychological forces (e.g. aggression), non-social factors (climate or technology), or reified social constructs (social facts). Since most contemporary sociologists reject the first two, the discussion here will be concerned with the third.

Berger (1966) has accused much Sociology of viewing society as a 'prison' or as a 'puppet-theatre'. According to the former position, society is external to men and constrains them through the operation of impersonal social facts; according to the latter, society enters into the minds of men through the process of socialization which gives them their social roles and determines how they will in future respond. 'That this sort of intellectual edifice is inviting to many orderly minds', he remarks, 'is demonstrated by the appeal that positivism in all its forms has had since its inception' (p. 190). None the less, there is an alternative view. Society may be seen as populated by living actors and its institutions regarded as dramatic conventions depending on the cooperation of the actors in maintaining a definition of the situation. As he puts it, the way in which this position 'opens up a passage out of the rigid determinism into which sociological thought originally led us' (p. 160), is best illustrated by the methodology of Weber.

Weber stands firmly against the reification of concepts by the observer. The State, for instance, does not itself act; it is merely a representation of certain meanings held by actors and is reducible to those meanings. When these meanings change, the State changes: 'for sociological purposes there is no such thing as a collective personality which "acts". When reference is made in a sociological context to a "state" [. . .] a "corporation" [or] a "family" [. . .] what is meant is [. . .] *only* a certain kind of development of actual or possible social actions of individual persons' (Weber, 1964, p. 102). Such sets of meanings constrain only in the sense that they are objectified by actors who orient their actions to them: 'The social relationship thus *consists* entirely and exclusively in the existence of a *probability* that there will be, in some meaningfully understandable sense, a course of social action' (p. 118, his italics). He goes on: 'It is vital to be continually clear about this in order to avoid the reification of these concepts.'

In attributing a causative role to the constructs of the observer (system needs, system dynamics) and losing sight of the meanings which actors attach to their actions, many contemporary sociologists have cheated themselves of a rich source of data. Parsons, in his introduction to Weber's most substantial work, accuses him of failing to use the insights of a functionalist system perspective ; but it is clear that Weber very sharply saw the difficulties involved in explanations in terms of the nature of the whole and, in particular, its need for survival.[12]

The Action frame of reference and the Systems approach

The Systems approach tends to regard behaviour as a reflection of the characteristics of a social system containing a series of impersonal processes which are external to actors and constrain them. In emphasizing that action derives from the meanings that men attach to their own and each other's acts, the Action frame of reference argues that man is constrained by the way in which he socially constructs his reality. On the one hand, it seems, Society makes man, on the other, Man makes society. It is hardly surprising, therefore, that each approach should appear to stress merely one side or another of the same coin. When the relative merits of the two approaches are discussed, it is usually suggested that they are complementary to each other. This appears to be the argument in a recent work by Percy Cohen (1968).

Cohen distinguishes a 'holistic' from an 'atomistic' approach: the former seeks to explain the action of parts of a system in terms of the nature of the whole, while the latter views the system as an *outcome* of the action of the parts. The tension between the two is provided by

12. Weber notes that sociologists have used an organic analogy in discussing society and goes on: 'this functional frame of reference is convenient for purposes of practical illustration and for provisional orientation . . . at the same time, if its cognitive value is overestimated and its concepts illegitimately "reified", it can be *highly dangerous*' (1964, p. 103, my emphasis). Similarly, Berger and Luckmann term functionalism 'a theoretical legerdemain' and suggest that: 'A purely structural sociology is endemically in danger of reifying social phenomena ' (1966, p. 170).

the fact that knowledge of the social system does not tell one everything about the action of its parts, just as information about its human parts does not in itself provide a complete description of the nature of the system. Cohen argues that this is because the members of society have biological and other characteristics which are separate from the nature of the whole system. Secondly, individuals have choice over which aspect of the whole to respond to, especially where it makes demands which are mutually inconsistent (Cohen, 1968, p. 14).[13] Thus both approaches have difficulty in explaining facts which the other is able to take for granted: the Action approach tends to assume an existing system in which action occurs but cannot successfully explain the nature of this system, while the Systems approach is unable to explain satisfactorily why particular actors act as they do.

The way in which each approach is affected by these sort of limitations has been taken up in a paper by Wagner (1964). Wagner distinguishes two sorts of atomistic model: 'Reductionist' theories explain the behaviour of the parts in terms of their individual biological or psychological make-up and, because they apply the same general laws to the parts and the whole, have no difficulty in also explaining the characteristics of society. Social action theories, on the other hand, are concerned with explanations in terms of interpersonal human action and are, therefore, best fitted to explain 'micro' problems involving particular patterns of action. When they seek to comprehend 'macro' processes, action theorists at once come up against 'the apparent machine-like character of large social systems which seem to follow their own mechanical laws'. It is almost impossible, in this situation, 'to submit adequate interpretations of large-scale societal structures and processes, without resorting to non-voluntaristic (i.e. positivist) explanations' (Wagner, 1964, p. 583). Attempts to do so, from an action position, inevitably raise the problem of what he calls 'a displacement of scope'.

As Touraine puts it, however, the view that: 'The action approach says little about the characteristics of the social system' (1964, p. 7) and, therefore, 'does not attempt to substitute for an analysis of social systems but to complement it' (p. 11), is severely challenged by several of the writers who have been discussed in this chapter. The work of Berger, Luckmann and Pullberg, for instance, supports the argument

13. The same point is made by Rose (1962), who argues that actors possess choice especially where a culture is internally inconsistent. Of course, if reality is socially constructed, then the maintenance of any definition of a situation is the outcome of choice by the actors – however much they may experience the situation as constraining.

that, by its examination of the sense in which society *does* make man, the Action approach can offer a means of explanation of the nature of social systems and need not depend on Systems analysis for, as it were, the other half of the picture. 'The paradox,' as Berger and Luckmann note, 'is that man is capable of producing a world that he then experiences as something other than a human product' (1966, p. 57).

The possibility that Action and Systems explanations offer conflicting rather than complementary frames of reference is strengthened by the view that they are concerned with different types of problem. Cohen argues that holism and atomism are alternative means of coming to grips with the same basic issue: the problem of moral order. However, as Dawe (1969) suggests, contemporary sociology is also concerned with a second problem – 'the exertion of human control over hitherto-inviolable institutions' (Dawe, 1969, p. 116). This latter issue was a major concern, as he points out, of the Enlightenment and it underlies Berger and Pullberg's discussion of 'objectivation' and reification.[13] A commitment to the insights of phenomenology may in practice prove difficult to reconcile with an acceptance of the positivist position. Even if both approaches are ultimately concerned with social order, their views of its nature and consequences are very different.

13. While the problem of order 'gave rise to a social system approach', Dawe remarks, '. . . the problem of control gave rise to a social action approach, with its emphasis on the actor's definition of and attempts to control his situation, and upon a distinctively "social science" view of the nature of social inquiry' (1969, pp. 116–17).

References

BERGER, P. L. (1966), *Invitation to Sociology*, Penguin.
BERGER, P. L., and LUCKMANN, T. (1967), *The Social Construction of Reality: A Treatise in the Sociology of Knowledge*, Allen Lane, the Penguin Press.
BERGER, P. L. and PULLBERG, S. (1966), 'Reification and the socological critique of consciousness', *New Left Rev.*, vol. 35, no. 1, pp. 56–71.
BLUMER, H. (1962), a paper in A. M. Rose (ed.), *Human Behaviour and Social Processes: An Interactionist Approach*, Houghton Mifflin.
CICOUREL, A. V. (1964), *Method and Measurement in Sociology*, Free Press.
COHEN, P. S. (1968), *Modern Social Theory*, Heinemann.
DAHENDORF, R. (1968), *Essays in the Theory of Society*, Stanford University Press.
DAWE, A. (1969), book review, *Sociology*, 3, no. 1, pp. 115–17.
GOFFMAN, E. (1959), *The Presentation of Self in Everyday Life*, Doubleday.
LAING, R. D. (1967), *The Politics of Experience*, Penguin.
PARSONS, T. (1951), *The Social System*, Free Press.
ROSE, A. M. (ed.) (1962), *Human Behaviour and Social Processes: An Interactionist Approach*, Houghton Mifflin.
SCHUTZ, A. (1964), *Collected Papers* (in three volumes, edited by M. Natanson), Nijhoff.

TOURAINE, A. (1964), 'Pour une sociologie actionnaliste', *Europ. J. Sociol.*, vol. 5, no. 1, pp. 1–24.

WAGNER, H. R. (1964), 'Displacement of scope: a problem of the relationship between small-scale and large-scale sociological theories', *Amer. J. Sociol.*, vol. 69, no. 6, pp. 571–84.

WEBER, M. (1964), *The Theory of Social and Economic Organization*, Free Press.

WHYTE, W. F. (1959), 'An interaction approach to the theory of organizations', in M. Haire (ed.), *Modern Organization Theory*, Wiley.

WRONG, D. W. (1967), 'The over-socialized conception of man', in N. J. Demerath and R. A. Peterson (eds.), *System, Change and Conflict*, Free Press.

Acknowledgements

Permission to reproduce the Readings in this volume
is acknowledged to the following sources:

1 Heinemann Educational Books Ltd
2 Chapman & Hall Ltd
3 Routledge & Kegan Paul Ltd
4a C. A. Watts & Co. Ltd
4b C. A. Watts & Co. Ltd
4c C. A. Watts & Co. Ltd
4d C. A. Watts & Co. Ltd
5a Free Press
5b Oxford University Press Inc
6a Free Press
6b Free Press
7a Free Press
7b Free Press
8 University of California Press
9 Free Press
10 University of Chicago Press and Anselm L. Strauss
11 Collier-Macmillan
12 University of Chicago Press
13 American Anthropological Association
14 Free Press
15 John Wiley & Sons Inc.
16a Doubleday & Co. Inc. and Lewis S. Feuer
16b C. A. Watts & Co. Ltd
17 Oxford University Press Inc.
18 Free Press
19 C. A. Watts & Co. Ltd
20 Heinemann Educational Books Ltd
21 Routledge & Kegan Paul Ltd and University of California
   Press
22 Routledge & Kegan Paul Ltd and Free Press
23 Routledge & Kegan Paul Ltd and Free Press
24 *British Journal of Sociology* and Frank Parkin
25 Basil Blackwell & Mott Ltd
26 George Allen & Unwin Ltd and Harper & Row Inc.

27 Macmillan Co.
28 Rand McNally & Co.
29a George Allen & Unwin Ltd and Charles Scribner's Sons
29b Free Press
29c Methuen & Co. Ltd and Beacon Press
30 *Social Research*
31 *Journal of Social Issues* and Robert N. Bellah
33 Collier-Macmillan
34 Faber & Faber Ltd and Doubleday & Co. Inc.
35 *Journal of the Scientific Study of Religion*
36 Random House Inc.
37 University of Pennsylvania Press and Ernest Nagel
38 *Journal of Philosophy*
39 Prentice-Hall Inc.
40 Princeton University Press
41 George Allen & Unwin Ltd and Norwegian
    Universities Press
42 A. D. Peters & Co.
43 Allen Lane The Penguin Press and
    Doubleday & Co. Inc.
44 Heinemann Educational Books Ltd

Author Index

Subject Index

Academic sociology, 15–17
Action, frame of reference, 562–79
Agendas, 177
Alienation, 54–62
  alienated labour, 51–62
Altercasting, 170
Anomie, 305, 309
Aristocracy, 48–9
Art, 96
Asceticism, 397–80, 413, 420
Authority, 114, 271
  legal, traditional and charismatic,
  68–75

Bakunism, 78–9
Behaviourism, 483
Bourgeoisie, 48–9, 238–44, 276–7,
  290–91
Bureaucracy, 70–79, 503–4
  and power, 67–79

Calvinism, 411–13, 425–8
Capitalism, 49–51, 64, 235–360,
  408–13, 418–30
Caste, 258–9, 290
China
  Confucianism in, 414–17
  stratification in, 284–6
Church
  and sect, 374, 379–83, 392–5, 506
  the universal, 384–5
Civil society, 44, 246–8
Civilization, 30, 95–7
Class, 48–9, 51, 237–362
  conflict, 245–9, 265–6, 273–5
  in Communist societies, 285,
  331–47, 348–60
  ruling, 275–87, 379
  situation, 251–4, 259
  status and party, 250–64
  struggle, 237, 243, 252, 254–6

Cognitive processes in interaction,
  163
Communication, 147–8, 190–91, 193
Communism, as religion, 369–70
Communist Party, 348, 350, 352
  Manifesto of the, 237–44, 265
Community, 151, 251
Comparative method, 34, 42
Concept and theory formation,
  482–500
Confucianism and puritanism,
  414–17
Consciousness, 46–9, 246
Control, social, 325, 549–53
Converge of stratification systems,
  331–46, 348
Cult, the, 390–91, 394

Data collection, 518–41
Deference and demeanour, 188–208
Definition
  problems of, 365–73
  of religion, 365–78
Definition of the situation, 161, 174
Denomination, 386
Deprivation, 395–406
  relative, 299–315
Division of labour, 32, 48, 94–105,
  241, 246, 267–8, 332
Domain assumptions, 15–17
Dyad and triad, 80–82

Ecclesia, the, 385
Education, 292, 322–4, 351, 357
Egalitarianism, 308–9, 317, 322,
  325, 350, 352, 354
Elite, 278–87, 333, 350, 356, 359
  governing, 278, 281
  power, 279–83
Elitism, 320–30
Enlightenment, the age of, 547–8